James Legge

The Chinese Classics with a Translation, Critical and Exegetical Notes, Prolegomena, and Copious Indexes

Confucian analects, the Great learning, and the doctrine of the mean. 1

James Legge

The Chinese Classics with a Translation, Critical and Exegetical Notes, Prolegomena, and Copious Indexes
Confucian analects, the Great learning, and the doctrine of the mean. 1

ISBN/EAN: 9783742822581

Manufactured in Europe, USA, Canada, Australia, Japa

Cover: Foto ©Andreas Hilbeck / pixelio.de

Manufactured and distributed by brebook publishing software
(www.brebook.com)

James Legge

The Chinese Classics with a Translation, Critical and Exegetical Notes, Prolegomena, and Copious Indexes

PREFACE.

The author arrived in the East as a Missionary towards the end of 1839, and was stationed at Malacca for between three and four years. Before leaving England, he had enjoyed the benefit of a few months' instruction in Chinese from the late Professor Kidd at the University of London, and was able in the beginning of 1840 to commence the study of the first of the Works in the present publication. It seemed to him then—and the experience of one and twenty years gives its sanction to the correctness of the judgment—that he should not be able to consider himself qualified for the duties of his position, until he had thoroughly mastered the Classical Books of the Chinese, and had investigated for himself the whole field of thought through which the sages of China had ranged, and in which were to be found the foundations of the moral, social, and political life of the people. Under this conviction he addressed himself eagerly to the reading of the Confucian Analects, and proceeded from them to the other Works. Circumstances occurred in the Mission at Malacca to throw various engagements upon him, which left him little time to spend at his books, and he consequently sought about for all the assistance which he could find from the labours of men who had gone before.

In this respect he was favourably situated, the charge of the Anglo-Chinese College having devolved upon him, so that he had free access to all the treasures in its Library. He had translations and dictionaries in abundance, and they facilitated his progress. Yet he desiderated some Work upon the Classics, more critical, more full and exact, than any which he had the opportunity of consulting, and he sketched to himself the plan of its execution. This was distinctly before him in 1841, and for several years he hoped to hear that some experienced Chinese scholar was preparing to give to the public something of the kind. As time went on, and he began to feel assured as to his own progress in the language, it occurred to him that he might venture on such an undertaking himself. He studied, wrote out translations, and made notes, with the project in his mind. He hopes he can say that it did not divert him from the usual active labours of a Missionary in preaching and teaching, but it did not allow him to rest satisfied in any operations of the time then being.

In 1856, he first talked with some of his friends about his purpose, and among them was the Rev. Josiah Cox, of the Wesleyan Missionary Society. The question of the expense of publication came up. The author's idea was that by-and-by he would be able to digest his materials in readiness for the press, and that then he would be likely, on application, to meet with such encouragement from the British and other foreign merchants in China, as would enable him to go forward with his plan. Mr. Cox, soon after, without the slightest intimation of his intention, mentioned the whole matter to his friend, Mr. Joseph Jardine. In consequence of what he reported of Mr. Jardine's sentiments, the author had an interview with that gentleman, when he very generously undertook to bear the expense of carrying the Work through the press. His lamented death leaves the author at liberty to speak more freely on this point than he would otherwise have done. Mr. Jardine expressed himself favourably of the plan, and said, "I know the liberality of the merchants in China, and that many of them would readily give their help to such an undertaking, but you need not have the trouble of canvassing the community. If you are prepared for the toil of the publication, I will bear the expense of it. We make our money in China, and we should be glad to assist in whatever promises to be of benefit to it."

The author could not but be grateful to Mr. Jardine for his proffer, nor did he hesitate to accept it. The interruption of missionary labours, consequent on the breaking out of hostilities in the end of 1856, was favourable to retired and literary work, and he immediately set about preparing some of his materials for the press. A necessary visit to England in 1857, which kept him absent from the Colony for eighteen months, proved a serious interruption, but the first-fruits of his labours are now in a state to be presented to the public.

The first conception of the present work and the circumstances under which it is published have thus been detailed. Of the style and manner of its execution it is for others to judge. It originated in the author's feeling of his own wants. He has translated, annotated, and reasoned, always in the first place to satisfy himself. He hopes that the volumes will be of real service to Missionaries and other students of the Chinese language and literature. They have been foremost in his mind as those whom he wished to benefit. But he has thought also of the general reader. The Chinese is the largest family of mankind. Thoughtful minds in other parts of the world cannot but be anxious to know what the minds of this many-millioned people have had to live upon for thousands of years. The Work will enable them to draw their own conclusions on the subject. The author will give his views on the scope and value of their contents in his prolegomena to the several volumes. Some will agree with his opinions, and others will probably differ from them. He only hopes that he will be found to advance no judgment for which he does not render a reason. To think freely and for himself is a source to him of much happiness; his object is to supply to others the means of realizing the same for themselves, so far as the subjects here investigated are concerned. He hopes also that the time is not very remote, when among the Chinese themselves there will be found many men of intelligence, able and willing to read without prejudice what he may say about the teachings of their sages.

The title-page says that the Work will be in seven volumes,—two, that is, for the Four Books, and one for each of the Five King. It will be necessary, however, from their size, to publish more than one of the latter in two or more parts, so that to the eye the Work will present the appearance perhaps of ten volumes. Should life and health be spared, the author would like to give a supplementary volume or two, so as to embrace all the Books in "The Thirteen King." The second volume is two-thirds printed, and will appear, God willing, before the end of the present year He must then be permitted to rest for a time, before proceeding with the Shoo-king or The Book of History. His directly missionary labours are the chief business of his life, and require of course his chief attention. The fact that the Work is inscribed to the memory of Mr. Jardine impresses him deeply with the frailty of life and the uncertainty of all human plans. While he has been putting the finishing hand to this first volume, the same solemn truth has been still more realizingly forced upon him by the news of the death of his own eldest brother, the thought of giving pleasure to whom by the publication was one of the greatest stimuli under the toil of its preparation. Whether he shall be permitted to accomplish what he contemplates, the future alone can determine.

It would have been an easy matter to swell the volume now presented to double the size. In the Chinese Commentators he had abundant materials to do so; but the author's object has been to condense rather than expand. He has not sought to follow Choo He or any other authority. The text, and not the commentary, has been his study. He has read the varying views of scholars extensively, but only that he might the better understand what was written in the Book. He has also consulted the renderings of other translators, but never till he had made his own. He may have sometimes altered his own to adopt a happier expression from them, but the translation is independent. He has not made frequent mention in his notes of the labours of other scholars,—not because he undervalues them, but because there was no necessity to call attention to the circumstance, where he agreed with them, and where he differed, he thought it more seemly to avoid "doubtful disputations."

In expressing the sounds of proper names, the author has followed the orthography of Morrison and Medhurst; and in the index of Chinese characters he has given, in addition, that of Mr. Wade, taken from his "Peking Syllabary." Yet he is afraid that Mr. Wade may find some characters incorrectly represented, as the author could only fix their pronunciation by the analogy of others. It may seem strange also to some scholars, that where he has spoken in the notes of the tones of characters, he has assumed that in the Court dialect there are eight tones in the same way as in the dialect of Canton Province. The author has not paid sufficient attention to the Court dialect to justify his speaking on this point with positiveness. If K'ang-he's dictionary were to determine the question, it could be shown that a distinction of "upper" and "lower" is made in all the tones, and not in the first or "even" one only. The author, moreover, has fancied that he could detect that distinction in the pronunciation of teachers of the Court dialect. On this subject, however, he speaks with submission.

There are many deficiencies in the present volume in point of typographical execution, for which the author ventures to ask the indulgence of the reader. The only workmen employed upon it have been Chinese. He is under great obligation to his excellent friend, Mr. Hwang Shing, the superintendent of the Mission Printing Office; but well-skilled as he is in the English language, he could not perform the duties of proof-reader. The work of correction has mainly devolved on the author himself or members of his family, and has been done when the mind was otherwise occupied, or amid constant interruptions. The errors would have been much more numerous than they are but for the great kindness of Mr. Jeffrey, formerly of the "China Mail" Office, who has read nearly all the sheets before their finally going to press. To Mr. Low, of the same Office, and latterly to Mr. Dixson, the proprietor of the "China Mail," the author is glad to take this opportunity of expressing his thanks for their advice and help in many typographical matters. The more serious mistakes will be found corrected, it is hoped, in the subjoined lists. For others of smaller importance the circumstances just mentioned may form some apology; and where the sound of a Chinese character may in a few instances have been represented somewhat incorrectly, the character itself in a foot-note, or its sound in the 7th Index, will supply the necessary correction. The author has likewise to thank his friend, and former colleague in the Mission at Hongkong, the Rev. Mr. Chalmers, for the compilation of the indexes of Subjects and Proper Names.

HONGKONG, 26*th March* 1861.

CONTENTS.

I. THE PROLEGOMENA.

CHAPTER I.

OF THE CHINESE CLASSICS GENERALLY.

SECTION		PAGE
I.	Books included under the name of the Chinese Classics, ...	1
II.	The Authority of the Chinese Classics, ...	8

CHAPTER II.

OF THE CONFUCIAN ANALECTS.

SECTION		PAGE
I.	Formation of the Text of the Analects by the Scholars of the Han dynasty, ...	12
II.	At what time, and by whom, the Analects were written; their Plan; and Authenticity, ...	14
III.	Of Commentaries upon the Analects, ...	18
IV.	Of Various Readings, ...	21

CHAPTER III.

OF THE GREAT LEARNING.

SECTION		PAGE
I.	History of the Text, and the different Arrangements of it which have been proposed,	22
II.	Of the Authorship, and division of the text into Classical Text and Commentary,	26
III.	Its Scope and Value, ...	27

CHAPTER IV.

THE DOCTRINE OF THE MEAN.

SECTION		PAGE
I.	Its place in the Le Ke, and its Publication separately, ...	35
II.	Its Author; and some account of him, ...	36
III.	Its Integrity, ...	43
IV.	Its Scope and Value, ...	44

CHAPTER VI.

LIST OF THE PRINCIPAL WORKS WHICH HAVE BEEN CONSULTED IN THE PREPARATION OF THIS VOLUME.

II. THE BODY OF THE VOLUME.

III. INDEXES.

ERRATA.

I. IN THE CHINESE TEXT.

Page.	Column.		Page.	Column.	
3,	2,	for 人 read 仁.	185,	9,	for 湼 read 涅.
21,	1,	日 is inverted.	199,	8,	耘 „ 芸.
70,	9,	for 祇 read 祗.	228,	6,	之 „ 知.
92,	4,	transpose 右左.	230,	4,	𡖅 „ 爽.
101,	2,	for 體 read 禮.	237,	9,	母 „ 毋.
114,	5,	仁 „ 人.	256,	1,	致 „ 至.
116,	2,	巳 „ 矣.	273,	6,	事 „ 士.
„	6,	𡿺 „ 訥.	283,	2,	transpose 內外.
130,	10,	日 is inverted.	283,	2,	for 泄 read 洩.
142,	10,	for 䟽 read 疏.	290,	4,	after 質 insert 諸.
143,	8,	舞 „ 無.	293,	4,	for 日 read 曰.
181,	7,	舆 „ 與.			

PAGE 11, between the 6th and 7th Columns, for 𥳑 read 節.
„ 23,.................. „ „ .... „ dele 二節.
„ 24,..................1st and 2d............ „ 二節.
„ „ ....4th and 5th............for 三 read 二.
„ 73,..................3d and 4th............by 成 insert 三節.
„ 116,..................6th and 7th............after 乎 „ 三節.
„ 238,..................3d and 4th, ...for 二 read 三.
„ 293,.................. „ „ „ .... „ 五 „ 四

II. CHINESE CHARACTERS IN THE NOTES.

Page.	Line.	Column.			Page.	Line.	Column.	
3,	28,	ii,	for 安 read 晏.		182,	22,	i,	for 明 read 日 月.
7,	10,	"	" 約 " 倚.		193,	2,	"	" 以 " 矣.
49,	1,	"	" 再 " 冉.		197,	4,	"	" 沒 " 醪.
52,	3,	i,	" 再 " 冉.		207,	1,	ii,	" 酒 " 洒.
88,	4,	ii,	" 未 " 末.		227,	10,	"	" 献 " 獻.
102,	9,	"	" 漪 " 譪.		250,	12,	" read,	" 尼 " 尼.
117,	6,	"	" 讚 " 譖.		257,	8,	"	" 照 " 昭.
128,	2,	"	" 扉 " 運.		264,	12,	i,	" 栽 " 裁.
141,	3,	"	" 堯 " 澆.		268,	18,	"	" 縣 " 虞.
152,	5,	"	" 恩 " 怨.		283,	15,	"	" 貉 " 貊.
160,	3,	i,	" 狛 " 秋.		284,	5,	"	" 日 " 但.
173,	16,	ii,	" 蕭 " 藺.		—,	6,	ii,	" 盧 " 慮.

III. IN THE PROLEGOMENA.

Page.	Line.		Page.	Line.	
2,	21,	for Kuh Leang-ch'ih read Kuh-leang Ch'ih.	20,	11,	for P'ing read ... ... Ping.
4,	6,	for 4... ... " ... ... 6.	40,	34,	" transpose " K'ang and Sung.
10,	21,	" Liang " ... ... Lew.	67,	14,	" who " ... ... which.
18,	13,	" 490 ... " ... ... 430.	85,	16,	" ages " ... ... sages.

IV. IN THE TRANSLATION AND NOTES.

Page.	Line.		Page.	Line.	
1,	3,	for pleasant read ... delightful.	26,	17, col. ii,	for 640 read ... 642.
130,	5,	" government " governments.	"	18, " "	" p'a " ... pa.
153,	6,	refer to char. 厲, Index vii.	168,	26, " i,	" HEAD " ... HAND.
183,	1,	for bing read ... ...sing.	269,	6, " i,	" ships " ... ... slips.
201,	9,	" no body " ... ... nobody.	271,	23, " ii,	" *Not, Lin, Sin,* read *Nat, Lin, Sin.*

PROLEGOMENA.

CHAPTER I.

OF THE CHINESE CLASSICS GENERALLY.

SECTION I.

BOOKS INCLUDED UNDER THE NAME OF THE CHINESE CLASSICS.

1. The Books now recognized as of highest authority in China are comprehended under the denominations of "The five *King*,"[1] and "The four *Shoo*."[2] The term *King* is of textile origin, and signifies the warp threads of a web, and their adjustment. An easy application of it is to denote what is regular and insures regularity. As used with reference to books, it indicates their authority on the subjects of which they treat. "The five *King*" are the five *canonical* Works, containing the truth upon the highest subjects from the sages of China, and which should be received as law by all generations. The term *Shoo* simply means *Writings* or *Books*.

2. The five King are:—the *Yih*,[3] or, as it has been styled, "The Book of Changes;" the *Shoo*,[4] or "The Book of History;" the *She*,[5] or "The Book of Poetry;" the Le Ke,[6] or "Record of Rites;" and the Ch'un Ts'ew,[7] or "Spring and Autumn," a chronicle of events, extending from 721 to 480, B.C. The authorship, or compilation rather, of all these works is loosely attributed to Confucius. But much of the Le Ke is from later hands. Of the Yih, the Shoo, and the She, it is only in the first that we find additions from the philosopher himself, in the shape of appendixes. The Ch'un Ts'ew is the only one of the five King which can rightly be described as of his own "making."

[1] 五經. [2] 四書. [3] 易經. [4] 書經. [5] 詩經. [6] 禮記. [7] 春秋.

"The four Books" is an abbreviation for "The Books of the four Philosophers."[8] The first is the Lun Yu,[9] or "Digested Conversations," being occupied chiefly with the sayings of Confucius. He is the philosopher to whom it belongs. It appears in this Work under the title of "Confucian Analects." The second is the Ta Hëŏ,[10] or "Great Learning," now commonly attributed to Tsăng Sin,[11] a disciple of the sage. He is the philosopher of it. The third is the Chung Yung,[12] or "Doctrine of the Mean," ascribed to K'ung Keih,[13] the grandson of Confucius. He is the philosopher of it. The fourth contains the works of Mencius.

3. This arrangement of the Classical Books, which is commonly supposed to have originated with the scholars of the Sung dynasty, is defective. The *Great Learning* and the *Doctrine of the Mean* are both found in the Record of Rites, being the forty-second and thirty-first Books respectively of that compilation, according to the usual arrangement of it.

4. The oldest enumerations of the Classical Books specify only *the five King*. The Yŏ Ke, or "Record of Music,"[14] the remains of which now form one of the Books in the Le Ke, was sometimes added to those, making with them the *six King*. A division was also made into *nine King*, consisting of the Yih, the She, the Shoo, the Chow Le,[15] or "Ritual of Chow," the E Le,[16] or "Ceremonial Usages," the Le Ke, and the three annotated editions of the Ch'un Ts'ew,[17] by Tso-k'ew Ming,[18] Kung-yang Kaou,[19] and Kuh Lëang-ch'ih.[20] In the famous compilation of the classical Books, undertaken by order of T'ae-tsung, the second emperor of the T'ang dynasty (A.D. 627–649), and which appeared in the reign of his successor, there are *thirteen King*; viz., the Yih, the She, the Shoo, the three editions of the Ch'un Ts'ew, the Le Ke, the Chow Le, the E Le, the Confucian Analects, the Urh Ya,[21] a sort of ancient dictionary, the Heaou King,[22] or "Classic of Filial Piety," and the works of Mencius.

5. A distinction, however, was made among the Works thus comprehended under the same common name, and Mencius, the Lun Yu, the Ta Hëŏ, the Chung Yung, and the Heaou King were spoken of as the seaou King, or "smaller Classics." It thus appears,

[8] 四子之書. [9] 論語. [10] 大學. [11] 曾參. [12] 中庸. [13] 孔伋. [14] 樂記. [15] 周禮. [16] 儀禮. [17] 春秋三傳. [18] 左丘明. [19] 公羊高. [20] 穀梁赤. [21] 爾雅. [22] 孝經.

contrary to the ordinary opinion on the subject, that the Ta Hëŏ and Chung Yung had been published as separate treatises before the Sung dynasty, and that the Four Books, as distinguished from the greater King, had also previously found a place in the literature of China.[23]

SECTION II.

THE AUTHORITY OF THE CHINESE CLASSICS.

1. This subject will be discussed in connection with each separate Work, and it is only designed here to exhibit generally the evidence on which the Chinese Classics claim to be received as genuine productions of the time to which they are referred.

2. In the memoirs of the Former Han dynasty (B.C. 201—A.D. 24), we have one chapter which we may call the History of Literature.[1] It commences thus:—"After the death of Confucius,[2] there was an end of his exquisite words; and when his seventy disciples had passed away, violence began to be done to their meaning. It came about that there were five different editions of the Ch'un Ts'ew, four of the She, and several of the Yih. Amid the disorder and collision of the warring States (B.C. 480–221), truth and falsehood were still more in a state of warfare, and a sad confusion marked the words of the various scholars. Then came the calamity inflicted under the Ts'in dynasty (B.C. 220–200), when the literary monuments were destroyed by fire, in order to keep the people in ignorance. But, by-and-by, there arose the Han dynasty, which set itself to remedy the evil wrought by the Ts'in. Great efforts were made to collect slips and tablets,[3] and the way was thrown wide open for the bringing in of Books. In the time of the emperor Heaou-woo[4] (B.C. 139–86), portions of Books being wanting and tablets lost, so that ceremonies and music were suffering great

23 For the statements in the two last paragraphs, see 西河合集·大學證文·卷一.

1 前漢書·本志·第十卷·藝文志. 2 仲尼. 3 篇籍,—slips and tablets on bamboo, which supplied in those days the place of paper. 4 世宗孝武皇帝.

damage, he was moved to sorrow, and said, 'I am very sad for this.' He therefore formed the plan of Repositories, in which the Books might be stored, and appointed officers to transcribe Books on an extensive scale, embracing the works of the various scholars, that they might all be placed in the Repositories. The emperor Shing[5] (B.C. 31–4), finding that a portion of the Books still continued dispersed or missing, commissioned Ch'in Nung, the superintendent of guests,[6] to search for undiscovered Books throughout the empire, and by special edict ordered the chief of the Banqueting House, Lew Heang,[7] to examine the classical Works, along with the commentaries on them, the writings of the scholars, and all poetical productions; the master-controller of infantry, Jin Hwang, to examine the Books on the art of war; the grand historiographer, Yin Hëen,[8] to examine the Books treating of the art of numbers (*i.e.*, divination); and the imperial physician, Le Ch'oo-kŏ,[10] to examine the books on medicine. Whenever any Book was done with, Heang forthwith arranged it, indexed it, and made a digest of it, which was presented to the emperor. While the undertaking was in progress, Heang died, and the emperor Gae (B.C. 5—A.D.) appointed his son, Hin,[11] a master of the imperial carriages, to complete his father's work. On this, Hin collected all the books, and presented a report of them, under seven divisions."

The first of these divisions seems to have been a general catalogue,[12] containing perhaps only the titles of the works included in the other six. The second embraced the classical Works.[13] From the abstract of it, which is preserved in the chapter referred to, we find that there were 294 collections of the Yih-king, from 13 different individuals or editors;[14] 412 collections of the Shoo-king, from 9 different individuals; 416 volumes of the She-king, from 6 different individuals;[15] of the Books of Rites, 555 collections, from 13

5 孝成皇帝. 6 謁者陳農. 7 光祿大夫劉向. 8 步兵校尉任宏. 9 太史令尹咸. 10 侍醫李柱國. 11 侍中奉車都尉歆. 12 輯略. 13 六藝略. 14 凡易十三家二百九十四篇. How much of the whole Work was contained in each 篇, it is impossible for us to ascertain. P. Regis says:—"*Pien, quemadmodum Gallice diceres 'des pièces d'éloquence, de poésie.'*" 15 詩六家四百一十六卷. The collections of the She-king are mentioned under the name of *Keuen*, 'sections,' 'portions.' Had *pëen* been used, it might have been understood of individual odes. This change of terms shows that by *pëen* in the other summaries, we are not to understand single blocks or chapters.

different individuals: of the Books on Music, 165 collections, from 6 different editors; 948 collections of History, under the heading of the Ch'un Ts'ew, from 23 different individuals; 229 collections of the Lun Yu, including the Analects and kindred fragments, from 12 different individuals; of the Heaou-king, embracing also the Urh Ya, and some other portions of the ancient literature, 59 collections, from 11 different individuals; and finally of the Lesser Learning, being works on the form of the characters, 45 collections, from 11 different individuals. The Works of Mencius were included in the second division,[16] among the Writings of what were deemed orthodox scholars,[17] of which there were 836 collections, from 53 different individuals.

3. The above important document is sufficient to show how the emperors of the Han dynasty, as soon as they had made good their possession of the empire, turned their attention to recover the ancient literature of the nation, the Classical Books engaging their first care, and how earnestly and effectively the scholars of the time responded to the wishes of their rulers. In addition to the facts specified in the preface to it, I may relate that the ordinance of the Ts'in dynasty against possessing the Classical Books (with the exception, as will appear in its proper place, of the Yih-king) was repealed by the second sovereign of the Han, the emperor Heaou Hwuy,[18] in the 4th year of his reign, B.C. 190, and that a large portion of the Shoo-king was recovered in the time of the third emperor, B.C. 178–156, while in the year B.C. 135, a special Board was constituted, consisting of literati who were put in charge of the five *King*.[19]

4. The collections reported on by Lew Hin suffered damage in the troubles which began A.D. 8, and continued till the rise of the second or eastern Han dynasty in the year 25. The founder of it (A.D. 25–57) zealously promoted the undertaking of his predecessors, and additional repositories were required for the books which were collected. His successors, the emperors, Heaou-ming[20] (58–75), Heaou-chang[21] (76–88), and Heaou-hwo[22] (89–105), took a part themselves in the studies and discussions of the literary tribunal,

16 諸子略. 17 儒家者流. 18 孝惠皇帝. 19 武帝建元五年,初置五經博士. 20 顯宗孝明皇帝. 21 肅宗孝章皇帝. 22 孝和皇帝.

and the emperor Heaou-ling,[23] between the years 172–178, had the text of the five *King*, as it had been fixed, cut in slabs of stone, in characters of three different forms.

5. Since the Han, the successive dynasties have considered the literary monuments of the country to be an object of their special care. Many of them have issued editions of the classics, embodying the commentaries of preceding generations. No dynasty has distinguished itself more in this line than the present Manchow possessors of the Empire. In fine, the evidence is complete that the Classical Books of China have come down from at least a century before our Christian era, substantially the same as we have them at present.

6. But it still remains to inquire in what condition we may suppose the Books were, when the scholars of the Han dynasty commenced their labours upon them. They acknowledge that the tablets—we cannot here speak of *manuscripts*—were mutilated and in disorder. Was the injury which they had received of such an extent that all the care and study put forth on the small remains would be of little use? This question can be answered satisfactorily, only by an examination of the evidence which is adduced for the text of each particular Classic; but it can be made apparent that there is nothing, in the nature of the case, to interfere with our believing that the materials were sufficient to enable the scholars to execute the work intrusted to them.

7. The burning of the ancient Books by order of the founder of the Ts'in dynasty is always referred to as the greatest disaster which they sustained, and with this is coupled the slaughter of many of the Literati by the same monarch.

The account which we have of these transactions in the Historical Records is the following:—[24]

"In his 34th year," (the 34th year, that is, after he had ascended the throne of Ts'in. It was only the 8th after he had been acknowledged Sovereign of the empire, coinciding with B.C. 212), the emperor, returning from a visit to the south, which had extended as far as Yuĕ, gave a feast in the palace of Heen-yang, when the Great

23 孝靈皇帝. 24 I have thought it well to endeavour to translate the whole of the passages. Father de Mailla merely constructs from them a narrative of his own; see *L'Histoire Générale de la Chine*, tome II., pp. 399-402. The 通鑑綱目 avoids the difficulties of the original by giving an abridgment of it.

Scholars, amounting to seventy men, appeared and wished him long life.[25] One of the principal ministers, Chow Ts'ing-shin,[26] came forward and said, 'Formerly, the State of Ts'in was only 1,000 le in extent, but Your Majesty, by your spirit-like efficacy and intelligent wisdom, has tranquillized and settled the whole empire, and driven away all barbarous tribes, so that, wherever the sun and moon shine, all appear before you as guests acknowledging subjection. You have formed the States of the various princes into provinces and districts, where the people enjoy a happy tranquillity, suffering no more from the calamities of war and contention. This condition of things will be transmitted for 10,000 generations. From the highest antiquity there has been no one in awful virtue like Your Majesty.'

"The Emperor was pleased with this flattery, when Shun Yu-yuĕ,[27] one of the great scholars, a native of Ts'e, advanced and said, 'The sovereigns of Yin and Chow, for more than a thousand years, invested their sons and younger brothers, and meritorious ministers, with domains and rule, and could thus depend upon them for support and aid;—that I have heard. But now Your Majesty is in possession of all within the seas, and your sons and younger brothers are nothing but private individuals. The issue will be that some one will arise to play the part of T'een Chang,[28] or of the six nobles *of Tsin*. Without the support *of your own family*, where will you find the aid which you may require? That a state of things not modelled from the lessons of antiquity can long continue;—that is what I have not heard. Ts'ing is now showing himself to be a flatterer, who increases the errors of Your Majesty, and not a loyal minister.'

"The Emperor requested the opinions of others on this representation, when the premier, Le Sze,[29] said, 'The five emperors were not one the double of the other, nor did the three dynasties accept one another's ways. Each had a peculiar system of government, not for the sake of the contrariety, but as being required by the changed times. Now, Your Majesty has laid the foundations of imperial sway, so that it will last for 10,000 generations. This is

25 博士七十人前爲壽. The 博士 were not only 'great scholars,' but had an official rank. There was what we may call a college of them, consisting of seventy members. 26 僕射周青臣. 27 淳于越. 28 田常,—常 should probably be 恆, as it is given in the T'ung Këen. 29 丞相李斯.

indeed beyond what a stupid scholar can understand. And, moreover, Yuë only talks of things belonging to the Three Dynasties, which are not fit to be models to you. At other times, when the princes were all striving together, they endeavoured to gather the wandering scholars about them; but now, the empire is in a stable condition, and laws and ordinances issue from one *supreme authority.* Let those of the people who abide in their homes give their strength to the toils of husbandry, and those who become scholars should study the various laws and prohibitions. Instead of doing this, however, the scholars do not learn what belongs to the present day, but study antiquity. They go on to condemn the present time, leading the masses of the people astray, and to disorder.

"At the risk of my life, I, the prime minister, say,—Formerly, when the empire was disunited and disturbed, there was no one who could give unity to it. The princes therefore stood up together; constant references were made to antiquity to the injury of the present state; baseless statements were dressed up to confound what was real, and men made a boast of their own peculiar learning to condemn what their rulers appointed. And now, when Your Majesty has consolidated the empire, and, distinguishing black from white, has constituted it a stable unity, they still honour their peculiar learning, and combine together; they teach men what is contrary to your laws. When they hear that an ordinance has been issued, every one sets to discussing it with his learning. In the court, they are dissatisfied in heart; out of it, they keep talking in the streets. While they make a pretence of vaunting their Master, they consider it fine to have extraordinary views of their own. And so they lead on the people to be guilty of murmuring and evil speaking. If these things are not prohibited, Your Majesty's authority will decline, and parties will be formed. The best way is to prohibit them. I pray that all the Records in charge of the Historiographers be burned, excepting those of Ts'in; that, with the exception of those officers belonging to the Board of Great Scholars, all throughout the empire who presume to keep copies of the She-king, or of the Shoo-king, or of the books of the Hundred Schools, be required to go with them to the officers in charge of the several districts, and burn them;[20] that all who may dare to speak together

[20] 悉詣守尉雜燒之

about the She and the Shoo be put to death, and their bodies exposed in the market place; that those who make mention of the past, so as to blame the present, be put to death along with their relatives; that officers who shall know of the violation of those rules and not inform against the offenders, be held equally guilty with them; and that whoever shall not have burned their Books within thirty days after the issuing of the ordinance, be branded and sent to labour on the wall for four years. The only Books which should be spared are those on medicine, divination, and husbandry. Whoever wants to learn the laws may go to the magistrates and learn of them.'

"The imperial decision was—'Approved.'"

The destruction of the scholars is related more briefly. In the year after the burning of the Books, the resentment of the emperor was excited by the remarks and flight of two scholars who had been favourites with him, and he determined to institute a strict inquiry about all of their class in Hëen-yang, to find out whether they had been making ominous speeches about him, and disturbing the minds of the people. The investigation was committed to the Censors,[31] and it being discovered that upwards of 460 scholars had violated the prohibitions, they were all buried alive in pits,[32] for a warning to the empire, while degradation and banishment were employed more strictly than before against all who fell under suspicion. The emperor's eldest son, Foo-soo, remonstrated with him, saying that such measures against those who repeated the words of Confucius and sought to imitate him, would alienate all the people from their infant dynasty, but his interference offended his father so much that he was sent off from court, to be with the general who was superintending the building of the great wall.

8. No attempts have been made by Chinese critics and historians to discredit the record of these events, though some have questioned the extent of the injury inflicted by them on the monuments of their ancient literature.[33] It is important to observe that the edict against the Books did not extend to the Yih-king, which was

[31] 御史悉案問諸生. 諸生傳相告引. [32] 自除犯禁者. 四百六十餘人. 皆阬之咸陽. The meaning of this passage as a whole is sufficiently plain, but I am unable to make out the force of the phrase 自除. [33] See the remarks of Chʻing Këä-tse (夾際鄭氏), of the Sung dynasty, on the subject, in the 文獻通考, Bk. clxxiv. p. 5.

excepted as being a work on divination, nor did it extend to the other classics which were in charge of the Board of Great Scholars. It is still more important to note that the burning took place only three years before the death of the tyrant who commanded it. He died B.C. 209, and the feeble reign of his second son, who succeeded him, lasted only three years. A brief season of disorder and struggling between different chiefs for the supreme authority ensued, but the reign of the founder of the Han dynasty dates from B.C. 201. Thus, eleven years were all which intervened between the order for the burning of the Books and the rise of that family, which signalized itself by the care which it bestowed for their recovery; and from the edict of the tyrant of Ts'in against private individuals having copies in their keeping, to its express abrogation by the emperor Heaou Hwuy, there were only 22 years. We may believe, indeed, that vigorous efforts to carry the edict into effect would not be continued longer than the life of its author,—that is, not for more than about three years. The calamity inflicted on the ancient Books of China by the House of Ts'in could not have approached to anything like a complete destruction of them. There would be no occasion for the scholars of the Han dynasty, in regard to the bulk of their ancient literature, to undertake more than the work of recension and editing.

9. The idea of forgery by them on a large scale is out of the question. The catalogues of Lëang Hin enumerated more than 13,000 volumes of a larger or smaller size, the productions of nearly 600 different writers, and arranged in 38 subdivisions of subjects.[34] In the third catalogue, the first subdivision contained the orthodox writers,[35] to the number of 53, with 836 Works or portions of their Works. Between Mencius and K'ung Keih, the grandson of Confucius, eight different authors have place. The second subdivision contained the Works of the Taouist school,[36] amounting to 993 collections, from 37 different authors. The sixth subdivision contained the Mihist writers,[37] to the number of 6, with their productions in 86 collections. I specify these two subdivisions, because they embraced the Works of schools or sects antagonist to that of Confucius, and some of them still hold a place in Chinese literature,

[34] 凡書六略三十八種。五百九十六家。萬三千二百六十九卷。 [35] 儒家者流。 [36] 道家者流。 [37] 墨家者流。

and contain many references to the five Classics, and to Confucius and his disciples.

10. The inquiry pursued in the above paragraphs conducts us to the conclusion that the materials from which the Classics, as they have come down to us, were compiled and edited in the two centuries preceding our Christian era, were genuine remains, going back to a still more remote period. The injury which they sustained from the dynasty of Ts'in was, I believe, the same in character as that to which they were exposed, during all the time of "the Warring States." It may have been more intense in degree, but the constant warfare which prevailed for some centuries among the different States which composed the empire was eminently unfavourable to the cultivation of literature. Mencius tells us how the princes had made away with many of the records of antiquity, from which their own usurpations and innovations might have been condemned.[38] Still the times were not unfruitful, either in scholars or statesmen, to whom the ways and monuments of antiquity were dear, and the space from the rise of the Ts'in dynasty to Confucius was not very great. It only amounted to 258 years. Between these two periods Mencius stands as a connecting link. Born probably in the year B.C. 371, he reached, by the intervention of K'ung Keih, back to the sage himself, and as his death happened B.C. 288, we are brought down to within nearly half a century of the Ts'in dynasty. From all these considerations we may proceed with confidence to consider each separate Work, believing that we have in these Classics and Books what the great sage of China and his disciples gave to their country more than 2,000 years ago.

38. See Mencius, V, Pt. II. ii. 2.

CHAPTER II.

OF THE CONFUCIAN ANALECTS.

SECTION I.

FORMATION OF THE TEXT OF THE ANALECTS BY THE SCHOLARS OF THE HAN DYNASTY.

1. When the work of collecting and editing the remains of the Classical Books was undertaken by the scholars of Han, there appeared two different copies of the Analects, one from Loo, the native State of Confucius, and the other from Ts'e, the State adjoining. Between these there were considerable differences. The former consisted of twenty Books or Chapters, the same as those into which the Classic is now divided. The latter contained two Books in addition, and in the twenty Books, which they had in common, the chapters and sentences were somewhat more numerous than in the Loo exemplar.

2. The names of several individuals are given, who devoted themselves to the study of those two copies of the Classic. Among the patrons of the Loo copy are mentioned the names of Shing, the prince of Hea, grand-tutor of the heir-apparent, who died at the age of 90, and in the reign of the emperor Seuen (B.C. 72—48);[1] Seaou Wang-che,[2] a general officer, who died in the reign of the emperor Yuen, (B.C. 47–32); Wei Heen, who was premier of the empire from B.C. 70–66; and his son Heuen-shing.[3] As patrons of the Ts'e, copy, we have Wang K'ing, who was a censor in the year B.C. 99;[4] Yung Shang,[5] and Wang Keih,[6] a statesman who died in the beginning of the reign of the emperor Yuen.

3. But a third copy of the Analects was discovered about B.C. 150. One of the sons of the emperor King was appointed king of Loo,[7] in the year B.C. 153, and some time after, wishing to enlarge his palace, he proceeded to pull down the house of the K'ung family, known as that where Confucius himself had lived. While doing so,

[1] 太子大傅夏侯勝. [2] 前將軍蕭望之. [3] 丞相韋賢, 及子玄成. [4] 王卿. [5] 庸生. [6] 中尉王吉. [7] 魯王共 (or 恭).

there were found in the wall copies of the Shoo-king, the Ch'un Ts'ew, the Heaou-king, and the Lun Yu or Analects, which had been deposited there, when the edict for the burning of the Books was issued. They were all written, however, in the most ancient form of the Chinese character,[8] which had fallen into disuse, and the king returned them to the K'ung family, the head of which, K'ung Gan-kwŏ,[9] gave himself to the study of them, and finally, in obedience to an imperial order, published a Work called "The Lun Yu, with Explanations of the Characters, and Exhibition of the Meaning."[10]

4. The recovery of this copy will be seen to be a most important circumstance in the history of the text of the Analects. It is referred to by Chinese writers, as "The old Lun Yu." In the historical narrative which we have of the affair, a circumstance is added which may appear to some minds to throw suspicion on the whole account. The king was finally arrested, we are told, in his purpose to destroy the house, by hearing the sounds of bells, musical stones, lutes, and harpsichords, as he was ascending the steps that led to the ancestral hall or temple. This incident was contrived, we may suppose, by the K'ung family, to preserve the house, or it may have been devised by the historian to glorify the sage, but we may not, on account of it, discredit the finding of the ancient copies of the Books. We have K'ung Gan-kwŏ's own account of their being committed to him, and of the ways which he took to decipher them. The work upon the Analects, mentioned above, has not indeed come down to us, but his labours on the Shoo-king still remain.

5. It has been already stated, that the Lun Yu of Ts'e contained two Books more than that of Loo. In this respect, the old Lun Yu agreed with the Loo exemplar. Those two books were wanting in it as well. The last book of the Loo Lun was divided in it, however, into two, the chapter beginning, "Yaou said," forming a whole Book by itself, and the remaining two chapters formed another Book beginning "Tsze-chang." With this trifling difference, the old and the Loo copies appear to have agreed together.

8 科斗文字,—lit. 'tadpole characters.' They were, it is said, the original forms devised by Ts'ang-Kee, with large heads and fine tails, like the creature from which they were named. See the notes to the preface to the Shoo-king in 'The thirteen Classics.' 9 孔安國. 10 論語訓解. See the Preface to the Lun Yu in 'The thirteen King.' It has been my principal authority in this Section.

6. Chang Yu, prince of Gan-ch'ang, who died B.C. 4, after having sustained several of the highest offices of the empire, instituted a comparison between the exemplars of Loo and Ts'e, with a view to determine the true text. The result of his labours appeared in twenty-one Books, which are mentioned in Lew Hin's catalogue. They were known as the Lun of the prince Chang,[12] and commanded general approbation. To Chang Yu is commonly ascribed the ejecting from the Classic the two additional books which the Ts'e exemplar contained, but Ma Twan-lin prefers to rest that circumstance on the authority of the old Lun, which we have seen was without them.[13] If we had the two Books, we might find sufficient reason from their contents to discredit them. That may have been sufficient for Chang Yu to condemn them as he did, but we can hardly suppose that he did not have before him the old Lun, which had come to light about a century before he published his Work.

7. In the course of the second century, a new edition of the Analects, with a commentary, was published by one of the greatest scholars which China has ever produced, Ch'ing Heuen, known also as Ch'ing K'ang-shing.[14] He died in the reign of the emperor Heen (A.D. 190–220) at the age of 74, and the amount of his labours on the ancient classical literature is almost incredible. While he adopted the Loo Lun as the received text of his time, he compared it minutely with those of Ts'e and the old exemplar. In the last section of this chapter will be found a list of the readings in his commentary different from those which are now acknowledged, in deference to the authority of Choo He, of the Sung dynasty. They are not many, and their importance is but trifling.

8. On the whole, the above statements will satisfy the reader of the care with which the text of the Lun Yu was fixed during the dynasty of Han.

SECTION II.

AT WHAT TIME, AND BY WHOM, THE ANALECTS WERE WRITTEN; THEIR PLAN; AND AUTHENTICITY.

1 At the commencement of the notes upon the first Book, under the heading—"The Title of the Work," I have given the received

11 安昌侯張禹. 12 張侯論. 13 文獻通考, Bk. clxxiv, p. 3.
14 鄭玄, 字康成. 15 孝獻皇帝.

account of its authorship, taken from the "History of Literature" of the western Han dynasty. According to that, the Analects were compiled by the disciples of Confucius, coming together after his death, and digesting the memorials of his discourses and conversations which they had severally preserved. But this cannot be true. We may believe, indeed, that many of the disciples put on record conversations which they had had with their master, and notes about his manners and incidents of his life, and that these have been incorporated with the Work which we have, but that Work must have taken its present form at a period somewhat later.

In Book VIII., chapters iii. and iv., we have some notices of the last days of Ts'ăng Sin, and are told that he was visited on his death-bed by the officer Măng King. Now *King* was the posthumous title of Chung-sun Tsëĕ,[1] and we find him alive, (Le Ke, II. Pt. II. ii. 2) after the death of duke To of Loo,[2] which took place B.C. 490, about fifty years after the death of Confucius.

Again, Book XIX. is all occupied with the sayings of the disciples. Confucius personally does not appear in it. Parts of it, as chapters iii., xii., and xviii., carry us down to a time when the disciples had schools and followers of their own, and were accustomed to sustain their teachings by referring to the lessons which they had heard from the sage.

Thirdly, there is the second chapter of Book XI., the second paragraph of which is evidently a note by the compilers of the Work, enumerating ten of the principal disciples, and classifying them according to their distinguishing characteristics. We can hardly suppose it to have been written while any of the ten were alive. But there is among them the name of Tsze-hea, who lived to the age of about a hundred. We find him, B.C. 406, three quarters of a century after the death of Confucius, at the court of Wei, to the prince of which he is reported to have presented some of the Classical Books.[3]

2. We cannot therefore accept the above account of the origin of the Analects,—that they were compiled by the disciples of Confucius. Much more likely is the view that we owe the work to their disciples. In the note on I. ii. 1, a peculiarity is pointed out in the

1 See Choo He's commentary, in loc.—孟敬子. 魯大夫. 仲孫氏. 名捷. 2 悼公. 3 晉魏斯受經於卜子夏; see the 歷代統紀表, Bk. I. p. 77.

use of the surnames of Yew Jŏ and Tsăng Sin, which has made some Chinese critics attribute the compilation to their followers. But this conclusion does not stand investigation. Others have assigned different portions to different schools. Thus, Book V. is given to the disciples of Tsze-kung; Book XI, to those of Min Tsze-k'een; Book XIV, to Yuen Heen; and Book XVI has been supposed to be interpolated from the Analects of Ts'e. Even if we were to acquiesce in these decisions, we should have accounted only for a small part of the Work. It is better to rest in the general conclusion, that it was compiled by the disciples of the disciples of the sage, making free use of the written memorials concerning him which they had received, and the oral statements which they had heard, from their several masters. And we shall not be far wrong, if we determine its date as about the end of the fourth, or the beginning of the fifth century before Christ.

3. In the critical work on the Four Books, called "Record of Remarks in the village of Yung,"[4] it is observed, "The Analects, in my opinion, were made by the disciples, just like this record of remarks. There they were recorded, and afterwards came a first-rate hand, who gave them the beautiful literary finish which we now witness, so that there is not a character which does not have its own indispensable place."[5] We have seen that the first of these statements contains only a small amount of truth with regard to the materials of the Analects, nor can we receive the second. If one hand or one mind had digested the materials provided by many, the arrangement and style of the work would have been different. We should not have had the same remark appearing in several Books, with little variation, and sometimes with none at all. Nor can we account on this supposition for such fragments as the last chapters of the 9th, 10th, and 16th Books, and many others. No definite plan has been kept in view throughout. A degree of unity appears to belong to some Books more than others, and in general to the first ten more than to those which follow, but there is no progress of thought or illustration of subject from Book to Book. And even in those where

4 榕村語錄.—榕村, 'the village of Yung,' is, I conceive, the writer's *nom de plume*.

5 論語想是門弟子,如語錄一般,記在那裏,後來有一高手,鍊成文理,這樣妙,下字無一不確.

the chapters have a common subject, they are thrown together at random more than on any plan.

4. When the Work was first called the Lun Yu, we cannot tell.[6] The evidence in the preceding section is sufficient to prove that when the Han scholars were engaged in collecting the ancient Books, it came before them, not in broken tablets, but complete, and arranged in Books or Sections, as we now have it. The old Lun was found deposited in the wall of the house which Confucius had occupied, and must have been placed there not later than B.C. 211, distant from the date which I have assigned to the compilation, not much more than a century and a half. That copy, written in the most ancient characters, was, possibly, the autograph of the compilers.

We have the Writings, or portions of the Writings, of several authors of the third and fourth centuries before Christ. Of these, in addition to "The Great Learning," "The Doctrine of the Mean," and "The Works of Mencius," I have looked over the Works of Seun K'ing[7] of the orthodox school, of the philosophers Chwang and Lëĕ of the Tauuist school,[8] and of the heresiarch Mih.[9]

In The Great Learning, Commentary, chapter iv., we have the words of Ana. XII. xiii. In The Doctrine of the Mean, ch. iii., we have Ana. VI. xxvii.; and in ch. xxviii. 5, we have Ana. III. xxiv. In Mencius, II. Pt. I. ii. 19, we have Ana. VII. xxxiii., and in vii. 2, Ana. IV. i.; in III. Pt. I. iv. 11, Ana. VIII. xviii., xix.; in IV. Pt. I. xiv. 1, Ana. XI. xvi. 2; V. Pt. II. vii. 9, Ana. X. xiii. 4.; and in VII. Pt. II. xxxvii. 1, 2, 8, Ana. V. xxi., XIII. xxi., and XVII. xiii. These quotations, however, are introduced by "The Master said," or "Confucius said," no mention being made of any book called "The Lun Yu," or Analects. In The Great Learning, Commentary, x. 15, we have the words of Ana. IV. iii., and in Mencius, III. Pt. II. vii. 3, those of Ana. XVII. i, but without any notice of quotation.

6 In the continuation of the "General Examination of Records and Scholars (續文獻通考), Bk. ccxviii. p. 17, it is said, indeed, on the authority of Wang Ch'ung (王充), a scholar of the 1st century, that when the Work came out of the wall it was named a Chuen or Record (傳), and that it was when K'ung Gan-kwŏ instructed a native of Ts'in, named Foo-k'ing, in it, that it first got the name of Lun Yu:—武帝得論語于孔壁中.皆名曰傳.孔安國以古論教齊人扶卿.始曰論語. If it were so, it is strange the circumstance is not mentioned in Ho An's preface. 7 荀卿. 8 莊子.列子. 9 墨子.

In the Writings of Seun K'ing, Book I. page 2, we find the words of Ana. XV. xxx; p. 6, those of XIV. xxv. In Book VIII. p. 13. we have the words of Ana. II. xvii. But in these three instances there is no mark of quotation.

In the Writings of Chwang, I have noted only one passage where the words of the Analects are reproduced. Ana. XVIII. v. is found, but with large additions, and no reference of quotation, in his treatise on "The state of Men in the world, Intermediate,"[10] placed, that is, between Heaven and Earth. In all those Works, as well as in those of Lëë and Mih, the references to Confucius and his disciples, and to many circumstances of his life, are numerous.[11] The quotations of sayings of his not found in the Analects are likewise many, especially in the Doctrine of the Mean, in Mencius, and in the works of Chwang. Those in the latter are mostly burlesques, but those by the orthodox writers have more or less of classical authority. Some of them may be found in the Kea Yu,[12] or "Family Sayings," and in parts of the Le Ke, while others are only known to us by their occurrence in these Writings. Altogether, they do not supply the evidence, for which I am in quest, of the existence of the Analects as a distinct Work, bearing the name of the Lun Yu, prior to the Ts'in dynasty. They leave the presumption, however, in favour of those conclusions, which arises from the facts stated in the first section, undisturbed. They confirm it rather. They show that there was abundance of materials at hand to the scholars of Han, to compile a much larger Work with the same title, if they had felt it their duty to do the business of compilation, and not that of editing.

SECTION III.

OF COMMENTARIES UPON THE ANALECTS.

1. It would be a vast and unprofitable labour to attempt to give a list of the Commentaries which have been published on this Work. My object is merely to point out how zealously the business of interpretation was undertaken, as soon as the text had been recovered by the scholars of the Han dynasty, and with what industry it has been persevered in down to the present time.

10 人間世. 11 In Mih's chapter against the Literati, he mentions some of the characteristics of Confucius, in the very words of the 10th Book of the Analects. 12 家語.

2. Mention has been made, in Section I. 6, of the Lun of prince Chang, published in the half century before our era. Paou Heen,[1] a distinguished scholar and officer, of the reign of Kwang-woo,[2] the first emperor of the Eastern Han dynasty, A.D. 25–57, and another scholar of the surname Chow,[3] less known but of the same time, published Works, containing arrangements of this into chapters and sentences, with explanatory notes. The critical work of K'ung Gan-kwŏ on the old Lun Yu has been referred to. That was lost in consequence of suspicions under which Gan-kwŏ fell towards the close of the reign of the emperor Woo, but in the time of the emperor Shun, A.D. 126–144, another scholar, Ma Yung,[4] undertook the exposition of the characters in the old Lun, giving at the same time his views of the general meaning. The labours of Ch'ing Heuen in the second century have been mentioned. Not long after his death, there ensued a period of anarchy, when the empire was divided into three governments, well known from the celebrated historical romance, called "The Three States." The strongest of them, the House of Wei, patronized literature, and three of its high officers and scholars, Ch'in K'eun, Wang Suh, and Chow Shang-lëĕ,[5] in the first half, and probably the second quarter, of the third century, all gave to the world their notes on the Analects.

Very shortly after, five of the chief ministers of the Government of Wei, Sun Yung, Ch'ing Ch'ung, Tsaou He, Seun K'ae, and Ho An,[6] united in the production of one great Work, entitled, "A Collection of Explanations of the Lun Yu."[7] It embodied the labours of all the writers which have been mentioned, and having been frequently reprinted by succeeding dynasties, it still remains. The preface of the five compilers, in the form of a memorial to the emperor, so called, of the House of Wei, is published with it, and has been of much assistance to me in writing these sections. Ho An was the leader among them, and the work is commonly quoted as if it were the production of him alone.

1 包咸· 2 光武· 3 周氏· 4 至順帝時,南郡太守,馬融,亦為之訓說· 5 司農,陳羣;太常,王肅;博士,周生烈· 6 光祿大夫,關內侯,孫邕;光祿大夫,鄭沖;散騎常侍,中領軍,安鄉亭侯,曹羲;侍中,荀顗;尚書,駙馬都尉,關內侯,何晏· 7 論語集解·

3. From Ho An downwards, there has hardly been a dynasty which has not contributed its labourers to the illustration of the Analects. In the Leang, which occupied the throne a good part of the sixth century, there appeared the "Comments of Wang K'an,"[8] who to the seven authorities cited by Ho An added other thirteen, being scholars who had deserved well of the Classic during the intermediate time. Passing over other dynasties, we come to the Sung, A.D. 960–1279. An edition of the Classics was published by imperial authority, about the beginning of the 11th century, with the title of "The correct Meaning." The principal scholar engaged in the undertaking was Hing P'ing.[9] The portion of it on the Analects[10] is commonly reprinted in "The Thirteen Classics," after Ho An's explanations. But the names of the Sung dynasty are all thrown into the shade by that of Choo He, than whom China has not produced a greater scholar. He composed, in the 12th century, three Works on the Analects:—the first called "Collected Meanings,"[11] the second, "Collected Comments;"[12] and the third, "Queries."[13] Nothing could exceed the grace and clearness of his style, and the influence which he has exerted on the literature of China has been almost despotic.

The scholars of the present dynasty, however, seem inclined to question the correctness of his views and interpretations of the Classics, and the chief place among them is due to Maou K'e-ling,[14] known by the *nom de plume* of Se-ho.[15] His writings, under the name of "The collected Works of Se-ho,"[16] have been published in 80 volumes, containing between three and four hundred books or sections. He has nine treatises on The Four Books, or parts of them, and deserves to take rank with Ch'ing Heuen and Choo He at the head of Chinese scholars, though he is a vehement opponent of the latter. Most of his writings are to be found also in the great Work called "A collection of Works on the Classics, under the Imperial dynasty of Ts'ing,"[17] which contains 1,400 sections, and is a noble contribution by the present rulers of China to the illustration of its ancient literature.

8 皇侃論語疏. 9 邢昺. 10 論語正義. 11 論語集義. 12 論語集註. 13 論語或問. 14 毛奇齡 15 西河. 16 西河全集. 17 皇清經解.

SECTION IV.

OF VARIOUS READINGS.

In "The Collection of Supplementary Observations on The Four Books,"[1] the second chapter contains a general view of commentaries on the Analects, and from it I extract the following list of various readings of the text found in the comments of Ch'ing Heuen, and referred to in the first section of this chapter.

Book II. i., 拱 for 共; viii., 餕 for 饌; xix., 措 for 錯; xxiii. 1, 十世可知 without 也, for 十世可知也. Book III. vii., in the clause 必也射乎, he makes a full stop at 也; xxi. 1, 主 for 社. Book IV. x., 敵 for 適, and 慕 for 莫. Book V. xxi., he puts a full stop at 子. Book VI. vii., he has not the characters 則吾. Book VII. iv., 晏 for 燕; xxxiv., 子疾 simply, for 子疾病. Book IX. ix., 弁 for 冕. Book XI. xxv. 7, 僎 for 撰, and 饋 for 歸. Book XIII. iii. 6, 于往 for 迂; xviii. 1, 弓 for 躬. Book XIV. xxxi., 謗 for 方; xxxiv. 1, 何是栖栖者與 for 何為是栖栖者與. Book XV. i. 2, 粻 for 糧. Book XVI. i. 13, 封 for 邦. Book XVII. i., 饋 for 歸; xxiv. 2, 絞 for 徼. Book XVIII. iv., 饋 for 歸; viii. 1, 侏 for 朱.

These various readings are exceedingly few, and in themselves insignificant. The student who wishes to pursue this subject at length, is provided with the means in the Work of Teih (? Chih) Keaou-show,[2] expressly devoted to it. It forms sections 449–473 of the Works on the Classics, mentioned at the close of the last section.

[1] 四書摭餘說. [2] 翟教授,四書考異.

CHAPTER III.

OF THE GREAT LEARNING.

SECTION I.

HISTORY OF THE TEXT, AND THE DIFFERENT ARRANGEMENTS OF IT WHICH HAVE BEEN PROPOSED.

1. It has already been mentioned that "The Great Learning" forms one of the Chapters of the Le Ke, or "Record of Rites," the formation of the text of which will be treated of in its proper place. I will only say here, that the Book, or Books, of Rites had suffered much more, after the death of Confucius, than the other ancient Classics which had been collected and digested by him. They were in a more dilapidated condition at the time of the revival of the ancient literature under the Han dynasty, and were then published in three collections, only one of which—the Record of Rites—retains its place among the *King*.

The Record of Rites consists, according to the current arrangement, of 49 Chapters or Books. Lew Heang (see ch. I. sect. II. 2.) took the lead in its formation, and was followed by the two famous scholars, Tae Tih,[1] and his relative, Tae Shing.[2] The first of these reduced upwards of 200 chapters, collected by Heang, to 89, and Shing reduced these again to 46. The three other Books were added in the second century of our era, The Great Learning being one of them, by Ma Yung, mentioned in the last chapter, section III. 2. Since his time, the Work has not received any further additions.

2. In his note appended to what he calls the chapter of "Classical Text," Choo He says that the tablets of the "old copies" of the rest of The Great Learning were considerably out of order. By those old copies, he intends the Work of Ch'ing Heuen, who published his commentary on the Classic, soon after it was completed by the additions of Ma Yung; and it is possible that the tablets were in confusion, and had not been arranged with sufficient care; but such a thing

[1] 戴德. [2] 戴聖. Shing was the son of a cousin of Tih's.

does not appear to have been suspected until the 12th century, nor can any authority from ancient monuments be adduced in its support.

I have related how the ancient Classics were cut on slabs of stone by imperial order, A.D. 175, the text being that which the various literati had determined, and which had been adopted by Ch'ing Heuen. The same work was performed about seventy years later, under the so-called dynasty of Wei, between the years 240 and 248, and the two sets of slabs were set up together. The only difference between them was, that whereas the Classics had been cut in the first instance in three different forms, called, the Seal character, the Pattern style, and the Imperfect form, there was substituted for the latter in the slabs of Wei the oldest form of the characters, similar to that which has been described in connection with the discovery of the old Lun Yu in the wall of Confucius' house. Amid the changes of dynasties, the slabs both of Han and Wei had perished, before the rise of the T'ang dynasty, A.D. 624; but under one of its emperors, in the year 836, a copy of the Classics was again cut on stone, though only in one form of the character. These slabs we can trace down through the Sung dynasty, when they were known as the tablets of Shen.[3] They were in exact conformity with the text of the Classics adopted by Ch'ing Heuen in his commentaries.

The Sung dynasty did not accomplish a similar work itself, nor has any one of the three which have followed it thought it necessary to engrave in stone in this way the ancient Classics. About the middle of the 16th century, however, the literary world in China was startled by a report that the slabs of Wei which contained The Great Learning had been discovered. But this was nothing more than the result of an impudent attempt at an imposition, for which it is difficult to a foreigner to assign any adequate cause. The treatise, as printed from these slabs, has some trifling additions, and many alterations in the order of the text, but differing from the arrangements proposed by Choo He, and by other scholars. There seems to be now no difference of opinion among Chinese critics that the whole affair was a forgery. The text of The Great Learning, as it appears in the Book of Rites with the commentary of Ch'ing

[3] 陝碑

Henen, and was thrice engraved on stone, in three different dynasties, is, no doubt, that which was edited in the Han dynasty by Ma Yung.

3. I have said, that it is possible that the tablets containing the text were not arranged with sufficient care by him, and indeed, any one who studies the treatise attentively, will probably come to the conclusion that the part of it forming the first six chapters of commentary in the present Work is but a fragment. It would not be a difficult task to propose an arrangement of the text different from any which I have yet seen; but such an undertaking would not be interesting out of China. My object here is simply to mention the Chinese scholars who have rendered themselves famous or notorious in their own country, by what they have done in this way. The first was Ch'ing Haou, a native of Loh-yang in Ho-nan province, in the 11th century.[4] His designation was Pih-shun, but since his death he has been known chiefly by the style of Ming-taou,[5] which we may render the Wise-in-doctrine. The eulogies heaped on him by Choo He and others are extravagant, and he is placed immediately after Mencius in the list of great scholars. Doubtless he was a man of vast literary acquirements. The greatest change which he introduced into The Great Learning, was to read *sin*[6] for *ts'in*,[7] at the commencement, making the second object proposed in the treatise to be the *renovation* of the people, instead of *loving* them. This alteration and his various transpositions of the text are found in Maou Se-ho's treatise on "The attested text of The Great Learning."[8]

Hardly less illustrious than Ch'ing Haou was his younger brother Ch'ing E, known by the style of Ching-shuh,[9] and since his death by that of E-ch'uen.[10] He followed Haou in the adoption of the reading "*to renovate*," instead of "*to love*." But he transposed the text differently, more akin to the arrangement afterwards made by Choo He, suggesting also that there were some superfluous sentences in the old text which might conveniently be erased. The Work, as proposed to be read by him, will be found in the volume of Maou just referred to.

We come to the name of Choo He who entered into the labours of the brothers Ch'ing, the younger of whom he styles his Master, in his introductory note to The Great Learning. His arrangement of

[4] 程子顥·字伯淳·河南洛陽人· [5] 明道· [6] 新· [7] 親· [8] 大學證文· [9] 程子頤·字正叔·明道之弟· [10] 伊川·

the text is that now current in all the editions of the Four Books, and it had nearly displaced the ancient text altogether. The sanction of Imperial approval was given to it during the Yuen and Ming dynasties. In the editions of the five *king* published by them, only the names of The Doctrine of the Mean and The Great Learning were preserved. No text of these Books was given, and Se-ho tells us that in the reign of Kea-tsing,[11] the most flourishing period of the Ming dynasty (A.D. 1522–1566), when Wang Wăn-shing,[12] published a copy of The Great Learning, taken from the T'ang edition of the Thirteen *King*, all the officers and scholars looked at one another in astonishment, and were inclined to suppose that the Work was a forgery. Besides adopting the reading of *sin* for *ts'in* from the Ch'ing, and modifying their arrangements of the text, Choo He made other innovations. He first divided the whole into one chapter of Classical text, which he assigned to Confucius, and ten chapters of Commentary, which he assigned to the disciple Tsăng. Previous to him, the whole had been published, indeed, without any specification of chapters and paragraphs. He undertook, moreover, to supply one whole chapter, which he supposed, after his master Ch'ing, to be missing.

Since the time of Choo He, many scholars have exercised their wit on The Great Learning. The Work of Maou Se-ho contains four arrangements of the text, proposed respectively by the scholars Wang Loo-chae,[13] Ke P'ang-san,[14] Kaou King-yih,[15] and Kŏ Hoo-chen.[16] The curious student may examine them there.

Under the present dynasty, the tendency has been to depreciate the labours of Choo He. The integrity of the text of Ch'ing Heuen is zealously maintained, and the simpler method of interpretation employed by him is advocated in preference to the more refined and ingenious schemes of the Sung scholars. I have referred several times in the notes to a Work published a few years ago, under the title of "The Old Text of the sacred *King*, with Commentary and Discussions, by Lo Chung-fan of Nan-hae."[17] I knew the man seventeen years ago. He was a fine scholar, and had taken the second degree, or that of *Keu-jin*. He applied to me in 1843 for Christian baptism, and offended by my hesitancy went and enrolled himself

11 嘉靖. 12 王文成. 13 王魯齋. 14 季彭山. 15 高景逸. 16 葛屺瞻. 17 聖經古本.南海羅仲藩註辨.

among the disciples of another Missionary. He soon, however, withdrew into seclusion, and spent the last years of his life in literary studies. His family have published the work on The Great Learning, and one or two others. He most vehemently impugns nearly every judgment of Choo He, but in his own exhibitions of the meaning he blends many ideas of the Supreme Being and of the condition of human nature, which he had learned from the Christian Scriptures.

SECTION II.

OF THE AUTHORSHIP, AND DISTINCTION OF THE TEXT INTO CLASSICAL TEXT AND COMMENTARY.

1. The authorship of The Great Learning is a very doubtful point, and one on which it does not appear possible to come to a decided conclusion. Choo He, as I have stated in the last section, determined that so much of it was *king*, or Classic, being the very words of Confucius, and that all the rest was *chuen*, or Commentary, being the views of Tsăng Sin upon the sage's words, recorded by *his* disciples. Thus, he does not expressly attribute the composition of the Treatise to Tsăng, as he is generally supposed to do. What he says, however, as it is destitute of external support, is contrary also to the internal evidence. The 4th chapter of commentary commences with "The Master said." Surely, if there were anything more, directly from Confucius, there would be an intimation of it in the same way. Or, if we may allow that short sayings of Confucius might be interwoven with the Work, as in the 15th paragraph of the 10th chapter, without referring them expressly to him, it is too much to ask us to receive the long chapter at the beginning as being from him. With regard to the Work having come from the disciples of Tsăng Sin, recording their master's views, the paragraph in chapter 6th, commencing with "The disciple Tsăng said," seems to be conclusive against that hypothesis. So much we may be sure is Tsăng's, and no more. Both of Choo He's judgments must be set aside. We cannot admit either the distinction of the contents into Classical text and Commentary, or that the Work was the production of Tsăng's disciples.

2. Who then was the author? An ancient tradition attributes it to K'ung Keih, the grandson of Confucius. In a notice published, at the time of their preparation, about the stone slabs of Wei, the following statement by Kea Kwei, a noted scholar of the 1st century is found:—"When K'ung Keih was living, and in straits, in Sung, being afraid lest the lessons of the former sages should become obscure, and the principles of the ancient emperors and kings fall to the ground, he therefore made The Great Learning as the warp of them, and The Doctrine of the Mean, as the woof."[1] This would seem, therefore, to have been the opinion of that early time, and I may say the only difficulty in admitting it is that no mention is made of it by Ch'ing Heuen. There certainly is that agreement between the two treatises, which makes their common authorship not at all unlikely.

3. Though we cannot positively assign the authorship of The Great Learning, there can be no hesitation in receiving it as a genuine monument of the Confucian school. There are not many words in it from the sage himself, but it is a faithful reflection of his teachings, written by some of his followers, not far removed from him by lapse of time. It must synchronize pretty nearly with the Analects, and may be safely referred to the fifth century before our era.

SECTION III.

ITS SCOPE AND VALUE.

1. The worth of The Great Learning has been celebrated in most extravagant terms by many Chinese writers, and there have been foreigners who have not yielded to them in their estimation of it. Pauthier, in the "Argument Philosophique," prefixed to his translation of the Work, says:—"It is evident that the aim of the Chinese philosopher is to exhibit the duties of political government as those of the perfecting of self, and of the practice of virtue by all men. He felt that he had a higher mission than that with which the greater part of ancient and modern philosophers have contented

[1] 唐氏奏疏有曰、虞松校刻石經于魏表、引賈逵之言、曰、孔伋窮居于宋、懼先聖之學不明、而帝王之道墜、故作大學以經之、中庸以緯之; see the 大學證文, 一, p. 5.

themselves; and his immense love for the happiness of humanity, which dominated over all his other sentiments, has made of his philosophy a system of social perfectionating, which, we venture to say, has never been equalled."

Very different is the judgment passed upon the treatise by a writer in the Chinese Repository:—"The *Ta Hëŏ* is a short politico-moral discourse. *Ta Hëŏ*, or 'Superior Learning,' is at the same time both the name and the subject of the discourse; it is the *summum bonum* of the Chinese. In opening this Book, compiled by a disciple of Confucius, and containing his doctrines, we might expect to find a Work like Cicero's *De Officiis;* but we find a very different production, consisting of a few commonplace rules for the maintenance of a good government."[1]

My readers will perhaps think, after reading the present section, that the truth lies between these two representations.

2. I believe that the Book should be styled *T'ae Hëŏ*, and not *Ta Hëŏ*, and that it was so named as setting forth the higher and more extensive principles of moral science, which come into use and manifestation in the conduct of government. When Choo He endeavours to make the title mean—"The principles of Learning, which were taught in the higher schools of antiquity," and tells us how at the age of 15, all the sons of the emperor, with the legitimate sons of the nobles, and high officers, down to the more promising scions of the common people, all entered these seminaries, and were taught the difficult lessons here inculcated, we pity the ancient youth of China. Such "strong meat" is not adapted for the nourishment of youthful minds. But the evidence adduced for the existence of such educational institutions in ancient times is unsatisfactory, and from the older interpretation of the title we advance more easily to contemplate the object and method of the Work.

3. The *object* is stated definitely enough in the opening paragraph: —"What The Great Learning teaches, is—to illustrate illustrious virtue; to love the people; and to rest in the highest excellence." The political aim of the writer is here at once evident. He has before him on one side, *the people*, the masses of the empire, and over against them are those whose work and duty, delegated by Heaven,

1 Chinese Repository, vol. iii, p. 98. 2 太學, not 大學. See the note on the title of the Work, p. 219.

is to govern them, culminating, as a class, in "the son of Heaven,"[3] "the one man,"[4] the emperor. From the 4th and 5th paragraphs, we see that if the lessons of the treatise be learned and carried into practice, the result will be that "illustrious virtue will be illustrated throughout the empire," which will be brought, through all its length and breadth, to a condition of happy tranquillity. This object is certainly both grand and good; and if a reasonable and likely method to secure it were proposed in the Work, language would hardly supply terms adequate to express its value.

4. But the above account of the object of The Great Learning leads us to the conclusion that the student of it should be an emperor. What interest can an ordinary man have in it? It is high up in the clouds, far beyond his reach. This is a serious objection to it, and quite unfits it for a place in schools, such as Choo He contends it once had. Intelligent Chinese, whose minds were somewhat quickened by Christianity, have spoken to me of this defect, and complained of the difficulty they felt in making the book a practical directory for their conduct. "It is so vague and vast," was the observation of one man. The writer, however, has made some provision for the general application of his instructions. He tells us that, from the emperor down to the mass of the people, all must consider the cultivation of the person to be the root, that is, the first thing to be attended to.[5] As in his method, moreover, he reaches from the cultivation of the person to the tranquillization of the Empire, through the intermediate steps of the regulation of the family, and the government of the State,[6] there is room for setting forth principles that parents and rulers generally may find adapted for their guidance.

5. The method which is laid down for the attainment of the great object proposed, consists of seven steps:—the investigation of things; the completion of knowledge; the sincerity of the thoughts; the rectifying of the heart; the cultivation of the person; the regulation of the family; and the government of the State. These form the steps of a climax, the end of which is the empire tranquillized. Pauthier calls the paragraphs where they occur instances of the sorites, or abridged syllogism. But they belong to *rhetoric*, and not to *logic*.

3 天子, Cl. Text, par. 6, 2. 4 一人, Comm. ix. 3. 5 Cl. Text, par. 6. 6 Cl. Text, parr. 4, 5.

6. In offering some observations on these steps, and the writer's treatment of them, it will be well to separate them into those preceding the cultivation of the person, and those following it; and to deal with the latter first.—Let us suppose that the cultivation of the person is all attained, every discordant mental element having been subdued and removed. It is assumed that the regulation of the family will necessarily flow from this. Two short paragraphs are all that are given to the illustration of the point, and they are vague generalities on the subject of men's being led astray by their feelings and affections.

The family being regulated, there will result from it the government of the State. First, the virtues taught in the family have their correspondencies in the wider sphere. Filial piety will appear as loyalty. Fraternal submission will be seen in respect and obedience to elders and superiors. Kindness is capable of universal application. Second, "From the loving example of one family, a whole State becomes loving, and from its courtesies the whole State becomes courteous."[7] Seven paragraphs suffice to illustrate these statements, and short as they are, the writer goes back to the topic of self-cultivation, returning from the family to the individual.

The State being governed, the whole empire will become peaceful and happy. There is even less of connection, however, in the treatment of this theme, between the premiss and the conclusion, than in the two previous chapters. Nothing is said about the relation between the whole empire, and its component States, or any one of them. It is said at once, "What is meant by 'The making the whole empire peaceful and happy depends on the government of the State,' is this.—When the sovereign behaves to his aged, as the aged should be behaved to, the people become filial; when the sovereign behaves to his elders, as elders should be behaved to, the people learn brotherly submission; when the sovereign treats compassionately the young and helpless, the people do the same."[8] This is nothing but a repetition of the preceding chapter, instead of that chapter's being made a step from which to go on to the splendid consummation of the good government of the whole empire.

The words which I have quoted are followed by a very striking enunciation of the golden rule in its negative form, and under the

7 See Comm. ix. 3. 8 See Comm. x. 1.

name of *the measuring square*, and all the lessons of the chapter are connected more or less closely with that. The application of this principle by a ruler, whose heart is in the first place in loving sympathy with the people, will guide him in all the exactions which he lays upon them, and in the selection of ministers, in such a way that he will secure the affections of his subjects, and his throne will be established, for "by gaining the people, the kingdom is gained, and, by losing the people, the kingdom is lost."[9] There are in this part of the treatise many valuable sentiments, and counsels for all in authority over others. The objection to it is, that, as the last step of the climax, it does not rise upon all the others with the accumulated force of their conclusions, but introduces us to new principles of action, and a new line of argument. Cut off the commencement of the first paragraph which connects it with the preceding chapters, and it would form a brief but admirable treatise by itself on the art of government.

This brief review of the writer's treatment of the concluding steps of his method will satisfy the reader that the execution is not equal to the design; and, moreover, underneath all the reasoning, and more especially apparent in the 8th and 9th chapters of commentary (according to the ordinary arrangement of the work), there lies the assumption that example is all but omnipotent. We find this principle pervading all the Confucian philosophy. And doubtless it is a truth, most important in education and government, that the influence of example is very great. I believe, and will insist upon it hereafter in these prolegomena, that we have come to overlook this element in our conduct of administration. It will be well if the study of the Chinese Classics should call attention to it. Yet in them the subject is pushed to an extreme, and represented in an extravagant manner. Proceeding from the view of human nature that it is entirely good, and led astray only by influences from without, the sage of China and his followers attribute to personal example and to instruction a power which we do not find that they actually possess.

7. The steps which precede the cultivation of the person are more briefly dealt with than those which we have just considered. "The cultivation of the person results from the rectifying the heart

[9] Comm. x. 5.

or mind."[10] True, but in The Great Learning very inadequately set forth.

"The rectifying of the mind is realized when the thoughts are made sincere."[11] And the thoughts are sincere, when no self-deception is allowed, and we move without effort to what is right and wrong, "as we love what is beautiful, and as we hate a bad smell."[12] How are we to attain to this state? Here the Chinese moralist fails us. According to Choo He's arrangement of the Treatise, there is only one sentence from which we can frame a reply to the above question. "Therefore," it is said, "the superior man must be watchful over himself when he is alone."[13] Following Choo's 6th chapter of commentary, and forming, we may say, part of it, we have in the old arrangement of The Great Learning all the passages which he has distributed so as to form the previous five chapters. But even from the examination of them, we do not obtain the information which we desire on this momentous inquiry.

6. Indeed, the more I study the Work, the more satisfied I become, that from the conclusion of what is now called the chapter of Classical text to the sixth chapter of Commentary, we have only a few fragments, which it is of no use trying to arrange, so as fairly to exhibit the plan of the author. According to his method, the chapter on the connection between making the thoughts sincere and so rectifying the mental nature, should be preceded by one on the completion of knowledge as the means of making the thoughts sincere, and that again by one on the completion of knowledge by the investigation of things, or whatever else the phrase *kih wuh* may mean. I am less concerned for the loss and injury which this part of the Work has suffered, because the subject of the connection between intelligence and virtue is very fully exhibited in The Doctrine of the Mean, and will come under my notice in the review of that Treatise. The manner in which Choo He has endeavoured to supply the blank about the perfecting of knowledge by the investigation of things is too extravagant. "The Learning for Adults," he says, "at the outset of its lessons, instructs the learner, in regard to all things in the world, to proceed from what knowledge he has of their principles, and pursue his investigation of them, till he reaches the extreme point. After exerting himself for a long time, he will

10 Comm. vii. 1. 11 Comm. Ch. vi. 12 Comm. vi. 1. 13 Comm. vi. 2.

suddenly find himself possessed of a wide and far-reaching penetration. Then, the qualities of all things, whether external or internal, the subtle or the coarse, will be apprehended, and the mind, in its entire substance and its relations to things, will be perfectly intelligent. This is called the investigation of things. This is called the perfection of knowledge."[14] And knowledge must be thus perfected before we can achieve the sincerity of our thoughts, and the rectifying of our hearts! Verily this would be learning not for adults only, but even Methuselahs would not be able to compass it. Yet for centuries this has been accepted as the orthodox exposition of the Classic. Lo Chung-fan does not express himself too strongly when he says that such language is altogether incoherent. The author would only be "imposing on himself and others."

9. The orthodox doctrine of China concerning the connection between intelligence and virtue is most seriously erroneous, but I will not lay to the charge of the author of The Great Learning the wild representations of the commentator of the twelfth century, nor need I make here any remarks on what the doctrine really is. After the exhibition which I have given, my readers will probably conclude that the Work before us is far from developing, as Pauthier asserts, "a system of social perfectionating which has never been equalled."

10. The Treatise has undoubtedly great merits, but they are not to be sought in the severity of its logical processes, or the large-minded prosecution of any course of thought. We shall find them in the announcement of certain seminal principles, which, if recognized in government and the regulation of conduct, would conduce greatly to the happiness and virtue of mankind. I will conclude these observations by specifying four such principles.

First, The writer conceives nobly of the object of government, that it is to make its subjects happy and good. This may not be a sufficient account of that object, but it is much to have it so clearly laid down to "all kings and governors," that they are to love the people, ruling not for their own gratification, but for the good of those over whom they are exalted by Heaven. Very important also is the statement that rulers have no divine right but what springs from the discharge of their duty. "The decree does not always rest

14 Suppl. to Comm. Ch. v.

on them. Goodness obtains it, and the want of goodness loses it."[15]

Second, The insisting on personal excellence in all who have authority in the family, the State, and the empire, is a great moral and social principle. The influence of such personal excellence may be overstated, but by the requirement of its cultivation the writer deserved well of his country.

Third, Still more important than the requirement of such excellence, is the principle that it must be rooted in the state of the heart, and be the natural outgrowth of internal sincerity. "As a man thinketh in his heart, so is he." This is the teaching alike of Solomon and the author of The Great Learning.

Fourth, I mention last the striking exhibition which we have of the golden rule, though only in its negative form. "What a man dislikes in his superiors, let him not display in the treatment of his inferiors; what he dislikes in inferiors, let him not display in his service of his superiors; what he dislikes in those who are before him, let him not therewith precede those who are behind him; what he dislikes in those who are behind him, let him not therewith follow those who are before him; what he dislikes to receive on the right, let him not bestow on the left; what he dislikes to receive on the left, let him not bestow on the right:—this is what is called the principle with which, as with a measuring square, to regulate one's conduct."[16]

The Work which contains those principles cannot be thought meanly of. They are "commonplace," as the writer in the Chinese Repository calls them, but they are at the same time eternal verities.

15 Comm. x. 11. 16 Comm. x. 2.

CHAPTER IV.

THE DOCTRINE OF THE MEAN.

SECTION I.

ITS PLACE IN THE LE KE, AND ITS PUBLICATION SEPARATELY.

1. The Doctrine of the Mean was one of the treatises which came to light in connection with the labours of Lew Heang, and its place as the 31st Book in the Le Ke was finally determined by Ma Yung and Ch'ing Heuen.

2. But while it was thus made to form a part of the great collection of Works on Ceremonies, it maintained a separate footing of its own. In Lew Hin's catalogue of the Classical Works, we find "Two *p'ëen* of Observations on the Chung Yung."[1] In the Records of the dynasty of Suy (A.D. 589–617), in the chapter on the History of Literature,[2] there are mentioned three Works on the Chung Yung;—the first called "The Record of the Chung Yung," in two *keuen*, attributed to Tae Yung, a scholar who flourished about the middle of the 5th century; the second, "A Paraphrase and Commentary on the Chung Yung," attributed to the emperor Woo (A.D. 502–549) of the Leang dynasty, in one *keuen*, and the third, "A Private Record, Determining the Meaning of the Chung Yung," in five *keuen*, the author, or supposed author, of which is not mentioned.[3]

It thus appears, that the Chung Yung had been published and commented on separately, long before the time of the Sung dynasty. The scholars of that, however, devoted special attention to it, the way being led by the famous Chow Lëen-k'e.[4] He was followed by the two brothers Ch'ing, but neither of them published upon it. At last came Choo He, who produced his Work called "The Chung

1 中庸說二篇. 2 隋書,卷三十二,志第二十七,經籍一, p. 12. 3 禮記中庸傳,二卷,宋散騎常侍戴顒撰; 中庸講疏,一卷,梁武帝撰; 私記制旨中庸義,五卷. 4 周濂溪.

Yung, in Chapters and Sentences,"[3] which was made the text book of the Classic at the literary examinations, by the fourth Emperor of the Yuen dynasty (A.D. 1312–1320), and from that time the name merely of the Treatise was retained in editions of the Le Ke. Neither text nor ancient commentary was given.

Under the present dynasty it is not so. In the superb edition of "The Five *King*" edited by a numerous committee of scholars towards the end of K'ang He's reign, the Chung Yung is published in two parts, the ancient commentaries from "The Thirteen *King*" being given side by side with those of Choo He.

SECTION II.

ITS AUTHOR; AND SOME ACCOUNT OF HIM.

1. The composition of the Chung Yung is attributed to K'ung Keih, the grandson of Confucius. Chinese inquirers and critics are agreed on this point, and apparently on sufficient grounds. There is indeed no internal evidence in the Work to lead us to such a conclusion. Among the many quotations of Confucius' words and references to him, we might have expected to find some indication that the sage was the grandfather of the author, but nothing of the kind is given. The external evidence, however, or that from the testimony of authorities, is very strong. In Sze-ma Ts'een's Historical Records, published B.C. 103, it is expressly said that "Tsze-sze made the Chung Yung."[1] And we have a still stronger proof, a century earlier, from Tsze-sze's own descendant, K'ung Foo, whose words are, "Tsze-sze compiled the Chung Yung in 49 *p'ëen*."[2] We may, therefore, accept the received account without hesitation.

2. As Keih, spoken of chiefly by his designation of Tsze-sze, thus occupies a distinguished place in the classical literature of China, it

[3] 中庸章句

[1] 子思作中庸; see the 史記四十七孔子世家. [2] This K'ung Foo (孔鮒) was that descendant of Confucius, who hid several books in the wall of his house, on the issuing of the imperial edict for their burning. He was a writer himself, and his Works are referred to under the title of 孔叢子. I have not seen them, but the statement given above is found in the 四書摭餘說, art. 中庸—孔叢子云子思撰中庸之書四十九篇.

may not be out of place to bring together here a few notices of him gathered from reliable sources.

He was the son of Le, whose death took place B.C. 482, four years before that of the sage, his father. I have not found it recorded in what year he was born. Sze-ma Ts'een says he died at the age of 62. But this is evidently wrong, for we learn from Mencius that he was high in favour with the duke Muh of Loo,[3] whose accession to that principality dates in B.C. 408, seventy years after the death of Confucius. In the "Plates and Notices of the Worthies, sacrificed to in the Sage's Temples,"[4] it is supposed that the 62 in the Historical Records should be 82.[5] It is maintained by others that Tsze-sze's life was protracted beyond 100 years.[6] This variety of opinions simply shows that the point cannot be positively determined. To me it seems that the conjecture in the Sacrificial Canon must be pretty near the truth.[7]

During the years of his boyhood, then, Tsze-sze must have been with his grandfather, and received his instructions. It is related, that one day, when he was alone with the sage, and heard him sighing, he went up to him, and, bowing twice, inquired the reason of his grief. "Is it," said he, "because you think that your descendants, through not cultivating themselves, will be unworthy of you? Or is it that, in your admiration of the ways of Yaou and Shun, you are vexed that you fall short of them?" "Child," replied Confucius, "how is it that you know my thoughts?" "I have often," said Tsze-sze, "heard from you the lesson, that when the father has gathered and prepared the firewood, if the son cannot carry the bundle, he is to be pronounced degenerate and unworthy. The remark comes frequently into my thoughts, and fills me with great apprehensions." The sage was delighted. He smiled and said, "Now, indeed, shall

3 魯穆公. 4 聖廟祀典圖考. 5 或以六十二爲八十二之誤. 82 and 62 may more easily be confounded, as written in Chinese than with the Roman figures. 6 See the 四書集證, on the preface to the Chung Yung.—年百餘歲卒. 7 Le himself was born in Confucius' 21st year, and if Tsze-sze had been born in Le's 21st year, he must have been 103 at the time of duke Muh's accession. But the tradition is, that Tsze-sze was a pupil of Tsang Sin who was born B.C. 504. We must place his birth therefore considerably later, and suppose him to have been quite young when his father died. I was talking once about the question with a Chinese friend, who observed:—"Le was 50 when he died, and his wife married again into a family of Wei. We can hardly think, therefore, that she was any thing like that age. Le could not have married so soon as his father did. Perhaps he was about 40 when Keih was born."

I be without anxiety! My undertakings will not come to nought. They will be carried on and flourish."[8]

After the death of Confucius, Keih became a pupil, it is said, of the philosopher Tsăng. But he received his instructions with discrimination, and in one instance which is recorded in the Le Ke, the pupil suddenly took the place of the master. We there read:—"Tsăng said to Tsze-sze, 'Keih, when I was engaged in mourning for my parents, neither congee nor water entered my mouth for seven days.' Tsze-sze answered, 'In ordering their rules of propriety, it was the design of the ancient kings that those who would go beyond them should stoop and keep by them, and that those who could hardly reach them should stand on tiptoe to do so. Thus it is that the superior man, in mourning for his parents, when he has been three days without water or congee, takes a staff to enable himself to rise."[9]

While he thus condemned the severe discipline of Tsăng, Tsze-sze appears in various incidents which are related of him, to have been himself more than sufficiently ascetic. As he was living in great poverty, a friend supplied him with grain, which he readily received. Another friend was emboldened by this to send him a bottle of wine, but he declined to receive it. "You receive your corn from other people," urged the donor, "and why should you decline my gift, which is of less value? You can assign no ground in reason for it, and if you wish to show your independence, you should do so completely." "I am so poor," was the reply, "as to be in want, and being afraid lest I should die and the sacrifices not be offered to my ancestors, I accept the grain as an alms. But the wine and the dried flesh which you offer to me are the appliances of a feast. For a poor man to be feasting is certainly unreasonable. This is the ground of my refusing your gift. I have no thought of asserting my independence."[10]

To the same effect is the account of Tsze-sze, which we have from Lew Heang. That scholar relates:—"When Keih was living in Wei, he wore a tattered coat, without any lining, and in 30 days had only 9 meals. T'ëen Tsze-fang having heard of his distress, sent a messenger to him with a coat of fox-fur, and being afraid that he might

8 See the 四書集證, in the place just quoted from. For the incident we are indebted to Kung Foo; see note 2. 9. Le Ke, II. Pt. I. ii. 7. 10, 11 See the 四書集證, as above.

not receive it, he added the message,—'When I borrow from a man, I forget it; when I give a thing, I part with it freely as if I threw it away.' Tsze-sze declined the gift thus offered, and when Tsze-fang said, 'I have, and you have not; why will you not take it?' he replied, 'You give away so rashly, as if you were casting your things into a ditch. Poor as I am, I cannot think of my body as a ditch, and do not presume to accept your gift."[11]

Tsze-sze's mother married again, after Le's death, into a family of Wei. But this circumstance, which is not at all creditable in Chinese estimation, did not alienate his affections from her. He was in Loo when he heard of her death, and proceeded to weep in the temple of his family. A disciple came to him and said, "Your mother married again into the family of the Shoo, and do you weep for her in the temple of the K'ung?" "I am wrong," said Tsze-sze, "I am wrong;" and with these words he went to weep elsewhere.[12]

In his own married relation he does not seem to have been happy, and for some cause, which has not been transmitted to us, he divorced his wife, following in this, it would appear, the example of Confucius. On her death, her son, Tsze-shang,[13] did not undertake any mourning for her. Tsze-sze's disciples were surprised and questioned him. "Did not your father," they asked, "mourn for his mother who had been divorced?" "Yes," was the reply. "Then why do you not cause Pih[14] to mourn for his mother?" Tsze-sze answered, "My father failed in nothing to pursue the proper path. His observances increased or decreased as the case required. But I cannot attain to this. While she was my wife, she was Pih's mother; when she ceased to be my wife, she ceased to be Pih's mother." The custom of the K'ung family not to mourn for a mother who had left it herself, or been divorced, took its rise from Tsze-sze.[15]

These few notices of K'ung Keih in his more private relations bring him before us as a man of strong feeling and strong will, independent, and with a tendency to asceticism in his habits.

As a public character, we find him at the ducal courts of Wei, Sung, Loo, and Pe, and at each of them held in high esteem by the

12 See the Le Ke, II. Pt. II. iii. 13. 庶氏之母死 must be understood as I have done above, and not with Ch'ing Heuen,—"Your mother was born a Miss Shoo." 13 子上,—this was the designation of Tsze-sze's son. 14 白,—this was Tsze-shang's name. 15 See the Le Ke, II. Pt. I. i. 1.

rulers. To Wei he was carried probably by the fact of his mother having married into that State. We are told that the prince of Wei received him with great distinction and lodged him honourably. On one occasion he said to him, "An officer of the State of Loo, you have not despised this small and narrow Wei, but have bent your steps hither to comfort and preserve it;—vouchsafe to confer your benefits upon me." Tsze-sze replied, "If I should wish to requite your princely favour with money and silks, your treasuries are already full of them, and I am poor. If I should wish to requite it with good words, I am afraid that what I should say would not suit your ideas, so that I should speak in vain, and not be listened to. The only way in which I can requite it, is by recommending to your notice men of worth." The duke said, "Men of worth is exactly what I desire." "Nay," said Keih, "you are not able to appreciate them." "Nevertheless," was the reply, "I should like to hear whom you consider deserving that name." Tsze-sze replied, "Do you wish to select your officers for the name they may have, or for their reality?" "For their reality, certainly," said the duke. His guest then said, "In the eastern borders of your State, there is one Le Yin, who is a man of real worth." "What were his grandfather and father?" asked the duke. "They were husbandmen," was the reply, on which the duke broke into a loud laugh, saying, "I do not like husbandry. The son of a husbandman cannot be fit for me to employ. I do not put into office all the cadets of those families even in which office is hereditary." Tsze-sze observed, "I mention Le Yin because of his abilities; what has the fact of his forefathers being husbandmen to do with the case? And moreover, the duke of Chow was a great sage, and K'ang-shuh was a great worthy. Yet if you examine their beginnings, you will find that from the business of husbandry they came forth to found their States. I did certainly have my doubts that in the selection of your officers you did not have regard to their real character and capacity." With this the conversation ended. The duke was silent.[16]

Tsze-sze was naturally led to K'ung, as the Sung family originally sprang from that principality. One account, quoted in "The Four

16 See the 氏姓譜·卷一百二·孔氏·孔伋.

Books, Text and Commentary, with Proofs and Illustrations,"[17] says that he went thither in his 16th year, and having foiled an officer of the State, named Yŏ Sŏ, in a conversation on the Shoo-king, his opponent was so irritated at the disgrace put on him by a youth, that he listened to the advice of evil counsellors, and made an attack on him to put him to death. The duke of Sung, hearing the tumult, hurried to the rescue, and when Keih found himself in safety, he said, "When king Wăn was imprisoned in Yew-le, he made the Yih of Chow. My grandfather made the Ch'un Ts'ew after he had been in danger in Ch'in and Ts'ae. Shall I not make something when rescued from such a risk in Sung?" Upon this he made the Chung Yung in 49 *p'ëen*.

According to this account, the Chung Yung was the work of Tsze-sze's early manhood, and the tradition has obtained a wonderful prevalence. The notice in "The Sacrificial Canon" says, on the contrary, that it was the work of his old age, when he had finally settled in Loo, which is much more likely.[18]

Of Tsze-sze in Pe, which could hardly be said to be out of Loo, we have only one short notice,—in Mencius, V. Pt. II. iii. 3, where the duke Hwuy of Pe is introduced as saying, "I treat Tsze-sze as my master."

We have fuller accounts of him in Loo where he spent all the latter years of his life, instructing his disciples to the number of several hundred,[19] and held in great reverence by the duke Muh. The duke indeed wanted to raise him to the highest office, but he declined this, and would only occupy the position of a "guide, philosopher, and friend." Of the attention which he demanded, however, instances will be found in Mencius, II. Pt. II. xi. 3; V. Pt. II. vi. 5, and vii. 3. In his intercourse with the duke he spoke the truth to him fearlessly. In the "Cyclopaedia of Surnames,"[20] I find the following conversations, but I cannot tell from what source they are extracted into that Work.—"One day, the duke said to Tsze-sze, 'The officer

17 This is the Work so often referred to as the 四書集證, the full title being 四書經註集證. The passage here translated from it will be found in the place several times referred to in this section. 18 The author of the 四書摭餘說 adopts the view that the Work was composed in Sung. Some have advocated this from ch. xxviii. 5, compared with Ana. III. ix., "it being proper," they say, "that Tsze-sze, writing in Sung, should not depreciate it as Confucius had done, out of it!" 19 See in the 'Sacrificial Canon,' on Tsze-sze. 20 This is the Work referred to in note 14.

Heen told me that you do good without wishing for any praise from men;—is it so?' Tsze-sze replied, 'No, that is not my feeling. When I cultivate what is good, I wish men to know it, for when they know it and praise me, I feel encouraged to be more zealous in the cultivation. This is what I desire, and am not able to obtain. If I cultivate what is good, and men do not know it, it is likely that in their ignorance they will speak evil of me. So by my good-doing I only come to be evil spoken of. This is what I do not desire, but am not able to avoid. In the case of a man, who gets up at cock-crowing to practise what is good, and continues sedulous in the endeavour till midnight, and says at the same time that he does not wish men to know it, lest they should praise him, I must say of such a man, that if he be not deceitful he is stupid.'"

Another day, the duke asked Tsze-sze saying, "Can my State be made to flourish." "It may," was the reply. "And how?" Tsze-sze said, "O prince, if you and your ministers will only strive to realize the government of the duke of Chow and of Pih-k'in; practising their transforming principles, sending forth wide the favours of your ducal house, and not letting advantages flow in private channels;—if you will thus conciliate the affections of the people, and at the same time cultivate friendly relations with neighbouring States, your kingdom will soon begin to flourish."

On one occasion, the duke asked whether it had been the custom of old for ministers to go into mourning for a prince whose service and State they had left. Tsze-sze replied to him, "Of old, princes advanced their ministers to office according to propriety, and dismissed them in the same way, and hence there was that rule. But now-a-days, princes bring their ministers forward as if they were going to take them on their knees, and send them away as if they would cast them into an abyss. If they do not treat them as their greatest enemies, it is well.—How can you expect the ancient practice to be observed in such circumstances?"[21]

These instances may suffice to illustrate the character of Tsze-sze, as it was displayed in his intercourse with the princes of his time. We see the same independence which he affected in private life, and a dignity not unbecoming the grandson of Confucius. But we miss the reach of thought and capacity for administration which belonged

[21] This conversation is given in the Le Ke, II. Pt. II. ii. 1.

to the Sage. It is with him, however, as a thinker and writer that we have to do, and his rank in that capacity will appear from the examination of the Chung Yung in the section that follows. His place in the temples of the Sage has been that of one of his four assessors, since the year 1267. He ranks with Yen Hwuy, Tsăng Sin, and Mencius, and bears the title of "The Philosopher Tsze-sze, Transmitter of the Sage."[23]

[23] 述聖子思子.

SECTION III.

ITS INTEGRITY.

1. In the testimony of K'ung Foo, which has been adduced to prove the authorship of the Chung Yung, it is said that the Work consisted originally of 49 *p'ëen*. From this statement it is argued by some, that the arrangement of it in 33 chapters, which originated with Choo He, is wrong;[1] but this does not affect the question of integrity, and the character *p'ëen* is so vague and indefinite, that we cannot affirm that K'ung Foo meant to tell us by it that Tsze-sze himself divided his Treatise into so many paragraphs or chapters.

It is on the entry in Lew Hin's catalogue, quoted Section 1,—"Two *p'ëen* of observations on the Chung Yung," that the integrity of the present Work is called in question. Yen Sze-koo, of the T'ang dynasty, has a note on that entry to the effect:—"There is now the Chung Yung in the Le Ke in one *p'ëen*. But that is not the original Treatise here mentioned, but only a branch from it."[2] Wang Wei, a writer of the Ming dynasty, says:—"Anciently, the Chung Yung consisted of two *p'ëen*, as appears from the History of Literature of the Han dynasty, but in the Le Ke we have only one *p'ëen*, which Choo He, when he made his 'Chapters and Sentences,' divided into 33 chapters. The old Work in two *p'ëen* is not to be met with now."[3]

[1] See the 四書摭餘說, art. 中庸. [2] 顏師古曰, 今禮記有中庸一篇, 亦非本禮經, 蓋此之流. [3] 王氏禕曰, 中庸古有二篇, 見漢藝文志, 而在禮記中者一篇而已, 朱子為章句, 因其一篇者, 分為三十三章, 而古所謂二篇者不可見矣.

These views are based on a misinterpretation of the entry in the Catalogue. It does not speak of two *p'ëen* of the Chung Yung, but of *two p'ëen of Observations* thereon. The Great Learning carries on its front the evidence of being incomplete, but the student will not easily believe that the Doctrine of the Mean is so. I see no reason for calling its integrity in question, and no necessity therefore to recur to the ingenious device employed in the edition of the five *king* published by the imperial authority of K'ang He, to get over the difficulty which Wang Wei supposes. It there appears in two *p'ëen*, of which we have the following account from the author of "Supplemental Remarks upon the Four Books:"—"The proper course now is to consider the first 20 chapters in Choo He's arrangement as making up the first *p'ëen*, and the remaining 13 as forming the second. In this way we retain the old form of the Treatise, and do not come into collision with the views of Choo. For this suggestion we are indebted to Loo Wang-chae" (an author of the Sung dynasty).[4]

4 See the 四書摭餘說, art. 中庸.

SECTION IV.

ITS SCOPE AND VALUE.

1. The Doctrine of the Mean is a work not easy to understand. "It first," says the philosopher Ch'ing, "speaks of one principle; it next spreads this out and embraces all things; finally, it returns and gathers them up under the one principle. Unroll it, and it fills the universe; roll it up, and it retires and lies hid in secrecy."[1] There is this advantage, however, to the student of it, that, more than most other Chinese Treatises, it has a beginning, a middle, and an end. The first chapter stands to all that follows in the character of a text, containing several propositions of which we have the expansion or development. If that development were satisfactory, we should be able to bring our own minds *en rapport* with that of the author. Unfortunately it is not so. As a writer he belongs to the intuitional school more than to the logical. This is well put in the "Continuation of the General Examination of Literary Monuments and Learned Men,"—"The philosopher Tsăng reached his conclusions by following in the train of things, watching and examining;

1 See the Introductory note, pp. 246, 247.

whereas Tsze-sze proceeds directly and reaches to Heavenly virtue. His was a mysterious power of discernment, approaching to that of Yen Hwuy."[2] We must take the Book and the author, however, as we have them, and get to their meaning, if we can, by assiduous examination and reflection.

2. "Man has received his *nature* from *Heaven*. Conduct in accordance with that nature constitutes what is right and true,—is a pursuing of the proper *path*. The cultivation or regulation of that path is what is called *instruction*." It is with these axioms that the Treatise commences, and from such an introduction we might expect that the writer would go on to unfold the various principles of duty, derived from an analysis of man's moral constitution.

Confining himself, however, to the second axiom, he proceeds to say that "the path may not for an instant be left, and that the superior man is cautious and careful in reference to what he does not see, and fearful and apprehensive in reference to what he does not hear. There is nothing more visible than what is secret, and nothing more manifest than what is minute, and therefore the superior man is watchful over his *aloneness*." This is not all very plain. Comparing it with the 6th chapter of Commentary in the Great Learning, it seems to inculcate what is there called "making the thoughts sincere." The passage contains an admonition about equivalent to that of Solomon,—"Keep thy heart with all diligence, for out of it are the issues of life."

The next paragraph seems to speak of *the nature* and *the path* under other names. "While there are no movements of pleasure, anger, sorrow, or joy, we have what may be called the state of *equilibrium*. When those feelings have been moved, and they all act in the due degree, we have what may be called the state of *harmony*. This equilibrium is the great root of the world and this harmony is its universal path." What is here called "the state of equilibrium," is the same as the nature given by Heaven, considered absolutely in itself, without deflection or inclination. This nature acted on from without, and responding with the various emotions, so as always "to hit"[3] the mark with entire correctness, produces the state of harmony,

2 See the 續文獻通考, Bk. ccix., art. 子思,—曾子得之于閱事省察,而子思之學,則直達天德,庶幾顏氏之妙悟.
3 中節.

and such harmonious response is the path along which all human activities should proceed.

Finally, "Let the states of equilibrium and harmony exist in perfection, and a happy order will prevail throughout heaven and earth, and all things will be nourished and flourish." Here we pass into the sphere of mystery and mysticism. The language, according to Choo He, "describes the meritorious achievements and transforming influence of sage and spiritual men in their highest extent." From the path of duty, where we tread on solid ground, the writer suddenly raises us aloft on wings of air, and will carry us we know not where, and to we know not what.

3. The paragraphs thus presented, and which constitute Choo He's first chapter, contain the sum of the whole Work. This is acknowledged by all;—by the critics who disown Choo He's interpretations of it, as freely as by him.[4] Revolving them in my own mind often and long, I collect from them the following as the ideas of the author:—1st, Man has received from Heaven a moral nature by which he is constituted a law to himself; 2d, Over this nature man requires to exercise a jealous watchfulness; and 3d, As he possesses it, absolutely and relatively, in perfection, or attains to such possession of it, he becomes invested with the highest dignity and power, and may say to himself—"I am a god; yea, I sit in the seat of God." I will not say here that there is blasphemy in the last of these ideas; but do we not have in them the same combination which we found in The Great Learning,—a combination of the ordinary and the extraordinary, the plain and the vague, which is very perplexing to the mind, and renders the Book unfit for the purposes of mental and moral discipline?

And here I may inquire whether we do right in calling the Treatise by any of the names which foreigners have hitherto used for it? In the note on the title, pp. 246, 247, I have entered a little into this question. The Work is not at all what a reader must expect to find in what he supposes to be a treatise on "The Golden Medium," "The Invariable Mean," or "The Doctrine of the Mean." These names are descriptive only of a portion of it. Where the phrase *Chung Yung*

4 Compare Choo He's language in his concluding note to the 1st chapter:—楊氏所謂一篇之體要 and Maou Se-ho's, in his 中庸說卷一, p. 11:—此中庸一書之綱要也.

occurs in the quotations from Confucius, in nearly every chapter from the 2d to the 11th, we do well to translate it by "the course of the Mean," or some similar terms; but the conception of it in Tsze-sze's mind was of a different kind, as the preceding analysis of the first chapter sufficiently shows.

4. I may return to this point of the proper title for the Work again, but in the mean time we must proceed with the analysis of it.—The ten chapters from the 2d to the 11th constitute the second part, and in them Tsze-sze quotes the words of Confucius, "for the purpose," according to Choo He, "of illustrating the meaning of the first chapter." Yet, as I have just intimated, they do not to my mind do this. Confucius bewails the rarity of the practice of the Mean, and graphically sets forth the difficulty of it. "The empire, with its component States and families, may be ruled; dignities and emoluments may be declined; naked weapons may be trampled under foot; but the course of the Mean can not be attained to."[5] "The knowing go beyond it, and the stupid do not come up to it."[6] Yet some have attained to it. Shun did so, humble and ever learning from people far inferior to himself;[7] and Yen Hway did so, holding fast whatever good he got hold of, and never letting it go?[8] Tsze-loo thought the Mean could be taken by storm, but Confucius taught him better.[9] And in fine, it is only the sage who can fully exemplify the Mean.[10]

All these citations do not throw any light on the ideas presented in the first chapter. On the contrary they interrupt the train of thought. Instead of showing us how virtue, or the path of duty is in accordance with our Heaven-given nature, they lead us to think of it as a mean between two extremes. Each extreme may be a violation of the law of our nature, but that is not made to appear. Confucius' sayings would be in place in illustrating the doctrine of the Peripatetics, "which placed all virtue in a medium between opposite vices."[11] Here in the Chung Yung of Tsze-sze I have always felt them to be out of place.

5. In the 12th chapter Tsze-sze speaks again himself, and we seem at once to know the voice. He begins by saying that "the way of the superior man reaches far and wide, and yet is secret,"

5 Ch. ix. 6 Ch. iv. 7 Ch. iv. 8 Ch. viii. 9 Ch. x. 10 Ch. xi. 11 Encyclopædia Britannica, Preliminary Dissertation, p. 316, latest edition.

ly which he means to tell us that the path of duty is to be pursued everywhere and at all times, while yet the secret spring and rule of it is near at hand, in the Heaven-conferred nature, the individual consciousness, with which no stranger can intermeddle. Choo He, as will be seen in the notes, gives a different interpretation of the utterance. But the view which I have adopted is maintained convincingly by Maou Se-ho in the second part of his "Observations on the Chung Yung." With this chapter commences the third part of the Work, which embraces also the eight chapters which follow. "It is designed," says Choo He, "to illustrate what is said in the first chapter that "the path may not be left." But more than that one sentence finds its illustration here. Tsze-sze had reference in it also to what he had said—"The superior man does not wait till he sees things to be cautious, nor till he hears things to be apprehensive. There is nothing more visible than what is secret, and nothing more manifest than what is minute. Therefore, the superior man is watchful over himself when he is alone."

It is in this portion of the Chung Yung that we find a good deal of moral instruction which is really valuable. Most of it consists of sayings of Confucius, but the sentiments of Tsze-sze himself in his own language are interspersed with them. The sage of China has no higher utterances than those which are given in the 13th chapter. —"The path is not far from man. When men try to pursue a course which is far from the common indications of consciousness, this course cannot be considered *the path*. In the Book of Poetry it is said—

'In hewing an axe-handle, in hewing an axe-handle,
The pattern is not far off.'

We grasp one axe-handle to hew the other, and yet if we look askance from the one to the other, we may consider them as apart. Therefore, the superior man governs men according to their nature, with what is proper to them; and as soon as they change what is wrong, he stops. When one cultivates to the utmost the moral principles of his nature, and exercises them on the principle of reciprocity, he is not far from the path. What you do not like when done to yourself, do not do to others.

"In the way of the superior man there are four things, to none of which have I as yet attained.—To serve my father as I would require my son to serve me: to this I have not attained; to serve my elder brother as I would require my younger brother to serve me: to this I have not attained; to serve my prince as I would require my minister to serve me: to this I have not attained; to set the example in behaving to a friend as I would require him to behave to me: to this I have not attained. Earnest in practising the ordinary virtues, and careful in speaking about them; if in his practice he has anything defective, the superior man dares not but exert himself, and if in his words he has any excess, he dares not allow himself such license. Thus his words have respect to his actions, and his actions have respect to his words;—is it not just an entire sincerity which marks the superior man?"

We have here the golden rule in its negative form expressly propounded:—"What you do not like when done to yourself, do not do to others." But in the paragraph which follows we have the rule virtually in its positive form. Confucius recognizes the duty of taking the initiative,—of behaving himself to others in the first instance as he would that they should behave to him. There is a certain narrowness, indeed, in that the sphere of its operations seems to be confined to the relations of society, which are spoken of more at large in the 20th chapter, but let us not grudge the tribute of our warm approbation to the sentiments.

This chapter is followed by two from Tsze-sze, to the effect that the superior man does what is proper in every change of his situation, always finding his rule in himself; and that in his practice there is an orderly advance from step to step,—from what is near to what is remote. Then follow five chapters from Confucius: —the first, on the operation and influence of spiritual beings, to show "the manifestness of what is minute, and the irrepressibleness of sincerity;" the second, on the filial piety of Shun, and how it was rewarded by Heaven with the empire, with enduring fame, and with long life; the third and fourth, on the kings Wăn and Woo, and the duke of Chow, celebrating them for their filial piety and other associate virtues; and the fifth, on the subject of government. These chapters are interesting enough in themselves, but when I go back from them, and examine whether I have from them any better understanding of the paragraphs in the first chapter which they are said to illustrate, I do not find that I have. Three of them, the 17th, 18th, and 19th, would be more in place in the Classic of Filial Piety than here in the Chung Yung. The meaning of the 16th is shadowy and undefined. After all the study which I have directed to it, there are some points in reference to which I have still doubts and difficulties.

The 20th chapter which concludes the third portion of the Work contains a full exposition of Confucius' views on government, though professedly descriptive only of that of the kings Wăn and Woo. Along with lessons proper for a ruler there are many also of universal application, but the mingling of them perplexes the mind. It tells us of "the five duties of universal application,"—those between sovereign and minister, husband and wife, father and son, elder and younger brother, and friends; of "the three virtues by which those duties are carried into effect," namely, knowledge, benevolence, and energy; and of "the one thing, by which those virtues are practised," which is singleness or sincerity.[10] It sets forth in detail the "nine standard rules for the administration of government," which are "the cultivation by the ruler of his own character; the honouring men of virtue and talents; affection to his relatives; respect towards the great ministers; kind and considerate treatment of the whole body of officers; cherishing the mass of the people as children; encouraging all classes of artizans; indulgent treatment of men from a distance; and the kindly cherishing of the princes of the States."[11] There are these and other equally interesting topics in this chapter; but, as they are in the Work, they distract the mind, instead of making the author's great object more clear to it, and I will not say more upon them here.

6. Doubtless it was the mention of "singleness," or "sincerity," in the 20th chapter, which made Tsze-sze introduce it into this Treatise, for from those terms he is able to go on to develope what he intended in saying that "if the states of Equilibrium and Harmony exist in perfection, a happy order will prevail throughout heaven and earth, and all things will be nourished and flourish." It is here, that now we are astonished at the audacity of the writer's assertions, and now lost in vain endeavours to ascertain his meaning. I have quoted the words of Confucius that it is "singleness," by which the three virtues of knowledge, benevolence, and energy are able to carry into practice the duties of universal obligation. He

10 Par. 8. 11 Par. 12.

says also that it is this same "singleness" by which "the nine standard rules of government" can be effectively carried out.[12] This "singleness" is just a name for "the states of Equilibrium and Harmony existing in perfection." It denotes a character absolutely and relatively good, wanting nothing in itself, and correct in all its outgoings. "Sincerity" is another term for the same thing, and in speaking about it, Confucius makes a distinction between sincerity absolute and sincerity acquired. The former is born with some, and practised by them without any effort; the latter is attained by study and practised by strong endeavour.[13] The former is "the way of Heaven;" the latter is "the way of men."[14] "He who possesses sincerity,"—absolutely, that is,—"is he who without effort hits what is right, and apprehends without the exercise of thought;—he is the sage who naturally and easily embodies the right way. He who attains to sincerity, is he who chooses what is good and firmly holds it fast. And to this attainment there are requisite the extensive study of what is good, accurate inquiry about it, careful reflection on it, the clear discrimination of it, and the earnest practice of it."[15] In these passages Confucius unhesitatingly enunciates his belief that there are some men who are absolutely perfect, who come into the world as we may conceive the first man was, when he was created by God "in His own image," full of knowledge and righteousness, and who grow up as we know that Christ did, "increasing in wisdom and in stature." He disclaimed being considered to be such an one himself,[16] but the sages of China were such. And moreover, others who are not so naturally may make themselves to become so. Some will have to put forth more effort and to contend with greater struggles, but the end will be the possession of the knowledge and the achievement of the practice.

I need not say that these sentiments are contrary to the views of human nature which are presented in the Bible. The testimony of Revelation is that "there is not a just man upon earth that doeth good and sinneth not." "If we say that we have no sin," and in writing this term, I am thinking here not of sin against God, but, if we can conceive of it apart from that, of failures in regard to what ought to be in our regulation of ourselves, and in our behaviour to others;—"if we say that we have no sin, we deceive ourselves, and

12 Par. 15. 13 Par. 9. 14 Par. 18. 15 Parr. 18, 19. 16 Ana. VII. xix.

the truth is not in us." This language is appropriate in the lips of the learned as well as in those of the ignorant, to the highest sage as to the lowest child of the soil. Neither the scriptures of God nor the experience of man know of individuals absolutely perfect. The other sentiment that men can make themselves perfect is equally wide of the truth. Intelligence and goodness by no means stand to each other in the relation of cause and effect. The sayings of Ovid, "*Video meliora proboque, deteriora sequor,*" "*Nitimur in vetitum semper, cupimusque negata,*" are a more correct expression of the facts of human consciousness and conduct than the high-flown phrases of Confucius.

7. But Tsze-sze adopts the dicta of his grandfather without questioning them, and gives them forth in his own style at the commencement of the fourth part of his Treatise. "When we have intelligence resulting from sincerity, this condition is to be ascribed to nature; when we have sincerity resulting from intelligence, this condition is to be ascribed to instruction. But given the sincerity, and there shall be the intelligence; given the intelligence, and there shall be the sincerity."[17]

Tsze-sze does more than adopt the dicta of Confucius. He applies them in a way which the sage never did, and which he would probably have shrunk from doing. The sincere, or perfect man of Confucius is he who satisfies completely all the requirements of duty in the various relations of Society, and in the exercise of government; but the sincere man of Tsze-sze is a potency in the universe. "Able to give its full development to his own nature, he can do the same to the nature of other men. Able to give its full development to the nature of other men, he can give their full development to the natures of animals and things. Able to give their full development to the natures of creatures and things, he can assist the transforming and nourishing powers of Heaven and Earth. Able to assist the transforming and nourishing powers of Heaven and Earth, he may with Heaven and Earth form a ternion."[18] Such are the results of sincerity natural. The case below this—of sincerity acquired, is as follows,—"The individual cultivates its shoots. From these he can attain to the possession of sincerity. This sincerity becomes apparent. From being apparent, it becomes manifest.

17 Ch. xxi. 18 Ch. xxii.

From being manifest, it becomes brilliant. Brilliant, it affects others. Affecting others, they are changed by it. Changed by it, they are transformed. It is only he who is possessed of the most complete sincerity that can exist under heaven, who can transform."[19] It may safely be affirmed, that when he thus expressed himself, Tsze-sze understood neither what he said nor whereof he affirmed. Maou Se-ho and some other modern writers explain away many of his predicates of sincerity, so that in their hands they become nothing but extravagant hyperboles, but the author himself would, I believe, have protested against such a mode of dealing with his words. True, his structures are castles in the air, but he had no idea himself that they were so.

In the 24th chapter there is a ridiculous descent from the sublimity of the two preceding. We are told that the possessor of entire sincerity is like a spirit and can foreknow, but the foreknowledge is only a judging by the milfoil and tortoise and other auguries! But the author recovers himself, and resumes his theme about sincerity as conducting to self-completion, and the completion of other men and things, describing it also as possessing all the qualities which can be predicated of Heaven and earth. Gradually the subject is made to converge to the person of Confucius, who is the ideal of the sage, as the sage is the ideal of humanity at large. An old account of the object of Tsze-sze in the Chung Yung is that he wrote it to celebrate the virtue of his grandfather."[20] He certainly contrives to do this in the course of it. The 30th, 31st, and 32d chapters contain his eulogium, and never has any other mortal been exalted in such terms. "He may be compared to heaven and earth in their supporting and containing, their overshadowing and curtaining all things; he may be compared to the four seasons in their alternating progress, and to the sun and moon in their successive shining." "Quick in apprehension, clear in discernment, of far-reaching intelligence, and all-embracing knowledge, he was fitted to exercise rule; magnanimous, generous, benign, and mild, he was fitted to exercise forbearance; impulsive, energetic, firm, and enduring, he was fitted to maintain a firm hold; self-adjusted, grave, never swerving from

19 Ch. xxiii. 20 唐陸德明釋文,謂孔子之孫子思作此以昭明祖德: see the 中庸唐說,—p 1.

the Mean, and correct, he was fitted to command reverence; accomplished, distinctive, concentrative, and searching, he was fitted to exercise discrimination." "All-embracing and vast, he was like heaven; deep and active as a fountain, he was like the abyss." "Therefore his fame overspreads the Middle kingdom, and extends to all barbarous tribes. Wherever ships and carriages reach; wherever the strength of man penetrates; wherever the heavens overshadow and the earth sustains; wherever the sun and moon shine; wherever frosts and dews fall;—all who have blood and breath unfeignedly honour and love him. Hence it is said,—He is the equal of Heaven!" "Who can know him but he who is indeed quick in apprehension, clear in discernment, of far-reaching intelligence, and all-embracing knowledge, possessing all heavenly virtue?"

8. We have arrived at the concluding chapter of the Work, in which the author, according to Choo He, "having carried his descriptions to the highest point in the preceding chapters, turns back and examines the source of his subject; and then again from the work of the learner, free from all selfishness and watchful over himself when he is alone, he carries out his description, till by easy steps he brings it to the consummation of the whole empire tranquillized by simple and sincere reverentialness. He moreover eulogizes its mysteriousness, till he speaks of it at last as without sound or smell."[31] Between the first and last chapters there is a correspondency, and each of them may be considered as a summary of the whole treatise. The difference between them is, that in the first a commencement is made with the mention of Heaven as the conferrer of man's nature, while in this the progress of man in virtue is traced, step by step, till at last it is equal to that of High Heaven.

9. I have thus in the preceding paragraphs given a general and somewhat copious review of this Work. My object has been to seize, if I could, the train of thought, and to hold it up to the reader. Minor objections to it, arising from the confused use of terms and singular applications of passages from the older Classics, are noticed in the notes subjoined to the translation. I wished here that its scope should be seen, and the means be afforded of judging how far it is worthy of the high character attributed to it. "The relish of it," says the younger Ch'ing, "is inexhaustible. The whole of it is solid

31 See the concluding note by Choo He.

learning. When the skilful reader has explored it with delight till he has apprehended it, he may carry it into practice all his life, and will find that it cannot be exhausted."[23]

My own opinion of it is much less favourable. The names by which it has been called in translations of it have led to misconceptions of its character. Were it styled "The states of Equilibrium and Harmony," we should be prepared to expect something strange and probably extravagant. Assuredly we should expect nothing more strange or extravagant than what we have. It begins sufficiently well, but the author has hardly enunciated his preliminary apothegms, when he conducts into an obscurity where we can hardly grope our way, and when we emerge from that, it is to be bewildered by his gorgeous but unsubstantial pictures of sagely perfection. He has eminently contributed to nourish the pride of his countrymen. He has exalted their sages above all that is called God or is worshipped, and taught the masses of the people that with them they have need of nothing from without. In the mean time it is antagonistic to Christianity. By-and-by, when Christianity has prevailed in China, men will refer to it as a striking proof how their fathers by their wisdom knew neither God nor themselves

23 The Introductory note, p. 217.

CHAPTER V.

CONFUCIUS AND HIS IMMEDIATE DISCIPLES.

SECTION I.

LIFE OF CONFUCIUS.

His ancestry.

1. "And have you foreigners surnames as well?" This question has often been put to me by Chinese. It marks the ignorance which belongs to the people of all that is external to themselves, and the pride of antiquity which enters largely as an element into their character. If such a pride could in any case be justified, we might allow it to the family of the K'ung, the descendants of Confucius. In the reign of K'ang-he, twenty-one centuries and a half after the death of the sage, they amounted to eleven thousand males. But their ancestry is carried back through a period of equal extent, and genealogical tables are common, in which the descent of Confucius is traced down from Hwang-te, the inventor of the cycle, B.C. 2637.[1]

The more moderate writers, however, content themselves with exhibiting his ancestry back to the commencement of the Chow dynasty, B.C. 1121. Among the relatives of the tyrant Chow, the last emperor of the Yin dynasty, was an elder brother, by a concubine, named K'e,[2] who is celebrated by Confucius, Ana. XVIII. i., under the title of the viscount of Wei. Foreseeing the impending ruin of their family, K'e withdrew from the court; and subsequently, he was invested by the emperor Shing, the second of the house of Chow, with the principality of Sung, which embraced the eastern portion of the present province of Ho-nan, that he might there continue the sacrifices to the emperors of Yin. K'e was followed as duke of Sung by a younger brother, in whose line the succession

1 See Memoires concernant les Chinois, Tome XII, p. 447, et seq. Father Amiot states, p. 501, that he had seen the representative of the family, who succeeded to the dignity of 衍聖公 in the 9th year of K'ien-lung, A.D. 1744. It is hardly necessary that I should say here, that the name Confucius is merely the Chinese characters 孔夫子 (K'ung Foo-tsze, 'The master, K'ung') latinized. 2 啓.

continued. His great-grandson, the duke Min,[3] was followed, B.C. 908, by a younger brother, leaving, however, two sons Fuh-foo Ho,[4] and Fang-sze.[5] Fuh Ho[6] resigned his right to the dukedom in favour of Fang-sze, who put his uncle to death in B.C. 893, and became master of the State. He is known as the duke Le,[7] and to his elder brother belongs the honour of having the sage among his descendants.

Three descents from Fuh Ho, we find Ching K'au-foo,[8] who was a distinguished officer under the dukes Tae, Woo, and Seuen[9] (B.C. 799—728). He is still celebrated for his humility, and for his literary tastes. We have accounts of him as being in communication with the Grand-historiographer of the empire, and engaged in researches about its ancient poetry, thus setting an example of one of the works to which Confucius gave himself.[10] K'aou gave birth to K'ung-foo Kea,[11] from whom the surname of K'ung took its rise. Five generations had now elapsed since the dukedom was held in the direct line of his ancestry, and it was according to the rule in such cases that the branch should cease its connection with the ducal stem, and merge among the people under a new surname. K'ung Kea was Master of the Horse in Sung, and an officer of well known loyalty and probity. Unfortunately for himself, he had a wife of surpassing beauty, of whom the chief minister of the State, by name Hwa Tuh,[12] happened on one occasion to get a glimpse. Determined to possess her, he commenced a series of intrigues, which ended, B.C. 709, in the murder of Kea and the reigning duke Shang.[13] At the same time, Tuh secured the person of the lady, and hastened to his palace with the prize, but on the way she had strangled herself with her girdle.

An enmity was thus commenced between the two families of K'ung and Hwa which the lapse of time did not obliterate, and the latter being the more powerful of the two, Kea's great-grandson withdrew into the State of Loo to avoid their persecution. There he was appointed commandant of the city of Fang,[14] and is known in history

3 湣公. 4 弗父何. 5 鮒 (al. 方) 祀. 6 I drop here the 父 (sp. 3d tone), which seems to have been used in those times in a manner equivalent to our Mr. 7 厲公. 8 正考甫; 甫 is used in the same way as 父; see note 6. 9 戴, 武, 宣 三公. 10 See the 國語, and 商頌詩序; quoted in Keang Yung's (江永) Life of Confucius, which forms a part of the 鄉黨圖考. 11 孔父嘉. 12 華督. 13 殤公. 14 防.

by the name of Fang-shuh.[15] Fang-shuh gave birth to Pih-hea,[16] and from him came Shuh-leang Heih,[17] the father of Confucius. Heih appears in the history of the times as a soldier of great prowess and daring bravery. In the year B.C. 562, when serving at the siege of a place called Peih-yang,[18] a party of the assailants made their way in at a gate which had purposely been left open, and no sooner were they inside than the portcullis was dropped. Heih was just entering, and catching the massive structure with both his hands, he gradually by dint of main strength raised it and held it up, till his friends had made their escape.

Thus much on the ancestry of the sage. Doubtless he could trace his descent in the way which has been indicated up to the imperial house of Yin, nor was there one among his ancestors during the rule of Chow to whom he could not refer with satisfaction. They had been ministers and soldiers of Sung and Loo, all men of worth, and in Ching K'aou, both for his humility and literary researches, Confucius might have special complacency.

From his birth to his first public employments. B.C. 551—531.

2. Confucius was the child of Shuh-leang Heih's old age. The soldier had married in early life, but his wife brought him only daughters,—to the number of nine, and no son. By a concubine he had a son, named Măng-p'e and also Pih-ne,[1] who proved a cripple, so that, when he was over seventy years, Heih sought a second wife in the Yen family,[2] from which came subsequently Yen Hwuy, the favourite disciple of his son. There were three daughters in the family, the youngest being named Ching-tsae.[3] Their father said to them, "Here is the commandant of Tsow. His father and grandfather were only scholars, but his ancestors before them were descendants of the sage emperors. He is a man ten feet high,[4] and of extraordinary prowess, and I am very desirous of his alliance. Though he is old and austere, you need have no misgivings about him. Which of you three will be his wife?" The two elder daughters were silent, but Ching-tsae said, "Why do you ask us, father? It is for you to determine." "Very well," said her father in reply, "you will do."

15 防叔. 16 伯夏. 17 叔梁紇. 18 偪陽.

1 孟皮一字伯尼. 2 顏氏. 3 徵在. 4 其人身長十尺. See, on the length of the ancient foot, Ana. VIII. vi., but the point needs a more sifting investigation than it has yet received.

Ching-tsae, accordingly, became Heih's wife, and in due time gave birth to Confucius, who received the name of K'ew, and was subsequently styled Chung-ne.[5] The event happened on the 21st day of the 10th month of the 21st year of the duke Seang, of Loo, being the 20th year of the emperor Ling, B.C. 551. The birth-place was in the district of Tsow, of which Heih was the governor. It was somewhere within the limits of the present department of Yen-chow in Shan-tung, but the honour of being the exact spot is claimed for two places in two different districts of the department.

The notices which we have of Confucius' early years are very scanty. When he was in his third year his father died. It is related of

5 名邱字仲尼. The legends say that Ching-tsae, fearing lest she should not have a son, in consequence of her husband's age, privately ascended the Ne-k'ew hill to pray for the boon, and that when she had obtained it, she commemorated the fact in the names—K'ew and Chung-ne. But the cripple, Mang-pe, had previously been styled Pih-ne. There was some reason, previous to Confucius' birth, for using the term ne in the family. As might be expected, the birth of the sage is surrounded with many prodigious occurrences. One account is, that the husband and wife prayed together for a son in a dell of mount Ne. As Ching-tsae went up the hill, the leaves of the trees and plants all erected themselves, and bent downwards on her return. That night she dreamt the Black *Te* appeared, and said to her, 'You shall have a son, a sage, and you must bring him forth in a hollow mulberry tree.' One day during her pregnancy, she fell into a dreamy state, and saw five old men in the hall, who called themselves the essences of the five planets, and led an animal which looked like a small cow with one horn, and was covered with scales like a dragon. This creature knelt before Ching-tsae, and cast forth from its mouth a slip of gem, on which was the inscription,—'The son of the essence of water shall succeed to the withering Chow, and be a throneless king.' Ching-tsae tied a piece of embroidered ribbon about its horn, and the vision disappeared. When Heih was told of it, he said, 'The creature must be the K'e-lin.' As her time drew near, Ching-tsae asked her husband if there was any place in the neighbourhood called 'The hollow mulberry tree.' He told her there was a dry cave in the south hill, which went by that name. Then she said, 'I will go and be confined there.' Her husband was surprised, but when made acquainted with her former dream, he made the necessary arrangements. On the night when the child was born, two dragons came and kept watch on the left and right of the hill, and two spirit-ladies appeared in the air, pouring out fragrant odours, as if to bathe Ching-tsae; and as soon as the birth took place, a spring of clear warm water bubbled up from the floor of the cave, which dried up again when the child had been washed in it. The child was of an extraordinary appearance; with a mouth like the sea, ox lips, a dragon's back, &c., &c. On the top of his head was a remarkable formation, in consequence of which he was named K'ew, &c. See the 列國志, Bk. lxxviii.—Sze-ma Ts'een seems to make Confucius to have been illegitimate, saying that Heih and Miss Yen cohabited in the wilderness (野合). Keang Yung says that the phrase has reference simply to the disparity of their ages.

6 Sze-ma Ts'een says that Confucius was born in the 22d year of duke Seang, B.C. 550. He is followed by Choo He in the short sketch of Confucius' life prefixed to the Lun Yu, and by 'The Annals of the Empire' (歷代統紀表), published with imperial sanction in the reign of Kea-k'ing. (To this latter work I have generally referred for my dates.) The year assigned in the text above rests on the authority of Kuh-leang and Kung-yang, the two commentators on the Ch'un Ts'ew. With regard to the month, however, the 10th is that assigned by Kuh-leang, while Kung-yang names the 11th. 7 Tsow is written 郰, 鄹, 陬, and 鄒.

him, that as a boy he used to play at the arrangement of sacrificial vessels, and at postures of ceremony. Of his schooling we have no reliable account. There is a legend, indeed, that at seven he went to school to Gan P'ing-chung,[8] but it must be rejected as P'ing-chung belonged to the State of Ts'e. He tells us himself that at fifteen he bent his mind to learning;[9] but the condition of the family was one of poverty. At a subsequent period, when people were astonished at the variety of his knowledge, he explained it by saying "When I was young, my condition was low, and therefore I acquired my ability in many things; but they were mean matters."[10]

When he was nineteen, he married a lady from the State of Sung, of the Këen-kwan family,[11] and in the following year his son Le was born. On the occasion of this event, the duke Ch'aou sent him a present of a couple of carp. It was to signify his sense of his prince's favour, that he called his son Le (*The Carp*), and afterwards gave him the designation of Pih-yu[12] (*Fish Primus*). No mention is made of the birth of any other children, though we know, from Ana. V. i., that he had at least one daughter. The fact of the duke of Loo's sending him a gift on the occasion of Le's birth, shows that he was not unknown, but was already commanding public attention and the respect of the great.

It was about this time, probably in the year after his marriage, that Confucius took his first public employment, as keeper of the stores of grain,[13] and in the following year he was put in charge of the public fields and lands.[14] Mencius adduces these employments in illustration of his doctrine that the superior man may at times take office on account of his poverty, but must confine himself in such a case to places of small emolument, and aim at nothing but the discharge of their humble duties. According to him, Confucius as keeper of stores, said, "My calculations must all be right:—that is all I have to care about;" and when in charge of the public fields, he said, "The oxen and sheep must be fat and strong and superior:—that is all I have to care about."[15] It does not appear whether

8 晏平仲. 9 Ana. II. iv. 10 Ana. IX. vi. 11 娶宋之亓官氏. 12 名曰鯉而字伯魚. 13 爲委吏. This is Mencius' account. Sze-ma Ts'ëen says 嘗爲季氏史, but his subsequent words 料量平 show that the office was the same. 14 Mencius calls this office 乘田, while Sze-ma Ts'ëen says 爲司職吏.

15 Mencius, V. Pt. II. v. 4.

these offices were held by Confucius in the direct employment of the State, or as a dependent of the Ke family in whose jurisdiction he lived. The present of the carp from the duke may incline us to suppose the former.

3. In his twenty-second year, Confucius commenced his labours as a public teacher, and his house became a resort for young and enquiring spirits, who wished to learn the doctrines of antiquity.

Commencement of his labours as a teacher. The death of his mother. Æt. 22—26.

However small the fee his pupils were able to afford, he never refused his instructions.[1] All that he required, was an ardent desire for improvement, and some degree of capacity. "I do not open up the truth," he said, "to one who is not eager to get knowledge, nor help out any one who is not anxious to explain himself. When I have presented one corner of a subject to any one, and he cannot from it learn the other three, I do not repeat my lesson."[2]

His mother died in the year B.C. 528, and he resolved that her body should lie in the same grave with that of his father, and that their common resting place should be in Fang, the first home of the K'ung in Loo. But here a difficulty presented itself. His father's coffin had been for twenty years, where it had first been deposited, off the road of *The Five Fathers*, in the vicinity of Tsow:—would it be right in him to move it? He was relieved from this perplexity by an old woman of the neighbourhood, who told him that the coffin had only just been put into the ground, as a temporary arrangement, and not regularly buried. On learning this, he carried his purpose into execution. Both coffins were conveyed to Fang, and put in the ground together, with no intervening space between them, as was the custom in some States. And now came a new perplexity. He said to himself, "In old times, they had graves, but raised no tumulus over them. But I am a man, who belongs equally to the north and the south, the east and the west. I must have something by which I can remember the place." Accordingly he raised a mound, four feet high, over the grave, and returned home, leaving a party of his disciples to see everything properly completed. In the mean time there came on a heavy storm of rain, and it was a considerable time before the disciples joined him.

1 Ana. VII. vii. 2 Ana. VII. viii.

"What makes you so late?" he asked. "The grave in Fang fell down," they said. He made no reply, and they repeated their answer three times, when he burst into tears, and said, "Ah! they did not make their graves so in antiquity."[3]

Confucius mourned for his mother the regular period of three years,—three years nominally, but in fact only twenty-seven months. Five days after the mourning was expired, he played on his lute but could not sing. It required other five days before he could accompany an instrument with his voice.[4]

Some writers have represented Confucius as teaching his disciples important lessons from the manner in which he buried his mother, and having a design to correct irregularities in the ordinary funeral ceremonies of the time. These things are altogether "without book." We simply have a dutiful son paying the last tribute of affection to a good parent. In one point he departs from the ancient practice, raising a mound over the grave, and when the fresh earth gives way from a sudden rain, he is moved to tears, and seems to regret his innovation. This sets Confucius vividly before us,—a man of the past as much as of the present, whose own natural feelings were liable to be hampered in their development by the traditions of antiquity which he considered sacred. It is important, however, to observe the reason which he gave for rearing the mound. He had in it a presentiment of much of his future course. He was "a man of the north, the south, the east, and the west." He might not confine himself to any one State. He would travel, and his way might be directed to some "wise ruler," whom his counsels would conduct to a benevolent sway that would break forth on every side till it transformed the empire.

He learns music; visits the court of Chow; and returns to Loo. B.C. 526—517.

4. When the mourning for his mother was over, Confucius remained in Loo, but in what special capacity we do not know. Probably he continued to encourage the resort of inquirers to whom he communicated instruction, and pursued his own researches into the history, literature, and institutions of the empire. In the year B.C. 524, the chief of the small State of T'an,[1]

3 Le Ke, II. Pt. I. i. 10; Pt. II. iii. 30; Pt. I. i. 6. See also the discussion of these passages in Keang Yung's 'Life of Confucius.' 4 Le Ke, II. Pt. I. i. 22.

1 See the Ts'un Ts'ew, under the 7th year of duke Ch'aou.—秋.郯子來朝.

made his appearance at the court of Loo, and discoursed in a wonderful manner, at a feast given to him by the duke, about the names which the most ancient sovereigns, from Hwang-te downwards, gave to their ministers. The sacrifices to the emperor Shaou-haou, the next in descent from Hwang-te, were maintained in T'an, so that the chief fancied that he knew all about the abstruse subject on which he discoursed. Confucius, hearing about the matter, waited on the visitor, and learned from him all that he had to communicate.[2]

To the year B.C. 523, when Confucius was twenty-nine years old, is referred his studying music under a famous master of the name of Sëang.[3] He was approaching his 30th year when, as he tells us, "he stood"[4] firm, that is, in his convictions on the subjects of learning to which he had bent his mind fifteen years before. Five years more, however, were still to pass by, before the anticipation mentioned in the conclusion of the last paragraph began to receive its fulfilment,[5] though we may conclude from the way in which it was brought about that he was growing all the time in the estimation of the thinking minds in his native State.

In the 24th year of duke Ch'aou, B.C. 517, one of the principal ministers of Loo, known by the name of Măng He, died. Seventeen years before, he had painfully felt his ignorance of ceremonial observances, and had made it his subsequent business to make himself acquainted with them. On his deathbed, he addressed his chief officer, saying, "A knowledge of propriety is the stem of a man. Without it he has no means of standing firm. I have heard that there is one K'ung Kew, who is thoroughly versed in it. He is a descendant of Sages, and though the line of his family was extinguished in Sung, among his ancestors there were Fuh-foo Ho, who resigned the dukedom to his brother, and Ching K'aou-foo, who was

2 This rests on the respectable authority of Tso-k'ew Ming's annotations on the Ch'un Ts'ew, but I must consider it apocryphal. The legend-writers have fashioned a journey to T'an. The slightest historical intimation becomes a text with them, on which they enlarge to the glory of the sage. Amiot has reproduced and expanded their romancings, and others, such as Pauthier (Chine, pp. 121-183) and Thornton (History of China, vol. I. pp. 151-215) have followed in his wake. 3 師襄. See the 'Family Sayings,' 卷三, art. 辯樂解; but the account there given is not more credible than the chief of T'an's expositions. 4 Ana. II. iv.

5 The journey to Chow is placed by Sze-ma Ts'een before Confucius' holding of his first official employments, and Choo He and most other writers follow him. It is a great error, and arises from a misunderstanding of the passage from the 左氏傳 upon the subject.

distinguished for his humility. Tsang Heih has observed that if sage men of intelligent virtue do not attain to eminence, distinguished men are sure to appear among their posterity. His words are now to be verified, I think, in K'ung K'ew. After my death, you must tell Ho-ke to go and study proprieties under him."[6] In consequence of this charge, Ho-ke,[7] Mang He's son, who appears in the Analects under the name of Mang E,[8] and a brother, or perhaps only a near relative, named Nan-kung King-shuh,[9] became disciples of Confucius. Their wealth and standing in the State gave him a position which he had not had before, and he told King-shuh of a wish which he had to visit the court of Chow, and especially to confer on the subject of ceremonies and music with Laou Tan. King-shuh represented the matter to the duke Ch'aou, who put a carriage and a pair of horses at Confucius' disposal for the expedition.[10]

At this time the court of Chow was in the city of Lŏ,[11] in the present department of Ho-nan of the province of the same name. The reigning emperor is known by the title of King,[12] but the sovereignty was little more than nominal. The state of China was then analogous to that of one of the European kingdoms during the prevalence of the feudal system. At the commencement of the dynasty, the various States of the empire had been assigned to the relatives and adherents of the reigning family. There were thirteen principalities of greater note, and a large number of smaller dependencies. During the vigorous youth of the dynasty, the emperor or lord paramount exercised an effective control over the various chiefs, but with the lapse of time there came weakness and decay. The chiefs—corresponding somewhat to the European dukes, earls, marquises, barons, &c.,—quarreled and warred among themselves, and the stronger among them barely acknowledged their subjection to the emperor. A similar condition of things prevailed in each particular State. There there were hereditary ministerial families, who were continually encroaching on the authority of their rulers, and the heads of those families again were frequently hard pressed by their inferior officers. Such was the state of China in Confucius' time. The

6 See 左氏傳昭公七年. 7 何忌. 8 孟懿子. 9 南宮敬叔. 10 The 家語 makes King-shuh accompany Confucius to Chow. It is difficult to understand this, if King-shuh were really a son of Mang He who had died that year. 11 洛. 12 敬王 (B.C. 518–475).

reader must have it clearly before him, if he would understand the position of the sage, and the reforms which, we shall find, it was subsequently his object to introduce.

Arrived at Chow, he had no intercourse with the court or any of the principal ministers. He was there not as a politician, but an inquirer about the ceremonies and maxims of the founders of the dynasty. Laou Tan,[13] whom he had wished to see, the acknowledged founder of the Taouists, or Rationalistic sect which has maintained its ground in opposition to the followers of Confucius, was then a treasury-keeper. They met and freely interchanged their views, but no reliable account of their conversations has been preserved. In the 5th Book of the Le Ke, which is headed, "The philosopher Tsăng asked," Confucius refers four times to the views of Laou-tsze on certain points of funeral ceremonies, and in the "Family Sayings," Book XXIV., he tells Ke K'ang what he had heard from him about "The Five Tes," but we may hope their conversation turned also on more important subjects. Sze-ma Ts'een, favourable to Laou-tsze, makes him lecture his visitor in the following style:—"Those whom you talk about are dead, and their bones are mouldered to dust; only their words remain. When the superior man gets his time, he mounts aloft; but when the time is against him, he moves as if his feet were entangled. I have heard that a good merchant, though he has rich treasures deeply stored, appears as if he were poor, and that the superior man whose virtue is complete, is yet to outward seeming stupid. Put away your proud air and many desires, your insinuating habit and wild will.[14] These are of no advantage to you. This is all which I have to tell you." On the other hand, Confucius is made to say to his disciples, "I know how birds can fly, how fishes can swim, and how animals can run. But the runner may be snared, the swimmer may be hooked, and the flyer may be shot by the arrow. But there is the dragon. I cannot tell how he mounts on the wind through the clouds, and rises to heaven. To-day I have seen Laou-tsze, and can only compare him to the dragon."[15]

13 According to Sze-ma Ts'een, Tan was the posthumous epithet of this individual, whose surname was Le (李), name Urh (耳), and designation Pih-yang (伯陽). 14 逸態與淫志. 15 See the 史記列傳第三, and compare the remarks attributed to Laou-tsze in the account of the K'ung family near the beginning.

While at Lô, Confucius walked over the grounds set apart for the great sacrifices to Heaven and Earth; inspected the pattern of the Hall of Light, built to give audience in to the princes of the empire; and examined all the arrangements of the ancestral temple and the court. From the whole he received a profound impression. "Now," said he with a sigh, "I know the sage wisdom of the duke of Chow, and how the house of Chow attained to the imperial sway."[16] On the walls of the Hall of Light were paintings of the ancient sovereigns from Yaou and Shun downwards, their characters appearing in the representations of them, and words of praise or warning being appended. There was also a picture of the duke of Chow sitting with his infant nephew, the king Shing, upon his knees, to give audience to all the princes. Confucius surveyed the scene with silent delight, and then said to his followers, "Here you see how Chow became so great. As we use a glass to examine the forms of things, so must we study antiquity in order to understand the present."[17] In the hall of the ancestral temple, there was a metal statue of a man with three clasps upon his mouth, and his back covered over with an enjoyable homily on the duty of keeping a watch upon the lips. Confucius turned to his disciples and said, "Observe it, my children. These words are true, and commend themselves to our feelings."[18]

About music he made inquiries at Ch'ang Hwang, to whom the following remarks are attributed:—"I have observed about Chung-ne many marks of a sage. His has river eyes and a dragon forehead,—the very characteristics of Hwang-te. His arms are long, his back is like a tortoise, and he is nine feet six inches in height,—the very semblance of T'ang the Completer. When he speaks, he praises the ancient kings. He moves along the path of humility and courtesy. He has heard of every subject, and retains with a strong memory. His knowledge of things seems inexhaustible.—Have we not in him the rising of a sage?"[19]

I have given these notices of Confucius at the court of Chow, more as being the only ones I could find, than because I put much faith in them. He did not remain there long, but returned the same year to Loo, and continued his work of teaching. His fame

16, 17, 18 See the 家語, 卷二, art. 觀周. 19 Quoted by Keang Yung from 'The Family Sayings.'

was greatly increased; disciples came to him from different parts, till their number amounted to three thousand. Several of those who have come down to us as the most distinguished among his followers, however, were yet unborn, and the statement just given may be considered as an exaggeration. We are not to conceive of the disciples as forming a community, and living together. Parties of them may have done so. We shall find Confucius hereafter always moving amid a company of admiring pupils; but the greater number must have had their proper avocations and ways of living, and would only resort to the master, when they wished specially to ask his counsel or to learn of him.

He withdraws to Ts'e, and returns to Loo the following year. B.C. 516, 515.

5. In the year succeeding the return to Loo, that State fell into great confusion. There were three Families in it, all connected irregularly with the ducal house, who had long kept the rulers in a condition of dependency. They appear frequently in the Analects as the Ke clan, the Shuh, and the Măng; and while Confucius freely spoke of their usurpations,[1] he was a sort of dependent of the Ke family, and appears in frequent communication with members of all the three. In the year B.C. 516, the duke Ch'aou came to open hostilities with them, and being worsted, fled into Ts'e, the State adjoining Loo on the north. Thither Confucius also repaired, that he might avoid the prevailing disorder of his native State. Ts'e was then under the government of a duke, afterwards styled King,[2] who "had a thousand teams, each of four horses, but on the day of his death the people did not praise him for a single virtue."[3] His chief minister, however, was Gan Ying,[4] a man of considerable ability and worth. At his court the music of the ancient sage-emperor, Shun, originally brought to Ts'e from the State of Ts'in,[5] was still preserved.

According to the "Family Sayings," an incident occurred on the way to Ts'e, which I may transfer to these pages as a good specimen of the way in which Confucius turned occurring matters to account, in his intercourse with his disciples. As he was passing by the side of the T'ae mountain, there was a woman weeping and wailing by a grave. Confucius bent forward in his carriage, and

1 See Analects, III. i., ii., *et al.* 2 景公. 3 Ana. XVI. xii. 4 晏嬰. This is the same who was afterwards styled 晏平仲. 5 陳.

after listening to her for some time, sent Tsze-loo to ask the cause of her grief. "You weep, as if you had experienced sorrow upon sorrow," said Tsze-loo. The woman replied, "It is so. My husband's father was killed here by a tiger, and my husband also; and now my son has met the same fate." Confucius asked her why she did not remove from the place, and on her answering, "There is here no oppressive government," he turned to his disciples, and said, "My children, remember this. Oppressive government is fiercer than a tiger."[6]

As soon as he crossed the border from Loo, we are told he discovered from the gait and manners of a boy, whom he saw carrying a pitcher, the influence of the sage's music, and told the driver of his carriage to hurry on to the capital.[7] Arrived there, he heard the strain, and was so ravished with it, that for three months he did not know the taste of flesh. "I did not think," he said, "that music could have been made so excellent as this."[8] The duke King was pleased with the conferences which he had with him,[9] and proposed to assign to him the town of Lin-k'ew, from the revenues of which he might derive a sufficient support; but Confucius refused the gift, and said to his disciples, "A superior man will only receive reward for services which he has done. I have given advice to the duke King, but he has not yet obeyed it, and now he would endow me with this place! Very far is he from understanding me."[10]

On one occasion the duke asked about government, and received the characteristic reply, "There is government when the prince is prince, and the minister is minister; when the father is father, and the son is son."[11] I say that the reply is characteristic. Once, when Tsz-loo asked him what he would consider the first thing to be done if entrusted with the government of a State, Confucius answered, "What is necessary is to rectify names."[12] The disciple thought the

6 See the 家語, 卷四, art. 正論解. I have translated, however, from the Le Ke, II. Pt II. iii, 10, where the same incident is given, with some variations, and without saying when or where it occurred. 7 See the 說苑, 卷十九, p. 18. 8 Ana. VII. xiii.

9 Some of these are related in the Family Sayings;—about the burning of the ancestral shrine of the emperor 釐, and a one-footed bird which appeared hopping and flapping its wings in Ts'e. They are plainly fabulous, though quoted in proof of Confucius' sage wisdom. This reference to them is more than enough. 10 家語, 卷二, 六本. 11. Ana. XII. xi.

12 Ana. XIII. iii.

reply wide of the mark, but it was substantially the same with what he said to the duke King. There is a sufficient foundation in nature for government in the several relations of society, and if those be maintained and developed according to their relative significancy, it is sure to obtain. This was a first principle in the political ethics of Confucius.

Another day the duke got to a similar inquiry the reply that the art of government lay in an economical use of the revenues; and being pleased, he resumed his purpose of retaining the philosopher in his State, and proposed to assign to him the fields of Ne-k'e. His chief minister Gan Ying dissuaded him from the purpose, saying, "Those scholars are impracticable, and cannot be imitated. They are haughty and conceited of their own views, so that they will not be content in inferior positions. They set a high value on all funeral ceremonies, give way to their grief, and will waste their property on great burials, so that they would only be injurious to the common manners. This Mr K'ung has a thousand peculiarities. It would take generations to exhaust all that he knows about the ceremonies of going up and going down. This is not the time to examine into his rules of propriety. If you, prince, wish to employ him to change the customs of Ts'e, you will not be making the people your primary consideration."[13]

I had rather believe that these were not the words of Gan Ying, but they must represent pretty correctly the sentiments of many of the statesmen of the time about Confucius. The duke of Ts'e got tired ere long of having such a monitor about him, and observed, "I cannot treat him as I would the chief of the Ke family. I will treat him in a way between that accorded to the chief of the Ke, and that given to the chief of the Măng family." Finally he said, "I am old; I cannot use his doctrines."[14] These observations were made directly to Confucius, or came to his hearing.[15] It was not consistent with his self-respect to remain longer in Ts'e, and he returned to Loo.[16]

6. Returned to Loo, he remained for the long period of about

13 See the 史記孔子世家, p. 2. 14 Ana. XVIII. iii. 15 Sze-ma Ts'een makes the first observation to have been addressed directly to Confucius. 16 According to the above account Confucius was only once, and for a portion of two years, in Ts'e. For the refutation of contrary accounts, see Keang Yung's Life of the sage.

fifteen years without being engaged in any official employment. It was a time, indeed, of great disorder. The duke Ch'aou continued a refugee in Ts'e, the government being in the hands of the great Families, up to his death in B.C. 509, on which event the rightful heir was set aside, and another member of the ducal house, known to us by the title of Ting,[1] substituted in his place. The ruling authority of the principality became thus still more enfeebled than it had been before, and, on the other hand, the chiefs of the Ke, the Shuh, and the Măng, could hardly keep their ground against their own officers. Of those latter the two most conspicuous were Yang Hoo,[2] called also Yang Ho,[3] and Kung-shan Fuh-jaou.[4] At one time Ke Hwan, the most powerful of the chiefs, was kept a prisoner by Yang Hoo, and was obliged to make terms with him in order to secure his liberation. Confucius would give his countenance to none, as he disapproved of all, and he studiously kept aloof from them. Of how he comported himself among them we have a specimen in the incident related in the Analects, XVII. i.—"Yang Ho wished to see Confucius, but Confucius would not go to see him. On this, he sent a present of a pig to Confucius, who, having chosen a time when Ho was not at home, went to pay his respects for the gift. He met him, however, on the way. 'Come, let me speak with you,' said the officer. 'Can he be called benevolent, who keeps his jewel in his bosom, and leaves his country to confusion?' Confucius replied, 'No.' 'Can he be called wise, who is anxious to be engaged in public employment, and yet is constantly losing the opportunity of being so?' Confucius again said, 'No.' The other added, 'The days and months are passing away; the years do not wait for us.' Confucius said, 'Right; I will go into office.'" Chinese writers are eloquent in their praises of the sage for the combination of propriety, complaisance, and firmness, which they see in his behaviour in this matter. To myself there seems nothing remarkable in it but a somewhat questionable dexterity. But it was well for the fame of Confucius that his time was not occupied during those years with official services. He turned them to better account, prosecuting his researches into the poetry, history, ceremonies, and music of the empire. Many disciples continued to resort to him, and the legendary

He remains without office in Lou, B.C. 516–501.

[1] 定公. [2] 陽虎. [3] 陽貨. [4] 公山弗擾(史記,狃).

writers tell us how he employed their services in digesting the results of his studies. I must repeat, however, that several of them, whose names are most famous, such as Tsăng Sin, were as yet children, and Min Sun[5] was not born till B.C. 500.

To this period we must refer the almost single instance which we have of the manner of Confucius' intercourse with his son Le. "Have you heard any lessons from your father different from what we have all heard?" asked one of the disciples once of Le. "No," said Le. "He was standing alone once, when I was passing through the court below with hasty steps, and said to me, 'Have you read the Odes?' On my replying, 'Not yet,' he added, 'If you do not learn the Odes, you will not be fit to converse with.' Another day, in the same place and the same way, he said to me, 'Have you read the rules of Propriety?' On my replying, 'Not yet,' he added, 'If you do not learn the rules of Propriety, your character cannot be established.' I have heard only these two things from him." The disciple was delighted and observed, "I asked one thing, and I have got three things. I have heard about the Odes. I have heard about the rules of Propriety. I have also heard that the superior man maintains a distant reserve towards his son."[6]

I can easily believe that this distant reserve was the rule which Confucius followed generally in his treatment of his son. A stern dignity is the quality which a father has to maintain upon his system. It is not to be without the element of kindness, but that must never go beyond the line of propriety. There is too little room left for the play and development of natural affection.

The divorce of his wife must also have taken place during these years, if it ever took place at all, which is a disputed point. The curious reader will find the question discussed in the notes on the second Book of the Le Ke. The evidence inclines, I think, against the supposition that Confucius did put his wife away. When she died, at a period subsequent to the present, Le kept on weeping aloud for her after the period for such a demonstration of grief had expired, when Confucius sent a message to him that his sorrow must be subdued, and the obedient son dried his tears.[7] We are glad to know that on one occasion—the death of his favourite disciple, Yen

5 閔損. 6. Ana XVI. xiii. 7 See the Le Ke II. Pt I. i. 27.

Hwuy—the tears of Confucius himself would flow over and above the measure of propriety.[6]

7 We come to the short period of Confucius' official life. In the year B.C. 501, things had come to a head between the chiefs of the three Families and their ministers, and had resulted in the defeat of the latter. In B.C. 500, the resources of Yang Hoo were exhausted, and he fled into Ts'e, so that the State was delivered from its greatest troubler, and the way was made more clear for Confucius to go into office, should an opportunity occur. It soon presented itself. Towards the end of that year he was made chief magistrate of the town of Chung-too.[1]

He holds office. B.C. 500-496.

Just before he received this appointment, a circumstance occured of which we do not well know what to make. When Yang-hoo fled into Ts'e, Kung-shan Fuh-jaou, who had been confederate with him, continued to maintain an attitude of rebellion, and held the city of Pe against the Ke family. Thence he sent a message to Confucius inviting him to join him, and the sage seemed so inclined to go that his disciple Tsze-loo remonstrated with him, saying, "Indeed you cannot go! why must you think of going to see Kung-shan?" Confucius replied, "Can it be without some reason that he has invited me? If any one employ me, may I not make an eastern Chow?"[2] The upshot, however, was that he did not go, and I cannot suppose that he had ever any serious intention of doing so. Amid the general gravity of his intercourse with his followers, there gleam out a few instances of quiet pleasantry, when he amused himself by playing with their notions about him. This was probably one of them.

As magistrate of Chung-too he produced a marvellous reformation of the manners of the people in a short time. According to the "Family Sayings," he enacted rules for the nourishing of the living and all observances to the dead. Different food was assigned to the old and the young, and different burdens to the strong and the weak. Males and females kept apart from each other in the streets. A

6 Ana. XI. ix.

1 中都宰. Amiot says this was 'la ville même où le Souverain tenait sa Cour' (Vie de Confucius, p. 117). He is followed of course by Thornton and Pauthier. My reading has not shown me that such was the case. In the notes to K'ang-he's edition of the 'Five King,' Le Ke, II. Pt. I. iii. 4, it is simply said—'Chung-too,—the name of a town of Loo. It afterwards belonged to Ts'e when it was called P'ing-luh (平陸).' 2 Ana. XVII. v.

thing dropt on the road was not picked up. There was no fraudulent carving of vessels. Inner coffins were made four inches thick, and the outer ones five. Graves were made on the high grounds, no mounds being raised over them, and no trees planted about them. Within twelve months, the princes of the States all about wished to imitate his style of administration.[3]

The duke Ting, surprised at what he saw, asked whether his rules could be employed to govern a whole State, and Confucius told him that they might be applied to the whole empire. On this the duke appointed him assistant-superintendent of Works,[4] in which capacity he surveyed the lands of the State, and made many improvements in agriculture. From this he was quickly made minister of Crime,[5] and the appointment was enough to put an end to crime. There was no necessity to put the penal laws in execution. No offenders showed themselves.[6]

These indiscriminating eulogies are of little value. One incident, related in the annotations of Tso-k'ew on the Ts'un Ts'ew,[7] commends itself at once to our belief, as in harmony with Confucius' character. The chief of the Ke, pursuing with his enmity the duke Ch'aou, even after his death, had placed his grave apart from the graves of his predecessors; and Confucius surrounded the ducal cemetery with a ditch so as to include the solitary resting-place, boldly telling the chief that he did it to hide his disloyalty.[8] But he signalized himself most of all, in B.C. 499, by his behaviour at an interview between the dukes of Loo and Ts'e, at a place called Shih-k'e,[9] and Këä-kuh,[10] in the present district of Lae-woo, in the department of T'ae-gan.[11] Confucius was present as master of ceremonies on the part of Loo, and the meeting was professedly pacific. The two princes were to form a covenant of alliance. The principal officer on the part of Ts'e, however, despising Confucius as "a man of ceremonies, without courage," had advised his sovereign to make the duke of Loo a prisoner, and for this purpose a band of the half-savage original inhabitants of the place advanced with weapons to the stage where the two dukes were met. Confucius understood

3 家語, Bk I. 4 司空. This office, however, was held by the chief of the Mang family. We must understand that Confucius was only an assistant to him, or perhaps acted for him. 5 大司寇. 6 家語, Bk I. 7 左傳, 定公元年. 8 家語, Bk I. 9 祝其. 10 夾谷. 11 泰安府, 萊蕪縣.

the scheme, and said to the opposite party, "Our two princes are met for a pacific object. For you to bring a band of savage vassals to disturb the meeting with their weapons, is not the way in which Ts'e can expect to give law to the princes of the empire. These barbarians have nothing to do with our Great Flowery land. Such vassals may not interfere with our covenant. Weapons are out of place at such a meeting. As before the spirits, such conduct is unpropitious. In point of virtue, it is contrary to right. As between man and man, it is not polite." The duke of Ts'e ordered the disturbers off, but Confucius withdrew, carrying the duke of Loo with him. The business proceeded, notwithstanding, and when the words of the alliance were being read on the part of Ts'e,—"So be it to Loo, if it contribute not 300 chariots of war to the help of Ts'e, when its army goes across its borders," a messenger from Confucius added,—"And so be it to us, if we obey your orders, unless you return to us the fields on the south of the Wăn." At the conclusion of the ceremonies, the prince of Ts'e wanted to give a grand entertainment, but Confucius demonstrated that such a thing would be contrary to the established rules of propriety, his real object being to keep his sovereign out of danger. In this way the two parties separated, they of Ts'e filled with shame at being foiled and disgraced by "the man of ceremonies," and the result was that the lands of Loo which had been appropriated by Ts'e were restored.[12]

For two years more Confucius held the office of minister of Crime. Some have supposed that he was further raised to the dignity of chief minister of the State,[13] but that was not the case. One instance of the manner in which he executed his functions is worth recording. When any matter came before him, he took the opinion of different individuals upon it, and in giving judgment would say, "I decide according to the view of so and so." There was an approach to our jury system in the plan, Confucius' object being to enlist general sympathy, and carry the public judgment with him in his administration of justice. A father having brought some charge against his son, Confucius kept them both in prison for three months, without

12 This meeting at Këă-kuh is related in Sze-ma Ts'een, the Family Sayings, and Kuh-leang, with many exaggerations. I have followed 左氏傳.定公十年. 13 The 家語 says, Bk II., 孔子爲攝司寇.攝相事. But he was a 相 only in the sense of an assistant of ceremonies, as at the meeting in Këă-kuh, described above.

making any difference in favour of the father, and then wished to dismiss them both. The head of the Ke was dissatisfied, and said, "You are playing with me, Sir minister of Crime. Formerly you told me that in a State or a family filial duty was the first thing to be insisted on. What hinders you now from putting to death this unfilial son as an example to all the people?" Confucius with a sigh replied, "When superiors fail in their duty, and yet go to put their inferiors to death, it is not right. This father has not taught his son to be filial;—to listen to his charge would be to slay the guiltless. The manners of the age have been long in a sad condition; we cannot expect the people not to be transgressing the laws."[14]

At this time two of his disciples, Tsze-loo and Tsze-yew, entered the employment of the Ke family, and lent their influence, the former especially, to forward the plans of their master. One great cause of disorder in the State was the fortified cities held by the three chiefs, in which they could defy the supreme authority, and were in turn defied themselves by their officers. Those cities were like the castles of the barons of England in the time of the Norman kings. Confucius had their destruction very much at heart, and partly by the influence of persuasion, and partly by the assisting counsels of Tsze-loo, he accomplished his object in regard to Pe,[15] the chief city of the Ke, and How,[16] the chief city of the Shuh.

It does not appear that he succeeded in the same way in dismantling Shing,[17] the chief city of the Mang;[18] but his authority in the State greatly increased. "He strengthened the ducal House and weakened the private Families. He exalted the sovereign, and depressed the ministers. A transforming government went abroad. Dishonesty and dissoluteness were ashamed and hid their heads. Loyalty and good faith became the characteristics of the men, and chastity and docility those of the women. Strangers came in crowds from other States."[19] Confucius became the idol of the people, and flew in songs through their mouths.[20]

14 See the 家語, Bk II. 15 費. 16 郈. 17 成. 18 In connection with these events, the Family Sayings and Sze-ma Ts'een mention the summary punishment inflicted by Confucius on an able but unscrupulous and insidious officer, the Shaou-ching, Maou (少正卯). His judgment and death occupy a conspicuous place in the legendary accounts. But the Analects, Tsze-sze, Mencius, and Tso-k'ew Ming are all silent about it, and Keang Yung rightly rejects it, as one of the many narratives invented to exalt the sage. 19 See the 家語, Bk II. 20 See 孔叢子, quoted by Keang Yung.

But this sky of bright promise was soon overcast. As the fame of the reformations in Loo went abroad, the neighbouring princes began to be afraid. The duke of Ts'e said, "With Confucius at the head of its government, Loo will become supreme among the States, and Ts'e which is nearest to it will be the first swallowed up. Let us propitiate it by a surrender of territory." One of his ministers proposed they should first try to separate between the sage and his sovereign, and to effect this, they hit upon the following scheme. Eighty beautiful girls, with musical and dancing accomplishments, were selected, and a hundred and twenty of the finest horses that could be found, and sent as a present to duke Ting. They were put up at first outside the city, and Ke Hwan having gone in disguise to see them, forgot the lessons of Confucius, and took the duke to look at the bait. They were both captivated. The women were received, and the sage was neglected. For three days the duke gave no audience to his ministers. "Master," said Tsze-loo to Confucius, "it is time for you to be going." But Confucius was very unwilling to leave. The spring was coming on, when the great sacrifice to Heaven would be offered, and he determined to wait and see whether the solemnity of that would bring the duke back to his right mind. No such result followed. The ceremony was hurried through, and portions of the offerings were not sent round to the various ministers, according to the established custom. Confucius regretfully took his departure, going away slowly and by easy stages.[21] He would have welcomed a messenger of recall. The duke continued in his abandonment, and the sage went forth to thirteen weary years of homeless wandering.

He wanders from State to State. B.C. 496—483.

6. On leaving Loo, Confucius first bent his steps westward to the State of Wei, situate about where the present provinces of Chih-le and Ho-nan adjoin. He was now in his 56th year, and felt depressed and melancholy. As he went along, he gave expression to his feelings in verse:—

"Fain would I still look towards Loo,
But this Kwei hill cuts off my view.
With an axe, I'd hew the thickets through.:—
Vain thought! 'gainst the hill I nought can do;"

[21] 史記.孔子世家. p. 5. See also Mencius, V. Pt. II. i. 4; et al.

and again,—

"Through the valley howls the blast,
Drizzling rain falls thick and fast.
Homeward goes the youthful bride,
O'er the wild, crowds by her side.
How is it, O azure Heaven,
From my home I thus am driven,
Through the land my way to trace,
With no certain dwelling-place?
Dark, dark, the minds of men!
Worth in vain comes to their ken.
Hastens on my term of years;
Old age, desolate, appears."[1]

A number of his disciples accompanied him, and his sadness infected them. When they arrived at the borders of Wei, at a place called E, the warden sought an interview, and on coming out from the sage, he tried to comfort the disciples, saying, "My friends, why are you distressed at your Master's loss of office? The empire has been long without the principles of truth and right; Heaven is going to use your master as a bell with its wooden tongue."[2] Such was the thought of this friendly stranger. The bell did indeed sound, but few had ears to hear.

Confucius' fame, however, had gone before him, and he was in little danger of having to suffer from want. On arriving at the capital of Wei, he lodged at first with a worthy officer, named Yen Ch'ow-yew.[3] The reigning duke, known to us by the epithet of Ling,[4] was a worthless, dissipated man, but he could not neglect a visitor of such eminence, and soon assigned to Confucius a revenue of 60,000 measures of grain.[5] Here he remained for ten months, and then for some reason left it to go to Ch'in.[6] On the way he had to pass by K'wang,[7] a place probably in the present department of K'ae-fung in Ho-nan, which had formerly suffered from Yang-hoo. It so happened that Confucius resembled Hoo, and the attention of the people being called to him by the movements of his carriage-driver, they thought it was their old enemy, and made an attack upon him. His

1 See Keang Yung's Life of Confucius, 去衍周遊考. 2 Ana. III. xxiv. 3 顏讎由. See Mencius, V. Pt. I, viii. 2. 4 靈公. 5 See the 史記孔子世家, p 3. 6 陳國. 7 匡.

followers were alarmed, but he was calm, and tried to assure them by declaring his belief that he had a divine mission. He said to them, "After the death of king Wăn, was not the cause of truth lodged here in me? If Heaven had wished to let this cause of truth perish, then I, a future mortal, should not have got such a relation to that cause. While Heaven does not let the cause of truth perish, what can the people of K'wang do to me?"[8] Having escaped from the hands of his assailants, he does not seem to have carried out his purpose of going to Ch'in, but returned to Wei.

On the way, he passed a house where he had formerly been lodged, and finding that the master was dead, and the funeral ceremonies going on, he went in to condole and weep. When he came out, he told Tsze-kung to take one of the horses from his carriage, and give it as a contribution to the expenses of the occasion. "You never did such a thing," Tsze-kung remonstrated, "at the funeral of any of your disciples; is it not too great a gift on this occasion of the death of an old host?" "When I went in," replied Confucius, "my presence brought a burst of grief from the chief mourner, and I joined him with my tears. I dislike the thought of my tears not being followed by any thing. Do it, my child."[9]

On reaching Wei, he lodged with Keu Pih-yuh, an officer of whom honourable mention is made in the Analects.[10] But this time he did not remain long in the State. The duke was married
B.C. 495. to a lady of the house of Sung, known by the name of Nan-tsze, notorious for her intrigues and wickedness. She sought an interview with the sage, which he was obliged unwillingly to accord.[11] No doubt he was innocent of thought or act of evil, but it gave great dissatisfaction to Tsze-loo that his master should have been in company with such a woman, and Confucius, to assure him, swore an oath, saying, "Wherein I have done improperly, may Heaven reject me! May Heaven reject me!"[12] He could not well abide, however, about such a court. One day the duke rode out through the streets of his capital in the same carriage with Nan-tsze, and made Confucius follow them in another. Perhaps

8 Ana. IX. v. In Ana. XI. xxii., there is another reference to this time, in which Yen Hwuy is made to appear. 9 See the Le Ke, II. Pt. I. ii. 16. 10 Ana. XIV. xxvi.; XV. vi. 11 See the account in the 史記.孔子世家 p. 6. 12 Ana. VI. xxvi.

he intended to honour the philosopher, but the people saw the incongruity, and cried out, "Lust in the front; virtue behind!" Confucius was ashamed, and made the observation, "I have not seen one who loves virtue as he loves beauty."[13] Wei was no place for him. He left it, and took his way towards Ch'in.

Ch'in which formed part of the present province of Ho-nan, lay south from Wei. After passing the small State of Ts'aou,[14] he approached the borders of Sung, occupying the present prefecture of Kwei-tih, and had some intentions of entering it, when an incident occurred, which it is not easy to understand from the meagre style in which it is related, but which gave occasion to a remarkable saying. Confucius was practising ceremonies with his disciples, we are told, under the shade of a large tree. Hwan T'uy, an ill-minded officer of Sung, heard of it, and sent a band of men to pull down the tree, and kill the philosopher, if they could get hold of him. The disciples were much alarmed, but Confucius observed, "Heaven has produced the virtue that is in me;—what can Hwan T'uy do to me?"[15] They all made their escape, but seem to have been driven westwards to the State of Ch'ing,[16] on arriving at the gate conducting into which from the east, Confucius found himself separated from his followers. Tsze-kung had arrived before him, and was told by a native of Ch'ing that there was a man standing by the east gate, with a forehead like Yaou, a neck like Kaou-yaou, his shoulders on a level with those of Tsze-ch'an, but wanting, below the waist, three inches of the height of Yu, and altogether having the disconsolate appearance of a stray dog." Tsze-kung knew it was the master, hastened to him, and repeated to his great amusement the description which the man had given. "The bodily appearance," said Confucius, "is but a small matter, but to say I was like a stray dog—capital! capital!"[17] The stay they made at Ch'ing was short, and by the end of B.C. 495, Confucius was in Ch'in.

All the next year he remained there lodging with the warder of the city wall, an officer of worth, of the name of Ching,[18] and we have no accounts of him which deserve to be related here.[19]

13 Ana. IX. xvii. 14 曹. 15 Ana. IX. xxii. 16 鄭. 17 See the 史記, 孔子世家, p 6. 18 司城貞子. See Mencius, V, Pt I, viii, 3. 19 Keang Yung digests in this place two foolish stories,—about a large bone found in the State of Yue, and a bird which appeared in Ch'in and died, shot through with a remarkable arrow. Confucius knew all about them.

In B.C. 493, Ch'in was much disturbed by attacks from Woo,[20] a large State, the capital of which was in the present department of Soo-chow, and Confucius determined to retrace his steps to Wei. On the way he was laid hold of at a place called P'oo,[21] which was held by a rebellious officer against Wei, and before he could get away, he was obliged to engage that he would not proceed thither. Thither, notwithstanding, he continued his route, and when Tsze-kung asked him whether it was right to violate the oath he had taken, he replied, "It was a forced oath. The spirits do not hear such."[22] The duke Ling received him with distinction, but paid no more attention to his lessons than before, and Confucius is said then to have uttered his complaint, "If there were any of the princes who would employ me, in the course of twelve months I should have done something considerable. In three years the government would be perfected."[23]

A circumstance occurred to direct his attention to the State of Tsin,[24] which occupied the southern part of the present Shan-se, and extended over the Yellow river into Ho-nan. An invitation came to Confucius, like that which he had formerly received from Kung-shan Fuh-jaou. Peih Heih, an officer of Tsin, who was holding the town of Chung-mow against his chief, invited him to visit him, and Confucius was inclined to go. Tsze-loo was always the mentor on such occasions. He said to him, "Master, I have heard you say, that when a man in his own person is guilty of doing evil, a superior man will not associate with him. Peih Heih is in rebellion; if you go to him, what shall be said?" Confucius replied, "Yes, I did use those words. But is it not said that if a thing be really hard, it may be ground without being made thin; and if it be really white, it may be steeped in a dark fluid without being made black? Am I a bitter gourd? Am I to be hung up out of the way of being eaten?"[25]

These sentiments sound strangely from his lips. After all, he did not go to Peih Heih; and having travelled as far as the Yellow river that he might see one of the principal ministers of Tsin, he heard of the violent death of two men of worth, and returned to

20 吳. 21 蒲. 22. This is related by Sze-ma Ts'een, 孔子世家, p. 7, and also in the Family Sayings. I would fain believe it is not true. The wonder is, that no Chinese critic should have set about disproving it. 23. Ana. XIII. x. 24 晉. 25 Ana. XVII. vii.

Wei, lamenting the fate which prevented him from crossing the stream, and trying to solace himself with poetry as he had done on leaving Loo. Again did he communicate with the duke, but as ineffectually, and disgusted at being questioned by him about military tactics, he left and went back to Ch'in.

He resided in Ch'in all the next year, B.C. 491, without anything occurring there which is worthy of note.[26] Events had transpired in Loo, however, which were to issue in his return to his native State. The duke Ting had deceased B.C. 494, and Ke Hwan, the chief of the Ke family, died in this year. On his deathbed, he felt remorse for his conduct to Confucius, and charged his successor, known to us in the Analects as Ke K'ang, to recall the sage; but the charge was not immediately fulfilled. Ke K'ang, by the advice of one of his officers, sent to Ch'in for the disciple Yen K'ew instead. Confucius willingly sent him off, and would gladly have accompanied him. "Let me return!" he said, "Let me return!"[27] But that was not to be for several years yet.

In B.C. 490, accompanied, as usual, by several of his disciples, he went from Ch'in to Ts'ae, a small dependency of the great fief of Ts'oo, which occupied a large part of the present provinces of Hoonan and Hoo-pih. On the way, between Ch'in and Ts'ae, their provisions became exhausted, and they were cut off somehow from obtaining a fresh supply. The disciples were quite overcome with want, and Tsze-loo said to the master, "Has the superior man indeed to endure in this way?" Confucius answered him, "The superior man may indeed have to endure want; but the mean man, when he is in want, gives way to unbridled license."[28] According to the "Family Sayings," the distress continued seven days, during which time Confucius retained his equanimity, and was even cheerful, playing on his lute and singing.[29] He retained, however, a strong impression of the perils of the season, and we find him afterwards recurring to it, and lamenting that of the friends that were with him in Ch'in and Ts'ae, there were none remaining to enter his door.[30]

Escaped from this strait, he remained in Ts'ae over B.C. 489, and in the following year we find him in She, another district of

26 Tso-k'ew Ming, indeed, relates a story of Confucius, on the report of a fire in Loo, telling whose ancestral temple had been destroyed by it. 27 Ana. V. xxi. 28 Ana. XV. i. 2, 3.
29 家語,卷二在厄二十篇. 30 Ana. XI. ii.

Ts'oo, the chief of which had usurped the title of duke. Puzzled about his visitor, he asked Tsze-loo what he should think of him, but the disciple did not venture a reply. When Confucius heard of it, he said to Tsze-loo, "Why did you not say to him,—He is simply a man who in his eager pursuit of knowledge forgets his food, who in the joy of its attainment forgets his sorrows, and who does not perceive that old age is coming on?"[31] Subsequently, the duke, in conversation with Confucius, asked him about government, and got the reply, dictated by some circumstances of which we are ignorant, "Good government obtains, when those who are near are made happy, and those who are far off are attracted."[32]

After a short stay in Shě, according to Sze-ma Ts'een, he returned to Ts'ae, and having to cross a river, he sent Tsze-loo to inquire for the ford of two men who were at work in a neighbouring field. They were recluses,—men who had withdrawn from public life in disgust at the waywardness of the times. One of them was called Ch'ang-tseu, and instead of giving Tsze-loo the information he wanted, he asked him, "Who is it that holds the reins in the carriage there?" "It is K'ung Kew." "K'ung Kew of Loo?" "Yes," was the reply, and then the man rejoined, "*He* knows the ford."

Tsze-loo applied to the other, who was called Këě-neih, but got for answer the question, "Who are you, Sir?" He replied, "I am Chung Yew." "Chung Yew, who is the disciple of K'ung Kew of Loo?" "Yes," again replied Tsze-loo, and Këě-neih addressed him, "Disorder, like a swelling flood, spreads over the whole empire, and who is he that will change it for you? Than follow one who merely withdraws from this one and that one, had you not better follow those who withdraw from the world altogether?" With this he fell to covering up the seed, and gave no more heed to the stranger. Tsze-loo went back and reported what they had said, when Confucius vindicated his own course, saying, "It is impossible to associate with birds and beasts as if they were the same with us. If I associate not with these people,—with mankind,—with whom shall I associate? If right principles prevailed through the empire, there would be no use for me to change its state."[33]

About the same time he had an encounter with another recluse, who was known as "The madman of Ts'oo." He passed by the

31 Ana. VII. xviii. 32 Ana. XIII. xvi. 33 Ana. XVIII. vi.

carriage of Confucius, singing out "O FUNG, O FUNG, how is your virtue degenerated! As to the past, reproof is useless, but the future may be provided against. Give up, give up your vain pursuit." Confucius alighted and wished to enter into conversation with him, but the man hastened away.[34]

But now the attention of the ruler of Ts'oo—king, as he styled himself—was directed to the illustrious stranger who was in his dominions, and he met Confucius and conducted him to his capital, which was in the present district of E-shing, in the department of Sëang-yang,[35] in Hoo-pih. After a time, he proposed endowing the philosopher with a considerable territory, but was dissuaded by his prime minister, who said to him, "Has your majesty any officer who could discharge the duties of an ambassador like Tsze-kung? or any one so qualified for a premier as Yen Hwuy? or any one to compare as a general with Tsze-loo? The kings Wăn and Woo, from their hereditary dominions of a hundred *le*, rose to the sovereignty of the empire. If K'ung K'ew, with such disciples to be his ministers, get the possession of any territory, it will not be to the prosperity of Ts'oo?[36] On this remonstrance the king gave up his purpose, and when he died in the same year, Confucius left the State, and went back again to Wei.

The duke Ling had died four years before, soon after Confucius
B.C. 489. had last parted from him, and the reigning duke, known to us by the title of Ch'uh,[37] was his grandson, and was holding the principality against his own father. The relations between them were rather complicated. The father had been driven out in consequence of an attempt which he had instigated on the life of his mother, the notorious Nan-tsze, and the succession was given to his son. Subsequently, the father wanted to reclaim what he deemed his right, and an unseemly struggle ensued. The duke Ch'uh was conscious how much his cause would be strengthened by the support of Confucius, and hence when he got to Wei, Tsze-loo could say to him, "The prince of Wei has been waiting for you, in order with you to administer the government;—what will you consider the first thing to be done?"[38] The opinion of the philosopher, however,

34 Ana. XVII. v. 35 襄陽府宜城縣. 36 See the 史記·孔子世家, p. 10. 37 出公. 38 Ana. XIII. iii. In the notes on this passage, I have given Choo He's opinion as to the time when Tsze-loo made this remark. It seems more correct, however, to refer it to Confucius' return to Wei from Ts'oo, as is done by Keang Yung.

was against the propriety of the duke's course,[39] and he declined taking office with him, though he remained in Wei for between five and six years. During all that time there is a blank in his history. In the very year of his return, according to the "Annals of the Empire," his most beloved disciple, Yen Hwuy died, on which occasion he exclaimed, "Alas! Heaven is destroying me! Heaven is destroying me!"[40] The death of his wife is assigned to B.C. 484, but nothing else is related which we can connect with this long period.

From his return to Loo to his death. B.C. 483—478.

9. His return to Loo was brought about by the disciple Yen Yew, who, we have seen, went into the service of Ke K'ang, in B.C. 491. In the year B.C. 483, Yew had the conduct of some military operations against Ts'e, and being successful, Ke K'ang asked him how he had obtained his military skill;—was it from nature, or by learning? He replied that he had learned it from Confucius, and entered into a glowing eulogy of the philosopher. The chief declared that he would bring Confucius home again to Loo. "If you do so," said the disciple, "see that you do not let mean men come between you and him." On this K'ang sent three officers with appropriate presents to Wei, to invite the wanderer home, and he returned with them accordingly.[1]

This event took place in the 11th year of the duke Gae,[2] who succeeded to Ting, and according to K'ung Foo, Confucius' descendant, the invitation proceeded from him.[3] We may suppose that while Ke K'ang was the mover and director of the proceeding, it was with the authority and approval of the duke. It is represented in the chronicle of Tso-k'ew Ming as having occurred at a very opportune time. The philosopher had been consulted a little before by K'ung Wăn,[4] an officer of Wei, about how he should conduct a feud with another officer, and disgusted at being referred to on such a subject, had ordered his carriage and prepared to leave the State, exclaiming, "The bird chooses its tree. The tree does not chase the bird." K'ung Wăn endeavoured to excuse himself, and to prevail on Confucius

39 Ana. VII. xiv. 40 Ana. XI. viii. In the notes on Ana. XI. vii. I have adverted to the chronological difficulty connected with the dates assigned respectively to the deaths of Yen Hwuy and Confucius' own son, Le. Keang Yung assigns Hwuy's death to B.C. 481.

1 See the 史記孔子世家. 2 哀公. 3 See Keang Yung's memoir, in loc. 4 孔文子, the same who is mentioned in the Analects, V. xiv.

to remain in Wei, and just at this juncture the messengers from Loo arrived.[5]

Confucius was now in his 69th year. The world had not dealt kindly with him. In every State which he had visited he had met with disappointment and sorrow. Only five more years remained to him, nor were they of a brighter character than the past. He had, indeed, attained to that state, he tells us, in which "he could follow what his heart desired without transgressing what was right,"[6] but other people were not more inclined than they had been to abide by his counsels. The duke Gae and Ke K'ang often conversed with him, but he no longer had weight in the guidance of State affairs, and wisely addressed himself to the completion of his literary labours. He wrote a preface to the Shoo-king; carefully digested the rites and ceremonies determined by the wisdom of the more ancient ages and kings; collected and arranged the ancient poetry; and undertook the reform of music.[7] He has told us himself, "I returned from Wei to Loo, and then the music was reformed, and the pieces in the Imperial Songs and Praise Songs found all their proper place."[8] To the Yih-king he devoted much study, and Sze-ma Ts'een says that the leather thongs by which the tablets of his copy were bound together were thrice worn out. "If some years were added to my life," he said, "I would give fifty to the study of the Yih, and then I might come to be without great faults."[9] During this time also, we may suppose that he supplied Tsăng Sin with the materials of the classic of Filial Piety. The same year that he returned, Ke K'ang sent Yen Yew to ask his opinion about an additional impost which he wished to lay upon the people, but Confucius refused to give any reply, telling the disciple privately his disapproval of the proposed measure. It was carried out, however, in the following year, by the agency of Yen, on which occasion, I suppose, it was that Confucius said to the other disciples, "He is no disciple of mine; my little children, beat the drum and assail him."[10] The year B.C. 482 was marked by the death of his son Le, which he seems to have borne with more equanimity than he did that of his disciple Yen Hwuy, which some writers assign to the following year, though I have already mentioned it under the year B.C. 488.

5 See the 左傳.哀公十一年. 6 Ana. II. iv. 6. 7 See the 史記, 孔子世家, p. 12. 8 Ana. IX. xiv. 9 Ana. VII. xvi. 10 Ana. XI. xvi.

In the spring of B.C. 480, a servant of Ke K'ang caught a k'e-lin on a hunting excursion of the duke in the present district of Këa-ts'eang.[11] No person could tell what strange animal it was, and Confucius was called to look at it. He at once knew it to be a *lin*, and the legend-writers say that it bore on one of its horns the piece of ribbon, which his mother had attached to the one that appeared to her before his birth. According to the chronicle of Kung-yang, he was profoundly affected. He cried out, "For whom have you come? For whom have you come?" His tears flowed freely, and he added, "The course of my doctrines is run."[12]

Notwithstanding the appearance of the lin, the life of Confucius was still protracted for two years longer, though he took occasion to terminate with that event his history of the Ts'un Ts'ew. This Work according to Sze-ma Ts'een was altogether the production of this year, but we need not suppose that it was so. In it, from the standpoint of Loo, he briefly indicates the principal events occurring throughout the empire, every term being expressive, it is said, of the true character of the actors and events described. Confucius said himself, "It is the Spring and Autumn which will make men know me, and it is the Spring and Autumn which will make men condemn me."[13] Mencius makes the composition of it to have been an achievement as great as Yu's regulation of the waters of the deluge.—"Confucius completed the Spring and Autumn, and rebellious ministers and villainous sons were struck with terror."[14]

Towards the end of this year, word came to Loo that the duke of Ts'e had been murdered by one of his officers. Confucius was moved with indignation. Such an outrage, he felt, called for his solemn interference. He bathed, went to court, and represented the matter to the duke, saying, "Ch'in Hăng has slain his sovereign, I beg that you will undertake to punish him." The duke pleaded his incapacity, urging that Loo was weak compared with Ts'e, but Confucius replied, "One half the people of Ts'e are not consenting to the deed. If you add to the people of Loo one half the people of Ts'e, you are sure to overcome." But he could not infuse his spirit into the duke, who told him to go and lay the matter before the chiefs of the three Families. Sorely against his sense of propriety,

11 兗州府嘉祥縣. 12 公羊傳, 哀公十四年. According to Kung-yang, however, the lin was found by some wood-gatherers. 13 Mencius III. Pt. II. ix. 8. 14 Men., III. Pt. II. ix. 11.

he did so, but they would not act, and he withdrew with the remark, "Following in the rear of the great officers, I did not dare not to represent such a matter."[15]

In the year B.C. 479, Confucius had to mourn the death of another of his disciples, one of those who had been longest with him,—the well-known Tsze-loo. He stands out a sort of Peter in the Confucian school, a man of impulse, prompt to speak and prompt to act. He gets many a check from the master, but there is evidently a strong sympathy between them. Tsze-loo uses a freedom with him on which none of the other disciples dares to venture, and there is not one among them all, for whom, if I may speak from my own feeling, the foreign student comes to form such a liking. A pleasant picture is presented to us in one passage of the Analects. It is said, "The disciple Min was standing by his side, looking bland and precise; Tsze-loo (named Yew), looking bold and soldierly; Yen Yew and Tsze-kung, with a free and straightforward manner. The master was pleased, but he observed, 'Yew there!—he will not die a natural death.'"[16]

This prediction was verified. When Confucius returned to Loo from Wei, he left Tsze-loo and Tsze-kaou[17] engaged there in official service. Troubles arose. News came to Loo, B.C. 479, that a revolution was in progress in Wei, and when Confucius heard it, he said, "Ch'ae will come here, but Yew will die."[18] So it turned out. When Tsze-kaou saw that matters were desperate he made his escape, but Tsze-loo would not forsake the chief who had treated him well. He threw himself into the melee, and was slain. Confucius wept sore for him, but his own death was not far off. It took place on the 11th day of the 4th month in the following year, B.C. 478.[19]

Early one morning, we are told, he got up, and with his hands behind his back, dragging his staff, he moved about by his door, crooning over,—

"The great mountain must crumble;
The strong beam must break;
And the wise man wither away like a plant."

15 See the 左傳.哀公十四年, and Analects, XIV. xxii. 16 Ana. XI. xii. 17 子羔, by surname Kaou (高), and name Ch'ae (柴). 18 See the 左傳.哀公十五年. 19 See the 左傳.哀公十六年, and Keang Yung's Life of Confucius, in loc.

After a little, he entered the house and sat down opposite the door. Tsze-kung had heard his words, and said to himself, "If the great mountain crumble, to what shall I look up? If the strong beam break, and the wise man wither away, on whom shall I lean? The master, I fear, is going to be ill." With this he hastened into the house. Confucius said to him, "Ts'ze, what makes you so late? According to the statutes of Hea, the corpse was dressed and coffined at the top of the eastern steps, treating the dead as if he were still the host. Under the Yin, the ceremony was performed between the two pillars, as if the dead were both host and guest. The rule of Chow is to perform it at the top of the western steps, treating the dead as if he were a guest. I am a man of Yin, and last night I dreamt that I was sitting with offerings before me between the two pillars. No intelligent monarch arises; there is not one in the empire that will make me his master. My time has come to die." So it was. He went to his couch, and after seven days expired.[20]

Such is the account which we have of the last hours of the great philosopher of China. His end was not unimpressive, but it was melancholy. He sunk behind a cloud. Disappointed hopes made his soul bitter. The great ones of the empire had not received his teachings. No wife nor child was by to do the kindly offices of affection for him. Nor were the expectations of another life present with him as he passed through the dark valley. He uttered no prayer, and he betrayed no apprehensions. Deep-treasured in his own heart may have been the thought that he had endeavoured to serve his generation by the will of God, but he gave no sign. "The mountain falling came to nought, and the rock was removed out of his place. So death prevailed against him and he passed; his countenance was changed, and he was sent away."

10. I flatter myself that the preceding paragraphs contain a more correct narrative of the principal incidents in the life of Confucius than has yet been given in any European language. They might easily have been expanded into a volume, but I did not wish to exhaust the subject, but only to furnish a sketch, which, while it might satisfy the general reader, would be of special assistance to the careful student of the classical Books. I had taken many notes of the manifest errors in regard to chronology and other matters in the

20 See the Le Ke, II. Pt. I. ii. 20.

"Family Sayings," and the chapter of Sze-ma Ts'een on the K'ung family, when the digest of Keang Yung, to which I have made frequent reference, attracted my attention. Conclusions to which I had come were confirmed, and a clue was furnished to difficulties which I was seeking to disentangle. I take the opportunity to acknowledge here my obligations to it. With a few notices of Confucius' habits and manners, I shall conclude this section.

Very little can be gathered from reliable sources on the personal appearance of the sage. The height of his father is stated, as I have noted, to have been ten feet, and though Confucius came short of this by four inches, he was often called "the tall man." It is allowed that the ancient foot or cubit was shorter than the modern, but it must be reduced more than any scholar I have consulted has yet done, to bring this statement within the range of credibility. The legends assign to his figure "nine-and-forty remarkable peculiarities,"[1] a tenth part of which would have made him more a monster than a man. Dr Morrison says that the images of him, which he had seen in the northern parts of China, represent him as of a dark swarthy colour.[2] It is not so with those common in the south. He was, no doubt, in size and complexion much the same as many of his descendants in the present day.

But if his disciples had nothing to chronicle of his personal appearance, they have gone very minutely into an account of many of his habits. The tenth book of the Analects is all occupied with his deportment, his eating, and his dress. In public, whether in the village, the temple, or the court, he was the man of rule and ceremony, but "at home he was not formal." Yet if not formal, he was particular. In bed even he did not forget himself;—"he did not lie like a corpse," and "he did not speak." "He required his sleeping dress to be half as long again as his body." "If he happened to be sick, and the prince came to visit him, he had his face to the east, made his court robes be put over him, and drew his girdle across them."

He was nice in his diet,—"not disliking to have his rice dressed fine, nor to have his minced meat cut small." "Anything at all

1 四十九表. 2 Chinese and English Dictionary, char. 孔. Sir John Davis also mentions seeing a figure of Confucius, in a temple near the Po-yang Lake, of which the complexion was 'quite black.' (The Chinese, vol II. p. 66).

gone he would not touch." "He must have his meat cut properly, and to every kind its proper sauce; but he was not a great eater." "It was only in wine that he laid down no limit to himself, but he did not allow himself to be confused by it." "When the villagers were drinking together, on those who carried staves going out, he went out immediately after." There must always be ginger at the table, and "when eating, he did not converse." "Although his food might be coarse rice and poor soup, he would offer a little of it in sacrifice, with a grave respectful air."

"On occasion of a sudden clap of thunder, or a violent wind, he would change countenance. He would do the same, and rise up moreover, when he found himself a guest at a loaded board." "At the sight of a person in mourning, he would also change countenance, and if he happened to be in his carriage, he would bend forward with a respectful salutation." "His general way in his carriage was not to turn his head round, nor talk hastily, nor point with his hands." He was charitable. "When any of his friends died, if there were no relations who could be depended on for the necessary offices, he would say, 'I will bury him.'"

The disciples were so careful to record these and other characteristics of their master, it is said, because every act, of movement or of rest, was closely associated with the great principles which it was his object to inculcate. The detail of so many small matters, however, does not impress a foreigner so favourably. There is a want of freedom about the philosopher. Somehow he is less a sage to me, after I have seen him at his table, in his undress, in his bed, and in his carriage.

SECTION II.

HIS INFLUENCE AND OPINIONS.

Homage rendered to Confucius by the emperors of China.

1. Confucius died, we have seen, complaining that of all the princes of the empire there was not one who would adopt his principles and obey his lessons. He had hardly passed from the stage of life, when his merit began to be acknowledged. When the duke Gae heard of his death, he pronounced his eulogy in the words, "Heaven has not left to me the aged man. There is none now to

assist me on the throne. Woe is me! Alas! O venerable Ne!"[1] Tsze-kung complained of the inconsistency of this lamentation from one who could not use the master when he was alive, but the duke was probably sincere in his grief. He caused a temple to be erected, and ordered that sacrifice should be offered to the sage, at the four seasons of the year.[2]

The emperors of the tottering dynasty of Chow had not the intelligence, nor were they in a position, to do honour to the departed philosopher, but the facts detailed in the first chapter of these prolegomena, in connection with the attempt of the founder of the Ts'in dynasty to destroy the monuments of antiquity, show how the authority of Confucius had come by that time to prevail through the empire. The founder of the Han dynasty, in passing through Loo, B.C. 194, visited his tomb and offered an ox in sacrifice to him. Other emperors since then have often made pilgrimages to the spot. The most famous temple in the empire now rises over the place of the grave. K'ang-he, the second and greatest of the rulers of the present dynasty, in the 23d year of his reign, there set the example of kneeling thrice, and each time laying his forehead thrice in the dust, before the image of the sage.

In the year of our Lord 1, began the practice of conferring honorary designations on Confucius by imperial authority. The emperor P'ing[3] then styled him—"The duke Ne, all-complete and illustrious."[4] This was changed, in A.D. 492, to—"The venerable Ne, the accomplished Sage."[5] Other titles have supplanted this. Shun-che,[6] the first of the Man-chow dynasty, adopted, in his second year, A.D. 645, the style,—"K'ung, the ancient Teacher, accomplished and illustrious, all-complete, the perfect Sage;"[7] but twelve years later, a shorter title was introduced,—"K'ung, the ancient Teacher, the perfect Sage."[8] Since that year no further alteration has been made.

At first, the worship of Confucius was confined to the country of Loo, but in A.D. 57 it was enacted that sacrifices should be offered to him in the imperial college, and in all the colleges of the principal

1 Le Ke, II. Pt. I, iii. 43. This eulogy is found at greater length in the 左傳, immediately after the notice of the sage's death. 2 See the 聖廟祀典圖考, 卷一, art. on Confucius. I am indebted to this for most of the notices in this paragraph. 3 平帝. 4 成宣尼公. 5 文聖尼父. 6 順治. 7 大成至聖文宣先師孔子. 8 至聖先師孔子.

territorial divisions throughout the empire. In those sacrifices he was for some centuries associated with the duke of Chow, the legislator to whom Confucius made frequent reference, but in A.D. 609 separate temples were assigned to them, and in 628 our sage displaced the older worthy altogether. About the same time began the custom, which continues to the present day, of erecting temples to him,—separate structures, in connection with all the colleges, or examination-halls, of the country.

The sage is not alone in those temples. In a hall behind the principal one occupied by himself are the tablets—in some cases, the images—of several of his ancestors, and other worthies; while associated with himself are his principal disciples, and many who in subsequent times have signalized themselves as expounders and exemplifiers of his doctrines. On the first day of every month, offerings of fruits and vegetables are set forth, and on the fifteenth there is a solemn burning of incense. But twice a year, in the middle months of spring and autumn, when the first *ting* day* of the month comes round, the worship of Confucius is performed with peculiar solemnity. At the imperial college the emperor himself is required to attend in state, and is in fact the principal performer. After all the preliminary arrangements have been made, and the emperor has twice knelt and six times bowed his head to the earth, the presence of Confucius' spirit is invoked in the words, "Great art thou, O perfect sage! Thy virtue is full; thy doctrine is complete. Among mortal men there has not been thine equal. All kings honour thee. Thy statutes and laws have come gloriously down. Thou art the pattern in this imperial school. Reverently have the sacrificial vessels been set out. Full of awe, we sound our drums and bells."[10]

The spirit is supposed now to be present, and the service proceeds through various offerings, when the first of which has been set forth, an officer reads the following,[11] which is the prayer on the occasion:—"On this....month of this....year, I, *A.B.*, the emperor, offer a sacrifice to the philosopher K'ung, the ancient Teacher, the perfect Sage, and say,—O Teacher, in virtue equal to Heaven and Earth, whose doctrines embrace the past time and the present, thou didst digest and transmit the six classics, and didst hand down lessons for all generations!

* 上丁日. 10, 11 See the 大清通禮, 卷十二.

Now in this second month of spring (or autumn), in reverent observance of the old statutes, with victims, silks, spirits, and fruits, I carefully offer sacrifice to thee. With thee are associated the philosopher Yen, continuator of thee; the philosopher Tsăng, exhibiter of thy fundamental principles; the philosopher Tsze-sze, transmitter of thee; and the philosopher Măng, second to thee. May'st thou enjoy the offerings."

I need not go on to enlarge on the homage which the emperors of China render to Confucius. It could not be more complete. It is worship and not mere homage. He was unreasonably neglected when alive. He is now unreasonably venerated when dead. The estimation with which the rulers of China regard their sage, leads them to sin against God, and is a misfortune to the empire.

General appreciation of Confucius.

2. The rulers of China are not singular in this matter, but in entire sympathy with the mass of their people. It is the distinction of this empire that education has been highly prized in it from the earliest times. It was so before the era of Confucius, and we may be sure that the system met with his approbation. One of his remarkable sayings was,—"To lead an uninstructed people to war is to throw them away."[1] When he pronounced this judgment, he was not thinking of military training, but of education in the duties of life and citizenship. A people so taught, he thought, would be morally fitted to fight for their government. Mencius, when lecturing to the duke of T'ăng on the proper way of governing a kingdom, told him that he must provide the means of education for all, the poor as well as the rich. "Establish," said he, "*ts'eang*, *seu*, *heŏ*, and *heaou*,—all those educational institutions,—for the instruction of the people."[2]

At the present day, education is widely diffused throughout China. In no other country is the schoolmaster more abroad, and in all schools it is Confucius who is taught. The plan of competitive examinations, and the selection for civil offices only from those who have been successful candidates,—good so far as the competition is concerned, but injurious from the restricted range of subjects with which an acquaintance is required,—have obtained for more than twelve centuries. The classical works are the text books. It is from them almost exclusively that the themes proposed to determine

1 Ana. XIII. 30. 2 Mencius, III. Pt. I. iii 10.

the knowledge and ability of the students are chosen. The whole of the magistracy of China is thus versed in all that is recorded of the sage, and in the ancient literature which he preserved. His thoughts are familiar to every man in authority, and his character is more or less reproduced in him.

The official civilians of China, numerous as they are, are but a fraction of its students, and the students, or those who make literature a profession, are again but a fraction of those who attend school for a shorter or longer period. Yet so far as the studies have gone, they have been occupied with the Confucian writings. In many schoolrooms there is a tablet or inscription on the wall, sacred to the sage, and every pupil is required, on coming to school on the morning of the 1st and 15th of every month, to bow before it, the first thing, as an act of worship.[3] Thus all in China who receive the slightest tincture of learning do so at the fountain of Confucius. They learn of him and do homage to him at once. I have repeatedly quoted the statement that during his life-time he had three thousand disciples. Hundreds of millions are his disciples now. It is hardly necessary to make any allowance in this statement for the followers of Taouism and Buddhism, for, as Sir John Davis has observed, "whatever the other opinions or faith of a Chinese may be, he takes good care to treat Confucius with respect."[4] For two thousand years he has reigned supreme, the undisputed teacher of this most populous land.

3. This position and influence of Confucius are to be ascribed, I conceive, chiefly to two causes:—his being the preserver, namely of the monuments of antiquity, and the exemplifier and expounder of the maxims of the golden age of China; and the devotion to him of his immediate disciples and their early followers. The national and the personal are thus blended in him, each in its highest degree of excellence. He was a Chinese of the Chinese; he is also represented, and all now believe him to have been, the *beau ideal* of humanity in its best and noblest estate.

The causes of his influence.

4. It may be well to bring forward here Confucius' own estimate of himself, and of his doctrines. It will serve to illustrate the

3 During the present dynasty, the tablet of 文昌帝君, the god of literature, has to a considerable extent displaced that of Confucius in schools. Yet the worship of him does not clash with that of the other. He is 'the father' of composition only.

4 The Chinese, vol. II, p. 45.

His own estimate of himself and of his doctrines.

statements just made. The following are some of his sayings.—"The sage and the man of perfect virtue;—how dare I rank myself with them? It may simply be said of me, that I strive to become such without satiety, and teach others without weariness." "In letters I am perhaps equal to other men; but the character of the superior man, carrying out in his conduct what he professes, is what I have not yet attained to." "The leaving virtue without proper cultivation; the not thoroughly discussing what is learned; not being able to move towards righteousness of which a knowledge is gained; and not being able to change what is not good;—these are the things which occasion me solicitude." "I am not one who was born in the possession of knowledge; I am one who is fond of antiquity and earnest in seeking it there." "A transmitter and not a maker, believing in and loving the ancients, I venture to compare myself with our old P'ang."[1]

Confucius cannot be thought to speak of himself in these declarations more highly than he ought to do. Rather we may recognize in them the expressions of a genuine humility. He was conscious that personally he came short in many things, but he toiled after the character, which he saw, or fancied that he saw, in the ancient sages whom he acknowledged; and the lessons of government and morals which he laboured to diffuse were those which had already been inculcated and exhibited by them. Emphatically he was "a transmitter and not a maker." It is not to be understood that he was not fully satisfied of the truth of the principles which he had learned. He held them with the full approval and consent of his own understanding. He believed that if they were acted on, they would remedy the evils of his time. There was nothing to prevent rulers like Yaou and Shun and the great Yu from again arising, and a condition of happy tranquillity being realized throughout the empire under their sway.

If in any thing he thought himself "superior and alone," having attributes which others could not claim, it was in his possessing a divine commission as the conservator of ancient truth and rules. He does not speak very definitely on this point. It is noted that

1 All these passages are taken from the VIIth Book of the Analects. See chh. xxxiii; xxxii.; iii.; xix.; and i.

"the appointments of Heaven was one of the subjects on which he rarely touched."[2] His most remarkable utterance was that which I have already given in the sketch of his Life:—"When he was put in fear in K'wang, he said, 'After the death of king Wăn, was not the cause of truth lodged here in me? If Heaven had wished to let this cause of truth perish, then I, a future mortal, should not have got such a relation to that cause. While Heaven does not let the cause of truth perish, what can the people of Kwang do to me?'"[3] Confucius, then, did feel that he was in the world for a special purpose. But it was not to announce any new truths, or to initiate any new economy. It was to prevent what had previously been known from being lost. He followed in the wake of Yaou and Shun, of T'ang, and king Wăn. Distant from the last by a long interval of time, he would have said that he was distant from him also by a great inferiority of character, but still he had learned the principles on which they all happily governed the empire, and in their name he would lift up a standard against the prevailing lawlessness of his age.

Estimate of him by his disciples and their early followers.

5. The language employed with reference to Confucius by his disciples and their early followers presents a striking contrast with his own. I have already, in writing of the scope and value of "The Doctrine of the Mean," called attention to the extravagant eulogies of his grandson Tsze-sze. He only followed the example which had been set by those among whom the philosopher went in and out. We have the language of Yen Yuen, his favourite, which is comparatively moderate, and simply expresses the genuine admiration of a devoted pupil.[1] Tsze-kung on several occasions spoke in a different style. Having heard that one of the chiefs of Loo had said that he himself—Tsze-kung—was superior to Confucius, he observed, "Let me use the comparison of a house and its encompassing wall. My wall only reaches to the shoulders. One may peep over it, and see whatever is valuable in the apartments. The wall of my master is several fathoms high. If one do not find the door and enter by it, he cannot see the rich ancestral temple with its beauties, nor all the officers in their rich array. But I may assume

2 Ana. IX. i. 3 Ana. IX. iii.
1 Ana. IX. x.

that they are few who find the door. The remark of the chief was only what might have been expected."[2]

Another time, the same individual having spoken revilingly of Confucius, Tsze-kung said, "It is of no use doing so. Chung-ne cannot be reviled. The talents and virtue of other men are hillocks and mounds which may be stept over. Chung-ne is the sun or moon, which it is not possible to step over. Although a man may wish to cut himself off from the sage, what harm can he do to the sun and moon? He only shows that he does not know his own capacity."[3]

In conversation with a fellow-disciple, Tsze-kung took a still higher flight. Being charged by Tsze-k'in with being too modest, for that Confucius was not really superior to him, he replied, "For one word a man is often deemed to be wise, and for one word he is often deemed to be foolish. We ought to be careful indeed in what we say. Our master cannot be attained to, just in the same way as the heavens cannot be gone up to by the steps of a stair. Were our master in the position of the prince of a State, or the chief of a Family, we should find verified the description which has been given of a sage's rule:—He would plant the people, and forthwith they would be established; he would lead them on, and forthwith they would follow him; he would make them happy, and forthwith multitudes would resort to his dominions; he would stimulate them, and forthwith they would be harmonious. While he lived, he would be glorious. When he died, he would be bitterly lamented. How is it possible for him to be attained to?"[4]

From these representations of Tsze-kung, it was not a difficult step for Tsze-sze to make in exalting Confucius not only to the level of the ancient sages, but as "the equal of Heaven." And Mencius took up the theme. Being questioned by Kung-sun Ch'ow, one of his disciples, about two acknowledged sages, Pih-e and E Yin, whether they were to be placed in the same rank with Confucius, he replied, "No. Since there were living men until now, there never was another Confucius;" and then he proceeded to fortify his opinion by the concurring testimony of Tsae Go, Tsze-kung and Yew Jŏ, who all had wisdom, he thought, sufficient to know their master. Tsae Go's opinion was, "According to my view of our master, he is

2 Ana. XIX. xxiii. 3 Ana. XIX. xxiv. 4 Ana. XIX. xxv.

far superior to Yaou and Shun." Tsze-kung said, "By viewing the ceremonial ordinances of a prince, we know the character of his government. By hearing his music, we know the character of his virtue. From the distance of a hundred ages after, I can arrange, according to their merits, the kings of a hundred ages;—not one of them can escape me. From the birth of mankind till now, there has never been another like our master." Yew Jŏ said, "Is it only among men that it is so? There is the k'e-lin among quadrupeds; the fung-hwang among birds; the T'ae mountain among mounds and ant-hills; and rivers and seas among rain-pools. Though different in degree, they are the same in kind. So the sages among mankind are also the same in kind. But they stand out from their fellows, and rise above the level; and from the birth of mankind till now, there never has been one so complete as Confucius."[5] I will not indulge in further illustration. The judgment of the sage's disciples, of Tsze-sze, and of Mencius, has been unchallenged by the mass of the scholars of China. Doubtless it pleases them to bow down at the shrine of the sage, for their profession of literature is thereby glorified. A reflection of the honour done to him falls upon themselves. And the powers that be, and the multitudes of the people, fall in with the judgment. Confucius is thus, in the empire of China, the one man by whom all possible personal excellence was exemplified, and by whom all possible lessons of social virtue and political wisdom are taught.

Subjects on which Confucius did not treat.—That he was unreligious, unspiritual, and open to the charge of insincerity.

6. The reader will be prepared by the preceding account not to expect to find any light thrown by Confucius on the great problems of the human condition and destiny. He did not speculate on the creation of things or the end of them. He was not troubled to account for the origin of man, nor did he seek to know about his hereafter. He meddled neither with physics nor metaphysics.[1] The testimony of the Analects about the subjects of his

5 Mencius, II. Pt. I. ii. 23—28.

1 The contents of the Yih-king, and Confucius' labours upon it, may be objected in opposition to this statement, and I must be understood to make it with some reservation. Six years ago, I spent all my leisure time for twelve months in the study of that Work, and wrote out a translation of it, but at the close I was only groping my way in darkness to lay hold of its scope and meaning, and up to this time I have not been able to master it so as to speak positively about it. It will come in due time, in its place, in the present Publication, and I do not think that what I here say of Confucius will require much, if any, modification.

teaching is the following:—"His frequent themes of discourse were the Book of Poetry, the Book of History, and the maintenance of the rules of Propriety." "He taught letters, ethics, devotion of soul, and truthfulness." "Extraordinary things; feats of strength; states of disorder; and spiritual beings; he did not like to talk about."[2]

Confucius is not to be blamed for his silence on the subjects here indicated. His ignorance of them was to a great extent his misfortune. He had not learned them. No report of them had come to him by the ear; no vision of them by the eye. And to his practical mind the toiling of thought amid uncertainties seemed worse than useless.

The question has, indeed, been raised, whether he did not make changes in the ancient creed of China,[3] but I cannot believe that he did so consciously and designedly. Had his idiosyncrasy been different, we might have had expositions of the ancient views on some points, the effect of which would have been more beneficial than the indefiniteness in which they are now left, and it may be doubted so far, whether Confucius was not unfaithful to his guides. But that he suppressed or added, in order to bring in articles of belief originating with himself, is a thing not to be charged against him.

I will mention two important subjects in regard to which there is a growing conviction in my mind that he came short of the faith of the older sages. The first is the doctrine of God. This name is common in the She-king, and Shoo-king. *Te* or *Shang Te* appears there as a personal being, ruling in heaven and on earth, the author of man's moral nature, the governor among the nations, by whom kings reign and princes decree justice, the rewarder of the good, and the punisher of the bad. Confucius preferred to speak of Heaven. Instances have already been given of this. Two others may be cited: —"He who offends against Heaven has none to whom he can pray?"[4] "Alas!" said he, "there is no one that knows me." Tsze-kung said, "What do you mean by thus saying that no one knows you?" He replied, "I do not murmur against Heaven. I do not grumble against men. My studies lie low, and my penetration rises high. But there is Heaven;—that knows me!"[5] Not once throughout the

2. Ana. VII. xvii; xxiv; xx. 3 See Hardwick's 'Christ and other Masters,' Part III. pp. 18, 19, with his reference in a note to a passage from Meadows' 'The Chinese and their Rebellions.' 4 Ana. III. xiii. 5 Ana. XIV. xxxvii.

Analects does he use the personal name. I would say that he was unreligious rather than irreligious; yet by the coldness of his temperament and intellect in this matter, his influence is unfavourable to the development of true religious feeling among the Chinese people generally, and he prepared the way for the speculations of the literati of mediæval and modern times, which have exposed them to the charge of atheism.

Secondly, Along with the worship of God there existed in China, from the earliest historical times, the worship of other spiritual beings,—especially, and to every individual, the worship of departed ancestors. Confucius recognized this as an institution to be devoutly observed. "He sacrificed to the dead as if they were present; he sacrificed to the spirits as if the spirits were present. He said, 'I consider my not being present at the sacrifice as if I did not sacrifice.'"[6] The custom must have originated from a belief of the continued existence of the dead. We cannot suppose that they who instituted it thought that with the cessation of this life on earth there was a cessation also of all conscious being. But Confucius never spoke explicitly on this subject. He tried to evade it. "Ke Loo asked about serving the spirits of the dead, and the master said, 'While you are not able to serve men, how can you serve their spirits?' The disciple added, 'I venture to ask about death,' and he was answered, 'While you do not know life, how can you know about death.'"[7] Still more striking is a conversation with another disciple, recorded in the "Family Sayings." Tsze-kung asked him, saying, "Do the dead have knowledge (of our services, that is), or are they without knowledge?" The master replied, "If I were to say that the dead have such knowledge, I am afraid that filial sons and dutiful grandsons would injure their substance in paying the last offices to the departed; and if I were to say that the dead have not such knowledge, I am afraid lest unfilial sons should leave their parents unburied. You need not wish, Ts'ze, to know whether the dead have knowledge or not. There is no present urgency about the point. Hereafter you will know it for yourself."[8] Surely this was not the teaching proper to a sage. He said on one occasion that he had

6 Ana. III. xii. 7 Ana. XI. xi. 8 家語, 卷二. art. 致思, towards the end.

no concealments from his disciples.[9] Why did he not candidly tell his real thoughts on so interesting a subject? I incline to think that he doubted more than he believed. If the case were not so, it would be difficult to account for the answer which he returned to a question as to what constituted wisdom. "To give one's-self earnestly," said he, "to the duties due to men, and, while respecting spiritual beings, to keep aloof from them, may be called wisdom."[10] At any rate, as by his frequent references to Heaven, instead of following the phraseology of the older sages, he gave occasion to many of his professed followers to identify God with a principle of reason and the course of nature; so, in the point now in hand, he has led them to deny, like the Sadducees of old, the existence of any spirit at all, and to tell us that their sacrifices to the dead are but an outward form, the mode of expression which the principle of filial piety requires them to adopt, when its objects have departed this life.

It will not be supposed that I wish to advocate or to defend the practice of sacrificing to the dead. My object has been to point out how Confucius recognized it, without acknowledging the faith from which it must have originated, and how he enforced it as a matter of form or ceremony. It thus connects itself with the most serious charge that can be brought against him,—the charge of insincerity. Among the four things which it is said he taught, "truthfulness" is specified,[11] and many sayings might be quoted from him, in which "sincerity" is celebrated as highly and demanded as stringently as ever it has been by any Christian moralist; yet he was not altogether the truthful and true man to whom we accord our highest approbation. There was the case of Măng Che-fan, who boldly brought up the rear of the defeated troops of Loo, and attributed his occupying the place of honour to the backwardness of his horse. The action was gallant, but the apology for it was weak and wrong. And yet Confucius saw nothing in the whole but matter for praise.[12] He could excuse himself from seeing an unwelcome visitor on the ground that he was sick, when there was nothing the matter with him.[13] These perhaps were small matters, but what shall we say to the incident which I have given in the sketch of his Life, p. 80,—his deliberately breaking the oath which

9 Ana. VII. xxiii. 10 Ana. VI. xx. 11 See above, near the beginning of this paragraph. 12 Ana. VI. xiii. 13 Ana. XVII. xx.

he had sworn, simply on the ground that it had been forced from him? I should be glad if I could find evidence on which to deny the truth of that occurrence. But it rests on the same authority as most other statements about him, and it is accepted as a fact by the people and scholars of China. It must have had, and it must still have, a very injurious influence upon them. Foreigners charge, and with reason, a habit of deceitfulness upon the nation and its government. For every word of falsehood and every act of insincerity, the guilty party must bear his own burden, but we cannot but regret the example of Confucius in this particular. It is with the Chinese and their sage, as it was with the Jews of old and their teachers. He that leads them has caused them to err, and destroyed the way of their paths.[14]

But was not insincerity a natural result of the un-religion of Confucius? There are certain virtues which demand a true piety in order to their flourishing in the corrupt heart of man. Natural affection, the feeling of loyalty, and enlightened policy, may do much to build up and preserve a family and a State, but it requires more to maintain the love of truth, and make a lie, spoken or acted, to be shrunk from with shame. It requires in fact the living recognition of a God of truth, and all the sanctions of revealed religion. Unfortunately the Chinese have not had these, and the example of him to whom they bow down as the best and wisest of men, encourages them to act, to dissemble, to sin.

His views on government.

7. I go on to a brief discussion of Confucius' views on government, or what we may call his principles of political science. It could not be in his long intercourse with his disciples but that he should enunciate many maxims bearing on character and morals generally, but he never rested in the improvement of the individual. "The empire brought to a state of happy tranquillity"[1] was the grand object which he delighted to think of; that it might be brought about as easily as "one can look upon the palm of his hand," was the dream which it pleased him to indulge in.[2] He held that there was in men an adaptation and readiness to be governed, which only needed to be taken advantage of in the proper way. There must be the right administrators, but given those, and "the

14 Isaiah, III. 12.

1 天下平. See the 大學經, parr. 4, 5; &c. 2 Ana. III. xi; et al.

growth of government would be rapid, just as vegetation is rapid in the earth; yea, their government would display itself like an easily-growing rush."[3] The same sentiment was common from the lips of Mencius. Enforcing it one day, when conversing with one of the petty princes of his time, he said in his peculiar style, "Does your Majesty understand the way of the growing grain? During the seventh and eighth months, when drought prevails, the plants become dry. Then the clouds collect densely in the heavens, they send down torrents of rain, and the grain erects itself as if by a shoot. When it does so, who can keep it back?"[4] Such, he contended, would be the response of the mass of the people to any true "shepherd of men." It may be deemed unnecessary that I should specify this point, for it is a truth applicable to the people of all nations. Speaking generally, government is by no device or cunning craftiness; human nature demands it. But in no other family of mankind is the characteristic so largely developed as in the Chinese. The love of order and quiet, and a willinguess to submit to "the powers that be", eminently distinguish them. Foreign writers have often taken notice of this, and have attributed it to the influence of Confucius' doctrines as inculcating subordination; but it existed previous to his time. The character of the people moulded his system, more than it was moulded by it.

This readiness to be governed arose, according to Confucius, from "the duties of universal obligation, or those between sovereign and minister, between father and son, between husband and wife, between elder brother and younger, and those belonging to the intercourse of friends."[5] Men as they are born into the world, and grow up in it, find themselves existing in those relations. They are the appointment of Heaven. And each relation has its reciprocal obligations, the recognition of which is proper to the Heaven-conferred nature. It only needs that the sacredness of the relations be maintained, and the duties belonging to them faithfully discharged, and the "happy tranquillity" will prevail all under heaven. As to the institutions of government, the laws and arrangements by which, as through a thousand channels, it should go forth to carry plenty and prosperity through the length and breadth of the country, it did not belong to Confucius, "the throneless king," to set them forth minutely. And

3 中庸, xx 3. 4 Mencius, I. Pt. I. vi. 6. 5 中庸, xx. 8

indeed they were existing in the records of "the ancient sovereigns." Nothing new was needed. It was only requisite to pursue the old paths, and raise up the old standards. "The government of Wăn and Woo," he said, "is displayed in the records,—the tablets of wood and bamboo. Let there be the men, and the government will flourish, but without the men, the government decays and ceases."[6] To the same effect was the reply which he gave to Yen Hwuy when asked by him how the government of a State should be administered. It seems very wide of the mark, until we read it in the light of the sage's veneration for ancient ordinances, and his opinion of their sufficiency. "Follow," he said, "the seasons of Hea. Ride in the state-carriages of Yin. Wear the ceremonial cap of Chow. Let the music be the Shaou with its pantomimes. Banish the songs of Ch'ing, and keep far from specious talkers."[7]

Confucius' idea then of a happy, well-governed State did not go beyond the flourishing of the five relations of society which have been mentioned; and we have not any condensed exhibition from him of their nature, or of the duties belonging to the several parties in them. Of the two first he spoke frequently, but all that he has said on the others would go into small compass. Mencius has said that "between father and son there should be affection; between sovereign and minister righteousness; between husband and wife attention to their separate functions; between old and young, a proper order; and between friends, fidelity."[8] Confucius, I apprehend, would hardly have accepted this account. It does not bring out sufficiently the authority which he claimed for the father and the sovereign, and the obedience which he exacted from the child and the minister. With regard to the relation of husband and wife, he was in no respect superior to the preceding sages who had enunciated their views of "propriety" on the subject. We have a somewhat detailed exposition of his opinions in the "Family Sayings."—"Man," said he, "is the representative of Heaven, and is supreme over all things. Woman yields obedience to the instructions of man, and helps to carry out his principles.[9] On this account she can determine nothing of herself, and is subject to the rule of the three

6 中庸, xx. 2. 7 Ana. XV. x. 8 Mencius, III. Pt. I. iv. 8. 9 男子者,任天道而長萬物者也;女子者,順男子之道,而長其理者也.

obediences. When young, she must obey her father and elder brother; when married, she must obey her husband; when her husband is dead, she must obey her son. She may not think of marrying a second time. No instructions or orders must issue from the harem. Woman's business is simply the preparation and supplying of wine and food. Beyond the threshold of her apartments she should not be known for evil or for good. She may not cross the boundaries of the State to accompany a funeral. She may take no step on her own motion, and may come to no conclusion on her own deliberation. There are five women who are not to be taken in marriage:—the daughter of a rebellious house; the daughter of a disorderly house; the daughter of a house which has produced criminals for more than one generation; the daughter of a leprous house; and the daughter who has lost her father and elder brother. A wife may be divorced for seven reasons, which may be overruled by three considerations. The grounds for divorce are disobedience to her husband's parents; not giving birth to a son; dissolute conduct; jealousy (of her husband's attentions, that is, to the other inmates of his harem); talkativeness; and thieving. The three considerations which may overrule these grounds are—first, if, while she was taken from a home, she has now no home to return to; second, if she have passed with her husband through the three years' mourning for his parents; third, if the husband have become rich from being poor. All these regulations were adopted by the sages in harmony with the natures of man and woman, and to give importance to the ordinance of marriage."[10]

With these ideas—not very enlarged—of the relations of society, Confucius dwelt much on the necessity of personal correctness of character on the part of those in authority, in order to secure the right fulfilment of the duties implied in them. This is one grand peculiarity of his teaching. I have adverted to it in the review of "The Great Learning," but it deserves some further exhibition, and there are three conversations with the chief Ke K'ang, in which it is very expressly set forth. "Ke K'ang asked about government, and Confucius replied, 'To govern means to rectify. If you lead on the people with correctness, who will dare not to be correct?'" "Ke K'ang, distressed about the number of thieves in the State, inquired

10 家語卷三·本命解·

of Confucius about how to do away with them. Confucius said, 'If you, sir, were not covetous, though you should reward them to do it, they would not steal.'" "Ke K'ang asked about government, saying, 'What do You say to killing the unprincipled for the good of the principled?' Confucius replied, 'Sir, in carrying on your government, why should you use killing at all? Let your evinced desires be for what is good, and the people will be good. The relation between superiors and inferiors is like that between the wind and the grass. The grass must bend, when the wind blows across it.'"[11]

Example is not so powerful as Confucius in these and many other passages represented it, but its influence is very great. Its virtue is recognized in the family, and it is demanded in the church of Christ. "A bishop"—and I quote the term with the simple meaning of overseer—"must be blameless." It seems to me, however, that in the progress of society in the West we have come to think less of the power of example in many departments of State than we ought to do. It is thought of too little in the army and the navy. We laugh at the "self-denying ordinance," and the "new model" of 1644, but there lay beneath them the principle which Confucius so broadly propounded,—the importance of personal virtue in all who are in authority. Now that Great Britain is the governing power over the masses of India, and that we are coming more and more into contact with tens of thousands of the Chinese, this maxim of our sage is deserving of serious consideration from all who bear rule, and especially from those on whom devolves the conduct of affairs. His words on the susceptibility of the people to be acted on by those above them ought not to prove as water spilt on the ground.

But to return to Confucius.—As he thus lays it down that the mainspring of the well-being of society is the personal character of the ruler, we look anxiously for what directions he has given for the cultivation of that. But here he is very defective. "Self-adjustment and purification," he said, "with careful regulation of his dress, and the not making a movement contrary to the rules of propriety;—this is the way for the ruler to cultivate his person."[12] This is laying too much stress on what is external; but even to attain to this

11 Analects, XII. xvii.; xviii.; xix. 12 中 庸, xx. 14.

is beyond unassisted human strength. Confucius, however, never recognized a disturbance of the moral elements in the constitution of man. The people would move, according to him, to the virtue of their ruler as the grass bends to the wind, and that virtue would come to the ruler at his call. Many were the lamentations which he uttered over the degeneracy of his times; frequent were the confessions which he made of his own shortcomings. It seems strange that it never came distinctly before him, that there is a power of evil in the prince and the peasant, which no efforts of their own and no instructions of sages are effectual to subdue.

The government which Confucius taught was a despotism, but of a modified character. He allowed no "*jus divinum*," independent of personal virtue and a benevolent rule. He has not explicitly stated, indeed, wherein lies the ground of the great relation of the governor and the governed, but his views on the subject were, we may assume, in accordance with the language of the Shoo-king:—"Heaven and Earth are the parents of all things, and of all things men are the most intelligent. The man among them most distinguished for intelligence becomes chief ruler, and ought to prove himself the parent of the people."[13] And again, "Heaven, protecting the inferior people, has constituted for them rulers and teachers, who should be able to be assisting to God, extending favour and producing tranquillity throughout all parts of the empire."[14] The moment the ruler ceases to be a minister of God for good, and does not administer a government that is beneficial to the people, he forfeits the title by which he holds the throne, and perseverance in oppression will surely lead to his overthrow. Mencius inculcated this principle with a frequency and boldness which are remarkable. It was one of the things about which Confucius did not like to talk. Still he held it. It is conspicuous in the last chapter of "The Great Learning." Its tendency has been to check the violence of oppression, and maintain the self-respect of the people, all along the course of Chinese history.

I must bring these observations on Confucius' views of government to a close, and I do so with two remarks. First, they are adapted to a primitive, unsophisticated state of society. He is a good counsellor for the father of a family, the chief of a clan, and even the head of a small principality. But his views want the comprehen-

13, 14 See the Shoo-king, V. I. Sect. I. 2, 7.

sion which would make them of much service in a great empire. Within three centuries after his death, the government of China passed into a new phase. The founder of the Ts'in dynasty conceived the grand idea of abolishing all its feudal Kingdoms, and centralizing their administration in himself. He effected the revolution, and succeeding dynasties adopted his system, and gradually moulded it into the forms and proportions which are now existing. There has been a tendency to advance, and Confucius has all along been trying to carry the nation back. Principles have been needed, and not "proprieties." The consequence is that China has increased beyond its ancient dimensions, while there has been no corresponding development of thought. Its body politic has the size of giant, while it still retains the mind of a child. Its hoary age is but senility.

Second, Confucius makes no provision for the intercourse of his country with other and independent nations. He knew indeed of none such. China was to him "The middle Kingdom,"[15] "The multitude of Great States,"[16] "All under heaven."[17] Beyond it were only rude and barbarous tribes. He does not speak of them bitterly, as many Chinese have done since his time. In one place he contrasts them favourably with the prevailing anarchy of the empire, saying, "The rude tribes of the east and north have their princes, and are not like the States of our great land which are without them."[18] Another time, disgusted with the want of appreciation which he experienced, he was expressing his intention to go and live among the nine wild tribes of the east. Some one said, "They are rude. How can you do such a thing?" His reply was, "If a superior man dwelt among them, what rudeness would there be?"[19] But had he been an emperor-sage, he would not only have influenced them by his instructions, but brought them to acknowledge and submit to his sway, as the great Yu did.[20] The only passage of Confucius' teachings from which any rule can be gathered for dealing with foreigners, is that in the "Doctrine of the Mean," where "indulgent treatment of men from a distance" is laid down as one of the nine standard rules for the government of the empire.[21] But "the men from a distance" are understood to be *pin* and *leu*[22] simply,— "guests," that is, or officers of one State seeking employment in

15 中國. 16 諸夏: Ana. III. v. 17 天下: *passim*. 18 Ana. III. v. 19 Ana. IX. xiii. 20 書經. III. ii. 10; *et al.* 21 柔遠人. 22 賓旅.

another, or at the imperial court; and "visitors," or travelling merchants. Of independent nations the ancient classics have not any knowledge, nor has Confucius. So long as merchants from Europe and other parts of the world could have been content to appear in China as suppliants, seeking the privilege of trade, so long the government would have ranked them with the barbarous hordes of antiquity, and given them the benefit of the maxim about "indulgent treatment," according to its own understanding of it. But when their governments interfered, and claimed to treat with that of China on terms of equality, and that their subjects should be spoken to and of as being of the same clay with the Chinese themselves, an outrage was committed on tradition and prejudice, which it was necessary to resent with vehemence.

I do not charge the contemptuous arrogance of the Chinese government and people upon Confucius; what I deplore, is that he left no principles on record to check the development of such a spirit. His simple views of society and government were in a measure sufficient for the people while they dwelt apart from the rest of mankind. His practical lessons were better than if they had been left, which but for him they probably would have been, to fall a prey to the influences of Taouism and Buddhism, but they could only subsist while they were left alone. Of the earth earthy, China was sure to go to pieces when it came into collision with a Christianly-civilized power. Its sage had left it no preservative or restorative elements against such a case.

It is a rude awakening from its complacency of centuries which China has now received. Its ancient landmarks are swept away. Opinions will differ as to the justice or injustice of the grounds on which it has been assailed, and I do not feel called to judge or to pronounce here concerning them. In the progress of events, it could not be but that the collision should come; and when it did come, it could not be but that China should be broken and scattered. Disorganization will go on to destroy it more and more, and yet there is hope for the people, with their veneration of the relations of society, with their devotion to learning, and with their habits of industry and sobriety;—there is hope for them, if they will look away from all their ancient sages, and turn to Him, who sends them, along with the dissolution of their ancient state, the knowledge of Himself, the only living and true God, and of Jesus Christ whom He hath sent.

8. I have little more to add on the opinions of Confucius. Many of his sayings are pithy, and display much knowledge of character; but as they are contained in the body of the Work, I will not occupy the space here with a selection of those which have struck myself as most worthy of notice. The fourth Book of the Analects, which is on the subject of *jin*, or perfect virtue, has several utterances which are remarkable.

Thornton observes:—"It may excite surprise, and probably incredulity, to state that the golden rule of our Saviour, 'Do unto others as you would that they should do unto you,' which Mr. Locke designates as 'the most unshaken rule of morality, and foundation of all social virtue,' had been inculcated by Confucius, almost in the same words, four centuries before."[1] I have taken notice of this fact in reviewing both "The Great Learning," and "The Doctrine of the Mean." I would be far from grudging a tribute of admiration to Confucius for it. The maxim occurs also twice in the Analects. In Book XV. xxiii., Tsze-kung asks if there be one word which may serve as a rule of practice for all one's life, and is answered, "Is not reciprocity such a word? What you do not want done to yourself do not do to others." The same disciple appears in Book V. xi., telling Confucius that he was practising the lesson. He says, "What I do not wish men to do to me, I also wish not to do to men;" but the master tells him, "Ts'ze, you have not attained to that." It would appear from this reply, that he was aware of the difficulty of obeying the precept; and it is not found, in its condensed expression at least, in the older classics. The merit of it is Confucius' own.

When a comparison, however, is drawn between it and the rule laid down by Christ, it is proper to call attention to the positive form of the latter,—"All things whatsoever ye would that men should do unto you, do ye even so to them." The lesson of the gospel commands men to do what they feel to be right and good. It requires them to commence a course of such conduct, without regard to the conduct of others to themselves. The lesson of Confucius only forbids men to do what they feel to be wrong and hurtful. So far as the point of priority is concerned, moreover, Christ adds, "This is the law and the prophets." The maxim was to be found substantially in the earlier revelations of God.

1 History of China, vol. I. p. 209.

But the worth of the two maxims depends on the intention of the enunciators in regard to their application. Confucius, it seems to me, did not think of the reciprocity coming into action beyond the circle of his five relations of society. Possibly, he might have required its observance in dealings even with the rude tribes, which were the only specimens of mankind besides his own countrymen of which he knew anything, for on one occasion, when asked about perfect virtue, he replied, "It is, in retirement, to be sedately grave; in the management of business, to be reverently attentive; in intercourse with others, to be strictly sincere. Though a man go among the rude uncultivated tribes, these qualities may not be neglected."[2] Still, Confucius delivered his rule to his countrymen only, and only for their guidance in their relations of which I have had so much occasion to speak. The rule of Christ is for man as man, having to do with other men, all with himself on the same platform, as the children and subjects of the one God and Father in heaven.

How far short Confucius came of the standard of Christian benevolence, may be seen from his remarks when asked what was to be thought of the principle that injury should be recompensed with kindness. He replied, "With what then will you recompense kindness? Recompense injury with justice, and recompense kindness with kindness."[3] The same deliverance is given in one of the Books of the Le Ke, where he adds that "he who recompenses injury with kindness is a man who is careful of his person."[4] Ch'ing Heuen, the commentator of the second century, says that such a course would be "incorrect in point of propriety."[5] This "propriety" was a great stumbling-block in the way of Confucius. His morality was the result of the balancings of his intellect, fettered by the decisions of men of old, and not the gushings of a loving heart, responsive to the promptings of Heaven, and in sympathy with erring and feeble humanity.

This subject leads me on to the last of the opinions of Confucius which I shall make the subject of remark in this place. A commentator observes, with reference to the inquiry about recompensing injury with kindness, that the questioner was asking only about trivial matters, which might be dealt with in the way he mentioned,

2 Analects, XIII. xix. 3 Ana. XIV. xxxvi. 4 禮記,表記, par. 12. 5 非禮之正.

while great offences such as those against a sovereign or a father, could not be dealt with by such an inversion of the principles of justice.[6] In the second Book of the Le Ke there is the following passage:—"With the slayer of his father, a man may not live under the same heaven; against the slayer of his brother, a man must never have to go home to fetch a weapon; with the slayer of his friend, a man may not live in the same State."[7] The *lex talionis* is here laid down in its fullest extent. The Chow Le tells us of a provision made against the evil consequences of the principle, by the appointment of a minister called "The Reconciler."[8] The provision is very inferior to the cities of refuge which were set apart by Moses for the manslayer to flee to from the fury of the avenger. Such as it was, however, it existed, and it is remarkable that Confucius, when consulted on the subject, took no notice of it, but affirmed the duty of blood-revenge in the strongest and most unrestricted terms. His disciple Tsze-hea asked him, "What course is to be pursued in the case of the murder of a father or mother?" He replied, "The son must sleep upon a matting of grass, with his shield for his pillow; he must decline to take office; he must not live under the same heaven with the slayer. When he meets him in the market-place or the court, he must have his weapon ready to strike him." "And what is the course on the murder of a brother?" "The surviving brother must not take office in the same State with the slayer; yet if he go on his prince's service to the State where the slayer is, though he meet him, he must not fight with him." "And what is the course on the murder of an uncle or a cousin?" "In this case the nephew or cousin is not the principal. If the principal on whom the revenge devolves can take it, he has only to stand behind with his weapon in his hand, and support him."[9]

Sir John Davis has rightly called attention to this as one of the objectionable principles of Confucius.[10] The bad effects of it are evident even in the present day. Revenge is sweet to the Chinese. I have spoken of their readiness to submit to government, and wish to live in peace, yet they do not like to resign even to government the "inquisition for blood." Where the ruling authority is feeble,

6 See notes in loc., p. 132. 7 禮記, I. Pt. I. v. 10. 8 周禮, 卷之十四, pp. 14–16. 9 禮記, II. Pt. I. ii. 24. See also the 家語, 卷四, 子貢問. 10 The Chinese, vol. II. p. 41.

as it is at present, individuals and clans take the law into their own hands, and whole districts are kept in a state of constant feud and warfare.

But I must now leave the sage. I hope I have not done him injustice; but after long study of his character and opinions, I am unable to regard him as a great man. He was not before his age, though he was above the mass of the officers and scholars of his time. He threw no new light on any of the questions which have a world-wide interest. He gave no impulse to religion. He had no sympathy with progress. His influence has been wonderful, but it will henceforth wane. My opinion is, that the faith of the nation in him will speedily and extensively pass away.

SECTION III.

HIS IMMEDIATE DISCIPLES.

Sze-ma Ts'een makes Confucius say:—"The disciples who received my instructions, and could comprehend them, were seventy-seven individuals. They were all scholars of extraordinary ability."[1] The common saying is, that the disciples of the sage were three thousand, while among them there were seventy-two worthies. I propose to give here a list of all those whose names have come down to us, as being his followers. Of the greater number it will be seen that we know nothing more than their names and surnames. My principal authorities will be the "Historical Records," the "Family Sayings," "The Sacrificial Canon for the Sage's Temple, with Plates," and the chapter on "The Disciples of Confucius" prefixed to the "Four Books, Text and Commentary, with Proofs and Illustrations." In giving a few notices of the better-known individuals, I will endeavour to avoid what may be gathered from the Analects.

1. Yen Hwuy, by designation Tsze-yuen (顏回.字子淵). He was a native of Loo, the favourite of his master, whose junior he was by 30 years, and whose disciple he became when he was quite a youth. "After I got Hwuy," Confucius remarked, "the disciples came closer to me." We are told that once, when he found himself on the Nung hill with Hwuy, Tsze-loo, and Tsze-kung, Confucius

[1] 孔子曰.受業身通者.七十有七人.皆異能之士也.

asked them to tell him their different aims, and he would choose between them. Tsze-loo began, and when he had done, the master said, "It marks your bravery." Tsze-kung followed, on whose words the judgment was, "They show your discriminating eloquence." At last came Yen Yuen, who said, "I should like to find an intelligent king and sage ruler whom I might assist. I would diffuse among the people instructions on the five great points, and lead them on by the rules of propriety and music, so that they should not care to fortify their cities by walls and moats, but would fuse their swords and spears into implements of agriculture. They should send forth their flocks without fear into the plains and forests. There should be no sunderings of families, no widows or widowers. For a thousand years there would be no calamity of war. Yew would have no opportunity to display his bravery, or Ts'ze to display his oratory." The master pronounced, "How admirable is this virtue!"

When Hwuy was 29, his hair was all white, and in three years more he died. He was sacrificed to, along with Confucius, by the first emperor of the Han dynasty. The title which he now has in the sacrificial Canon,—"Continuator of the Sage," was conferred in the 9th year of the emperor, or, to speak more correctly, of the period, Kea-tsing, A.D. 1530. Almost all the present sacrificial titles of the worthies in the temple were fixed at that time. Hwuy's place is the first of the four Assessors, on the east of the sage.[8]

2. Min Sun, styled Tsze-k'een, (閔損字子騫). He was a native of Loo, 15 years younger than Confucius, according to Sze-ma

8 I have referred briefly, at p. 93, to the temples of Confucius. The principal hall, called 大成殿, or 'Hall of the Great and Complete One,' is that in which is his own statue or the tablet of his spirit, having on each side of it, within a screen, the statues, or tablets, of his 'four Assessors.' On the east and west, along the walls of the same apartment are the two 序, the places of the 十二哲, or 'twelve Wise Ones,' those of his disciples, who, next to the 'Assessors,' are counted worthy of honour. Outside this apartment, and running in a line with the two 序, but along the external wall of the sacred inclosure, are the two 廡, or side-galleries, which I have sometimes called the ranges of the outer court. In each there are 64 tablets of the disciples and other worthies, having the same title, as the Wise Ones, that of 先賢, or 'Ancient Worthy,' or the inferior title of 先儒, 'Ancient Scholar.' Behind the principal hall is the 崇聖祠殿, sacred to Confucius' ancestors, whose tablets are in the centre, fronting the south, like that of Confucius. On each side are likewise the tablets of certain 'ancient Worthies,' and 'ancient Scholars.'

Ts'een, but 50 years younger, according to the "Family Sayings," which latter authority is followed in "The Annals of the Empire." When he first came to Confucius, we are told, he had a starved look,[1] which was by-and-by exchanged for one of fulness and satisfaction.[2] Tsze-kung asked him how the change had come about. He replied, "I came from the midst of my reeds and sedges into the school of the master. He trained my mind to filial piety, and set before me the examples of the ancient kings. I felt a pleasure in his instructions, but when I went abroad, and saw the people in authority, with their umbrellas and banners, and all the pomp and circumstance of their trains, I also felt pleasure in that show. These two things assaulted each other in my breast. I could not determine which to prefer, and so I wore that look of distress. But now the lessons of our master have penetrated deeply into my mind. My progress also has been helped by the example of you my fellow-disciples. I now know what I should follow and what I should avoid, and all the pomp of power is no more to me than the dust of the ground. It is on this account that I have that look of fulness and satisfaction." Tsze-k'een was high in Confucius' esteem. He was distinguished for his purity and filial affection. His place in the temple is the first, east, among "The Wise Ones," immediately after the four assessors. He was first sacrificed to along with Confucius, as is to be understood of the other "Wise Ones," excepting in the case of Yew Jŏ, in the 8th year of the style K'ae-yuen of the sixth emperor of the T'ang dynasty, A.D. 720. His title, the same as that of all but the Assessors is—"The ancient Worthy, the philosopher Min."

3. Yen Kăng, styled Pih-new (冉耕字白[*al.*, 百]牛). He was a native of Loo, and Confucius' junior only by seven years. When Confucius became Minister of Crime, he appointed Pih-new to the office, which he had himself formerly held, of commandant of Chung-too. His tablet is now fourth among "The Wise Ones," on the west.

4. Yen Yung, styled Chung-kung (冉雍字仲弓). He was of the same clan as Yen Kăng, and 29 years younger than Confucius. He had a bad father, but the master declared that was not to be counted to him, to detract from his admitted excellence. His place is among "The Wise Ones," the second, east.

[1] 菜色. [2] 芻豢之色.

5. Yen K'ew, styled Tsze-yew (冉求.字子有). He was related to the two former, and of the same age as Chung-kung. He was noted among the disciples for his versatile ability and many acquirements. Tsze-kung said of him, "Respectful to the old, and kind to the young; attentive to guests and visitors; fond of learning and skilled in many arts; diligent in his examination of things:—these are what belong to Yen K'ew." It has been noted in the life of Confucius that it was by the influence of Tsze-yew that he was finally restored to Loo. He occupies the third place, west, among "The Wise ones."

6. Chung Yew, styled Tsze-loo and Ke-loo (仲由.字子路.又字季路). He was a native of P'ëen (卞) in Loo, and only 9 years younger than Confucius. At their first interview, the master asked him what he was fond of, and he replied, "My long sword." Confucius said, "If to your present ability there were added the results of learning, you would be a very superior man." "Of what advantage would learning be to me?" asked Tsze-loo. "There is a bamboo on the southern hill, which is straight itself without being bent. If you cut it down and use it, you can send it though a rhinoceros' hide;—what is the use of learning?" "Yes," said the master; "but if you feather it and point it with steel, will it not penetrate more deeply?" Tsze-loo bowed twice, and said, "I will reverently receive your instructions." Confucius was wont to say, "From the time that I got Yew, bad words no more came to my ears." For some time Tsze-loo was chief magistrate of the district of P'oo (蒲), where his administration commanded the warm commendations of the master. He died finally in Wei, as has been related above, p. 87. His tablet is now the fourth, east, from those of the Assessors.

7. Tsae Yu, styled Tsze-go (宰予.字子我). He was a native of Loo, but nothing is mentioned of his age. He had "a sharp mouth," according to Sze-ma Ts'een. Once, when he was at the court of Ts'oo on some commission, the king Ch'aou offered him an easy carriage adorned with ivory for his master. Yu replied, "My master is a man who would rejoice in a government where right principles were carried out, and can find his joy in himself when that is not the case. Now right principles and virtue are as it were in a state of slumber. His wish is to rouse and put them in motion. Could he find a prince really anxious to rule according to them, he would walk on foot to his court, and be glad to do so. Why need

he receive such a valuable gift as this from so great a distance?" Confucius commended this reply; but where he is mentioned in the Analects, Tsze-go does not appear to great advantage. He took service in the State of Ts'e, and was chief magistrate of Lin-tsze, where he joined with T'een Chang in some disorderly movement,[1] which led to the destruction of his kindred, and made Confucius ashamed of him. His tablet is now the second, west, among "The Wise Ones."

8. Twan-muk Ts'ze, styled Tsze-kung (端木賜, 字子貢 [*al.*, 子贛]), whose place is now third, east, from the Assessors. He was a native of Wei (衛), and 31 years younger than Confucius. He had great quickness of natural ability, and appears in the Analects as one of the most forward talkers among the disciples. Confucius used to say, "From the time that I got Ts'ze, scholars from a distance came daily resorting to me." Several instances of the language which he used to express his admiration of the master have been given in the last section. Here is another:—The duke King of Ts'e asked Tsze-kung how Chung-ne was to be ranked as a sage. "I do not know," was the reply. "I have all my life had the heaven over my head, but I do not know its height, and the earth under my feet, but I do not know its thickness. In my serving of Confucius, I am like a thirsty man who goes with his pitcher to the river, and there he drinks his fill, without knowing the river's depth." He took leave of Confucius to become commandant of Sin-yang (信陽宰); when the master said to him, "In dealing with your subordinates, there is nothing like impartiality; and when wealth comes in your way, there is nothing like moderation. Hold fast these two things, and do not swerve from them. To conceal men's excellence is to obscure the worthy; and to proclaim people's wickedness is the part of a mean man. To speak evil of those whom you have not sought the opportunity to instruct, is not the way of friendship and harmony." Subsequently Tsze-kung was high in office both in Loo and Wei, and finally died in Ts'e. We saw how he was in attendance on Confucius at the time of the sage's death. Many of the disciples built huts near the master's grave, and mourned for him three years, but Tsze-kung remained sorrowing alone for three years more.

9. Yen Yen, styled Tsze-yew (言偃, 字子游), now the 4th in the western range of "The Wise Ones." He was a native of Woo

[1] 與田常作亂. See above, p. 7.

(吳), 45 years younger than Confucius, and distinguished for his literary acquirements. Being made commandant of Woo-shing, he transformed the character of the people by "proprieties" and music, and was praised by the master. After the death of Confucius, Ke K'ang asked Yen how that event had made no sensation in Loo like that which was made by the death of Tsze-ch'an, when the men laid aside their bowstring rings and girdle ornaments, and the women laid aside their pearls and ear-rings, and the voice of weeping was heard in the lanes for three months. Yen replied, "The influences of Tsze-ch'an and my master might be compared to those of overflowing water and the fattening rain. Wherever the water in its overflow reaches, men take knowledge of it, while the fattening rain falls unobserved."

10. Puh Shang, styled Tsze-hea (卜商, 字子夏). It is not certain to what State he belonged, his birth being assigned to Wei (衞), to Wei (魏), and to Wăn (溫). He was 45 years younger than Confucius, and lived to a great age, for we find him, B.C. 406, at the court of the prince Wăn of Wei (魏), to whom he gave copies of some of the classical Books. He is represented as a scholar extensively read and exact, but without great comprehension of mind. What is called Maou's She-king (毛詩) is said to contain the views of Tsze-hea. Kung-yang Kaou and Kuh-lëang Ch'ih are also said to have studied the Ch'un Ts'ew with him. On the occasion of the death of his son he wept himself blind. His place is the 5th, east, among "The Wise Ones."

11. Twan-sun Sze, styled Tsze-chang (顓孫師, 字子張), has his tablet, corresponding to that of the preceding, on the west. He was a native of Ch'in (陳), and 48 years younger than Confucius. Tsze-kung said, "Not to boast of his admirable merit; not to signify joy on account of noble station; neither insolent nor indolent; showing no pride to the dependent:—these are the characteristics of Twan-sun Sze." When he was sick, he called Shin Ts'ëang to him, and said, "We speak of his *end* in the case of a superior man, and of his *death* in the case of a mean man. May I think that it is going to be the former with me to-day?"

12. Tsăng Sin [or Ts'an], styled Tsze-yu (曾參, 字子輿, [*al.*, 子與]). He was a native of south Woo-shing, and 46 years younger than Confucius. In his 16th year he was sent by his father into

Ts'oo, where Confucius then was, to learn under the sage. Excepting perhaps Yen Hwuy, there is not a name of greater note in the Confucian school. Tsze-kung said of him, "There is no subject which he has not studied. His appearance is respectful. His virtue is solid. His words command credence. Before great men he draws himself up in the pride of self-respect. His eyebrows are those of longevity." He was noted for his filial piety, and after the death of his parents, he could not read the rites of mourning without being led to think of them, and moved to tears. He was a voluminous writer. Ten Books of his composition are said to be contained in the "Rites of the elder Tae" (大戴禮). The classic of Filial Piety he is said to have made under the eye of Confucius. On his connection with "The Great Learning," see above, Ch. III. Sect. II. He was first associated with the sacrifices to Confucius in A.D. 668, but in 1267 he was advanced to be one of the sage's four Assessors. His title—"Exhibiter of the Fundamental Principles of the Sage," dates from the period of Kea-tsing, as mentioned in speaking of Yen Hwuy.

13. Tan-t'ae Mëë-ming, styled Tsze-yu (澹臺滅明. 字子羽). He was a native of Woo-shing, 39 years younger than Confucius, according to the "Historical Records," but 49, according to the "Family Sayings." He was excessively ugly, and Confucius thought meanly of his talents in consequence, on his first application to him. After completing his studies, he travelled to the south as far as the Yang-tsze. Traces of his presence in that part of the country are still pointed out in the department of Soo-chow. He was followed by about three hundred disciples, to whom he laid down rules for their guidance in their intercourse with the princes. When Confucius heard of his success, he confessed how he had been led by his bad looks to misjudge him. He, with nearly all the disciples whose names follow, first had a place assigned to him in the sacrifices to Confucius in A.D. 739. The place of his tablet is the second, east, in the outer court, beyond that of the "Assessors" and "Wise Ones."

14. Corresponding to the preceding, on the west, is the tablet of Fuk Puh-ts'e, styled Tsze-tseen (宓 [*al.*, 密 and 虙, all=伏] 不齊. 字子賤). He was a native of Loo, and, according to different accounts, 30, 40, and 49 years younger than Confucius. He was commandant of Tan-foo (單父宰), and hardly needed to put forth any personal effort. Wo-ma K'e had been in the same office, and

had succeeded by dint of the greatest industry and toil. He asked Puh-ts'e how he managed so easily for himself, and was answered, "I employ men; you employ men's strength." People pronounced Fuh to be a superior man. He was also a writer, and his works are mentioned in Lew Hin's catalogue.

15. Next to that of Mëë-ming is the tablet of Yuen Hëen, styled Tsze-sze (原憲,字子思) a native of Sung, or, according to Ch'ing Heuen, of Loo, and younger than Confucius by 36 years. He was noted for his purity and modesty, and for his happiness in the principles of the master amid deep poverty. After the death of Confucius, he lived in obscurity in Wei. In the notes to Ana. VI. iii., I have referred to an interview which he had with Tsze-kung.

16. Kung-yay Chang [al., Che], styled Tsze-Ch'ang [al., Tsze-che], (公冶長 [al., 芝], 字子長, [al., 子之]), has his tablet next to that of Pih-ts'e. He was son-in-law to Confucius. His nativity is assigned both to Loo and to Ts'e.

17. Nan-kung Kwŏ, styled Tsze-yung (南宮括 [al., 适, and, in the "Family Sayings," 縚 (T'aou)], 字子容), has the place at the east next to Yuen Hëen. It is a question much debated whether he was the same with Nan-kung King-shuh, who accompanied Confucius to the court of Chow, or not. On occasion of a fire breaking out in the palace of duke Gae, while others were intent on securing the contents of the Treasury, Nan-kung directed his efforts to save the Library, and to him was owing the preservation of the copy of the Chow Le which was in Loo, and other ancient monuments.

18. Kung-seih Gae, styled Ke-ts'ze [al., Ke-ch'in] (公晳哀,字季次 [al., 季沉]). His tablet follows that of Kung-yay. He was a native of Loo, or of Ts'e. Confucius commended him for refusing to take office with any of the Families which were encroaching on the authority of the princes of the States, and for choosing to endure the severest poverty rather than sacrifice a tittle of his principles.

19. Tsăng Tëen, styled Seih (曾蒧 [al., 點] 字晳). He was the father of Tsăng Ts'an. His place in the temples is the hall to Confucius' ancestors, where his tablet is the first, west.

20. Yen Woo-yaou, styled Loo (顏無繇字路). He was the father of Yen Hwuy, younger than Confucius by six years. His sacrificial place is the first, east, in the same hall as the last.

21. Following the tablet of Nan-kung Kwŏ is that of Shang Keu,

styled Tsze-muh (商瞿, 字子木). To him, it is said, we are indebted for the preservation of the Yih-king, which he received from Confucius. Its transmission step by step, from Keu down to the Han dynasty, is minutely set forth.

22. Next to Kung-seih Gae is the place of Kaou Ch'ae, styled Tsze-kaou and Ke-kaou (高柴, 字子羔, [al., 季羔; for 羔 moreover, we find 皋, and 睾]), a native of Ts'e, according to the "Family Sayings," but of Wei, according to Sze-ma Ts'een and Ch'ing Heuen. He was 30 (some say 40) years younger than Confucius, dwarfish and ugly, but of great worth and ability. At one time he was criminal judge of Wei, and in the execution of his office condemned a prisoner to lose his feet. Afterwards that same man saved his life, when he was flying from the State. Confucius praised Ch'ae for being able to administer stern justice with such a spirit of benevolence as to disarm resentment.

23. Shang Keu is followed by Tseih-teaou K'ae [prop. K'e], styled Tsze-k'ae, Tsze-jŏ, and Tsze-sew (漆雕開 [pr. 啟], 字子開, 子若, and 子脩), a native of Ts'ae (蔡), or, acc. to Heuen, of Loo. We only know him as a reader of the Shoo-king, and refusing to go into office.

24. Kung-pih Leaou, styled Tsze-chow (公伯僚, 字子周). He appears in the Analects XIV. xxxiii., slandering Tsze-loo. It is doubtful whether he should have a place among the disciples.

25. Sze-ma Kăng, styled Tsze-new (司馬耕, 字子牛), follows Tseih-teaou K'ae. He was a great talker, a native of Sung, and a brother of Hwan T'uy, to escape from whom seems to have been the labour of his life.

26. The place next Kaou Ch'ae is occupied by Fan Seu, styled Tsze-ch'e (樊須, 字子遲), a native of Ts'e, or, acc. to others, of Loo, and whose age is given as 36 or 46 years younger than Confucius. When young, he distinguished himself in a military command under the Ke family.

27. Yew Jŏ, styled Tsze-jŏ (有若, 字子若). He was a native of Loo, and his age is stated very variously. He was noted among the disciples for his great memory and fondness for antiquity. After the death of Confucius, the rest of the disciples, because of the likeness of Jŏ's voice to the Master's, wished to render the same observances to him which they had done to Confucius, but on

Tsăng Sin's demurring to the thing, they abandoned the purpose. The tablet of Tsze-jŏ is now the 6th, east, among "The Wise Ones," to which place it was promoted in the 3d year of K'ëen-lung of the present dynasty. This was done in compliance with a memorial from the president of one of the Boards, who said he was moved by a dream to make the request. We may suppose that his real motives were—a wish to do justice to the merits of Tsze-jŏ, and to restore the symmetry of the tablets in the "Hall of the Great and Complete One," which had been disturbed by the introduction of the tablet of Choo He in the preceding reign.

28. Kung-se Ch'ih, styled Tsze-hwa (公西赤 字子華), a native of Loo, younger than Confucius by 42 years, whose place is the 4th, west, in the outer court. He was noted for his knowledge of ceremonies, and the other disciples devolved on him all the arrangements about the funeral of the Master.

29. Woo-ma She [or K'e], styled Tsze-K'e (巫馬施[*al.*, 期],字子期[*al.*, 子旗]), a native of Ch'in, or, acc. to Ch'ing Heuen, of Loo, 30 years younger than Confucius. His tablet is on the east, next to that of Sze-ma Kăng. It is related that on one occasion, when Confucius was about to set out with a company of the disciples on a walk or journey, he told them to take umbrellas. They met with a heavy shower, and Woo-ma asked him, saying, "There were no clouds in the morning, but after the sun had risen, you told us to take umbrellas. How did you know that it would rain?" Confucius said, "The moon last evening was in the constellation Peih, and is it not said in the She-king, 'When the moon is in Peih, there will be heavy rain?' It was thus I knew it."

30. Lëang Chen [*al.*, Le], styled Shuh-yu (梁鱣[*al.* 鯉] 字 叔魚), occupies the eighth place, west, among the tablets of the outer court. He was a man of Ts'e, and his age is stated as 29 and 39 years younger than Confucius. The following story is told in connection with him.—When he was thirty, being disappointed that he had no son, he was minded to put away his wife. "Do not do so," said Shang Keu to him. "I was 38 before I had a son, and my mother was then about to take another wife for me, when the Master proposed sending me to Ts'e. My mother was unwilling that I should go, but Confucius said, 'Don't be anxious. Keu will have five sons

after he is forty.' It has turned out so, and I apprehend it is your fault, and not your wife's, that you have no son yet." Chen took this advice, and in the second year after, he had a son.

31. Yen Hing [*al.*, Sin, Lew, and Wei], styled Tsze-lew (顏幸 [*al.* 辛, 柳, and 韋], 字子柳), occupies the place, east, after Woo-ma She. He was a native of Loo, and 46 years younger than Confucius.

32. Leang Chen is followed on the west by Yen Joo, styled Tsze-Loo [*al.*, Tsze-tsăng and Tsze-yu] (冉孺 [*al.*, 儒] 字子魯 [*al.*, 子曾 and 子魚]), a native of Loo, and 50 years younger than Confucius.

33. Yen Hing is followed on the east by Ts'aou Seuh, styled Tsze-seun (曹卹 字子循), a native of Ts'oe, 50 years younger than Confucius.

34. Next on the west is Pih K'ëen, styled Tsze-seih, or, in the current copies of the "Family Sayings," Tsze-k'ëae (伯虔 字子晳 [*al.*, 子析] or 子楷), a native of Loo, 50 years younger than Confucius.

35. Following Tsze-seun is Kung-sun Lung [*al.*, Ch'ung], styled Tsze-shih (公孫龍 [*al.* 寵], 字子石) whose birth is assigned by different writers to Wei, Ts'oo, and Chaou (趙). He was 53 years younger than Confucius. We have the following account:—"Tsze-kung asked Tsze-shih, saying, 'Have you not studied the Book of Poetry?' Tsze-shih replied, 'What leisure have I to do so? My parents require me to be filial; my brothers require me to be submissive; and my friends require me to be sincere. What leisure have I for anything else?' 'Come to my Master,' said Tsze-kung, 'and learn of him.'"

Sze-ma Ts'een here observes:—"Of the thirty-five disciples which precede, we have some details. Their age and other particulars are found in the Books and Records. It is not so, however, in regard to the fifty-two which follow."

36. Yen Ke, styled Tsze-ch'an [*al.* Ke-ch'an and Tsze-tă], (冉季, 字子產 [*al.* 季產 and 子達]), a native of Loo whose place is the eleventh, west, next to Pih K'ëen.

37. Kung-tsoo Kow-tsze or simply Tsze, styled Tsze-che (公祖句茲 [or simply 茲], 字子之), a native of Loo. His tablet is the 23d, east, in the outer court.

38. Ts'in Tsoo, styled Tsze-nan (秦祖, 字子南), a native of Ts'in. His tablet precedes that of the last, two places.

39. Tseih-teaou Ch'e, styled Tsze-lëen (漆雕哆[*al.*, 侈], 字子斂), a native of Loo. His tablet is the 13th, west.

40. Yen Kaou, styled Tsze-Keaou (顏高字子驕). According to the "Family Sayings," he was the same as Yen K'ih (刻, or 尅) who drove the carriage, when Confucius rode in Wei after the duke and Nan-tsze. But this seems doubtful. Other authorities make his name Ch'an (產), and style him Tsze-tsing (子精). His tablet is the 13th, east.

41. Tseih-teaou T'oo-foo [*al.*, Ts'ung], styled Tsze-yew, Tsze-k'e and Tsze-wăn], 漆雕徒父[*al.* 從], 字子有 or 子友 [*al.*, 子期 and 子文]) a native of Loo, whose tablet precedes that of Tseih-teaou Ch'e.

42. Jang Sze-ch'ih, styled Tsze-t'oo, or Tsze-ts'ung (壤[*al.* 穰]駟赤, 字子徒[*al.* 子從]), a native of Ts'in. Some consider Jang-sze (壤駟) to be a double surname. His tablet comes after that of No. 40.

43. Shang Tsih, styled Tsze-ke and Tsze-sew (商澤, 字子季[*al.*, 子秀]), a native of Loo. His tablet is immediately after that of Fan Seu, No. 26.

44. Shih Tsŏ [*al.*, Che and Tsze]-shuh, styled Tsze-ming (石作[*al.*, 之 and 子]蜀, 字子明). Some take Shih-tsŏ (石作) as a double surname. His tablet follows that of No. 42.

45. Jin Puh-ts'e, styled Seuen (任不齊, 字選), a native of Ts'oo, whose tablet is next to that of No. 28.

46. Kung Leang Joo, styled Tsze-ching (公良孺[*al.*, 儒], 字子正), a native of Ch'in, follows the preceding in the temples. The "Sacrificial Canon" says:—"Tsze-ching was a man of worth and bravery. When Confucius was surrounded and stopt in P'oo, Tsze-ching fought so desperately, that the people of P'oo were afraid, and let the Master go, on his swearing that he would not proceed to Wei."

47. How [*al.*, Shih] Ch'oo [*al.*, K'ëen], styled Tsze-le [*al.*, Le-che], (后[*al.*, 石]處[*al.*, 虔], 字子里[*al.*, 里之]), a native of Ts'e, having his tablet the 17th, east.

48. Ts'in Yen, styled K'ae (秦冉, 字開), a native of Ts'ae. He is not given in the list of the "Family Sayings," and on this account his tablet was put out of the temples in the 9th year of Kea-tsing. It was restored, however, in the second year of Yung-ching, A.D. 1724, and is the thirty-third, east, in the outer court.

49. Kung-hea Show, styled Shing [and Tsze-shing], (公夏首 [*al.*, 守], 字乘 [and 子乘]), a native of Loo, whose tablet is next that of No. 44.

50. He Yung-tëen [or simply Tëen,] styled Tsze-seih [*al.*, Tsze-keae, and Tsze-k'eae], (奚容蒧 [or 點], 字子晳 [*al.*, 子偕 and 子楷]), a native of Wei, having his tablet the 18th, east.

51. Kung Këen-ting [*al.*, Kung Yew], styled Tsze-chung (公肩 [*al.*, 堅] 定 [*al.*, 公有], 字子仲, [*al.*, 中, and 忠]). His nativity is assigned to Loo, to Wei, and to Tsin (晉). He follows No. 46.

52. Yen Tsoo [*al.*, Seang], styled Seang, and Tsze-seang (顏祖 [*al.*, 相], 字襄, and 子襄), a native of Loo, with his tablet following that of No. 50.

53. Heaou Tan [*al.*, Woo], styled Tsze-këa (鄡單 [*al.*, 鄔], 字子家), a native of Loo. His place is next to that of No. 51.

54. Keu [*al.*, Kow] Tsing-keang [and simply Tsing] styled Tsze-keang [*al.*, Tsze-keae and Tsze-mäng], (句 [*al.*, 勾 and 鉤] 井疆 [and simply 井], 字子疆 [*al.*, 子界, and 子孟]), a native of Wei, following No. 52.

55. Han [*al.*, Tsae]-foo Hih, styled Tsze-hih [*al.*, Tsze-sŏ and Tsze-soo], (罕 [*al.*, 宰] 父黑, 字子黑 [*al.*, 子索, and 子素]), a native of Loo, whose tablet is next to that of No. 53.

56. Ts'in Shang, styled Tsze-p'ei [*al.*, P'ei-tsze, and Puh-tsze], (秦商, 字子丕 [*al.*, 丕茲, and 不茲]), a native of Loo, or, according to Ch'ing Heuen, of Ts'oo. He was 40 years younger than Confucius. One authority, however, says he was only 4 years younger, and that his father and Confucius' father were both celebrated for their strength. His tablet is the 12th, east.

57. Shin Tang, styled Chow (申黨字周). In the "Family Sayings" there is a Shin Tseih, styled Tsze-chow (申績, 字子周). The name is given by others as T'ang (堂 and 儻), and Tsuh (續), with the designation Tsze-tsuh (子續). These are probably the same person mentioned in the Analects as Shin Ch'ang (申棖). Prior to the Ming dynasty they were sacrificed to as two, but in A.D. 1530, the name of Tang was expunged from the sacrificial list, and only that of Ch'ang left. His tablet is the 31st, east.

58. Yen Che-puh, styled Tsze-shuh [or simply Shuh], (顏之僕, 字子叔 [or simply 叔]), a native of Loo, who occupies the 29th place, east.

59. Yung K'e, styled Tsze-k'e [*al.*, Tsze-yen], (榮旂 [or 祈] 字子旗 or 子祺 [*al.*, 子期]), a native of Loo, whose tablet is the 20th, west.

60. Hëen Shing, styled Tsze-k'e [*al.*, Tsze-hwang], (縣成 字子祺 [*al.*, 子横]), a native of Loo. His place is the 22d, east.

61. Tso Jin-ying, [or simply Ying], styled Hing and Tsze-hing (左人郢 [or simply 郢], 字行 and 子行), a native of Loo. His tablet follows that of No. 59.

62. Yen Keih, styled Yin [*al.*, Tsze-sze], (燕伋 [or 級], 字思 [*al.*, 子思], a native of Ts'in. His tablet is the 24th, east.

63. Ch'ing Kwŏ, styled Tsze-t'oo (鄭國 字子徒), a native of Loo. This is understood to be the same with the Sëë Pang, styled Tsze-ts'ung (薛邦字子從), of the "Family Sayings." His tablet follows No. 61.

64. Ts'in Fei, styled Tsze-che (秦非 字子之), a native of Loo, having his tablet the 31st, west.

65. She Che-chang, styled Tsze-hăng [*al.*, chang], 施之常 字子恆 [*al.*, 常]), a native of Loo. His tablet is the 30th, east.

66. Yen K'wae, styled Tsze-shing, (顏噲 字子聲), a native of Loo. His tablet is the next to that of No. 64.

67. Poo Shuh-shing, styled Tsze-keu (步叔乘 [in the "Family Sayings" we have 椉, an old form of 乘], 字子車), a native of Ts'e. Sometimes for Poo (步) we find Shaou (少). His tablet is the 30th, west.

68. Yuen K'ang, styled Tsze-tseih (原亢 字子籍), a native of Loo. Sze-ma Ts'een calls him Yuen K'ang-tseih, not mentioning any designation. The "Family Sayings" makes him Yuen K'ang (抗), styled Tseih. His tablet is the 23d, west.

69. Yŏ Kae [*al.*, Hin], styled Tsze-shing, (樂欬 [*al.*, 欣], 字子聲), a native of Loo. His tablet is the 25th, east.

70. Lëen Këĕ, styled Yung and Tsze-yung [*al.*, Tsze-ts'aou], (廉潔 字庸 and 子庸 [*al.*, 子曹]), a native of Wei, or of Ts'e. His tablet is next to that of No. 68.

71. Shuh-chung Hwuy [*al.*, K'wae], styled Tsze-k'e (叔仲會 [*al.*, 噲], 字子期), a native of Loo, or, according to Ch'ing Heuen, of Tsin. He was younger than Confucius by 54 years. It is said that he and another youth, called K'ung Seuen (孔璇), attended by turns with their pencils, and acted as amanuenses to the sage, and

when Măng Woo-pih expressed a doubt of their competency, Confucius declared his satisfaction with them. He follows Lëen Këë in the temples.

72. Yen Ho, styled Yen (顏何字冉), a native of Loo. The present copies of the "Family Sayings" do not contain this name, and in A.D. 1588 Yen was displaced from his place in the temples. His tablet, however, has been restored during the present dynasty. It is the 33d, west.

73. Teih Hih, styled Chĕ [*al.*, Tsze-chĕ and Chĕ-che] (狄黑字晳 [*al.*, 子晳 and 哲之]), a native of Wei, or of Loo. His tablet is the 26th, east.

74. Kwei [*al.*, Pang] Sun, styled Tsze-lëen [*al.*, Tsze-yin] (邽 [*al.*, 邦] 巽字子歛 [*al.*, 子欽]), a native of Loo. His tablet is the 27th, west.

75. K'ung Chung, styled Tsze-mëë (孔忠字子蔑). This was the son, it is said, of Confucius' elder brother, the cripple Măng-p'e. His tablet is next to that of No. 73. His sacrificial title is "The ancient Worthy, the philosopher Mëë."

76. Kung-se Yu-joo [*al.*, Yu], styled Tsze-shang (公西輿如 [*al.*, 輿], 字子上), a native of Loo. His place is the 26th, west.

77. Kung-se Tëen, styled Tsze-shang (公西蒧 [or 點], 字子上 [*al.*, 子尙]), a native of Loo. His tablet is the 28th, east.

78. Kin Chang [*al.*, Laou], styled Tsze-k'ae (琴張 [*al.*, 牢], 字子開), a native of Wei. His tablet is the 29th, west.

79. Ch'in K'ang, styled Tsze-k'ang [*al.*, Tsze-k'in] (陳亢字子亢 [*al.*, 子禽]), a native of Ch'in. See notes on Ana. I. x.

80. Hëen Tan [*al.*, T'an-foo, and Fung], styled Tsze-seang (縣亶 [*al.*, 亶父, and 豐], 字子象]), a native of Loo. Some suppose that this is the same as No. 53. The advisers of the present dynasty in such matters, however, have considered them to be different, and in 1724, a tablet was assigned to Heen Tan, the 34th, west.

The three preceding names are given in the "Family Sayings."

The research of scholars has added about twenty others.

81. Lin Fang, styled Tsze-k'ew (林放字子邱), a native of Loo. The only thing known of him is from the Ana. III. iv. His tablet was displaced under the Ming, but has been restored by the present dynasty. It is the first, west.

82. Keu Yuen, styled Pih-yuh (蘧瑗字伯玉), an officer of

Wei, and, as appears from the Analects and Mencius, an intimate friend of Confucius. Still his tablet has shared the same changes as that of Lin Fang. It is now the first, east.

83. and 84. Shin Ch'ang (申棖), and Shin T'ang (申堂). See No. 57.

85. Muh Pei (牧皮), mentioned by Mencius, VII. Pt. II. xxxvii. 4. His entrance into the temple has been under the present dynasty. His tablet is the 34th, east.

86. Tso-k'ew Ming or Tso K'ew-ming (左丘明) has the 32d place, east. His title was fixed in A.D. 1530 to be—"The Ancient Scholar," but in 1642 it was raised to that of "Ancient Worthy." To him we owe the most distinguished of the annotated editions of the Ch'un Ts'ew. But whether he really was a disciple of Confucius, and in presonal communication with him, is much debated.

The above are the only names and surnames of those of the disciples who now share in the sacrifices to the sage. Those who wish to exhaust the subject, mention in addition, on the authority of Tso-k'ew Ming, Chung-sun Ho-ke (仲孫何忌), a son of Măng He (see p. 63), and Chung-sun Shwŏ (仲孫說), also a son of Măng He, supposed by many to be the same with No. 17; Joo Pei, (孺悲), mentioned in the Analects XVII. xx., and in the Le Ke, XVIII. Pt. II. ii. 21; Kung-wang Che-k'ew (公罔之裘) and Tseu Tëen (序點), mentioned in the Le Ke, XLI. 7; Pin-mow Këa (賓牟賈), mentioned in the Le Ke, XVII. iii. 16; K'ung Seuen (孔琁) and Hwuy Shuh-lan (惠叔蘭), on the authority of the Family Sayings; Chang Ke (常季), mentioned by Chwang-tsze; Keŭh Yu (鞠語), mentioned by Gan-tsze (晏子); Leen-yu (廉瑀), and Loo Tseun (魯峻), on the authority of 文翁石室; and finally Tsze-fuk Ho (子服何), the Tsze-fuk King-pih (子服景伯) of the Analects, XIV. xxxviii.

CHAPTER VI.

LIST OF THE PRINCIPAL WORKS WHICH HAVE BEEN CONSULTED IN THE PREPARATION OF THIS VOLUME.

SECTION I.

CHINESE WORKS, WITH BRIEF NOTICES.

十三經註疏. "The Thirteen King, with Commentary and Explanations." This is the great repertory of ancient lore upon the Classics. On the Analects, it contains the "Collection of Explanations of the Lun Yu," by Ho An and others (see p. 19), and "The Correct Meaning," or Paraphrase of Hing Ping (see p. 20). On the Great Learning and the Doctrine of the Mean, it contains the comments and glosses of Ch'ing Heuen, and K'ung Ying-tă (孔穎達) of the T'ang dynasty.

新刻批點四書讀本. "A new edition of the Four Books, Punctuated and Annotated, for Reading." This work was published in the 7th year of Taou-kwang (1827) by a Kaou Lin (高琳). It is the finest edition of the Four Books which I have seen, in point of typographical execution. It is indeed a volume for reading. It contains the ordinary "Collected Comments" of Choo He on the Analects, and his "Chapters and Sentences" of the Great Learning and Doctrine of the Mean. The editor's own notes are at the top and bottom of the page, in rubric.

四書朱子本義匯參. "The Proper Meaning of the Four Books as determined by Choo He, Compared with, and Illustrated from, other Commentators." This is a most voluminous work, published in the tenth year of K'ëen-lung, A.D. 1745, by Wang Poots'ing (王步靑), a member of the Han-lin College. On the Great Learning and the Doctrine of the Mean, the "Queries" (或問) of Choo He are given in the same text as the standard commentary.

四書經註集證. "The Four Books, Text and Commentary, with Proofs and Illustrations." The copy of this Work which I have was edited by a Wang T'ing-ke (汪廷機), in the 3d year of

Këa-k'ing, A.D. 1798. It may be called a commentary on the commentary. The research in all matters of Geography, History, Biography, Natural History, &c., is immense.

四書諸儒輯要, "A Collection of the most important Comments of Scholars on the Four Books." By Le Pei-lin (李沛霖); published in the 57th year of K'ang-he, A.D. 1718. This Work is about as voluminous as the 滙參, but on a different plan. Every chapter is preceded by a critical discussion of its general meaning, and the logical connection of its several paragraphs. This is followed by the text, and Choo He's standard commentary. We have then a paraphrase, full and generally perspicuous. Next, there is a selection of approved comments, from a great variety of authors; and finally, the reader finds a number of critical remarks and ingenious views, differing often from the common interpretation, which are submitted for his examination.

四書翼註論文, "A Supplemental Commentary, and Literary Discussions, on the Four Books." By Chang K'ëen-t'aou [*al.*, T'eih-gan] (張甄陶 [*al.*, 惕菴]), a member of the Han-lin college, in the early part, apparently, of the reign of K'ëen-lung. The work is on a peculiar plan. The reader is supposed to be acquainted with Choo He's commentary, which is not given; but the author generally supports his views, and defends them against the criticisms of some of the early scholars of this dynasty. His own exercitations are of the nature of essays more than of commentary. It is a book for the student who is somewhat advanced, rather than for the learner. I have often perused it with interest and advantage.

四書遵註合講, "The Four Books, according to the Commentary, with Paraphrase." Published in the 8th year of Yung Ching, A.D. 1730, by Ung Fuh [*al.*, K'ih-foo] (翁復 [*al.*, 克夫]). Every page is divided into two parts. Below, we have the text and Choo He's commentary. Above, we have an analysis of every chapter, followed by a paraphrase of the several paragraphs. To the paraphrase of each paragraph are subjoined critical notes, digested from a great variety of scholars, but without the mention of their names. A list of 116 is given who are thus laid under contribution. In addition, there are maps and illustrative figures at the commencement; and to each Book there are prefixed biographical notices, explanations of peculiar allusions, &c.

新增四書補註附考備旨, "The Four Books, with a complete Digest of Supplements to the Commentary, and additional Suggestions. A new edition, with Additions." By Too Ting-ke (杜定基). Published A.D. 1779. The original of this Work was by T'ăng Lin (鄧林), a scholar of the Ming dynasty. It is perhaps the best of all editions of the Four Books for a learner. Each page is divided into three parts. Below, is the text divided into sentences and members of sentences, which are followed by short glosses. The text is followed by the usual commentary, and that by a paraphrase, to which are subjoined the Supplements and Suggestions. The middle division contains a critical analysis of the chapters and paragraphs; and above, there are the necessary biographical and other notes.

四書味根錄, "The Four Books, with the Relish of the Radical Meaning." This is a new Work, published in 1852. It is the production of Kin Ch'ing, styled Ts'ew-t'an (金澂, 字秋潭), an officer and scholar, who, returning, apparently to Canton province, from the North in 1836, occupied his retirement with reviewing his literary studies of former years, and employed his sons to transcribe his notes. The writer is fully up in all the commentaries on the classics, and pays particular attention to the labours of the scholars of the present dynasty. To the Analects, for instance, there is prefixed Keang Yung's History of Confucius, with criticisms on it by the author himself. Each chapter is preceded by a critical analysis. Then follows the text with the standard commentary, carefully divided into sentences, often with glosses, original and selected, between them. To the commentary there succeeds a paraphrase, which is not copied by the author from those of his predecessors. After the paraphrase we have Explanations (解). The Book is beautifully printed, and in small type, so that it is really a *multum in parvo*, with considerable freshness.

日講四書義解, "A Paraphrase for Daily Lessons, Explaining the Meaning of the Four Books." This work was produced in 1677, by a multitude of the members of the Han-lin college, in obedience to an Imperial rescript. The paraphrase is full, perspicuous, and elegant.

御製周易折中;書經傳說彙纂;詩經傳說彙纂;禮記義疏;春秋傳說彙纂. These works form together a superb edition of the Five King, published by imperial authority in the reigns of K'ang-he and his successor, Yung-ching. They contain the standard views (傳); various opinions (說); critical decisions of the editors (案); prolegomena; plates or cuts; and other apparatus for the student.

毛西河先生全集. "The Collected Writings of Maou Se-ho." See prolegomena, p. 20. The voluminousness of his Writings is understated there. Of 經集, or Writings on the Classics, there are 236 sections, while his 文集, or other literary compositions, amount to 257 sections. His treatises on the Great Learning and the Doctrine of the Mean have been especially helpful to me. He is a great opponent of Choo He, and would be a much more effective one, if he possessed the same graces of style as that "prince of literature."

四書摭餘說, "A collection of Supplemental Observations on the Four Books." The preface of the author, Ts'aou Che-shing (曹之升), is dated in 1795, the last year of the reign of K'ëen-lung. The work contains what we may call prolegomena on each of the Four Books, and then excursus on the most difficult and disputed passages. The tone is moderate, and the learning displayed? extensive and solid. The views of Choo He are frequently well defended from the assaults of Maou Se-ho. I have found the Work very instructive.

鄉黨圖考, "On the Tenth Book of the Analects, with Plates." This Work was published by the author, Keang Yung (江永), in the 21st year of K'ëen-lung, A.D. 1761, when he was 76 years old. It is devoted to the illustration of the above portion of the Analects, and is divided into ten Sections, the first of which consists of woodcuts and tables. The second contains the Life of Confucius, of which I have largely availed myself in the last Chapter. The whole is a remarkable specimen of the minute care with which Chinese scholars have illustrated the Classical Books.

四書釋地;四書釋地續;四書釋地又續;四書釋地三續. We may call these volumes—"The Topography of the Four Books; with three Supplements." The Author's name is Yen Jŏ-keu (閻若璩). The first volume was published in 1698, and the second in 1700. I have not been able to find the dates of publication of the other two, in which there is more biographical and general matter than topographical. The author apologizes for the inappropriateness of their titles by saying that he could not help calling them Supplements to the Topography, which was his "first love."

皇清經解, "Explanations of the Classics, under the Imperial dynasty of Ts'ing." See above, p. 20. The Work, however, was not published, as I have there supposed, by Imperial authority, but under the superintendence, and at the expense (aided by other officers), of Yuen Yuen (阮元), Governor-general of K'wang-tung and K'wang-se, in the 9th year of the last reign, 1829. The publication of so extensive a Work shows a public spirit and zeal for literature among the high officers of China, which should keep foreigners from thinking meanly of them.

孔子家語, "Family Sayings of Confucius." Family is to be taken in the sense of Sect or School. In Lew Hin's Catalogue, in the subdivision devoted to the Lun Yu, we find the entry:—"Family Sayings of Confucius, 27 Books," with a note by Yen Sze-koo of the T'ang dynasty,—"Not the existing Work called the Family Sayings." The original Work was among the treasures found in the wall of Confucius' old house, and was deciphered and edited by K'ung Gan-kwŏ. The present Work is by Wang-suh of the Wei (魏) dynasty, grounded professedly on the older one, the blocks of which had suffered great dilapidation during the intervening centuries. It is allowed also, that, since Suh's time, the Work has suffered more than any of the acknowledged Classics. Yet it is a very valuable fragment of antiquity, and it would be worth while to incorporate it with the Analects. My copy is the edition of Le Yung (李容), published in 1780.

聖廟祀典圖考, "Sacrificial Canon of the Sage's Temples, with Plates." This Work, published in 1826, by Koo Yuen, styled Seang-chow (顧沅字湘舟), is a very pains-taking account of all the Names sacrificed to in the temples of Confucius, the dates of their attaining to that honour, &c. There are appended to it Memoirs of Confucius and Mencius, which are not of so much value.

十子全書, "The complete Works of the Ten *Tsze*." See Morrison's Dictionary, under the character 子. I have only had occasion, in connection with this Work, to refer to the writings of Chwang-tsze (莊子) and Lëĕ-tsze (列子). My copy is an edition of 1804.

歷代名賢列女氏姓譜. "A Cyclopædia of Surnames, or Biographical Dictionary, of the Famous Men and Virtuous Women of the successive Dynasties." This is a very notable work of its class; published in 1793, by 蕭智漢, and extending through 157 chapters or Books.

文獻通考. "General Examination of Records and Scholars." This astonishing Work, which cost its author, Ma Twan-lin (馬端臨), twenty years' labour, was first published in 1321. Remusat says—"This excellent Work is a library in itself, and if Chinese literature possessed no other, the language would be worth learning for the sake of reading this alone." It does indeed display all but incredible research into every subject connected with the Government, History, Literature, Religion, &c., of the empire of China. The author's researches are digested in 348 Books. I have had occasion to consult principally those on the Literary Monuments, embraced in 76 Books, from the 174th to the 249th.

續文獻通考. "A Continuation of the General Examination of Records and Scholars." This Work, which is in 254 Books, and nearly as extensive as the former, was the production of Wang K'e (王圻), who dates his preface in 1586, the 14th year of Wan-leih, the style of the reign of the 14th emperor of the Ming dynasty. Wang K'e brings down the Work of his predecessor to his own times. He also frequently goes over the same ground, and puts things in a clearer light. I have found this to be the case in the chapters on the classical and other Books.

二十三史. "The twenty-three Histories." These are the imperially-authorized records of the empire, commencing with the "Historical Records," the work of Sze-ma Ts'een, and ending with the History of the Ming dynasty, which appeared in 1742, the result of the joint labours of 145 officers and scholars of the present dynasty. The extent of the collection may be understood from this, that my copy, bound in English fashion, makes fifty-five volumes, each one larger than this. No nation has a history so thoroughly digested; and on the whole it is trustworthy. In preparing this volume, my necessities have been confined mostly to the Works of Sze-ma Ts'een, and his successor, Pan Koo (班固), the Historian of the first Han dynasty.

歷代統記表. "The Annals of the Empire." Published by imperial authority in 1803, the 8th year of Kea-k'ing. This Work is invaluable to a student, being, indeed, a collection of chronological tables, where every year from the rise of the Chow dynasty, B.C. 1121, has a distinct column to itself, in which, in different compartments, the most important events are noted. Beyond that date, it ascends to the commencement of the cycles in the 61st year of Hwang-te, giving not every year, but the years of which any thing has been mentioned in history. From Hwang-te also, it ascends through the dateless ages up to P'wan-koo, the first of mortals.

歷代疆域表. "The Boundaries of the Empire in the successive Dynasties." This Work by the same author, and published in 1817, does for the boundaries of the empire the same service which the preceding renders to its chronology.

SECTION II.

TRANSLATIONS AND OTHER WORKS.

CONFUCIUS SINARUM PHILOSOPHUS; sive Scientia Sinensis Latine Exposita. Studio et opera Prosperi Intorcetta, Christiani Herdritch, Francisci Rougemont, Philippi Couplet, Patrum Societatis JESU. Jussu Ludovici Magni. Parisiis: MDCLXXXVII.

THE WORKS OF CONFUCIUS; containing the Original Text, with a Translation. Vol. I. By J. Marshman. Serampore: 1809.

THE FOUR BOOKS, Translated into English, by Rev. David Collie, of the London Missionary Society. Malacca: 1828.

L'INVARIABLE MILIEU, Ouvrage Moral de Tseu-sse, en Chinois et en Mandchou, avec une Version littérale Latine, une Traduction Françoise, &c., &c. Par M. Abel-Rémusat. A Paris: 1817.

LE TA HIO, OU LA GRANDE ETUDE: Traduit en François, avec une Version Latine, &c. Par G. Pauthier. Paris: 1837.

Y-KING, Antiquissimus Sinarum Liber, quem ex Latina Interpretatione P. Regis, aliorumque ex Soc. JESU PP. edidit Julius Mohl. 1839: Stuttgartiæ et Tubingæ.

MEMOIRES concernant L'Histoire, Les Sciences, Les Arts, Les Mœurs, Les Usages, &c., des Chinois. Par les Missionnaires de Pekin. A Paris: 1776—1814.

HISTOIRE GENERALE DE LA CHINE; ou Annales de cet Empire, Traduites du Tong-Kien-Kang-Mou. Par le feu Pere Joseph-Annie-Marie de Moyriac de Mailla, Jesuite François, Missionnaire a Pekin. A Paris: 1776—1785.

NOTITIA LINGUÆ SINICÆ. Auctore P. Premare. Malaccæ: cura Academiæ Anglo-Sinensis. MDCCCXXXI.

THE CHINESE REPOSITORY. Canton, China. 20 vols. 1832—1851.

DICTIONNAIRE DES NOMS, Anciens et Modernes, des Villes et Arrondissements de Premier, Deuxieme, et Troisieme ordre, compris dans L'Empire Chinois, &c. Par Edouard Biot, Membre du Conseil de la Société Asiatique. Paris: 1842.

THE CHINESE. By John Francis Davis, Esq., F.R.S., &c. In two volumes. London: 1836.

CHINA: its State and Prospects. By W. H. Medhurst, D.D., of the London Missionary Society. London: 1838.

L'UNIVERS: Histoire et Description des tous les Peuples. Chine. Par M. G. Pauthier. Paris: 1838.

HISTORY OF CHINA, from the earliest Records to the Treaty with Great Britain in 1842. By Thomas Thornton, Esq., Member of the Royal Asiatic Society. In two volumes. London: 1844.

THE MIDDLE KINGDOM: A Survey of the Geography, Government, Education, Social Life, Arts, Religion, &c., of the Chinese Empire. By S. Wells Williams, LL.D. In two volumes. New York and London: 1848.

THE RELIGIOUS CONDITION OF THE CHINESE. By Rev. Joseph Edkins, B. A., of the London Missionary Society. London: 1859.

CHRIST AND OTHER MASTERS. By Charles Hardwick, M.A., Christian Advocate in the University of Cambridge. Part III. Religions of China, America, and Oceanica. Cambridge: 1858.

CONFUCIAN ANALECTS.

BOOK I. HEŎ URH.

論語

學而第一

一章 子曰、[1]學而時習之、不亦說乎。[2]有朋自遠方來、不亦樂乎。[3]人不知而不慍、不亦君子乎。

CHAPTER I. 1. The Master said, "Is it not pleasant to learn with a constant perseverance and application?

2. "Is it not pleasant to have friends coming from distant quarters?

3. "Is he not a man of complete virtue, who feels no discomposure though men may take no note of him?"

TITLE OF THE WORK.—論語, 'Discourses and Dialogues;' that is, the discourses or discussions of Confucius with his disciples and others on various topics, and his replies to their inquiries. Many chapters, however, and one whole book, are the sayings, not of the sage himself, but of some of his disciples. The characters may also be rendered 'Digested Conversations,' and this appears to be the more ancient signification attached to them, the account being, that, after the death of Confucius, his disciples collected together and compared the memoranda of his conversations which they had severally preserved, digesting them into the twenty books which compose the work. Hence the title—論語, 'Discussed Sayings,' or 'Digested Conversations.' See 論語註疏解經序. I have styled the work 'Confucian Analects,' as being more descriptive of its character than any other name I could think of.

HEADING OF THIS BOOK.—學而第一. The two first characters in the book, after the introductory—'The Master said,' are adopted as its heading. This is similar to the custom of the Jews, who name many books in the Bible from the first word in them. 第一, 'The first;' that is, of the twenty books composing the whole work. In some of the books we find a unity or analogy of subjects, which evidently guided the compilers in grouping the chapters together. Others seem devoid of any such principle of combination. The sixteen chapters of this book are occupied, it is said, with the fundamental subjects which ought to engage the attention of the learner, and the great matters of human practice. The word 學, '*learn*,' rightly occupies the forefront in the studies of a nation, of which its educational system has so long been the distinction and glory.

1. THE WHOLE WORK AND ACHIEVEMENT OF THE LEARNER, FIRST PERFECTING HIS KNOWLEDGE, THEN ATTRACTING BY HIS FAME LIKE-MINDED INDIVIDUALS, AND FINALLY COMPLETE IN HIMSELF. 1. 子, at the commencement, indicates Confucius. 子, 'a son,' is also the common designation of males,—especially of virtuous men. We find it, in conversations, used in the same way as our 'Sir.' When it *follows* the surname, it is equivalent to our 'Mr.,' or may be rendered 'the philosopher,' 'the scholar,' 'the officer,' &c. Often, however, it is better to leave it untranslated. When it *precedes* the surname, it indicates that the person spoken of was the master of the writer, as 子沈子, 'my master, the philosopher 沈.' Standing single and alone, as in the text, it denotes Confucius, *the philosopher*, or, rather, *the master*. If we render the term by Confucius, as all preceding translators have done, we miss the indication which it gives of the handiwork of his disciples, and the reverence

二 有子曰、其爲人也孝弟、而好犯上者鮮矣、不好犯上、而好作亂者、未之有也。二君子務本、本立、而道生、孝

CHAPTER II. 1. The philosopher Yew said, "They are few who, being filial and fraternal, are fond of offending against their superiors. There have been none, who, not liking to offend against their superiors, have been fond of stirring up confusion.

2. "The superior man bends his attention to what is radical. That being established, all practical courses naturally grow up.

which it bespeaks for him. 學, in the old commentators, is explained by 誦, 'to read chantingly,' 'to discuss.' Choo He interprets it by 效, 'to imitate,' and makes its results to be 明善而復初, 'the understanding of all excellence, and the bringing back original goodness.' Subsequent scholars profess, for the most part, great admiration of this explanation. It is an illustration, to my mind, of the way in which Choo He and his followers are continually being wise above what is written in the classical books. 習 is the rapid and frequent motion of the wings of a bird in flying, used for 'to repeat,' 'to practise.' 之 is the obj. of the third pers. pronoun, and its antecedent is to be found in the pregnant meaning of 學. 不亦 is explained by 豈不, 'is it not?' See 四書補註備旨. To bring out the force of 'also' in 亦, some say thus:—'The occasions for pleasure are many, *is this not also one?*' 說, read *yuĕ*, as always when it has the 4th tone marked, stands for 悅. What is learned becomes by practice and application one's own, and hence arises complacent pleasure in the mastering mind. 悅 as distinguished from 樂, *lŏ*, in the next par., is the internal, individual, feeling of pleasure, and the other, its external manifestation, implying also companionship. 2. 朋, properly, 'fellow-students;' but, generally, individuals of the same class and character, like-minded. 3. 君子 I translate here—'a man of complete virtue.' Literally, it is—'a princely man.' See on 子, above. It is a technical term in Chin. moral writers, for which there is no exact correspondency in English, and which cannot be rendered always in the same way. See Morrison's Dictionary, char. 子. Its opposite is 小人, 'a small, mean, man.' 人不知, 'Men do not know him,' but anciently some explained—'men do not know,' that is, are stupid under his teaching. The interpretation in the text is doubtless the correct one.

2. FILIAL PIETY AND FRATERNAL SUBMISSION ARE THE FOUNDATION OF ALL VIRTUOUS PRACTICE. 1. Yew, named 若, and styled 子有, and 子若, a native of 魯, was famed among the other disciples of Confucius for his strong memory, and love for the doctrines of antiquity. In personal appearance he resembled the sage. See Mencius, III. Pt. II. iv. 13. 有子 is 'Yew, the philosopher,' and he and Tsăng Ts'an (or Sin) are the only two of Confucius' disciples who are mentioned in this style in the *Lun Yu*. This has led to an opinion on the part of some, that the work was compiled by their disciples. This may not be sufficiently supported, but I have not found the peculiarity pointed out satisfactorily explained. The tablet of Yew's spirit is now in the same apartment of the sage's temples as that of the sage himself, occupying the 6th place in the eastern range of 'the wise ones.' To this position it was promoted in the 3d year of Keen-lung of the present dynasty. A degree of activity enters into the meaning of 爲 in 爲人,—'playing the man,' 'as men, showing themselves filial,' &c. 弟, here = 悌, 'to be submissive as a younger brother,' is in the low. 3d tone. With its proper signification, it was anciently in the 2d tone. 而 = 'and yet,' different from its simple conjunctive use = 'and,' in the prec. ch. 好, a verb, 'to love,' in the up. 3d tone, diff. from the same char. in the 2d tone, an adj., = 'good.' 鮮, up. 2d tone, = 'few.' On the idiom—未之有, see Premare's gram. p. 156. 2.

弟也者、其爲人之本與。子曰、巧言令色、鮮矣仁。曾子曰、吾日三省吾身、爲人謀、而不忠乎、與朋友交、而不信乎、傳不習乎。

Filial piety and fraternal submission!—are they not the root of all benevolent actions?"

CHAPTER III. The Master said, "Fine words and an insinuating appearance are seldom associated with true virtue."

CHAPTER IV. The philosopher Tsăng said, "I daily examine myself on three points:—whether, in transacting business for others, I may have been not faithful;—whether, in intercourse with friends, I may have been not sincere;—whether I may have not mastered and practised the instructions of my teacher."

君子 has a less intense signification here than in the last chap. I translate—'The superior man,' for want of a better term. 本, 'the root,' 'what is radical,' is here said of filial and fraternal duties, and 道, 'ways' or 'courses,' of all that is intended by 爲(=行) 仁, below. The particles 也者 resume the discourse about 孝弟, and introduce some further description of them. See Prem., p. 158. 與, in the lower 1st tone, is half interrogative, an answer in the affirmative being implied. 仁 is explained here as 'the principle of love,' 'the virtue of the heart.' Mencius says—仁也者人也, '仁 is man,' in accordance with which, Julien translates it by *humanitas*. *Benevolence* often comes near it, but, as has been said before of 君子, we cannot give a uniform rendering of this term.

3. FAIR APPEARANCES ARE SUSPICIOUS. 巧言令色,—see Shoo-king, II. iii. 2. 巧, 'skill in workmanship;' then, 'skill,' 'cleverness,' generally, and sometimes with a bad meaning, as here, ='artful,' 'hypocritical.' 令 'a law,' 'an order,' also 'good,' and here like 巧, with a bad meaning, ='pretending to be good.' 色, 'the manifestation of the feelings in the colour of the countenance,' is here used for the appearance generally.

4. HOW THE PHILOSOPHER TSANG DAILY EXAMINED HIMSELF, TO GUARD AGAINST HIS BEING GUILTY OF ANY IMPOSITION. *Tsăng*, whose name was 參 (*Ts'an*, now commonly read *Sin*,) and his designation 子輿, was one of the principal disciples of Confucius. A follower of the sage from his 16th year, though inferior in natural ability to some others, by his filial piety and other moral qualities, he entirely won the Master's esteem, and by persevering attention mastered his doctrines. Confucius employed him in the composition of the 孝經, or 'Classic of Filial Piety.' The authorship of the 大學, 'The Great Learning,' is also ascribed to him, though incorrectly, as we shall see. Ten books, moreover, of his composition are preserved in the *Le-ke*. His spirit tablet among the sage's four assessors, occupying the first place on the west, has precedence of that of Mencius. 省, read *sing*, 'to examine.' 三省 is naturally understood of 'three times,' but the context and consent of commentators make us assent to the interpretation—'on three points.' 身, 'the body,' 'one's personality;' 吾身=*myself*. 爲 is in low. 3d tone,='for.' So, frequently, below. 忠, from 中, 'middle,' 'the centre,' and 心, 'the heart,'=loyalty, faithfulness, action with and from the heart. 朋, see ch. 1. 友, 'two hands joined,' denoting union. 朋友, 'friends.' 傳不習 is very enigmatical. The translation follows Choo He. 何安 explained quite differently:—'whether I have given instruction in what I had not studied and practised?' It does seem more correct to take

（五）子曰、道千乘之國、敬事而信、節用而愛人、使民以時。

（六）子曰、弟子、入則孝、出則弟、謹而信、汎愛衆、而親仁、行有餘力、則以學文。

（七）子夏曰、賢賢易色、事父母、能竭其力、事君、能致其身、

CHAPTER V. The Master said, "To rule a country of a thousand chariots, there must be reverent attention to business, and sincerity; economy in expenditure, and love for men; and the employment of the people at the proper seasons."

CHAPTER VI. The Master said, "A youth, when at home, should be filial, and, abroad, respectful to his elders. He should be earnest and truthful. He should overflow in love to all, and cultivate the friendship of the good. When he has time and opportunity, after the performance of these things, he should employ them in polite studies."

CHAPTER VII. Tsze-hea said, "If a man withdraws his mind from the love of beauty, and applies it as sincerely to the love of the virtuous; if, in serving his parents, he can exert his utmost

傳 actively, 'to give instruction,' rather than passively, 'to receive instruction.' See 四書改錯, XV. 17.

5. FUNDAMENTAL PRINCIPLES FOR THE GOVERNMENT OF A LARGE STATE. 道 is used for 導, 'to rule,' 'to lead,' and is marked in the 3d tone, to distinguish it from 道, the noun, which was anciently read with the 3d tone. It is diff. from 治, which refers to the actual business of government, while 導 is the duty and purpose thereof, apprehended by the prince. The standpoint of the principles is the prince's mind. 乘, in low, 3d tone, 'a chariot,' diff. from its meaning in the 1st tone, 'to ride.' A country of 1000 chariots is one of the largest fiefs of the empire, which could bring such an armament into the field. The last principle,—使民以時, means that the people should not be called from their husbandry at improper seasons, to do service on military expeditions and public works.

6. RULES FOR THE TRAINING OF THE YOUNG:—DUTY FIRST AND THEN ACCOMPLISHMENTS. 弟子, 'younger brothers and sons,' taken together,=youths, a youth. The 2d 弟 is for 悌, as in ch. 2. 入出, 'coming in, going out,'=at home, abroad. 汎 is explained by Choo He by 廣, 'wide,' 'widely;' its proper meaning is 'the rush or overflow of water.' 力, 'strength,' here embracing the idea of *leisure*. 學文, not *literary studies* merely, but all the accomplishments of a gentleman also:—ceremonies, music, archery, horsemanship, writing, and numbers.

7. TSZE-HEA'S VIEWS OF THE SUBSTANCE OF LEARNING. Tsze-hea was the designation of 卜商, another of the sage's distinguished disciples, and now placed 5th in the eastern range of 'the wise ones.' He was greatly famed for his learning, and his views on the *She-king* and the *Ch'un Ts'ew* are said to be preserved in the comm. of 毛, and of 公羊高 and 穀梁赤. He wept himself blind on the death of his son, but lived to a great age, and was much esteemed by the people and princes of the time. With regard to the scope of this chapter, there

與朋友交、言而有信、雖曰未學、吾必謂之學矣。

〔八〕子一曰、君子不重、則不威、學則不固。二主忠信。三無友不如己者。四過則勿憚改。

〔九〕曾子曰、慎終追遠、民德歸厚矣。

strength, if, in serving his prince, he can devote his life; if, in his intercourse with his friends, his words are sincere;—although men say that he has not learned, I will certainly say that he has."

CHAPTER VIII. 1. The Master said, "If the scholar be not grave, he will not call forth any veneration, and his learning will not be solid.

2. "Hold faithfulness and sincerity as first principles.

3. "Have no friends not equal to yourself.

4. "When you have faults, do not fear to abandon them."

CHAPTER IX. The philosopher Tsăng said, "Let there be a careful attention *to perform the funeral rites* to parents, and let them be followed when long gone *with the ceremonies of sacrifice*;—then the virtue of the people will resume its proper excellence."

is some truth in what the comm. Woo, 吳, says,—that Tsze-hea's words may be wrested to depreciate learning, while those of the Master in the prec. ch. hit exactly the due medium. The 2d 賢 is a concrete noun. Written in full, 賢, it is composed of the characters for a *minister*, *loyal*, and a *precious shell*. It conveys the ideas of *talents* and *worth* in the concrete, but it is not easy to render it uniformly by any one term of another language. The 1st 賢 is a verb, ='to treat as a hëen.' 色 has a diff. meaning from that in the 3d ch. Here it means 'sensual pleasure.' Literally rendered, the first sentence would be, 'esteeming properly the virtuous, and changing the love of woman,' and great fault is found by some, as in 四書改錯, XIII. 1. with Choo He's interpretation which I have followed; but there is force in what his adherents say, that the passage is not to be understood as if the individual spoken of had ever been given to pleasure, but simply signifies the sincerity of his love for the virtuous. 致 here =委, 'to give to,' 'to devote.'

8. PRINCIPLES OF SELF-CULTIVATION. 1. 君子 has here its lightest meaning,=*a student*, one who wishes to be a *keun-tsze*. 孔安國, of the Han dynasty, in the 1st half of the 2d century, took 固, in the sense of 'obscured,' 'dulled,' and interprets—'Let him learn, and he will not fall into error.' The received interpretation, as in the transl., is better. 2. 主, as a verb, 'to hold to be chief.' It is often used thus. 3. The object of friendship, with Chinese moralists, is to improve one's knowledge and virtue;—hence, this seemingly selfish maxim.

9. THE GOOD EFFECT OF ATTENTION ON THE PART OF PRINCES TO THE OFFICES TO THE DEAD:—AN ADMONITION OF TSANG SIN. 終, 'the end,' =death, and 遠, 'distant,' have both the force of adjectives,='the dead,' and 'the departed,' or 'the long gone.' 慎 and 追 mean, 'to be careful of,' 'to follow,' but their application is as in the translation. 厚, 'thick,' in opposition to 薄, 'thin;' metaphorically,=*good*, *excellent*. The force of 歸, 'to return,' is to shew that this virtue is naturally proper to the people.

十 子禽問於子貢曰、夫子至於是邦也、必聞其政、求之與、抑與之與。二 子貢曰、夫子溫、良、恭、儉、讓、以得之、夫子之求之也、其諸異乎人之求之與。

十一 子曰、父在、觀其志、父沒、觀其行、三年無改於父之道、可謂孝矣。

CHAPTER X. 1. Tsze-k'in asked Tsze-kung, saying, "When our master comes to any country, he does not fail to learn all about its government. Does he ask his information? or is it given to him?"

2. Tsze-kung said, "Our master is benign, upright, courteous, temperate, and complaisant, and thus he gets his information. The Master's mode of asking information!—is it not different from that of other men?"

CHAPTER XI. The Master said, "While a man's father is alive, look at the bent of his will; when his father is dead, look at his conduct. If for three years he does not alter from the way of his father, he may be called filial."

10. CHARACTERISTICS OF CONFUCIUS, AND THEIR INFLUENCE ON THE PRINCES OF THE TIME. 1. Tsze-k'in, and Tsze-k'ang (亢), are designations of 陳亢, one of the minor disciples of Confucius. His tablet occupies the 28th place, on the west, in the outer hall of the temple. A good story is related of him. On the death of his brother, his wife and major-domo wished to bury some living persons with him, to serve him in the regions below. The thing being referred to Tsze-k'in, he proposed that the wife and steward should themselves submit to the immolation, which made them stop the matter. Tsze-kung, with the double surname 端木, and named 賜, occupies a higher place in the Confucian ranks, and is now the third on the east, among 'the wise ones.' He is conspicuous in this work for his readiness and smartness in reply, and displayed on several occasions practical and political ability. 夫, 'a general designation for males,'=a man. 夫子,—a common designation for a teacher or master. 是邦, 'this country'=any country. 必, 'must,'=does not fail to. The antecedent to both the 之 is the whole clause 聞其政. Obs. the diff. in 與, up. 2d tone,='to give,' and often a preposition, 'with,' 'to,' and 與, low. 1st tone, as in ch. 2. 2. The force of 其諸 is well enough expressed by the dash in English, the previous 也 indicating a pause in the discourse, which the 其, 'it,' resumes.

11. ON FILIAL DUTY. 行 is in the low. 3d tone, explained by 行迹, 'traces of walking,'=conduct. It is to be understood that the way of the father had not been very bad. An old interpretation, that the three years are to be understood of the three years of mourning for the father, is now rightly rejected.

十二 有子曰、禮之用、和爲貴、先王之道、斯爲美、小大由之。二 有所不行、知和而和、不以禮節之、亦不可行也。

十三 有子曰、信近於義、言可復也、恭近於禮、遠恥辱也、因不失其親、亦可宗也。

十四 子曰、君子食無求

CHAPTER XII. 1. The philosopher Yew said, "In practising the rules of propriety, a natural ease is to be prized. In the ways prescribed by the ancient kings, this is the excellent quality, and in things small and great we follow them.

2. "Yet it is not to be observed in all cases. If one, knowing *how* such ease *should be prized*, manifests it, without regulating it by the rules of propriety, this likewise is not to be done."

CHAPTER XIII. The philosopher Yew said, "When agreements are made according to what is right, what is spoken can be made good. When respect is shown according to what is proper, one keeps far from shame and disgrace. When the parties upon whom a man leans are proper persons to be intimate with, he can make them his guides and masters."

CHAPTER XIV. The Master said, "He who aims to be a man of complete virtue, in his food does not seek to gratify his appetite,

12. IN CEREMONIES A NATURAL EASE IS TO BE PRIZED, AND YET TO BE SUBORDINATE TO THE END OF CEREMONIES,—THE REVERENTIAL OBSERVANCE OF PROPRIETY. 1. 禮 is not easily rendered in another language. There underlies it the idea of *what is proper*. It is 事之宜, 'the fitness of things,' what reason calls for in the performance of duties towards superior beings, and between man and man. Our term 'ceremonies' comes near its meaning here. 道 is here a name for 禮, as indicating the course or ways to be pursued by men. In 小大由之, the antecedent to 之 is not 和, but 禮 or 道. 2. Obs. the force of the 亦, 'also,' in the last clause, and how it affirms the general principle enunciated in the first paragraph.

13. TO SAVE FROM FUTURE REPENTANCE, WE MUST BE CAREFUL IN OUR FIRST STEPS. A diff. view of the scope of this ch. is taken by Ho An. It illustrates, according to him, the difference between being sincere and righteousness, between being respectful and propriety, and how a man's conduct may be venerated. The latter view commends itself, the only difficulty being with 近於, 'near to,' which we must accept as a *variant* for 合乎, 'agreeing with.' 約=信約, 'a covenant,' 'agreement.' 遠, up. 3d tone, 'to keep away from.' The force of the 亦='he can go on to make them his masters,' 宗 being taken as an active verb.

14. WITH WHAT MIND ONE AIMING TO BE A KEUN-TSZE PURSUES HIS LEARNING. He may be well, even luxuriously, fed and lodged, but,

飽、居無求安、敏於事、而愼於言、就有道、而正焉、可謂好學也已。

〔十五〕子貢曰、貧而無諂、富而無驕、何如。子曰、可也、未若貧而樂、富而好禮者也。子貢曰、詩云、如切如磋、如琢如磨、其斯之謂與。子曰、賜也、始可與言詩

nor in his dwelling-place does he seek the appliances of ease; he is earnest in what he is doing, and careful in his speech; he frequents the company of men of principle that he may be rectified:—such a person may be said indeed to love to learn."

CHAPTER XV. 1. Tsze-kung said, "What do you pronounce concerning the poor man who yet does not flatter, and the rich man who is not proud?" The Master replied, "They will do; but they are not equal to him, who, though poor, is yet cheerful, and to him, who, though rich, loves the rules of propriety."

2. Tsze-kung replied, "It is said in the Book of Poetry, 'As you cut and then file, as you carve and then polish.'—The meaning is the same, I apprehend, as that which you have just expressed."

3. The Master said, "With one like Tsze, I can begin to talk about the Odes. I told him one point, and he knew its proper sequence."

with his higher aim, these things are not his seeking,—無求. A nominative to 可謂 must be supposed,—*all this*, or *such a person*. The closing particles, 也已, give emphasis to the preceding sentence,=*yes indeed*.

15. AN ILLUSTRATION OF THE SUCCESSIVE STEPS IN SELF-CULTIVATION. 1. Tsze-kung had been poor, and then did not cringe. He became rich, and was not proud. He asked Confucius about the style of char. to which he had attained. Conf. allowed its worth, but sent him to higher attainments. 而, here,='and yet.' 何如, 'what as?'='what do you say— what is to be thought,—of this?' Obs. the force of the 未, 'not yet.' 2. The ode quoted is the first of the songs of Wei (衞), praising the prince Woo, who had dealt with himself as an ivory-worker who first cuts the bone, and then files it smooth, or a lapidary whose hammer and chisel are followed by all the appliances for smoothing and polishing. See the She-king, I. v. Ode I. st. 2. 2. In 其斯之謂, the antecedent to 其 is the passage of the ode, and that to 斯 is the reply of Confucius. 之謂, see Premare, p. 156. 3. Intorcetta and his co-adjutors translate this par. as if 賜 were in the 2d person. But the Chin. comm. put it in the 3d, and correctly. Premare, on the char. 也, says, '*Fere semper adjungitur nominibus propriis. Sic in libro Lun Yu, Confucius loquens de suis discipulis, Yeou, Kieou, Hoei, vel quem alloquens, dicit* 由也, 求也, 回也.' With the example in III. 17, before us, it is not to be denied that the name before 也 is sometimes in the 2d person, but generally it is in the 3d, and the force of the

已矣、告諸往而知來者。

十六 子曰、不患人之不己知、患不知人也。

CHAPTER XVI. The Master said, "I will not be afflicted at men's not knowing me; I will be afflicted that I do not know men."

也=quasi 賜也, quasi Tsze. 已矣, nearly=也已, in ch. 14. 已, the final part. (see Prolem. p. 185), is thus marked with a tone, to distinguish it from 己, 'self,' as in next ch. The last clause may be given—'Tell him the past, and he knows the future,' but the connection determines the meaning as in the translation. 諸, as in ch. 10, is a particle, a mere 語助, as it is called, 'a helping' or supporting sound.

16. PERSONAL ATTAINMENT SHOULD BE OUR CHIEF AIM. Comp. ch. 1. p. 3. Obs. the transposition in 己知, which is more elegant than 知己 would be. 己, 'self,' the person depending on the context. We cannot translate 'do not be afflicted,' because 不 is not used imperatively, like 勿. A nominative to 患 has to be assumed,—我, 'I,' or 君子, 'the superior man.'

BOOK II. WEI CHING.

爲政第二

一 子曰、爲政以德、譬如北辰、居其所、而衆星共之。

CHAPTER I. The Master said, "He who exercises government by means of his virtue, may be compared to the north polar star, which keeps its place and all the stars turn towards it."

HEADING OF THIS BOOK.—爲政第二. This second book contains twenty-four chapters, and is named 爲政, 'The practice of government.' That is the object to which learning, treated of in the last book, should lead, and here we have the qualities which constitute, and the character of the men who administer, good government.

1. THE INFLUENCE OF VIRTUE IN A RULER. 德 is explained by 得, but the old comm. say 物得以生謂之德, 'what creatures get in order to their birth is called their virtue,' while Choo He makes it=行道而有得於心, 'the practice of truth and acquisition thereof in the heart.' Choo's view of the comparison is that it sets forth the illimitable influence which virtue in a ruler exercises without his using any effort. This is extravagant. His opponents say that virtue is the polar star, and the various departments of government the other stars. This is far-fetched. We must be content to accept the vague utterance without minutely determining its meaning. 北辰 is, no doubt, 'the north polar star,' anciently believed to coincide exactly with the place of the real pole. 共 is up. 3d tone, used for 拱, 'to fold the hands in saluting,' here='to turn respectfully towards.'

二 子曰、詩三百、一言以蔽之、曰、思無邪。

三 子曰、一道之以政、齊之以刑、民免而無恥。二道之以德、齊之以禮、有恥且格。

四 子曰、一吾十有五、而志于學。二三十而立。三四十而不惑。四五

CHAPTER II. The Master said, "In the Book of Poetry are three hundred pieces, but the design of them all may be embraced in one sentence—'Have no depraved thoughts.'"

CHAPTER III. 1. The Master said, "If the people be led by laws, and uniformity sought to be given them by punishments, they will try to avoid *the punishment*, but have no sense of shame.

2. "If they be led by virtue, and uniformity sought to be given them by the rules of propriety, they will have the sense of shame, and moreover will become good."

CHAPTER IV. 1. The Master said, "At fifteen, I had my mind bent on learning.

2. "At thirty, I stood firm.

3. "At forty, I had no doubts.

2. THE PURE DESIGN OF THE BOOK OF POETRY. The number of compositions in the She-king is rather more than the round number here given. 一言=一句, 'one sentence.' 蔽=蓋, 'to cover,' 'to embrace.' 思無邪, see She-king, IV. ii. I. st. 4. The sentence there is indicative, and in praise of the duke He, who had no depraved thoughts. The sage would seem to have been intending his own design in compiling the She. Individual pieces are calculated to have a diff. effect.

3. HOW RULERS SHOULD PREFER MORAL APPLIANCES. 1. 道, as in I. 5. 之, 'them,' ref. to 民, below. 政, as oppos. to 德,=laws and prohibitions. 齊, 'corn earing evenly;' hence, what is level, equal, adjusted, and here with the corresponding verbal force. 民免, 'The people will avoid,' that is, avoid breaking the laws thro. fear of the punishment. 2. 格 has the signif. of 'to come to,' and 'to correct,' from either of which the text may be explained,—'will come to good,' or 'will correct themselves.' Obs. the diff. of 且 and 而 in p. 1. 而='but;' 且='moreover.'

4. CONFUCIUS' OWN ACCOUNT OF HIS GRADUAL PROGRESS AND ATTAINMENTS. Chin. comm. are perplexed with this ch. Holding of Confucius that 生而知之,安而行之, 'he was born with knowledge, and did what was right with entire ease,' they say that he here conceals his sagehood, and puts himself on the level of common men, to set before them a stimulating example. We may believe that the compilers of the Analects, the sage's immediate disciples, did not think of him so extravagantly as later men have done. It is to be wished, however, that he had been more definite and diffuse in his account of himself. 1. 有, in low. 3d tone,='and.' The 'learning,' to which, at 15, Conf. gave himself, is to be understood of the subjects of the 'Superior Learning.' See Choo He's preliminary essay to the Ta Heö. 2. The 'standing firm' probably indicates that he no more needed to bend his will. 3. The 'no doubts' may have been concerning what was proper in all circumstances and

十而知天命。六十而耳順。七十而從心所欲、不踰矩。

孟懿子問孝、子曰、無違。樊遲御、子告之曰、孟孫問孝於我、我對曰、無違。樊遲曰、何謂也。子曰、生事之以禮、死葬之以禮、祭之以禮。

4. "At fifty, I knew the decrees of heaven.

5. "At sixty, my ear was an obedient organ *for the reception of truth*.

6. "At seventy, I could follow what my heart desired, without transgressing what was right".

CHAPTER V. Măng E asked what filial piety was. The Master said, "It is not being disobedient."

2. *Soon after*, as Fan Ch'e was driving him, the Master told him, saying, 'Măng-sun asked me what filial piety was, and I answered him,—'not being disobedient."

3. Fan Ch'e said, "What did you mean?" The Master replied, "That parents, when alive, should be served according to propriety; that, when dead, they should be buried according to propriety; and that they should be sacrificed to according to propriety."

events. 4. 'The decrees of Heaven,'=the things decreed by Heaven, the constitution of things making what was proper to be so. 5. 'The ear obedient' is the mind receiving as by intuition the truth from the ear. 6. 矩, 'an instrument for determining the square.' 不踰矩, 'without transgressing the square.'

5. FILIAL PIETY MUST BE SHOWN ACCORDING TO THE RULES OF PROPRIETY. 1. Mang E was a great officer of the state of Loo, by name Ho-ke (何忌), and the chief of one of the three great families by which in the time of Conf. the authority of that state was grasped. Those families were descended from three brothers, the sons by a concubine of the duke Hwan (B. C. 710-693), who were distinguished at first by the prenomens of 仲, 叔, and 季. To these was subsequently added the character 孫 'grandson,' to indicate their princely descent, and 仲孫, 叔孫, and 季孫 became the respective surnames of the families. 仲孫 was changed into 孟孫, by the father of Mang E, on a principle of humility, as he thereby only claimed to be the eldest of the inferior sons or their representatives, and avoided the presumption of seeming to be a younger full brother of the reigning duke. 懿 'mild and virtuous,' was the posthumous honorary title given to Ho-ke. On 子, see I. I. 1. Fan, by name 須, and designated 子遲, was a minor disciple of the sage. Conf. repeated his remark to Fan, that he might report the explanation of it to his friend Mang E, or Mang-sun, and thus prevent him from supposing that all the sage intended was disobedience to parents.

六 孟武伯問孝、子曰、父母唯其疾之憂。

七 子游問孝、子曰、今之孝者、是謂能養、至於犬馬、皆能有養、不敬、何以別乎。

八 子夏問孝、子曰、色難、有事、弟子服其勞、有酒食、先生饌、曾是以爲孝乎。

CHAPTER VI. Măng Woo asked what filial piety was. The Master said, "Parents are anxious lest their children should be sick."

CHAPTER VII. Tsze-yew asked what filial piety was. The Master said, "The filial piety of now-a-days means the support of one's parents. But dogs and horses likewise are able to do something in the way of support;—without reverence, what is there to distinguish the one support given from the other?"

CHAPTER VIII. Tsze-hea asked what filial piety was. The Master said, "The difficulty is with the countenance. If, when *their elders* have any *troublesome* affairs, the young take the toil of them, and if, when *the young* have wine and food, they set them before their elders, is THIS to be considered filial piety?"

6. THE ANXIETY OF PARENTS ABOUT THEIR CHILDREN AN ARGUMENT FOR FILIAL PIETY. This enigmatical sentence has been interpreted in two ways. Choo He takes 唯 (=惟) not in the sense of 'only,' but of 'thinking anxiously.'—'Parents have the sorrow of thinking anxiously about their—i. e. their children's—being unwell. Therefore children should take care of their persons.' The old comm. again take 唯 in the sense of 'only.'—'Let parents have only the sorrow of their children's illness. Let them have no other occasion for sorrow. This will be filial piety.' Mang Woo (the hon. epithet,='Bold and of straightforward principle,') was the son of Mang E, and by name 彘. 伯 merely indicates that he was the eldest son.

HOW THERE MUST BE REVERENCE IN FILIAL DUTY. Tsze-yew was the designation of 言偃, a native of 吳, and distinguished among the disciples of Conf. for his knowl. of the rules of propriety, and for his learning. He is now 4th on the west among 'the wise ones.' 養 is in low. 3d tone,='to minister support to,' the act of an inferior to a superior. In low. 3d tone, it='to nourish,' 'bring up.' Choo He gives a different turn to the sentiment,—'But dogs and horses likewise manage to get their support.' The other and older interpr. is better. 至於, 'Coming to,'=as to, *quoad*. 別, up. 4th tone, 'to discriminate,' 'distinguish.' In low. tone, 別='to leave,' 'separate from.'

8. THE DUTIES OF FILIAL PIETY MUST BE PERFORMED WITH A CHEERFUL COUNTENANCE. 色, here, nearly analogous to I. 8. 事 followed by 勞,=the '*troublesome* affairs' in the transl. 弟子, as in I. 6. The use of the phrase here extends filial duty to elders generally,—to the 父兄 as well as to the 父母. We have in transl. to supply their respective nom. to the two 有. 食, read *tsze*, 'rice,' and then, food generally. 先生饌,=與先生 (earlier born=elders) 饌之. 曾, low. 1st tone,=則.

【第九章】子曰、吾與回言終日、不違、如愚、退而省其私、亦足以發、回也不愚。

【第十章】子曰、視其所以。【二】觀其所由。【三】察其所安。【四】人焉廋哉、人焉廋哉。

【第十一章】子曰、溫故而知新、可以爲師矣。

CHAPTER IX. The Master said, "I have talked with Hwuy for a whole day, and he has not made any objection *to any thing I said*;—as if he were stupid. He has retired, and I have examined his conduct when away from me, and found him able to illustrate *my teachings*. Hwuy!—He is not stupid."

CHAPTER X. 1. The Master said, "See what a man does.

2. "Mark his motives.

3. "Examine in what things he rests.

4. "How can a man conceal his character!

5. "How can a man conceal his character!"

CHAPTER XI. The Master said, "If a man keeps cherishing his old knowledge, so as continually to be acquiring new, he may be a teacher of others."

'then,' a transition particle. To these diff. interrogatories about filial duty, the sage, we are told, made answer according to the character of the questioner, as each one needed instruction.

9. THE QUIET RECEPTIVITY OF THE DISCIPLE HWUY. Yen Hwuy (顏回), styled 子淵, was Confucius' favourite disciple, and is now honoured with the first place east among his four assessors in his temples, and with the title of 復聖顏子, 'The second sage, the philosopher Yen.' At 29 his hair was entirely white, and at 33 he died to the excessive grief of the sage. The subject of 退 is 回, and that of 省 (as in I. 4.) is 吾. 其私, 'his privacy,' not meaning his conduct in secret, but only his way when not with the master. 亦 'also,' takes up 如愚,—He was so, and also so. 回也, see I. 15.

10. HOW TO DETERMINE THE CHARACTERS OF MEN. 1. 以 is explained as 行, or 行用, 'does.' The same, tho' not its comm. meaning, is the first given to it in the Dict. For the noun to which the three 其 refer, we must go down to 人 in the 4th par. There is a climax in 所以, 所由 ('what from'), and 所安, and a corresponding one in the verbs 視, 觀, and 察. 4. 焉, gen. a final particle, in low. 1st tone, is here in up. 1st., an interrogative=how? Its interrog. force blends with the exclamatory of 哉 at the end.

11. TO BE ABLE TO TEACH OTHERS ONE MUST FROM HIS OLD STORES BE CONTINUALLY DEVELOPING THINGS NEW. 溫 is exp. in the Dict. by 燖 and, with ref. to this very pass. it is said, 'one's old learning being thorough, again constantly to practise it, is called 溫.' Mod. comm. say that the 'new learning is in the old.' The idea probably is that of assimilating old acquisitions and new, the mind's harmonizing them. Comp. 中庸, XXVII. 1.

十二 子曰、君子不器。

十三 子貢問君子、子曰、先行其言、而後從之。

十四 子曰、君子周而不比、小人比而不周。

十五 子曰、學而不思則罔、思而不學則殆。

十六 子曰、攻乎異端、斯害也已。

CHAPTER XII. The Master said, "The accomplished scholar is not an utensil."

CHAPTER XIII. Tsze-kung asked what constituted the superior man. The Master said, "He acts before he speaks, and afterwards speaks according to his actions."

CHAPTER XIV. The Master said, "The superior man is catholic and no partizan. The mean man is a partizan and not catholic."

CHAPTER XV. The Master said, "Learning without thought is labour lost; thought without learning is perilous."

CHAPTER XVI. The Master said, "The study of strange doctrines is injurious indeed!"

12. THE GENERAL APTITUDE OF THE KEUN-TSZE. This is not like our Eng. saying, that 'such a man is a machine,'—a blind instrument. A utensil has its particular use. It answers for that and no other. Not so with the superior man, who is *ad omnia paratus*.

13. HOW WITH THE SUPERIOR MAN WORDS FOLLOW ACTIONS. The reply is literally;—'He first acts his words and afterwards follows them.' A translator's diffic. is with the latter clause. What is the antecedent to 之? It would seem to be 其言, but in that case there is no room for words at all. Nor is there according to the old comm. In the interpretation I have given, Choo He follows the famous Chow Leen-k'e, (周濂溪).

14. THE DIFFERENCE BETWEEN THE KEUN-TSZE AND THE SMALL MAN. 比, here low. 3d tone, 'partial,' 'partizanly.' The sent. is this—'With the Keun-tsze, it is principles not men; with the small man, the reverse.'

15. IN LEARNING, READING AND THOUGHT MUST BE COMBINED. 罔, 'a net,' used also in the sense of 'not,' as an adverb, and here as an adj. The old comm. makes 殆, 'perilous,' simply='wearisome to the body.'

16. STRANGE DOCTRINES ARE NOT TO BE STUDIED. 攻, often 'to attack,' as an enemy, here='to apply one's-self to,' 'to study.' 端, 'correct;' then, 'beginnings,' 'first principles;' here='doctrines.' 也已, as in I. 14. In Conf. time Buddhism was not in China, and we can hardly suppose him to intend Taouism. Indeed, we are ignorant to what doctrines he referred, but his maxim is of gen. application.

十七 子曰、由、誨女知之乎、知之爲知之、不知爲不知、是知也。

十八 子張學干祿。子曰、多聞闕疑、愼言其餘、則寡尤、多見闕殆、愼行其餘、則寡悔、言寡尤、行寡悔、祿在其中矣。

CHAPTER XVII. The Master said, "Yew, shall I teach you what knowledge is? When you know a thing, to hold that you know it; and when you do not know a thing, to allow that you do not know it;—this is knowledge."

CHAPTER XVIII. 1. Tsze-chang was learning with a view to official emolument.

2. The Master said, "Hear much and put aside the points of which you stand in doubt, while you speak cautiously at the same time of the others:—then you will afford few occasions for blame. See much and put aside the things which seem perilous, while you are cautious at the same time in carrying the others into practice:—then you will have few occasions for repentance. When one gives few occasions for blame in his words, and few occasions for repentance in his conduct, he is in the way to get emolument."

17. THERE SHOULD BE NO PRETENSE IN THE PROFESSION OF KNOWLEDGE, OR THE DENIAL OF IGNORANCE. 由, by surname 仲, and generally known by his designation of *Tsze-lu* (子路), was one of the most famous disciples of Confucius, and now occupies in the temples the 4th place east in the sage's own hall. He was noted for his courage and forwardness, a man of impulse rather than reflection. Conf. had foretold that he would come to an untimely end, and so it happened. He was killed through his own rashness in a revolution in the state of Wei. The tassel of his cap being cut off when he received his death-wound, he quoted a saying—'The superior man must not die without his cap,' tied on the tassel, adjusted the cap, and expired. This action—結纓禮全, is much lauded. Of the six 知, the 1st and 6th are knowledge subjective, the other four are knowledge objective. The first 知之=知之之道. In the other two cases, 之='any one thing.' 爲=以爲, 'to take to be,' 'to consider,' 'to allow.' 女, thus marked with a tone, is used for 汝, 'you.'

18. THE END IN LEARNING SHOULD BE ONE'S OWN IMPROVEMENT, AND NOT EMOLUMENT. 1. Tsze-chang, named 師, with the double surname 顓孫, a native of Ch'in (陳), was not undistinguished in the Confucian school. Tsze-kung praised him as a man of merit without boasting, humble in a high position, and not arrogant to the helpless. From this ch., however, it would appear that inferior motives did sometimes rule him. 學='was learning,' i. e., at some particular time. 干=求, 'to seek for.' 2. 闕 is explained in the comm. as in transl.,—姑舍置, but this meaning of it is not found in the Dict. 祿在其中, 'Emolument is herein,' i. e., it will come without

〔十九〕哀公問曰、何爲則民服。孔子對曰、擧直錯諸枉、則民服、擧枉錯諸直、則民不服。〔二十〕季康子問使民敬忠以勸、如之何。子曰、臨之以莊、則敬、孝慈、則忠、擧善而教不能、則勸。〔二十一〕或謂孔子曰、子奚

CHAPTER XIX. The duke Gae asked, saying, "What should be done in order to secure the submission of the people?" Confucius replied, "Advance the upright and set aside the crooked, then the people will submit. Advance the crooked and set aside the upright, then the people will not submit."

CHAPTER XX. Ke K'ang asked how to cause the people to reverence *their ruler*, to be faithful to him, and to urge themselves to virtue. The Master said, "Let him preside over them with gravity;—then they will reverence him. Let him be filial and kind to all;—then they will be faithful to him. Let him advance the good and teach the incompetent;—then they will eagerly seek to be virtuous."

CHAPTER XXI. 1. Some one addressed Confucius, saying, "Sir, why are you not engaged in the government?"

seeking: the individual is on the way to it. The lesson is that we are to do what is right, and not be anxious about temporal concerns.

19. HOW A PRINCE BY THE RIGHT EMPLOYMENT OF HIS OFFICERS MAY SECURE THE REAL SUBMISSION OF HIS SUBJECTS. Gae was the honorary epithet of 蔣, duke of Loo (B. C. 494-367). Conf. died in his 16th year. According to the laws for posthumous titles, 哀 denotes 'the respectful and benevolent, early cut off.' 哀公='The to-be-lamented duke.' 錯, up. 3d tone,=置, 'to set aside.' 諸 is partly euphonious, but also indicates the plural. 孔子對曰, 'The philosopher K'ung replied.' Here, for the first time, the sage is called by his surname, and, 對 is used, as indicating the reply of an inferior to a superior.

20. EXAMPLE IN SUPERIORS IS MORE POWERFUL THAN FORCE. K'ang, 'easy and pleasant, people-soother,' was the honorary epithet of Ke-sun Fei (肥), the head of one of the three great families of Loo; see ch. 5. His idea is seen in 使, 'to cause,' the power of *force*; that of Conf. appears in 則, 'then,' the power of influence. In 以勸, 以 is said to=與, 'together with,' 'mutually.' 勸, 'to advise,' 'to teach,' has also in the Dict. the meaning—'to rejoice to follow,' which is its force here, 爲善, 'the practice of goodness,' being understood.

21. CONFUCIUS' EXPLANATION OF HIS NOT BEING IN ANY OFFICE. 1. 或謂孔子,—The surname indic. that the questioner was not a disciple. Conf. had his reason for not being in office at the time, but it was not expedient to tell. He replied therefore, as in par. 2. See Shoo-king xxi. 1. But the text is neither correctly applied nor exactly quoted. The old

不爲政。二子曰、書云孝乎、惟孝友于兄弟、施於有政、是亦爲政、奚其爲爲政。

二十二子曰、人而無信、不知其可也、大車無輗、小車無軏、其何以行之哉。

二十三子張問十世、可知也。二子曰、殷因於夏禮、

2. The Master said, "What does the Shoo-king say of filial piety?—'You are filial, you discharge your brotherly duties. These qualities are displayed in government.' This then also constitutes the exercise of government. Why must there be THAT to make one be in the government."

CHAPTER XXII. The Master said, "I do not know how a man without truthfulness is to get on. How can a large carriage be made to go without the cross bar for yoking the oxen to, or a small carriage without the arrangement for yoking the horses?"

CHAPTER XXIII. 1. Tsze-chang asked whether *the affairs of* ten ages *after* could be known.

2. Confucius said, "The Yin dynasty followed the regulations of the Hea: wherein it took from or added to them may be known. The Chow dynasty has followed the regulations of the Yin: wherein it took from or added to them may be known. Some other may follow the Chow, but though it be should be at the distance of a hundred ages, its affairs may be known."

Inter. read in one sentence 孝乎惟孝, 'O filial piety! nothing but filial piety!' Choo He, however, pauses at 乎, and commences rightly the quotation with 惟孝. A western may think that the philosopher might have made a happier evasion. 奚其爲爲政, the 1st 爲=以爲, and 其 referring to the thought in the man's question, that *office* was necessary to one's being in government.

22. THE NECESSITY TO A MAN OF BEING TRUTHFUL AND SINCERE. 輗 and 軏 are explained in the Dict. in the same way—'the cross bar at the end of the carriage pole.' But there was a difference. Choo He says, 'In the light carriage the end of the pole curved upwards, and the cross bar was suspended from a hook.' This would give it more elasticity.

23. THE GREAT PRINCIPLES GOVERNING SOCIETY ARE UNCHANGEABLE. 1. 世 may be taken as an age='a century,' or as a generation=30 years, which is its radical meaning, being formed from *three tens* and *one* (卅 and 一). Both meanings are in the Dict. Conf. made no pretension to supernatural powers, and all comm. are agreed that the things here asked about were not what we would call contingent or indifferent events. He merely says that the great principles of morality and relations of society had continued the same and would ever do so. 也=乎. 2. The Hea, Yin, and Chow are now spoken of as the 三代. 'The three

所損益、可知也。周因於殷禮、所損益、可知也。其或繼周者、雖百世、可知也。

〔二十四章〕子曰、非其鬼而祭之、諂也。見義不爲、無勇也。

CHAPTER XXIV. 1. The Master said, "For a man to sacrifice to a spirit which does not belong to him is flattery."

2. "To see what is right and not to do it is want of courage."

changes,' i.e., the three great dynasties. The first Emperor of the Hea was 'The great Yu,' B.C. 2204, of the Yin, T'ang, B.C. 1765, and of Chow, Woo, B.C. 1121.

24. NEITHER IN SACRIFICE NOR IN OTHER PRACTICE MAY A MAN DO ANYTHING BUT WHAT IS RIGHT. 1. 人神曰鬼, 'The human spirit (i.e., of the dead) is called 鬼.' The 鬼 of which a man may say that they are his, are those only of his ancestors, and to them only he may sacrifice. The ritual of China provides for sacrifices to three classes of objects—天神, 地示, 人鬼, 'spirits of heaven, of the earth, of men.' This ch. is not to be extended to all the three. It has reference only to the manes of departed men.

BOOK III. PĂ YIH.

八佾第三

〔一章〕孔子謂季氏、八佾舞於庭、是可忍也、孰不可忍也。

CHAPTER I. Confucius said of the head of the Ke family, who had eight rows of pantomimes in his area, "If he can bear to do this, what may he not bear to do?"

HEADING OF THIS BOOK.—八佾第三. The last book treated of the practice of government, and therein no things, according to Chinese ideas, are more important than ceremonial rites and music. With these topics therefore, the twenty six chapters of this book are occupied, and 'eight rows,' the principal words in the first chapter, are adopted as its heading.

1. CONFUCIUS' INDIGNATION AT THE USURPATION OF IMPERIAL RITES. 季氏, by contraction for 季孫氏; see II. 5. 氏 and 姓 are now used without distinction, meaning 'surname,' only that the 氏 of a woman is always spoken of, and not her 姓. Originally the 氏 appears to have been used to denote the branch families of one surname. 季氏, 'The Ke family,' with special reference to its head, '*The* Ke,' as we should say. 佾, 'a row of dancers,' or pantomimes rather, who kept time in the temple services, in the 庭, the front space before the raised portion in the principal hall, moving or brandishing feathers, flags, or other articles. In his ancestral temple, the Emperor had 8 rows, each row consisting of eight men, a duke or prince had 6, and a great officer only 4. For the Ke, therefore, to use 8 rows was a

二 三家者、以雍徹。子曰、相維辟公、天子穆穆、奚取於三家之堂。

三 子曰、人而不仁、如禮何、人而不仁、如樂何。

四 林放問禮之本。二 子曰、大哉問。禮、與其奢也、寧

CHAPTER II. The three families used the YUNG ode, while the vessels were being removed, *at the conclusion of the sacrifice.* The Master said, "'Assisting are the princes;—the emperor looks profound and grave:'—what application can these words have in the hall of the three families?"

CHAPTER III. The Master said, "If a man be without the virtues proper to humanity, what has he to do with the rites of propriety? If a man be without the virtues proper to humanity, what has he to do with music?"

CHAPTER IV. Lin Fang asked what was the first thing to be attended to in ceremonies.

2. The Master said, "A great question indeed!"

usurpation, for tho' it may be argued, that to the ducal family of Loo imperial rites were conceded, and that the offshoots of it (II. 5) might use the same, still great officers were confined to the ordinances proper to their rank. 謂 is used here, as frequently, in the sense—'to speak of.' Conf. remark may also be translated, 'If this be endured, what may not be endured?' And this is probably the correct interpretation, for there is force in the observations of the author of the 四書翼註, that this remark and the following must be assigned to the sage during the short time that he held high office in Loo.

2. AGAINST AGAINST USURPED RITES. 三家者, '*Those* belonging to the three families.' They assembled together, as being the descendants of duke Hwan (II. 5), in one temple. To this temple belonged the 庭 in the last ch., which is called 季氏庭, because circumstances had concurred to make the Ke the chief of the three families; see 四書改錯, viii. 7. For the Yung ode, see She-king, [illegible] Bk. II. st. 7. It was, properly, sung in the imperial temples of the Chow dynasty, at the 徹, 'the clearing away,' of the sacrificial apparatus, and contains the lines quoted by Confucius, which of course were quite inappropriate to the circumstances of the three families. 辟,—up. 4th tone, without an aspirate. 相,—up. 3d tone, 'assistant,' 'assisting.'

3. CEREMONIES AND MUSIC VAIN WITHOUT VIRTUE. 仁, see I. 2. I don't know how to render it here, otherwise than in the transla. Comm. define it—心之全德, 'the entire virtue of the heart.' As referred to 禮, it indicates the feeling of reverence; as referred to 樂 (*yŏ*), it indicates harmoniousness.

4. THE OBJECT OF CEREMONIES SHOULD REGULATE THEM:—AGAINST FORMALISM. 1. Lin Fang, styled 子邱, was a man of Loo, supposed to have been a disciple of Conf., and whose tablet is now placed first, on the west, in the outer court of the temples. He is known only by the question in this ch. Acc. to Choo He, 本 here is not 根本, 'the radical idea,' 'the essence;' but as 初, 'the beginning,' opposed to 末,—'the first thing to be attended to.' 2. 禮 has not the gen. meaning of the char. in the 1st par. As opposed to 喪 (up. 1st tone), it must indicate the festive or fortunate (吉) ceremonies,—capping, marriage, and sacrifices.

儉、喪、與其易也、寧戚。

五 子曰、夷狄之有君、不如諸夏之亡也。

六 季氏旅於泰山。子謂冉有曰、女弗能救與。對曰、不能。子曰、嗚呼、曾謂泰山、不如林放乎。

3. In *festive* ceremonies, it is better to be sparing than extravagant. In the ceremonies of mourning, it is better that there be deep sorrow than a minute attention to observances."

CHAPTER V. The Master said, "The rude tribes of the east and north have their princes, and are not like the States of our great land which are without them."

CHAPTER VI. The chief of the Ke family was about to sacrifice to the T'ae mountain. The Master said to Yen-yew, "Can you not save him from this?" He answered, "I cannot." Confucius said, "Alas! will you say that the T'ae mountain is not so discerning as Lin Fang?"

易, read *e*, low 3d tone. Choo He explains it by 治, as in Mencius—易其田疇, 'to cleanse and dress the fields,' and interprets as in the transl. The old comm. take the meaning—和易, 'harmony and ease,' *i. e.*, not being overmuch troubled.

5. THE ANARCHY OF CONFUCIUS' TIME. The 夷 were the barbarians on the east of China, and 狄, those on the north. See 禮記, 王制, iii. 14. The two are here used for the barbarous tribes about China generally. 諸夏 is a name for China because of the *multitude* of its people (諸), and its *greatness* (夏). 華夏, 'The flowery and great,' is still a common designation of it. Choo He takes 如 as simply = 似, and hence the sentiment in the transl. Ho An's comm. is to this effect:—'The rude tribes with their princes are still not equal to China with its anarchy.' 亡, read as, and = 無.

6. ON THE FOLLY OF USURPED SACRIFICES. 旅 is said to be the name appropriate to sacrifices to mountains, but we find it applied also to sacrifices to God. The T'ae mountain is the first of the 'five mountains' (五嶽), which are celebrated in Chinese literature, and have always received religious honours. It was in Loo, or rather on the borders between Loo and Ts'e, about 2 miles north of the present district city of T'ae-gan (泰安), in the department of Tse-nan (濟南), in Shan-tung. According to the ritual of China, sacrifice could only be offered to these mountains by the emperor, and princes in whose States any of them happened to be. For the chief of the Ke family, therefore, to sacrifice to the T'ae mountain, was a great usurpation. 女 as in II. 7, = 汝, and 曾 as in II. 8, = 則, or we may take it as = 經. 'Have you said,' &c. 泰山 = 泰山之神, 'The spirit of the T'ae mountain.' Lin Fang,—see ch. 4, from which the reason of this reference to him may be understood. Yen Yew, named (求), and by designation 子有, was one of the disciples of Conf., and is now third, in the hall, on the west. He entered the service of the Ke family, and was a man of ability and resources.

七 子曰、君子無所爭、必也射乎、揖讓而升、下而飲、其爭也君子。

八 一 子夏問曰、巧笑倩兮、美目盼兮、素以爲絢兮、何謂也。二 子曰、繪事後素。三 曰、禮後乎。子曰、起予者商也、始可與言詩已矣。

CHAPTER VII. The Master said, "The student of virtue has no contentions. If it be said he cannot avoid them, shall this be in archery? *But* he bows complaisantly *to his competitors;* thus he ascends *the hall,* descends, and exacts the forfeit of drinking. In his contention, he is still the Keun-tsze."

CHAPTER VIII. 1. Tsze-hea asked, saying, "What is the meaning of the passage—'The pretty dimples of her artful smile! The well defined black and white of her eye! The plain ground for the colours?'"

2. The Master said, "The business of laying on the colours follows the preparation of the plain ground."

3. "Ceremonies then are a subsequent thing." The Master said, "It is Shang who can bring out my meaning! Now I can begin to talk about the odes with him"

7. THE SUPERIOR MAN AVOIDS ALL CONTENTIOUS STRIVING. Here 君子=尙德之人, 'the man who prefers virtue.' 必也射乎 lit., 'if he must, shall it be archery?' 揖讓, according to Choo He, extend over all the verbs, 升, 下, 飲. 下 is marked in the 3d tone, anciently appropriate to it as a verb. 飲, up. 3d tone, 'to give to drink,' here=to exact from the vanquished the forfeit cup. In Conf. time there were three principal exercises of archery:—the great archery, under the eye of the Emperor, the guests' archery, which might be at the imperial court or at the visits of the princes among themselves, and the festive archery, for amusement. The regulations for the archers were substantially the same in them all, and served to prove their virtue, instead of giving occasion to quarrelling. There is no end to the controversies among comm. on minor points.

8. CEREMONIES ARE SECONDARY AND ORNAMENTAL. 1. The sentences quoted by Tsze-hea are from a 逸詩, one of the poems which Conf. did not admit into the She-king. The two first lines, however, are found in it, I. v. 3. The disciple's inquiry turns on the meaning of 以爲 in the last line, which he took to mean—'The plain ground is to be regarded as the colouring.' 2. Conf., in his reply, makes 後 a verb, governing 素,='comes after the plain ground.' 3. 禮後乎. Tsze-hea's remark is an exclamation rather than a question. 起予者, 'He who stirs me up,'='He who brings out my meaning.' On the last sentence, see I. 15.—The above interpretation, especially as to the meaning of 繪事後素, after Choo He, is quite the opposite of that of the old interpreters. Their view is of course strongly supported by the author of 四書改錯, VIII. 3.

〔九章〕子曰、夏禮吾能言之、杞不足徵也、殷禮吾能言之、宋不足徵也、文獻不足故也、足、則吾能徵之矣。

〔十章〕子曰、禘自既灌而往者、吾不欲觀之矣。

〔十一章〕或問禘之說。子曰、不知也、知其說者、之於天下也、其如示諸

CHAPTER IX. The Master said, "I am able to describe the ceremonies of the Hea dynasty, but Ke cannot sufficiently attest my words. I am able to describe the ceremonies of the Yin dynasty, but Sung cannot sufficiently attest my words. They cannot do so because of the insufficiency of their records and wise men. If those were sufficient, I could adduce them in support of my words."

CHAPTER X. The Master said, "At the great sacrifice, after the pouring out of the libation, I have no wish to look on."

CHAPTER XI. Some one asked the meaning of the great sacrifice. The Master said, "I do not know. He who knew its meaning would

9. THE DECAY OF THE MONUMENTS OF ANTIQUITY. Of Hea and Yin, see II. 23. In the small state of Ke (originally what is now the district of the same name in K'ae-fung dep. in Ho-nan, but in Conf. time a part of Shan-tung), the sacrifices to the emperors of the Hea dynasty were maintained by their descendants. So with the Yin dynasty and Sung, a part of the present Ho-nan. But the 文, 'literary monuments' of those countries, and their 獻 (=賢, so in the Shoo-king, v. vii. 5, *et al.*) 'wise men' had become few. Had Conf. therefore delivered all his knowledge about the two dynasties, he would have exposed his truthfulness to suspicion. 徵, in the sense of 證, 'to witness,' and, at the end, 'to appeal to for evidence.' The old comm., however take 徵 in the sense of 成, 'to complete,' and interpret the whole differently.—We see from the chapter how in the time of Confucius many of the records of antiquity had perished.

10. THE SAGE'S DISSATISFACTION AT THE WANT OF PROPRIETY OF AND IN CEREMONIES. 禘 is the name belonging to different sacrifices, but here indicating the 大祭, 'great sacrifice,' which could properly be celebrated only by the Emperor. The individual sacrificed to in it was the remotest ancestor from whom the founder of the reigning dynasty traced his descent. As to who were his assessors in the sacrifice and how often it was offered;—these are disputed points. See K'ang-he's dict. char. 禘. Comp. also 四書改錯, vii. 8, and 四書摭餘說, I. 15. An imperial rite, its use in Loo was wrong (see next ch.), but there was something in the service after the early act of libation inviting the descent of the spirits, which more particularly moved the anger of Conf. 而往=以後, diff. from 往 in I. 15.

11. THE PROFOUND MEANING OF THE GREAT SACRIFICE. This ch. is akin to II. 21. Conf. evades replying to his questioner, it being contrary to Chinese propriety to speak in a country of the faults of its government or rulers. If he had entered into an account of the 禘 sacrifice, he must have condemned the use of an imperial rite in Loo. 說 'explanation,' commentary. The antecedent to the second 其 is the whole of the preceding clause:—'The relation to the empire of him who knew its meaning;—

斯乎。指其掌。〔十二〕祭如在、祭神如神在。〔二〕子曰、吾不與祭、如不祭。〔十三〕王孫賈問曰、與其媚於奧、寧媚於竈、何謂也、〔二〕子曰、不然、獲罪於天、無所禱也。

find it as easy to govern the empire as to look on this;"—pointing to his palm.

CHAPTER XII. 1. He sacrificed *to the dead*, as if they were present. He sacrificed to the spirits, as if the spirits were present.

2. The Master said, "I consider my not being present at the sacrifice, as if I did not sacrifice."

CHAPTER XIII. 1. Wang-sun Kea asked, saying, "What is the meaning of the saying, 'It is better to pay court to the furnace than to the south-west corner'?"

2 The Master said, "Not so. He who offends against Heaven has none to whom he can pray."

that would be as to look on this.' 乎, interjective, more than interrogative. 示=視, 'to see.' 天下, 'under heaven,' an ambitious designation for the Chinese empire, as ἡ οἰκουμένη and *orbis* were used by the Greeks and Romans.

12. CONFUCIUS' OWN SINCERITY IN SACRIFICING. 1. 祭 here is historical and not to be translated in the imperative. We have to supply an object to the first 祭, viz. 先祖, *the dead*, his forefathers, as contrasted with 神 in the next clause, = all the 'spirits' to which in his official capacity he would have to sacrifice. 2. Obs. 與 in low 3d tone, 'to be present at,' 'to take part in.'

13. THAT THERE IS NO RESOURCE AGAINST THE CONSEQUENCES OF VIOLATING THE RIGHT. 1. Kea was a great officer of Wei (衛), and having the power of the state in his hands insinuated to Confucius that it would be for his advantage to pay court to him. The 奧, or south west corner, was from the structure of ancient houses the coziest nook, and the place of honour. Choo He explains the proverb by reference to the customs of sacrifice. The furnace was comparatively a mean place, but when the spirit of the furnace was sacrificed to, then the rank of the two places was changed for the time, and the proverb quoted was in vogue. But there does not seem much force in this explanation. The *door*, or *well*, or any other of the five things in the regular sacrifices, might take the place of the *furnace*. The old explanation which makes no reference to sacrifice is simpler. 奧 might be the more retired and honourable place, but the 竈 was the more important for the support and comfort of the household. The prince and his immediate attendants might be more honourable than such a minister as Kea, but more benefit might be got from him. 媚, from *woman* and *eyebrows*, = 'to ogle,' 'to flatter.' 2. Confucius' reply was in a high tone. Choo He says, 天則理也, 'Heaven means principle.' But why should Heaven mean principle, if there were not in such a use of the term an instinctive recognition of a supreme government of intelligence and righteousness? We find 天 explained in the 摭餘說 by 高高在上者, 'The lofty one who is on high.'

[十四]子曰、周監於二代、郁郁乎文哉、吾從周。

[十五]子入大廟、每事問。或曰、孰謂鄹人之子知禮乎、入大廟、每事問。子聞之曰、是禮也。

[十六]子曰、射不主皮、爲力不同科、古之道也。

CHAPTER XIV. The Master said, "Chow had the advantage of viewing the two past dynasties. How complete and elegant are its regulations! I follow Chow."

CHAPTER XV. The Master, when he entered the grand temple, asked about every thing. Some one said, "Who will say that the son of the man of Tsow knows the rules of propriety. He has entered the grand temple and asks about every thing." The Master heard the remark, and said, "This is a rule of propriety."

CHAPTER XVI. The Master said, "In archery it is not *going through* the leather which is the principal thing;—because people's strength is not equal. This was the old way."

14. THE COMPLETENESS AND ELEGANCE OF THE INSTITUTIONS OF THE CHOW DYNASTY. By the 周 we are specially to understand the founders of the power and polity of the dynasty—the kings Wan and Woo, and the duke of Chow. The two past dynasties are of course the Hea and the Shang or Yin. 文 is an adj.

15. CONFUCIUS IN THE GRAND TEMPLE. 大 (=太) 廟 was the temple dedicated to the duke of Chow (周公), and where he was worshipped with imperial rites. The thing is supposed to have taken place, at the begin. of Conf. official service in Loo, when he went into the temple with other officers to assist at the sacrifice. He had studied all about ceremonies, and was famed for his knowledge of them, but he thought it a mark of sincerity and earnestness to make minute inquiries about them on the occasion spoken of. 鄹 was the name of the town in Loo of which Conf' father had been governor, who was known therefore as 'the man of Tsow.' We may suppose that Conf. would be styled as in the text, only in his early life, or by very ordinary people.

16. HOW THE ANCIENTS MADE ARCHERY A DISCIPLINE OF VIRTUE. We are not to understand 射不主皮 of all archery among the ancients. The char. are found in the 儀禮. 鄉射, par. 815, preceded by the char. 禮. There were trials of archery where the strength was tested. Probably Conf. was speaking of the 禮射 of his times, when the strength which could go through the 皮, 'skin,' or leather, in the middle of the target, was esteemed more than the skill which could hit it.

十七 子貢欲去告朔之餼羊。子曰、賜也、爾愛其羊、我愛其禮。

十八 子曰、事君盡禮、人以爲諂也。

十九 定公問、君使臣、臣事君、如之何。孔子對曰、君使臣以禮、臣事君以忠。

二十 子曰、關雎樂而不淫、哀而不傷。

CHAPTER XVII. 1. Tsze-kung wished to do away with the offering of a sheep connected with the inauguration of the first day of each month.

2. The Master said, "Tsze, you love the sheep; I love the ceremony."

CHAPTER XVIII. The Master said, "The full observance of the rules of propriety in serving one's prince is accounted by people to be flattery."

CHAPTER XIX. The duke Ting asked how a prince should employ his ministers, and how ministers should serve their prince. Confucius replied, "A prince should employ his ministers according to the rules of propriety; ministers should serve their prince with faithfulness."

CHAPTER XX. The Master said, "The Kwan Ts'eu is expressive of enjoyment without being licentious, and of grief without being hurtfully excessive."

17. HOW CONFUCIUS CLEAVED TO ANCIENT RITES. 1. The emperor in the last month of the year gave out to the princes a calendar for the 1st days of the 12 months of the year ensuing. This was kept in their ancestral temples, and on the 1st of every month, they offered a sheep and announced the day, requesting sanction for the duties of the month. This idea of requesting sanction is indicated by 告, read *kuh*, up. 4th tone. The dukes of Loo neglected now their part of this ceremony, but the sheep was still offered:—a meaningless formality, it seemed to Tsze-kung. Conf., however, thought that while any part of the cer. was retained, there was a better chance of restor. the whole. 去, up. 3d tone, an act. verb, 'to put away.' It is disputed whether 餼, in the text, mean a *living* sheep, or a sheep killed but not roasted. 2. 愛, in the sense of 愛惜, 'to grudge,' it is said. But this is hardly necessary.

18. HOW PRINCES SHOULD BE SERVED:—AGAINST THE SPIRIT OF THE TIMES.

19. THE GUIDING PRINCIPLES IN THE RELATION OF PRINCE AND MINISTER. 定, 'Greatly anxious, tranquillizer of the people,' was the posthumous epithet of 宋, prince of Loo, B.C. 508-494. 如之何, 'As it what,' 之 referring to the two points inquired about.

20. THE PRAISE OF THE FIRST OF THE ODES. 關雎 is the name of the first ode in the Shoo-king, and may be translated—'The murmuring of the ts'eu.' See Shi-king, I. i. 1.

二十一 哀公問社於宰我。宰我對曰、夏后氏以松、殷人以栢、周人以栗、曰、使民戰栗。二子聞之曰、成事不說、遂事不諫、既往不咎。

二十二 子曰、管仲之器小哉。或曰、管仲儉乎。曰、管氏有三歸、

CHAPTER XXI. The duke Gae asked Tsae Go about the altars of the spirits of the land. Tsae Go replied, "The Hea sovereign used the pine tree; the man of the Yin used the cypress; and the man of the Chow used the chestnut tree, meaning thereby to cause the people to be in awe."

2. When the Master heard it, he said, "Things that are done, it is needless to speak about; things that have had their course, it is needless to remonstrate about; things that are past, it is needless to blame."

CHAPTER XXII. The Master said, "Small indeed was the capacity of Kwan Chung!"

2. Some one said, "Was Kwan Chung parsimonious?" "Kwan," was the reply, "had the *San Kwei*, and his officers performed no double duties; how can he be considered parsimonious?"

21. A RASH REPLY OF TSAE GO ABOUT THE ALTARS TO THE SPIRITS OF THE LAND, AND LAMENT OF CONFUCIUS THEREON. 哀公, see II. 19. Tsae Go, by name 予, and styled 子我, was an eloquent disciple of the sage, a native of Loo. His place is the second west among 'the wise ones.' 社, from 示, K'e, 'spirit or spirits of the earth,' and 土, 'the soil,' means 土地神主, 'the resting place or altars of the spirits of the land or ground.' Go simply tells the duke that the founders of the several dynasties planted such and such trees about those altars. The reason was that the soil suited such trees, but as 栗, 'the chestnut tree,' the tree of the existing dynasty, is used in the sense of 慄, 'to be afraid,' he suggested a reason for its planting which might lead the duke to severe measures against his people to be carried into effect at the altars. Comp. Shoo-king, IV. ii. 5, 'I will put you to death before the 社.' 夏后氏 is the Great Yu, called 后, to distinguish him from his predecessors, the 帝, and 夏氏, to distinguish him from 舜, who was 虞氏, while they were descended from the same ancestor. See ch. I, on 氏. 殷人 and 周人, in parallelism with 夏后氏, must mean the founders of those dynasties; why they are simply styled 人, 'man,' or 'men,' I have not found clearly explained, though comm. feel it necess. to say something on the point. 2. This is all directed against Go's reply. He had spoken, and his words could not be recalled.

22. CONFUCIUS' OPINION OF KWAN-CHUNG:—AGAINST HIM. 1. Kwan-chung, by name 夷吾, is one of the most famous names in Chin. history. He was chief minister to the duke 桓 of 齊 (B. C. 683-640), the first and greatest of the five *p'a* (伯 or 霸), leaders of the princes of the empire under the Chow dynasty. In the times of Conf. and Men., people thought

官事不攝、焉得儉。然則管仲知禮乎。曰、邦君樹塞門、管氏亦樹塞門、邦君爲兩君之好、有反坫、管氏亦有反坫、管氏而知禮、孰不知禮。

[二十三] 子語魯大師樂曰、樂其可知也。始作、翕如也、從之、純如也、皦如也、繹如也、以成。

3. "Then, did Kwan Chung know the rules of propriety?" The Master said, "The princes of states have a screen intercepting the view at their gates. Kwan had likewise a screen at his gate. The princes of states on any friendly meeting between two of them, had a stand on which to place their inverted cups. Kwan had also such a stand. If Kwan knew the rules of propriety, who does not know them?"

CHAPTER XXIII. The Master instructing the Grand music-master of Loo said, "How to play music may be known. At the commencement of the piece, all the parts should sound together. As it proceeds, they should be in harmony, severally distinct and flowing without break, and thus on to the conclusion."

more of Kwan, than those sages, no hero-worshippers, would allow. 器 see II. 12, but its signif. here is different,—our measure or *capacity*. 2. 三歸, in the Dict., and the approved comm. of Choo He, was the name of an extravagant tower built by Kwan. There are other views of the phrase, the oldest, and the best supported appar., being that it means 'three wives.' (A woman's marriage is called 歸.) The *San Kwei* and having no pluralists among his officers proved suff. that he could not be parsimonious. 焉, up. 1st tone, 'how.' 3. 樹 'a tree,' here in the sense of 屏, 'a screen,' the screen of a prince, usurped by Kwan, who was only entitled to the 簾 of a great officer. 好 up. 3d tone,=好會, 'a friendly meeting.' The 坫 from 土 and 占, was a stand, made originally of earth and turf. Kwan usurped the use of it, as he did of the screen. This showed him to be as regardless of prescribed forms, as in par. 2 he appears of expense, and he came far short therefore of the Confucian idea of the *Keun-tsze*.

23. ON THE PLAYING OF MUSIC. 語, low. 3d tone,=告, 'to tell,' 'to instruct.' 大(=太)師樂, was the title of the grand music-master. 樂其可知也, 'music, it may be known,' but the subject is not of the principles, but the performance of music. Observe the 如. Premare says, '*adjectivis additum sensum auget et exprimit modum*.' It is our *ly* or *like*,—翕如, 'blended-like.' 從, up. 3d tone, the same as 縱=放, 'let go,' i.e., proceeding, swelling on.

〔二十四〕儀封人請見、曰、君子之至於斯也、吾未嘗不得見也。從者見之。出曰、二三子、何患於喪乎、天下之無道也久矣、天將以夫子爲木鐸。

〔二十五〕子謂韶、盡美矣、又盡善也、謂武、盡美矣、未盡善也。

〔二十六〕子曰、居上不寬、爲禮

CHAPTER XXIV. The border-warden at E requested to be introduced to the Master, saying, "When men of superior virtue have come to this, I have never been denied the privilege of seeing them." The followers *of the sage* introduced him, and when he came out from the interview, he said, "My friends, why are you distressed by your master's loss of office? The empire has long been without the principles *of truth and right;* Heaven is going to use your master as a bell with its wooden tongue."

CHAPTER XXV. The Master said of the Shaou that it was perfectly beautiful and also perfectly good. He said of the Woo that it was perfectly beautiful but not perfectly good.

CHAPTER XXVI. The Master said, "High station filled without indulgent generosity; ceremonies performed without reverence; mourning conducted without sorrow;—wherewith should I contemplate such ways?"

24. A STRANGER'S VIEW OF THE VOCATION OF CONFUCIUS. E was a small town on the borders of Wei, referred to a place in the present dis. of 蘭陽, dep. 開封, Honan prov. Conf. was retiring from Wei, the prince of which could not employ him. This was the 喪 (op. 3d tone),=失位. The 1st and 3d 見 are read *heen*, low. 3d tone,=通使得見, 'to introduce,' or 'to be introduced.' 之 in 君子之至於斯也, has its prop. poss. power,—'In the case of a Keun-tsze's coming to this.' 從, low. 3d tone, 'to attend upon.' 二三子, 'Two or three sons,' or 'gentlemen,'=' my friends.' The same idiom occurs elsewhere. The 木鐸 was a metal bell with a wooden tongue, shaken to call attention to announcements, or along the ways to call people together. Heaven would employ Conf. to proclaim and call men's attention to the truth and right (道).

25. THE COMPARATIVE MERITS OF THE MUSIC OF SHUN AND WOO. 韶 was the name of the music made by Shun, perfect in melody and sentiment. 武 was the music of king Woo, also perfect in melody, but breathing the martial air, indicative of its author.

26. THE DISREGARD OF WHAT IS ESSENTIAL VITIATES ALL SERVICES. The meaning of the ch. turns upon 何以=何有, or 以何者, 'wherewith.' 寬 is ess. to rulers, 敬 to ceremonies, and 哀 to mourning. If they be wanting, one has no standpoint to view what are only shams or semblances.

不敬、臨喪不哀、吾何以觀之哉。

BOOK IV. LE JIN.

里仁第四

〔第一章〕子曰、里仁爲美、擇不處仁、焉得知。

〔第二章〕子曰、不仁者、不可以久處約、不可以長處樂、仁者安仁、知者利仁。

CHAPTER I. The Master said, "It is virtuous manners which constitute the excellence of a neighbourhood. If a man in selecting a residence, do not fix on one where such prevail, how can he be wise?"

CHAPTER II. The Master said, "Those who are without virtue, cannot abide long either in a condition of poverty and hardship, or in a condition of enjoyment. The virtuous rest in virtue; the wise desire virtue."

HEADING OF THIS BOOK.—里仁第四. 'Virtue in a neighbourhood.—No. IV.'—Such is the title of this fourth Book, which is mostly occupied with the subject of 仁. To render that term invariably by *benevolence*, would by no means suit many of the chapters. See II. 1, 2. *Virtue*, as a general term, would answer better. The embodiment of virtue demands an acquaintance with ceremonies and music, treated of in the last book: and this, it is said, is the reason why the one subject immediately follows the other.

1. RULE FOR THE SELECTION OF A RESIDENCE. According to the 周禮, 5 families made a 鄰, and 5 鄰 a 里, which we might style, therefore, *a hamlet or village*. There are other estimates of the number of its component households. 處, up. 2d tone, a verb, 'to dwell in.' 知, up. 3d tone, is the same as 智, 'wise,' 'wisdom.' So, not unfrequently, below. Friendship, we have seen, is for the aid of virtue (I. 8, 3), and the same should be the object desired in selecting a residence.

2. ONLY TRUE VIRTUE ADAPTS A MAN FOR THE VARIED CONDITIONS OF LIFE. 約, 'to bind,' is used for what binds, as an oath, a covenant; and here, the metaphor being otherwise directed, it denotes a condition of poverty and distress. 利, 'gain,' 'profit,' used as a verb,=貪, 'to desire,' 'to covet.' 安仁, 'to rest in virtue,' being virtuous without effort. 利仁, 'to desire virtue,' being virtuous because it is the best policy. Obs. how 者 following 仁 and 知 makes these terms adjectives. 不可, 'may not,'=不能, 'cannot.' The inability is moral.

三子曰、惟仁者、能好人、能惡人。

四子曰、苟志於仁矣、無惡也。

五一子曰、富與貴、是人之所欲也、不以其道得之、不處也。貧與賤、是人之所惡也、不以其道得之、不去也。二君子去仁、惡乎成名。三君子無終食之間

CHAPTER III. The Master said, "It is only the truly virtuous man, who can love, or who can hate, others."

CHAPTER IV. The Master said, "If the will be set on virtue, there will be no practice of wickedness."

CHAPTER V. 1. The Master said, "Riches and honours are what men desire. If it cannot be obtained in the proper way, they should not be held. Poverty and meanness are what men dislike. If it cannot be obtained in the proper way, they should not be avoided.

2. "If a superior man abandon virtue, how can he fulfil the requirements of that name?

3. "The superior man does not, even for the space of a single meal, act contrary to virtue. In moments of haste, he cleaves to it. In seasons of danger, he cleaves to it."

3. ONLY IN THE GOOD MAN ARE EMOTIONS OF LOVE AND HATRED RIGHT. This ch., containing an important truth, is incorporated with the 大學傳, x. 15. 好 and 惡 (read wû) are both verbs, up. 3d tone.

4. THE VIRTUOUS WILL PRESERVES FROM ALL WICKEDNESS. 苟=誠, not merely—'if,' but 'if really.' Comp. the apostle's sentiment, I. John, iii. 9, 'Whosoever is born of God doth not commit sin.'

5. THE DEVOTION OF THE KEUN-TSZE TO VIRTUE. 1. For the antecedent to 之 in the recurring 得之, we are to look to the foll. verbs, 處 (up. 2d tone) and 去. We might translate the first 不以道得之, 'if they cannot be obtained, &c.,' but this would not suit the second case. 其道, 'the way,' i.e., the proper way. If we supply a nom. to 處 and 去, it must be 君子.—He will not 'abide in,' nor 'go away from,' riches and honours. 2. 惡, read woo, up. 1st tone, 'how.' 名, 'name,' not reputation, but the name of a *keun-tsze*, which he bears. 3. 終食之間, 'The space in which a meal can be *finished*;' 造次 (interch. with 草次) and 顛沛 are well-known expressions, the former for haste and confusion, the latter for change and danger, but it is not easy to trace the attaching of these meanings to the characters. 顛, 'to fall down,' and 沛, the same, but the for. with the face up, the other with the face down. 必於是, Comp. Horace's '*Omnis in hoc sum*.'

違仁、造次必於是、顚沛必於是。

六 子曰、我未見好仁者、惡不仁者、好仁者、無以尙之、惡不仁者、其爲仁矣、不使不仁者、加乎其身。二 有能一日用其力於仁矣乎、我未見力不足者。三 蓋有之矣、我未之見也。

七 子曰、人之過也、各於其黨、觀過、斯知仁矣。

CHAPTER VI. 1. The Master said, "I have not seen a person who loved virtue, or one who hated what was not virtuous. He who loved virtue, would esteem nothing above it. He who hated what is not virtuous, would practise virtue in such a way that he would not allow any thing that is not virtuous to approach his person.

2. "Is any one able for one day to apply his strength to virtue? I have not seen the case in which his strength would be insufficient.

3. "Should there possibly be any such case, I have not seen it."

CHAPTER VII. The Master said, "The faults of men are characteristic of the class to which they belong. By observing a man's faults, it may be known that he is virtuous."

6. A LAMENT BECAUSE OF THE RARITY OF THE LOVE OF VIRTUE; AND ENCOURAGEMENT TO PRACTISE VIRTUE. 1. The first four 者 belong to the verbs 好 and 惡, and give them the force of participles. In 使不仁者, 者 belongs to 不仁, and 不仁者=不仁之事. Commonly, 者='he or those who,' but sometimes also='that or those things which.' 尙=加, 'to add to.' Morr., char. 尙, translates the sentence wrongly—'He who loves virtue and benevolence can have nothing more said in his praise.' 3. 蓋 here is 疑辭, 'a particle of doubt.' 未之有, a transpos., as in I. 2.

7. A MAN IS NOT TO BE UTTERLY CONDEMNED BECAUSE HE HAS FAULTS. Such is the sentiment found in this ch., in which we may say, however, that Conf. is liable to the charge brought against Tsze-hea, I. 7. 人之過也 stands absolutely,—'As to the faults of men.' 各=各人, and 於=從,—'Each man follows his class.' Obs. the force of 過, 'what goes beyond.' The faults are the excesses of the general tendencies. Comp. Goldsmith's line, 'And even his failings leaned to virtue's side.'

〔八〕子曰、朝聞道、夕死、可矣。

〔九〕子曰、士志於道、而恥惡衣惡食者、未足與議也。

〔十〕子曰、君子之於天下也、無適也、無莫也、義之與比。

〔十一〕子曰、君子懷德、小人懷土、君子懷刑、小

CHAPTER VIII. The Master said, "If a man in the morning hear the right way, he may die in the evening without regret."

CHAPTER IX. The Master said, "A scholar, whose mind is set on truth, and who is ashamed of bad clothes and bad food, is not fit to be discoursed with."

CHAPTER X. The Master said, "The superior man, in the world, does not set his mind either for any thing, or against any thing; what is right he will follow."

CHAPTER XI. The Master said, "The superior man thinks of virtue; the small man thinks of comfort. The superior man thinks of the sanctions of law; the small man thinks of favours *which he may receive.*"

8. THE IMPORTANCE OF KNOWING THE RIGHT WAY. One is perplexed to translate 道 here. Chû defines it—事物當然之理 'the principles of what is right in events and things.' Better is the expl. in 四書翼註,—道即率性之道, '道 is the path,—*i. e., of action,*—which is in accordance with our nature.' Man is formed for this, and if he die without coming to the knowledge of it, his death is no better than that of a beast. One would fain recognize, in such sentences as this, a vague apprehension of some higher truth or 道, than Chi. sages have been able to propound. —Ho An takes a diff. view of the whole ch., and makes it a lament of Confucius that he was likely to die without hearing of right principles prevailing in the world.—'Could I once hear of the prevalence of right principles, I could die the same evening.'

9. THE PURSUIT OF TRUTH SHOULD RAISE A MAN ABOVE BEING ASHAMED OF POVERTY. 與議,—'to be discoursed with,' *i. e.,* about 道, or 'truth,' which perhaps is the best translation of the term in places like this.

10. RIGHTEOUSNESS IS THE RULE OF THE KEUN-TSZE'S PRACTICE. 君子之云云, 'The relation of the *keun-tsze* to the world,' *i. e.,* to all things presenting themselves to him. 適, read *tîh,* is explained by 專主, 'to set the mind exclusively on.' We may take the last clause thus:—'his is the according with, and keeping near to (比, low. 3d tone, = 從 or 親) righteousness.' This gives each char. its signification.

11. THE DIFFERENT MINDINGS OF THE SUPERIOR AND THE SMALL MAN. 懷 is here emphatic, = 'cherishes and plans about.' 土, 'earth,' 'the ground,' is here defined—所處之安, 'the rest or comforts one dwells amidst.' May it not be used somewhat in our sense of earthly?—'thinks of what is earthly.'

人懷惠。

十二 子曰、放於利而行、多怨。

十三 子曰、能以禮讓爲國乎、何有、不能以禮讓爲國、如禮何。

十四 子曰、不患無位、患所以立、不患莫己知、求爲可知也。

十五 一 子曰、參乎、吾道一以貫之。曾子曰、唯。二 子出、門人問

CHAPTER XII. The Master said, "He who acts with a constant view to his own advantage will be much murmured against."

CHAPTER XIII. The Master said, "Is *a prince* able to govern his kingdom with the complaisance proper to the rules of propriety, what difficulty will he have? If he cannot govern it with that complaisance, what has he to do with the rules of propriety?"

CHAPTER XIV. The Master said, "*A man should say*, I am not concerned that I have no place, I am concerned how I may fit myself for one. I am not concerned that I am not known, I seek to be worthy to be known."

CHAPTER XV. 1. The Master said, "Sin, my doctrine is that of an all-pervading unity." The disciple Tsăng replied, "Yes."

2. The Master went out, and the *other* disciples asked, saying,

12. THE CONSEQUENCE OF SELFISH CONDUCT. 放, up. 2d tone,=依, 'to accord with,' 'to lie alongside.'—'He who acts along the line of gain.'

13. THE INFLUENCE IN GOVERNMENT OF CEREMONIES OBSERVED IN THEIR PROPER SPIRIT. 禮讓字是二非一, i. e., they are a hendiadys. 讓=禮之實, 'the sincer. and subs. of cer.,' the *spirit of* it, as we should say. Comp. 和 in I. 12. 爲=治, 'to govern.' This mean. is found in the Dict. 如禮何, see III. 3.

14. ADVISING TO SELF-CULTIVATION. Comp. I. 16. Here, as there, 不 not being imper. we must supply a nominative. 位, 'a place,' i. e. an official situation. 所以立 is to be completed 所以立乎其位.

15. CONFUCIUS' DOCTRINE THAT OF A PERVADING UNITY. This chap. is said to be the most profound in the *Lun Yü*. 1. 吾道一以貫之:—To myself it occurs to translate, 'my doctrines have one thing which goes thro. them,' but such an expos. has not been approved by any Chin. comm. 一以貫之 are made to contain the copula and predicate of 吾道, and 之, it is said, 指萬事萬物, 'refers to all affairs and all things.' The 2d par. shows us clearly enough what the one thing or unity intended by Conf. was. It was the heart, man's nature, of which all the relations and duties of life are only the development and outgo-

曰、何謂也。曾子曰、夫子之道、忠恕而已矣。

十六 子曰、君子喻於義、小人喻於利。

十七 子曰、見賢思齊焉、見不賢而內自省也。

十八 子曰、事父母幾諫、見志不從、又敬

"What do his words mean?" Tsăng said, "The doctrine of our master is to be true to the principles of our nature and the benevolent exercise of them to others,—this and nothing more."

CHAPTER XVI. The Master said, "The mind of the superior man is conversant with righteousness; the mind of the mean man is conversant with gain."

CHAPTER XVII. The Master said, "When we see men of worth, we should think of equalling them; when we see men of a contrary character, we should turn inwards and examine ourselves."

CHAPTER XVIII. The Master said, "In serving his parents, *a son* may remonstrate with them, but gently; when he sees that they do not incline to follow *his advice*, he shows an increased degree of reverence, but does not abandon *his purpose;* and should they punish him, he does not allow himself to murmur."

ings. 忠 and 恕, which seem to be two things, are both formed from 心, 'the heart,' 忠 being compounded of 中, 'middle,' 'centre,' and 心, and 恕 of 如 'as,' and 心. The 'centre heart'=I, the ego, and the 'as heart'=the I in sympathy' with others. 忠 is duty-doing, on a consideration, or from the impulse, of one's own self; 恕 is duty doing, on the principle of reciprocity. The ch. is important, showing that Conf. only claimed to unfold and enforce duties indicated by man's natural constitution. He was simply a moral philosopher. Obs. 唯, up. 2d tone,='yes.' Some say that 門人 must mean Tsang's own disciples, and that had they been those of Conf., we should have read 弟子. The criticism can't be depended on. 而已矣 is a very emphatic—'and nothing more.'

16. HOW RIGHTEOUSNESS AND SELFISHNESS DISTINGUISH THE SUPERIOR MAN AND THE SMALL MAN. 喻＝曉, 'to understand.' 於 is here to be dwelt on and may be compared with the Hebrew *eth*.

17. THE LESSONS TO BE LEARNED FROM OBSERVING MEN OF DIFFERENT CHARACTERS. Of the final particles 焉 and 也, it is said, 二字頗有抑揚警醒意, 'they have something of a repressive, expansive, warning force.'

18. HOW A SON MAY REMONSTRATE WITH HIS PARENTS ON THEIR FAULTS. See the 禮記, XII. i. 15. 幾, up. 1st tone, 'mildly,'=the 下氣, 怡色, 柔聲 of the 內則. 志 is the will of the parents. 又敬＝更加孝敬, 'again increasing his filial reverence,' the 起敬起孝 of the 內則. 不違 is not abandoning his purpose of remonstrance, and not as 包咸 says in the

不違、勞而不怨。

[十九章] 子曰、父母在、不遠遊、遊必有方。

[二十章] 子曰、三年無改於父之道、可謂孝矣。

[二十一章] 子曰、父母之年、不可不知也、一則以喜、一則以懼。

[二十二章] 子曰、古者言之不出、恥躬之不逮也。

[二十三章] 子曰、以約失之者鮮矣。

CHAPTER XIX. The Master said, "While his parents are alive, *the son* may not go abroad to a distance. If he does go abroad, he must have a fixed place to which he goes."

CHAPTER XX. The Master said, "If the son for three years does not alter from the way of his father, he may be called filial."

CHAPTER XXI. The Master said, "The years of parents may by no means not be kept in the memory, as an occasion at once for joy and for fear."

CHAPTER XXII. The Master said, "The reason why the ancients did not readily give utterance to their words, was that they feared lest their actions should not come up to them."

CHAPTER XXIII. The Master said, "The cautious seldom err."

comment given by Ho An, 不敢違父母意, 'not daring to go against the mind of his parents.' 勞 = 'toiled and pained,' what the 內則 says, 撻之流血, 'should they beat him till the blood flows.'

19. A SON OUGHT NOT TO GO TO A DISTANCE WHERE HE WILL NOT BE ABLE TO PAY THE DUE SERVICES TO HIS PARENTS. 方 = 一定向, 'a fixed direction or quarter,' whence he may be recalled, if necessary.

20. A REPETITION OF PART OF I. 11.

21. WHAT EFFECT THE AGE OF PARENTS SHOULD HAVE ON THEIR CHILDREN. 知, it is said, conveys here 念念不忘意, 'the meaning of unforgetting thoughtfulness.'

22. THE VIRTUE OF THE ANCIENTS SEEN IN THEIR SLOWNESS TO SPEAK. Obs. the force of the two 之.—'The not coming forth of the words of the ancients was shame about the not coming up to them of their actions.'

23. ADVANTAGE OF CAUTION. Collie's version, which I have adopt., is here happy. 約, see ch. 2. The 'binding' here is of one's-self, self-restraint, = 'caution.' 失之, 'loses it,' 之 referring to whatev. bus. the cautious may be engaged in. 之, foll. an act. verb, often makes it neuter; at least, a neuter verb renders the expression best in English.

廿四 子曰、君子欲訥於言、而敏於行。

廿五 子曰、德不孤、必有鄰。

廿六 子游曰、事君數、斯辱矣、朋友數、斯疏矣。

CHAPTER XXIV. The Master said, "The superior man wishes to be slow in his words and earnest in his conduct."

CHAPTER XXV. The Master said, "Virtue is not left to stand alone. *He who practises it* will have neighbours."

CHAPTER XXVI. Tsze-yew said, "In serving a prince, frequent remonstrances lead to disgrace. Between friends, frequent reproofs make the friendship distant."

24. RULE OF THE KEUN-TSZE ABOUT HIS WORDS AND ACTIONS.

25. THE VIRTUOUS ARE NOT LEFT ALONE:—AN ENCOURAGEMENT TO VIRTUE. 孤, 'fatherless;' here—solitary, friendless. 德不孤=德無孤立之理, 'It is not the nature of virtue to be left to stand alone.' 鄰, see ch. 1; here, generally, for friends, associates of like mind.

26. A LESSON TO COUNSELLORS AND FRIENDS. 數, up. 4th tone, read *shŏ*, 'frequently,' understood here in ref. to remonstrating or reproving.

BOOK V. KUNG-YAY CH'ANG.

公冶長第五

一 子謂公冶長、可妻也、雖在縲絏之中、非其罪也。以其子妻之。二 子謂南容、

CHAPTER I. 1. The Master said of Kung-yay Ch'ang that he might be wived; although he was put in bonds, he had not been guilty of any crime. *Accordingly*, he gave him his own daughter to wife.

2. Of Nan Yung he said that if the country were well governed, he

HEADING OF THIS BOOK.—公冶長第五. Kung-yay Ch'ang, the surname and name of the first individual spoken of in it, heads this book, which is chiefly occupied with the judgment of the sage on the character of several of his disciples and others. As the decision frequently turns on their being possessed of that *jin*, or perfect virtue, which is so conspicuous in the last book, this is the reason, it is said, why the one immediately follows the other. As Tsze-kung appears in the book several times, some have fancied that it was compiled by his disciples.

邦有道不廢、邦無道免於刑戮。以其兄之子妻之。

二 子謂子賤、君子哉若人、魯無君子者、斯焉取斯。

三 子貢問曰、賜也何如。子曰、女器也。曰、何器也。曰、瑚璉也。

would not be out of office, and if it were ill governed, he would escape punishment and disgrace. He gave him the daughter of his own elder brother to wife.

CHAPTER II. The Master said, of Tsze-tseen, "Of superior virtue indeed is such a man! If there were not virtuous men in Loo, how could this man have acquired this character?"

CHAPTER III. Tsze-kung asked, "What do you say of me, Tsze? The Master said, "You are an utensil." "What utensil?" "A gemmed sacrificial utensil."

1. CONFUCIUS IN MARRIAGE-MAKING WAS GUIDED BY CHARACTER, AND NOT BY FORTUNE. 1. Of Kung-yay Ch'ang, tho' the son-in-law of Conf., nothing certain is known, and his tablet is only 3d on the west, among the *seen heen*. Silly legends are told of his being put in prison from his bringing suspicion on himself by his knowl. of the language of birds. Choo He approves the interpr. of 縲 as mean. 'a black rope,' with which criminals were anciently bound (絏) in prison. 妻, and in par. 2, up. 3d tone, 'to wive,' 'to give to to wife.' 子, in both par.,='a daughter.' 2. Nan Yung, another of the disciples, is now 4th, east, in the outer hall. The discussions about who he was, and whether he is to be identified with 南宮适, and several other *aliases*, are very perplexing. See 四書改錯, I. 10,11, and 摭餘說, I. 24. 廢, 'to lay, or be laid aside,' here, *i.e., from office*. 戮, 'to put to death,' has also the lighter meaning of 'disgrace.' We cannot tell whether Conf. is giving his impress. of Yung's char., or referring to events that had taken place.

2. THE KEUN-TSZE FORMED BY INTERCOURSE WITH OTHER KEUN-TSZE. Tsze-tseen, by surname 宓 (=虙, and said to be i. q. 伏), and named 不齊, appears to have been of some note among the disci. of Conf., both as an administrator and writer, tho' his tablet is now only 2d west, in the outer hall. What chiefly disting. him, as appears here, was his cultivation of the friendship of men of ability and virtue. 若人 is more than '*this man*.' It is 若此人, 'a man such as this.' See the 註疏 *in loc*. The first 斯 is 'this man;' the second, 'this *virtue*.' The paraphrasts complete the last clause thus:—斯將何所取以成斯德乎, 'what friends could this man have chosen to complete this virtue?'

3. WHERETO TSZE-KUNG HAD ATTAINED. See I. 10, II. 12. The 瑚璉 were vessels richly adorned, used to contain grain-offerings in the Imper. ancestral temples. Under the Hea dyn., they were called 瑚, and 璉, under the Yin. See the *Le Ke*, XIV. 27. While the sage did not grant to Tsze that he was a *Keun-tsze* (II. 12), he made him 'a vessel of honour,' valuable and fit for use on high occasions.

四 或曰、雍也仁、而不佞。子曰、焉用佞、禦人以口給、屢憎於人、不知其仁、焉用佞。

五 子使漆雕開仕。對曰、吾斯之未能信。子說。

六 子曰、道不行、乘桴浮于海、從我者、

CHAPTER IV. 1. Some one said, "Yung is truly virtuous, but he is not ready with his tongue."

2. The Master said, "What is the good of being ready with the tongue? They who meet men with smartnesses of speech, for the most part procure themselves hatred. I know not whether he be truly virtuous, but why should he show readiness of the tongue?"

CHAPTER V. The Master was wishing Tseih-teaou K'ae to enter on official employment. He replied, "I am not yet able to rest in the assurance of THIS." The Master was pleased.

CHAPTER VI. The Master said, "My doctrines make no way. I will get upon a raft, and float about on the sea. He that will accompany me will be Yew, I dare to say." Tsze-loo hearing this was

4. OF YEN YUNG. READINESS WITH THE TONGUE NO PART OF VIRTUE. 1. 冉雍, styled 仲弓, has his tablet the second, on the east of Conf. own tablet, among 'the wise ones.' His father was a worthless character (see VI. 4), but he himself was the opposite. 佞 means 'ability,' generally, then 'ability of speech,' often, though not here, with the bad sense of artfulness and flattery. 2. Conf. would not grant that Yung was 仁, but his not being 佞 was in his favour rather than otherwise. 口給 (read *keë*. See Dict.), 'smartnesses of speech.' 焉 is here 'why,' rather than 'how.' The first 焉用仁 is a gen. statement, not having, like the sec., special reference to Yen Yung. In the 註疏 不知其仁焉用佞 is read as one sentence;—'I do not know how the virtuous should also use readiness of speech.' This is not so good as the received interpretation.

5. TSEIH-TEAOU K'AE'S OPINION OF THE QUALIFICATIONS NECESSARY TO TAKING OFFICE. Tseih-teaou, now 6th, on the east, in the out. hall, was styled 子若. His name originally was 啟, changed into 開, on the accession of the Emperor 孝景, A. D. 156, whose name was also 啟. The diff. in the ch. is with 斯—what does it refer to? and with 信—what is its force? In the ch. about the disciples in the 家語, it is said that K'ae was reading in the Shoo-king, when Conf. spoke to him about taking office, and he pointed to the book, or some particular passage in it, saying, 'I am not yet able to rest in the assurance of (信=眞知確見) this.' It may have been so. Obs. the force of the 之,—'There is as yet my want of faith of this.'

6. CONFUCIUS PROPOSING TO WITHDRAW FROM THE WORLD:—A LESSON TO TSZE-LOO. Tsze-loo supposed his master really meant to leave the world, and the idea of floating along the coasts, pleased his ardent temper, while he was delighted with the compliment paid to himself. But Conf. only expressed in this way his regret at the backwardness of men to receive his doctrines. 無所取材 is diff. of interpretation. Choo He takes 材 as being for 裁, 'to cut out clothes,' 'to estimate, discrimi-

其由與。子路聞之喜。子曰、由也、好勇過我、無所取材。

[七章] 孟武伯問子路仁乎。子曰、不知也。又問。子曰、由也、千乘之國、可使治其賦也、不知其仁也。求也何如。子曰、求也、千室之邑、百乘之家、可使爲之宰也、不知其仁也。赤也何如。子曰、赤也、束帶立於朝、可使與賓客言也、不知其仁也。

glad, upon which the Master said, "Yew is fonder of daring than I am. He does not exercise his judgment upon matters."

CHAPTER VII. 1. Măng Woo asked about Tsze-loo, whether he was perfectly virtuous. The Master said, "I do not know."

2. He asked again, when the Master replied, "In a kingdom of a thousand chariots, Yew might be employed to manage the military levies, but I do not know whether he be perfectly virtuous."

3. "And what do you say of K'ew?" The Master replied, "In a city of a thousand families, or a house of a hundred chariots, K'ew might be employed as governor, but I do not know whether he is perfectly virtuous."

4. "What do you say of Ch'ih?" The Master replied, "With his sash girt and standing in a court, Ch'ih might be employed to converse with the visitors and guests, but I do not know whether he is perfectly virtuous."

mate,' and hence the mean. in the transl. An old comm., 鄭玄, keeping the mean. of 材, explains—無所取於桴材,—'my meaning is not to be found in the raft.' Another old writer makes 材=哉, and putting a stop at 勇 expl.—'Yew is fond of daring; He cannot go beyond himself to find my meaning.' 與, here='I dare to say.'

7. OF TSZE-LOO, TSZE-YEW, AND TSZE-HWA

1. 孟武伯. See II. 6. 2. 千乘之國, see I. 5. 賦, properly, 'revenues,' 'taxes,' but the quota of soldiers contributed being regul. by the amt. of the rev., the term is used here for the forces, or military levies. 3. 求 see III. 6. 百乘之家, in opp. to 千乘之國, was the secondary fief, the territory appropriated to the highest nobles or officers in a 國 or state, suppos. also to comprehend 1000 fami-

子謂子貢曰、女與回也、孰愈。對曰、賜也、何敢望回、回也、聞一以知十、賜也、聞一以知二。子曰、弗如也、吾與女、弗如也。

宰予晝寢。子曰、朽木不可雕也、糞土之牆、不可杇也、於予與何誅。子曰、始吾於人也、聽其言而信其行、今吾於人也、

CHAPTER VIII. 1. The Master said to Tsze-kung, "Which do you consider superior, yourself or Hwuy?"

2. Tsze-kung replied, "How dare I compare myself with Hwuy? Hwuy hears one point and knows all about a subject; I hear one point and know a second."

3. The Master said, "You are not equal to him. I grant you, you are not equal to him."

CHAPTER IX. 1. Tsae Yu being asleep during the day time, the Master said, "Rotten wood cannot be carved; a wall of dirty earth will not receive the trowel. This Yu!—what is the use of my reproving him?"

2. The Master said, "At first, my way with men was to hear their words, and give them credit for their conduct. Now my way is to hear their words, and look at their conduct. It is from Yu that I have learned to make this change."

lit. 爲之宰, 'To be its governor.' This is a pec. idiom. 4. Ch'ih, surnamed 公西, and styled 子華, having now the 14th place, west, in the cat. hall, was famous among the disciples for his knowl. of rules of cer., and those especially relating to dress and intercourse. 朝, low. 1st tone. 賓 and 客 may be distinguished, the former indicating neighbouring princes visiting the court, the lat. ministers and officers of the state present as guests.

8. SUPERIORITY OF YEN HWUY TO TSZE-KUNG. 2. 望, 'to look to,' 'to look up to,' here = 比, 'to compare with.' 'One' is the begin. of numbers, and 'ten' the completion; hence the mean. of 聞一以知十, as in the transl. 3. 與 = 許, 'to allow,' 'to grant to.' Ho An gives here the comm. of 包咸, (about A. D. 50), who interprets strangely,—'I and you are both not equal to him,' saying that Conf. thus comforted Tsze-kung.

9. THE IDLENESS OF TSAE YU AND ITS REPROOF. 1. 於予與, 'in the case of Yu?' 與 has here the force of an exclam.; so below. 誅, a strong term, to mark the severity of the reproof. 2. 子曰 is superfluous. The char. were probably added by a transcriber. If not, they should head another chapter.

聽其言而觀其行、於予與改是。

十 子曰、吾未見剛者。或對曰、申棖。子曰、棖也慾、焉得剛。

十一 子貢曰、我不欲人之加諸我也、吾亦欲無加諸人。子曰、賜也、非爾所及也。

十二 子貢曰、夫子之文章、

CHAPTER X. The Master said, "I have not seen a firm and unbending man." Some one replied, "There is Shin Ch'ang." "Ch'ang," said the Master, "is under the influence of his passions; how can he be pronounced firm and unbending?"

CHAPTER XI. Tsze-kung said, "What I do not wish men to do to me, I also wish not to do to men." The Master said, "Tsze, you have not attained to that."

CHAPTER XII. Tsze-kung said, "The Master's *personal* displays *of his principles*, and *ordinary* descriptions of them may be heard. His discourses about *man's* nature, and the way of Heaven, cannot be heard."

10. UNBENDING VIRTUE CANNOT CO-EXIST WITH INDULGENCE OF THE PASSIONS. Shin Ch'ang (there are several *aliases*, but they are disputed,) was one of the minor disciples, of whom little or nothing is known. He was styled 子周, and his place is 31st, east, in the out. ranges. 剛 is to be understood with *reference* to virtue. 慾 is 情所好, 'what the passions love,' 'lusts.' 焉得 are said to = 不是, and not 不能. I have transl. accordingly.

11. THE DIFFICULTY OF ATTAINING TO THE NOT WISHING TO DO TO OTHERS AS WE WISH THEM NOT TO DO TO US. It is said—此章見無我之不易及, 'this ch. shows that the no *I* (freed. from selfishness) is not easily reached.' In the 中庸, XIII. 3, it is said—施諸己而不願亦勿施諸人, 'what you do not like when done to yourself, do not do to others.' The diff. between it and the sent. here is said to be that of 恕, 'reciprocity,' and 仁, 'benevolence,' or the highest virtue, appar. in the adv. 勿 and 無, the one prohibitive, and the other a simple, unconstrained, negation. The golden rule of the Gospel is higher than both,—'Do ye unto others as ye would that others should do unto you.' 諸 = 於; 加諸, or 加於, 'to add upon,' 'to do to.'

12. THE GRADUAL WAY IN WHICH CONFUCIUS COMMUNICATED HIS DOCTRINES. So the lesson of this ch. is summed up, but there is hardly another more perplexing to a transl. 文章 is the comm. name for essays, elegant literary compositions. Of course that mean. is out of the question. Whatever is *figured* and *brilliant* is 文, whatever is *orderly* and *defined* is 章. The comm., accordingly, make 文 to be the deportment and manners of the sage, and 章 his ordin. discourses, but 聞 is an inapprop. term

可得而聞也、夫子之言性與天道、不可得而聞也。

十三 子路有聞、未之能行、唯恐有聞。

十四 子貢問曰、孔文子、何以謂之文也。子曰、敏而好學、不恥下問、是以謂之文也。

十五 子謂子產、有君子之道四焉、其行己也恭、其事上也敬、其養民也惠、其使民

CHAPTER XIII. When Tsze-loo heard anything, if he had not yet carried it into practice, he was only afraid lest he should hear *something else.*

CHAPTER XIV. Tsze-kung asked saying, "On what ground did Kung-wăn get that title of WAN?" The Master said, "He was of an active nature and yet fond of learning, and he was not ashamed to ask *and learn of* his inferiors!—On these grounds he has been styled WAN."

CHAPTER XV. The Master said of Tsze-ch'an that he had four of the characteristics of a superior man:—in his conduct of himself, he was humble; in serving his superiors, he was respectful; in nourishing the people, he was kind; in ordering the people, he was just."

with reference to the former. These things, however, were level to the cap. of the discl. generally, and they had the benefit of them. As to his views about man's nature, the gift of Heaven, and the way of Heaven generally;—these he only commun. to those who were prepared to receive them, and Tsze-kung is supposed to have expressed himself thus, after being on some occasion so privileged.

13. THE ARDOUR OF TSZE-LOO IN PRACTISING THE MASTER'S INSTRUCTIONS. The concl. 唯恐有聞 is to be completed 唯恐復有所聞, as in the translation.

14. AN EXAMPLE OF THE PRINCIPLE ON WHICH HONORARY POSTHUMOUS TITLES WERE CONFERRED. 文, corresponding nearly to our 'accomplished,' was the posthum. title given to 子圉, an officer of the state of Wei, and a contempor. of Conf. Many of his actions had been of a doubtful char., which made Tsze-kung stumble at the applica. to him of so hon. an epithet. But Conf. shows that, whatever he might otherwise be, he *had* those qualities, which justified his being so denominated. The rule for posth. titles in China has been, and is, very much,—'*De mortuis nil nisi bonum.*'

15. THE EXCELLENT QUALITIES OF TSZE-CH'AN. Tsze-ch'an, named 公孫僑, was the chief min. of the state of Ching (鄭), the ablest perhaps, and most upright, of all the statesmen among Conf. contemporaries. The sage wept when he heard of his death. The old interpret. take 使 in the sense of 'employing,' but it seems to express more, and = 'ordering,' 'regulating.'

也義。

子曰、晏平仲、善與人交、久而敬之。

子曰、臧文仲、居蔡、山節藻梲、何如其知也。

子張問曰、令尹子文、三仕爲令尹、無喜色、三已之、無慍色、舊令尹之政、必以告新令尹、何如。子曰、忠矣。曰、仁矣乎。曰、

CHAPTER XVI. The Master said, "Gan P'ing knew well how to maintain friendly intercourse. The acquaintance might be long, but he showed the *same* respect *as at first*."

CHAPTER XVII. The Master said, "Tsang Wăn kept a large tortoise in a house, on the capitals of the pillars of which he had hills made, with representations of duckweed on the small pillars *above the beams supporting the rafters*.—Of what sort was his wisdom?"

CHAPTER XVIII. 1. Tsze-chang asked, saying, "The minister Tsze-wăn, thrice took office, and manifested no joy in his countenance. Thrice he retired from office, and manifested no displeasure. He made it a point to inform the new minister of the way in which he had conducted the government;—what do you say of him?" "The Master replied, "He was loyal." "Was he perfectly virtuous?" "I do not know. How can he be pronounced perfectly virtuous?"

16. HOW TO MAINTAIN FRIENDSHIP. 'Familiarity breeds contempt,' and with contempt friendship ends. It was not so with Gan P'ing, another of the worthies of Confucius' times. He was a prin. minister of Ts'e (齊), by name 嬰. P'ing (='Ruling and averting calamity') was his posth. title. If we were to render 仲, the name would be 'Gan P'ing, secundus.' Obs. the antecd. to 之 is 人.

17. THE SUPERSTITION OF TSANG WAN. Tsang Wăn (wăn is the hon. epithet, and 仲, see last ch.) had been a great off. in Loo, and left a reputation for wisdom, which Conf. did not think was deserved. His full name was 臧孫辰. He was descended from the duke 孝 (B.C. 794-767), whose son was styled 子臧. This Tsang was taken by his descendants as their surname. This is mentioned to shew one of the ways in which surnames were formed among the Chinese. 蔡 'a large tortoise,' so called, because the state of that name was famous for its tortoises. 居 is used as an act. verb,=藏. The 節=柱頭斗栱 'the capitals of the pillars.' The 梲 may be seen in any Ch. house. There being no ceilings, the whole structure of the roof is displayed, and these small pillars are very conspicuous. The old interpr. make the keep. such a tortoise an act of usurpat. on the part of Tsang Wan. Choo He finds the point of Conf. words in the keeping it in such a style.

18. THE PRAISE OF PERFECT VIRTUE IS NOT TO BE LIGHTLY ACCORDED. 1. Ling yin, lit., 'good corrector,' was the name given to the chief min. of Tsoo (楚). 尹 is still applied to officers;

未知、焉得仁。二 崔子弒齊君、陳文子有馬十乘、棄而違之、至於他邦、則曰、猶吾大夫崔子也、違之、之一邦、則又曰、猶吾大夫崔子也、違之、何如。子曰、清矣。曰、仁矣乎。曰、未知、焉得仁。

十九 季文子三思而後行。子聞之曰、再斯可矣。

二十 子曰、甯武子、邦有道、則

2. *Tsze-chang* proceeded, "When the officer Ts'uy killed the prince of Ts'e, Ch'in Wăn, though he was the owner of forty horses, abandoned them and left the country. Coming to another state, he said, 'They are here like our great officer, Ts'uy,' and left it. He came to a second state, and with the same observation left it also;—what do you say of him?" The Master replied, "He was pure." "Was he perfectly virtuous?" "I do not know. How can he be pronounced perfectly virtuous?"

CHAPTER XIX. Ke Wăn thought thrice, and then acted. When the Master was informed of it, he said, "Twice may do."

CHAPTER XX. The Master said, "When good order prevailed in his country, Ning Woo acted the part of a wise man. When his country was in disorder, he acted the part of a stupid man. Others may equal his wisdom, but they cannot equal his stupidity."

e. g., the prefect of a department is called 府尹. Tsze-wăn, surnamed 鬬, and named 穀於菟 ('suckled by a tiger'), had been noted for the things mentioned by Tsze-chang, but the sage would not concede that he was therefore 仁. 2. 崔 was a great officer of Ts'e. Gan P'ing (ch. 16), distinguished himself on the occasion of the murder (B. C. 547) here referred to. Ch'in Wăn was likewise an officer of Ts'e. 之一邦. 之 is a verb, = 往. 乘, low. 3d tone, as in I. 5, but with a diff. meaning, 'a team of four horses.'

19. PROMPT DECISION GOOD. Wăn was the posth. title of 季行父, a faithful and distinguished officer of Loo. 三, up. 3d tone, 'three times,' but some say it = 二 三, 'again and again.' Comp. Robert Hall's remark,—'In matters of conscience first thoughts are best.'

20. THE UNCOMMON BUT ADMIRABLE STUPIDITY OF NING WOO. Ning Woo (武, hon. ep. See II. 6), was an officer of Wei in the times of Wăn, (B. C. 635-627), the second of the five pa, (III. 22). In the first part of his official life, the state was quiet and prosperous, and he 'wisely' acquitted himself of his duties. Afterwards came confusion. The prince was driven from the throne, and Ning Yu (俞 was his name) might, like other wise men, have retired from the danger. But he 'foolishly,' as it seem-

知、邦無道、則愚、其知可及也、其愚不可及也。

二十一 子在陳曰、歸與歸與、吾黨之小子、狂簡、斐然成章、不知所以裁之。

二十二 子曰、伯夷叔齊、不念舊惡、怨是用希。

二十三 子曰、孰謂微生高

CHAPTER XXI. When the Master was in Ch'in, he said, "Let me return! Let me return! The little children of my school are ambitious and too hasty. They are accomplished and complete so far, but they do not know how to restrict and shape themselves."

CHAPTER XXII. The Master said, "Pih-e and Shuh-ts'e did not keep the former wickednesses of men in mind, and hence the resentments directed towards them were few."

CHAPTER XXIII. The Master said, "Who says of Wei-shang Kaou that he is upright? One begged some vinegar of him, and he begged it of a neighbour and gave it him."

ed, chose to follow the fortunes of his prince, and yet adroitly brought it about in the end, that the prince was reinstated and order restored.

21. THE ANXIETY OF CONFUCIUS ABOUT THE TRAINING OF HIS DISCIPLES. Confucius was thrice in Ch'in. It must have been the 3d time, when he thus expressed himself. He was then over 60 years, and being convinced that he was not to see for himself the triumph of his principles, he became the more anxious about their transmission, and the train. of the disci. in order to that. Such is the com. view of the ch. Some say, however, that it is not to be understood of all the disciples. Comp. Mencius, VII. ii. 37. 吾黨之小子, an affectionate way of speaking of the disciples. 狂, 'mad,' also, 'extravagant,' 'highminded.' The 狂 are naturally 簡, hasty and careless of minutiæ. 斐然, 'accomplished-like.' 章, see ch. 12. 成章, 'something complete.' 裁, see ch. 6, but its applica. here is somewhat diff. The anteced. to 之 is all the preced. description.

22. THE GENEROSITY OF PIH-E AND SHUH-TS'E, AND ITS EFFECTS. These were ancient worthies of the closing period of the Shang dynasty. Comp. Mencius, II.i.2,9, *et al.* They were brothers, sons of the king of Koo-chuh (孤竹), named respectively 允 and 致. E and Ts'e are their hon. epithets, and 伯 and 叔 only indicate their relation to each other as elder and younger. Pih-e and Shuh-ts'e, however, are in effect their names in the mouths and writings of the Chinese. Koo-chuh was a small state, included in the pres. depart. of 永平, in Pih-chih-le. Their father left his kingdom to Shuh-ts'e, who refused to take the place of his elder brother. Pih-e in turn declined the throne, so they both abandoned it, and retired into obscurity. When king Woo was taking his measures against the tyrant Chow, they made their appearance, and remonstrated against his course. Finally, they died of hunger, rather than live under the new dynasty. They were celebrated for their purity, and aversion to men whom they considered bad, but Conf. here brings out their generosity. 怨是用希=怨是以希, 'Resentments thereby were few.'

23. SMALL MEANNESSES INCONSISTENT WITH UPRIGHTNESS. It is implied that Kaou gave the vinegar as from himself.

直、或乞醯焉、乞諸其鄰而與之。

〔二十四〕子曰、巧言令色、足恭、左丘明恥之、丘亦恥之、匿怨而友其人、左丘明恥之、丘亦恥之。

〔二十五〕顏淵季路侍。子曰、盍各言爾志。子路曰、願車馬、衣輕裘、與朋友共、敝之而無憾。顏淵曰、願無

CHAPTER XXIV. The Master said, "Fine words, an insinuating appearance, and excessive respect;—Tso-k'ew Ming was ashamed of them. I also am ashamed of them. To conceal resentment against a person, and appear friendly with him;—Tso-k'ew Ming was ashamed of such conduct. I also am ashamed of it."

CHAPTER XXV. 1. Yen Yuen and Ke Loo being by his side, the Master said to them, "Come, let each of you tell his wishes."

2. Tsze-loo said, "I should like, having chariots and horses, and light fur dresses, to share them with my friends, and though they should spoil them, I would not be displeased."

3. Yen Yuen said, "I should like not to boast of my excellence, nor to make a display of my meritorious deeds."

4. Tsze-loo then said, "I should like, sir, to hear your wishes." The Master said, "*They are*, in regard to the aged, to give them rest; in regard to friends, to show them sincerity; in regard to the young, to treat them tenderly."

24. PRAISE OF SINCERITY, AND OF TSO-K'EW MING. 巧言令色, see I. 3. 足恭, 'excessive respect.' 足 being in 3d tone, read *tseu*. Some of the old comm., keeping the usual tone and meaning of 足, interpret the phrase of movements of the 'feet' to indicate respect. The discussions about Tso-k'ew Ming are endless. See 摭餘說, I. 30. It is sufficient for us to rest in the judgment of the comm. 程, that 'he was an ancient of reputation.' It is not to be received that he was a disciple of Conf. 丘 was the name of Conf. The Chinese decline pronouncing it, always substituting *mow* (某), 'such an one,' for it.

25. THE DIFFERENT WISHES OF YEN YUEN, TSZE-LOO, AND CONFUCIUS. 1. 盍各言爾志, 'why not each tell your will?' 2. A student is apt to translate—'I should like to have chariots and horses, &c.' but 共 is the import. word in the par., and under the regimen of 願. 衣, up. 3d tone, 'to wear.' Several writers carry the reg. of 願 on to 之, and removing the comma at 共, read 共敝 together, but this constr. is not so good. 3. In Ho An's compilation 施勞 is interpr.—'not to impose troublesome affairs on others.' Choo He's view is better. Comp. the Yih-king, 繫

伐善、無施勞。子路曰、願聞子之志。子曰、老者安之、朋友信之、少者懷之。

二十六 子曰、已矣乎、吾未見能見其過、而內自訟者也。

二十七 子曰、十室之邑、必有忠信、如丘者焉、不如丘之好學也。

CHAPTER XXVI. The Master said, "It is all over! I have not yet seen one who could perceive his faults, and inwardly accuse himself."

CHAPTER XXVII. The Master said, "In a hamlet of ten families, there may be found one honourable and sincere as I am, but not so fond of learning."

辭 I. ii. 10. 4. 信之＝與之以信, 'To be with them with sincerity.'—The Master and the disci., it is said, agreed in being devoid of selfishness. Hwuy's, however, was seen in a higher style of mind and object than Yew's. In the sage, there was an unconsciousness of self, and without any effort, he propos. acting in regard to his classification of men just as they ought severally to be acted to.

26. A LAMENT OVER MEN'S PERSISTENCE IN ERROR. The 乎 has an exclamat. force. 訟, 'to litigate.' 內自訟者, 'one who brings himself before the bar of his conscience.' The remark affirms a fact, inexplicable on Conf. view of the nature of man. But perhaps such an exclamation should not be pressed too closely.

27. THE HUMBLE CLAIM OF CONFUCIUS FOR HIMSELF. 邑 (人聚會之稱也) is 'the designation of the place where men are collected together,' and may be applied from a hamlet upwards to a city. 忠＝忠厚, 'honourable,' 'substantial.' Confucius thus did not claim higher natural and moral qualities than others, but sought to perfect himself by learning.

BOOK VI. YUNG YAY.

雍也第六

一 子曰、雍也、可使南面。二 仲弓問子桑伯子。子曰、可也、簡。三 仲弓曰、居敬而行簡、以臨其民、不亦可乎、居簡而行簡、無乃大簡乎。四 子曰、雍之言然。

CHAPTER I. 1. The Master said, "There is Yung!—He might occupy the place of a prince."

2. Chung-kung asked about Tsze-sang Pih-tsze. The Master said, "He may pass. He does not mind small matters."

3. Chung-kung said, "If a man cherish in himself a reverential feeling *of the necessity of attention to business*, though he may be easy in small matters, in his government of the people, that may be allowed. But if he cherish in himself that easy feeling, and also carry it out in his practice, is not such an easy mode of procedure excessive?"

4. The Master said, "Yung's words are right."

HEADING OF THIS BOOK.—雍也第六. 'There is Yung!' commences the first ch., and stands as the title of the book. Its subjects are much akin to those of the preceding book, and therefore, it is said, they are in juxtaposition.

1. THE CHARACTERS OF YEN YUNG AND TSZE-SANG PIH-TSZE, AS REGARDS THEIR ADAPTATION FOR GOVERNMENT. 1. 可使南面, 'might be employed with his face to the south.' In China, the emperor sits facing the south. So did the princes of the states in their several courts in Conf. time. An explan. of the practice is attempted in the Yih-King, 說卦 ch. 9, 離也者明也、萬物皆相見、南方之卦也、聖人南面而聽天下、嚮明而治、蓋取此也, 'The diagram Le conveys the idea of brightness, when all things are exhibited to one another. It is the diagram of the south. The custom of the sages (i. e., monarchs) to sit with their faces to the south, *and listen to the representations* of the empire, governing towards the bright region, was taken from this.' 2. Obs. Chung-kung was the designation of Yen Yung, see V. 4. 簡 has here substantially the same meaning as in V. 21,—不煩 'not troubling,' i. e., one's self about small matters. With ref. to that place, however, the Dict., after the old comm., explains it by 大, 'great.' 3. Of Tsze-sang Pih-tsze, we know nothing certain but what is here stated. Choo He seems to be wrong in approving the identifica. of him with a Tsze-sang Hoo. 居敬, 'to dwell in respect,' to have the mind imbued with it. 敬=敬事 in I. 5.

二 哀公問弟子孰爲好學。孔子對曰、有顏回者好學、不遷怒、不貳過、不幸短命死矣、今也則亡、未聞好學者也。

三 子華使於齊、冉子爲其母請粟。子曰、與之釜。請益。曰、與之庾。冉子與之粟五秉。子曰、赤之適齊也、乘肥馬、衣輕裘、吾

CHAPTER II. The duke Gae asked which of the disciples loved to learn. Confucius replied to him, "There was Yen Hwuy; HE loved to learn. He did not transfer his anger; he did not repeat a fault. Unfortunately, his appointed time was short and he died; and now there is not *such another*. I have not yet heard of any one who loves to learn *as he did*."

CHAPTER III. 1. Tsze-hwa being employed on a mission to Ts'e, the disciple Yen requested grain for his mother. The Master said, "Give her a *foo*." *Yen* requested more. "Give her an *yu*," said the Master. Yen gave her five *ping*.

2. The Master said, "When Ch'ih was proceeding to Ts'e, he had fat horses to his carriage, and wore light furs. I have heard

2. THE RARITY OF A TRUE LOVE TO LEARN. HWUY'S SUPERIORITY TO THE OTHER DISCIPLES. In 有顏回者, 者 = 'that.'—'There was that Yen Hwuy.' 'He did not transfer his anger,' *i. e.*, his anger was no tumultuary passion in the mind, but was excited by some specific cause, to which alone it was directed. 短命死矣,—'He died an early death,' but 命 conveys also the idea in the transl. The two last clauses are completed thus:—今也則亡 (read as, and = 無) 是人,未聞如是之好學者也.

3. DISCRIMINATION OF CONFUCIUS IN REWARDING OR SALARYING OFFICERS. 1. 使, up. 3d tone, 'to commission,' or 'to be commissioned.' Choo He says the commission was a private one from Confucius, but this is not likely. The old interpretation makes it a public one from the court of Loo; see 四書改錯, III. 9. 冉子, 'The disciple Yen'; see III. 6. Yen is here styled 子, like 有子, in I. 2, but only in narrative, not as introducing any wise utterance. A *foo* contained 6 *tow* (斗), and 4 *shing* (升), or 64 *shing*. The *Yu* contained 160 *shing*, and the *ping* 16 *hŭ* (斛), or 1600 *shing*. A *shing* of the present day is about 1/9th less than an English pint. 2. The 之 in 吾聞之, refers to what follows. 3. In Ho An's edition, another chapter commences here. Yuen Sze, named 憲, is now the third, east, in the outer hall of the temples. He was noted for his pursuit of truth, and carelessness of worldly advantages. After the death of Conf., he withdrew into retirement in Wei. It is related that Tsze-kung, high in official station, came one day in great style to visit him. Sze received him in a tattered coat, and Tsze-kung asking

聞之也、君子周急、不
繼富。原思爲之宰、與
之粟九百、辭。子曰、毋
以與爾鄰里鄉黨乎。
四 子謂仲弓曰、犂牛
之子、騂且角、雖欲勿
用、山川其舍諸。
五 子曰、回也、其心三
月不違仁、其餘、則日
月至焉而已矣。

that a superior man helps the distressed, but does not add to the wealth of the rich."

3. Yuen Sze being made governor *of his town by the Master*, he gave him nine hundred measures of grain, but Sze declined them.

4. The Master said, "Do not decline them. May you not give them away in the neighbourhoods, hamlets, towns, and villages?"

CHAPTER IV. The Master, speaking of Chung-kung, said, "If the calf of a brindled cow be red and horned, although men may not wish to use it, would *the spirits of* the mountains and rivers put it aside?"

CHAPTER V. The Master said, "Such was Hwuy that for three months there would be nothing in his mind contrary to perfect virtue. The others may attain to this on some days or in some months, but nothing more."

him if he were ill, he replied, 'I have heard that to have no money is to be poor, and that to study truth and not be able to find it is to be ill.' This answer sent Tsze-kung away in confusion. The 900 measures (whatever they were) was the proper allowance for an officer of Sze's station. 爲之宰, See V. 7, though it is not easy to give the 之 the same reference here as in that passage. 4. According to ancient statutes, a *lin*, a *le*, a *heang*, and a *tang*, have each their specific number of component families, but the meaning is no more than—'the poor about you.' 乎 makes the remark=' may you not, &c.'

4. THE VICES OF A FATHER SHOULD NOT DISCREDIT A VIRTUOUS SON. The father of Chung-kung (see V. 4) was a man of bad character, and some would have visited this upon his son, which drew forth Conf. remark. 'The rules of the Chow dyn. required that sacrific. victims should be red, and have good horns. An animal with those qual., tho' it might spring from one not possessing them, would certainly not be unacceptable on that account to the spirits sacrificed to. I translate 子 by 'calf,' but is is not implied that the victim was young. 舍, up. 3d tone,=捨, 'to lay aside,' 'to put away.' 其舍諸=其舍之乎.

5. THE SUPERIORITY OF HWUY TO THE OTHER DISCIPLES. It is impossible to say whether we should translate here about Hwuy in the past or present tense. 違 here is not 違背, 'to oppose,' but 違去, 'to depart from.' 日月至, 'come to it,' i.e., the line of perfect virtue, 'in the course of a day, or a month.' 日月 may also be, 'for a day or a month.' So in the 註疏.

六 季康子問仲由、可使從政也與。子曰、由也果、於從政乎何有。曰、賜也、可使從政也與。曰、賜也達、於從政乎何有。曰、求也、可使從政也與。曰、求也藝、於從政乎何有。

七 季氏使閔子騫爲費宰、閔子騫曰、善爲我辭焉、如有復我者、則吾必在汶上矣。

CHAPTER VI. Ke K'ang asked, "Is Chung-yew fit to be employed as an officer of government?" The Master said, "Yew is a man of decision; what difficulty would he find in being an officer of government?" *K'ang* asked, "Is Tsze fit to be employed as an officer of government?" and was answered, "Tsze is a man of intelligence; what difficulty would he find in being an officer of government?" And to the same question about K'ew the Master gave the same reply, saying, "K'ew is a man of various ability."

CHAPTER VII. The chief of the Ke family sent to ask Min Tsze-k'een to be governor of Pe. Min Tsze-k'een said, "Decline the offer for me politely. If any one come again to me with a second invitation, I shall be *obliged to go and live* on the banks of the Wăn."

6. THE QUALITIES OF TSZE-LOO, TSZE-KUNG, AND TSZE-YEW, AND THEIR COMPETENCY TO ASSIST IN GOVERNMENT. The prince is called 爲政者, 'the *doer* of government;' his ministers and officers are styled 從政者, 'the *followers* of government.' 也與 and 何有 are set, the one expression against the other, the former indicating a doubt of the competency of the disciples, the latter affirming their more than competency.

7. MIN TSZE-K'EEN REFUSES TO SERVE THE KE FAMILY. The tablet of Tsze-k'een (his name was 損) is now the first on the east among 'the wise ones' of the temple. He was among the foremost of the disciples. Conf. praises his filial piety, and we see here, how he could stand firm in his virtue, and refuse the proffers of powerful but unprincipled families of his time. 使=使人來召, in the transl., and in 復 (*fow*, low. 3d tone) 我者, we must similarly understand, 復來召我者. 費, read *Pe*, was a place belonging to the Ke family. Its name is still preserved in 費縣 in the depart. of 沂州, in Shan-tung. The Wăn stream divided Ts'e and Loo. Tsze-k'een threatens, if he should be troubled again to retreat to Ts'e, where the Ke family could not reach him.

[八]伯牛有疾、子問之、自牖執其手、曰、亡之、命矣夫、斯人也、而有斯疾也、斯人也、而有斯疾也。

[九]子曰、賢哉回也、一簞食、一瓢飲、在陋巷、人不堪其憂、回也不改其樂、賢哉回也。

[十]冉求曰、非不說子之道、力不足也。子曰、力不

CHAPTER VIII. Pih-new being sick, the Master went to ask for him. He took hold of his hand through the window, and said, "It is killing him. It is the appointment *of Heaven*, alas! That such a man should have such a sickness! That such a man should have such a sickness!"

CHAPTER IX. The Master said, "Admirable indeed was the virtue of Hwuy! With a single bamboo dish of rice, a single gourd dish of drink, and living in his mean narrow lane, while others could not have endured the distress, he did not allow his joy to be affected by it. Admirable indeed was the virtue of Hwuy!"

CHAPTER X. Yen K'ew said, "It is not that I do not delight in your doctrines, but my strength is insufficient." The Master said, "Those whose strength is insufficient give over in the middle of the way, but now you limit yourself."

8. LAMENT OF CONFUCIUS OVER THE MORTAL SICKNESS OF PIH-NEW. Pih-new, 'elder or uncle New,' was the denomination of 冉耕, who had an honourable place among the disciples of the sage. In the old interpr., his sickness is said to have been 惡疾, 'an evil disease,' by which name leprosy, called 癩, is intended, though that char. is now employed for 'itch.' Suffering from such a disease, Pih-new would not see people, and Confucius took his hand through the window. A differ. explanation of that circumstance is given by Choo He. He says that sick persons were usually placed on the north side of the apartment, but when the prince visited them, in order that he might appear to them with his face to the south (see ch. 1), they were moved to the south. On this occasion, Pih-new's friends wanted to receive Conf. after this royal fashion, which he avoided by not entering the house. 亡 appears as an act. verb 亡之, 'It is killing him.' 夫, low. 1st tone, generally an initial particle='now.' It is here final, and='alas!'

9. THE HAPPINESS OF HWUY INDEPENDENT OF POVERTY. The 簞 was simply a piece of the stem of a bamboo, and the 瓢 half of a gourd cut into two. 食, see II. 8. The eulogy turns much on 其 in 其樂, as opposed to 其憂. '*his* joy,' the delight which he had in the doctrines of his master, contrasted with the grief others would have felt under such poverty.

10. A HIGH AIM AND PERSEVERANCE PROPER TO A STUDENT. Conf. would not admit K'ew's apology for not attempting more than he did. 'Give over in the middle of the way,' i. e., they go as long and as far as they can, they are pursuing when they stop.

足者、中道而廢、今女畫。

〔十一〕子謂子夏曰、女爲君子儒、無爲小人儒。

〔十二〕子游爲武城宰、子曰、女得人焉耳乎。曰、有澹臺滅明者、行不由徑、非公事、未嘗至於偃之室也。

〔十三〕子曰、孟之反不伐、奔而殿、將入門、策其馬、曰、非敢後也、馬不進也。

CHAPTER XI. The Master said to Tsze-hea, "Do you be a scholar after the style of the superior man, and not after that of the mean man."

CHAPTER XII. Tsze-yew being governor of Woo-shing, the Master said to him, "Have you got *good* men *there?*" He answered, "There is Tan-t'ae Mëë-ming, who never in walking takes a short cut, and never comes to my office, excepting on public business."

CHAPTER XIII. The Master said, "Măng Che-fan does not boast of his merit. Being in the rear on an occasion of flight, when they were about to enter the gate, he whipt up his horse saying, 'It is not that I dare to be last. My horse would not advance.'"

11. HOW LEARNING SHOULD BE PURSUED. 君子 and 小人 here = adjectives, qualifying 儒. The 君子, it is said, learns 爲己, for his own real improvement and from duty; the 小人 learning 爲人, 'for men,' with a view to their opinion, and for his own material benefit.

12. THE CHARACTER OF TAN-T'AE MEE-MING. The ch. shows, according to Chinese comm., the advantage to people in authority of their having good men about them. In this way after their usual fashion, they seek for a profound meaning in the remark of Conf. Tan-t'ae Mëë-ming, who was styled 子羽, has his tablet the 2d east outside the hall. The accounts of him are very conflicting. Acc. to one, he was very good-looking, while another says he was so bad-looking that Conf. at first formed an unfavourable opinion of him, an error which he afterwards confessed on Mëë-ming's becoming eminent. He travelled southwards with not a few followers, and places near Soo-chow and elsewhere retain names indicative of his presence. 焉耳乎, three particles coming together are said to indicate the slow and deliberate manner in which the sage spoke. 滅明者, Comp. 顏回者 in ch. 2. 室 is said to = 公堂.

13. THE VIRTUE OF MANG CHE-FAN IN CONCEALING HIS MERIT. But where was his virtue in deviating from the truth? And how could Conf. commend him for doing so? These questions have never troubled the commentators. Mang Che-fan, named 側 was an officer of Loo. The defeat, after which he thus distinguished himself was in the 11th year of duke Gae, B. C. 483. To lead the van of an army is called 啟, to bring up the rear is 殿. In retreat, the rear is of course the place of honour. 伐, see V. 25, 4.

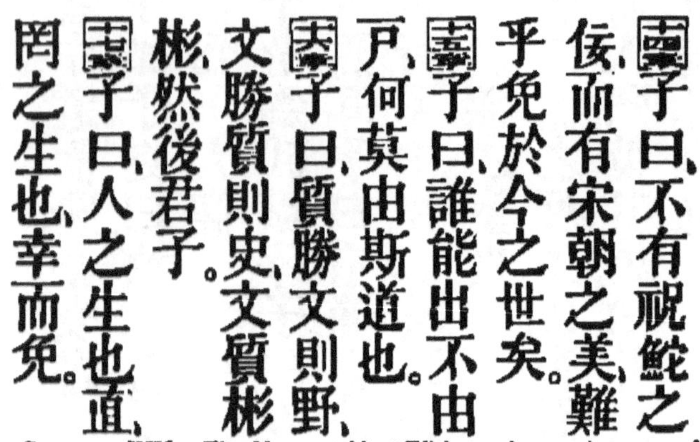

〔十四〕子曰、不有祝鮀之佞、而有宋朝之美、難乎免於今之世矣。〔十五〕子曰、誰能出不由戶、何莫由斯道也。〔十六〕子曰、質勝文則野、文勝質則史、文質彬彬、然後君子。〔十七〕子曰、人之生也直、罔之生也、幸而免。

CHAPTER XIV. The Master said, "Without the specious speech of the litanist T'o, and the beauty of *the prince* Chaou of Sung, it is difficult to escape in the present age."

CHAPTER XV. The Master said, "Who can go out but by the door? How is it that men will not walk according to these ways?"

CHAPTER XVI. The Master said, "Where the solid qualities are in excess of accomplishments, we have rusticity; where the accomplishments are in excess of the solid qualities, we have the manners of a clerk. When the accomplishments and solid qualities are equally blended, we then have the man of complete virtue."

CHAPTER XVII. The Master said, "Man is born for uprightness. If a man lose his uprightness, and yet live, his escape *from death* is the effect of mere good fortune."

14. THE DEGENERACY OF THE AGE ESTEEMING GLIBNESS OF TONGUE AND BEAUTY OF PERSON. 祝, 'to pray,' 'prayers;' here, in the concrete, the officer charged with the prayers in the ancestral temple. I have coined the word *litanist* to come as near to the meaning as possible. This T'o was an officer of the state of Wei, styled 子魚. Prince Chaou had been guilty of incest with his sister Nan-tsze (see ch. 26), and afterwards, when she was married to the duke Ling of Wei, he served as an officer there, carrying on his wickedness. He was celebrated for his beauty of person. 而 is a simple connective, =與, and the 不 is made to belong to both clauses. This seems the correct construction, tho' unusual. The old comm. construe differently:—'If a man have not the speech of To, though he may have the beauty of Chaou, &c.,' making the degeneracy of the age all turn on its fondness for specious talk. This can't be right.

15. A LAMENT OVER THE WAYWARDNESS OF MEN'S CONDUCT. 斯道, 'These ways,' is a moral sense;—not deep doctrines, but rules of life.

16. THE EQUAL BLENDING OF SOLID EXCELLENCE AND ORNAMENTAL ACCOMPLISHMENTS IN A COMPLETE CHARACTER. 史, 'an historian,' an officer of importance in China. The term, however, is to be understood here of 'a clerk,' 'a scrivener in a public office,' one that is of a class sharp and well informed, but insincere.

17. LIFE WITHOUT UPRIGHTNESS IS NOT TRUE LIFE, AND CANNOT BE CALCULATED ON. 'No more serious warning than this,' says one comm., 'was ever addressed to men by Confucius.' A distinction is made by Choo He and others between the two 生, that the 1st is 始生, 'birth,' or 'the beginning of life,' and the 2d is 生存, 'preservation in life.' 人之生也直, 'The being born of man is upright,' which may mean either that man at his birth is upright, or that he is born for uprightness. I prefer the latter view. 罔之生也, 'The living without it,' if we take 罔=無, or 'to

〔十八〕子曰、知之者、不如好之者、好之者、不如樂之者。

〔十九〕子曰、中人以上、可以語上也、中人以下、不可以語上也。

〔二十〕樊遲問知。子曰、務民之義、敬鬼神而遠之、可謂知矣。問仁。曰、仁者先難而後獲、可

CHAPTER XVIII. The Master said, "They who know *the truth* are not equal to those who love it, and they who love it are not equal to those who find pleasure in it."

CHAPTER XIX. The Master said, "To those whose talents are above mediocrity, the highest subjects may be announced. To those who are below mediocrity, the highest subjects may not be announced."

CHAPTER XX. Fan Ch'e asked what constituted wisdom. The Master said, "To give one's-self earnestly to the duties due to men, and, while respecting spiritual beings, to keep aloof from them, may be called wisdom." He asked about perfect virtue. The Master said, "The man of virtue makes the difficulty *to be overcome* his first business, and success only a subsequent consideration;—this may be called perfect virtue."

defame it,' 罔 = 誣. We long here as elsewhere for more perspicuity and fuller development of view. An important truth struggles here for expression, but only finds it imperfectly. Without uprightness the end of man's existence is not fulfilled, but his preservation in such case is not merely a fortunate accident.

18. DIFFERENT STAGES OF ATTAINMENT. The four 之 have all one reference, which must be 道 or 理, the subject spoken of.

19. TEACHERS MUST BE GUIDED IN COMMUNICATING KNOWLEDGE BY THE SUSCEPTIVITY OF THE LEARNERS. In 以上, 上 is read up. 2d tone, a verbal word, and not the prep. 'upon,' so the 下 in 以下 is also verbal as in III. 7. The 中人, 'or mediocre people,' may have all classes of subjects announced to them, I suppose.

20. CHIEF ELEMENTS IN WISDOM AND VIRTUE. The modern comm. take 民 here as = 人, and 民之義 as = 人道之宜, 'what is right according to the principles of humanity.' With some hesitation, I have assented to this view, though 民 properly means 'the multitude,' 'the people,' and the old interpr. explain—'Strive to perfect the righteousness of the people.' We may suppose from the second clause that Fan Ch'e was striving after what was uncommon and superhuman. For a full exhibition of the phrase 鬼神, see 中庸, XVI. Here [illegible] 'spiritual beings,' manes and others. 遠, up. 3d tone. 遠之, 'Keep at a distance from them,' not 'keep them at a distance.' The sage's advice therefore is—'attend to what are plainly human duties, and do not be superstitious.' 先 and 後 are, as frequently elsewhere, verbs, 'put first,' 'put last.' The old interpreters take them differently, but not so well.

謂仁矣。

二十一 子曰、知者樂水、仁者樂山。知者動、仁者靜。知者樂、仁者壽。

二十二 子曰、齊一變、至於魯、魯一變、至於道。

二十三 子曰、觚不觚、觚哉觚哉。

二十四 宰我問曰、仁者雖告之曰、井有仁焉、其從之

CHAPTER XXI. The Master said, "The wise find pleasure in water; the virtuous find pleasure in hills. The wise are active; the virtuous are tranquil. The wise are joyful, the virtuous are long-lived."

CHAPTER XXII. The Master said, "Ts'e, by one change, would come to the state of Loo. Loo, by one change, would come to a state where true principles predominated."

CHAPTER XXIII. The Master said, "A cornered vessel without corners.—A strange cornered vessel! A strange cornered vessel!"

CHAPTER XXIV. Tsae Go asked, saying, "A benevolent man, though it be told him,—'There is a man in the well,' will go in after him, I suppose." Confucius said, "Why should he do so? A supe-

21. CONTRASTS OF THE WISE AND THE VIRTUOUS. The two first 樂 are read *ngaou*, low. 3d tone,=喜好, 'to find pleasure in.' The wise or knowing are active and restless, like the waters of a stream, ceaselessly flowing and advancing. The virtuous are tranquil and firm, like the stable mountains. The pursuit of knowledge brings joy. The life of the virtuous may be expected to glide calmly on and long. After all, the saying is not very comprehensible.

22. THE CONDITION OF THE STATES TS'E AND LOO. Ts'e and Loo were both within the present Shan-tung. Ts'e lay along the coast on the north, embracing the present dep. of 青州 and other territory. Loo was on the south, the larger portion of it being formed by the present dep. of 兖州. At the rise of the Chow dynasty, king Woo invested 太公望, 'the great duke Wang,' with the principality of Ts'e, while his successor, king Ching, constituted the son of his uncle, the famous duke of Chow, prince of Loo. In Conf. time, Ts'e had degenerated more than Loo. 道 is 先王盡善盡美之道, 'the entirely good and admirable ways of the former kings.'

23. THE NAME WITHOUT THE REALITY IS FOLLY. This was spoken (see the 註疏) with ref. to the governments of the time, retaining ancient names without ancient principles. The 觚 was a drinking vessel; others say a wooden tablet. The latter was a later use of the term. It was made with corners as appears from the composition of the character, which is formed from 角, 'a horn,' 'a sharp corner.' In Conf. time, the form was changed, while the name was kept.

24. THE BENEVOLENT EXERCISE THEIR BENEVOLENCE WITH PRUDENCE. Tsae Go could see no limitation to acting on the impulses of benevolence. We are not to suppose with modern

也。子曰、何爲其然也、君子可逝也、不可陷也、可欺也、不可罔也。

二十五 子曰、君子博學於文、約之以禮、亦可以弗畔矣夫。

二十六 子見南子、子路不說、夫子矢之曰、予所否者、天厭之、天厭之。

二十七 子曰、中庸之爲德也、其至矣乎、民鮮久矣。

rior man may be made to go *to the well*, but he cannot be made to go down into it. He may be imposed upon, but he cannot be befooled."

CHAPTER XXV. The Master said, "The superior man, extensively studying all learning, and keeping himself under the restraint of the rules of propriety, may thus likewise not overstep what is right."

CHAPTER XXVI. The Master having visited Nan-tsze, Tsze-loo was displeased, on which the Master swore, saying, "Wherein I have done improperly, may Heaven reject me! may Heaven reject me!"

CHAPTER XXVII. The Master said, "Perfect is the virtue which is according to the Constant Mean! Rare for a long time has been its practice among the people."

comm. that he wished to show that benevolence was impracticable. 雖 belongs to the whole following clause, especially to the mention of a well. The second 仁 is for 人. 其—也 indicate some doubt in Go's mind. Obs. the *hophal* force of 逝 and 陷.

25. THE HAPPY EFFECT OF LEARNING AND PROPRIETY COMBINED. 君子 has here its lighter meaning,='the student of what is right and true.' The 之 in 約之 we naturally refer to 文, but comparing IX. 10, 2—約我以禮,—we may assent to the observa. that 我指己身, '*I* refers to the learner's own person.' See note on IV. 23. 畔, 'the boundary of a field;' then, 'to overstep that boundary.' 矣夫, as in V. 26, but the force here is more 'ah!' than 'alas!'

26. CONFUCIUS VINDICATES HIMSELF FOR VISITING THE UNWORTHY NAN-TSZE. Nan-tsze was the wife of the duke of Wei, and sister of prince Chaou, mentioned ch. 14. Her lewd character was well known, and hence Tsze-loo was displeased, thinking an interview with *her* was disgraceful to the Master. Great pains are taken to explain the incident. 'Nan-tsze,' says one, 'sought the interview from the stirrings of her natural conscientiousness.' 'It was a rule,' says another, 'that officers in a state should visit the prince's wife.' 'Nan-tsze,' argues a third, 'had all influence with her husband, and Confucius wished to get currency by her means for his doctrines.' Whether 矢 is to be understood in the sense of 'to swear,'=誓, or 'to make a declaration'=陳, is much debated. Evidently, the thing is an oath, or solemn protestation against the suspicions of Tsze-loo.

27. THE DEFECTIVE PRACTICE OF THE PEOPLE IN CONFUCIUS' TIME. See 中庸, III.

廿八 子貢曰、如有博施於民、而能濟衆、何如、可謂仁乎。子曰、何事於仁、必也聖乎、堯舜其猶病諸。二 夫仁者、己欲立而立人、己欲達而達人。三 能近取譬、可謂仁之方也已。

CHAPTER XXVIII. 1. Tsze-kung said, "Suppose the case of a man extensively conferring benefits on the people, and able to assist all, what would you say of him? Might he be called perfectly virtuous?" The Master said, "Why speak only of virtue in connection with him? Must he not have the qualities of a sage? Even Yaou and Shun were still solicitous about this.

2. "Now the man of perfect virtue, wishing to be established himself, seeks also to establish others; wishing to be enlarged himself, he seeks also to enlarge others.

3. "To be able to judge *of others* by what is nigh *in ourselves*;—this may be called the art of virtue."

28. THE TRUE NATURE AND ART OF VIRTUE. There are no higher sayings in the Analects than we have here. 1. 施, up 3d tone, 'to confer benefits.' 聖乎,—乎 is said to be 'a particle of doubt and uncertainty,' but it is rather the interrogative affirmation of opinion. Tsze-kung appears to have thought that great doings were necessary to virtue, and propounds a case which would transcend the achievements of Yaou and Shun. From such extravagant views the Master recalls him. 2. This is the description of 仁者之心體, 'the mind of the perfectly virtuous man' as void of all selfishness. 3. It is to be wished that the idea intended by 能近取譬 had been more clearly expressed. Still we seem to have here a near approach to a positive enunciation of 'the golden rule.'

BOOK VII. SHUH URH.

述而第七

一 子曰、述而不作、信而好古、竊比於我老彭。

二 子曰、默而識之、學而不厭、誨人不倦、何有於我哉。

三 子曰、德之不脩、學之不講、聞義不能徙、不善不能改、

CHAPTER I. The Master said, "A transmitter and not a maker, believing in and loving the ancients, I venture to compare myself with our old P'ang."

CHAPTER II. The Master said, "The silent treasuring up of knowledge; learning without satiety; and instructing others without being wearied:—what one of these things belongs to me?"

CHAPTER III. The Master said, "The leaving virtue without proper cultivation; the not thoroughly discussing what is learned; not being able to move towards righteousness of which a knowledge is gained; and not being able to change what is not good:—these are the things which occasion me solicitude."

HEADING OF THIS BOOK.—述而第七. 'A transmitter, and ——Book VII.' We have in this book much information of a personal character about Confucius, both from his own lips, and from the descriptions of his disciples. The two preceding books treat of the disciples and other worthies, and here, in contrast with them, we have the sage himself exhibited.

1. CONFUCIUS DISCLAIMS BEING AN ORIGINATOR OR MAKER. 述=傳舊而已, 'simply to hand down the old.' Comm. say the master's language here is from his extreme humility. But we must hold that it expresses his true sense of his position and work. Who the individual called endearingly 'our old P'ang' was, can hardly be ascertained. Choo He adopts the view that he was a worthy officer of the Shang dynasty. But that individual's history is a mass of fables. Others make 老彭 to be Laou-tsze, the founder of the Taou sect, and others again make two individuals, one this Laou-tsze, and the other that 彭祖.

2. CONFUCIUS' HUMBLE ESTIMATE OF HIMSELF. 識, here by most scholars read *che*, up. 3d tone, 'to remember.' 之 refers, it is said, to 理, 'principles,' the subjects of the silent observation and reflection. 何有於我哉, cannot be—'what difficulty do these occasion me?' but—何者能有於我, as in the transl. 'The language,' says Choo He, 'is that of humility upon humility.' Some insert, in their expl., 此外 before 何—'Besides these, what is there in me?' But this is quite arbitrary. The profession may be inconsistent with what we find in other passages, but the inconsistency must stand rather than violence be done to the language. Ho An gives the singular exposition of 鄭康成 (about A.D. 150—200)—'Other men have not these things, I only have them.'

3. CONFUCIUS' ANXIETY ABOUT HIS SELF-CULTIVATION:—ANOTHER HUMBLE ESTIMATE OF HIMSELF. Here again, comm. find only the expressions of humility, but there can be no reason why we should not admit that Confucius was anxious lest these things, which are only put forth as possibilities, should become in his case actual

是吾憂也。

〔四〕子之燕居、申申如也、夭夭如也。

〔五〕子曰、甚矣吾衰也、久矣吾不復夢見周公。

〔六〕子曰、志於道、〇二 據於德、〇三 依於仁、〇四 游於藝。

CHAPTER IV. When the Master was unoccupied with business, his manner was easy, and he looked pleased.

CHAPTER V. The Master said, "Extreme is my decay. For a long time, I have not dreamed, as I was wont to do, that I saw the duke of Chow."

CHAPTER VI. 1. The Master said, "Let the will be set on the path of duty.

2. "Let every attainment in what is good be firmly grasped.

3. "Let perfect virtue be accorded with.

4. "Let relaxation and enjoyment be found in the polite arts."

facts. 講 is in the sense explained in the Dict. by the terms 習 and 究, 'practising,' 'examining.'

4. THE MANNER OF CONFUCIUS WHEN UNOCCUPIED. The first clause, which is the subject of the other two, is literally—'The master's dwelling at ease.' Obs. 燕, up. 3d tone; 夭, up. 1st tone; 如, as in III, 23.

5. HOW THE DISAPPOINTMENT OF CONFUCIUS' HOPES AFFECTED EVEN HIS DREAMS. 周公 (Chow-kung) is now to all intents a proper name, but the characters mean 'the duke of Chow.' Chow was the name of the seat of the family from which the dynasty so called sprang, and on the enlargement of this territory, king Wăn divided the original seat between his sons 旦 (Tan) and 奭 (Shih). Tan was *Chow kung*, in wisdom and politics what his elder brother, the first emperor, Woo, was in arms. Confucius had longed to bring the principles and institutions of Chow-kung into practice, and in his earlier years, while hope animated him, had often dreamt of the former sage. The orig. territory of Chow was what is now the dis. of Ke-shan (岐山), dep. of Fung-tseang (鳳翔), in Shen-se.

6. RULES FOR THE FULL MOULDING OF CHARACTER. 3. 德 might be translated virtue, but 仁='perfect virtue' following, we require another term. 4. 游, 'to ramble for amusement,' here='to seek recreation.' 藝, see note on 文, in I. 6. A full enumeration makes 'six arts,' viz., ceremonies, music, archery, charioteering, the study of characters or language, and figures or arithmetic. The ceremonies were ranged in five classes: lucky or sacrifices, unlucky or the mourning cer., military, those of host and guest, and festive. Music required the study of the music of Hwang-te, of Yaou, of Shun, of Yu, of Tang, and of Woo. Archery had a five-fold classification. Charioteering had the same. The study of the characters required the examination of them, to determine whether there predominated in their formation resemblance to the object, combination of ideas, indication of properties, a phonetic principle, a principle of contrariety, or metaphorical accommodation. Figures were managed according to nine rules, as the object was the measurement of land, capacity, &c. These six subjects were the business of the highest and most liberal education, but we need not suppose that Conf. had them all in view here.

七 子曰、自行束脩以上、吾未嘗無誨焉。

八 子曰、不憤不啟、不悱不發、舉一隅、不以三隅反、則不復也。

九 子食於有喪者之側、未嘗飽也。二 子於是日哭、則不歌。

十 子謂顏淵曰、用之則行、舍之則藏、惟我

CHAPTER VII. The Master said, "From the man bringing his bundle of dried flesh *for my teaching* upwards, I have never refused instruction to any one."

CHAPTER VIII. The Master said, "I do not open up the truth to one who is not eager *to get knowledge*, nor help out any one who is not anxious to explain himself. When I have presented one corner of a subject to any one, and he cannot from it learn the other three, I do not repeat my lesson."

CHAPTER IX. 1. When the Master was eating by the side of a mourner, he never ate to the full.

2. He did not sing on the same day in which he had been weeping.

CHAPTER X. 1. The Master said to Yen Yuen, "When called to office to undertake its duties; when not so called, to lie retired; —it is only I and you who have attained to this."

7. THE READINESS OF CONFUCIUS TO IMPART INSTRUCTION. It was the rule anciently that when one party waited on another, he should carry some present or offering with him. Pupils did so when they first waited on their teacher. Of such offerings, one of the lowest was a bundle of 脩, 'dried flesh.' The wages of a teacher are now called 脩金, 'the money of the dried flesh.' However small the offering brought to the sage, let him only see the indication of a wish to learn, and he imparted his instructions. 以上, may be translated 'upwards,' i. e., 'to such a man and others with larger gifts,' 上 being up. 2d tone, or the char. may be understood in the sense of 'attending my instructions,' with its usual tone. I prefer the former interpretation.

8. CONFUCIUS REQUIRED A REAL DESIRE AND ABILITY IN HIS DISCIPLES. The last ch. tells of the sage's readiness to teach, this shows that he did not teach where his teaching was likely to prove of no avail. 悱, in the comm. and dict., is explained 口欲言而未能之貌 'the appearance of one with mouth wishing to speak and yet not able to do so.' This being the meaning, we might have expected the character to be 啡. 反, 'to turn,' is explained 還以相證之義 'going round for mutual testimony.' 不復=不復有所告, 'I tell him nothing more.'

9. CONFUCIUS' SYMPATHY WITH MOURNERS. The weeping is understood to be on occasion of offering his condolences to a mourner, which was 'a rule of propriety.'

10. THE ATTAINMENTS OF HWUY LIKE THOSE OF CONFUCIUS. THE EXCESSIVE BOLDNESS OF TSZE-LOO. 1. In 用之, 舍之, 之 is ex-

與爾有是夫。二子路曰、子行三軍則誰與。三子曰、暴虎馮河、死而無悔者、吾不與也。必也臨事而懼、好謀而成者也。

十一子曰、富而可求也、雖執鞭之士、吾亦爲之、如不可求、從吾所好。

十二子之所慎、齊、戰、疾。

2. Tsze-loo said, "If you had the conduct of the armies of a great state, whom would you have to act with you?"

3. The Master said, "I would not have him to act with me, who will unarmed attack a tiger, or cross a river without a boat, dying without any regret. My associate must be the man who proceeds to action full of solicitude, who is fond of adjusting his plans, and then carries them into execution."

CHAPTER XI. The Master said, "If the search for riches is sure to be successful, though I should become a groom with whip in hand to get them, I will do so. As the search may not be successful, I will follow after that which I love."

CHAPTER XII. The things in reference to which the Master exercised the greatest caution were—fasting, war, and sickness.

plained by 我, but we have seen that 之 foll. active verbs imparts to them a sort of neuter signification. 用之 = 'used.' 舍之 = 'neglected.' 2. A *Keun*, acc. to the 周禮, consisted of 12,500 men. The imperial forces consisted of six such bodies, and those of a great state of three. 3. 暴虎馮河, see She-king, II. ii. 1, st. 6. 懼 does not indicate *timidity*, but *solicitude*.—Tsze-loo, it would appear, was jealous of the praise conferred on Hwuy, and pluming himself on his bravery, put in for a share of the Master's approbation. But he only brought on himself this rebuke.

11. THE UNCERTAINTY AND FOLLY OF THE PURSUIT OF RICHES. It occurs to a student to understand the first clause—'If it be *proper* to search for riches,' and the third—'I will do it.' But the transl. is acc. to the modern comm., and the conclusion agrees better with it. In expl. 執鞭之士, some refer us to the attendants who cleared the street with their whips when the prince went abroad, but we need not seek any particular allusion of the kind. Obs. 而 = 若, 'if,' and then, 如 = 'since.'—An objection to the pursuit of wealth may be made on the ground of righteousness, or on that of its uncertainty. It is the latter on which Confucius here rests.

12. WHAT THINGS CONFUCIUS WAS PARTICULARLY CAREFUL ABOUT. 齊, read *Chae*, and = 齋, 'to fast,' or, rather, denoting the whole religious adjustment, enjoined before the offering of sacrifice, and extending over the ten days previous to the great sacrificial seasons. 齊 means 'to equalize' (see II. 8), and the effect of those previous exercises was 齊不齊以

十三 子在齊聞韶、三月不知肉味、曰、不圖爲樂之至於斯也。

十四 冉有曰、夫子爲衛君乎。子貢曰、諾、吾將問之。二 入曰、伯夷叔齊、何人也。曰、古之賢人也。曰、怨乎。曰、求仁而得仁、又何怨。出曰、夫子不爲也。

CHAPTER XIII. When the Master was in Ts'e, he heard the Shaou, and for three months did not know the taste of flesh. "I did not think," he said, "that music could have been made so excellent as this."

CHAPTER XIV. 1. Yen Yew said, "Is our Master for the prince of Wei?" Tsze-kung said, "Oh! I will ask him."

2. He went in *accordingly*, and said, "What sort of men were Pih-e and Shuh-ts'e?" "They were ancient worthies," said the Master. "Did they have any repinings *because of their course?*" The Master again replied, "They sought to act virtuously, and they did so; what was there for them to repine about?" On this, *Tsze-kung* went out and said, "Our Master is not for him."

致齊, 'to adjust what was not adjusted, to produce a perfect adjustment.' Sacrifices presented in such a state of mind were sure to be acceptable. Other people, it is said, might be heedless in refer. to sacrifices, to war, and to sickness, but not so the sage.

13. THE EFFECT OF MUSIC ON CONFUCIUS. The *shaou*, see III. 25. This incident must have happened in the 36th year of Conf., when he followed the duke Ch'aou in his flight from Loo to Ts'e. As related in the 史記, 'Historical Records,' before the characters 三月, we have 學之, 'he learned it three months,' which may relieve us from the necessity of extending the three months over all the time in which he did not know the taste of his food. In Ho An's compilation, the 不知 is expl. by 忽忘, 'he was careless about and forgot.' The last clause is also explained there—'I did not think that this music had reached this country of Ts'e.'

14. CONFUCIUS DID NOT APPROVE OF A SON OPPOSING HIS FATHER. 1. The eldest son of duke Ling of Wei had planned to kill his mother (? stepmother), the notorious Nan-tsze (VI. 26). For this he had to flee the country, and his son, on the death of Ling, became duke (出公), and subsequently opposed his father's attempts to wrest the sovereignty from him. This was the matter argued among the disciples,—Was Confucius for (爲 low. 3d tone), the son, the reigning duke? 2. In Wei it would not have been acc. to *propriety* to speak by name of its ruler, and therefore Tsze-kung put the case of Pih-e and Shuh-ts'e, see V. 22. They having given up a throne, and finally their lives, rather than do what they thought wrong, and Confucius fully approving of their conduct, it was plain he could not approve of a son's holding by force what was the rightful inheritance of the father. 求仁而得仁, 'They sought for virtue, and they got virtue;' i. e., such was the character of their conduct.

〔十五〕子曰、飯疏食飲水、曲肱而枕之、樂亦在其中矣、不義而富且貴、於我如浮雲。

〔十六〕子曰、加我數年、五十以學易、可以無大過矣。

〔十七〕子所雅言、詩、書、執禮、皆雅言也。

CHAPTER XV. The Master said, "With coarse rice to eat, with water to drink, and my bended arm for a pillow;—I have still joy in the midst of these things. Riches and honours acquired by unrighteousness are to me as a floating cloud."

CHAPTER XVI. The Master said, "If some years were added to my life, I would give fifty to the study of the Yih, and then I might come to be without great faults."

CHAPTER XVII. The Master's frequent themes of discourse were—the Odes, the History, and the maintenance of the Rules of propriety. On all these he frequently discoursed.

15. THE JOY OF CONFUCIUS INDEPENDENT OF OUTWARD CIRCUMSTANCES. 飯, low. 3d tone, 'a meal,' also, as here, a verb, 'to eat.' 枕, up. 3d tone, 'to pillow,' 'to use as a pillow.' Critics call attention to 亦, making the sentiment—'*My joy is everywhere. It is amid other circumstances. It is also here.*' 不義云云,—'By unrighteousness I might get riches and honours, but such riches and honours are to me as a floating cloud. It is vain to grasp at them, so uncertain and unsubstantial.'

16. THE VALUE WHICH CONFUCIUS SET UPON THE STUDY OF THE YIH. Choo He supposes that this was spoken when Conf. was about seventy, as he was in his 68th year when he ceased his wanderings, and settled in Loo to the adjustment and compilation of the Yih and other *king*. If the remark be referred to that time, an error may well be found in 五十, for he would hardly be speaking at 70 of having 50 years added to his life. Choo also mentions the report of a certain individual that he had seen a copy of the Lun Yu, which read 假 for 加, and 卒 for 卆. Amended thus, the meaning would be—'If I had some more years to finish the study of the Yih, &c.' Ho An interprets the chapter quite differently. Referring to the saying, II. 4, 4, 'At fifty, I knew the decrees of heaven,' he supposes this to have been spoken when Conf. was 47, and explains—'In a few years more I will be fifty, and have finished the Yih, when I may be without great faults.'—One thing remains upon both views:—Confucius never claimed, what his followers do for him, to be a perfect man.

17. CONFUCIUS' MOST COMMON TOPICS. 書, 'The History,' i. e., the historical documents which he compiled into the Shoo-king that has come down to us in a mutilated condition. 詩 also, and much less 禮, must not be understood of the now existing She-king and Le-ke. Choo He explains 雅 (low. 3d tone) by 常, 'constantly.' The old interpr. Ch'ing, explains it by 正 'correctly,'—'Conf. would speak of the Odes, &c., with attention to the correct enunciation of the characters.' This does not seem so good.

〔十八〕葉公問孔子於子路、子路不對。〔二〕子曰、女奚不曰、其爲人也、發憤忘食、樂以忘憂、不知老之將至云爾。

〔十九〕子曰、我非生而知之者、好古、敏以求之者也。

〔二十〕子不語、怪、力、亂、神。

CHAPTER XVIII. 1. The duke of Shě asked Tsze-loo about Confucius, and Tsze-loo did not answer him.

2. The Master said, "Why did you not say to him,—He is simply a man, who in his eager pursuit of knowledge forgets his food, who in the joy *of its attainment* forgets his sorrows, and who does not perceive that old age is coming on?"

CHAPTER XIX. The Master said, "I am not one who was born in the possession of knowledge; I am one who is fond of antiquity, and earnest in seeking it *there*."

CHAPTER XX. The subjects on which the Master did not talk, were—extraordinary things, feats of strength, disorder, and spiritual beings.

18. CONFUCIUS' DESCRIPTION OF HIS CHARACTER, AS BEING SIMPLY A MOST EARNEST LEARNER. 1. 葉 (read *shě*) was a district of Ts'oo (楚), the governor or prefect of which had usurped the title of *kung*. Its name is still preserved in a district of the dep. of 南陽, in the south of Ho-nan. 2. 云 sometimes finishes a sentence (Premare, '*claudit sententiam*'), as here. The 爾 after it = 耳, imparting to all the preceding description a meaning indicated by our *simply* or *only*.

19. CONFUCIUS' KNOWLEDGE NOT CONNATE, BUT THE RESULT OF HIS STUDY OF ANTIQUITY. Here again, acc. to comm., is a wonderful instance of the sage's humility disclaiming what he really had. The comment of 尹和靖, subjoined to Choo He's own, is to the effect that the knowledge born with a man is only 義 and 理, while ceremonies, music, names of things, history, &c., must be learned. This would make what we may call connate or innate knowledge the moral sense, and those intuitive principles of reason, on and by which all knowledge is built up. But Confucius could not mean to deny his being possessed of these. 'I love antiquity;' i. e., the ancients and all their works.

20. SUBJECTS AVOIDED BY CONFUCIUS IN CONVERSATION. 亂, 'confusion,' meaning rebellious disorder, parricide, regicide, and such crimes. Choo He makes 神 here=鬼神造化之迹 'the mysterious, or spiritual operations apparent in the course of nature.' 王肅 (died A. D. 266), as given by Ho An, simply says—鬼神之事, 'the affairs of spiritual beings.' For an instance of Conf. avoiding such a subject, see XI. 11.

〔廿一〕子曰、三人行、必有我師焉、擇其善者而從之、其不善者而改之。

〔廿二〕子曰、天生德於予、桓魋其如予何。

〔廿三〕子曰、二三子、以我爲隱乎、吾無隱乎爾、吾無行而不與二三子者、是丘也。

〔廿四〕子以四教。文、行、忠、信。

CHAPTER XXI. The Master said, "When I walk along with two others, they may serve me as my teachers. I will select their good qualities and follow them, their bad qualities and avoid them."

CHAPTER XXII. The Master said, "Heaven produced the virtue that is in me. Hwan T'uy—what can he do to me?"

CHAPTER XXIII. The Master said, "Do you think, my disciples, that I have any concealments? I conceal nothing from you. There is nothing which I do that is not shown to you, my disciples;—that is my way."

CHAPTER XXIV. There were four things which the Master taught,—letters, ethics, devotion of soul, and truthfulness.

21. HOW A MAN MAY FIND INSTRUCTORS FOR HIMSELF. 三人行, 'Three men walking;' but it is implied that the speaker is himself one of them. The comm. all take 擇 in the sense of 'to distinguish,' 'to determine,'—'I will determine the one who is good, and follow him, &c.' I prefer to understand as in the translation. 改之, 'change them,' i. e., correct them in myself, avoid them.

22. CONFUCIUS CALM IN DANGER, THROUGH THE ASSURANCE OF HAVING A DIVINE MISSION. Acc. to the historical accounts, Conf. was passing through Sung in his way from Wei to Ch'in, and was practising ceremonies with his disciples under a large tree, when they were set upon by emissaries of Hwan T'uy, a high officer of Sung. These pulled down the tree, and wanted to kill the sage. His disciples urged him to make haste and escape, when he calmed their fears by these words. At the same time, he disguised himself till he had got past Sung. This story may be apocryphal, but the saying remains,—a remarkable one.

23. CONFUCIUS PRACTISED NO CONCEALMENT WITH HIS DISCIPLES. 二三子, see III. 24. 與 is explained by Choo He by 示, 'to show,' as if the meaning were, 'There is not one of my doings in which I am not showing my doctrines to you.' But the common signif. of 與 may be retained, as in Ho An,—'which is not given to, shared with, you.' To what the concealment has reference we cannot tell. Observe the force of 者 *foll.* by 也 at the end;—'To have none of my actions not shared with you,—*that* is I, Hew.'

24. THE SUBJECTS OF CONFUCIUS'S TEACHING. 以四教, 'took four things and taught.' There were four things which—or four ways in which—Confucius taught. 文 here—our use *of letters*. 行=人倫日用, 'what is daily used in the relations of life.' 忠=無一念之不盡, 'not a single thought not ex-

二十五 子曰、聖人吾不得而見之矣、得見君子者、斯可矣。(二)子曰、善人吾不得而見之矣、得見有恆者、斯可矣。(三)亡而爲有、虛而爲盈、約而爲泰、難乎有恆矣。

二十六 子釣而不綱、弋不射宿。

二十七 子曰、蓋有不知而作

CHAPTER XXV. 1. The Master said, "A sage it is not mine to see; could I see a man of real talent and virtue, that would satisfy me."

2. The Master said, "A good man it is not mine to see; could I see a man possessed of constancy, that would satisfy me.

3. "Having not and yet affecting to have, empty and yet affecting to be full, straitened and yet affecting to be at ease:—it is difficult with such characteristics to have constancy."

CHAPTER XXVI. The Master angled,—but did not use a net. He shot,—but not at birds perching.

CHAPTER XXVII. The Master said, "There may be those who act without knowing why. I do not do so. Hearing much and selecting what is good and following it, seeing much and keeping it in memory:—this is the second style of knowledge."

hausted,' 倘=無一事之不實, 'not a single thing without its reality.' These are the explanations in the 四書備旨. I confess to apprehend but vaguely the two latter subjects as distinguished from the second.

25. THE PAUCITY OF TRUE MEN IN, AND THE PRETENTIOUSNESS OF, CONFUCIUS' TIME. 子曰, par. 3, is supposed by some to be an addition to the text. That being so, we have in the ch. a climax of character:—the man of constancy, or the single-hearted, stedfast man; the good man, who on his single-heartedness has built up his virtue; the *Keun-tsze*, the man of virtue in large proportions, and intellectually able besides; and the sage, or highest style of man. 聖, from 耳, 口, and 壬, 'ear, mouth, and good,'=intuitively apprehensive of truth, and correct in utterance and action. Comp. Mencius, VII. ii. 25.

26. THE HUMANITY OF CONFUCIUS. 綱 is properly the large rope attached to a net, by means of which it may be drawn so as to sweep a stream. 弋, 'to shoot with a string tied to the arrow, by which it may be drawn back again.' 射, applied to such shooting, lower 4th tone, read *shih*. Confucius would only destroy what life was necessary for his use, and in taking that he would not take advantage of the inferior creatures. This ch. is said to be descriptive of him in his early life.

27. AGAINST ACTING HEEDLESSLY. Paou Heen, in Ho An, says that this was spoken with ref. to heedless compilers of records. Choo He makes 作之 simply=作事, 'to do things,' 'to act.' The paraphrasts make the latter part descriptive of Confucius—'I hear much, &c.' This is not necessary, and the transl. had better be as indefinite as the original.

之者、我無是也。多聞、擇其善者而從之、多見而識之、知之次也。

廿八 互鄉難與言、童子見、門人惑。子曰、與其進也、不與其退也、唯何甚、人潔己以進、與其潔也、不保其往也、

廿九 子曰、仁遠乎哉、我欲仁、斯仁至矣。

三十 陳司敗問昭公知禮乎。孔子曰、知禮。孔子退、揖巫馬期而進

CHAPTER XXVIII. 1. It was difficult to talk with the people of Hoo-heang, and a lad of that place having had an interview with the Master, the disciples doubted.

2. The Master said, "I admit people's approach to me without committing myself *as to what they may do* when they have retired. Why must one be so severe? If a man purify himself to wait upon me, I receive him so purified, without guaranteeing his past conduct."

CHAPTER XXIX. The Master said, "Is virtue a thing remote? I wish to be virtuous, and lo! virtue is at hand."

CHAPTER XXX. 1. The minister of crime of Ch'in asked whether the duke Ch'aou knew propriety, and Confucius said, "He knew propriety."

28. THE READINESS OF CONFUCIUS TO MEET APPROACHES TO HIM THOUGH MADE BY THE UNLIKELY. 1. In 互鄉 the 鄉 appears to be like our local termination *ham*,—'The people of Hoo-ham.' Its site is now sought in three different places. 2. Choo He would here transpose the order of the text, and read 人潔己云云 immediately after 子曰. He also supposes some characters lost in the sentence 唯何甚. This is hardly necessary. 與, as in V. 8, 3,=許, 'to allow,' 'to concede to.'

29. VIRTUE IS NOT FAR TO SEEK. 哉, after 乎, implies the negative answer to be given.

30. HOW CONFUCIUS ACKNOWLEDGED HIS ERROR. 1. Ch'in, one of the states of China in Conf. time, is to be referred probably to the present department of Ch'in-chow in Ho-nan province. 司敗 was the name given in Ch'in and Tsoo to the minister elsewhere called 司寇, which terms Morrison and Medhurst translate—'criminal judge.' But *judge* does not come up to his functions, which were legislative as well as executive. He was the adviser of his sovereign on all matters relating to

之、曰、吾聞君子不黨、君子亦黨乎、君取於吳爲同姓、謂之吳孟子。君而知禮、孰不知禮。巫馬期以告。子曰、丘也幸、苟有過、人必知之。

三十一 子與人歌、而善、必使反之、而後和之。

三十二 子曰、文、莫吾猶人

2. Confucius having retired, the minister bowed to Woo-ma K'e to come forward, and said, "I have heard that the superior man is not a partizan. May the superior man be a partizan also? The prince married a daughter of *the house of* Woo, of the same surname with himself, and called her,—'The elder *lady* Tsze of Woo'. If the prince knew propriety, who does not know it?"

3. Woo-ma K'e reported these remarks, and the Master said, "I am fortunate! If I have any errors, people are sure to know them."

CHAPTER XXXI. When the Master was in company with a person who was singing, if he sang well, he would make him repeat the song, while he accompanied it with his own voice.

CHAPTER XXXII. The Master said, "In letters I am perhaps equal to other men, but *the character of* the superior man, carrying out in his conduct what he professes, is what I have not yet attained to."

crime. See the 周禮,秋官司寇. Ch'aou was the hon. ep. of Chow (稠), duke of Loo, B.C. 541-509. He had a reputation for the knowledge and observance of ceremonies, and Conf. answered the minister's question accordingly, the more readily that he was speaking to the officer of another state, and was bound, therefore, to hide any failings that his own sovereign might have had. 2. With all his knowledge of proprieties, the duke Ch'aou had violated an import. rule,—that which forbids the intermarriage of parties of the same surname. The ruling houses of Loo and Woo were branches of the imperial house of Chow, and consequently had the same surname—*Ke* (姬). To conceal his violation of the rule, Ch'aou called his wife by the surname *Tsze* (子), as if she had belonged to the ducal house of Sung. 取, up. 3d tone = 娶. 3. Conf. takes the criticism of his questioner very lightly.

31. THE GOOD FELLOWSHIP OF CONFUCIUS. On this chapter, see the 四書合講, which states very distinctly the interpretation which I have followed, making only two singings and not three. 和, lower 3d tone, here = 'to sing in unison with.'

32. ACKNOWLEDGMENT OF CONFUCIUS IN ESTIMATING HIMSELF. 莫 here occasions some difficulty. Ho An takes it, as it often is, = 無, and explains, 'I am not better than others in letters.' In the dict., with ref. to this pass., it is explained by 强, so that the meaning would be—'By effort, I can equal other men in letters.' Choo He makes it 疑辭, a 'particle of doubt,' = 'perhaps.' But this is forced for the occasion. 躬行君子, 'an-in-person-acting *superior-man*.'

也、躬行君子、則吾未之有得。

三十三子曰、若聖與仁、則吾豈敢、抑爲之不厭、誨人不倦、則可謂云爾已矣。公西華曰、正唯弟子不能學也。

三十四子疾病。子路請禱。子曰、有諸。子路對曰、有之、誄曰、禱爾于上下神祇。子曰、丘之禱久矣。

CHAPTER XXXIII. The Master said, "The sage and the man of perfect virtue;—how dare I *rank myself with them?* It may simply be said of me, that I strive to become such without satiety, and teach others without weariness." Kung-se Hwa said, "This is just what we, the disciples, cannot imitate you in."

CHAPTER XXXIV. The Master being very sick, Taze-loo asked leave to pray for him. He said, "May such a thing be done?" Taze-loo replied, "It may. In the Prayers it is said, 'Prayer has been made to the spirits of the upper and lower worlds.'" The Master said, "My praying has been for a long time."

33. WHAT CONFUCIUS DECLINED TO BE CONSIDERED, AND WHAT HE CLAIMED. 若 and 抑 are said to be correlatives, in which case they=our 'although' and 'yet.' More naturally, we may join 若 directly with 聖與人, and take 抑 as=our 'but.' 云爾, see ch. 18, 2. 已矣, added to 云爾, increases its emphasis,—'just this and nothing more.'

34. CONFUCIUS DECLINES TO BE PRAYED FOR. 疾病 together mean 'very sick.' 有諸, 諸 is interrogative, as we find it frequently in Mencius. 誄, 'To write a eulogy, and confer the posthumous honorary title;' also, 'to eulogise in prayer,' *i. e.*, to recite one's excellencies as the ground of supplication. Tsze-loo must have been referring to some well known collection of such prayers. In 禱爾, 爾 seems rather to be an expletive than the pronoun. 上下=heaven and earth, 神 being the approp. desig. of the spirits of the former, and 祇 of the latter.—Choo He says, 'Prayer is the expression of repentance and promise of amendment, to supplicate the help of the spirits. If there may not be those things, then there is no need for praying. In the case of the sage, he had committed no errors, and admitted of no amendment. In all his conduct he had been in harmony with the spiritual intelligences, and therefore he said,—*my praying has been for a long time.*' We may demur to some of these expressions, but the declining to be prayed for, and concluding remark, do indicate the satisfaction of Confucius with himself. Here, as in other places, we wish that our information about him were not so stinted and fragmentary.

三十五 子曰、奢則不孫、儉則固、與其不孫也、寧固。

三十六 子曰、君子坦蕩蕩、小人長戚戚。

三十七 子溫而厲、威而不猛、恭而安。

CHAPTER XXXV. The Master said, "Extravagance leads to insubordination, and parsimony to meanness. It is better to be mean than to be insubordinate."

CHAPTER XXXVI. The Master said, "The superior man is satisfied and composed; the mean man is always full of distress."

CHAPTER XXXVII. The Master was mild, and yet dignified; majestic, and yet not fierce; respectful, and yet easy.

35. MEANNESS NOT SO BAD AS INSUBORDINATION. 孫, read *sun*, like 遜, and with the same meaning.

36. CONTRAST IN THEIR FEELINGS BETWEEN THE KEUN-TSZE AND THE MEAN MAN. 坦, 'a level plain' used adverbially with 然,—'lightsomely.' This is its force here. 長=常時, 'constantly.'

37. HOW VARIOUS ELEMENTS MODIFIED ONE ANOTHER IN THE CHARACTER OF CONFUCIUS.

BOOK VIII. T'AE-PIH.

泰伯第八

一 子曰、泰伯其可謂至德也已矣、三以天下讓、民無得而稱焉。

CHAPTER I. The Master said, "T'ae-pih may be said to have reached the highest point of virtuous action. Thrice he declined the empire, and the people *in ignorance of his motives* could not express their approbation of his conduct."

THE HEADING OF THIS BOOK.—泰伯第八, 'T'ae-pih, Book eighth.' As in other cases, the first words of the book give name to it. The subjects of the chapter are miscellaneous, but it begins and ends with the character and deeds of ancient sages and worthies, and on this account it follows the seventh chapter, where we have Confucius himself described.

1. THE EXCEEDING VIRTUE OF T'AE-PIH. T'ae-pih was the eldest son of king T'ae (大), the grandfather of Wan, the founder of the Chow dynasty. T'ae had formed the intention of upsetting the Yin dyn., of which T'ae-pih disapproved. T'ae moreover, because of the sage virtues of his grandson Ch'ang (昌), who afterwards became king Wan, wished to hand

二 子曰、恭而無禮則勞、愼而無禮則葸、勇而無禮則亂、直而無禮則絞。君子篤於親、則民興於仁、故舊不遺、則民不偷。

三 曾子有疾、召門弟子曰、啟予

CHAPTER II. 1. The Master said, "Respectfulness, without the rules of propriety, becomes laborious bustle; carefulness, without the rules of propriety, becomes timidity; boldness, without the rules of propriety, becomes insubordination; straightforwardness, without the rules of propriety, becomes rudeness.

2. "When those who are in high stations perform well all their duties to their relations, the people are aroused to virtue. When old friends are not neglected by them, the people are preserved from meanness."

CHAPTER III. The philosopher Tsăng being sick, he called to him the disciples of his school, and said, "Uncover my feet, uncover my hands. It is said in the Book of Poetry, 'We should be apprehensive and cautious, as if on the brink of a deep gulf, as if treading on thin ice,' *and so have I been.* Now and hereafter, I know my escape *from all injury to my person*, O ye, my little children."

down his principality to his 3d son, Ch'ang's father. T'ae-pih observing this, and to escape opposing his father's purpose, retired with his second brother among the barbarous tribes of the south, and left their youngest brother in possession of the state. The motives of his conduct T'ae-pih kept to himself, so that the people 不得而稱之, 'could not find how to praise him.' There is a difficulty in making out the refusal of the empire *three* times, there being different accounts of the times and ways in which he did so. Chow He cuts the knot, by making 'thrice' = 'firmly,' in which solution we may acquiesce. There is as great difficulty to find out a declining of the empire in T'ae-pih's withdrawing from the petty state of Chow. It may be added that king Woo, the first emperor of the Chow dyn., subsequently conferred on T'ae-pih the posthumous title of Chief of Woo (吳), the country to which he had withdrawn, and whose rude inhabitants gathered round him. His second brother succeeded him in the government of them, and hence the ruling house of Woo had the same surname as the imperial house of Chow, that namely of Tsze (子). See VII. 30. 也已矣 give emphasis to the preceding declaration. Comp. I. 14.

2. THE VALUE OF THE RULES OF PROPRIETY; AND OF EXAMPLE IN THOSE IN HIGH STATIONS. 1. We must bear in mind that the ceremonies, or rules of propriety, spoken of in these books, are not mere conventionalities, but the ordinations of man's moral and intelligent nature in the line of what is *proper*. 絞, 'to strangle,' is here explained by Chow He by 急切. Ho An, after Ma Yung (early part of 2d century), makes it =絞刺, 'sarcasm.' 2. There does not seem any connection between the for. paragraph and this, and hence this is by many considered to be a new chap., and assigned to the philosopher Tsăng. 君子, diff. here from its previous usage, having reference more to the 位 or station of the individuals indicated, than to their 德 or virtue. 故舊=舊臣,故交, 'old ministers and old intimacies' 偷, often a verb, 'to steal;' here an adj., 'mean.'

3. THE PHILOSOPHER TSĂNG'S FILIAL PIETY SEEN IN HIS CARE OF HIS PERSON. We get our bodies perfect from our parents, and should so preserve them to the last. This is a great branch of filial piety with the Ch., and this ch. is said to illustrate how Tsăng-tsze had made

足、啟予手、詩云、戰戰兢兢、如臨深淵、如履薄氷、而今而後、吾知免夫、小子。

四 曾子有疾、孟敬子問之。曾子言曰、鳥之將死、其鳴也哀、人之將死、其言也善。君子所貴乎道者三、動容貌、斯遠暴慢矣、正顏色、斯近信矣、出辭氣、斯遠鄙倍矣、籩豆之事、則有司存。

CHAPTER IV. 1. The philosopher Tsăng being sick, Mang King went to ask how he was.

2. Tsăng said to him, "When a bird is about to die, its notes are mournful; when a man is about to die, his words are good.

3. "There are three principles of conduct which the man of high rank should consider specially important:—that in his deportment and manner he keep from violence and heedlessness; that in regulating his countenance he keep near to sincerity; and that in his words and tones he keep far from lowness and impropriety. As to such matters as attending to the sacrificial vessels, there are the proper officers for them."

this his life-long study. He made the disci. uncover his hands and feet to show them in what preservation those members were. 詩云,—see the Shi-king, II. v. i. st. 6. In 而今, we must take 而 = 自. The whole clause indicates, comm. say, not so much Tsăng's satisfaction in the preservation of his person, as the anxiety which he had had, and would continue to have, if life were prolonged, in preserving it.

4. THE PHILOSOPHER TSANG'S DYING COUNSELS TO A MAN OF HIGH RANK. 1. 敬 was the hon. epi. of 仲孫捷, a great officer of Loo, and son of Mang-woo, II. 6. From the conclusion of this chapter, we may suppose that he descended to small matters below his rank. 之 refers to 疾. 2. 言, in 曾子言曰, intimates that Tsăng commenced the conversation. 3. 動, 正, and 出 are all verbs governing the nouns following. 倍 is read like 背, and with the same meaning, 'to rebel against,' 'to be contrary to,' that here opposed being 道, 'the truth and right.' 籩 was a bamboo dish with a stand, made to hold fruits and seeds at sacrifice; 豆 was like it, and of the same size, only made of wood, and used to contain pickled vegetables and sauces. 君子 is used as in ch. 2.—In Ho An's compilation, the three clauses, begin. 斯遠, are taken differently, and—'thus he will not suffer from men's being violent and insulting, &c., &c.' I prefer the modern view.

[五]曾子曰、以能問於不能、以多問於寡、有若無、實若虛、犯而不校、昔者吾友、嘗從事於斯矣。

[六]曾子曰、可以託六尺之孤、可以寄百里之命、臨大節、而不可奪也、君子人與、君子人也。

[七]曾子曰、士、不可以不弘毅、任重而道遠。仁以爲己

CHAPTER V. The philosopher Tsăng said, "Gifted with ability, and yet putting questions to those who were not so; possessed of much, and yet putting questions to those possessed of little; having, as though he had not; full, and yet counting himself as empty; offended against, and yet entering into no altercation:—formerly I had a friend who pursued this style of conduct."

CHAPTER VI. The philosopher Tsăng said, "Suppose that there is an individual who can be entrusted with the charge of a young orphan *prince*, and can be commissioned with authority over *a state of* a hundred *le*, and whom no emergency however great can drive from his principles:—is such a man a superior man? He is a superior man indeed."

CHAPTER VII. 1. The philosopher Tsăng said, "The scholar may not be without breadth of mind and vigorous endurance. His burden is heavy and his course is long.

5. THE ADMIRABLE SIMPLICITY AND FREEDOM FROM EGOTISM OF A FRIEND OF THE PHILOSOPHER TSANG. This friend is supposed to have been Yen Yuen. 校, 'imprisonment by means of wood,' 'stocks.' The Dict., after the old interpr., explains it with reference to this passage, by [illegible]也, 報也 'altercation,' 'recompensing.' 從事於斯, lit., 'followed things in this way.'

6. A COMBINATION OF TALENTS AND VIRTUE CONSTITUTING A KEUN TSZE. 六尺之孤, 'an orphan of six cubits.' By a comparison of a passage in the Chow Le and other references to the subject, it seems to be established that 'of six cubits' is here equivalent to 'of 15 years,' and that for every cubit more or less we should add or deduct five years. See the 釋註集證, where it is also said that the ancient cubit was shorter than the modern, and only=7.4 in., so that 6 cubits=4.44 cubits of the present day. But this estimate of the ancient cubit is probably still too high. King Wăn, it is said, was 10 cubits high, i. e., 7.4 modern cubits or more than 8½ English feet. 百里之命, see Men. V. ii. 2. 與 amounts nearly to a question, and is answered by 也,—'Yes, indeed.'

7. THE NECESSITY TO THE SCHOLAR OF COMPASS AND VIGOUR OF MIND. 士, 'a learned

任、不亦重乎、死而後已、不亦遠乎。

八章 子曰、興於詩。二立於禮。三成於樂。

九章 子曰、民可使由之、不可使知之。

十章 子曰、好勇疾貧、亂也、人而不仁、疾之已甚、亂也。

2. "Perfect virtue is the burden which he considers it is his to sustain;—is it not heavy? Only with death does his course stop;—is it not long?"

CHAPTER VIII. 1. The Master said, "It is by the Odes that the mind is aroused.

2. "It is by the Rules of propriety that the character is established.

3. "It is from Music that the finish is received."

CHAPTER IX. The Master said, "The people may be made to follow a path of action, but they may not be made to understand it."

CHAPTER X. The Master said, "The man who is fond of daring and is dissatisfied with poverty, will proceed to insubordination. So will the man who is not virtuous, when you carry your dislike of him to an extreme."

man,' 'a scholar,' but in all ages learning has been the qualification for, and passport to, official employment in China, hence it is also a general designation for 'an officer.' 任, low. 3d tone, a noun,—'an office,' 'a burden borne;' with the 1st tone, it is the verb 'to bear.'

8. THE EFFECTS OF POETRY, PROPRIETIES, AND MUSIC. These three short sentences are in form like the four, 志於道, &c., in VII. 6, but must be interpreted differently. There the first term in each sentence is a verb in the imperative mood; here it is in the indicative. There the 於 is to be joined closely to the 1st character and here to the 3d. There it = our prepos. to; here it = by. The terms 詩, 禮, 樂, have all specific reference.

9. WHAT MAY, AND WHAT MAY NOT BE ATTAINED TO WITH THE PEOPLE. According to Choo He, the first 之 is 理之所當然,—duty, what principles require, and the second is 理之所以然, 'the principle of duty.' He also takes 可 and 不可 as = 能 and 不能. If the meaning were so, then the sentiment would be much too broadly expressed. See 四書改錯, XVI. 15. As often in other places, the 翼註 gives the meaning here happily; viz., that a knowledge of the reasons and principles of what they are called to do need not be required from the people,—不可責之民.

10. DIFFERENT CAUSES OF INSUBORDINATION —A LESSON TO RULERS.

十一 子曰、如有周公之才之美、使驕且吝、其餘不足觀也已。

十二 子曰、三年學、不至於穀、不易得也。

十三 一 子曰、篤信好學、守死善道。二 危邦不入、亂邦不居、天下有道則見、無道則隱。三 邦有道、貧且賤焉、恥也、邦無道、富且貴焉、恥也。

CHAPTER XI. The Master said, "Though a man have abilities as admirable as those of the duke of Chow, yet if he be proud and niggardly, those other things are really not worth being looked at."

CHAPTER XII. The Master said, "It is not easy to find a man who has learned for three years without coming to be good."

CHAPTER XIII. 1. The Master said, "With sincere faith he unites the love of learning; holding firm to death, he is perfecting the excellence of his course.

2. "*Such an one* will not enter a tottering state, nor dwell in a disorganized one. When right principles of government prevail in the empire, he will show himself; when they are prostrated, he will keep concealed.

3. "When a country is well governed, poverty and a mean condition are things to be ashamed of. When a country is ill governed, riches and honour are things to be ashamed of."

11. THE WORTHLESSNESS OF TALENT WITHOUT VIRTUE. 'The duke of Chow;'—see VII. 5. 其餘, 'the overplus,' 'the superfluity,' referring to the 'talents,' and indicating that ability is not the 本, or root of character, not what is essential. 也已, as in ch. 1.

12. HOW QUICKLY LEARNING LEADS TO GOOD. This is the interpretation of K'ung Gan-kwŏ, who takes 穀 in the sense of 善. Choo He takes the term in the sense of 祿, 'emolument,' and would change 至 into 志, making the whole a lamentation over the rarity of the disinterested pursuit of learning. But we are not at liberty to admit alterations of the text, unless, as received, it be absolutely unintelligible.

13. THE QUALIFICATIONS OF AN OFFICER, WHO WILL ALWAYS ACT RIGHT IN ACCEPTING AND DECLINING OFFICE. 1. This par. is to be taken as descriptive of character, the effects of whose presence we have in the next, and of its absence in the last. 2. 見 in oppos. to 隱, read *hëen*, low. 3d tone. The whole ch. seems to want the warmth of generous principle and feeling. In fact, I doubt whether its parts bear the relation and connection which they are supposed to have.

子曰、不在其位、不謀其政。

子曰、師摯之始、關雎之亂、洋洋乎、盈耳哉。

子曰、狂而不直、侗而不愿、悾悾而不信、吾不知之矣。

子曰、學如不及、猶恐失之。

子曰、巍巍乎、舜禹之

CHAPTER XIV. The Master said, "He who is not in any particular office, has nothing to do with plans for the administration of its duties."

CHAPTER XV. The Master said, "When the music-master, Che, first entered on his office, the finish with the Kwan Ts'eu was magnificent;—how it filled the ears!"

CHAPTER XVI. The Master said, "Ardent and yet not upright; stupid and yet not attentive; simple and yet not sincere:—such persons I do not understand."

CHAPTER XVII. The Master said, "Learn as if you could not reach your object, and were *always* fearing also lest you should lose it."

CHAPTER XVIII. The Master said, "How majestic was the manner in which Shun and Yu held possession of the empire, as if it were nothing to them!"

14. EVERY MAN SHOULD MIND HIS OWN BUSINESS. So the sentiment of this ch. is generalized by the paraphrasts, and perhaps correctly. Its letter, however, has doubtless operated to prevent the spread of right notions about political liberty in China.

15. THE PRAISE OF THE MUSIC-MASTER CHE. Neither Morrison nor Medhurst gives what appears to be the meaning of 亂 in this ch. K'ang-he's dict. has it—樂之卒章曰亂. 'The last part in the musical services is called *lwan*.' The programme on those occasions consisted of four parts, in the last of which a number of pieces from the *fung* or national songs was sung, commencing with the *Kwan-ts'eu*. The name *lwan* was also given to a sort of refrain, at the end of each song.—The old interpreters explain differently, — 'when the music-master Che first corrected the confusion of the Kwan-ts'eu,' &c.

16. A LAMENTATION OVER MORAL ERROR ADDED TO NATURAL DEFECT. 吾不知之, 'I do not know them,' that is, any common, natural defects of endowment are generally associated with certain redeeming qualities, as hastiness with straightforwardness, &c. In the parties Conf. had in view, these redeeming qualities were absent. He did not understand them, and could do nothing for them.

17. WITH WHAT EARNESTNESS AND CONTINUOUSNESS LEARNING SHOULD BE PURSUED.

18. THE LOFTY CHARACTER OF SHUN AND YU. Shun received the empire from Yaou, B.C. 2254, and Yu received it from Shun, B.C. 2204. The throne came to them not by inheritance. They were called to it by their talents and virtue. And yet the possession of empire did not affect them at all. 不與,—'It did not concern them,' was as if nothing to them. He

有天下也、而不與焉。〔十九章〕子曰、大哉、堯之爲君也、巍巍乎、唯天爲大、唯堯則之、蕩蕩乎、民無能名焉。〔二節〕巍巍乎、其有成功也、煥乎、其有文章。〔二十章〕舜有臣五人、而天下治。〔二節〕武王曰、予有亂臣十人。〔三節〕孔子曰、才難、不其然乎、唐虞之際、於斯爲盛、

CHAPTER XIX. 1. The Master said, "Great indeed was Yaou as a sovereign! How majestic was he! It is only Heaven that is grand, and only Yaou corresponded to it. How vast *was his virtue!* The people could find no name for it.

2. "How majestic was he in the works which he accomplished! How glorious in the elegant regulations which he instituted!"

CHAPTER XX. 1. Shun had five ministers, and the empire was well governed.

2. King Woo said, "I have ten able ministers."

3. Confucius said, "Is not *the saying* that talents are difficult to find, true? *Only* when the dynasties of T'ang and Yu met, were they more abundant than in this *of Chow, yet* there was a woman among them. *The able ministers* were no more than nine men."

An takes 與=求—'They had the empire without seeking for it.' This is not according to usage.

19. THE PRAISE OF YAOU. 1. No doubt, Yaou, as he appears in Chinese annals, is a fit object of admiration, but if Confucius had had a right knowledge of, and reverence for, Heaven, he could not have spoken as he does here. Grant that it is only the visible heaven over-spreading all, to which he compares Yaou, even that is sufficiently absurd. 則之, not simply=法之, 'imitated it,' but 能與之準, 'could equalize with it.' 2. 其有成功=其所有之成功, the great achievements of his government. 文章 (see V. 12)=the music, ceremonies, &c., of which he was the author.

20. THE SCARCITY OF MEN OF TALENT, AND PRAISE OF THE HOUSE OF CHOW. 1. Shun's five ministers were 禹, superintendent of works, 稷, superintendent of agriculture, 契 (sëe), minister of instruction, 臯陶, minister of justice, and 伯益, warden of woods and marshes. Those five, as being eminent above all their compeers, are mentioned. 2. See the Shoo-king, V. I. sect. ii. 6. 亂臣, 'governing, *i. e.*, able ministers.' In the dict., the first meaning given of 亂 is 'to regulate,' and the second is just the opposite,—'to confound,' 'confusion.' Of the ten ministers, the most distinguished of course was the duke of Chow. One of them, it is said next par., was a woman, but whether she was the mother of king Wan, or his wife, is much disputed. 3. Instead of the usual 'the master said,' we have here 孔子曰, 'The philosopher K'ung said.' This

有婦人焉、九人而已。四三分天下有其二、以服事殷、周之德、其可謂至德也已矣。

二十一 子曰、禹吾無間然矣、菲飲食、而致孝乎鬼神、惡衣服、而致美乎黻冕、卑宮室、而盡力乎溝洫、禹吾無間然矣。

4. "*King Wăn* possessed two of the three parts of the empire, and with those he served the dynasty of Yin. The virtue of the house of Chow may be said to have reached the highest point indeed."

CHAPTER XXI. The Master said, "I can find no flaw in the character of Yu. He used himself coarse food and drink, but displayed the utmost filial piety towards the spirits. His ordinary garments were poor, but he displayed the utmost elegance in his sacrificial cap and apron. He lived in a low mean house, but expended all his strength on the ditches and water-channels. I can find nothing like a flaw in Yu."

is accounted for on the ground that the words of king Woo having been quoted immediately before, it would not have done to crown the sage with his usual title of 'the *Master*.' The style of the whole chapter, however, is different from that of any previous one, and we may suspect that it is corrupted. 才難 is a sort of proverb, or common saying, which Conf. quotes and illustrates. 唐虞之際, (Yaou is called T'ang, having ascended the throne from the marquisate of that name, and Yu became the accepted surname or style of Shun.) 於斯爲盛 is understood by Choo He as in the transl., while the old comm. take exactly the opposite view. The whole is obscure. 4. This par. must be spoken of King Wăn.

21. THE PRAISE OF YU. 間, read *Këen*, up. 3d tone, 'a crevice,' 'a crack.' 禹吾無間然矣, '*In Yu, I find* no crevice so,' i. e., I find nothing in him to which I can point as a flaw. 鬼神 is interpreted of the spirits of heaven and earth, as well as those sacrificed to in the ancestral temple, but the saying that the rich offerings were filial (孝) would seem to restrict the phrase to the latter. The 黻 was an apron made of leather, and coming down over the knees, and the 冕 was a sort of cap or crown, flat on the top, and projecting before and behind, with a long fringe on which gems and pearls were strung. They were both used in sacrificing. 溝洫, generally the water-channels by which the boundaries of the fields were determined, and provision made for their irrigation, and to carry off the water of floods. The 洫 were 4 cubits wide and deep, and arranged so as to flow into the 溝, which were double the size.

BOOK IX. TSZE HAN.

子罕第九

[一] 子罕言、利、與命、與仁。

[二] 1. 達巷黨人曰、大哉孔子、博學而無所成名。2. 子聞之、謂門弟子曰、吾何執、執御乎、執射乎、吾執御矣。

CHAPTER I. The subjects of which the Master seldom spoke were—profitableness, and also the appointments *of Heaven*, and perfect virtue.

CHAPTER II. 1. A man of the village of Tă-heang said, "Great indeed is the philosopher K'ung! His learning is extensive, and yet he does not render his name famous by any *particular* thing."

2. The Master heard the observation, and said to his disciples, "What shall I practise? Shall I practise charioteering, or shall I practise archery? I will practise charioteering."

HEADING OF THIS BOOK.—子罕第九. 'The Master seldom, No. 9.' The thirty chapters of this Book are much akin to those of the seventh. They are mostly occupied with the doctrine, character, and ways of Confucius himself.

1. SUBJECTS SELDOM SPOKEN OF BY CONFUCIUS. 利 is mostly taken here in a good sense, not as selfish gain, but as it is defined under the first of the diagrams in the Yih-king,—義之和, 'the harmoniousness of all that is righteous;' that is, how what is right is really what is truly profitable. Comp. Mencius, I. i. 1. Yet even in this sense Conf. seldom spoke of it, as he would not have the consideration of the profitable introduced into conduct at all. With his not speaking of 仁 there is a difficulty which I know not how to solve. The IVth book is nearly all occupied with it, and no doubt it was a prominent topic in Conf. teachings. 命 is not our *fate*, unless in the primary meaning of that term,—'*Fatum est quod dii fantur*.' Nor is it *decree*, or antecedent purpose and determination, but the decree embodied and realized in its object.

2. AMUSEMENT OF CONFUCIUS AT THE REMARK OF AN IGNORANT MAN ABOUT HIM. Comm., old and new, say that the ch. shows the exceeding humility of the sage, educed by his being praised, but his observation on the man's remark was evidently ironical. 1. For want of another word, I render 黨 'by village.' According to the statutes of Chow, 'five families made a 比, four *pe* a 閭, and five *lü* or 500 families a *tang*.' Who the villager was is not recorded, though some would have him to be the same with 項橐, the boy of whom it is said in the 三字經, 昔仲尼師項橐, 'of old Confucius was a scholar to Heang T'o.' The man was able to see that Confucius was very extensively learned, but his idea of fame, common to the age, was that it must be acquired by excellence in some one particular art. In his lips, 孔子 was not more than our 'Mr. K'ung.'

三 子曰、麻冕、禮也、今也純、儉、吾從衆。二 拜下、禮也、今拜乎上、泰也、雖違衆、吾從下。

四 子絕四、毋意、毋必、毋固、毋我。

五 子畏於匡。二 曰、文王既沒、文不在茲乎。三 天之將喪斯文也、後死者、不得與於斯文也、

CHAPTER III. 1. The Master said, "The linen cap is that prescribed by the rules of ceremony, but now a silk one is worn. It is economical, and I follow the common practice.

2. "The rules of ceremony prescribe the bowing below *the hall*, but now the practice is to bow *only* after ascending it. That is arrogant. I *continue to* bow below the hall, though I oppose the common practice."

CHAPTER IV. There were four things from which the Master was entirely free. He had no foregone conclusions, no arbitrary predeterminations, no obstinacy, and no egoism.

CHAPTER V. 1. The Master was put in fear in K'wang.

2. He said, "After the death of king Wăn, was not the cause of truth lodged here *in me*?

3. SOME COMMON PRACTICES INDIFFERENT AND OTHERS NOT. 1. The cap here spoken of was that prescribed to be worn in the ancestral temple, and made of very fine linen dyed of a deep dark colour. There are long discussions about the number of threads that went into its warp. It had fallen into disuse, and was superseded by a simpler one of silk. Rather than be singular, Confucius gave in to a practice which involved no principle of right, and was economical. 2. Choo He explains the 拜下, 拜乎上, thus:—'In the ceremonial intercourse between ministers and their prince, it was proper for them to bow below the raised hall. This the prince declined, on which they ascended and completed the homage.' See this illustrated in the 釋註集證, *in loc.* The prevailing disregard of the first part of the cer., Conf. considered inconsistent with the proper distance to be observed between prince and minister, and therefore he would be singular in adhering to the rule.

4. FRAILTIES FROM WHICH CONFUCIUS WAS FREE. 毋, it is said, is not prohibitive here, but simply negative,=無. This criticism is made to make it appear that it was not by any effort, as 絕 and 毋 would naturally suggest, that Confucius attained to these things.

5. CONFUCIUS ASSURED IN A TIME OF DANGER BY HIS CONVICTION OF A DIVINE MISSION. Comp. VII. 22, but the adventure to which this ch. refers is placed in the sage's history before the other, and seems to have occurred in his 57th year, not long after he had resigned office, and left Loo. 1. There are different opinions as to what state K'wang belonged to. The most likely is that it was a border town of Ch'ing, and its site is now to be found in the dep. of K'ae-fung in Ho-nan. The account is that K'wang had suffered from 陽虎, an officer of Loo, to whom Conf. bore a resemblance. As he passed by the place moreover, a disciple, 顏剋, who had been associated with Yang Foo in his operations against K'wang, was driving him. These circum. made the people think that Conf. was their old enemy, so they attacked him, and kept him prisoner for five days. The accounts of his escape vary, some of them being evidently

天之未喪斯文也、匡人其如予何。

[六] 一 大宰問於子貢曰、夫子聖者與、何其多能也。二 子貢曰、固天縱之將聖、又多能也。三 子聞之曰、大宰知我乎、吾少也賤、故多能、鄙事、君子多乎哉、不多也。四 牢曰、子云、吾不試、故藝。

3. "If Heaven had wished to let this cause of truth perish, then I, a future mortal, should not have got such a relation to that cause. While Heaven does not let the cause of truth perish, what can the people of K'wang do to me?"

CHAPTER VI. 1. A high officer asked Tsze-kung saying, "May we not say that your Master is a sage? How various is his ability!"

2. Tsze Kung said, "Certainly Heaven has endowed him unlimitedly. He is about a sage. And, moreover, his ability is various."

3. The Master heard of the conversation and said, "Does the high officer know me? When I was young, my condition was low, and therefore I acquired my ability in many things, but they were mean matters. Must the superior man have such variety of ability? He does not need variety of ability."

4. Laou said, "The Master said, 'Having no official employment, I acquired many arts.'"

fabulous. The disciples were in fear. 畏 would indicate that Confucius himself was so, but this is denied. 2. 文,—I render by 'the cause of truth.' More exactly, it is the truth embodied in literature, ceremonies, &c., and its use instead of 道, 'truth in its principles,' is attributed to Conf. modesty. 在茲, 'in this,' ref. to himself. 3. There may be modesty in his use of 文, but he here identifies himself with the line of the great sages, to whom Heaven has intrusted the instruction of men. In all the six centuries between himself and king Wăn, he does not admit of such another. 後死者, 'he who dies afterwards,'—a future mortal.

6. ON THE VARIOUS ABILITY OF CONFUCIUS:—HIS SAGEHOOD NOT THEREIN. 1. According to the 周禮, the 大宰 was the chief of the six great officers of state, but the use of the designation in Conf. times was confined to the states of Woo and Sung, and hence the officer in the text must have belonged to one of them. See the 註疏, *in loc.* The force of 與 is as appears in the transl. 2. 與 is responded to by Tsze-kung with 固, 'certainly,' while yet by the use of 將 he gives his answer an air of hesitancy. 縱之, 'lets him go,' i. e., does not restrict him at all. The officer had found the sagehood of Conf. in his various ability;—by

〔七〕子曰、吾有知乎哉、無知也、有鄙夫問於我、空空如也、我叩其兩端而竭焉。

〔八〕子曰、鳳鳥不至、河不出圖、吾已矣夫。

〔九〕子見齊衰者、冕衣裳者、與瞽者、見之、雖少必作、過之必趨。

CHAPTER VII. The Master said, "Am I indeed possessed of knowledge? I am not knowing. But if a mean person, who appears quite empty-like, ask anything of me, I set it forth from one end to the other, and exhaust it."

CHAPTER VIII. The Master said, "The FUNG bird does not come; the river sends forth no map:—it is all over with me."

CHAPTER IX. When the Master saw a person in a mourning dress, or any one with the cap and upper and lower garments of full dress, or a blind person, on observing them *approaching*, though they were younger than himself, he would rise up, and if he had to pass by them, he would do so hastily.

the 又, 'moreover,' Tsze-kung makes that ability only an addit. circum. 3. Conf. explains his possess. of various ability, and repudiates its being essen. to the sage, or even to the *Keun-tsze*. 4. Laou was a disciple, by surname K'in (琴), and styled Tsze-k'ae (子開), or Tsze-chang (子張). It is supposed that when these conversations were being digested into their present form, some one remembered that Laou had been in the habit of mentioning the remark given, and accordingly it was appended to the chapter. 子云 indicates that it was a frequent saying of Confucius.

7. CONFUCIUS DISCLAIMS THE KNOWLEDGE ATTRIBUTED TO HIM, AND DECLARES HIS EARNESTNESS IN TEACHING. The first sentence here was probably an exclamation with reference to some remark upon himself as having extraordinary knowledge. 叩其兩端, 'exhibit (叩=發動, 'to agitate,') its two ends,' i. e., discuss it from beginning to end.

8. FOR WANT OF AUSPICIOUS OMENS, CONFUCIUS GIVES UP THE HOPE OF THE TRIUMPH OF HIS DOCTRINES. The *fung* is the male of a fabulous bird, which has been called the Chinese phenix, said to appear when a sage ascends the throne or when right principles are going to triumph thro' the empire. The female is called 凰. In the days of Shun, they gambolled in his hall, and were heard singing on mount K'e in the time of king Wan. The river and the map carry us farther back still,—to the time of Fuh-he, to whom a monster with the head of a dragon, and the body of a horse, rose from the water, being marked on the back so as to give that first of the sages the idea of his diagrams. Conf. indorses these fables. 吾已矣夫,—see V. 26, and obs. how 乎 and 夫 are interchanged.

9. CONFUCIUS' SYMPATHY WITH SORROW, RESPECT FOR RANK, AND PITY FOR MISFORTUNE. 齊, read *tsze*, is 'the lower edge of a garment' and joined with 衰, read *ts'uy*, 'mourning garments,' the two char. indicate the mourning of the second degree of intensity, where the edge is unhemmed, but cut *even*, instead of being ragged, the terms for which are 斬衰. The phrase, however, seems to be for 'in mourning' generally. 少, up. 3d tone, 'young.'

〔十〕〔一〕顏淵喟然歎曰、仰之
彌高、鑽之彌堅、瞻之在
前、忽焉在後。〔二〕夫子循循
然善誘人、博我以文、約
我以禮。〔三〕欲罷不能、既竭
吾才、如有所立卓爾、雖
欲從之、末由也已。
〔十一〕〔一〕子疾病、子路使門人
爲臣。〔二〕病閒曰、久矣哉、由
之行詐也、無臣而爲有

CHAPTER X. 1. Yen Yuen, *in admiration of the Master's doctrines,* sighed and said, "I looked up to them, and they *seemed to become* more high; I tried to penetrate them, and they *seemed to become* more firm; I looked at them before me, and suddenly they *seemed to be* behind.

2. "The Master, by orderly method, skilfully leads men on. He enlarged my mind with learning, and taught me the restraints of propriety.

3. "When I wish to give over *the study of his doctrines,* I cannot do so, and having exerted all my ability, there seems something to stand right up before me; but though I wish to follow *and lay hold of it,* I really find no way to do so."

CHAPTER XI. 1. The Master being very ill, Tsze-loo wished the disciples to act as ministers to him.

2. During a remission of his illness, he said, "Long has the conduct of Yew been deceitful! By pretending to have ministers when I have them not, whom should I impose upon? Should I impose upon Heaven?

10. YEN YUEN'S ADMIRATION OF HIS MASTER'S DOCTRINES, AND HIS OWN PROGRESS IN THEM. 1. 喟然歎, 'sighingly sighed.' 仰 and the other verbs here are to be translated in the past tense, as the ch. seems to give an account of the progress of Hwuy's mind. 忽焉=忽然, 'suddenly.' 2. 誘=引進, 'to lead forward.' 博我云云,—comp. VI. 25. 3. 卓爾=卓然, an adv., 'uprightly,' 'loftily.' 從之, 'to follow it,' i. e., to advance thereupon to it.' 末, in the sense of 無. 末由=無所由以用其力, 'I have not the means whereby to use my strength.' 也已, 'yea, indeed.'—It was this which made him sigh.

11. CONFUCIUS' DISLIKE OF PRETENSION, AND CONTENTMENT WITH HIS CONDITION. 1. 使, 'was causing,' or wanted to cause. Conf. had been a great officer, and enjoyed the services of ministers, as in a petty court. Tsze-loo would have surrounded him in his great sickness (疾病), with the illusions of his former state, and

臣、吾誰欺、欺天乎。三且予與其死於臣之手也、無寧死於二三子之手乎、且予縱不得大葬、予死於道路乎。

十二子貢曰、有美玉於斯、韞匵而藏諸、求善賈而沽諸。子曰、沽之哉、沽之哉、我待賈者也。

十三子欲居九夷。二或曰、陋、如之何。子曰、君子居之、何陋之有。

十四子曰、吾自衛反魯、然後樂

3. "Moreover, than that I should die in the hands of ministers, is it not better that I should die in the hands of you, my disciples? And though I may not get a great burial, shall I die upon the road?"

CHAPTER XII. Tsze-kung said, "There is a beautiful gem here. Should I lay it up in a case and keep it? or should I seek for a good price and sell it?" The Master said, "Sell it! Sell it! But I would wait till the price was offered."

CHAPTER XIII. 1. The Master was wishing to go and live among the nine wild tribes of the east.

2. Some one said, "They are rude. How can you do such a thing?" The Master said, "If a superior man dwelt among them, what rudeness would there be?"

CHAPTER XIV. The Master said, "I returned from Wei to Loo, and then the music was reformed, and the pieces in the Imperial songs and Praise songs found all their proper place."

brought on himself this rebuke. 3. 縱=縱然, a conjunction, 'letting it be that,'=although.

12. HOW THE DESIRE FOR OFFICE SHOULD BE QUALIFIED BY SELF-RESPECT. 諸 is interrog. here, as in VII. 25. There being no nominative to 韞, like the 'I' in the transl., we might render, 'should it be put, &c.' 賈, read koo, up. 3d tone, = 價, 'price,' 'value.' The disciple wanted to elicit from Conf. why he declined office so much, and insinuated the subject in this way.

13. HOW BARBARIANS CAN BE CIVILIZED. This ch. is to be understood, it is said, like V. 6, not as if Conf. really wished to go among the E, but that he thus expressed his regret that his doctr. did not find accept. in China. 1. 夷, see III. 5. There were nine tribes or varieties (種) of them, the yellow, white, red, &c. 2. 如之何,—the 之 refers to his purpose to go among the E.

14. CONFUCIUS' SERVICES IN CORRECTING THE MUSIC OF HIS NATIVE STATE AND ADJUSTING THE

正、雅頌各得其所。

〔十五〕子曰、出則事公卿、入則事父兄、喪事不敢不勉、不爲酒困、何有於我哉。

〔十六〕子在川上曰、逝者如斯夫、不舍晝夜。

〔十七〕子曰、吾未見好德如好色者也。

〔十八〕子曰、譬如爲山、未成一簣、止、吾止也、譬如平地、雖

CHAPTER XV. The Master said, "Abroad, to serve the high ministers and officers; at home, to serve one's father and elder brother; in all duties to the dead, not to dare not to exert one's-self; and not to be overcome of wine:—what one of these things do I attain to?"

CHAPTER XVI. The Master standing by a stream, said, "It passes on just like this, not ceasing day or night!"

CHAPTER XVII. The Master said, "I have not seen one who loves virtue as he loves beauty."

CHAPTER XVIII. The Master said, "*The prosecution of learning* may be compared to what may happen in raising a mound. If there want but one basket *of earth* to complete the work, and I stop,

Book of Poetry. Conf. returned from Wei to Lû in his 69th year, and died 5 years after. The 雅 (read ya, low. 3d tone), and the 頌, are the names of two, or rather three, of the divisions of the She-king, the former being the 'elegant' or 'correct' odes, to be used with music at imperial festivals, and the praise-songs, celebrating principally the virtues of the founders of different dynasties, to be used in the services of the ancestral temple.

15. CONFUCIUS' VERY HUMBLE ESTIMATE OF HIMSELF. Comp. VII. 2, but the things which Confucius here disclaims are of a still lower char. than those there mentioned. Very remarkable is the last, as from the sage. The old interpr. treat 何有於我哉, as they do in VII. ii. 公卿 stand together, indicat. men of superior rank. If we disting. between them, the 公 may express the princes, high officers in the imperial court, and the 卿, the high officers in the princes' courts.

16. HOW CONFUCIUS WAS AFFECTED BY A RUNNING STREAM. What does the *it* in the transl. refer to? 者 and 如 indicate something in the sage's mind, suggested by the ceaseless move. of the water. Choo He makes it 天地之化, 'the course of nature.' In the 註疏 we find for it 時事, 'events,' 'the things of time.' Probably Choo He is correct. Comp. Mencius, IV. ii. 18.

17. THE RARITY OF A SINCERE LOVE OF VIRTUE. 色, as in I. 7.

18. THAT LEARNERS SHOULD NOT CEASE NOR INTERMIT THEIR LABOURS. This is a fragment, like many other chapters, of some conversation, and the subject thus illustrated must be supplied, after the mod. comm., as in the translation, or, after the old, by 'the following of virtue.' See the Shoo-king, V. v. 9, where the subject is virtuous consistency. We might expect 平 in 平地, to be a verb, like 爲

覆一簣、進、吾往也。

十九 子曰、語之而不惰者、其回也與。

二十 子謂顏淵曰、惜乎、吾見其進也、未見其止也。

廿一 子曰、苗而不秀者、有矣夫、秀而不實者、有矣夫。

廿二 子曰、後生可畏、焉知來者之不如今也、四十五十而無聞焉、斯亦不足畏也已。

the stopping is my own work. It may be compared to *throwing down the earth* on the level ground. Though *but* one basketful is thrown *at a time*, the advancing with it is my own going forward."

CHAPTER XIX. The Master said, "Never flagging when I set forth anything to him;—ah! that is Hwuy."

CHAPTER XX. The Master said of Yen Yuen, "Alas! I saw his constant advance. I never saw him stop in his progress."

CHAPTER XXI. The Master said, "There are cases in which the blade springs, but the plant does not go on to flower! There are cases where it flowers, but no fruit is subsequently produced!"

CHAPTER XXII. The Master said, "A youth is to be regarded with respect. How do we know that his future will not be equal to our present? If he reach the age of forty or fifty, and has not made himself heard of, then indeed he will not be worth being regarded with respect."

is 爲山, but a good sense cannot be made out by taking it so. 雖, as 'tho' only,' as many take it in VI. 26. The lesson of the ch. is—that repeated acquisitions individually small will ultimately amount to much, and that the learner is never to give over.

19. HWUY THE EARNEST STUDENT.

20. CONFUCIUS' FOND RECOLLECTION OF HWUY AS A MORAL STUDENT. This is said to have been spoken after Hwuy's death. 惜乎 looks as if it were so. The 未, 'not yet,' would rather make us think differently.

21. IT IS THE END WHICH CROWNS THE WORK.

22. HOW AND WHY A YOUTH SHOULD BE REGARDED WITH RESPECT. The same person is spoken of throughout the ch., as is shown by the 亦 in the last sentence. This is not very conclusive, but it brings out a good enough meaning. With Conf. remark compare that of John Trebonius, Luther's schoolmaster at Eisenach, who used to raise his cap to his pupils on entering the schoolroom, and gave as the reason—

子曰、法語之言、能無從乎、改之爲貴、巽與之言、能無說乎、繹之爲貴、說而不繹、從而不改、吾末如之何也已矣。

子曰、主忠信、毋友不如己者、過則勿憚改。

子曰、三軍可奪帥也、匹夫不可奪志也。

CHAPTER XXIII. The Master said, "Can men refuse to assent to the words of strict admonition? But it is reforming the conduct because of them which is valuable. Can men refuse to be pleased with words of gentle advice? But it is unfolding their aim which is valuable. If a man be pleased with these words, but does not unfold their aim, and assents to those, but does not reform his conduct, I can really do nothing with him."

CHAPTER XXIV. The Master said, "Hold faithfulness and sincerity as first principles. Have no friends not equal to yourself. When you have faults, do not fear to abandon them."

CHAPTER XXV. The Master said, "The commander of the forces of a large state may be carried off, but the will of even a common man cannot be taken from him."

'There are among these boys men of whom God will one day make burgomasters, chancellors, doctors, and magistrates. Although you do not yet see them with the badges of their dignity, it is right that you should treat them with respect.' 後生, 'after born,' a youth. See 先生, II. 8.

23. THE HOPELESSNESS OF THE CASE OF THOSE WHO ASSENT AND APPROVE WITHOUT REFORMATION OR SERIOUS THOUGHT. 法語之言, 'words of law-like admonition.' 巽, is the name of the diagram, to which the element of 'wind' is attached. Wind enters everywhere, hence the char. is interpreted by 'entering,' and also by 'mildness,' 'yielding.' 巽與之言, 'words of gentle insinuation.' In 繹之爲貴, an anteced. to 之 is readily found in the prec. 言, but in 改之爲貴, such an anteced. can only be found in a roundabout way. This is one of the cases which shows the inapplicability to Chinese composition of our strict syntactical apparatus. 末 as in ch. 10.

24. This is a repetition of part of I. 8.

25. THE WILL UNSUBDUABLE. 三軍, see VII. 10. 帥, read shwae, lower 3d tone, = 將帥, 'a general.' 匹, 'mate.' We find in the dict.—'Husband and wife of the common people are a pair (相匹),' and the applica. of the term being thus fixed, an individual man is called 匹夫, an individual woman 匹婦.

〔二十六〕子曰、衣敝縕袍、與衣狐貉者立、而不恥者、其由也與。〔二〕不忮不求、何用不臧。〔三〕子路終身誦之、子曰、是道也、何足以臧。

〔二十七〕子曰、歲寒、然後知松柏之後彫也。

〔二十八〕子曰、知者不惑、仁者不憂、勇者不懼。

〔二十九〕子曰、可與共學、未可與

CHAPTER XXVI. 1. The Master said, "Dressed himself in a tattered robe quilted with hemp, yet standing by the side of men dressed in furs, and not ashamed;—ah! it is Yew who is equal to this.

2. "'He dislikes none, he courts nothing;—what can he do but what is good?'"

3. Tsze-loo kept continually repeating these *words of the ode*, when the Master said, "Those things are by no means sufficient to constitute perfect excellence."

CHAPTER XXVII. The Master said, "When the year becomes cold, then we know how the pine and the cypress are the last to lose their leaves."

CHAPTER XXVIII. The Master said, "The wise are free from perplexities; the virtuous from anxiety; and the bold from fear."

CHAPTER XXIX. The Master said, "There are some with whom we may study in common, but we shall find them unable to go along with us to principles. *Perhaps* we may go on with them to prin-

26. TSZE-LOO'S BRAVE CONTENTMENT IN POVERTY, BUT FAILURE TO SEEK THE HIGHEST AIMS. 1. On the *structure* of this par., comp. ch. 19. The 狐 is the fox. The 貉, read *hŏ*, is probably the badger. It is described as nocturnal in its habits, yielding a soft, warm, fur. It sleeps much, and is carnivorous. This last characteristic is not altogether inapplicable to the badger. See the 本草, 獸部. 2. See the She-king, I. iii. 8. st. 4. 3. 終身, not 'all his life,' as frequently, but 'continually.' Tsze-loo was a man of impulse, with many fine points, but not sufficiently reflective.

27. MEN ARE KNOWN IN TIMES OF ADVERSITY. 後彫, 'the after-withering,' a meiosis for their being evergreens.

28. SEQUENCES OF WISDOM, VIRTUE, AND BRAVERY. 仁者不憂,—this is one of the sayings about virtue, which is only true of pious trust in God.

29. HOW DIFFERENT INDIVIDUALS STOP AT DIFFERENT STAGES OF PROGRESS. More literally rendered, this ch. would be—'It may be possible with *some parties* together to study, but it may not yet be possible with them to go on to principles, &c.' 權, the weight of a steel-yard,

適道、可與適道、未可與立、可與立、未可與權。

唐棣之華、偏其反而、豈不爾思、室是遠而。子曰、未之思也、夫何遠之有。

ciples, but we shall find them unable to get established in those along with us. Or if we may get so established along with them, we shall find them unable to weigh *occurring events* along with us."

CHAPTER XXX. 1. How the flowers of the aspen-plum flutter and turn! Do I not think of you? But your house is distant.

2. The Master said, "It is the want of thought about it. How is it distant?"

then 'to weigh.' It is used here with ref. to occurring events,—to weigh them and determine the application of principles to them. In the old comm., 權 is used here in opposition to 經, the latter being that which is always, and everywhere right, the former a deviation from that in particular circumstances, to bring things right. This meaning of the term here is denied. The ancients adopted it probably from their interpretation of the second clause in the next ch., which they made one with this.

30. THE NECESSITY OF REFLECTION. 1. This is from one of the pieces of poetry, which Conf. did not admit into his collection, and no more of it being preserved than what we have here, it is not altogether intelligible. There are long disputes about the 唐棣. Choo He makes it a kind of small plum or cherry tree, whose leaves are constantly quivering, even when there is no wind, and adopting a reading, in a book of the Tsin (晉) dyn., of 翩 for 偏, and changing 反 into 翻, he makes out the meaning in the transl. The old comm. keep the text, and interpret,—'How perversely contrary are the flowers of the Tang-tae!' saying that those flowers are first open and then shut. This view made them take 權 in the last ch., as we have noticed. Who or what is meant by 爾 in 爾思, we cannot tell. The two 而 are mere expletives, completing the rhythm. 2. With this par. Choo He compares VII. 30.—The whole ch. is like the 29th of the last book, and suggests the thought of its being an addition by another hand to the original compilation.

BOOK X. HEANG TANG.

鄉黨第十

一 孔子於鄉黨、恂恂如也、似不能言者。二 其在宗廟朝廷、便便言、唯謹爾。

一 朝、與下大夫言、侃侃如也、與上大夫言、誾誾如也。二 君在、踧踖如也、與與如也。

CHAPTER I. 1. Confucius, in his village, looked simple and sincere, and as if he were not able to speak.

2. When he was in the *prince's* ancestorial temple, or in the court, he spoke minutely on every point, but cautiously.

CHAPTER II. 1. When he was waiting at court, in speaking with the officers of the lower grade, he spake freely, but in a straightforward manner; in speaking with the officers of the higher grade, he did so blandly, but precisely.

2. When the prince was present, his manner displayed respectful uneasiness; it was grave, but self-possessed.

HEADING OF THIS BOOK.—鄉黨第十. 'The village, No 10.' This book is different in its character from all the others in the work. It contains hardly any sayings of Confucius, but is descriptive of his ways and demeanour in a variety of places and circumstances. It is not uninteresting, but, as a whole, it does not heighten our veneration for the sage. We seem to know him better from it, and to Western minds, after being viewed in his bedchamber, his undress, and at his meals, he becomes divested of a good deal of his dignity and reputation. There is something remarkable about the style. Only in one passage is he styled 子, '*The Master.*' He appears either as 孔子, 'The philosopher, K'ung,' or as 君子, 'The superior man.' A suspicion is thus raised that the chronicler had not the same relation to him as the compilers of the other books. Anciently, the book formed only one chapter, but it is now arranged under seventeen divisions. These divisions, for convenience in the translation, I continue to denominate chapters, which is done also in some native editions.

1. DEMEANOUR OF CONFUCIUS IN HIS VILLAGE, IN THE ANCESTRAL TEMPLE, AND IN THE COURT. 1. In the dict., quoting from a record of 'the former Han dyn., the 鄉 contained 2,500 families, and the 黨 only 500, but the two terms are to be taken here together, indicating the residence of the Sage's relatives. His native place in Loo is doubtless intended, and perhaps the original seat of his family in Sung. 恂恂如 is expl. by Wang Suh 'mild-like,' and by Choo He, as in the transl., thinking probably that, with that meaning, it suited the next clause better. 2. 便, read p'ëen, lower 1st tone =辯, 'to debate,' 'to discriminate accurately.' 爾=耳. In these two places of high ceremony and of government, it became the sage, it is said, to be precise and particular. Comp. III. 15.

2. DEMEANOUR OF CONFUCIUS AT COURT WITH OTHER OFFICERS, AND BEFORE THE PRINCE. 1. 朝 may be taken here as a verb, lit.='courting.' It was the custom for all the officers to repair at daybreak to the court, and wait for the prince to give them audience. 大夫, 'great officer,' was a general name, applicable

三 君召使擯、色勃如也、足躩如也。②揖所與立、左右手、衣前後、襜如也。③趨進、翼如也。④賓退、必復命曰、賓不顧矣。

四 入公門、鞠

CHAPTER III. 1. When the prince called him to employ him in the reception of a visitor, his countenance appeared to change, and his legs to bend beneath him.

2. He inclined himself to the *other officers* among whom he stood, moving his left or right arm, *as their position required*, but keeping the skirts of his robe before and behind evenly adjusted.

3. He hastened forward, *with his arms* like the wings of a bird.

4. When the guest had retired, he would report to the prince, "The visitor is not turning round any more."

CHAPTER IV. 1. When he entered the palace gate, he seemed to bend his body, as if it were not sufficient to admit him.

to all the higher ministers in a court. At the imperial court they were divided into three classes,—'highest,' 'middle,' and 'lowest,' 上, 中, 下, but the various princes had only the first and third. Of the first order there were properly three, the 卿 or nobles of the state, who were in Loo the chiefs of the 'three families.' Confucius belonged himself to the lower grade. 2. 踧踖, 'the feet moving uneasily,' indicating the respectful anxiety of the mind. 與, low. 1st tone, here appears in the phrase 與與如也, in a new sense.

3. DEMEANOUR OF CONFUCIUS AT THE OFFICIAL RECEPTION OF A VISITOR. 1. The visitor is supposed to be the prince of another state. On the occasion of two princes meeting there was much ceremony. The visitor having arrived, remained outside the front gate, and the host inside his reception room, which was in the ancestral temple. Messages passed between them by means of a number of officers called 介, on the side of the visitor, and 擯, on the side of the host, who formed a zigzag line of communication from the one to the other, and passed their questions and answers along, till an understanding about the visit was thus officially effected. 足躩如 is explained by 盤辟貌, 'the appearance of turning round and inclination.' I suppose I have expressed the idea in the transl. 2. This shows Conf. manner when engaged in the transmission of the messages between the prince and his visitor. The prince's agents, in immediate commun. with himself, was the 上擯, the next was the 承擯, and below were one or more 紹擯. Conf. must have been the *shing pin*, bowing to the right as he transmitted a message to the *shang pin*, who was an officer of the higher grade, and to the left as he transmitted one from him to the *shaou pin*. 3. The host having come out to receive his visitor, proceeded in with him, it is said, followed by all their internuncios in a line, and to his manner in this movement this par. is generally referred. But the duty of seeing the guest off, the subj. of next par., belonged to the *shang pin*, and could not be performed by Conf. as merely a *shing pin*. Hence arises a difficulty. Either it is true that Conf. was at one time raised to the rank of the highest dignitaries of the state, or he was temporarily employed, for his knowl. of ceremo., after the first act in the reception of visitors, to discharge the duties of one. Assuming this, the 趨進 is to be explained of some of his movements in the reception room. How could he hurry forward when walking in file with the other internuncios? See the [illegible]餘說, ii. 23. 4. 必復命, 'would return the commission,' i. e., he had seen the guest off, according to his duty, and reported it. The ways of China, it appears, were much the same anciently as now. A guest turns round and bows repeatedly in leaving, and the host can't return to his place, till these salutations are ended.

4. DEMEANOUR OF CONFUCIUS IN THE COURT AT AN AUDIENCE. 1. The imperial court consisted of five divisions, each having its peculiar

躬如也、如不容。〔二〕立不中門、行不履閾。〔三〕過位、色勃如也、足躩如也、其言似不足者。〔四〕攝齊升堂、鞠躬如也、屏氣似不息者。〔五〕出、降一等、逞顏色、怡怡如也、沒階、趨進、翼如也、復其位、踧踖如也。

〔五〕執圭、鞠躬如也、如

2. When he was standing, he did not occupy the middle of the gate-way; when he passed in or out, he did not tread upon the threshold.

3. When he was passing the *vacant* place *of the prince*, his countenance appeared to change, and his legs to bend under him, and his words came as if he hardly had breath to utter them.

4. He ascended the dais, holding up his robe with both his hands, and his body bent; holding in his breath also, as if he dared not breathe.

5. When he came out *from the audience*, as soon as he had descended one step, he began to relax his countenance, and had a satisfied look. When he had got to the bottom of the steps, he advanced rapidly to his place, *with his arms* like wings, and on occupying it, his manner *still* showed respectful uneasiness.

CHAPTER V. 1. When he was carrying the sceptre *of his prince*, he seemed to bend his body, as if he were not able to bear its weight. He did not hold it higher than the position of the hands in making

gate. That of a prince of a state consisted only of three, whose gates were named 庫, 雉 and 路. The 公門 is the *koo*, or first of these. The bending his body when passing through, high as the gate was, is supposed to indicate the great reverence which Conf. felt. 2. 不中門=不中於門. 'He did not stand opposite the middle of the gate-way.' Each gate had a post in the centre, called 闑, by which it was divided into two halves, appropriated to ingress and egress. The prince only could stand in the centre of either of them, and he only could tread on the threshold or sill. 3. At the early formal audience at day-break, when the prince came out of the inner apartment, and received the homage of the officers, he occupied a particular spot called 宁. This is the 位, now empty, which Confucius passes in his way to the audience in the inner apartment. 4. 齊 see IX.9. He is now ascending the steps to the 堂, 'the dais,' or raised platform in the inner apartment, where the prince held his council, or gave entertainments, and from which the family rooms of the palace branched off. 5. The audience is now over, and Conf. is returning to his usual place at the formal audience. K'ang Gan-kwŏ makes the 位 to be the 宁 in par. 3, but improperly. 進 after 趨 is an addition that has somehow crept into the ordinary text.

5. DEMEANOUR OF CONFUCIUS WHEN EMPLOYED ON A FRIENDLY EMBASSY. 1. 圭, may be

不勝、上如揖、下如授、勃如戰色、足蹜蹜如有循。享禮、有容色。私覿、愉愉如也。

六 君子不以紺緅飾。紅紫不以爲褻服。當暑、袗絺綌、必表而出之。緇衣羔裘、素衣麑裘、黃衣

a bow, nor lower than their position in giving anything to another. His countenance seemed to change, and look apprehensive, and he dragged his feet along as if they were held by something to the ground.

2. In presenting the presents *with which he was charged*, he wore a placid appearance.

3. At his private audience, he looked highly pleased.

CHAPTER VI. 1. The superior man did not use a deep purple, or a puce colour, in the ornaments of his dress.

2. Even in his undress, he did not wear anything of a red or reddish colour.

3. In warm weather, he had a single garment either of coarse or fine texture, but he wore it displayed over an inner garment.

4. Over lamb's fur he wore a garment of black; over fawn's fur one of white; and over fox's fur one of yellow.

translated 'sceptre,' in the sense simply of 'a badge of authority.' It was a precious stone, conferred by the emperor on the princes, and differed in size and shape, according to their rank. They took it with them when they attended the imper. court, and, acc. to Choo He, and the old interpr., it was carried also by their representatives, as their voucher, on occasions of embassies among themselves. In the 攟餘說, II. 53, however, it is contended, appar. on suff. grounds, that the sceptre then employed was different from the other. 勝, up. 1st tone, 'to be equal to,' 'able for.' 2. The prec. par. describes Conf. manner in the friendly court, at his first interview, showing his credentials, and delivering his message. That done, he had to deliver the various presents with which he was charged. This was called 享,—獻. 3. After all the public presents were delivered, the ambassador had others of his own to give, and his interview for that purpose was called 私覿.—Choo He remarks that there is no record of Confucius ever having been employed on such a mission, and supposes that this ch., and the preced., are simply summaries of the manner in which he used to say duties referred to in them ought to be discharged.

6. RULES OF CONFUCIUS IN REGARD TO HIS DRESS.—The discussions about the colours here mentioned are lengthy and tedious. I am not confident that I have given them all correctly in the transl. 1. 君子 used here to denote Confucius can hardly have come from the hand of a disciple. 紺,—深青揚赤色, 'a deep azure flushed with carnation.' 緅,—絳色, 'a deep red;' it was dipped thrice in a red dye, and then twice in a black.' 飾, 'for ornament,' i. e., for the edgings of the collar and sleeves. The last, it is said, by Choo He, after K'ung Gan-kwŏ, was worn in fasting, and the first in mourning, on which account Confucius would not use them. See this and the account of the colours dealt in the 攟餘說, in loc. 2. There are five colours which go by the name

狐裘。五褻裘長、短右袂。六必有寢衣、長一身有半。七狐貉之厚以居。八去喪、無所不佩。九非帷裳、必殺之。十羔裘玄冠不以弔。十一吉月、必朝服而朝。

5. The fur robe of his undress was long, with the right sleeve short.

6. He required his sleeping dress to be half as long again as his body.

7. When staying at home, he used thick furs of the fox or the badger.

8. When he put off mourning, he wore all the appendages of the girdle.

9. His under-garment, except when it was required to be of the curtain shape, was made of silk cut narrow above and wide below.

10. He did not wear lamb's fur, or a black cap, on a visit of condolence.

11. On the first day of the month, he put on his court robes, and presented himself at court.

of 正, 'correct,' viz., 青, 黃, 赤, 白, 黑, 'azure, yellow, carnation, white, and black;' others, among which are 紅 and 紫, go by the name of 閒, or 'intermediate.' See the 集證, in loc. Conf. would use only the correct colours, and moreover, Choo He adds, red and reddish-blue are liked by women and girls. 褻服, his dress, when in private. 3. 絺 and 綌 were made from the fibres of a creeping plant, the 葛. See the She-king, I. i. 2. 必表而出之, 'he must display and have it outwards.' The interpr. of this, as in the transl., after Choo He, tho' diff. from the old comm., seems to be correct. 4. The lamb's fur belonged to the court dress, the fawn's was worn on embassies, the fox's on occasions of sacrifice, &c. 5. Conf. knew how to blend comfort and convenience. 6. This par., it is supposed, belongs to the next ch., in which case it is not the usual sleeping garment of Conf. that is spoken of, but the one he used in fasting. 長, low. 3d tone, 'over,' 'overplus.' 7. These are the 褻裘 of par. 5. 8. The appendages of the girdle were, the handkerchief, a small knife, a spike for opening knots, &c. 去, up. 3d tone, 'to put away.' 9. The 裳 was the lower garment, reaching below the knees like a kilt or petticoat. For court and sac. dress, it was made curtain like, as wide at top as at bottom. In that worn on other occasions, Conf. saved the cloth in the way described. So, at least, says K'ung Gan-kwo. 殺, read shae, up. 3d tone. 10. Lamb's fur was worn black (par. 4), but white is the colour of mourning in China, and Conf. would not visit mourners, but in a sympathizing colour. 11. 吉月, 'the fortunate day of the moon,' i.e., the first of the month. This was Conf. practice, after he had ceased to be in office.

〔七〕一 齊、必有明衣、布。二 齊、必變食、居必遷坐。〔八〕一 食不厭精、膾不厭細。二 食饐而餲、魚餒而肉敗、不食。色惡不食。臭惡不食。失飪不食。不時不食。三 割不正不食。不得其醬不食。四 肉雖多、不使勝食氣。惟酒無量、不及亂。五 沽酒

CHAPTER VII. 1. When fasting, he thought it necessary to have his clothes, brightly clean, and made of linen cloth.

2. When fasting, he thought it necessary to change his food, and also to change the place where he commonly sat in the apartment.

CHAPTER VIII. 1. He did not dislike to have his rice finely cleaned, nor to have his minced meat cut quite small.

2. He did not eat rice which had been injured by heat or damp and turned sour, nor fish or flesh which was gone. He did not eat what was discoloured, or what was of a bad flavour, nor anything which was not in season.

3. He did not eat meat which was not cut properly, nor what was served without its proper sauce.

4. Though there might be a large quantity of meat, he would not allow what he took to exceed the due proportion for the rice. It was only in wine that he laid down no limit for himself, but he did not allow himself to be confused by it.

5. He did not partake of wine and dried meat, bought in the market.

7. RULES OBSERVED BY CONFUCIUS WHEN FASTING. 1. 齊, read *chai*, up 1st tone; see VII. 12. The 6th par. of last ch. should come in as the 2d here. 2. The fasting was not from all food, but only from wine or spirits, and from pot herbs. Observe the diff. between 變 and 遷, the former 'to change,' the lat. 'to change from,' 'to remove.'--The whole ch. may be compared with Matt. VI. 16-18.

8. RULES OF CONFUCIUS ABOUT HIS FOOD. 1. 膾, 'minced meat,' acc. to the comm., was made of beef, mutton, or fish, *uncooked*. 100 *ching* of paddy were reduced to 30, to bring it to the state of 精 rice. 2. 飪, in the dict., is 'overdone,' hence 失飪 = 'wrong in being overdone.' Some, however, make the phrase to mean 'badly cooked,' either, under-done, or overdone. 4. 食 (tsze) 氣, 'the breath of the rice,' or perhaps, 'the life-sustaining power of it,' but 氣 can hardly be translated here. 唯 = 惟, 'only,' showing, it is said, that in other things he had a limit, but the use of wine being to make glad, he could not before-hand set a limit to the quantity of it. 6. Lit., 'He did not take away ginger in eating.' 8. The prince, anciently (and it is still a custom),

市脯不食。[六]不撤薑食。[七]不多食。[八]祭於公、不宿肉。祭肉不出三日、出三日、不食之矣。[九]食不語、寢不言。[十]雖疏食菜羹、瓜祭、必齊如也。

[九章]席不正不坐。

[十章]鄉人飲酒、杖者出、斯出矣。[二]鄉人儺、朝服而立於阼階。

6. He was never without ginger when he ate.

7. He did not eat much.

8. When he had been *assisting* at the prince's sacrifice, he did not keep the flesh *which he received* over night. The flesh of his *family* sacrifice he did not keep over three days. If kept over three days, people could not eat it.

9. When eating, he did not converse. When in bed, he did not speak.

10 Although his food might be coarse rice and vegetable soup, he would offer *a little of it* in sacrifice with a grave respectful air.

CHAPTER IX. If his mat was not straight, he did not sit on it.

CHAPTER X. 1. When the villagers were drinking together, on those who carried staves going out, he went out immediately after.

2. When the villagers were going through their ceremonies to drive away pestilential influences, he put on his court robes and stood on the eastern steps.

distributed among the assisting ministers the flesh of his sacrifice. Each would only get a little, and so it could be used at once. 10. 瓜 should be changed into 必, according to Choo He. Ho An, however, retains it, and putting a comma after it, joins it with the two preced. specimens of spare diet. The 'sacrificing' refers to a custom something like our saying grace. The master took a few grains of rice, or part of the other provisions, and placed them on the ground, among the sacrificial vessels, a tribute to the worthy or worthies who first taught the art of cooking. The Buddhist priests in their monasteries have a custom of this kind, and on public occasions, as when Ke-ying gave an entertainment in Hongkong in 1845, something like it is sometimes observed, but any such ceremony is unknown among the common habits of the people. However poor might be his fare, Confucius always observed it. 齊 chae,=齋, the grave demeanour appropriate to fasting.

9. RULE OF CONFUCIUS ABOUT HIS MAT.

10. OTHER WAYS OF CONFUCIUS IN HIS VILLAGE. 1. At sixty, people carried staves. Conf. here showed his respect for age. 斯 has here an adverbial force,=卽. 2. There were three 儺 ceremonies every year, but that in the text was called 'the great no,' being observed in the winter season, when the officers led all the people of a village about, searching every house to expel demons, and drive away pestilence. It was conducted with great uproar, and little better than a play, but Conf. saw a good old idea in it, and when the mob was in his house, he stood on the eastern steps (the place of a host receiving guests) in full dress. Some make the steps those of his ancestral temple, and his standing there to be to assure the spirits of his shrine.

十一 問人於他邦、再拜而送之。二 康子饋藥、拜而受之、曰、丘未達、不敢嘗。

十二 廐焚、子退朝、曰、傷人乎、不問馬。

十三 君賜食、必正席、先嘗之、君賜腥、必熟而薦之、君賜生、必畜之。二 侍食於君、

CHAPTER XI. 1. When he was sending complimentary inquiries to any one in another state, he bowed twice as he escorted the messenger away.

2. *Ke* K'ang having sent him a present of physic, he bowed and received it, saying, "I do not know it. I dare not taste it."

CHAPTER XII. The stable being burned down, when he was at court, on his return he said, "Has any man been hurt?" He did not ask about the horses.

CHAPTER XIII. 1. When the prince sent him a gift of *cooked* meat, he would adjust his mat, *first* taste it, *and then give it away to others.* When the prince sent him a gift of undressed meat, he would have it cooked, and offer it *to the spirits of his ancestors.* When the prince sent him a gift of a living animal, he would keep it alive.

2. When he was in attendance on the prince and joining in the entertainment, the prince only sacrificed. He first tasted every thing.

11. TRAITS OF CONFUCIUS' INTERCOURSE WITH OTHERS. 1. The two bows were not to the messenger, but intended for the distant friend to whom he was being sent. 2. 康 was the 季康子 of II. 20, *et al.* Conf. accepted the gift, but thought it necessary to let the donor know he could not, for the present at least, avail himself of it.

12. HOW CONFUCIUS VALUED HUMAN LIFE. A 廐 was fitted to accommodate 216 horses. See the 集證, *in loc.* It may be used indeed for a private stable, but it is more natural to take it here for the 國 or state *kew*. This is the view in the 家語.

13. DEMEANOUR OF CONFUCIUS IN RELATION TO HIS PRINCE. 1. He would not offer the cooked meat to the spirits of his ancestors, not knowing but it might previously have been offered by the prince to the spirits of his. But he reverently tasted it, as if he had been in the prince's presence. He 'honoured' the gift of cooked food, 'glorified' the undressed, and 'was kind' to the living animal. 2. The 祭 here is that in ch. 8, 10. Among parties of equal rank, all performed the ceremony, but Conf., with his prince, held that the prince sacrificed for all. He tasted every thing, as if he had been a cook, it being the cook's duty to taste every dish, before the prince partook of it. 3. 首, upper 3d tone, 頭向, 'the direction of the head.' The head to the east was the proper position for a person in bed; a sick man might for comfort be lying differently, but Conf. would not see the prince but in the correct position, and also in the court dress, so far as he could accomplish it. 4. He would not wait a moment, but let his carriage follow him.

君祭、先飯。三 疾、君視之、東首、加朝服拖紳。四 君命召、不俟駕、行矣。

十四 入太廟每事問。

十五 朋友死、無所歸、曰、於我殯。二 朋友之饋、雖車馬、非祭肉不拜。三

十六 寢不尸、居不容。二 見齊衰者、雖狎必變。見冕者、與瞽者、雖褻必以貌。凶

3. When he was sick and the prince came to visit him, he had his head to the east, made his court robes be spread over him, and drew his girdle across them.

4. When the prince's order called him, without waiting for his carriage to be yoked, he went at once.

CHAPTER XIV. When he entered the ancestral temple of the state, he asked about everything.

CHAPTER XV. 1. When any of his friends died, if he had no relations who could be depended on for the necessary offices, he would say, "I will bury him."

2. When a friend sent him a present, though it might be a carriage and horses, he did not bow.

3. The only present for which he bowed was that of the flesh of sacrifice.

CHAPTER XVI. 1. In bed, he did not lie like a corpse. At home, he did not put on any formal deportment.

2. When he saw any one in a mourning dress, though it might be an acquaintance, he would change countenance; when he saw any one wearing the cap of full dress, or a blind person, though he might be in his undress, he would salute them in a ceremonious manner.

14. A repetition of III. 15. Comp. also ch. 2. These two passages make the explanation, given at III. 15, of the questioning being on his first entrance on office very doubtful.

15. TRAITS OF CONFUCIUS IN THE RELATION OF A FRIEND. 1. 殯, properly, 'the closing up of the coffin,' is here used for all the expenses and services necessary to interment. 2. Between friends there should be a community of goods. 'The flesh of sacrifice,' however, was that which had been offered by his friend to the spirits of his parents or ancestors. That demanded acknowledgment.

16. CONFUCIUS IN BED, AT HOME, HEARING THUNDER, &C. 2. Comp. IX. 9, which is here repeated, with heightening circumstances. 3. 式 is the front bar of a cart or carriage. In fact, the carriage of Confucius' time was

服者式之、式負版者。有盛饌、必變色而作。迅雷、風烈、必變。

升車、必正立、執綏。車中、不內顧、不疾言、不親指。

色斯舉矣、翔而後集。曰山梁雌雉、時哉時哉。子路共之、三嗅而作。

3. To any person in mourning he bowed forward to the cross-bar of his carriage; he bowed in the same way to any one bearing the tables of population.

4. When he was at an entertainment where there was an abundance of provisions set before him, he would change countenance and rise up.

5. On a sudden clap of thunder, or a violent wind, he would change countenance.

CHAPTER XVII. 1. When he was about to mount his carriage, he would stand straight, holding the cord.

2. When he was in the carriage, he did not turn his head quite round, he did not talk hastily, he did not point with his hands.

CHAPTER XVIII. 1. *Seeing* the countenance, it instantly rises. It flies round, and by and bye settles.

2. *The Master* said, "There is the hen-pheasant on the hill bridge. At its season! At its season!" Tsze-loo made a motion to it. Thrice it smelt him and then rose.

only what we call a cart. In saluting when riding, parties bowed forward to this bar. 4. He showed these signs, with reference to the generosity of the provider.

17. CONFUCIUS AT AND IN HIS CARRIAGE. 1. The 綏 was a strap or cord, attached to the carriage to assist in mounting it. 2. 不內顧, 'He did not look round within,' *i.e.*, turn his head quite round. See the Le Ke, I. I. 5. p. 43.

18. A fragment, which seemingly has no connect. with the rest of the book. Various corrections of characters are proposed, and various views of the meaning given. Ho An's view of the conclusion is this.—'Tsze-loo took it and served it up. The Master thrice smelt it and rose.' 共, up. 2d tone, = 向.

BOOK XI. SEEN TSIN.

先進第十一

子曰、先進於禮樂、野人也、後進於禮樂、君子也、如用之、則吾從先進。

子曰、從我於陳蔡者、皆不及門也。德行、顏淵、閔子騫、冉伯牛、仲弓。言語、宰我、子貢。政事、冉

CHAPTER I. 1. The Master said, "The men of former times, in the matters of ceremonies and music, were rustics, *it is said*, while the men of *these* latter times, in ceremonies and music, are accomplished gentlemen.

2. "If I have occasion to use those things, I follow the men of former times."

CHAPTER II. 1. The Master said, "Of those who were with me in Ch'in and Ts'ae, there are none to be found to enter my door."

2. Distinguished for their virtuous principles and practice, there were Yen Yuen, Min Tsze-k'een, Yen Pih-new, and Chung-kung; for their ability in speech, Tsae Go and Tsze-kung; for their adminis-

1. HEADING OF THIS BOOK.—先進第十一, 'The former men—No. XI.' With this Book there commences the second part of the Analects, commonly called the *Hea Lun* (下論). There is, however, no classical authority for this division. It contains 25 chapters, treating mostly of various disciples of the Master, and deciding the point of their worthiness. Min Tsze-K'een appears in it four times, and on this account some attribute the compilation of it to his disciples. There are indications in the style of a peculiar hand.

1. CONFUCIUS' PREFERENCE OF THE SIMPLER WAYS OF FORMER TIMES. 1. 先進, 後進, are said by Choo He to=先輩, 後輩. Literally, the expressions are,—'those who first advanced,' 'those who afterwards advanced,' *i.e.*, on the stage of the world. In Ho An, the chap. is said to speak of the disciples who had first advanced to office, and those who had advanced subsequently,—評其弟子之中仕進先後之輩. But the 2d par. is decidedly against this interpretation. 進 is not to be joined to the succeeding 於禮樂, but 於—*regard*. It is supposed that the characterising the 先進 as rustics, and their successors as *keun-tsze*, was a style of his times, which Conf. quotes ironically. We have in it a new instance of the various application of the name *keun-tsze*. In the 備旨, it is said, 'Of the words and actions of men in their mutual intercourse and in the business of government, whatever indicates *respect* is here included in *ceremonies*, and whatever is expressive of *harmony* is here included in *music*.'

2. CONFUCIUS' AFFECTIONATE MEMORY OF HIS DISCIPLES' FIDELITY. CHARACTERISTICS OF TEN OF THE DISCIPLES. 1. This utterance must have been made towards the close of Conf. life, when

有、季路。文學、子游、子夏。

三 子曰、回也、非助我者也、於吾言無所不說。

四 子曰、孝哉閔子騫、人不間於其父母昆弟之言。

五 南容三復白圭、孔子以其兄之子妻之。

trative talents, Yen Yew and Ke Loo; for their literary acquirements, Tsze-yew and Tsze-hea.

CHAPTER III. The Master said, "Hwuy gives me no assistance. There is nothing that I say in which he does not delight."

CHAPTER IV. The Master said, "Filial indeed is Min Tsze-k'een! Other people say nothing of him different from the report of his parents and brothers."

CHAPTER V. Nan Yung was frequently repeating the *lines about a* white sceptre-stone. Confucius gave him the daughter of his elder brother to wife.

many of his disciples had been removed by death, or separated from him by other causes. In his 62d year or thereabouts, as the accounts go, he was passing, in his wanderings from Ch'in to Ts'ae, when the officers of Ch'in, afraid that he would go on into Ts'ae, endeavoured to stop his course, and for several days he and the disciples with him were cut off from food. Both Ch'in and Ts'ae were in the present province of Ho-nan, and are referred to the departments of 陳州 and 汝寧. 2. This par. is to be taken as a note by the compilers of the book, enumerating the principal followers of Conf. on the occasion referred to, with their distinguishing qualities. They are arranged in four classes (四科), and, amounting to ten, are known as the 十哲. The 'four classes' and 'ten wise ones' are often mentioned in connection with the sage's school.

3. HWUY'S SILENT RECEPTION OF THE MASTER'S TEACHINGS. A teacher is sometimes *helped* by the doubts and questions of learners, which lead him to explain himself more fully. Comp. III. 8, 3. 說 for 悅 as in I. 1, 1, but K'ung Gan-kwŏ takes it in its usual pronuncia., = 解, 'to explain.'

4. THE FILIAL PIETY OF MIN TSZE-K'EEN. 間, as in VIII. 21, 'could pick out no crevice or flaw in the words, &c.' 陳羣 (about A.D. 240-250) as given in Ho An, explains—'men had no words of disparagement for his conduct in reference to his parents and brothers.' This is the only instance where Conf. calls a disciple by his designation. The use of 子騫 is supposed, in the 合講, to be a mistake of the compilers.

5. CONFUCIUS' APPROBATION OF NAN YUNG. Nan Yung, see V. 1. 三, as in V. 19. I have translated it by 'frequently,' but, in the 'Family Sayings,' it is related that Yung repeated the lines thrice in one day. 白圭, see the She-king, III. iii. 2, st. 5. The lines there are —'A flaw in a white sceptre-stone, may be ground away; but for a flaw in speech, nothing can be done.' In his repeating of these lines, we have, perhaps, the ground-virtue of the char. for which Yung is commended in V. 1. Obs. 孔子, where we might expect 子.

[六]季康子問弟子孰爲好學。孔子對曰、有顏回者好學、不幸短命死矣、今也則亡。

[七]顏淵死、顏路請子之車、以爲之椁。[二]子曰、才不才、亦各言其子也、鯉也死、有棺而無椁、吾不徒行以爲之椁、以吾從大夫之後、不可徒行也。

[八]顏淵死、子曰、噫、天喪予、天喪予。

CHAPTER VI. Ke K'ang asked which of the disciples loved to learn. Confucius replied to him, "There was Yen Hwuy; he loved to learn. Unfortunately his appointed time was short, and he died. Now there is no one *who loves to learn, as he did.*"

CHAPTER VII. 1. When Yen Yuen died, Yen Loo begged the carriage of the Master to get an outer shell for his *son's* coffin.

2. The Master said, "Every one calls his son his son, whether he has talents or has not talents. There was Le; when he died, he had a coffin but no outer shell. I would not walk on foot to get a shell for him, because, following after the great officers, it was not proper that I should walk on foot."

CHAPTER VIII. When Yen Yuen died, the Master said, "Alas! Heaven is destroying me! Heaven is destroying me!"

6. HOW HWUY LOVED TO LEARN. See VI. 2. where the same question is put by the duke Gae, and the same answer is returned, only in a more extended form.

7. HOW CONFUCIUS WOULD NOT SELL HIS CARRIAGE TO BUY A SHELL FOR YEN YUEN. 1. A great chronological difficulty belongs here. Hwuy, according to the 'Family Sayings,' and the 'Historical Records,' must have died several years before Confucius' son, Le. Either the dates in them are false, or this ch. is spurious.—Yen Loo, the father of Hwuy, had himself been a disciple of the sage in former years. 爲之椁 (*i.q.* char. in text),—this is the idiom noticed in V. 7, 3. 爲 would almost seem to be an active verb followed by a double objective. In burying, they used a coffin, called 棺, and an outer shell, without a bottom which was called 椁. 2. 吾從大夫之後, lit., 'I follow in rear of the great officers.' This is said to be an expression of humility. Confucius, retired from office, might still present himself at court, in the robes of his former dignity, and would still be consulted on emergencies. He would no doubt have a foremost place on such occasions.

8. CONFUCIUS FELT HWUY'S DEATH AS IF IT HAD BEEN HIS OWN. The old interpr. make this simply the exclamation of bitter sorrow. The moderns, perhaps correctly, make the chief in-

〔九〕顏淵死、子哭之慟、從者曰、子慟矣。曰、有慟乎。非夫人之爲慟而誰爲。

〔十〕顏淵死、門人欲厚葬之。子曰、不可。門人厚葬之。子曰、回也、視予猶父也、予不得視猶子也、非我也、夫二三子也。

〔十一〕季路問事鬼神。子曰、未能事人、焉能事鬼。敢

CHAPTER IX. 1. When Yen Yuen died, the Master bewailed him exceedingly, and the disciples who were with him said, "Sir, your grief is excessive?"

2. "Is it excessive?" said he.

3. "If I am not to mourn bitterly for this man, for whom should I mourn?"

CHAPTER X. 1. When Yen Yuen died, the disciples wished to give him a great funeral, and the Master said, "You may not do so."

2. The disciples did bury him in great style.

3. The Master said, "Hwuy behaved towards me as his father. I have not been able to treat him as my son. The fault is not mine; it belongs to you, O disciples."

CHAPTER XI. Ke Loo asked about serving the spirits *of the dead*. The Master said, "While you are not able to serve men, how can you serve *their* spirits?" *Ke Loo added*, "I venture to ask about death?" He was answered, "While you do not know life, how can you know about death?"

gredient in his grief that the man was gone to whom he looked most for the transmission of his doctrines.

9. CONFUCIUS VINDICATES HIS GREAT GRIEF FOR THE DEATH OF HWUY. 1. 哭 is the loud wail of grief. Moaning with tears is called 泣. 3. 夫人=斯人, 'This man.' The third definition of 夫 in the dict. is 有所指之辭 'a term of definite indication.'

10. CONFUCIUS' DISSATISFACTION WITH THE GRAND WAY IN WHICH HWUY WAS BURIED. 1. The old interpreters take 門人 as being the disciples of Yen Yuen. This is not natural, and yet we can hardly understand how the disciples of Confucius would act so directly contrary to his express wishes. Conf. objected to a grand funeral as inconsistent with the poverty of the family (see ch. 7). 3. 視, lit., '*regarded* me,' but that term would hardly suit the next clause. 夫, as in the last ch. This pass., indeed, is cited in the dict. in illustration of that use of the term. 二三子, see III. 24.

11. CONFUCIUS AVOIDS ANSWERING QUESTIONS ABOUT SERVING SPIRITS, AND ABOUT DEATH. 鬼神 are here to be taken together, and understood of the spirits of the dead. This appears

問死。曰、未知生、焉知死。

〔十二〕閔子侍側、誾誾如也、子路行行如也、冉有、子貢、侃侃如也。子樂。〔二〕若由也、不得其死然。

〔十三〕魯人爲長府。〔二〕閔子騫曰、仍舊貫、如之何、何必改作。〔三〕子曰、夫人不言、言必有中。

CHAPTER XII. 1. The disciple Min was standing by his side, looking bland and precise; Tsze-loo, looking bold and soldierly; Yen Yew and Tsze-kung, with a free and straightforward manner. The Master was pleased.

2. He said, "Yew there!—he will not die a natural death."

CHAPTER XIII. 1. Some parties in Loo were going to take down and rebuild the Long treasury.

2. Min Tsze-k'een said, "Suppose it were to be repaired after its old style;—why must it be altered, and made anew?"

3. The Master said, "This man seldom speaks; when he does, he is sure to hit the point."

from Confucius using only 鬼 in his reply, and from the opposition between 人 and 鬼. 人 is man alive, while 鬼 is man dead—a ghost, a spirit. Two views of the replies are found in commentators. The older ones say—'Confucius put off Ke Loo, and gave him no answer, because spirits and death are obscure and unprofitable subjects to talk about.' With this some modern writers agree, as the author of the 翼註, but others, and the majority, say—'Confucius answered the disciple profoundly, and showed him how he should prosecute his inquiries in the proper order. The service of the dead must be in the same spirit as the service of the living. Obedience and sacrifice are equally the expression of the filial heart. Death is only the natural termination of life. We are born with certain gifts and principles, which carry us on to the end of our course.' This is ingenious refining, but, after all, Confucius avoids answering the important questions proposed to him.

12. CONFUCIUS HAPPY WITH HIS DISCIPLES ABOUT HIM. HE WARNS TSZE-LOO. 1. 閔子, like 冉子, VI. 3, 1. 行, read *hang*, low. 3d tone. 2. There wanting here the 子曰 at the commencement, some would change the 樂 at the end of the 1st. par. into 曰, to supply the blank. 若由也,—若 is used with reference to the appearance and manner of Tsze-loo. 然, in the 註疏, is taken as = the final 焉. Some say that it indicates some uncertainty as to the prediction. But it was verified; see on 11. 17.

13. WISE ADVICE OF MIN SUN AGAINST USELESS EXPENDITURE. 1. 魯人, not 'the people of Loo,' but as in the transl.—certain officers, disapprobation of whom is indicated by simply calling them 人. The full meaning of

〔十四〕子曰、由之瑟、奚為於丘之門。門人不敬子路。子曰、由也、升堂矣、未入於室也。〔十五〕子貢問師與商也孰賢。子曰、師也過、商也不及。曰、然則師愈與。子曰、過猶不及。〔十六〕季氏富於周公、而求也為之聚斂而附

CHAPTER XIV. 1. The Master said, "What has the harpsichord of Yew to do in my door?"

2. The other disciples *began* not to respect Tsze-loo. The Master said, "Yew has ascended to the hall, though he has not yet passed into the inner apartments."

CHAPTER XV 1. Tsze-kung asked which of the two, Sze or Shang, was the superior. The Master said, "Sze goes beyond *the due mean*, and Shang does not come up to it."

2. "Then," said Tsze-kung, "the superiority is with Sze, I suppose."

3. The Master said, "To go beyond is as wrong as to fall short."

CHAPTER XVI. 1. The head of the Ke family was richer than the duke of Chow had been, and yet K'ew collected his imposts for him, and increased his wealth.

爲 is collected from the rest of the chapter. 府 is 'a treasury,' as distinguished from 倉, 'a granary,' and from 庫, 'an arsenal.' 'The Long treasury' was the name of the one in question. 2. The use of 貫 is perplexing. Choo He adopts the explanation of it by the old comm. as = 事, 'affair,' but with what propriety I do not see. The character means 'a string of cowries, or cash,' then 'to thread together,' 'to connect.' May not its force be here,—'suppose it were to be carried on—continued—as before'? 3. 夫 as in ch. 9. 中, up. 3d tone, a verb, 'to hit the mark,' as in shooting.

14. CONFUCIUS' ADMONITION AND DEFENCE OF TSZE-LOO. 1. The form of the harpsichord seems to come nearer to that of the *shih* than any other of our instruments. The 瑟 is a kindred instrument with the 琴, commonly called 'the scholar's lute.' See the Chinese Repository, vol. VIII. p. 38. The music made by Yew was more martial in its air than befitted the peace-inculcating school of the sage. 2. This contains a defence of Yew, and an illustration of his real attainments.

15. COMPARISON OF SZE AND SHANG. EXCESS AND DEFECT EQUALLY WRONG. 1. 賢, here = 勝, 'to overcome,' 'be superior to,' being interchanged with 愈 in par. 2. We find this meaning of the term also in the dictionary.

16. CONFUCIUS' INDIGNATION AT THE SUPPORT OF USURPATION AND EXTORTION BY ONE OF HIS DISCIPLES. 1. 季氏, see III. 1. Many illustrations might be collected of the encroachments of the Ke family, and its great wealth. 爲之聚斂, 'for him collected and ingathered,' *i. e.* all his imposts. This clause and the next imply that K'ew was aiding in the matter of laying imposts on the people. 2. 'Beat the

益之。子曰、非吾徒也、小子、鳴鼓而攻之、可也。

十七 一柴也愚、二參也魯、三師也辟、四由也喭。

十八 一子曰、回也其庶乎、屢空。二賜不受命、而貨殖焉、億則屢中。

十九 子張問善人之

2. The Master said, "He is no disciple of mine. My little children, beat the drum and assail him."

CHAPTER XVII. 1. Ch'ae is simple.

2. Sin is dull.

3. Sze is specious.

4. Yew is coarse.

CHAPTER XVIII. 1. The Master said, "There is Hwuy! He has nearly attained *to perfect virtue*. He is often in want."

2. "Tsze does not acquiesce in the appointments *of Heaven*, and his goods are increased by him. Yet his judgments are often correct."

CHAPTER XIX. Tsze-chang asked what were the characteristics of the GOOD man. The Master said, "He does not tread in the footsteps of others, but, moreover, he does not enter the chamber *of the sage*."

drum and assail him,'—this refers to the practice of executing criminals in the market place, and by beat of drum collecting the people to hear their crimes. Comm., however, say that the Master only required the disciples here to tell K'ew of his faults and recover him.

17. CHARACTERS OF THE FOUR DISCIPLES—CH'AE, SIN, SZE, AND YEW. It is supposed a 子曰 is missing from the beginning of this ch. Admitting this, the sentences are to be translated in the present tense, and not in the past which would be required, if the chap. were simply the record of the compilers. 1. Ch'ae, by surname 高, and styled 子羔 (of 羔 there are several other), has his tablet now the 5th west, in the outer court of the temples. He was small and ugly, but distinguished for his sincerity, filial piety, and justice. Such was the conviction of his impartial justice, that in a time of peril he was saved by a man, whom he had formerly punished with cutting off his feet. 3. 辟, read *p'eih*, is defined in the dict.,—'practising airs with little sincerity.'—Confucius certainly does not here flatter his followers.

18. HWUY AND TSZE CONTRASTED. In Ho An's compilation, this ch. is joined with the preceding as one. 1. 庶, here=近, 'nearly,' 'near to.' It is often found with 乎 following, both terms together being=our 'nearly.' To make out a meaning, the old comm. supply 聖道, 'the way or doctrines of the sages,' and the modern supply 道, 'the truth and right.' 空, up. 3d tone, 'emptied,' *i.e.*, brought to extremity, poor, distressed. Hwuy's being brought often to this state is mentioned merely as an additional circumstance about him, intended to show that he was happy in his deep poverty. Ho An preserves the comment of some one, which is worth giving here, and acc. to which, 空=虛中, 'empty—hearted,' free from all vanities and ambitions. Then 屢=每, 'always.' In this sense 屢空 was the formative element of Hwuy's character. 2. 受, 'to receive,' here='to acquiesce in.' 億=度, 'to form a judgment.'

19. THE GOOD MAN. Comp. VII. 23. By 善人 Choo He understands—質美而未

道。子曰、不踐迹、亦不入於室。

〔二十〕子曰、論篤是與、君子者乎、色莊者乎。

〔二十一〕子路問聞斯行諸、子曰、有父兄在、如之何其聞斯行之。冉有問聞斯行諸。子曰、聞斯行之。公西華曰、由也問聞斯行諸、子曰、有父兄在、求也

CHAPTER XX. The Master said, "If, because a man's discourse appears solid and sincere, we allow him *to be a good man*, is he *really* a superior man? or is his gravity only in appearance?"

CHAPTER XXI. Tsze-loo asked whether he should immediately carry into practice what he heard. The Master said, "There are your father and elder brothers *to be consulted*;—why should you act on that principle of immediately carrying into practice what you hear?" Yen Yew asked the same, whether he should immediately carry into practice what he heard, and the Master answered, "Immediately carry into practice what you hear." Kung-se Hwa said, "Yew asked whether he should carry immediately into practice what he heard, and you said, 'There are your father and elder brothers *to be consulted*.' K'ew asked whether he should immediately carry into practice what he heard, and you said, 'Carry it immediately into practice.' I, Ch'ih, am perplexed, and venture to ask you for an explanation." The Master said, "K'ew is retiring and slow; therefore, I urged him forward. Yew has more than his own share of energy; therefore, I kept him back."

善者, 'one of fine natural capacity, but who has not learned.' Such a man will in many things be a law to himself, and needs not to follow in the wake of others, but after all his progress will be limited. The text is rather enigmatical. 入室, comp. ch. 14, 2.

20. WE MAY NOT HASTILY JUDGE A MAN TO BE GOOD FROM HIS DISCOURSE. 論 is here 'speech,' 'conversation.' In Ho An, this ch. is joined to the preceding one, and is said to give additional characteristics of 'the good man,' mentioned on a diff. occasion.—The construction, however, on that view is all but inextricable.

21. AN INSTANCE IN TSZE-LOO AND YEN YEW OF HOW CONFUCIUS DEALT WITH HIS DISCIPLES ACCORDING TO THEIR CHARACTERS. On Tsze-loo's question, comp. V. 13. 聞斯行諸, 'Hearing this (=anything), should I do it at once or not?' 行諸=行之乎, like 舍諸, in VI. 4. 兼人,—兼 is explained by Choo He with 勝, 'to overcome,' 'to be superior to.' But we can well take it in its radical signification of 'to unite,' as a hand grasps two sheaves of corn. The phrase is equivalent to our English one in the transl. Similarly, the best pure gold is called 兼金.

聞斯行諸。子曰、聞斯行之。赤也惑、敢問。子曰、求也退、故進之。由也兼人、故退之。

廿二 子畏於匡、顏淵後。子曰、吾以女爲死矣。曰、子在、回何敢死。

廿三 季子然問仲由冉求、可謂大臣與。二 子曰、吾以子爲異之問、曾由與求之問。三 所謂大臣者、以道事君、不可則止。今由

CHAPTER XXII. The Master was put in fear in K'wang and Yen Yuen fell behind. The Master, *on his rejoining him*, said, "I thought you had died." *Hwuy* replied, "While you were alive, how should I presume to die?"

CHAPTER XXIII. 1. Ke Tsze-jen asked whether Chung-yew and Yen K'ew could be called great ministers.

2. The Master said, "I thought you would ask about some extraordinary individuals, and you only ask about Yew and K'ew!

3. "What is called a great minister, is one who serves his prince according to what is right, and when he finds he cannot do so, retires.

22. YEN YUEN'S ATTACHMENT TO CONFUCIUS, AND CONFIDENCE IN HIS MISSION. See IX. 5. If Hwuy's answer was anything more than pleasantry, we must pronounce it foolish. The comm., however, expand it thus:—'I knew that you would not perish in this danger, and therefore I would not rashly expose my own life, but preserved it rather, that I might continue to enjoy the benefit of your instructions.' If we inquire how Hwuy knew that Conf. would not perish, we are informed that he shared his master's assurance that he had a divine mission.—See VII. 22, IX. 5.

23. A GREAT MINISTER. CHUNG-YEW AND YEN K'EW ONLY ORDINARY MINISTERS. The paraphrasts sum up the contents thus:—'Conf. represses the boasting of Ke Tsze-jen, and indicates an acquaintance with his traitorous purposes.' 1. Ke Tsze-jen was a younger brother of Ke Hwan, who was the 季氏 of III. 1. Having an ambitious purpose on the dukedom of Loo, he was increasing his officers, and having got the two disciples to enter his service, he boastingly speaks to Conf. about them. 2. 吾以云云, lit., 'I supposed you were making a question of (=about) extraordinary men, and lo! it is a question about Yew and K'ew.' 曾=乃; its force is rather diff. from what it has in II. 8, but is much akin to that in III. 6. 4. 具臣 is explained 備臣數而已, 'simply filled to rank among the number of officers.' 具 often means what is merely 'official.' 具文, 'an official paper.' 具臣, 'mere officials.' 5. 之 supposes an antecedent, such as 主, 'their master.'

與求也、可謂具臣矣。曰、然則從之者與。子曰、弑父與君、亦不從也。

子路使子羔爲費宰。子曰、賊夫人之子。子路曰、有民人焉、有社稷焉、何必讀書、然後爲學。子曰、是故惡夫佞者。

子路、曾皙、冉有、公西華、侍坐。子曰、以吾一日

4. "Now, as to Yew and K'ew, they may be called ordinary ministers."

5. Tsze-jen said, "Then they will always follow their chief;—will they?"

6. The Master said, "In an act of parricide or regicide, they would not follow him."

CHAPTER XXIV. 1. Tsze-loo got Tsze-kaou appointed governor of Pe.

2. The Master said, "You are injuring a man's son."

3. Tsze-loo said, "There are (there) common people and officers; there are the altars of the spirits of the land and grain. Why must one read books before he can be considered to have learned?"

4. The Master said, "It is on this account that I hate your glib-tongued people."

CHAPTER XXV. 1. Tsze-loo, Tsăng Sih, Yen Yew, and Kung-se Hwa, were sitting by *the Master*.

2. He said to them, "Though I am a day or so older than you, don't think of that.

24. HOW PRELIMINARY STUDY IS NECESSARY TO THE EXERCISE OF GOVERNMENT:—A REPROOF OF TSZE-LOO. 1. 費,—see VI. 7. This commandantship is probably what Min Sun there refused. Tsze-loo had entered into the service of the Ke family (see last ch.), and recommended (使) Tsze-kaou as likely to keep the turbulent Pe in order, thereby withdrawing him from his studies with the Master. 2. 賊, in the sense of 害, 'to injure.' 夫 as in ch. 9, 2. It qualifies the whole phrase 人之子, and is not to be joined only with 人. By denominating Tsze-kaou—'a man's son,' Conf. intimates, I suppose, that the father was injured as well. His son ought not to be so dealt with. 3. The absurd defence of Tsze-loo. It is to this effect:—'The whole duty of man is in treating others men right, and rendering what is due to spiritual beings, and it may be learned practically without the study you require.' 4. 是故, 'on this account,' with reference to Tsze-loo's reply.

25. THE AIMS OF TSZE-LOO, TSANG SIH, YEN YEW, AND KUNG-SE HWA, AND CONFUCIUS' REMARKS ABOUT THEM. Comp. V. 7. 25. 1. The

長乎爾、毋吾以也。三居則曰、不吾知也、如或知爾、則何以哉。四子路率爾而對曰、千乘之國、攝乎大國之閒、加之以師旅、因之以饑饉、由也爲之、比及三年、可使有勇、且知方也。夫子哂之。五求、爾何如。對曰、方六七十、如五六十、求也爲之、比及三年、可使足民、如其禮樂、以

3. "From day to day you are saying, 'We are not known.' If some *prince* were to know you, what would you do?"

4. Tsze-loo hastily and lightly replied, "Suppose the case of a state of ten thousand chariots; let it be straitened between *other* large states; let it be suffering from invading armies; and to this let there be added a famine in corn and in all vegetables;—if I were intrusted with the government of it, in three years' time I could make the people to be bold, and to recognize the rules of righteous conduct." The Master smiled at him.

5. *Turning to Yen Yew, he said,* "K'ew, what are your wishes?" *K'ew* replied, "Suppose a state of sixty or seventy *le* square, or one of fifty or sixty, and let me have the government of it;—in three years' time, I could make plenty to abound among the people. As to *teaching them* the principles of propriety, and music, I must wait for the rise of a superior man *to do that.*"

disciples mentioned here are all familiar to us excepting Tsăng Sih. He was the father of the more celebrated Tsăng Sin, and himself by name Teen (點). The four are mentioned in the order of their age, and Teen would have answered immediately after Tsze-loo, but that Conf. passed him by, as he was occupied with his harpsichord. 2. 長, up 2d tone, 'senior.' Many understand 爾雖, 'ye,' as nom. to the first 以, but it is better with Choo He to take 以=雖, 'although.' 一日, 'one day,' would seem to indicate the importance which the disciples attached to the seniority of their Master, and his wish that they should attach no importance to it. In 毋吾以也 we have a not uncommon inversion. It = 毋以吾爲長, 'don't consider me to be your senior.' 3. 居=平居之時, 'the level, ordinary, course of your lives.' 何以哉=何以爲用哉, 'what would you consider to be your use?' i.e., what course of action would you pursue? 4. 率爾, an adv., ='hastily.' 攝, acc. to Choo He,=管束, acc. to Paou Heen,=迫, 'straitened,' 'urged.'

俟君子。(六節)赤、爾何如。對曰、非曰能之、願學焉、宗廟之事、如會同、端章甫、願爲小相焉。(七節)點、爾何如。鼓瑟希、鏗爾、舍瑟而作、對曰、異乎三子者之撰。子曰、何傷乎、亦各言其志也。曰、莫春者、春服既成、冠者五六人、童子六七人、浴乎沂、風乎舞雩、詠而歸。夫子喟然歎曰、吾與

6. "What are your wishes, Ch'ih," *said the Master next to Kung-se Hwa.* *Ch'ih* replied, "I do not say that my ability extends to these things, but I should wish to learn them. At the services of the ancestral temple, and at the audiences of the Princes with the Emperor, I should like, dressed in the dark squaremade robe and the black linen cap, to act as a small assistant."

7. *Last of all, the Master asked Tsang Sih,* "Teen, what are your wishes?" *Teen,* pausing as he was playing on his harpsichord, while it was yet twanging, laid the instrument aside, and rose. "My wishes," he said, "are different from the cherished purposes of these three gentlemen." "What harm is there in that?" said the Master; "do you also, as well as they, speak out your wishes." *Teen* then said, "In *this,* the last month of spring, with the dress of the season all complete, along with five or six young men who have assumed the cap, and six or seven boys, I would wash in the E, enjoy the breeze among the rain-altars, and return home singing." The Master heaved a sigh and said, "I give my approval to Teen."

In the Chow Le, 500 men make a 旅, and 5 旅, or 2,500 men, make a 師. The two terms together have here the meaning given in the transl. 爲之, 'managed it.' 比, lower 3d tone, blends its force with the foll. 及. 方＝向, 'towards.' 知方, 'know the quarter to which to turn, the way in which to go.' 5. At the beginning of this paragraph and the two following, we must supply 子曰. 如＝或, 'or.' 6. 能之,—之 refers to the 禮樂 in p. 5. 會 is the name for occasional or incidental interviews of the princes with the emperor, what are called 時見. 同 belongs to occasions when they all presented themselves together at court. The 端, (and from its colour called 元端), was a robe of ceremony, so called from its *straight* make, its component parts having no gathers nor slanting cuttings. 章甫 was the name of a cap of

點也。[八]三子者出、曾皙後、曾皙曰、夫三子者之言何如。子曰、亦各言其志也已矣。[九]曰、夫子何哂由也。[十]曰、爲國以禮、其言不讓、是故哂之。[十一]唯求則非邦也與。安見方六七十、如五六十、而非邦也者。[十二]唯赤則非邦也與。宗廟會同、非諸侯而何。赤也爲之小、孰能爲之大。

8. The three others having gone out, Tsăng Sih remained behind, and said, "What do you think of the words of these three friends?" The Master replied, "They simply told each one his wishes."

9. *Teen* pursued, "Master, why did you smile at Yew?"

10. He was answered, "The management of a state demands the rules of propriety. His words were not humble; therefore I smiled at him."

11. *Teen again said*, "But was it not a state which K'ew proposed for himself?" *The reply was*, "*Yes;* did you ever see a territory of sixty or seventy *le*, or one of fifty or sixty, which was not a state?"

12. *Once more, Teen inquired*, "And was it not a state which Ch'ih proposed for himself?" *The Master again replied*, "*Yes;* who but princes have to do with ancestral temples, and audiences with the Emperor? If Ch'ih were to be a small *assistant* in these *services*, who could be a great one?"

ceremony. It had different names under different dynasties. 甫 means a man. The cap was so named, as 'displaying the man.' 7. 希＝止, 'pausing,' 'stopping.' So, in the dict. 鏗, an adv., expressing the twanging sound of the instrument. 莫, read *moo*, low. 3d tone, the same as 暮, 'sunset,' 'the close of a period of time.' 冠 (up. 3d tone) 者, 'capped men.' Capping was in China a custom similar to the assuming the *toga virilis* among the Romans. It took place at 20. 浴 is not 'to bathe,' but is used with reference to some custom of washing the hands and clothes at some stream in the 3d month, to put away evil influences. 雩 was the name of a sacrifice, accompanied with prayer, for rain. Dancing movements were employed at it, hence the name—舞雩. 11. 曾皙曰 is to be supplied before 唯, and 子曰 before 安. Similar supplements must be made in the next paragraph.—It does not appear whether Teen, even at the last, understood why Conf. had laughed at Tsze-loo, and not at the others. 'It was not,' say the comm., 'because Tsze-loo was extravagant in his aims. They were all thinking of great things, yet not greater than they were able for. Tsze-loo's fault was in the levity with which he had proclaimed his wishes. That was his offence against *propriety*.'

BOOK XII. YEN YUEN.

顏淵第十二

[一] 顏淵問仁。子曰、克己復禮爲仁。一日克己復禮、天下歸仁焉。爲仁由己、而由仁乎哉。[二] 顏淵曰、請問其目。子曰、非禮勿視、非禮勿聽、非禮勿言、非禮勿動。顏淵曰、回雖不敏、請事斯語矣。

CHAPTER I. 1. Yen Yuen asked about perfect virtue. The Master said, "To subdue one's-self and return to propriety, is perfect virtue. If a man can for one day subdue himself and return to propriety, all under heaven will ascribe perfect virtue to him. Is the practice of perfect virtue from a man himself, or is it from others?"

2. Yen Yuen said, "I beg to ask the steps of that process." The Master replied, "Look not at what is contrary to propriety; listen not to what is contrary to propriety; speak not what is contrary to propriety; make no movement which is contrary to propriety." Yen Yuen *then* said, "Though I am deficient in intelligence and vigour, I will make it my business to practise this lesson."

HEADING OF THIS BOOK.—顏淵第十二, 'The twelfth Book, beginning with Yen Yuen.' It contains 24 chapters, conveying lessons on perfect virtue, government, and other questions of morality and policy, addressed in conversation by Confucius chiefly to his disciples. The different answers, given about the same subject to different questioners, show well how the sage suited his instructions to the characters and capacities of the parties with whom he had to do.

1. HOW TO ATTAIN TO PERFECT VIRTUE:—A CONVERSATION WITH YEN YUEN. 1. In Ho An, 克己 is explained by 約身, 'to restrain the body.' Choo He defines 克 by 勝, 'to overcome,' and 己 by 身之私欲, 'the selfish desires of the body.' In the 合講, it is said—己非卽是私,但私卽附身而存,故謂私爲己, '己 here is not exactly selfishness, but selfishness is what abides by being attached to the body, and hence it is said that selfishness is 己.' And again, 克己非克去其己,乃克去己中之私欲也, '克己 is not subduing and putting away the *self*, but subduing and putting away the selfish desires in *the self*.' This 'selfishness in the self' is of a three-fold character:—first, 氣稟, said by Morrison to be 'a person's natural constitution and disposition of mind;' it is, I think, very much the *ψυχικὸς ἄνθρωπος* or 'animal man;' second, 耳,目,口,鼻之欲, 'the desires of the ears, the eyes, the mouth, the nose;' *i. e.*, the dominating influences of the senses; and third, 爾我, 'Thou and I,' *i. e.*, the lust of superiority. More concisely, the 己 is said, in the

二 仲弓問仁。子曰、出門如見大賓、使民如承大祭、己所不欲、勿施於人、在邦無怨、在家無怨。仲弓曰、雍雖不敏、請事斯語矣。

三 司馬牛問仁。子曰、仁者其言

CHAPTER II. Chung-kung asked about perfect virtue. The Master said, "*It is*, when you go abroad, *to behave to every one* as if you were receiving a great guest; to employ the people as if you were assisting at a great sacrifice; not to do to others as you would not wish done to yourself; to have no murmuring against you in the country, and none in the family." Chung-kung said, "Though I am deficient in intelligence and vigour, I will make it my business to practise this lesson."

CHAPTER III. 1. Sze-ma New asked about perfect virtue.

2. The Master said, "The man of perfect virtue is cautious and slow in his speech."

翼註, to be the 人心 as opposed to the 道心, 'the mind of man' in opposition to the 'mind of reason.' See the Shoo-king II. ii. 9. This refractory 'mind of man,' it is said, 與生俱生, 'is innate,' or, perhaps, 'connate.' In all these statements, there is an acknowledgment of the fact—the morally abnormal condition of human nature—which underlies the Christian doctrine of original sin. With ref. to the above three-fold classification of selfish desires, the second par. shows that it was the second order of them—the influence of the senses, which Conf. specially intended. 復禮,—see note on 禮, VIII. 2. It is not here *ceremonies*. Choo He defines it—天理之節文, 'the specific divisions and graces of heavenly principle or reason.' This is continually being departed from, on the impulse of selfishness, but there is an ideal of it as *proper* to man, which is to be sought—'returned to'—by overcoming that. 歸 is explained by Choo He by 與, 'to allow.' The gloss of the 備旨 is—稱其仁, 'will praise his perfect virtue.' The whole sentence thus seems to become a mere platitude. Perhaps 天下 is only = our 'every body,' or 'any body.' In Ho An, *kwei* is taken in the sense of 'to return,'—'the empire will return to perfect virtue,' supposing the exemplifier to be a prince. In the next sentence, which is designed to teach that every man may attain to this virtue for himself, 而='or.' 2. 其 refers to 克己復禮. 目=條目, 'a list' or 'index.' 事 is used as an active verb;—'I beg to make my business these words.'

2. WHEREIN PERFECT VIRTUE IS REALIZED:—A CONVERSATION WITH CHUNG-KUNG. From this ch., it appears that reverence (敬) and reciprocity (恕), on the largest scale, are perfect virtue. 使民,—'ordering the people,' is apt to be done with haughtiness. This part of the answer may be compared with the apostle's precept—'Honour all men,' only the 'all men' is much more comprehensive there. 己所云云,—comp. V. 11. 在邦, 在家,='abroad,' 'at home.' Paou Heen, in Ho An, however, takes the former as denoting the 'prince of a state,' and the lat., 'the chief of a great officer's establishment.' This is like the interpr. of 歸 in last ch.—The answer, the same as that of Hwuy in last ch., seems to betray the hand of the compiler.

3. CAUTION IN SPEAKING A CHARACTERISTIC OF PERFECT VIRTUE:—A CONVERSATION WITH TSZE-NEW. 1. Tsze-new was the designation of Sze-ma Kang (耕, *alias* 犂), whose tablet is

也訒。三曰、其言也訒、斯謂之仁已乎。子曰、爲之難、言之得無訒乎。

四 司馬牛問君子。子曰、君子不憂不懼。二曰、不憂不懼、斯爲之君子矣乎。三子曰、內省不疚、夫何憂何懼。

五 司馬牛憂曰、人皆有兄弟、我獨亡。二子夏

3. "Cautious and slow in his speech!" said New;—"Is this what is meant by perfect virtue?" The Master said, "When a man feels the difficulty of doing, can he be other than cautious and slow in speaking?"

CHAPTER IV. 1. Sze-ma New asked about the superior man. The Master said, "The superior man has neither anxiety nor fear."

2. "Being without anxiety or fear!" said New;—"does this constitute what we call the superior man?"

3. The Master said, "When internal examination discovers nothing wrong, what is there to be anxious about, what is there to fear?"

CHAPTER V. 1. Sze-ma New, full of anxiety, said, "*Other* men all have their brothers, I only have not."

2. Tsze-hea said to him, "There is the following saying which I have heard:—

New the 7th can in the outer ranges of the disciples. He belonged to Sung, and was a brother of Hwan T'uy, VII. 22. Their ordinary surname was Heang (向), but that of Hwan could also be used by them, as they were descended from the duke so called. The office of 'Master of the horse' (司馬) had long been in the family, and that title appears here as if it were New's surname. 3. 訒＝言難出, 'the words coming forth with difficulty.' 3. 爲之, 言之,—comp. on 之 in the note on VII. 10, *et al.* —'Doing being difficult, can speaking be without difficulty of utterance?'

4. HOW THE KEUN-TSZE HAS NEITHER ANXIETY NOR FEAR, AND CONSCIOUS RECTITUDE FREES FROM THESE. 1. 憂 is our 'anxiety,' trouble about coming troubles; 懼 is 'fear,' when the troubles have arrived. 2. 疚, is 'a chronic illness;' here it is understood with ref. to the mind, *that* displaying no symptom of disease.

5. CONSOLATION OFFERED BY TSZE-HEA TO TSZE-NEW ANXIOUS ABOUT THE PERIL OF HIS BROTHER. 1. Tsze-new's anxiety was occasioned by the conduct of his eldest brother Hwan T'uy, who, he knew, was contemplating rebellion, which would probably lead to his death. 兄弟, 'elder brothers' and 'younger brothers,' but Tsze-new was himself the youngest of his family. The phrase simply = 'brothers.' 'All have their brothers,'—*i. e.*, all can rest quietly without anxiety in their relation. 2. It is naturally supposed that the author of the observation was Conf. 4. The 翼註 says that the expr.—'all within the four seas are brothers,' 不是通天譜, 'does not mean that all under heaven have the same genealogical register.' Chu He's

曰、商聞之矣。三死生有命、富貴在天。四君子敬而無失、與人恭而有禮、四海之內、皆兄弟也、君子何患乎無兄弟也。

〔六〕子張問明。子曰、浸潤之譖、膚受之愬、不行焉、可謂明也已矣、浸潤之譖、膚受之愬、不行焉、可謂遠也已矣。

3. "'Death and life have their determined appointment; riches and honours depend upon Heaven.'

4. "Let the superior man never fail reverentially to order his own conduct, and let him be respectful to others and observant of propriety:—then all within the four seas will be his brothers. What has the superior man to do with being distressed because he has no brothers?"

CHAPTER VI. Tsze-chang asked what constituted intelligence. The Master said, "He with whom neither slander that gradually soaks *into the mind*, nor statements that startle like a wound in the flesh, are successful, may be called intelligent indeed. Yea, he with whom neither soaking slander, nor startling statements, are successful, may be called far-seeing."

interpr. is that, when a man so acts, other men will love and respect him as a brother. This, no doubt, is the extent of the saying. I have found no satisfactory gloss on the phrase—'the four seas.' It is found in the Shoo-king, the She-king, and the Le-ke. In the 爾雅, a sort of Lexicon, very ancient, which was once reckoned among the *king*, it is explained as a territorial designation, the name of the dwelling-place of all the barbarous tribes. But the great Yu is represented as having made the four seas as four ditches, to which he drained the waters inundating 'the middle kingdom.' Plainly, the ancient conception was of their own country as the great habitable tract, north, south, east, and west of which were four seas or oceans, between whose shores and their own borders the intervening space was not very great, and occupied by wild hordes of inferior races. See the 四書釋地續, II. 24.—Comm. consider Tsze-hea's attempt at consolation altogether wide of the mark.

6. WHAT CONSTITUTES INTELLIGENCE:—ADDRESSED TO TSZE-CHANG. Tsze-chang, it is said, was always seeking to be wise about things lofty and distant, and therefore Conf. brings him back to things near at hand, which it was more necessary for him to attend to. 浸潤之譖, 'soaking, moistening, slander,' which unperceived sinks into the mind. 膚受之愬 (=and interchanged with 訴), 'statements of wrongs which startle like a wound in the flesh,' to which in the surprise credence is given. He with whom these things 不行,—are 'no go,' is intelligent,—yea, far-seeing. 遠=明之至. So, Choo He. The old interpr. differ in their view of 膚受之愬. The 註疏 says—'The skin receives dust which gradually accumulates.' This makes the phrase synonymous with the former.

七 子一貢問政。子曰、足食、足兵、民信之矣。子二貢曰、必不得已而去、於斯三者何先。曰、去兵。子三貢曰、必不得已而去、於斯二者何先。曰、去食、自古皆有死、民無信不立。

八 一棘子成曰、君子質而已矣、何以文爲。子二

CHAPTER VII. 1. Tsze-kung asked about government. The Master said, "*The requisites of government are* that there be sufficiency of food, sufficiency of military equipment, and the confidence of the people in their ruler."

2. Tsze-kung said, "If it cannot be helped, and one of these must be dispensed with, which of the three should be foregone first?" "The military equipment," said the Master.

3. Tsze-kung *again* asked, "If it cannot be helped, and one of the remaining two must be dispensed with, which of them should be foregone?" The Master answered, "Part with the food. From of old, death has been the lot of all men; but if the people have no faith *in their rulers*, there is no standing *for the state*."

CHAPTER VIII. 1. Kih Tsze-shing said, "In a superior man it is only the substantial qualities which are wanted;—why should we seek for ornamental accomplishments?"

7. REQUISITES IN GOVERNMENT:—A CONVERSATION WITH TSZE-CHANG. 1. 兵 primarily means 'weapons.' 'A soldier,' the bearer of such weapons, is a secondary meaning. There were no standing armies in Conf. time. The term is to be taken here, as='military equipment,' 'preparation for war.' 信之,—之 refers to 其上, 'their ruler.' 3. The difficulty here is with the concluding clause—無信不立. Transferring the mean. of 信 from par. 1, we naturally render as in the transl., and 不立=國不立, 'the state will not stand.' This is the view, moreover, of the old interpreters. Choo He and his followers, however, seek to make much more of 信. On the 1st par. he comments,—'The granaries being full, and the military preparation complete, then let the influence of instruction proceed. So shall the people have faith in their ruler, and will not leave him or rebel.' On the 3d par. he says,—'If the people be without food, they must die, but death is the inevitable lot of men. If they are without 信, though they live, they have not wherewith to establish themselves. It is better for them in such case to die. Therefore it is better for the ruler to die, not losing faith to his people, so that the people will prefer death rather than lose faith to him.'

8. SUBSTANTIAL QUALITIES AND ACCOMPLISHMENTS IN THE KEUN-TSZE. 1. Tsze-shing was an officer of the state of Wei, and, distressed by the pursuit in the times of what was merely external, made this not sufficiently well-considered remark, to which Tsze-kung replied, in, acc. to Choo He, an equally one-sided manner. 1. 何以文爲 is thus expanded in the 註疏,—何用文章乃爲君子, 'why use accomplishments in order to make a

貢曰、惜乎夫子之說、君子也、駟不及舌。三文猶質也、質猶文也、虎豹之鞟、猶犬羊之鞟。

九 哀公問於有若曰、年饑、用不足、如之何。二有若對曰、盍徹乎。三曰、二、吾猶不足、如之何其徹也。四對曰、百姓足、君孰與不足、百姓不足、君孰與足。

2. Tsze-kung said, "Alas! Your words, sir, show you to be a superior man, but four horses cannot overtake the tongue.

3. "Ornament is as substance; substance is as ornament. The hide of a tiger or leopard stript of its hair, is like the hide of a dog or goat stript of its hair."

CHAPTER IX 1. The duke Gae inquired of Yew Jŏ, saying, "The year is one of scarcity, and *the returns for* expenditure are not sufficient;—what is to be done?"

2. *Yew Jŏ* replied to him, "Why not simply tithe the people."

3. "With two tenths," said the duke, "I find them not enough;—how could I do with that system of one tenth?"

4. Yew Jŏ answered, "If the people have plenty, their prince will not be left to want alone. If the people are in want, their prince cannot enjoy plenty alone."

Keun-tsze? 2. We may interpret this par., as in the transl., putting a comma after 說. So, Choo He. But the old interpr. seem to have read right on, without any comma, to 也, in which case the par. would be—'alas! sir, for the way in which you speak of the superior man!' And this is the most natural construction. 3. The mod. comm. seem hypercritical in condemning Tsze-kung's language here. He shows the desirableness of the ornamental accomplishments, but does not necessarily put them on the same level with the substantial qualities.

9. LIGHT TAXATION THE BEST WAY TO SECURE THE GOVERNMENT FROM EMBARRASSMENT FOR WANT OF FUNDS. 2. By the statutes of the Chow dynasty, the ground was divided into allotments cultivated in common by the families located upon them, and the produce was divided equally, nine tenths being given to the farmers, and one tenth being reserved as a contribution to the state. This was called the law of 徹, which term=通, 'pervading,' 'general,' with ref., apparently, to the system of common labour. 3. A former duke of Loo, Seuen (B. C. 608-590), had imposed an additional tax of another tenth from each family's portion. 4. The meaning of this par. is given in the transl. Literally rendered, it is,—'The people having plenty, the prince—with whom not plenty? The people not having plenty, with whom can the prince have plenty?' Yew Jŏ wished to impress on the duke that a sympathy and common condition should unite him and his people. If he lightened his taxation to the regular tithe, then they would cultivate their allotments with so much vigour, that his receipts would be abundant. They would be able, moreover, to help their kind ruler in any emergency.

十 子張問崇德辨惑。子曰、主忠信、徙義、崇德也。愛之欲其生、惡之欲其死、既欲其生、又欲其死、是惑也。誠不以富、亦祇以異。

十一 齊景公問政於孔子。孔子對曰、君君、臣臣、父父、子子。公曰、善哉、信如君不君、臣不臣、父不父、子不子、雖有粟、吾得而食諸。

CHAPTER X. 1. Tsze-chang having asked how virtue was to be exalted, and delusions to be discovered, the Master said, "Hold faithfulness and sincerity as first principles, and be moving continually to what is right;—this is the way to exalt one's virtue.

2. "You love a man and wish him to live; you hate him and wish him to die. Having wished him to live, you also wish him to die. This is a case of delusion.

3. "'It may not be on account of her being rich, yet you come to make a difference.'"

CHAPTER XI. 1. The duke King, of Ts'e, asked Confucius about government.

2. Confucius replied, "*There is government*, when the prince is prince, and the minister is minister; when the father is father, and the son is son."

3. "Good!" said the duke; "if, indeed, the prince be not prince, the minister not minister, the father not father, and the son not son, although I have my revenue, can I enjoy it?"

10. HOW TO EXALT VIRTUE AND DISCOVER DELUSIONS. 1. 主忠信,—see I. 8. 2. The Master says nothing about the 辨, 'discriminating,' or 'discovering,' of delusions, but gives an instance of a twofold delusion. Life and death, it is said, are independent of our wishes. To desire for a man either the one or the other, therefore, is one delusion. And on the change of our feelings to change our wishes in reference to the same person, is another. 之,—此人.—But in this Confucius hardly appears to be the sage. 3. See the Shih-king, II. iv. 4. st. 3. I have translated according to the meaning in the Shih-king. The quotation may be twisted into some sort of accordance with the preceding par., as a case of delusion, but the comm. Ch'ing (程) is probably correct in supposing that it should be transferred to XVI. 12.

11. GOOD GOVERNMENT OBTAINS ONLY WHEN ALL THE RELATIVE DUTIES ARE MAINTAINED. 1. Conf. went to Ts'e in his 36th year, and finding the reigning duke—styled *King* after his death—overshadowed by his ministers, and thinking of setting aside his eldest son from the succes-

十二 子曰、片言可以折獄者、其由也與。子路無宿諾。

十三 子曰、聽訟、吾猶人也、必也、使無訟乎。

十四 子張問政。子曰、居之無倦、行之以忠。

十五 子曰、博學於文、約之以禮、亦可以弗畔矣夫。

CHAPTER XII. 1. The Master said, "Ah! it is Yew, who could with half a word settle litigations!"

2. Tsze-loo never slept over a promise.

CHAPTER XIII. The Master said, "In hearing litigations, I am like any other body. What is necessary, is to cause *the people* to have no litigations."

CHAPTER XIV. Tsze-chang asked about government. The Master said, "*The art of governing* is to keep *its affairs* before the mind without weariness, and to practise them with undeviating consistency."

CHAPTER XV. The Master said, "By extensively studying all learning, and keeping himself under the restraint of the rules of propriety, *one* may thus likewise not err from what is right."

sion, he shaped his answer to the question about government accordingly. 6 雖有粟, 'although I have the grain,' i.e., my revenue, the tithe of the produce of the country. 吾得而食諸 (食諸, comp. 行諸, XI. 21), 'shall I be able to eat it?'—intimating a sense of the danger he was exposed to from his insubordinate officers.

12. WITH WHAT EASE TSZE-LOO COULD SETTLE LITIGATIONS. 1. We translate here—'could,' and not—'can,' because Conf. is not referring to facts, but simply praising the disciple's character. 片言=半言, 'half a word.' 2. This par. is a note by the compilers, stating a fact about Tsze-loo, to illustrate what the Master said of him. 宿 is explained by Choo He by 留, 'to leave,' 'to let remain.' Its prim. mean. is—'to pass a night.' We have in English, as given in the transl., a corresponding idiom.—In Ho An, 片言 is taken as=偏言, 'one-sided words,' mean. that Tsze-loo could judge rightly on hearing half a case. 宿 again is explained by 豫, 'beforehand.'—'Tsze-loo made no promises beforehand.'

13. TO PREVENT BETTER THAN TO DETERMINE LITIGATIONS. See the 大學傳, IV. 訟, as oppos. to 獄 (prec. ch.) is used of civil causes (爭財曰訟), and the other of criminal (爭罪曰獄). Little stress is to be laid on the 'I.' 吾猶人 simply='One man is as good as another.' Much stress is to be laid on 使, as='to influence to.'

14. THE ART OF GOVERNING. 居, as oppos. to 行, must be an active verb, and is explained by Choo He as in the translation. 之 refers to 政, or, rather, that aspect of government about which Tsze-chang was inquiring. 無倦=始終如一, 'first and last the same;' 以忠=表裏如一, 'externally and internally the same.'

15. HARDLY DIFFERENT FROM VI. 25.

[十六]子曰、君子成人之美、不成人之惡、小人反是。

[十七]季康子問政於孔子。孔子對曰、政者正也、子帥以正、孰敢不正。

[十八]季康子患盜、問於孔子。孔子對曰、苟子之不欲、雖賞之不竊。

[十九]季康子問政於孔子、曰、如殺無道、以就有道、何如。

CHAPTER XVI. The Master said, "The superior man *seeks to* perfect the admirable qualities of men, and does not *seek to* perfect their bad qualities. The mean man does the opposite of this."

CHAPTER XVII. Ke K'ang asked Confucius about government. Confucius replied, "To govern means to rectify. If you lead on *the people* with correctness, who will dare not to be correct?"

CHAPTER XVIII. Ke K'ang distressed about the number of thieves *in the state*, inquired of Confucius *about how to do away with them*. Confucius said, "If you, sir, were not covetous, although you should reward them to do it, they would not steal."

CHAPTER XIX. Ke K'ang asked Confucius about government, saying, "What do you say to killing the unprincipled for the good of the principled?" Confucius replied, "Sir, in carrying on your government, why should you use killing at all? Let your *evinced*

16. OPPOSITE INFLUENCE UPON OTHERS OF THE SUPERIOR MAN AND THE MEAN MAN.

17. GOVERNMENT MORAL IN ITS END, AND EFFICIENT BY EXAMPLE.

18. THE PEOPLE ARE MADE THIEVES BY THE EXAMPLE OF THEIR RULERS. This is a good instance of Conf. boldness in reproving men in power. Ke K'ang had confirmed himself as head of the Ke family, and entered into all its usurpations, by taking off the infant nephew, who should have been its rightful chief. 不欲=不貪, 'did not covet,' i.e., a position and influence to which you have no right. 苟子之不欲, 'given the fact of your not being ambitious.' 賞之=賞民.

19. KILLING NOT TO BE TALKED OF BY RULERS; THE EFFECT OF THEIR EXAMPLE. In 就有道, 就 is an active verb,=成, or 成就, 'to complete,' 'to perfect.' 德 is used in a vague sense, not positive virtue, but='nature,' 'character.' Some for 上 would read 尙=加, 'to add upon,' but 上 itself must here have substantially that meaning. 草上之風=草加之以風, 'the grass, having the wind upon it.'

孔子對曰、子爲政、焉用殺、子欲善、而民善矣、君子之德風、小人之德草、草上之風、必偃。

二十章 一 子張問士何如、斯可謂之達矣。二 子曰、何哉、爾所謂達者。三 子張對曰、在邦必聞、在家必聞。四 子曰、是聞也、非達也。五 夫達也者、質直而好義、察言而觀色、慮以下人、在邦必達、在家必達。六 夫聞也者、色取仁而行

desires be for what is good, and the people will be good. The relation between superiors and inferiors, is like that between the wind and the grass. The grass must bend, when the wind blows across it."

CHAPTER XX. 1. Tsze-chang asked, "What must the officer be, who may be said to be distinguished?"

2. The Master said, "What is it you call being distinguished?"

3. Tsze-chang replied, "It is to be heard of through the state, to be heard of through the family."

4. The Master said, "That is notoriety, not distinction.

5. "Now, the man of distinction is solid and straightforward, and loves righteousness. He examines people's words, and looks at their countenances. He is anxious to humble himself to others. Such a man will be distinguished in the country; he will be distinguished in the family.

6. "As to the man of notoriety, he assumes the appearance of vir-

20. THE MAN OF TRUE DISTINCTION, AND THE MAN OF NOTORIETY. 1. 士 'a scholar,' 'an officer.' The two ideas blend together in China. 達=通達, 'to reach all round.' It includes here the ideas of being influential, and that influence being acknowledged. 3. If 士 be understood of 'an officer,' then 在邦 assumes him to be the minister of a prince of a state, and 在家, that he is only the minister of a great officer, who is the head of a family. If, however, 士 be understood of 'a scholar,' 邦 will=州里, 'the country,' 'people generally,' and 家 will=族黨, 'the circle of relatives and neighbours.' 5. 也者, see I. 2. 下人,—下 is the verb. The dict. explains it—降也, 自上而下也, 'to descend. From being on high to become low.' But it is here rather more still. 下人, 'to come down below *other* men.'

違、居之不疑、在邦必聞、在家必聞。

〔二一〕[一] 樊遲從遊於舞雩之下、曰、敢問崇德修慝辨惑。子[二] 曰、善哉問。[三] 先事後得、非崇德與、攻其惡、無攻人之惡、非修慝與、一朝之忿、忘其身以及其親、非惑與。

〔二二〕[一] 樊遲問仁。子曰、愛人。問

tue, but his actions are opposed to it, and he rests in this character without any doubts *about himself*. Such a man will be heard of in the country; he will be heard of in the family."

CHAPTER XXI. 1. Fan-ch'e rambling with the Master under *the trees* about the rain-altars, said, "I venture to ask how to exalt virtue, to correct cherished evil, and to discover delusions."

2. The Master said, "Truly a good question!

3. "If doing what is to be done be made the first business, and success a secondary consideration;—is not this the way to exalt virtue? To assail one's own wickedness and not assail that of others;—is not this the way to correct cherished evil? For a morning's anger, to disregard one's own life, and involve that of his parents;—is not this a case of delusion?"

CHAPTER XXII. 1. Fan Ch'e asked about benevolence. The Master said, "It is to love *all* men." He asked about knowledge. The Master said, "It is to know *all* men."

2. Fan Ch'e did not immediately understand *these answers.*

21. HOW TO EXALT VIRTUE, CORRECT VICE, AND DISCOVER DELUSIONS. Comp. ch. 10. Here, as there, under the last point of the inquiry, Conf. simply indicates a case of delusion, and perhaps that is the best way to teach how to discover delusions generally. 1. 舞雩, see XI. 25, 11; followed here by 之下, there must be reference to the trees growing about the altars. 慝, formed from 'heart' and 'to conceal,' =secret vice. 3. 先事後得,—comp. with 先難後獲, in VI. 20, which also is the report of a conversation with Fan Ch'e. 其惡,—其=己, 'himself,' 'his own.' 'A morning's anger' must be a small thing, but the consequences of giving way to it are very terrible. The case is one of great delusion.

22. ABOUT BENEVOLENCE AND WISDOM:—HOW KNOWLEDGE SUBSERVES BENEVOLENCE. Fan Ch'e might well deem the Master's replies enigmatical, and, with the help of Tsze-hea's explanations, the student still finds it difficult to

知。子曰、知人。二樊遲未達。三子曰、舉直錯諸枉、能使枉者直。四樊遲退、見子夏、曰、鄉也、吾見於夫子而問知。子曰、舉直錯諸枉、能使枉者直、何謂也。五子夏曰、富哉、言乎。六舜有天下、選於衆、舉皋陶、不仁者遠矣、湯有天下、選於衆、舉伊尹、不仁者遠矣。

二十三章子貢問友。子曰、忠告、而善道

3. The Master said, "Employ the upright and put aside all the crooked;—in this way, the crooked can be made to be upright."

4. Fan Ch'e retired, and seeing Tsze-hea, he said to him, "A little ago, I had an interview with our Master, and asked him about knowledge. He said, 'Employ the upright, and put aside all the crooked;—in this way, the crooked can be made to be upright.' What did he mean?"

5. Tsze-hea said, "Truly rich is his saying!

6. "Shun, being in possession of the empire, selected from among all the people and employed Kaou-yaou, on which all who were devoid of virtue disappeared. T'ang being in possession of the empire, selected from among all the people, and employed E-yin, and all who were devoid of virtue disappeared."

CHAPTER XXIII. Tsze-kung asked about friendship. The Master said, "Faithfully admonish *your friend*, and kindly try to lead him. If you find him impracticable, stop. Do not disgrace yourself."

understand the chapter. 1. 仁 here, being opposed to, or distinct from, 知, is to be taken as meaning 'benevolence,' and not as 'perfect virtue.' 2. 未, 'not yet,' i.e., not immediately. 3. See II. 19. 4. 鄉, up. 3d tone, in the dict. explained by 昔, 'formerly.' 6. Kaou-yaou, and E-yin,—see the Shoo-king, II. iii, and III. iv. Shun and T'ang showed their wisdom—their knowledge of men—in the selection of those ministers. That was their employment of the upright, and therefore all devoid of virtue disappeared. That was their making the crooked upright;—and so their love reached to all.

之、不可則止、毋自辱焉。

[二十四] 曾子曰、君子以文會友、以友輔仁。

CHAPTER XXIV. The philosopher Tsăng said, "The superior man on literary grounds meets with his friends, and by their friendship helps his virtue."

23. PRUDENCE IN FRIENDSHIP. 告 read *kuh*, as in III. 7, implying some degree of deference. 道 = 導, as in II. 3, 1.

24. THE FRIENDSHIP OF THE KEUN-TSZE. 以文, 'by means of letters,' i. e., common literary studies and pursuits.

BOOK XIII. TSZE-LOO.

子路第十三

[一] 子路問政。子曰、先之、勞之。請益。曰、無倦。

[二] 仲弓為季氏

CHAPTER I. 1. Tsze-loo asked about government. The Master said, "Go before the people *with your example*, and be laborious in their affairs."

2. He requested further instruction, and was answered, "Be not weary in these things."

CHAPTER II. 1. Chung-kung, being chief minister to the head of the Ke family, asked about government. The Master said, "Em-

HEADING OF THIS BOOK.—子路第十三, 'Tsze-loo.—Book XIII.' Here, as in the last book, we have a number of subjects touched upon, all bearing more or less directly on the government of the state, and the cultivation of the person. The book extends to thirty chapters.

1. THE SECRET OF SUCCESS IN GOVERNING IS THE UNWEARIED EXAMPLE OF THE RULERS:—A LESSON TO TSZE-LOO. 1. To what understood antecedents do the 之 refer? For the first, we may suppose 民,—先之 = 率民, or 道民, 'precede the people,' 'lead the people,' that is, do so by the example of your personal conduct. But we cannot in the second clause bring 之 (=民) in the same way under the regimen of 勞. 勞之 = 爲他勤勞, 'to be laborious for them;' that is, to set them the example of diligence in agriculture, &c. It is better, however, according to the idiom I have several times pointed out, to take 之 as giving a sort of neuter and general force to the preceding words, so that the expressions are = 'example and laboriousness.'—K'ung Gan-kwŏ understands the meaning differently:—'set the people an example, and then you may make them labour.' But this is not so good. 2. 無 in old copies is 毋. The meaning comes to the same.

宰、問政。子曰、先有司、赦小過、舉賢才。曰、焉知賢才而舉之。曰、舉爾所知、爾所不知、人其舍諸。

三 子路曰、衞君待子而爲政、子將奚先。子曰、必也、正名乎。子路曰、有是哉、子之迂也、奚其正。子曰、野哉、由也、君子於其所不知、蓋闕如也。名不

ploy first the services of your various officers, pardon small faults, and raise to office men of virtue and talents."

2. *Chung-kung* said, "How shall I know the men of virtue and talent, so that I may raise them to office?" He was answered, "Raise to office those whom you know. As to those whom you do not know, will others neglect them?"

CHAPTER III. 1. Tsze-loo said, "The prince of Wei has been waiting for you, in order with you to administer the government. What will you consider the first thing to be done?"

2. The Master replied, "What is necessary is to rectify names."

3. "So, indeed!" said Tsze-loo. "You are wide of the mark. Why must there be such rectification?"

4. The Master said, "How uncultivated you are, Yew! A superior man, in regard to what he does not know, shows a cautious reserve."

2. THE DUTIES CHIEFLY TO BE ATTENDED TO BY A HEAD MINISTER:—A LESSON TO YEN YUNG. 1. 先有司,—comp. VIII. 4, 3. The 有司 are the various smaller officers. A head minister should assign them their duties, and not be interfering in them himself. His business is to examine into the manner in which they discharge them. And in doing so, he should overlook small faults. 2. 人其舍諸,—comp. 山川其舍諸, in VI. 4, though the force of 舍 here is not so great as in that ch. Conf. meaning is, that Chung-kung need not trouble himself about *all* men of worth. Let him advance those he knew. There was no fear that the others would be neglected. Comp. what is said on 'knowing men,' in XII. 22.

3. THE SUPREME IMPORTANCE OF NAMES BEING CORRECT. 1. This conversation is assigned by Choo He to the 11th year of the duke Gae of Loo, when Conf. was 69, and he returned from his wanderings to his native state. Tsze-loo had then been some time in the service of the duke Ch'uh of Wei, who it would appear, had been wishing to get the services of the sage himself, and the disciple did not think that his Master would refuse to accept office, as he had not objected to *his* doing so. 2. 名 must have here a special reference, which Tsze-loo did not apprehend. Nor did the old interpr., for Ma Yung explains the 正名 by 正百事之名, 'to rectify the names of all things.' On this view, the reply would indeed be 'wide of the mark.' The answer is substantially the same as the reply to duke King of Tse about

正、則言不順、言不順、則
事不成。事不成、則禮樂
不興、禮樂不興、則刑罰
不中、刑罰不中、則民無
所措手足。故君子名之
必可言也、言之必可行
也、君子於其言、無所苟
而已矣。
〔四〕樊遲請學稼。子曰、吾
不如老農。請學爲圃。曰、

5. "If names be not correct, language is not in accordance with the truth of things. If language be not in accordance with the truth of things, affairs cannot be carried on to success.

6. "When affairs cannot be carried on to success, proprieties and music will not flourish. When proprieties and music do not flourish, punishments will not be properly awarded. When punishments are not properly awarded, the people do not know how to move hand or foot.

7. "Therefore a superior man considers it necessary that the names he uses may be spoken *appropriately*, and also that what he speaks may be carried out *appropriately*. What the superior man requires, is just that in his words there may be nothing incorrect."

CHAPTER IV 1. Fan Ch'e requested to be taught husbandry. The Master said, "I am not so good for that as an old husbandman." He requested *also* to be taught gardening, and was answered, "I am not so good for that as an old gardener."

govern. In XII. 11, that it obtains when the prince is prince, the father father, &c; that is, when each man in his relations is what the *name* of his relation would require. Now, the duke Ch'eh held the rule of Wei against his father: see VII. 14. Conf., from the necessity of the case and peculiarity of the circumstances, allowed his disciples, notwithstanding that, to take office in Wei; but at the time of this conversation, Ch'eh had been duke for nine years, and ought to have been so established that he could have taken the course of a filial son without subjecting the state to any risks. On this account, Conf. said he would begin with rectifying the name of the duke, that is, with requiring him to resign the dukedom to his father, and be what his name of *son* required him to be. See the 翼註, *in loc.* This view enables us to understand better the climax that follows, tho' its successive steps are still not without difficulty. 正名乎,—乎 may be taken as an exclamation, or as='is it not?' 4. 闕如,—闕 is used in the same sense as in II. 18. The phrase='is putting-aside-like,' *i.e.*, the sup. man reserves and revolves what he is in doubt about, and does not rashly speak. 6. 'Proprieties' here are not ceremonial rules, but as='*order*,' what such rules are designed to display and secure. So, 'music' is equivalent to 'harmony.' 中, 3d tone, is the verb; 不中 ='do not hit the mark.'

4. A RULER HAS NOT TO OCCUPY HIMSELF WITH WHAT IS PROPERLY THE BUSINESS OF THE PEOPLE. It is to be supposed that Fan Ch'e

吾不如老圃。樊遲出。子曰、小人哉、樊須也。上好禮、則民莫敢不敬。上好義、則民莫敢不服。上好信、則民莫敢不用情。夫如是、則四方之民、襁負其子而至矣、焉用稼。

[五] 子曰、誦詩三百、授之以政、不達。使於四方、不能專對。雖多、亦奚以爲。

2. Fan Ch'e having gone out, the Master said, "A small man, indeed, is Fan Seu!"

3. "If a superior love propriety, the people will not dare not to be reverent. If he love righteousness, the people will not dare not to submit *to his example*. If he love good faith, the people will not dare not to be sincere. Now, when these things obtain, the people from all quarters will come to him, bearing their children on their backs. What need has he of a knowledge of husbandry?"

CHAPTER V. The Master said, "Though a man may be able to recite the three hundred odes, yet if, when intrusted with a governmental charge, he knows not how to act, or if, when sent to any quarter on a mission, he cannot give his replies unassisted, notwithstanding the extent *of his learning*, of what practical use is it?"

was at this time in office somewhere, and thinking of the Master, as the villager and high officer did, IX. 2 and 6, that his knowledge embraced almost every subject, he imagined that he might get lessons from him on the two subjects he specifies, which he might use for the benefit of the people. 1. 稼 is properly the 'seed-sowing,' and 圃, 'a kitchen-garden,' but they are used generally, as in the transl. 3. 情, 'the feelings,' 'desires,' but sometimes, as here, in the sense of 'sincerity.' 襁, often joined with 褓, is a cloth with strings by which a child is strapped upon the back of its mother or nurse.—This par. shows what people in office should learn. Conf. intended that it should be repeated to Fan Ch'e.

5. LITERARY ACQUIREMENTS USELESS WITHOUT PRACTICAL ABILITY. 詩三百,—see II. 2. 誦, 'to croon over,' as Chinese students do; here,='to have learned.' 專=獨, 'alone,' i.e., unassisted by the individuals of his suite. 多, 'many,' refer. to the 300 odes. 亦, 'also,' here and in other places,=our 'yet,' 'after all.' 奚以爲—以, it is said,=用, 'use,' and 爲 is a mere expletive,—是語助詞, but each term may have its meaning, as in the translation.

[六] 子曰、其身正、不令而行、其身不正、雖令不從。

[七] 子曰、魯衛之政、兄弟也。

[八] 子謂衛公子荊善居室、始有、曰、苟合矣、少有、曰、苟完矣、富有、曰、苟美矣。

[九] 子適衛、冉有僕。二子曰、庶矣哉。三冉有曰、既庶矣、

CHAPTER VI. The Master said, "When a prince's personal conduct is correct, his government is effective without the issuing of orders. If his personal conduct is not correct, he may issue orders, but they will not be followed."

CHAPTER VII. The Master said, "The government of Loo and Wei are brothers."

CHAPTER VIII. The Master said of King, a scion of the ducal family of Wei, that he knew the economy of a family well. When he began to have means, he said, "Ha! here is a collection!" when they were a little increased, he said, "Ha! this is complete!" when he had become rich, he said, "Ha! this is admirable!"

CHAPTER IX. 1. When the Master went to Wei, Yen Yew acted as driver of his carriage.

2. The Master observed, "How numerous are the people!"

3. Yew said, "Since they are thus numerous, what more shall be done for them?" "Enrich them," was the reply.

6. HIS PERSONAL CONDUCT ALL IN ALL TO A RULER. A translator finds it impossible here to attain to the terse conciseness of his original.

7. THE SIMILAR CONDITION OF THE STATES OF LOO AND WEI. Comp. VI. 22. Loo's state had been from the influence of Chow-kung, and Wei was the fief of his brother Fung (封), commonly known as K'ang-shuh (康叔). They had, similarly, maintained an equal and brotherly course in their progress, or, as it was in Confucius' time, in their degeneracy. That portion of the present Ho-nan, which runs up and lies between Shan-se and Pih-chih-le, was the bulk of Wei.

8. THE CONTENTMENT OF THE OFFICER KING, AND HIS INDIFFERENCE IN GETTING RICH. King was a great officer of Wei, a scion of its ducal house. 善居室 is a difficult expression. Literally it is—'dwelt well in his house.' 室 implies that he was a married man, the head of a family. The 合講 says the phrase is equivalent to 處家, 'managed his family.' Choo He explains 苟 by 聊且粗畧之意,—'it is significant of indifference and carelessness.' Our word 'ha!' expressing surprise and satisfaction corresponds to it pretty nearly. The 備旨 says that the 曰 is not to be understood as if King really made these utterances, but that Conf. thus vividly represents how he felt.

又何加焉。曰、富之。四、曰、既富矣、又何加焉。曰、教之。

子曰、苟有用我者、朞月而已可也、三年有成。

子曰、善人爲邦百年、亦可以勝殘去殺矣、誠哉是言也。

子曰、如有王者、必世而後仁。

4. "And when they have been enriched, what more shall be done?" The Master said, "Teach them."

CHAPTER X. The Master said, "If there were any of the princes who would employ me, in the course of twelve months, I should have done something considerable. In three years, *the government* would be perfected."

CHAPTER XI. The Master said, "'If good men were to govern a country *in succession* for a hundred years, they would be able to transform the violently bad, and dispense with capital punishments.' True indeed is this saying!"

CHAPTER XII. The Master said, "If a truly royal ruler were to arise, it would *still* require a generation, and then virtue would prevail."

9. A PEOPLE NUMEROUS, WELL-OFF, AND EDUCATED, IS THE GREAT ACHIEVEMENT OF GOVERNMENT. 1. 僕, 'a servant,' but here with the mean. in the translation. That, indeed, is the second meaning of the char. given in the dict.

10. CONFUCIUS' ESTIMATE OF WHAT HE COULD DO, IF EMPLOYED TO ADMINISTER THE GOVERNMENT OF A STATE. 朞, is to be distinguished from 期, and = 'a revolution of the *year*.' There is a comma at 月, and 而已可 are read together. 而已 does not signify, as is often done, 'and nothing more,' but = 'and have,' 已 being 已經, a sign of the perfect tense, —'Given twelve months, and there would be a passable result. In three years, there would be a completion.'

11. WHAT A HUNDRED YEARS OF GOOD GOVERNMENT COULD EFFECT. Conf. quotes here a saying of his time, and approves of it. 勝, upper 1st tone, 'to be equal to.' 勝殘, 'would be equal to the violent,' that is, to transform them. 去殺, 'to do away with killing,' that is, with capital punishments, unnecessary with a transformed people.

12. IN WHAT TIME A ROYAL RULER COULD TRANSFORM THE EMPIRE. 王者, 'one who was a king.' The char. 王 is formed by three straight lines representing the three powers of Heaven, Earth, and Man, and a perpendicular line, going through and uniting them, and thus conveys the highest idea of power and influence. See the dict., char. 王. Here it means the highest wisdom and virtue in the highest place.

〔十三〕子曰、苟正其身矣、於從政乎何有、不能正其身、如正人何。〔十四〕冉子退朝、子曰、何晏也。對曰、有政。子曰、其事也、如有政、雖不吾以、吾其與聞之。〔十五〕定公問一言而可以興邦、有諸。孔子對曰、言不可以若是其

CHAPTER XIII. The Master said, "If a minister make his own conduct correct, what difficulty will he have in assisting in government? If he cannot rectify himself, what has he to do with rectifying others?"

CHAPTER XIV. The disciple Yen returning from the court, the Master said to him, "How are you so late?" He replied, "We had government business." The Master said, "It must have been *family* affairs. If there had been government business, though I am not *now* in office, I should have been consulted about it."

CHAPTER XV. 1. The duke Ting asked whether there was a single sentence which could make a country prosperous. Confucius replied, "Such an effect cannot be expected from one sentence.

2. "There is a saying, however, which people have—'To be a prince is difficult; to be a minister is not easy.'

世, 'a generation,' or thirty years. See note on II. 23, 1. The old interpr. take 仁 as=仁政, 'virtuous government.'—To save Conf. from the charge of vanity in what he says, in ch. 10, that he could accomplish in three years, it is said, that the perfection which he predicates there would only be the foundation for the virtue here realized.

13. THAT HE BE PERSONALLY CORRECT ESSENTIAL TO AN OFFICER OF GOVERNMENT. Comp. ch. 6. That the subject is here an officer of gov., and not the ruler, appears from the phrase 從政; see note on VI. 6. With reference to the other phraseology of the ch., the 備旨 says that 從政 embraces 正君, 'the rectification of the prince,' and 正民, 'the rectification of the people.'

14. AN INGENIOUS ADMONITION TO YEN YEW ON THE USURPING TENDENCIES OF THE KE FAMILY. The point of the ch. turns on the opposition of the phrases 有政 and 其事也:—at the court of the Ke family, that is, they had really been discussing matters of government, affecting the state, and proper only for the prince's court. Conf. affects not to believe it, and says that at the chief's court they could only have been discussing the affairs of his house. 不吾以,—an inversion, and 以=用, 'although I am now not employed.' 與, low. 3d tone.—'I should have been present and heard it.' Superannuated officers might go to court on occasions of emergency, and might also be consulted on such, though the gen. rule was to allow them to retire at 70. See the Le Ke, I. I. 28.

15. HOW THE PROSPERITY AND RUIN OF A COUNTRY MAY DEPEND ON THE RULER'S VIEW OF HIS POSITION, HIS FEELING ITS DIFFICULTY, OR ONLY CHERISHING A HEADSTRONG WILL. 1. I should suppose that 一言可以興邦, and

幾也。二人之言曰、爲君難、爲臣不易。三如知爲君之難也、不幾乎一言而興邦乎。四曰、一言而喪邦有諸。孔子對曰、言不可以若是其幾也、人之言曰、予無樂乎爲君、唯其言而莫予違也。五如其善、而莫之違也、不亦善乎。如不善、而莫之違也、不幾乎一言而喪邦乎。

[十六]一葉公問政。二子曰、近者說、遠

3. "If *a ruler* knows this,—the difficulty of being a prince,—may there not be expected from this one sentence the prosperity of his country?"

4. *The duke then* said, "Is there a single sentence which can ruin a country?" Confucius replied, "Such an effect as that cannot be expected from one sentence. There is, *however*, the saying which people have—'I have no pleasure in being a prince, only in that no one offer any opposition to what I say!'

5. "If *a ruler's* words be good, is it not also good that no one oppose them? But if they are not good, and no one opposes them, may there not be expected from this one sentence the ruin of his country?"

CHAPTER XVI. 1. The duke of Shè asked about government.

2. The Master said, "*Good government obtains, when* those who are near are made happy, and those who are far off are attracted."

the correspond. sent. below were comm. sayings, about which the duke asks, in a way to intimate his disbelief of them—有諸. 幾 is not here in the sense of 'a spring,' or '*primum mobile*,' but=期, in the sense of 'to expect,' 'to be expected from.' 一言=一句, as in II. 2. 2. It is only the first part of the saying on which Conf. dwells. That is called 主, the principal sentence; the other is only 帶說, 'an accessory.' 3. Some put a comma at the first 乎, but it is better to take that 乎 as a preposition;—'May it not be expected that *from* this one word, &c.?' Similarly, par. 4, 乎 is a prep.,=our *in*. 其言,—言 is used specially of the orders, rules, &c., which a ruler may issue.

16. GOOD GOVERNMENT SEEN FROM ITS EFFECTS. 1. 葉, read *shè*; see VII. 18. 2. Conf. is supposed to have in view the oppressive and aggressive govt. of Ts'oo, to which *Shè* belonged.

者來。

十七 子夏爲莒父宰，問政。子曰，無欲速，無見小利。欲速則不達，見小利則大事不成。

十八 一 葉公語孔子曰，吾黨有直躬者，其父攘羊，而子證之。二 孔子曰，吾黨之直者異於是，父爲子隱，子爲父隱，直在其中矣。

CHAPTER XVII. Tsze-hea, being governor of Keu-foo, asked about government. The Master said, "Do not be desirous to have things done quickly; do not look at small advantages. Desire to have things done quickly prevents their being done thoroughly. Looking at small advantages prevents great affairs from being accomplished."

CHAPTER XVIII. 1. The duke of Shě informed Confucius, saying, "Among us here there are those who may be styled upright in their conduct. If their father have stolen a sheep, they will bear witness to the fact."

2. Confucius said, "Among us, in our part of the country, those who are upright are different from this. The father conceals the misconduct of the son, and the son conceals the misconduct of the father. Uprightness is to be found in this."

17. HASTE AND SMALL ADVANTAGES NOT TO BE DESIRED IN GOVERNING. Keu-foo (*foo*, up. 3d tone) was a small city in the western borders of Loo. 無＝毋, the prohibitive particle.

18. NATURAL DUTY AND UPRIGHTNESS IN COLLISION. 1. 吾黨, 'our village,' 'our neighbourhood,' but 黨 must be taken vaguely, as in the transl.; comp. V. 21. We cannot say whether the duke is referring to one or more actual cases, or giving his opinion of what his people would do. Conf. reply would incline us to the latter view. In the 集證, accounts are quoted of such cases, but they are probably founded on this chap. 攘 is 'to steal on occasion,' *i. e.*, on some temptation, as where another person's animal comes into my grounds, and I appropriate it. 證 seems to convey here the idea of accusation, as well as of witnessing. 2. 直在其中,—comp. II. 18, 2. The expression does not absolutely affirm that this is upright, but that in this there is a better principle than in the other conduct.—Any body but a Chinese will say that both the duke's view of the subject and the sage's were incomplete.

〔十九〕樊遲問仁。子曰、居處恭、執事敬、與人忠、雖之夷狄、不可棄也。

〔二十〕子貢問曰、何如斯可謂之士矣。子曰、行己有恥、使於四方、不辱君命、可謂士矣。曰、敢問其次。曰、宗族稱孝焉、鄉黨稱弟焉。曰、敢問其次。曰、言必信、行必果、硜硜然、小

CHAPTER XIX. Fan Ch'e asked about perfect virtue. The Master said, "It is, in retirement, to be sedately grave; in the management of business, to be reverently attentive; in intercourse with others, to be strictly sincere. Though a man go among rude uncultivated tribes, these *qualities* may not be neglected."

CHAPTER XX. 1. Tsze-kung asked, saying, "What qualities must a man possess to entitle him to be called an officer?" The Master said, "He who in his conduct of himself maintains a sense of shame, and when sent to any quarter will not disgrace his prince's commission, deserves to be called an officer."

2. *Tsze-kung* pursued, "I venture to ask who may be placed in the next lower rank?" and he was told, "He whom the circle of his relatives pronounce to be filial, whom his fellow-villagers and neighbours pronounce to be fraternal."

3. *Again the disciple* asked, "I venture to ask about the class still next in order." *The Master* said, "They are determined to be sincere in what they say, and to carry out what they do. They are obstinate little men. Yet perhaps they may make the next class."

19. CHARACTERISTICS OF PERFECT VIRTUE. This is the third time that Fan Ch'e is represented as quest. the Master about 仁, and it is supposed by some to have been the first in order. 居處 (up. 3d tone), in oppos. to 執事,— 'dwelling alone,' 'in retirement.' 之 is a verb, as in V. 18, 2,=往, 'to go to.'

20. DIFFERENT CLASSES OF MEN WHO IN THEIR SEVERAL DEGREES MAY BE STYLED OFFICERS, AND THE INFERIORITY OF THE MASS OF THE OFFICERS OF CONFUCIUS' TIME. 1. 士,—comp. on XII. 20. Here it denotes—not the scholar, but the officer. 有恥, 'has shame,' i. e., will avoid all bad conduct which would subject him to reproach. 2. 宗族 is 'a designation for all who form one body having the same ancestor,'—是同宗共族之稱. These are also called 九族, 'nine branches of kindred,' being all of the same surname from the great-great-grandfather to the great-great-grandson. 弟=悌, not simply 'brotherly,' in the strict sense, but 'submissive,' giving due honour to all older than himself. 3. 硜, 'the sound of stones.'

人哉、抑亦可以爲次矣。四曰、今之從政者何如。子曰、噫、斗筲之人、何足算也。

二十一子曰、不得中行而與之、必也狂狷乎、狂者進取、狷者有所不爲也。

二十二子曰、南人有言曰、人而無恆、不可以作巫醫、善夫。二不恆其德、或承之

4. *Tsze-kung finally* inquired, "Of what sort are those of the present day, who engage in government?" The Master said, "Pooh! they are so many pecks and hampers, not worth being taken into account."

CHAPTER XXI. The Master said, "Since I cannot get men pursuing the due medium, to whom I might communicate *my instructions*, I must find the ardent and the cautiously-decided. The ardent will advance and lay hold *of truth*; the cautiously-decided will keep themselves from what is wrong."

CHAPTER XXII. 1. The Master said, "The people of the south have a saying—'A man without constancy cannot be either a wizard or a doctor.' Good!

2. "Inconstant in his virtue, he will be visited with disgrace."

硜硜然, 'stone like.' The dict., with ref. to this passage, explains it—小人貌, 'the appearance of a small man.' 4. 斗筲之人 i. e., mere utensils. Comp. on II. 12.

21. CONFUCIUS OBLIGED TO CONTENT HIMSELF WITH THE ARDENT AND CAUTIOUS AS DISCIPLES. Comp. V. 21, and Mencius VII. ii. 37. 與之 is explain. as in the transl.—以道傳之. The 註疏, however, gives simply—與之同處, 'dwell together with them,' and treats the ch. as if it had no reference to the transmission of the sage's doctrines, or to his disciples. 必也狂狷乎,—comp. ch. 3, 2. 狷 is explained in the dict. by 褊急, 'contracted and urgent.' Oppos. to 狂, it would seem to denote caution, but yet not a caution which may not be combined with decision. 有所不爲, 'have what they will not do.'

22. THE IMPORTANCE OF FIXITY AND CONSTANCY OF MIND. 1. I translate 巫 by 'wizard,' for want of a better term. In the Chow Le, Bk. XXVI, the 巫 appear sustaining a sort of official status, regularly called in to bring down spiritual beings, obtain showers, &c. They are distinguished as men and women, though 巫 is often feminine, 'a witch,' as opposed to 覡, 'a wizard.' Conf. use of the saying, &c. in Choo He, is this:—'Since such small people must have constancy, how much more ought others to have it!' The ranking of the doctors and wizards together sufficiently shows what was the position of the healing art in those days.—Ch'ing K'ang-shing interprets this par. quite inadmissibly:—'wizards and doctors

羞。三子曰、不占而已矣。

〔二十三〕子曰、君子和而不同、小人同而不和。

〔二十四〕子貢問曰、鄉人皆好之、何如。子曰、未可也。鄉人皆惡之、何如。子曰、未可也。不如鄉人之善者好之、其不善者惡之。

〔二十五〕子曰、君子易事而難說也、說之不以道、不說也、及

3. The Master said, "This arises simply from not prognosticating."

CHAPTER XXIII. The Master said, "The superior man is affable, but not adulatory; the mean is adulatory, but not affable."

CHAPTER XXIV. Tsze-kung asked saying, "What do you say of a man who is loved by all the people of his village?" The Master replied, "We may not for that accord our approval of him." "And what do you say of him who is hated by all the people of his village?" The Master said, "We may not for that conclude that he is bad. It is better than either of these cases that the good in the village love him, and the bad hate him."

CHAPTER XXV. The Master said, "The superior man is easy to serve and difficult to please. If you try to please him in any way which is not accordant with right, he will not be pleased. But in his employment of men, he uses them according to their capacity. The

cannot manage people who have no constancy.' 2. This is a quotation from the Yih-king, diagram 恆. 3. This is inexplicable to Choo He. Some bring out from it the mean. in the translation.—Ch'ing K'ang-shing says:—'By the Yih we prognosticate good and evil, but in it there is no prognostication of people without constancy.'

23. THE DIFFERENT MANNERS OF THE SUPERIOR AND THE MEAN MAN. Comp. II. 14, but here the parties are contrasted in their more private intercourse with others. 同, 'agreeing with,'—flattering.

24. HOW, TO JUDGE OF A MAN FROM THE LIKINGS AND DISLIKINGS OF OTHERS, WE MUST KNOW THE CHARACTERS OF THOSE OTHERS. 未可,—lit., 'not yet may.' The general mean. of a Chin. sentence is often plain, and yet we are puzzled to supply exactly the subjects, auxiliaries, &c., which other languages require. In rendering the phrase, I have followed many of the paraphrasts, who complete it thus:—未可信其爲賢也, and 未可信其爲惡也. In the 註疏, however, the second occurrence of it is expanded in the same way as the first.

25. DIFFERENCE BETWEEN THE SUPERIOR AND THE MEAN MAN IN THEIR RELATION TO THOSE EMPLOYED BY THEM. 易事而難說(=悅),—as in the transl., or we may render,—'is easily

其使人也、器之。小人難事而易說也。說之雖不以道、說也。及其使人也、求備焉。

〔二十六〕子曰、君子泰而不驕、小人驕而不泰。

〔二十七〕子曰、剛、毅、木、訥、近仁。

〔二十八〕子路問曰、何如斯可謂之士矣。子曰、切切、偲偲、怡怡如也、可謂士矣。朋友切切偲偲、兄弟怡怡。

mean man is difficult to serve, and easy to please. If you try to please him, though it be in a way which is not accordant with right, he may be pleased. But in his employment of men, he wishes them to be equal to everything."

CHAPTER XXVI. The Master said, "The superior man has a dignified ease without pride. The mean man has pride without a dignified ease."

CHAPTER XXVII. The Master said, "The firm, the enduring, the simple, and the modest, are near to virtue."

CHAPTER XXVIII. Tsze-loo asked saying, "What qualities must a man possess to entitle him to be called a scholar?" The Master said, "He must be thus,—earnest, urgent, and bland:—among his friends, earnest and urgent; among his brethren, bland."

served, but is pleased with difficulty.' 器之,—see II. 12, 器 being here a verb. 求備 is the opposite of 器之, and=以全材責備一人身上, 'he requires all capabilities from a single man.'

26. THE DIFFERENT AIR AND BEARING OF THE SUPERIOR AND THE MEAN MAN.

27. NATURAL QUALITIES WHICH ARE FAVOURABLE TO VIRTUE. 木, 'wood,' here an adj., but not our 'wooden.' It=質樸, 'simple,' 'plain.' 訥, see IV. 24. The gloss on it here is—遲鈍, 'slow and blunt.' 'Modest' seems to be the idea.

28. QUALITIES THAT MARK THE SCHOLAR IN SOCIAL INTERCOURSE. This is the same question as in ch. 20, 1, but 士 is here 'the scholar,' the gentleman of education, without reference to his being in office or not.

廿九 子曰、善人教民七年、亦可以即戎矣。

三十 子曰、以不教民戰、是謂棄之。

CHAPTER XXIX. The Master said, "Let a good man teach the people seven years, and they may then likewise be employed in war."

CHAPTER XXX. The Master said, "To lead an uninstructed people to war, is to throw them away."

29. HOW THE GOVERNMENT OF A GOOD RULER WILL PREPARE THE PEOPLE FOR WAR. 善人, 'a good man,'—spoken with reference to him as a ruler. The teaching is not to be understood of military training, but of the duties of life and citizenship; a people so taught are morally fitted to fight for their government. What military training may be included in the teaching, would merely be the hunting and drilling in the people's repose from the toils of agriculture. 戎, 'weapons of war.' 可以即戎,—'they may go to their weapons.'

30. THAT PEOPLE MUST BE TAUGHT, TO PREPARE THEM FOR WAR. Comp. the last ch. The lang. is very strong, and 教 being understood as in last ch., shows how Conf. valued education for all classes.

BOOK XIV. HËEN-WAN.

憲問第十四

一 憲問恥。子曰、邦有道穀、邦無道穀、恥也。

CHAPTER I. Hëen asked what was shameful. The Master said, "When good government prevails in a state, *to be thinking only of his* salary; and, when bad government prevails, *to be thinking, in the same way, only of his* salary;—this is shameful."

HEADING OF THIS BOOK.—憲問第十四, 'Hëen asked—No. XIV.' The glossarial Hing Ping (邢昺) says, 'In this Book we have the characters of the *Three Kings*, and *Two Chiefs*, the courses proper for princes and great officers, the practice of virtue, the knowledge of what is shameful, personal cultivation, and the tranquillising of the people;—all subjects of great importance in government. They are therefore collected together, and arranged after the last chapter which commences with an inquiry about government.' Some writers are of opinion that the whole book was compiled by Hëen or Yuen See, who appears in the first chapter.

1. IT IS SHAMEFUL IN AN OFFICER TO BE CARING ONLY ABOUT HIS EMOLUMENT. Hëen is the Yuen Sze of VI. 3, and if we suppose Conf. answer designed to have a practical application to himself, it is not easily reconcileable with what appears of his character, in that other place. 穀, here=祿, 'emolument,' but its meaning must be pregnant and intensive, as in the transl. If we do not take it so, the sentiment is contradictory to VIII. 13, 3. K'ung Gan-kwŏ, however, takes the following view of the reply:—'When a country is well governed, emolument is right; when a country is ill-governed! to take office and emolument is shameful.' I prefer the construction of Choo He, which appears in the translation.

二 克、伐、怨、欲、不行焉、可以爲仁矣。子曰、可以爲難矣、仁則吾不知也。

三 子曰、士而懷居、不足以爲士矣。

四 子曰、邦有道、危言危行、邦無道、危行言孫。

五 子曰、有德者、必有言、有言者、不必有德、仁者、必有勇、勇者、不必有仁。

CHAPTER II. 1. "When the love of superiority, boasting, resentments, and covetousness are repressed, may this be deemed perfect virtue?"

2. The Master said, "This may be regarded as the achievement of what is difficult. But I do not know that it is to be deemed perfect virtue."

CHAPTER III. The Master said, "The scholar who cherishes the love of comfort, is not fit to be deemed a scholar."

CHAPTER IV. The Master said, "When good government prevails in a state, language may be lofty and bold, and actions the same. When bad government prevails, the actions may be lofty and bold, but the language may be with some reserve."

CHAPTER V. The Master said, "The virtuous will be sure to speak *correctly*, but those whose speech is good may not always be virtuous. Men of principle are sure to be bold, but those who are bold may not always be men of principle."

2. THE PRAISE OF PERFECT VIRTUE IS NOT TO BE ALLOWED FOR THE REPRESSION OF BAD FEELINGS. In Ho An, this ch. is joined to the preceding, and Choo He also takes the first par. to be a question of Yuen Heen. 1. 克, 'overcoming,' *i.e.*, here = 'the love of superiority.' 伐, as in V. 25, 3. 不行, 'do not go,' *i. e.*, are not allowed to have their way, = are repressed. 2. 難, 'difficult,'—the doing what is difficult. 仁 is *good* 仁;—'as to its being perfect virtue, that I do not know.'

3. A SCHOLAR MUST BE AIMING AT WHAT IS HIGHER THAN COMFORT OR PLEASURE. Comp. IV. 11. The 懷居 here is akin to the 懷土 there. Comp. also IV. 9.

4. WHAT ONE DOES MUST ALWAYS BE RIGHT; WHAT ONE FEELS NEED NOT ALWAYS BE SPOKEN;—A LESSON OF PRUDENCE. 孫 for 遜, as in VII. 35. 危, 'terror from being in a high position,' then 'danger,' 'dangerous.' It is used here in a good sense, meaning 'lofty, and what may seem to be, or really be, dangerous,' under a bad government, where good principles do not prevail.

5. WE MAY PREDICATE THE EXTERNAL FROM THE INTERNAL, BUT NOT VICE VERSA. The 有言 must be understood of virtuous speaking

〔六〕南宮适問於孔子曰、羿善射、奡盪舟、俱不得其死然、禹稷躬稼、而有天下。夫子不答。南宮适出。子曰、君子哉若人、尙德哉若人。

〔七〕子曰、君子而不仁者有矣夫、未有小人而仁者也。

CHAPTER VI. Nan-kung Kwŏh, submitting an inquiry to Confucius, said, "E was skilful at archery, and Ngaou could move a boat along upon the land, but neither of them died a natural death. Yu and Tseih personally wrought at the toils of husbandry, and they became possessors of the empire." The Master made no reply; but when Nan-kung Kwŏh went out, he said, "A superior man indeed is this! An esteemer of virtue indeed is this!"

CHAPTER VII. The Master said, "Superior men, and yet not *always* virtuous, there have been, alas! But there never has been a mean man, and, *at the same time*, virtuous."

and 'virtuously,' or 'correctly,' be supplied to bring out the sense. A translator is puzzled to render 仁者 differently from 有德者. I have said 'men of principle,' the opposition being between moral and animal courage; yet the men of principle may not be without the other, in order to their doing justice to themselves.

6. EMINENT PROWESS CONDUCTING TO RUIN; EMINENT VIRTUE LEADING TO EMPIRE. THE MODESTY OF CONFUCIUS. Nan-kung Kwŏh is said by Choo He to have been the same as Nan Yung in V. 1. But this is doubtful. See on Nan Yung there. Kwŏh, it is said, insinuated in his remark an inquiry, whether Conf. was not like Yu or Tseih, and the great men of the time so many Es and Ngaous; and the sage was modestly silent upon the subject. E and Ngaou carry us back to the 22d century before Christ. The first belonged to a family of princelets, famous, from the time of the emperor 嚳 (B. C. 2432), for their archery, and dethroned the emperor How Seang (后相), B. C. 2115. E was afterwards slain by his minister, Han Tsuh, (寒浞), who then married his wife, and one of their sons (奡, *Keaou*) was the individual here named Ngaou, who was subsequently destroyed by the emperor Shaou-k'ang, the posthumous son of How-seang. Tseih was the son of the emperor 嚳, of whose birth many prodigies are narrated, and appears in the Shoo-king as 后稷, the minister of agriculture to Yaou and Shun, by name 棄. The Chow family traced their descent lineally from him, so that though the empire only came to his descendants more than a thousand years after his time, Nan-kung Kwŏh speaks as if he had got it himself, as Yu did. 君子哉若人,—comp. V. 2.

7. THE HIGHEST VIRTUE NOT EASILY ATTAINED TO, AND INCOMPATIBLE WITH MEANNESS. Comp. IV. 4. We must supply the 'always,' to bring out the meaning.

〔八〕子曰、愛之、能勿勞乎、忠焉、能勿誨乎。

〔九〕子曰、爲命、裨諶草創之、世叔討論之、行人子羽修飾之、東里子產潤色之。

〔十〕或問子產。子曰、惠人也。問子西。曰、彼哉彼哉。問管仲。曰、人也、奪伯氏駢邑三百、飯蔬食、沒齒、

CHAPTER VIII. The Master said, "Can there be love which does not lead to strictness with its object? Can there be loyalty which does not lead to the instruction of its object?"

CHAPTER IX. The Master said, "In preparing the governmental notifications, P'e Shin first made the rough draught; She-shuh examined and discussed its contents; Tsze-yu, the manager of Foreign intercourse, then made additions, or subtractions; and, finally, Tsze-ch'an of Tung-le gave it the proper elegance and finish."

CHAPTER X. 1. Some one asked about Tsze-ch'an. The Master said, "He was a kind man."

2. He asked about Tsze-se. The Master said, "That man! That man!"

3. He asked about Kwan Chung. "For him," said the Master, "the city of P'een, with three hundred families, was taken from the chief of the Pih family, who did not utter a murmuring word, though, till he was toothless, he had only coarse rice to eat."

8. A LESSON FOR PARENTS AND MINISTERS, THAT THEY MUST BE STRICT AND DECIDED. 勞, being ;| with 誨, is a verb, and conveys the meaning in the translation, diff. from the meaning of the term in XIII. 6. Kung Gan-kwŏ takes it in the sense of 'to soothe,' 'comfort,' low. 3d tone, but that does not suit the parallelism.

9. THE EXCELLENCE OF THE OFFICIAL NOTIFICATIONS OF CH'ING, OWING TO THE ABILITY OF FOUR OF ITS OFFICERS. The state of Ch'ing, small and surrounded by powerful neighbours, was yet fortunate in having able ministers, through whose mode of conducting its government it enjoyed considerable prosperity. 命, with ref. to this passage, is explained in the dict. by 政令盟會之辭 'the language of government orders, covenants, and conferences.' See the Chow Le, XXV. p. 11. Tsze-ch'an (see V. 15.) was the chief minister of the State, and in preparing such documents first used the services of P'e Shin, who was noted for his wise planning of matters. 'She-shuh' shows the relation of the officer indicated to the ruling family. His name was Yew-keih (游吉). The province of the 行人 was—主國使之禮, 'to superintend the ceremonies of communication with other states.' See the Chow Le, XXXIV. p. 13.

10. THE JUDGMENT OF CONFUCIUS CONCERNING TSZE-CH'AN, TSZE-SE, AND KWAN CHUNG. 1 See V. 15. 2. Tsze-se was the chief minister

無怨言。

十一 子曰、貧而無怨難、富而無驕易。

十二 子曰、孟公綽、爲趙魏老則優、不可以爲滕薛大夫。

十三 一 子路問成人。子曰、若臧武仲之知、公綽之不欲、卞莊子之勇、冉求之藝、文之以禮樂、亦可以爲成人矣。二 曰、今之成人者何必然、見

CHAPTER XI. The Master said, "To be poor without murmuring is difficult. To be rich without being proud is easy."

CHAPTER XII. The Master said, "Măng Kung-ch'ŏ is more than fit to be chief officer in the families of Chaou and Wei, but he is not fit to be minister to either of the states T'ăng or Sëē."

CHAPTER XIII. 1. Tsze-loo asked what constituted a COMPLETE man. The Master said, "Suppose a man with the knowledge of Tsang Woo-chung, the freedom from covetousness of Kung-ch'ŏ, the bravery of Chwang of Peen, and the varied talents of Yen K'ew; add to these the accomplishments of the rules of propriety and music:—such an one might be reckoned a COMPLETE man."

2. *He then* added, "But what is the necessity for a complete man of the present day to have all these things? The man, who in

of Tsin. He had refused to accept the nomination to the sovereignty of the state in preference to the rightful heir, but did not oppose the usurping tendencies of the rulers of Tsin. He had moreover opposed the wish of king Ch'aou to employ the sage. 3. Kwan Chung, —see III. 22. To reward his merits, the duke Hwan conferred on him the domain of the officer mentioned in the text, who had been guilty of some offence. His submitting, as he did, to his changed fortunes was the best tribute to Kwan's excellence.

11. IT IS HARDER TO BEAR POVERTY ARIGHT THAN TO CARRY RICHES. This sentiment may be controverted.

12. THE CAPACITY OF MANG KUNG-CH'Ŏ. Kung-ch'ŏ was the head of the Măng, or Chung-sun family, and, acc. to the 'Historical Records,' was regarded by Conf. more than any other great man of the times in Loo. His estimate of him however, as appears here, was not very high. In the sage's time, the government of the state of Tsin (晉) was in the hands of the three families, Chaou, Wei, and Han (韓), which afterwards divided the territory among themselves, and became, as we shall see in the times of Mencius, three independent principalities. 老,=家臣之長, 'head of the ministers of a family,' often called 家宰. T'ang was a small state, the place of which is seen in the district of the same name in the dep. of Yen-chow. Sëē was another small state adjacent to it.

13. OF THE COMPLETE MAN:—A CONVERSATION WITH TSZE-LOO. 1. Tsang Woo-chung had been an officer of Loo in the reign anterior to

利思義、見危授命、久要不忘平生之言、亦可以爲成人矣。

十四 子問公叔文子於公明賈曰、信乎、夫子不言、不笑、不取乎。二 公明賈對曰、以告者過也、夫子時然後言、人不厭其言、樂然後笑、人不厭其笑、義然後取、人不厭其取。子曰、其然、豈其然乎。

the view of gain thinks of righteousness; who in the view of danger is prepared to give up his life; and who does not forget an old agreement, however far back it extends:—such a man may be reckoned a COMPLETE man."

CHAPTER XIV. 1. The Master asked Kung-ming Kea about Kung-shuh Wăn, saying, "Is it true that your master speaks not, laughs not, and takes not?"

2. Kung-ming Kea replied, "This has arisen from the reporters going beyond *the truth*.—My master speaks when it is the time to speak, and so men do not get tired of his speaking. He laughs when there is occasion to be joyful, and so men do not get tired of his laughing. He takes when it is consistent with righteousness to do so, and so men do not get tired of his taking." The Master said, "So! But is it so with him?"

that in which Conf. was born. So great was his reputation for wisdom that the people gave him the title of a 聖人, or 'sage.' Woo was his honor. epithet, and 仲 denotes his family place, among his brothers. Chwang, it is said by Choo He, after Chow (周), one of the oldest commentators, whose surname only has come down to us, was 卞邑大夫, 'great officer of the city of Peen.' In the 'Great collection of Surnames,' a secondary branch of a family of the state of Tsaou (曹) having settled in Loo, and being gifted with Peen, its members took their surname thence. For the history of Chwang and of Woo-chung, see the 集證, in loc. 亦可云云,—亦 implies that there was a higher style of man still, to whom the epithet *complete* would be more fully applicable. 2. The 曰 is to be understood of Confucius, though some suppose that Tsze-loo is the speaker. 要 up. 1st tone, =約, 'an agreement,' 'a covenant;'—'a long agreement, he does not forget the words of his whole life.' The meaning is what appears in the translation.

14. THE CHARACTER OF KUNG-SHUH WAN, WHO WAS SAID NEITHER TO SPEAK, NOR LAUGH, NOR TAKE. 1. Wăn was the hon. epithet of the individual in question, by name Che (枝), or, as some say, Fă (發), an officer of the state of

子曰、臧武仲、以防求爲後於魯、雖曰不要君、吾不信也。

子曰、晉文公譎而不正、齊桓公正而不譎。

子路曰、桓公殺公子糾、召忽死之、管仲不死、

CHAPTER XV. The Master said, "Tsang Woo-chung, keeping possession of Fang, asked of *the duke of* Loo to appoint a successor to him *in his family*. Although it may be said that he was not using force with his sovereign, I believe he was."

CHAPTER XVI. The Master said, "The duke Wăn of Tsin was crafty and not upright. The duke Hwan of Ts'e was upright and not crafty."

CHAPTER XVII. 1. Tsze-loo said, "The duke Hwan caused his brother Kew to be killed, when Shaou Hwŭh died *with his master*, but Kwan Chung did not die. May not I say that he was wanting in virtue?"

Wei. He was descended from the duke 獻, and was himself the founder of the Kang-shuh family, being so designated, I suppose, because of his relation to the reigning duke. Of Kang-shing Kea nothing seems to be known. 2. 其然,—with reference to Kea's account of Kang-shuh Wan. 豈其然乎 intimates Conf. opinion that Kea was himself going beyond the truth.

15. CONDEMNATION OF TSANG WOO-CHUNG FOR FORCING A FAVOUR FROM HIS PRINCE. Woo-chung (see ch. 13) was obliged to fly from Loo, by the animosity of the Mang family, and took refuge in Choo (邾). As the head of the Tsang family, it devolved on him to offer the sacrifices in the ancestral temple, and he wished one of his half-brothers to be made the head of the family, in his room, that these might not be neglected. To strengthen the application for this, which he contrived to get made, he returned himself to the city of Fang, which belonged to his family, and thence sent a message to the court, which was tantamount to a threat that if the application were not granted, he would hold possession of the place. This was what Confucius condemned,—the 以防 in a matter which should have been left to the duke's grace. See all the circumstances in the 左傳, 襄公二十三年. 要, up. 1st tone, as in ch. 12, but with a diff. meaning,=脅, 'to force to do.'

16. THE DIFFERENT CHARACTERS OF THE DUKES WAN OF TSIN AND HWAN OF TS'E. Hwan and Wan were the two first of the five leaders of the princes of the empire, who play an important part in Chinese history, during the period of the Chow dynasty known as the Ch'un Ts'ew (春秋). Hwan ruled in Ts'e, B. C. 683-640, and Wan in Tsin B. C. 635-627. Of duke Hwan, see the next ch. The attributes mentioned by Conf. are not to be taken absolutely, but as respectively predominating in the two chiefs.

17. THE MERIT OF KWAN CHUNG;—A CONVERSATION WITH TSZE-LOO. 1. 公子糾, 'the duke's son Kew,' but, to avoid the awkwardness of that rendering, I say—'his brother.' Hwan (the hon. ep. His name was 小白.) and Kew had both been refugees in different states, the latter having been carried into Loo, away from the troubles and dangers of Ts'e, by the ministers, Kwan Chung and Shaou Hwuh. On the death of the prince of Ts'e, Hwan anticipated Kew, got to Ts'e, and took possession of the state. Soon after, he required the duke of Loo to put his brother to death, and to deliver up the two ministers, when Shaou (召 here=邵) Hwuh chose to dash his brains out, and die with his master, while Kwan Chung returned gladly to Ts'e, took service with Hwan, became

曰、未仁乎。二子曰、桓公九合諸侯、不以兵車、管仲之力也、如其仁、如其仁。十八子貢曰、管仲非仁者與、桓公殺公子糾、不能死、又相之。二子曰、管仲相桓公、霸諸侯、一匡天下、民到于今、受其賜、微管仲、吾其被髮左衽矣。三豈若匹夫匹婦之為諒也、

2. The Master said, "The duke Hwan assembled all the princes together, and that not with weapons of war and chariots:—it was all through the influence of Kwan Chung. Whose beneficence was like his? Whose beneficence was like his?"

CHAPTER XVIII. 1. Tsze-kung said, "Kwan Chung, I apprehend, was wanting in virtue. When the duke Hwan caused his brother Kew to be killed, Kwan Chung was not able to die with him. Moreover, he became prime minister to Hwan."

2. The Master said, "Kwan Chung acted as prime minister to the duke Hwan, made him leader of all the princes, and united and rectified the whole empire. Down to the present day, the people enjoy the gifts which he conferred. But for Kwan Chung, we should now be wearing our hair dishevelled, and the lappets of our coats buttoning on the left side.

his prime minister, and made him supreme arbiter among the various chiefs of the empire. Such conduct was condemned by Tsze-loo. 死之 is a peculiar expression. 2. Conf. defends Kwan Chung, on the ground of the services which he rendered, using 仁 in a different acceptation from that intended by the disciple. 九, upper 1st tone, explained in the dict. by 糾, synonymous with 合, though the 註疏 makes out more than nine assemblages of princes under the presidency of duke Hwan. 如其仁=誰如其仁者, as in the translation.

18. THE MERIT OF KWAN CHUNG:—A CONVERSATION WITH TSZE-KUNG. 1. Tsze-loo's doubts about Kwan Chung arose from his not dying with the prince Kew; Tsze-kung's turned principally on his subsequently becoming premier to Hwan. 2. 匡=正, 'to rectify,' 'reduce to order.' —— blends with 匡 its own verbal force,—'to unite.' 微=無, 'not,' 'if not.' 被 (p'e, low. 1st tone,) 髮,—see the Le-ke, III. iii. 14, where this is mentioned as a characteristic of the eastern barbarians. 左衽—see the Shoo-king, V. xxv. 13. A note in the 集證 says, that anciently the right was the position of honour, and the right hand, moreover, is the more convenient for use, but the practice of the barbarians was contrary to that of China in both points. The sent. of Conf. is, that but for Kwan Chung, his countrymen would have sunk

自經於溝瀆、而莫之知也。

[十九]公叔文子之臣、大夫僎、與文子同升諸公。子聞之曰、可以爲文矣。

[二十]子言衞靈公之無道也、康子曰、夫如是、奚而不喪。孔子曰、仲叔圉治賓客、祝鮀治

3. "Will you require from him the small fidelity of common men and common women, who would commit suicide in a stream or ditch, no one knowing any thing about them?"

CHAPTER XIX. 1. The officer, Sëen, who had been *family*-minister to Kung-shuh Wăn, ascended to the prince's *court* in company with Wăn.

2. The Master, having heard of it, said, "He deserves to be considered WAN."

CHAPTER XX. 1. The Master was speaking about the unprincipled course of the duke Ling of Wei, when *Ke* K'ang said, "Since he is of such a character, how is it he does not lose his throne?"

2. Confucius said, "The Chung-shuh, Yu, has the superinten-

to the state of the rude tribes about them. 3. 匹夫,匹婦,—see IX. 25. 諒=小信, 'small fidelity,' by which is intended the faithfulness of a married couple of the common people, where the husband takes no concubine in addition to his wife. The argument is this:—'Do you think Kwan Chung should have considered himself bound to Kew, as a common man considers himself bound to his wife? And would you have had him commit suicide, as common people will do on any slight occasion?' Commentators say that there is underlying the vindication this fact:—that Kwan Chung and Shaou Hwuh's adherence to Kew was wrong in the first place, Kew being the younger brother. Chung's conduct therefore was not to be judged as if Kew had been the senior. There is nothing of this, however, in Confucius' words. He vindicates Chung simply on the ground of his subsequent services, and his reference to 'the small fidelity' of husband and wife among the common people is very unhappy. 自經, 'to strangle one's-self,' but in connection with 溝瀆, the phrase must be understood generally,=' to commit suicide.'

19. THE MERIT OF KUNG-SHUH WAN IN RECOMMENDING TO OFFICE A MAN OF WORTH. 1. Kung-shuh Wăn,—see ch. 14. The par. is to be understood as intimating that Kung-shuh, seeing the worth and capacity of his minister, had recommended him to his sovereign, and afterwards was not ashamed to appear in the same rank with him at court. 公,=our 'duke's,' *i.e.*, the duke's court. 2. 文, as an honorary epithet, sometimes means—錫民爵位, 'He who confers on a common man rank and office.'

20. THE IMPORTANCE OF GOOD AND ABLE MINISTERS:—SEEN IN THE STATE OF WEI. 1. *Ling* was the hon. epithet of Yuen (元), duke of Wei, B. C. 533-492. He was the husband of Nan-tsze, VI. 26. 2. The Chung-shuh, Yu, is the K'ung Wăn of V. 14. 仲叔 express his family position, according to the degrees of kindred. 'The litanist, T'o,'—see VI. 14. Wang-sun Kea,—see III. 13.

宗廟、王孫賈治軍旅、夫如是、奚其喪。

〔二十一〕子曰、其言之不怍、則爲之也難。

〔二十二〕陳成子弑簡公。〔二〕孔子沐浴而朝、告於哀公曰、陳恆弑其君、請討之。〔三〕公曰、告夫三子。〔四〕孔子曰、以吾從大夫之後、不敢不告也、君

dence of his guests and of strangers; the litanist, T'o, has the management of his ancestral temple; and Wang-sun Kea has the direction of the army and forces:—with such officers as these, how should he lose his throne?"

CHAPTER XXI. The Master said, "He who speaks without modesty will find it difficult to make his words good."

CHAPTER XXII. 1. Ch'in Shing murdered the duke Këen *of Ts'e.*

2. Confucius bathed, went to court, and informed the duke Gae, saying, "Ch'in Hăng has slain his sovereign. I beg that you will undertake to punish him."

3. The duke said, "Inform the chiefs of the three families of it."

4. Confucius *retired, and* said, "Following in the rear of the great officers, I did not dare not to represent such a matter, and my prince says, 'Inform the chiefs of the three families of it.'"

21. EXTRAVAGANT SPEECH HARD TO BE MADE GOOD. Comp. IV. 22.

22. HOW CONFUCIUS WISHED TO AVENGE THE MURDER OF THE DUKE OF TS'E:—HIS RIGHTEOUS AND PUBLIC SPIRIT. 1. *Këen*,—'Indolent in not a single virtue,' and 'tranquil, not speaking unadvisedly,' are the meanings attached to 簡, as an hon. epithet, while 成 indicates, 'tranquilliser of the people, and establisher of government.' The murder of the duke Këen by his officer, Ch'in Hăng (恆), took place, B. C. 480, barely two years before Conf. death. 2. 沐浴 implies all the fasting and all the solemn preparation, as for a sacrifice or other great occasion. Properly, 沐 is to wash the hair with the water in which rice has been washed, and 浴 is to wash the body with hot water. 請討之,—acc. to the account of this matter in the 左傳, Conf. meant that the duke Gae should himself, with the forces of Loo, undertake the punish. of the regicide. Some mod. comm. cry out against this. The sage's advice, they say, would have been that the duke should report the thing to the emperor, and with his authority associate other princes with himself to do justice on the offender. 3. 告夫三子,—this is the use of 夫 in XI. 24, *et al.* 4. This is taken as the remark of Confucius, or his colloquy with himself, when he had gone out from the duke. 以吾從大夫之後,—see XI. 7. The 者 leaves the sentence incomplete;—'my prince says, Inform the three chiefs of it;—this circumstance.' The paraphrasts complete the sentence by 何耶,—'How is it

曰、告夫三子者。之三子告、不可、孔子曰、以吾從大夫之後、不敢不告也。

二十三 子路問事君。子曰、勿欺也、而犯之。

二十四 子曰、君子上達、小人下達。

二十五 子曰、古之學者爲己、今之學者爲人。

二十六 蘧伯玉使人於孔子。孔子與之坐而問焉、曰、夫子何爲。

5. He went to the chiefs, and informed them, but they would not act. Confucius *then* said, "Following in the rear of the great officers, I did not dare not to represent such a matter."

CHAPTER XXIII. Tsze-loo asked how a sovereign should be served. The Master said, "Do not impose on him, and, moreover, withstand him to his face."

CHAPTER XXIV. The Master said, "The progress of the superior man is upwards; the progress of the mean man is downwards."

CHAPTER XXV. The Master said, "In ancient times, men learned with a view to their own improvement. Now-a-days, men learn with a view to the approbation of others."

CHAPTER XXVI. 1. Keu Pih-yuh sent a messenger *with friendly inquiries* to Confucius.

2. Confucius sat with him, and questioned him. "What," said he, "is your master engaged in?" The messenger replied, "My

that the prince, &c.?' 5. 之三子,—之 is the verb—'to go to.' 孔子曰,云云,—This was spoken to the chiefs, to reprove them for their disregard of a crime, which concerned every public man.

23. HOW THE MINISTER OF A PRINCE MUST BE SINCERE AND BOLDLY UPRIGHT. 犯之 is well expressed by the phrase in the translation. See the Le-ke, II. i. 12, where it appears that to 犯 was required by the duty of a minister, but not allowed to a son.

24. THE DIFFERENT PROGRESSIVE TENDENCIES OF THE SUPERIOR MAN AND THE MEAN MAN. Ho An takes 達 in the sense of 曉, 'to understand.' The modern view seems better.

25. THE DIFFERENT MOTIVES OF LEARNERS IN OLD TIMES, AND IN THE TIMES OF CONFUCIUS. 爲己, 爲人, 'for themselves, for other men.' The meaning is as in the translation.

26. AN ADMIRABLE MESSENGER. 1. Pih-yuh was the designation of Keu Yuen (瑗), an

對曰、夫子欲寡其過、而未能也、使者出、子曰、使乎、使乎。

廿七 子曰、不在其位、不謀其政。

廿八 曾子曰、君子思不出其位。

廿九 子曰、君子恥其言而過其行。

三十 子一 曰、君子道者三、我無能焉、仁者不憂、知者不惑、勇者不懼。二 子貢曰、夫子自道也。

master is anxious to make his faults few, but he has not yet succeeded." He then went out, and the Master said, "A messenger indeed! A messenger indeed!"

CHAPTER XXVII. The Master said, "He who is not in any particular office, has nothing to do with plans for the administration of its duties."

CHAPTER XXVIII. The philosopher Tsăng said, "The superior man, in his thoughts, does not go out of his place."

CHAPTER XXIX. The Master said, "The superior man is modest in his speech, but exceeds in his actions."

CHAPTER XXX. 1. The Master said, "The way of the superior man is threefold, but I am not equal to it. Virtuous, he is free from anxieties; wise, he is free from perplexities; bold, he is free from fear."

2. Tsze-kung said, "Master, that is what you yourself say."

officer of the state of Wei, and a disciple of the sage. His place is now 1st east in the outer court of the temples. Conf. had lodged with him when in Wei, and it was after his return to Lû that Pih-yuh sent to inquire for him.

27. A repetition of VIII. 14.

28. THE THOUGHTS OF A SUPERIOR MAN IN HARMONY WITH HIS POSITION. Tsăng here quotes from the 象, or Illustration, of the 52d diagram of the Yih-king, but he leaves out one character,—以 before 思, and thereby alters the meaning somewhat. What is said in the Yih, is—'The superior man is thoughtful, and so does not go out of his place.'—The ch., it is said, is inserted here, from its analogy with the preceding.

29. THE SUPERIOR MAN MORE IN DEEDS THAN IN WORDS. 恥其言,—lit., 'is ashamed of his words.' Comp. ch. 21, and IV. 22.

30. CONFUCIUS' HUMBLE ESTIMATE OF HIMSELF, WHICH TSZE-KUNG DENIES. 1. We have the greatest part of this par. in IX. 28, but the translation must be somewhat different, as 仁者, 知者, 勇者, are here in apposition with 君子. 君子道者=君子所以爲道者, 'what the superior man takes to be his path.' 2. 道=言, 'to say.'

三十一 子貢方人、子曰、賜也賢乎哉、夫我則不暇。

三十二 子曰、不患人之不己知、患其不能也。

三十三 子曰、不逆詐、不億不信、抑亦先覺者、是賢乎。

三十四 微生畝謂孔子曰、丘何爲是栖栖者與、無乃爲佞乎。二 孔子曰、非敢爲佞也、疾固也。

CHAPTER XXXI. Tsze-kung was *in the habit of* comparing men together. The Master said, "Ts'ze must have reached a high pitch of excellence! Now, I have not leisure *for this.*"

CHAPTER XXXII. The Master said, "I will not be concerned at men's not knowing me; I will be concerned at my own want of ability."

CHAPTER XXXIII. The Master said, "He who does not anticipate attempts to deceive him, nor think beforehand of his not being believed, and yet apprehends these things readily when they occur;—is he not a man of superior worth?"

CHAPTER XXXIV. 1. We-shang Mow said to Confucius, "K'ew, how is it that you keep roosting about? Is it not that you are an insinuating talker?"

2. Confucius said, "I do not dare to play the part of such a talker, but I hate obstinacy."

31. ONE'S WORK IS WITH ONE'S-SELF:—AGAINST MAKING COMPARISONS. 賢乎哉—'Ha! is he not superior?' The remark is ironical.

32. CONCERN SHOULD BE ABOUT OUR PERSONAL ATTAINMENT, AND NOT ABOUT THE ESTIMATION OF OTHERS. See I. 16, *et al.* A critical canon is laid down here by Choo He:—'All passages, the same in meaning and in words, are to be understood as having been spoken only once, and their recurrence is the work of the compilers. Where the meaning is the same and the language a little different, they are to be taken as having been repeated by Confucius himself, with the variations.' According to this rule, the sentiment in this chapter was repeated by the master in four different utterances.

33. QUICK DISCRIMINATION WITHOUT SUSPICIOUSNESS IS HIGHLY MERITORIOUS. 逆, 'to be disobedient,' 'to rebel;' also, 'to meet,' and here 'to anticipate,' *i. e.*, in judgment. 抑亦 are XIII. 19, but the meaning is there 'perhaps,' while here the 抑 is adversative, and = 'but.' 先覺者 is used in opposition to 後覺者, and = 'a quick apprehender, one who understands things before others.' So, Choo He. K'ung Gan-kwŏ, however, takes 抑 as conjunctive, and 先覺 in apposition with the two preceding characteristics, and interprets the conclusion—'Is such a man of superior worth?' On Choo He's view, the 乎 is exclamatory.

34. CONFUCIUS NOT SELF-WILLED, AND YET NO GLIB-TONGUED TALKER:—DEFENCE OF HIMSELF FROM THE CHARGE OF AN AGED REPROVER. 1.

三十五 子曰、驥不稱其力、稱其德也。

三十六 或曰、以德報怨、何如。二 子曰、何以報德。三 以直報怨、以德報德。

三十七 子曰、莫我知也夫。二 子貢曰、何爲其莫知子也。子曰、不怨天、不尤人、下學

CHAPTER XXXV. The Master said, "A horse is called a *ke*, not because of its strength, but because of its *other* good qualities."

CHAPTER XXXVI. 1. Some one said, "What do you say concerning the principle that injury should be recompensed with kindness?"

2. The Master said, "With what then will you recompense kindness?

3. "Recompense injury with justice, and recompense kindness with kindness."

CHAPTER XXXVII. 1. The Master said, "Alas! there is no one that knows me."

2. Tsze-kung said, "What do you mean by thus saying—that no one knows you?" The Master replied, "I do not murmur against

From We-shang's addressing Conf. by his name, it is presumed that he was an old man. Such a liberty in a young man would have been impudence. It is presumed also, that he was one of those men who kept themselves retired from the world in disgust. 栖 'to perch or roost,' as a bird, used contemptuously with ref. to Conf. going about among the princes and wishing to be called to office. 2. 固=執一不通. 'holding to one idea without intelligence.'

35. VIRTUE, AND NOT STRENGTH, THE FIT SUBJECT OF PRAISE. 驥 was the name of a famous horse of antiquity who could run 1000 *le* in one day. See the dict. in voc. It is here used generally for 'a good horse.'

36. GOOD IS NOT TO BE RETURNED FOR EVIL; EVIL TO BE MET SIMPLY WITH JUSTICE. 1. 德=恩惠, 'kindness.' 怨, 'resentment,' 'hatred,' here put for what awakens resentment, 'wrong,' 'injury.' The phrase 以德報怨 is found in the 道德經 of Laou-tsze, II. 63, but it is likely that Conf. questioner simply consulted him about it as a saying which he had heard and was inclined to approve himself. 3. 以直, 'with straightness,' *i.e.*, with justice.—How far the ethics of Confucius fall below the Christian standard is evident from this chapter. The same expressions are attributed to Confucius in the Le-ke, XXXII. 11, and it is there added 子曰, 以德報怨, 則寬身之仁(=人), which is explained,—'He who returns good for evil is a man who is careful of his person,' *i.e.*, will try to avert danger from himself by such a course. The author of the 翼註 says, that the injuries intended by the questioner were only trivial matters, which perhaps might be dealt with in the way he mentioned, but great offences, as those against a sovereign, a father, may not be dealt with by such an inversion of the principles of justice. The Master himself, however, does not fence his deliverance in any way.

37. CONFUCIUS, LAMENTING THAT MEN DID NOT KNOW HIM, RESTS IN THE THOUGHT THAT HEAVEN KNEW HIM. 1. 莫我知,—the inversion for 莫知我, 'does not know me.' He referred, comm. say, to the way in which he pursued his course, simply 爲己, out of his own conviction of duty, and for his own improvement, without regard to success, or the

而上達、知我者其天乎。

三十八 公伯寮愬子路於季孫、子服景伯以告、曰、夫子固有惑志於公伯寮、吾力猶能肆諸市朝。二 子曰、道之將行也與、命也、道之將廢也與、命也、公伯寮其如命何。

Heaven. I do not grumble against men. My studies lie low, and my penetration rises high. But there is Heaven;—that knows me!"

CHAPTER XXXVIII. 1. The Kung-pih, Leaou, having slandered Tsze-loo to Ke-sun, Tsze-fuk King-pih informed Confucius of it, saying, "Our master is certainly being led astray by the Kung-pih, Leaou, but I have still power enough left to cut *Leaou* off, and expose his corpse in the market and in the court."

2. The Master said, "If *my* principles are to advance, it is so ordered. If they are to fall to the ground, it is so ordered. What can the Kung-pih, Leaou, do, where such ordering is concerned?"

opinions of others. 2. 何爲其莫知子也, 'what is that—no man knows you?' 下學, 上達,—'beneath I learn, above I penetrate;'—the meaning appears to be that he contented himself with the study of men and things, common matters as more ambitious spirits would deem them, but from these he rose to understand the high principles involved in them,—'the appointments of Heaven (天命),' according to one commentator. 知我者, 其天乎,—'He who knows me—is that Heaven?'

38. HOW CONFUCIUS RESTED, AS TO THE PROGRESS OF HIS DOCTRINES, ON THE ORDERING OF HEAVEN:—ON OCCASION OF TSZE-LOO'S BEING SLANDERED. 1. Leaou, called Kung-pih (lit., duke's uncle), probably from an affinity with the ducal house, is said by some to have been a disciple of the sage, but that is not likely, as we find him here slandering Tsze-loo, that he might not be able, in his official connection with the Ke family, to carry the Master's lessons into practice. 景 was the hon. ep. of Tsze-fuh Pih, an officer of Loo. 夫子 refers to Ke-sun. 有惑志,—'is having his will deceived.' Exposing the bodies (陳尸) of criminals, after their execution, was called 肆. The bodies of 'great officers' were so exposed in the court, and those of meaner criminals in the market-place. 市朝 came to be employed together, though the exposure could take place only in one place, just as we have seen 兄弟 used generally for 'brother.' 2. 與 makes the preceding clause conditional, = 'if.' 命 = 天命, 'Heaven's ordering.'

[三十九]子曰、賢者辟世。[二]其次辟地。[三]其次辟色。[四]其次辟言。

[四十]子曰、作者七人矣。

[四十一]子路宿於石門。晨門曰、奚自。子路曰、自孔氏。曰、是知其不可而爲之者與。

[四十二]子擊磬於衞、有荷蕢、而過孔氏之門者、

CHAPTER XXXIX. 1. The Master said, "*Some* men of worth retire from the world.

2. "Some retire from *particular* countries.

3. "Some retire because of *disrespectful* looks.

4. "Some retire because of *contradictory* language."

CHAPTER XL. The Master said, "Those who have done this are seven men."

CHAPTER XLI. Tsze-loo happening to pass the night in Shih-mun, the gate-keeper said to him, "Whom do you come from?" Tsze-loo said, "From Mr. K'ung." "It is he,—is it not?"—said the other, "who knows the impracticable nature of the times, and yet will be doing in them."

CHAPTER XLII. 1. The Master was playing, *one day*, on a musical stone in Wei, when a man, carrying a straw basket, passed the door

39. DIFFERENT CAUSES WHY MEN OF WORTH WITHDRAW FROM PUBLIC LIFE, AND DIFFERENT EXTENTS TO WHICH THEY SO WITHDRAW THEMSELVES. 1. 辟, pr. low, 3d tone,＝避. 2. 其次,—'the next class,' but comm. say that the meaning is no more than 'some,' and that the terms do not indicate any comparison of the parties on the ground of their worthiness. 3. The 'looks,' and 'language' in par. 4, are to be understood of the princes whom the worthies wished to serve.—It is observed in the 日講論語解義 that Conf. could never bear to withdraw himself entirely from the world.

40. THE NUMBER OF MEN OF WORTH WHO HAD WITHDRAWN FROM PUBLIC LIFE IN CONFUCIUS' TIME. This ch. is understood both by Choo He and the old commentators, in connection with the preceding, as appears in the translation. Choo, however, explains 作 by 起, 'have arisen.' The others explain it by 爲, 'have done this.' They also give the names of the seven men, which, acc. to Choo, is 鑿, 'chiselling,' i.e., forcing out an illustration of the text.

41. CONDEMNATION OF CONFUCIUS' COURSE IN SEEKING TO BE EMPLOYED, BY ONE WHO HAD WITHDRAWN FROM PUBLIC LIFE. The site of Shih-mun is referred to the district of Ch'ang-ts'ing, dep. Tse-nan, in Shan-tung. 晨門, 'morning gate,'—a designation of the keeper, as having to open the gate in the morning. He was probably one of the seven worthies, spoken of in the preced. chapter. We might translate 石門 by 'Stony-gate.' It seems to have been one of the frontier passes between Ts'e and Loo. 孔氏, 'the K'ung,' or Mr. K'ung. Observe the force of the final 與.

42. THE JUDGMENT OF A RETIRED WORTHY ON CONFUCIUS' COURSE, AND REMARK OF CONFUCIUS THEREON. 1. The *k'ing* was one of the eight musical instruments of the Chinese; see

曰、有心哉、擊磬乎。○二節既而曰、鄙哉、硜硜乎、莫己知也、斯已而已矣、深則厲、淺則揭。○三節子曰、果哉、末之難矣。

■子張曰、書云、高宗諒陰、三年不言、何謂也。○二節子曰、何必高宗、古之人皆然、君薨、百官總己、以聽於冢宰三年。

of the house where Confucius was, and said, "His heart is full who *so* beats the musical stone."

2. A little while after, he added, "How contemptible is the one-ideaed obstinacy *those sounds display!* When one is taken no notice of, he has simply at once to give over *his wish for public employment.* 'Deep water must be crossed with the clothes on; shallow water may be crossed with the clothes held up.'"

3. The Master said, "How determined is he in his purpose! *But* this is not difficult."

CHAPTER XLIII. 1. Tsze-chang said, "What is meant when the SHOO says that Kaou-tsung, while observing the usual imperial mourning, was for three years without speaking?"

2. The Master said, "Why must Kaou-tsung *be referred to as an example of this?* The ancients all did so. When the sovereign died, the officers all attended to their several duties, taking instructions from the prime minister for three years."

Medhurst's dict., in voc. 過, op. 1st tone, 'to go by.' Meaning 'to go beyond,' 'to exceed,' it is in the 3d tone. 有心哉擊磬乎 is to be read as one sentence, and understood as if there were a 之 after the 哉. 2. 硜硜乎,—see XIII. 21. 3. The 備旨 interprets this clause also, as if a 之 were after the 哉, and 硜硜 had reference to the sounds of the *King.* 深則云云,—see She-king I. iii. 9. st. 1. The quotation was intended to illustrate that we must act according to circumstances. 3. 末=無. 之 seems to be a mere expletive.

43. HOW GOVERNMENT WAS CARRIED ON DURING THE THREE YEARS OF SILENT MOURNING BY THE EMPEROR. 1. 書云,—see the Shoo-king, IV. viii. Sect I. 1, but the passage there is not exactly as in the text. It is there said that Kaou-tsung, after the three years' mourning still did not speak. 高宗 was the honorary epithet of the emperor Woo-ting (武丁), B. C. 1323–1263. 諒 (Shan, 亮) 陰 (read gan), acc. to the dict., means 'the shed where the mourner lived the three years.' Choo He says he does not know the meaning of the terms.—Tsze-chang was perplexed to know how government could be carried on during so long

四十四 子曰、上好禮、則民易使也、

四十五 子路問君子、子曰、脩己以敬。曰、如斯而已乎。曰、脩己以安人。曰、如斯而已乎。曰、脩己以安百姓、脩己以安百姓、堯舜其猶病諸。

四十六 原壤夷俟、子曰、幼

CHAPTER XLIV. The Master said, "When rulers love *to observe* the rules of propriety, the people respond readily to the calls on them for service."

CHAPTER XLV. Tsze-loo asked what constituted the superior man. The Master said, "The cultivation of himself in reverential carefulness." "And is this all?" said *Tsze-loo*. "He cultivates himself so as to give rest to others," was the reply. "And is this all?" *again* asked *Tsze-loo*. *The Master* said, "He cultivates himself so as to give rest to all the people. He cultivates himself so as to give rest to all the people:—even Yaou and Shun were still solicitous about this."

CHAPTER XLVI. Yuen Jang was squatting on his heels, and so waited *the approach of* the Master, who said to him, "In youth,

a period of silence. 2. 古之人,—the 人 embraces the emperors, and subordinate princes who had their own petty courts. 總己,—in the 備旨 it is said,—總,攝也,不敢放縱意也,'總 is to manage. The meaning is, that they did not dare to allow themselves any license.' The expression is not an easy one. I have followed the paraphrasts.

44. HOW A LOVE OF THE RULES OF PROPRIETY IN RULERS FACILITATES GOVERNMENT.

45. REVERENT SELF-CULTIVATION THE DISTINGUISHING CHARACTERISTIC OF THE KEUN-TSZE. 以敬, it is said, are not to be taken as the *wherewith* of the *Keun-tsze* in his cultivating himself, but as the chief thing which he keeps before him in the process. I translate 以, therefore, by in, but in the other sentences, it indicates the realizations, or consequences, of the 修己. 百姓,—'the *hundred surnames*,' as a designation for the mass of the people, occurs as early as in the Yaou *tien* (堯典). It is = 百家姓, 'the surnames of the hundred families, into which number the families of the people were perhaps divided at a very early time. The surnames of the Chinese now amount to several hundreds. The small work—百家姓帖, made in the Sung dynasty, contains nearly 450. In the 集證, *in loc.*, we find a ridiculous reason given for the surnames being a hundred, to the effect that the ancient sages gave a surname for each of the 5 notes of the scale in music, and of the 5 great relations of life and of the 4 seas; consequently, 5 × 5 × 4=100.' It is to be observed, that in the Shoo-king, we find 'a hundred surnames,' interchanged with 萬姓, 'ten thousand surnames,' and it would seem needless, therefore, to seek to attach a definite explanation to the number. 堯舜其猶病諸,—see VI. 28.

46. CONFUCIUS' CONDUCT TO AN UNMANNERLY OLD MAN OF HIS ACQUAINTANCE. Yuen Jang was an old acquaintance of Confucius, but had adopt-

而不孫弟、長而無述焉、老而不死、是為賊。以杖叩其脛。

四十七 闕黨童子將命、一 或問之曰、益者與。二 子曰、吾見其居於位也、見其與先生並行也、非求益者也、欲速成者也。

not humble as befits a junior; in manhood, doing nothing worthy of being handed down; and living on to old age:—this is to be a pest." With this he hit him on the shank with his staff.

CHAPTER XLVII. 1. A youth of the village of K'euĕh was employed by *Confucius* to carry the messages between him and his visitors. Some one asked about him, saying, "I suppose he has made great progress."

2. The Master said, "I observe that he is fond of occupying the seat *of a full-grown man;* I observe that he walks shoulder to shoulder with his elders. He is not one who is seeking to make progress *in learning.* He wishes quickly to become a man."

ed the principles of Laou-tsze, and gave himself extraordinary license in his behaviour.—See an instance in the Le-ke, II. Pt. II. iii. 24. 夷俟,—the dict. explains the two words together by 展足箕坐, but that is the meaning of 夷 alone, and 俟=待, 'to wait for.' So, the commentators, old and new. The use of 夷 in this sense is thus explained:—'The 鴟鳥 is fond of squatting, and is therefore called the squatting ch'e (蹲鴟), but it is called by some the ch'e e (鴟夷), and hence 夷 is used for 蹲, to squat!' See the 集證, *in loc.* 孫 for 遜, and 弟 for 悌. 賊,—in the sense of 賊害,—our 'pest,' rather than 'thief.' The address of Conf. might be translated in the 2d person, but it is perhaps better to keep to the 3d, leaving the application to be understood.

47. CONFUCIUS' EMPLOYMENT OF A FORWARD YOUTH. 1. 闕黨,—there is a tradition that Confucius lived and taught in 闕里, but it is much disputed. 將命謂傳賓主之言, '將命 means to convey the messages between visitors and the host.' 益者與,—the inquirer supposed that Conf. employment of the lad was to distinguish him for the progress which he had made. 2. According to the rules of ceremony, a youth must sit in the corner, the body of the room being reserved for fullgrown men. See the Le-ke, II. Pt. I. i. 17. In walking with an elder, a youth was required to keep a little behind him. See the Le-ke, III. v. 15. Confucius' employment of the lad, therefore, was to teach him the courtesies required by his years.

BOOK XV. WEI LING KUNG.

衛靈公第十五

〔一〕衛靈公問陳於孔子。孔子對曰、俎豆之事、則嘗聞之矣、軍旅之事、未之學也。明日遂行。〔二〕在陳絕糧、從者病、莫能興。〔三〕子路慍見曰、君子亦有窮乎。子曰、君子固窮、小人窮斯濫矣。

CHAPTER I. 1. The duke Ling of Wei asked Confucius about tactics. Confucius replied, "I have heard all about sacrificial vessels, but I have not learned military matters." On this, he took his departure the next day.

2. When he was in Ch'in, their provisions were exhausted, and his followers became so ill that they were unable to rise.

3. Tsze-loo, with evident dissatisfaction, said, "Has the superior man likewise to endure *in this way?*" The Master said, "The superior man may indeed have to endure want, but the mean man, when he is in want, gives way to unbridled license."

HEADING OF THIS BOOK.—衛靈公第十五, 'The duke, Ling, of Wei—Book XV.' The contents of the Book, contained in forty chapters, are as miscellaneous as those of the former. Rather they are more so, some chapters bearing on the public administration of government, several being occupied with the superior man, and others containing lessons of practical wisdom. 'All the subjects,' says Hing Ping, 'illustrate the feeling of the sense of shame and consequent pursuit of the correct course, and therefore the Book immediately follows the preceding one.'

1. CONFUCIUS REFUSES TO TALK ON MILITARY AFFAIRS. IN THE MIDST OF DISTRESS, HE SHOWS THE DISCIPLES HOW THE SUPERIOR MAN IS ABOVE DISTRESS. 1. 陳, read chin, low. 3d tone, 'the arrangement of the ranks of an army,' here=tactics, generally. 俎豆之事,—Comp. 籩豆之事, VIII. 4, 3. The 俎 was a dish, 18 inches long and 8 in. broad, on a stand, 8½ in. high, upon which the flesh of victims was laid, but the meaning is sacrificial vessels generally,=the business of ceremonies. It is said of Conf., in the 'Historical Records,' that when a boy, he was fond of playing at 俎 and 豆. He wished by his reply and departure, to teach the duke that the rules of propriety, and not war, were essential to the government of a state. 2. From Wei, Conf. proceeded to Ch'in, and there met with the distress here mentioned. It is probably the same which is referred to in XI. 2, 1, though there is some chronological difficulty about the subject. (See the note by Choo He in his preface to the Analects.) 3. 固 = 'yes, indeed,' with reference to Tsze-loo's question. Some take it in its sense of 'firm.'—'The superior man firmly endures want.'

二 子曰、賜也、女以予爲多學而識之者與。對曰、然、非與。曰、非也、予一以貫之。

三 子曰、由、知德者鮮矣。

四 子曰、無爲而治者、其舜也與、夫何爲哉、恭己正南面而已矣。

五 子張問行。子曰、言忠信、行篤敬、雖蠻貊之邦、

CHAPTER II. 1. The Master said, "Ts'ze, you think, I suppose, that I am one who learns many things and keeps them in memory?"

2. Tsze-kung replied, "Yes,—but perhaps it is not so?"

3. "No," was the answer; "I *seek* a unity all-pervading."

CHAPTER III. The Master said, "Yew, those who know virtue are few."

CHAPTER IV. The Master said, "May not Shun be instanced as having governed efficiently without exertion? What did he do? He did nothing but gravely and reverently occupy his imperial seat."

CHAPTER V. 1. Tsze-chang asked how a man might conduct himself, *so as to be everywhere appreciated.*

2. The Master said, "Let his words be sincere and truthful, and his actions honorable and careful;—such conduct may be practised among the rude tribes of the South or the North. If his words be

2. HOW CONFUCIUS AIMED AT THE KNOWLEDGE OF AN ALL-PERVADING UNITY. This chapter is to be compared with IV. 15, only, says Chu He, 'that is spoken with reference to practice, and this with reference to knowledge.' But the design of Conf. was probably the same in them both; and I understand the first par. here as meaning—'Ts'ze, do you think that I am aiming, by the exercise of memory, to acquire a varied and extensive knowledge?' Then the 3d paragraph is equivalent to:—'I am not doing this. My aim is to know myself,—the mind which embraces all knowledge, and regulates all practice.' This is the view of the chapter given in the 日講:—此一章發曾學貴乎知要, 'This chapter teaches that what is valuable in learning, is the knowledge of that which is important.'

3. FEW REALLY KNOW VIRTUE. This is understood as spoken with reference to the dissatisfaction manifested by Tsze-loo in ch. 1. If he had possessed a right knowledge of virtue, he would not have been so affected by distress.

4. HOW SHUN WAS ABLE TO GOVERN WITHOUT PERSONAL EFFORT. 恭己, 'made himself reverent.' 正南面, 'correctly adjusted his south-wards face;' see VI. 1. Shun succeeding Yaou, there were many ministers o great virtue and ability, to occupy all the offices of the government. All that Shun did, was by his grave and sage example. This is the lesson—the influence of a ruler's personal character.

5. CONDUCT THAT WILL BE APPRECIATED IN ALL PARTS OF THE WORLD. 1. We must supply a good deal to bring out the meaning here. Choo He compares the question with that other of Tsze-chang about the scholar who may be

行矣、言不忠信、行不篤敬、雖州里、行乎哉。三立則見其參於前也、在輿則見其倚於衡也、夫然後行。四子張書諸紳。

六子曰、直哉史魚、邦有道如矢、邦無道如矢。二君子哉蘧伯玉、邦有道則仕、邦無道、則可卷而懷之。

not sincere and truthful, and his actions not honorable and careful, will he, with such conduct, be appreciated, even in his neighbourhood?

3. "When he is standing, let him see those two things, as it were fronting him. When he is in a carriage, let him see them attached to the yoke. Then may he subsequently carry them into practice."

4. Tsze-chang wrote these counsels on the end of his sash.

CHAPTER VI. 1. The Master said, "Truly straightforward was the historiographer Yu. When good government prevailed in his state, he was like an arrow. When bad government prevailed, he was like an arrow.

2. "A superior man indeed is Keu Pih-yuh! When good government prevails in his state, he is to be found in office. When bad government prevails, he can roll his principles up, and keeps them in his breast."

called 蠻; see XII. 20. 2. 貊 is another name for the 北狄, the rude tribes on the north. 2,500 families made up a 州, and 25 made up a 里, but the meaning of the phrase is that given in the translation. 3. 其, 'them,' i.e., such words and actions.—Let him see them 參於前, 'before him, with himself making a trio.' 輿 is properly 'the bottom of a carriage,' planks laid over wheels, a simple 'hackery,' but here it='a carriage.' 4. 紳 denotes the ends of the sash that hang down.

6. THE ADMIRABLE CHARACTERS OF TSZE-YU AND KEU PIH-YUH. 1. 子魚 was the designation of 魚子, the historiographer of Wei, on his deathbed, he left a message for his prince, and gave orders that his body should be laid out in a place and manner likely to attract his attention when he paid the visit of condolence. It was so, and the message then delivered had the desired effect. Perhaps it was on hearing this that Confucius made this remark. 如矢, 'as an arrow,' i.e., straight and decided. 2. Keu Pih-yuh,—see XIV. 26. 可=能. 卷而懷之,—之 is to be understood as referring to 'his principles,' or perhaps the clause = 'he could roll himself up and keep himself to himself,' i.e., he kept aloof from office.—Comm. say that Tsze-yu's uniform straightforwardness was not equal to Pih-yuh's rightly adapting himself to circumstances.

〔七〕子曰、可與言、而不與之言、失人、不可與言、而與之言、失言、知者不失人、亦不失言。

〔八〕子曰、志士、仁人、無求生以害仁、有殺身以成仁。

〔九〕子貢問爲仁。子曰、工欲善其事、必先利其器、居是邦也、事其大夫之賢者、友其士之仁者。

〔十〕一顏淵問爲邦。二子曰、行夏之

CHAPTER VII. The Master said, "When a man may be spoken with, not to speak to him is to err in reference to the man. When a man may not be spoken with, to speak to him is to err in reference to our words. The wise err neither in regard to their man nor to their words."

CHAPTER VIII. The Master said, "The determined scholar and the man of virtue will not seek to live at the expense of injuring their virtue. They will even sacrifice their lives to preserve their virtue complete."

CHAPTER IX. Tsze-kung asked about the practice of virtue. The Master said, "The mechanic, who wishes to do his work well, must first sharpen his tools. When you are living in any state, take service with the most worthy among its great officers, and make friends of the most virtuous among its scholars."

CHAPTER X. 1. Yen Yuen asked how the government of a country should be administered.

7. THERE ARE MEN WITH WHOM TO SPEAK, AND MEN WITH WHOM TO KEEP SILENCE. THE WISE KNOW THEM. 失言 may be translated, literally and properly,—'to lose our words,' but in English we do not use 'to lose,' in connection with 'men,' in the same way.

8. HIGH NATURES VALUE VIRTUE MORE THAN LIFE. The 志士 and 仁人 are two different classes, the same described IV. 2,—仁者安仁, 知者利仁. 有殺身 is naturally translated—'They will kill themselves.' No doubt suicide is included in the expression (See the 疏 to Ho An), and Confucius here justifies that act, as in certain cases expressive of high virtue.

9. HOW INTERCOURSE WITH THE GOOD AIDS THE PRACTICE OF VIRTUE. Comp. Proverbs XXVII. 17, 'Iron sharpeneth iron; so a man sharpeneth the countenance of his friend.'

10. CERTAIN RULES, EXEMPLIFIED IN THE ANCIENT DYNASTIES, TO BE FOLLOWED IN GOVERNING:—A REPLY TO YEN YUEN. 1. The disciple

時。三乘殷之輅。四服周之冕。五樂則韶舞。六放鄭聲、遠佞人、鄭聲淫、佞人殆。

十一子曰、人無遠慮、必有近憂。

十二子曰、已矣乎、吾未見好德如好色者也。

十三子曰、臧文仲、其竊位者與、知柳下惠之

2. The Master said, "Follow the seasons of Hea.

3. "Ride in the state carriage of Yin.

4. "Wear the ceremonial cap of Chow.

5. "Let the music be the Shaou with its pantomimes.

6. "Banish the songs of Ch'ing, and keep far from specious talkers. The songs of Ch'ing are licentious; specious talkers are dangerous."

CHAPTER XI. The Master said, "If a man take no thought about what is distant, he will find sorrow near at hand."

CHAPTER XII. The Master said, "It is all over! I have not seen one who loves virtue as he loves beauty."

CHAPTER XIII. The Master said, "Was not Tsang Wăn like one who had stolen his situation? He knew the virtue and the talents

modestly put his question with reference to the government of a state (邦), but the Master answers it according to the disciple's ability, as if it had been about the ruling of the empire (治天下). 2. The three great ancient dynasties began the year at different times. According to an ancient tradition, 'Heaven was opened at the time 子; Earth appeared at the time 丑; and Man was born at the time 寅.' 子 commences in our December, at the winter solstice; 丑 a month later; and 寅 a month after 丑. The Chow dynasty began its year with 子; the Shang with 丑; and the Hea with 寅. As human life then commenced, the year, in reference to human labours, naturally proceeds from the spring, and Conf. approved the rule of the Hea dynasty. His decision has been the law of all dynasties since the Tsin. See the '*Discours Preliminaire, Chap. I*,' in Gaubil's Shoo King. 3. The state carriage of the Yin dynasty was plain and substantial, which Conf. preferred to the more ornamented ones of Chow. 4. Yet he does not object to the more elegant cap of that dynasty, 'the cap,' says Choo He, 'being a small thing, and placed over all the body.' 5. The shaou was the music of Shun; see III. 25. 舞,—the 'dancers,' or 'pantomimes,' who kept time to the music. See the Shoo-king II. ii. 21. 6. 鄭聲, 'the sounds of Ch'ing,' meaning both the songs of Ch'ing, and the appropriate music to which they were sung. These songs form the 7th book of the 1st division of the She-king, and are here characterized justly.

11. THE NECESSITY OF FORETHOUGHT AND PRECAUTION.

12. THE RARITY OF A TRUE LOVE OF VIRTUE. 已矣乎,—see V. 26; the rest is a repetition of IX. 17, said to have been spoken by Conf. when he was in Wei, and saw the duke riding out openly in the same carriage with Nan-tsze.

13. AGAINST JEALOUSY OF OTHERS' TALENTS;—THE CASE OF TSANG WAN, AND HWUY OF LEW-HEA. Tsang Wan-chung.—See V. 17. 竊位 is explained—如盜得而陰據之, 'as if he had got it by theft, and

賢、而不與立也。

〔十四〕子曰、躬自厚而薄責於人、則遠怨矣。

〔十五〕子曰、不曰如之何、如之何者、吾末如之何也已矣。

〔十六〕子曰、群居終日、言不及義、好行小慧、難矣哉。

〔十七〕子曰、君子義以爲質、禮以行之、孫以出之、信

of Hwuy of Lew-hea, and yet did not *procure that he should* stand with him *in court*."

CHAPTER XIV. The Master said, "He who requires much from himself and little from others, will keep himself from *being the object of* resentment."

CHAPTER XV. The Master said, "When a man is not *in the habit of* saying—'What shall I think of this? What shall I think of this?' I can indeed do nothing with him!"

CHAPTER XVI. The Master said, "When a number of people are together, for a whole day, without their conversation turning on righteousness, and when they are fond of carrying out *the suggestions of* a small shrewdness;—theirs is indeed a hard case."

CHAPTER XVII. The Master said, "The superior man *in everything* considers righteousness to be essential. He performs it according to the rules of propriety. He brings it forth in humility. He completes it with sincerity. This is indeed a superior man."

secretly held possession of it.' Tsang Wăn would not recommend Hwuy, because he was an abler and better man than himself. Hwuy is a famous name in China. He was an officer of Loo, so styled after death, whose name was 展獲, and designation 禽. He derived his revenue from a town called Lew-hea, though some say that it was a *lew* or willow tree, overhanging his house, which made him to be known as Lew-hea Hwuy—'Hwuy that lived under the willow tree.' See Mencius, II. i. 9.

14. THE WAY TO WARD OFF RESENTMENTS. 責, it is said, is here 'to require from,' and not 'to reprove,' but the one meaning passes insensibly into the other.

15. NOTHING CAN BE MADE OF PEOPLE WHO TAKE THINGS EASILY, NOT GIVING THEMSELVES THE TROUBLE TO THINK. Comp. VII. 8.

16. AGAINST FRIVOLOUS TALKERS AND SUPERFICIAL SPECULATORS. Choo He explains 難矣哉 by 無以入德而將有患害, 'they have no ground from which to become virtuous, and they will meet with calamity.' Ho An gives Ch'ing K'ang-shing's explanation:—終無成, 'they will never complete any thing.' Our nearly literal translation appears to convey the meaning. 'A hard case,' *i.e.*, they will make nothing out, and nothing can be made of them.

17. THE CONDUCT OF THE SUPERIOR MAN IS RIGHTEOUS, COURTEOUS, HUMBLE, AND SINCERE. 質, is explained by Choo He by 質幹, 'the substance and stem;' and in the 備旨 by

以成之、君子哉。

十八 子曰、君子病無能焉、不病人之不己知也。

十九 子曰、君子疾沒世而名不稱焉。

二十 子曰、君子求諸己、小人求諸人。

廿一 子曰、君子矜而不爭、群而不黨。

廿二 子曰、君子不以言舉人、不以

CHAPTER XVIII. The Master said, "The superior man is distressed by his want of ability. He is not distressed by men's not knowing him."

CHAPTER XIX. The Master said, "The superior man dislikes the thought of his name not being mentioned after his death."

CHAPTER XX. The Master said, "What the superior man seeks, is in himself. What the mean man seeks, is in others.

CHAPTER XXI. The Master said, "The superior man is dignified, but does not wrangle. He is sociable, but not a partizan."

CHAPTER XXII. The Master said, "The superior man does not promote a man *simply* on account of his words, nor does he put aside *good* words because of the man."

基址, 'foundation.' The antecedent to all the 之 is 義, or rather the thing, whatever it be, done righteously.

18. OUR OWN INCOMPETENCY, AND NOT OUR REPUTATION, THE PROPER BUSINESS OF CONCERN TO US. See XIV. 32, *et al.*

19. THE SUPERIOR MAN WISHES TO BE HAD IN REMEMBRANCE. Not, say the commentators, that the superior man cares about fame, but fame is the invariable concomitant of merit. He can't have been the superior man, if he be not remembered. 沒世,—see 大學傳, II. In the 備旨, 日講, and many other paraphrases, 沒世 is taken as=終身; 'all his life.'

20. HIS OWN APPROBATION IS THE SUPERIOR MAN'S RULE. THE APPROBATION OF OTHERS IS THE MEAN MAN'S. Comp. XIV. 25.

21. THE SUPERIOR MAN IS DIGNIFIED AND AFFABLE, WITHOUT THE FAULTS TO WHICH THOSE QUALITIES OFTEN LEAD. Comp. II. 14, and VII. 30. 矜 is here=莊以持己, 'grave in self-maintenance.'

22. THE SUPERIOR MAN IS DISCRIMINATING, IN HIS EMPLOYMENT OF MEN AND JUDGING OF STATEMENTS.

人廢言。

廿三 子貢問曰、有一言而可以終身行之者乎。子曰、其恕乎、己所不欲、勿施於人。

廿四 子曰、吾之於人也、誰毀、誰譽、如有所譽者、其有所試矣。二 斯民也、三代之所以直道而行也。

廿五 子曰、吾猶及史之闕文也、有馬者、借人乘之、今亡已夫。

CHAPTER XXIII. Tsze-kung asked, saying, "Is there one word which may serve as a rule of practice for all one's life?" The Master said, "Is not RECIPROCITY such a word? What you do not want done to yourself, do not do to others."

CHAPTER XXIV. 1. The Master said, "In my dealings with men, whose evil do I blame, whose goodness do I praise, beyond what is proper? If I do sometimes exceed in praise, there must be ground for it in my examination *of the individual.*

2. "This people supplied the ground why the three dynasties pursued the path of straightforwardness."

CHAPTER XXV. The Master said, "Even in my *early* days, a historiographer would leave a blank in his text, and he who had a horse would lend him to another to ride. Now, alas! there are no such things."

23. THE GREAT PRINCIPLE OF RECIPROCITY IS THE RULE OF LIFE. Comp. V. 11. It is singular that Tsze-kung professes there to act on the principle here recommended to him.

24. CONFUCIUS SHOWED HIS RESPECT FOR MEN BY STRICT TRUTHFULNESS IN AWARDING PRAISE OR CENSURE. 1. I have not marked 'beyond what is proper' with italics, because there is really that force in the verbs—毀 and 譽. 'Ground for it in my examination of the individual;'—*i. e.*, from examination of him I believe he will yet verify my words. 2. 斯民也, resumes the 人 of the 1st par., which the 也 indicates. 所以 is to be taken as='the reason why,' and 行 as a neuter verb, of general application. 三代, 'the three dynasties,' with special reference to their great founders, and the principles which they inaugurated.—The truth-approving nature of the people was a rule even to those sages. It was the same to Confucius.

25. INSTANCES OF THE DEGENERACY OF CONFUCIUS' TIMES. Most paraphrasts supply a 見 after 及;—'even in my time I have seen.'

〔二十六〕子曰、巧言亂德。小不忍、則亂大謀。〔二十七〕子曰、衆惡之、必察焉、衆好之、必察焉。〔二十八〕子曰、人能弘道、非道弘人。〔二十九〕子曰、過而不改、是謂過矣。〔三十〕子曰、吾嘗終日

CHAPTER XXVI. The Master said, "Specious words confound virtue. Want of forbearance in small matters confounds great plans."

CHAPTER XXVII. The Master said, "When the multitude hate a man, it is necessary to examine into the case. When the multitude like a man, it is necessary to examine into the case."

CHAPTER XXVIII. The Master said, "A man can enlarge the principles *which he follows;* those principles do not enlarge the man."

CHAPTER XXIX. The Master said, "To have faults and not to reform them,—this, indeed, should be pronounced having faults."

CHAPTER XXX. The Master said, "I have been the whole day

The appointment of the historiographer is referred to Hwang-te, or 'The Yellow emperor,' the inventor of the cycle. The statutes of Chow mention no fewer than five classes of such officers. They were attached also to the feudal courts, and what Confucius says, is that, in his early days, a historiographer, on any point about which he was not sure, would leave a blank; so careful were they to record only truth. 吾猶及 extends on to 有馬云云. This second sentence is explained in the 註:—'If any one had a horse which he could not tame, he would lend it to another to ride and exercise it!'—The commentator Hoo (胡氏) says well, that the meaning of the chapter must be left in uncertainty.

26. THE DANGER OF SPECIOUS WORDS, AND OF IMPATIENCE. 小不忍 is not 'a little impatience,' but impatience in little things: 'the hastiness,' it is said, 'of women and small people.'

27. IN JUDGING OF A MAN, WE MUST NOT BE GUIDED BY HIS BEING GENERALLY LIKED OR DISLIKED. Comp. XIII. 24.

28. PRINCIPLES OF DUTY AN INSTRUMENT IN THE HAND OF MAN. This sentence is quite mystical in its sententiousness. The 翼註 says:—'道 here is the path of duty, which all men, in their various relations, have to pursue, and man has the three virtues of knowledge, benevolence, and fortitude, wherewith to pursue that path, and so he enlarges it. That virtue remote, occupying an empty place, cannot enlarge man, needs not to be said.' That writer's account of 道 here is probably correct, and 'duty unapprehended.' 'in an empty place,' can have no effect on any man; but this is a mere truism. Duty apprehended is constantly enlarging, elevating, and energizing multitudes, who had previously been unconscious of it. 'The first clause of the chapter may be granted, but the second is not in accordance with truth.

29. THE CULPABILITY OF NOT REFORMING KNOWN FAULTS. Comp. I. 8. Choo He's commentary appears to make the meaning somewhat different. He says:—'If one having faults can change them, he comes back to the condition of having no faults. But if he do not change them, then they go on to their completion, and will never come to be changed.'

30. THE FRUITLESSNESS OF THINKING, WITHOUT READING. Comp. II. 15, where the dependence of acquisition and reflection on each other is set forth.—Many comm. say that Conf. merely transfers the things which he here mentions to himself for the sake of others, not that it ever was really thus with himself.

不食、終夜不寢、以思、無益、不如學也。

〖三十一〗子曰、君子謀道不謀食、耕也、餒在其中矣、學也、祿在其中矣、君子憂道、不憂貧。

〖三十二〗子曰、知及之、仁不能守之、雖得之、必失之。〖二〗知及之、仁能守之、不莊以涖之、則民不敬。〖三〗知及之、仁能守之、莊以涖之、動之不以禮、未善也。

without eating, and the whole night without sleeping:—occupied with thinking. It was of no use. The better plan is to learn."

CHAPTER XXXI. The Master said, "The object of the superior man is truth. Food is not his object. There is ploughing;—even in that there is *sometimes* want. So with learning;—emolument may be found in it. The superior man is anxious lest he should not get truth; he is not anxious lest poverty should come upon him."

CHAPTER XXXII. 1. The Master said, "When a man's knowledge is sufficient to attain, and his virtue is not sufficient to enable him to hold, whatever he may have gained, he will lose again.

2. "When his knowledge is sufficient to attain, and he has virtue enough to hold fast, if he cannot govern with dignity, the people will not respect him.

3. "When his knowledge is sufficient to attain, and he has virtue enough to hold fast; when he governs also with dignity, yet if he try to move the people contrary to the rules of propriety:—full excellence is not reached."

31. THE SUPERIOR MAN SHOULD NOT BE MERCENARY, BUT HAVE TRUTH FOR HIS OBJECT. Here again we translate 道 by 'truth,' as the best term that offers. 餒, 'hunger,'=want. 'Want may be in the midst of ploughing,'—*i.e.*, husbandry is the way to plenty, and yet despite the labours of the husbandman, a famine or scarcity sometimes occurs. The application of this to the case of learning, however, is not very apt. Is the emolument that sometimes comes with learning a calamity like famine?—Ch'ing K'ang-shing's view is:—'Although a man may plough, yet, not learning, he will come to hunger. If he learn, he will get emolument, and tho' he do not plough, he will not be in want. This is advising men to learn.'

32. HOW KNOWLEDGE WITHOUT VIRTUE IS NOT LASTING, AND TO KNOWLEDGE AND VIRTUE A RULER SHOULD ADD DIGNITY AND THE RULES OF PROPRIETY. 1. Here the various 之 and the

〔三十三〕子曰、君子不可小知、而可大受也、小人不可大受、而可小知也。〔三十四〕子曰、民之於仁也、甚於水火、水火吾見蹈而死者矣、未見蹈仁而死者也。〔三十五〕子曰、當仁、不讓於師。

CHAPTER XXXIII. The Master said, "The superior man cannot be known in little matters; but he may be intrusted with great concerns. The small man may not be intrusted with great concerns, but he may be known in little matters."

CHAPTER XXXIV. The Master said, "Virtue is more to man than either water or fire. I have seen men die from treading on water and fire, but I have never seen a man die from treading the course of virtue."

CHAPTER XXXV. The Master said, "Let every man consider virtue as what devolves on himself. He may not yield the performance of it *even* to his teacher."

two first in the other paragraphs, 指理言, 'have *li*, or principle, for their reference.' In Ho An, however, Paou Heen says:—'A man may have knowledge equal to the management of his office (治其官), but if he have not virtue which can hold it fast, though he get it, he will lose it.' 2. In 涖之, and 動之 below, 之指民言, 'the 之 have 民, or people, for their reference.' 3. The phrase—'to move the people' is analogous to several others, such as 鼓之, 舞之, 興之, 'to drum the people,' 'to dance them,' 'to rouse them.'

33. HOW TO KNOW THE SUPERIOR MAN AND THE MEAN MAN; AND THEIR CAPACITIES. Choo He says—知, 我知之, 'the knowing here is our knowing the individuals.' The 'little matters' are ingenious but trifling arts and accomplishments, in which a really great man may sometimes be deficient, while a small man will be familiar with them. The 'knowing' is not that the parties are *keun-tsze* and *seaou-jin*, but what attainments they have, and for what they are fit. The difficulty, on this view, is with the conclusion—而可小知.—Ho An gives the view of Wang Suh:—'The way of the *keun-tsze* is profound and far-reaching. He may not let his knowledge be small, and he may receive what is great. The way of the *seaou-jin* is shallow and near. He may let his knowledge be small, and he may not receive what is great.'

34. VIRTUE MORE TO MAN THAN WATER OR FIRE, AND NEVER HURTFUL TO HIM. 民 is here =人, 'man,' as in VI. 20. 民之於仁也—'the people's relation to, or dependence on, virtue.' The case is easily conceivable of men's suffering death on account of their virtue. There have been martyrs for their loyalty and other virtues, as well as for their religious faith. Choo He provides for this diff. in his remarks:—'The want of fire and water is hurtful only to man's body, but to be without virtue is to lose one's mind (the higher nature), and so it is more to him than water or fire.' See on IV. 8.

35. VIRTUE PERSONAL AND OBLIGATORY ON EVERY MAN. The old interpreters take 當 in the sense of 'ought.' Choo He certainly improves on them by taking it in the sense of 擔當, as in the translation. A student at first takes 當 to be in the 2d person, but the 不 following recalls him to the 3d.

三十六 子曰、君子貞、而不諒。

三十七 子曰、事君敬其事、而後其食。

三十八 子曰、有教、無類。

三十九 子曰、道不同、不相爲謀。

四十 子曰、辭達而已矣。

四十一 一 師冕見、及階、子曰、階也。及席、子曰、席也。

CHAPTER XXXVI. The Master said, "The superior man is correctly firm, and not firm merely."

CHAPTER XXXVII. The Master said, "A minister, in serving his prince, reverently discharges his duties, and makes his emolument a secondary consideration."

CHAPTER XXXVIII. The Master said, "There being instruction, there will be no distinction of classes."

CHAPTER XXXIX. The Master said, "Those whose courses are different cannot lay plans for one another."

CHAPTER XL. The Master said, "In language it is simply required that it convey the meaning."

CHAPTER XLI. 1. The Music-master, Meën, having called upon him, when they came to the steps, the Master said, "Here are the steps." When they came to the mat *for the guest* to sit upon, he

36. THE SUPERIOR MAN'S FIRMNESS IS BASED ON RIGHT. 貞 is used here in the sense which it has throughout the Yih-king. Both it and 諒 imply firmness, but 貞 supposes a moral and intelligent basis which may be absent from 諒; see XIV. 18, 3.

37. THE FAITHFUL MINISTER. The 其 refers not to 君, but to the individual who 事君. We have to supply the subject—'a minister.' 後, as in VI. 20.

38. THE EFFECT OF TEACHING. Choo He says on this:—'The nature of all men is good, but we find among them the different classes of good and bad. This is the effect of physical constitution and of practice. The superior man, in consequence, employs his teaching, and all may be brought back to the state of good, and there is no necessity (The lang. is 不當復論其類之惡) of speaking any more of the badness of some.' This is very extravagant. Teaching is not so omnipotent.—The old interpretation is simply that in teaching there should be no distinction of classes.

39. AGREEMENT IN PRINCIPLE NECESSARY TO CONCORD IN PLANS. 爲 is the 3d tone, but I do not see that there would be any great difference in the meaning, if it were read in its usual 1st tone.

40. PERSPICUITY THE CHIEF VIRTUE OF LANGUAGE. 辭 may be used both of speech and of style.

41. CONSIDERATION OF CONFUCIUS FOR THE BLIND. 1. 師,—i. e. 太師, III. 23. Anciently, the blind were employed in the offices of music, partly because their sense of hearing

皆坐、子告之曰、某在斯、某在斯。二 師冕出。子張問曰、與師言之道與。三 子曰、然、固相師之道也。

said, "Here is the mat." When all were seated, the Master informed him, saying, "So and so is here; so and so is here."

2. The Music-master, Mëen, having gone out, Tsze-chang asked, saying, "Is it the rule to tell those things to the Music-master?"

3. The Master said, "Yes. This is certainly the rule for those who lead the blind."

was more than ordinarily acute, and partly that they might be made of some use in the world; see the 樂記. 見,—low 3d tone. Mëen had come to Conf. house, under the care of a guide, but the sage met him, and undertook the care of him himself. 3. 之 is governed by 言, and refers to the words of Conf. to Mëen in the preceding paragraph.

BOOK XVI. KE SHE.

季氏第十六

一 季氏將伐顓臾。二 冉有季路見於孔子、曰、季氏將有事於顓臾。

CHAPTER I. 1. The head of the Ke family was going to attack Chuen-yu.

2. Yen Yew and Ke Loo had an interview with Confucius, and said, "*Our chief*, Ke, is going to commence operations against Chuen-yu."

HEADING OF THIS BOOK.—季氏第十六. 'The chief of the Ke—No XVI.' Throughout this Book, Confucius is spoken of as 孔子, 'The philosopher K'ung,' and never by the designation 子, or 'The Master.' Then, the style of several of the chapters (IV—XI) is not like the utterances of Confucius to which we have been accustomed. From these circumstances, one commentator, Hung Kwoh (洪适), supposed that it belonged to the Ts'e (齊) recension of these analects; the other books belonging to the Loo (魯) recension. This supposition, however, is not otherwise supported.

1. CONFUCIUS EXPOSES THE PRESUMPTUOUS AND IMPOLITIC CONDUCT OF THE CHIEF OF THE KE FAMILY IN PROPOSING TO ATTACK A MINOR STATE, AND REBUKES YEN YEW AND TSZE-LOO FOR ASSISTING THE DESIGN. 1. 季氏 and 季孫 below,—see III. 1. Chuen-yu was a

三節孔子曰、求、無乃爾是過與。四節夫顓臾、昔者先王以爲東蒙主、且在邦域之中矣、是社稷之臣也、何以伐爲。五節冉有曰、夫子欲之、吾二臣者、皆不欲也。六節孔子曰、求、周任有言曰、陳力就列、不能者止、危而不持、顚而不扶、則將焉用彼相矣。七節且爾言過矣、虎兕出於柙、龜玉毀於

3. Confucius said, "K'ew, is it not you who are in fault here?

4. "Now, in regard to Chuen-yu, long ago, a former king appointed it to preside over *the sacrifices to* the eastern Mung; moreover, it is in the midst of the territory of our state; and its ruler is a minister in direct connexion with the emperor:—What has *your chief* to do with attacking it?"

5. Yen Yew said, "Our master wishes the thing; neither of us two ministers wishes it."

6. Confucius said, "K'ew, there are the words of Chow Jin,—'When he can put forth his ability, he takes his place in the ranks *of office;* when he finds himself unable to do so, he retires from it. How can he be used as a guide to a blind man, who does not support him when tottering, nor raise him up when fallen?'

7. "And further, you speak wrongly. When a tiger or wild bull escapes from his cage; when a tortoise or gem is injured in its repository:—whose is the fault?"

small territory in Loo, whose ruler was of the 子, or 4th order of nobility. It was one of the states called 附庸, or 'attached,' whose chiefs could not appear in the presence of the emperor, excepting in the train of the prince within whose jurisdiction they were embraced. Their existence was not from a practice like the sub-infeudation, which belonged to the feudal system of Europe. They hold of the lord paramount or emperor, but with the restriction which has been mentioned, and with a certain subserviency also to their immediate superior. Its particular position is fixed by its proximity to P'e, and to the Mung hill. 伐 is not merely 'to attack,' but 'to attack and punish,' an exercise of judicial authority, which could emanate only from the emperor. The term is used here, to show the nefarious and presumptuous character of the contemplated operations. 2. There is some difficulty here, as, acc. to the 'Historical Records,' the two disciples were not in the service of the Ke family, at the same time. We may suppose, however, that Tsze-loo, returning with the sage from Wei on the invitation of duke Gae, took service a second time, and for a short period, with the Ke family, of which the chief was then Ke K'ang. This brings the time of the

櫝中、是誰之過與。八冉有曰、今夫顓臾固、而近於費、今不取、後世必爲子孫憂。九孔子曰、求、君子疾夫舍曰欲之、而必爲之辭。十丘也、聞有國有家者、不患寡、而患不均、不患貧、而患不安、蓋均無貧、和無寡、安無傾。十一夫如

8. Yen Yew said, "But at present, Chuen-yu is strong and near to Pe; if *our chief* do not now take it, it will hereafter be a sorrow to his descendants."

9. Confucius said, "K'ew, the superior man hates that declining to say—'I want such and such a thing,' and framing explanations *for the conduct*.

10. "I have heard that rulers of states and chiefs of families are not troubled lest their people should be few, but are troubled lest they should not keep their several places; that they are not troubled with fears of poverty, but are troubled with fears of a want of contented repose *among the people in their several places*. For when the people keep their several places, there will be no poverty; when harmony prevails, there will be no scarcity of people; and when there is such a *contented* repose, there will be no rebellious upsettings.

transaction to B. C. 483, or 482. 將有事, —lit., 'is going to have an affair.' 3. Conf. addresses himself only to K'ew, as he had been a considerable time, and very active, in the Ke service. 4. It was the prerogative of the princes to sacrifice to the hills and rivers within their jurisdictions;—here was the chief of Chuen-yu, imperially appointed (the 'former king' is probably 成, the second emperor of the Chow dynasty) to be the lord of the Mung mountain, that is, to preside over the sacrifices offered to it. This raised him high above any mere ministers or officers of Loo. The mountain Mung is in the present district of Pe, in the department of E-chow. It was called eastern, to distinguish it from another of the same name in Shen-se, which was the western Mung. 且在邦域之中,—this is mentioned, to show that Chuen-yu was so situated as to give Loo no occasion for apprehension. 社稷之臣, 'a minister of the altars to the spirits of the land and grain.' To those spirits only, the princes had the prerogative of sacrificing. The chief of Chuen-yu having this, how dared an officer of Loo to think of attacking him? The 臣 is used of his relation to the emperor. Chao Ke makes the phrase = 公家之臣, 'a minister of the ducal house,' saying that the three families had usurped all the dominions proper of Loo, leaving only the chiefs of the attached states to appear in the ducal court. I prefer the former interpretation. 何以伐爲 must be understood with reference to the Ke. 爲 appears to be an expletive, unless we conceive it joined with the 何, the two characters together being simply = 'why,' or 'how.' 5. 夫子, our 'master,' i. e., the chief of the

是、故遠人不服、則修文德以來之、既來之、則安之。十二 今由與求也、相夫子、遠人不服、而不能來也、邦分崩離析、而不能守也。十三 而謀動干戈於邦內、吾恐季孫之憂、不在顓臾、而在蕭牆之內也。

11. "So it is.—Therefore, if remoter people are not submissive, all the influences of civil culture and virtue are to be cultivated to attract them to be so; and when they have been so attracted, they must be made contented and tranquil.

12. "Now, here are you, Yew and K'ew, assisting your chief. Remoter people are not submissive, and, *with your help*, he cannot attract them to him. In his own territory there are divisions and downfalls, leavings and separations, and, *with your help*, he cannot preserve it.

13. "And yet he is planning these hostile movements within our state.—I am afraid that the sorrow of the Ke-sun *family* will not be on account of Chuen-yu, but will be found within the screen of their own court."

Ke family. 6. Chow Jin is by Choo He simply called—'a good historiographer of ancient times.' Some trace him back to the Shang dynasty, and others only to the early times of the Chow. There are other weighty utterances of his in vogue, besides that in the text. 7. Choo He explains 兕 by 野牛, 'a wild bull.' The dict. says it is like an ox, and goes on to describe it as 'one-horned.' The 本草獸部, says that 兕 and 犀 are different terms for the same animal, i. e., the rhinoceros. I cannot think that 龜 here is the living tortoise. That would not be kept in a 櫝, or 'coffer,' like a gem. Perhaps the term is, by mistake, for 圭. 9. The regimen of 疾 extends down to the end of the par. 夫,—as in XI. 24. 舍之辭 is the same idiom as 舍之宰, V. 7. 10. Conf. uses the term 患 here, with ref. to the 寡 in p. 8. 均, 'equality,' 謂各得其分, 'means—every one getting his own proper name and place.' From this point, Conf. speaks of the general disorganization of Loo under the management of the three families, and especially of the Ke. By 遠人 we certainly cannot understand the people of Chuen-yu. 11. 來 is to be understood with a hiphil force, 'to make to come,' 'to attract.' 12. 不能來, 不能守, are to be understood of the head of the Ke family, as controlling the government of Loo, and *as being assisted by the two disciples*, so that the reproof falls heavily on them. 13. 在蕭牆之內,—Choo He simply says 蕭牆, 屏也, '*seaou-ts'eang* means a screen.' In the dict., after Ch'ing K'ang-shing, *seaou* in this pass.=肅, 'reverent,' and 牆 alone means 'screen,' and the phrase is thus explained:—'Officers, on reaching the screen, which they had only to pass, to find themselves in the presence of their head, were supposed to become more reverential'; and hence, the expression in the text='among his own immediate officers.'

孔子曰、天下有道、則禮樂征伐、自天子出、天下無道、則禮樂征伐、自諸侯出、自諸侯出、蓋十世希不失矣、自大夫出、五世希不失矣、陪臣執國命、三世希不失矣。天下有道、則政不在大夫。天下有道、則庶人不議。

CHAPTER II. 1. Confucius said, "When good government prevails in the empire, ceremonies, music, and punitive military expeditions, proceed from the emperor. When bad government prevails in the empire, ceremonies, music, and punitive military expeditions proceed from the princes. When these things proceed from the princes, *as a rule*, the cases will be few in which they do not lose their power in ten generations. When they proceed from the great officers *of the princes, as a rule*, the cases will be few in which they do not lose their power in five generations. When the subsidiary ministers *of the great officers* hold in their grasp the orders of the kingdom, *as a rule*, the cases will be few in which they do not lose their power in three generations.

2. "When right principles prevail in the empire, government will not be in the hands of the great officers.

3. "When right principles prevail in the empire, there will be no discussions among the common people."

2. THE SUPREME AUTHORITY OUGHT EVER TO MAINTAIN ITS POWER. THE VIOLATION OF THIS RULE ALWAYS LEADS TO RUIN, WHICH IS SPEEDIER AS THE RANK OF THE VIOLATOR IS LOWER.—In these utterances, Conf. had reference to the disorganized state of the empire, when 'the son of Heaven' was fast becoming an empty name, the princes of states were in bondage to their great officers, and those again at the mercy of their family ministers. 1. 有道, 無道,—compare XIV. i. 征伐 are to be taken together, as in the transl. We read of four 征, i. e., expeditions,—east, west, north, and south; and of nine 伐, i. e., nine grounds on which the emperor might order such expeditions. On the imperial prerogatives, see the 中庸, XXVIII. 蓋, is here=大約 'generally speaking,' 'as a rule.' 陪臣=家臣, 'family-ministers,' 國命 are the same as the previous 禮, 樂, 征, 伐, but having been usurped by the princes, and now again snatched from them by their officers, they can no longer be spoken of as imperial affairs, but only as 國之事, 'state matters.' 3. 議=私議, 'private discussions;' i. e., about the said state of public affairs.

〔三〕孔子曰、祿之去公室、五世矣、政逮於大夫、四世矣、故夫三桓之子孫微矣。

〔四〕孔子曰、益者三友、損者三友、友直、友諒、友多聞、益矣、友便辟、友善柔、友便佞、損矣。

〔五〕孔子曰、益者三樂、損者三樂、樂節禮樂、

CHAPTER III. Confucius said, "The revenue *of the state* has left the ducal house, now for five generations. The government has been in the hands of the great officers for four generations. On this account, the descendants of the three Hwan are much reduced."

CHAPTER IV. Confucius said, "There are three friendships which are advantageous, and three which are injurious. Friendship with the upright; friendship with the sincere; and friendship with the man of much observation:—these are advantageous. Friendship with the man of specious airs; friendship with the insinuatingly soft; and friendship with the glib-tongued:—these are injurious."

CHAPTER V. Confucius said, "There are three things men find enjoyment in which are advantageous, and three things they find enjoyment in which are injurious. To find enjoyment in the discriminating study of ceremonies and music; to find enjoyment in

3. ILLUSTRATION OF THE PRINCIPLES OF THE LAST CHAPTER. In the year B.C. 608, at the death of duke Wăn, his rightful heir was killed, and the son of a concubine raised to the dukedom. He is in the annals as duke Seuen (宣), and after him came Ch'ing, Seang, Ch'aou, and Ting, in whose time this must have been spoken. These dukes were but shadows, pensionaries of their great officers, so that it might be said the revenue had gone from them. Obs. that here and in the prec. ch., 世 is used for 'a reign.' 'The three Hwan' are the three families, as being all descended from duke Hwan; see on II. 5. 故夫,—'therefore,' uttered with a sigh.—Choo He appears to have fallen into a mistake in enumerating the four heads of the Ke family who had administered the government of Loo as Woo, Taou, P'ing, and Hwan, as Taou (悼) died before his father, and would not be said therefore to have the government in his hands. The right enumeration is Wăn (文), Woo (武), P'ing (平), and Hwan (桓). See the 摭餘說, III. XXVI.

4. THREE FRIENDSHIPS ADVANTAGEOUS, AND THREE INJURIOUS. In the 備旨 it is said—三友下各友字俱作交字看, 是我去友人, 'after 三友, the character 友 is always verbal, and = 交, 'to have intercourse with.' It is as well to translate the term by 'friendship' throughout. 諒 is here 'sincere,' without the subtractions required in XIV. 18, 3, XV. 36. 便,—here = 習熟, 'practised.' 善柔,—善柔之工, 善 is skilfulness in being bland. 辟, as in XI. 17, 3.

5. THREE SOURCES OF ENJOYMENT ADVANTAGEOUS, AND THREE INJURIOUS. Here we have 樂 with three pronunciations and in three

樂道人之善、樂多賢友、益矣、樂驕樂、樂佚遊、樂宴樂、損矣。

〔六〕孔子曰、侍於君子有三愆、言未及之而言、謂之躁、言及之而不言、謂之隱、未見顏色而言、謂之瞽。

〔七〕孔子曰、君子有三戒、少之時、血氣未定、戒之

speaking of the goodness of others; to find enjoyment in having many worthy friends:—these are advantageous. To find enjoyment in extravagant pleasures; to find enjoyment in idleness and sauntering; to find enjoyment in the pleasures of feasting:—these are injurious."

CHAPTER VI. Confucius said, "There are three errors to which they who stand in the presence of a man of virtue and station are liable. They may speak when it does not come to them to speak;—this is called rashness. They may not speak when it comes to them to speak;—this is called concealment. They may speak without looking at the countenance *of their superior*;—this is called blindness."

CHAPTER VII. Confucius said, "There are three things which the superior man guards against. In youth, when the physical

different meanings. The leading word is read ngâo, low. 3d tone, 'to have enjoyment in,' as in VI. 21. In 禮樂, it is yŏ, 'music.' The two others are 樂, lŏ, 'joy,' 'to delight in.' 節禮樂,—節=節之, i.e., it is a verb, 'to discriminate;' 'to mark the divisions of.' The idea is that ceremonies and music containing in them the principles of propriety and harmony, the study of them could not but be beneficial to the student himself, as having to exemplify both of those things. 驕, primarily, a 'tall horse,' often used for 'proud'; here,=vain and extravagant self-indulgence. 宴, 'feasting,' including, says a gloss, 'eating, drinking, music, women, &c.'

6. THREE ERRORS IN REGARD TO SPEECH TO BE AVOIDED IN THE PRESENCE OF THE GREAT. 君子, according to Choo He, denotes here 'a man both of rank and virtue.' 'Without looking at the countenance,'—i.e., to see whether he is paying attention or not.—The general principle is that there is a time to speak. Let that be observed, and these three errors will be avoided.

7. THE VICES WHICH YOUTH, MANHOOD, AND AGE, HAVE TO GUARD AGAINST. 血氣, 'blood and breath.' In the 中庸, XXI. 凡有血氣者='all human beings.' Here the phrase is equivalent to 'the physical powers.' On 未定, 'not yet settled,' the gloss in the

在色、及其壯也、血氣方剛、戒之在鬬、及其老也、血氣既衰、戒之在得。

[八] 孔子曰、君子有三畏、畏天命、畏大人、畏聖人之言。小人不知天命而不畏也、狎大人、侮聖人之言。

[九] 孔子曰、生而知之者、上也、學而知之者、次也、

powers are not yet settled, he guards against lust. When he is strong, and the physical powers are full of vigour, he guards against quarrelsomeness. When he is old, and the animal powers are decayed, he guards against covetousness."

CHAPTER VIII. 1. Confucius said, "There are three things of which the superior man stands in awe. He stands in awe of the ordinances of Heaven. He stands in awe of great men. He stands in awe of the words of sages.

2. "The mean man does not know the ordinances of Heaven, and *consequently* does not stand in awe of them. He is disrespectful to great men. He makes sport of the words of sages."

CHAPTER IX. Confucius said, "Those who are born with the possession of knowledge are the highest class of men. Those who learn, and so, *readily*, get possession of knowledge, are the next.

備旨 is—方動之時, 'the time when they are moving most.' As to what causal relation Conf. may have supposed to exist between the state of the physical powers, and the several vices indicated, that is not developed. Hing Ping explains the first caution thus:—'Youth embraces all the period below 29. Then, the physical powers are still weak, and the sinews and bones have not reached their vigour, and indulgence in lust will injure the body.'

8. CONTRAST OF THE SUPERIOR AND THE MEAN MAN IN REGARD TO THE THREE THINGS OF WHICH THE FORMER STANDS IN AWE. 天命, according to Choo He, means the moral nature of man, conferred by Heaven. High above the nature of other creatures, it lays him under great responsibility to cherish and cultivate him. The old interpr. take the phrase to indicate Heaven's moral administration by rewards and punishments. The 'great men' are men high in position and great in wisdom and virtue, the royal instructors, who have been raised up by Heaven for the training and ruling of mankind. So, the commentators; but the 狎 suggests at once a more general and a lower view of the phrase.

9. FOUR CLASSES OF MEN IN RELATION TO KNOWLEDGE. On the 1st clause, see on VII. 19, where Conf. disclaims for himself being ranked in the first of the classes here mentioned. The modern commentators say, that men are differenced here by the difference of their 氣質, or 氣稟, on which see Morrison's dict., part, II. vol I. char. 質 困, in the dict., and by commentators, old and new, is explained by 不通, 'not thoroughly understanding.' It

困而學之、又其次也。困而不學、民斯爲下矣。

十 孔子曰、君子有九思、視思明、聽思聰、色思溫、貌思恭、言思忠、事思敬、疑思問、忿思難、見得思義。

十一 孔子曰、見善如不及、見不善如探湯、吾見其人矣、吾聞其語矣。二隱居

Those who are dull and stupid, and yet compass the learning are another class next to these. As to those who are dull and stupid and yet do not learn;—they are the lowest of the people."

CHAPTER X. Confucius said, "The superior man has nine things which are subjects with him of thoughtful consideration. In regard to the use of his eyes, he is anxious to see clearly. In regard to the use of his ears, he is anxious to hear distinctly. In regard to his countenance, he is anxious that it should be benign. In regard to his demeanour, he is anxious that it should be respectful. In regard to his speech, he is anxious that it should be sincere. In regard to his doing of business, he is anxious that it should be reverently careful. In regard to what he doubts about, he is anxious to question others. When he is angry, he thinks of the difficulties his anger may involve him in. When he sees gain to be got, he thinks of righteousness."

CHAPTER XI. 1. Confucius said, "Contemplating good, *and pursuing it*, as if they could not reach it; contemplating evil, *and shrinking from it*, as they would from thrusting the hand into boiling water:—I have seen such men, as I have heard such words.

is not to be joined with 學, as if the meaning were—'they learn with painful effort, although such effort will be required in the case of the 困.

10. NINE SUBJECTS OF THOUGHT TO THE SUPERIOR MAN:—VARIOUS INSTANCES OF THE WAY IN WHICH HE REGULATES HIMSELF. The conciseness of the text contrasts here with the verbosity of the translation, and yet the many words of the latter seem necessary.

11. THE CONTEMPORARIES OF CONFUCIUS COULD ESCHEW EVIL, AND FOLLOW AFTER GOOD, BUT NO ONE OF THE HIGHEST CAPACITY HAD APPEARED AMONG THEM. 1. The two first clauses here and in the next par., also, are quotations of old sayings, current in Confucius' time. Such men were several of the sage's own disciples. 2. 求其志, 'seeking for their aims;' i.e., meditating on them, studying them, fixing them, to be prepared to carry them out, as in the next clause. Such men among the ancients

以求其志、行義以達其道、吾聞其語矣、未見其人也。

十二 齊景公有馬千駟、死之日、民無德而稱焉、伯夷叔齊、餓于首陽之下、民到于今稱之。其斯之謂與。

十三 陳亢問於伯魚曰、子亦有異聞乎。對曰、未也、嘗獨立、鯉趨而過庭、曰、學詩乎。對曰、未也。不學詩、無以言。

2. "Living in retirement to study their aims, and practising righteousness to carry out their principles:—I have heard these words, but I have not seen such men."

CHAPTER XII. 1. The duke King of Ts'e had a thousand teams, each of four horses, but on the day of his death, the people did not praise him for a single virtue. P'ih-e and Shuh-ts'e died of hunger at the foot of the Show-yang mountain, and the people, down to the present time, praise them.

2. "Is not that saying illustrated by this?"

CHAPTER XIII. 1. Ch'in K'ang asked Pih-yu, saying, "Have you heard any lessons *from your father* different *from what we have all heard?*"

2. Pih-yu replied, "No. He was standing alone once, when I passed below the hall with hasty steps, and said to me, 'Have you learned the Odes?' On my replying 'Not yet,' *he added*, 'If you do not learn the Odes, you will not be fit to converse with.' I retired and studied the Odes.

were the great ministers E-yen and T'ae-kung. Such might the disciple Yen Hwuy have been, but an early death snatched him away before he could have an opportunity of showing what was in him.

12. WEALTH WITHOUT VIRTUE AND VIRTUE WITHOUT WEALTH;—THEIR DIFFERENT APPRECIATIONS. This chapter is plainly a fragment. As it stands, it would appear to come from the compilers and not from Confucius. Then the 2d par. implies a reference to something which has been lost. Under XII. 10, I have referred to the proposal to transfer to this place the last par. of that chapter which might be explained, so as to harmonize with the sentiment of this. —The duke King of Ts'e,—see XII. 11. P'ih-e and Shuh-ts'e,—see VI. 22. The mountain Show-yang is to be found probably in the dep. of 蒲州 in Shan-se.

13. CONFUCIUS' INSTRUCTION OF HIS SON NOT DIFFERENT FROM HIS INSTRUCTION OF THE DISCIPLES GENERALLY. 1. Ch'in K'ang is the Tsze-k'in of I. 10. When Confucius' eldest son was born, the duke of Loo sent the philosopher a present of a carp, on which account he named the child

鯉退而學詩。三 他日又獨立、鯉趨而過庭、曰、學禮乎。對曰、未也。不學禮、無以立。鯉退而學禮。四 聞斯二者。五 陳亢退而喜曰、問一得三、聞詩、聞禮、又聞君子之遠其子也。

十四 邦君之妻、君稱之曰夫人、夫人自稱、曰小童、邦人稱之、曰君夫人、稱

3. "Another day, he was in the same way standing alone, when I passed by below the hall with hasty steps, and said to me, 'Have you learned the rules of Propriety?' On my replying 'Not yet,' *he added*, 'If you do not learn the rules of Propriety, your character cannot be established.' I then retired, and studied the rules of Propriety.

4. "I have heard only these two things from him."

5. Ch'in K'ang retired, and, quite delighted, said, "I asked one thing, and I have got three things. I have heard about the Odes. I have heard about the rules of Propriety. I have also heard that the superior man maintains a distant reserve towards his son."

CHAPTER XIV. The wife of the prince of a State is called by him FOO-JIN. She calls herself SEAOU T'UNG. The people of the State call

鯉, (the carp), and afterwards gave him the designation of 伯魚. 子亦有異聞乎, 'Have you *also* (i. e., as being his son) heard different instructions?' 2. On 詩 here, and 禮, next par., see on VII. 17. Before 不學, here and below, we must supply a 曰. 3. 立,—see VIII. 8. 4. The force of the 者 is to make the whole—'what I have heard from him are only these two remarks.' 5. Confucius is, no doubt, intended by 君子, but it is best to translate it generally.

14. APPELLATIONS FOR THE WIFE OF A PRINCE. This chapter may have been spoken by Confucius to rectify some disorder of the times, but there is no intimation to that effect. The different appellations may be thus explained ;— 妻 is 與已齊者, 'she who is her husband's equal.' The 夫 in 夫人 is taken as =扶, 'to support,' 'to help,' so that that designation is equivalent to 'helpmeet.' 童 means either 'a youth,' or 'a girl.' The wife modestly calls herself 小童, 'the little girl.' The old interpreters take—most naturally—君夫人 as=君之夫人, 'our prince's help-meet,' but the modern comm. take 君 adjectively, as=主, with reference to the office of the wife to 'preside over the internal economy of the palace.' On this view 君夫人 is

諸異邦、曰寡小君、異邦人稱之、亦曰君夫人。

her KEUN FOO-JIN, and, to the people of other States, they call her K'WA SEAOU KEUN. The people of other states also call her KEUN FOO-JIN.

'the domestic help-meet.' The ambassador of a prince spoke of him by the style of 寡君. 'my prince of small virtue.' After that example of modesty, his wife was styled to the people of other States, 'our small prince of small virtue.' The people of other States had no reason to imitate her subjects in that, and so they styled her—'your prince's help-meet,' or 'the domestic help-meet.'

BOOK XVII. YANG HO.

陽貨第十七

一章 陽貨欲見孔子、孔子不見、歸孔子豚、孔子時其亡也、而往拜之。遇諸塗。謂孔子曰、來、予與爾言、曰、懷其寶而迷其邦、可謂仁乎。曰、不可。好從

CHAPTER I. 1. Yang Ho wished to see Confucius, but Confucius would not go to see him. *On this*, he sent a present of a pig to Confucius, who, having chosen a time when Ho was not at home, went to pay his respects *for the gift*. He met him, *however*, on the way.

2. *Ho* said to Confucius, "Come, let me speak with you." He then asked, "Can he be called benevolent, who keeps his jewel in his bo-

HEADING OF THIS BOOK.—陽貨第十七. 'Yang Ho, No. XVII.'—As the last Book commenced with the presumption of the Head of the Ke family, who kept his prince in subjection, this begins with an account of an officer, who did for the head of the Ke what he did for the duke of Loo. For this reason—some similarity in the subject matter of the first chapters—this Book, it is said, is placed after the former. It contains 26 chapters.

1. CONFUCIUS' POLITE BUT DIGNIFIED TREATMENT OF A POWERFUL, BUT USURPING AND UNWORTHY, OFFICER. 1. Yang Ho, known also as Yang Hoo (虎), was nominally the principal minister of the Ke family, but its chief was entirely in his hands, and he was scheming to arrogate the whole authority of the state of Loo to himself. He first appears in the Chronicles of Loo about the year B.C. 505, acting against the exiled duke Ch'aou; in B.C. 504, we find

事、而亟失時、可謂知乎。曰、不可。日月逝矣、歲不我與。孔子曰、諾、吾將仕矣。

〔二〕子曰、性相近也、習相遠也。

〔三〕子曰、唯上知與下愚不移。

som, and leaves his country to confusion?" *Confucius* replied, "No." "Can he be called wise, who is anxious to be engaged in public employment, and yet is constantly losing the opportunity of being so?" *Confucius again* said, "No." "The days and months are passing away; the years do not wait for us." Confucius said, "Right; I will go into office."

CHAPTER II. The Master said, "By nature, men are nearly alike; by practice, they get to be wide apart."

CHAPTER III. The Master said, "There are only the wise of the highest class, and the stupid of the lowest class, who cannot be changed."

him keeping his own chief. He Hwo was a prisoner, and, in 501, he is driven out, on the failure of his projects, a fugitive into Ts'e. At the time when the incidents in this ch. occurred, Yang Ho was anxious to get, or appear to get, the support of a man of Conf. reputation, and finding that the sage would not call on him, he adopted the expedient of sending him a pig, at a time when Conf. was out at home, the rules of ceremony requiring that when a great officer sent a present to a scholar, and the latter was not in his house on its arrival, he had to go to the officer's house to acknowledge it. See the Le-ke, XIII. iii. 20. 歸 is in the sense of 饋, 'to present food,' properly 'before a superior.' Confucius, however, was not to be entrapped. He also *timed* (時, as a verb) Hoo's being away from home (亡), and went to call on him. 2. 迷其邦, 'deludes, confuses, his country,' but the meaning is only negative, = 'leaves his country to confusion.' 亟, read *k'e*, up. 3d tone, 'frequently.' 日月—我與, —all this is to be taken as the remark of Yang Ho, and a 曰 supplied before 日, 我與; 與, in the dict., and by the old interpreters, is here explained, as in the translation by 待, 'to wait for.'

2. THE DIFFERENCES IN THE CHARACTERS OF MEN ARE CHIEFLY OWING TO HABIT. 性, it is contended, is here not the moral constitution of man, absolutely considered, but his complex, actual nature, with its elements of the material, the animal, and the intellectual, by association with which, the perfectly good moral nature is continually being led astray. The moral nature is the same in all, and though the material organism and disposition do differ in different individuals, they are, at first, more nearly alike than they subsequently become. In the 註疏, we read:—'The nature is the constitution received by man at birth, and is then still. While it has not been acted on by external things, men are all like one another; they are 近. After it has been acted on by external things, then practice forms, as it were, a second nature. He who practises what is good, becomes the superior man, and he who practises what is not good, becomes the mean man:—men become 相遠.'—No doubt, it is true that many—perhaps most—of the differences among men are owing to habit.

3. ONLY TWO CLASSES WHOM PRACTICE CANNOT CHANGE. This is a sequel to the last chapter with which it is incorporated in Ho An's edition. The case of the 下愚 would seem to be inconsistent with the doctrine of the perfect goodness of the moral nature of all men. Modern

四章 子之武城、聞絃歌之聲。二 夫子莞爾而笑曰、割雞焉用牛刀。三 子游對曰、昔者偃也、聞諸夫子曰、君子學道則愛人、小人學道則易使也。四 子曰、二三子、偃之言是也。前言戲之耳。

五章 公山弗擾以費畔、召、子欲往。二 子路不說、曰、末

CHAPTER IV. 1. The Master having come to Woo-hing, heard *there* the sound of stringed instruments and singing.

2. Well-pleased and smiling, he said, "Why use an ox-knife to kill a fowl?"

3. Tsze-yew replied, "Formerly, Master, I heard you say,—'When the man of high station is well instructed, he loves men; when the man of low station is well instructed, he is easily ruled.'"

4. The Master said, "My disciples, Yen's words are right. What I said was only in sport."

CHAPTER V. 1. Kung-shan Fuh-jaou, when he was holding Pe, and in an attitude of rebellion, invited the Master to visit him, who was rather inclined to go.

2. Tsze-loo was displeased, and said, "Indeed you cannot go! Why must you think of going to see Kung-shan?"

commentators, to get over the difficulty, say that they are the 自暴者 and 自棄者 of Mencius, IV. Pt. I. x.

4. HOWEVER SMALL THE SPHERE OF GOVERNMENT, THE HIGHEST INFLUENCES OF PROPRIETIES AND MUSIC SHOULD BE EMPLOYED. 1. Woo-shing was in the district of Pe. Tsze-yew appears as the commandant of it, in VI. 12. 弦, 'the silken string of a musical instrument,' used here for stringed instruments generally. In the 備旨 we read, 'The town was named Woo (武), from its position, precipitous and favourable to military operations, but Tsze-yew had been able, by his course, to transform the people, and make them change their mail and helmets for stringed instruments and singing. This was what made the Master glad.' 2. 莞 (read *wan*, up. 3d tone) 爾, 'smilingly.' 'An ox-knife,' a large instrument, and not necessary for the death of a fowl. Conf. intends by it the high principles of government employed by Tsze-yew. 3. 君子 and 小人 are here indicative of rank, and not of character. 易使 'are easily employed, i.e., 安分從上, 'they rest in their lot, and obey their superiors.' 4. 二三子, as in VII. 23, *et al.* Obs. the force of the final 耳,='only.'

5. THE LENGTHS TO WHICH CONFUCIUS WAS INCLINED TO GO, TO GET HIS PRINCIPLES CARRIED INTO PRACTICE. Kung-shan Fuh-jaou, called also Kung-shan Fuh-new (狃), by designation 子洩, was a confederate of Yang Ho (ch. I),

之也已、何必公山氏之之也。三子曰、夫召我者、而豈徒哉、如有用我者、吾其為東周乎。

六章 子張問仁於孔子、孔子曰、能行五者於天下為仁矣。請問之、曰、恭寬信敏惠、恭則不侮、寬則得衆、信則人任焉、敏則有功、惠則足以使人。

3. The Master said, "Can it be without some reason that he has invited ME? If any one employ me, may I not make an eastern Chow?"

CHAPTER VI. 1. Tsze-chang asked Confucius about perfect virtue. Confucius said, "To be able to practise five things everywhere under heaven constitutes perfect virtue." He begged to ask what they were, and was told, "Gravity, generosity *of soul*, sincerity, earnestness, and kindness. If you are grave, you will not be treated with disrespect. If you are generous, you will win all. If you are sincere, people will repose trust in you. If you are earnest, you will accomplish much. If you are kind, this will enable you to employ the services of others."

and acc. to K'ung Gan-kwŏ, and the 日講, it was after the imprisonment by them, in common, of Ke Hwan, that Fuh-jaou sent this invitation to Conf. Others make the invitation subsequent to Ho's discomfiture and flight to Ts'e. See the 歷代統紀表, B.C. 500. We must conclude, with Tsze-lun, that Conf. ought not to have thought of accepting the invitation of such a man. 2. The first and last 之 are the verb. 末－無. 末之也已,—'There is no going there. Indeed there is not.' 何必公山氏之之也, 'why must there be going to (之 here＝*to*) *that* (such is the force of 氏) Kung-shan?' 3. 夫召我者.—者 is to be taken here as referring expressly to Fuh-jaou, while its reference below is more general. The 我 in 用我, and 吾 are emphatic. The original seat of the Chow dynasty lay west from Loo, and the revival of the principles and government of Wăn and Woo in Loo, or even in Pe, which was but a part of it, might make an eastern Chow; so that Confucius would perform the part of king Wăn.—After all, the sage did not go to Pe.

6. FIVE THINGS THE PRACTICE OF WHICH CONSTITUTES PERFECT VIRTUE. 於天下, 'in under heaven' is simply＝'any where.' 信則人任.—任, low 3d tone, is explained by Choo He by 倚仗, 'to rely upon,' a meaning of the term not found in the dictionary. See XX. 1, 6.

七 佛肸召。子欲往。〇二子路曰、昔者由也聞諸夫子曰、親於其身爲不善者、君子不入也。佛肸以中牟畔、子之往也、如之何。〇三子曰、然。有是言也。不曰堅乎、磨而不磷、不曰白乎、涅而不緇。〇四吾豈匏瓜也哉、焉能繫而不食。

CHAPTER VII. 1. Peih Heih inviting him to visit him, the Master was inclined to go.

2. Tsze-loo said, "Master, formerly I have heard you say, 'When a man in his own person is guilty of doing evil, a superior man will not associate with him.' Peih Heih is in rebellion, holding possession of Chung-mow; if you go to him, what shall be said?"

3. The Master said, "Yes, I did use these words. But is it not said, that, if a thing be really hard, it may be ground without being made thin? Is it not said, that, if a thing be really white, it may be steeped in a dark fluid without being made black?

4. "Am I a bitter gourd! How can I be hung up out of the way of being eaten?"

7. CONFUCIUS, INCLINED TO RESPOND TO THE ADVANCES OF AN UNWORTHY MAN, PROTESTS AGAINST HIS CONDUCT BEING JUDGED BY ORDINARY RULES. Comp. ch. V; but the invitation of Peih Heih was subsequent to that of Kung-shan Fuh-jaou, and after Conf. had given up office in Loo. 1. 佛 (read Peih) 肸 Heih was commandant of Chung-mow, for the chief of the Chaou family, in the state of Tsin. 2. 親於其身爲不善者,—'he who himself, in his own person, does what is not good.' 不入,—acc. to K'ung Gan-kwŏ,=不入其國, 'does not enter his state;' acc. to Choo He, it=不入其黨, 'does not enter his party.' There were two places of the name of Chung-mow, one belonging to the state of Ch'ing, and the other to the state of Tsin (晉), which is that intended here, and is referred to the present district of 湯陰, dep. of 彰德, in Ho-nan province. 3. 不曰 is to be taken interrogatively, as in the translation. P'ing's paraphrase is—人豈不曰, 'do not men say?' 堅乎云云,—'Is a thing hard, then,' &c. 涅 is explained—'black earth in water, which may be used to dye a black colour.' The application of these strange proverbial sayings is to Conf. himself, as, from his superiority, incapable of being affected by evil communications. 4. This par. is variously explained. By some, 匏瓜 is taken as the name of a star; so that the meaning is—'Am I, like such and such a star, to be hung up, &c?' But we need not depart from the proper meaning of the characters. Choo He, with Ho An, takes 不食 actively;—'A gourd can be hung up, because it does not need to eat. But I must go about, north, south, east, and west, to get food.' This seems to me very unnatural. The expression is taken passively, as in the translation, in the 日講 and other works.

〔八〕子曰、由也、女聞六言六蔽矣乎。對曰、未也。二居、吾語女。三好仁不好學、其蔽也愚。好智不好學、其蔽也蕩。好信不好學、其蔽也賊。好直不好學、其蔽也絞。好勇不好學、其蔽也亂。好剛不好學、其蔽也狂。

CHAPTER VIII. 1. The Master said, "Yew, have you heard the six words to which are attached six becloudings?" Yew replied, "I have not."

2. "Sit down, and I will tell them to you.

3. "There is the love of being benevolent without the love of learning;—the beclouding here leads to a foolish simplicity. There is the love of knowing without the love of learning;—the beclouding here leads to dissipation of mind. There is the love of being sincere without the love of learning;—the beclouding here leads to an injurious disregard of consequences. There is the love of straightforwardness without the love of learning;—the beclouding here leads to rudeness. There is the love of boldness without the love of learning;—the beclouding here leads to insubordination. There is the love of firmness without the love of learning;—the beclouding here leads to extravagant conduct."

8. KNOWLEDGE, ACQUIRED BY LEARNING, IS NECESSARY TO THE COMPLETION OF VIRTUE, BY PRESERVING THE MIND FROM BEING BECLOUDED. 1. 六言是六字, 'The six 言 are six characters'; see the 備旨. They are, therefore, the benevolence, knowledge, sincerity, straight-forwardness, boldness, and firmness, mentioned below, all virtues, but yet each, when pursued without discrimination, tending to becloud the mind. 蔽=遮掩, 'to cover and screen;' the primary meaning of it is said to be 小艸 'small plants.' 2. 居='sit down.' Tsze-loo had risen, acc. to the rules of propriety, to give his answer: see the Le-ke, I. Pt. I. iii. 31; and Conf. tells him to resume his seat. 3. I give here the paraphrase of the 日講 on the first virtue and its beclouding, which may illustrate the manner in which the whole paragraph is developed:—'In all matters, there is a perfectly right and unchangeable principle, which men ought carefully to study, till they have thoroughly examined and apprehended it. Then their actions will be without error, and their virtue may be perfected. For instance, loving is what rules in benevolence. It is certainly a beautiful virtue, but if you only set yourself to love men, and do not care to study to understand the principle of benevolence, then your mind will be beclouded by that loving, and you will be following a man into a well to save him, so that both he and you will perish. Will not this be foolish simplicity?'

九 子曰、小子、何莫學夫詩。二 詩可以興。三 可以觀。四 可以群。五 可以怨。六 邇之事父、遠之事君。七 多識於鳥獸草木之名。

十 子謂伯魚曰、女爲周南召南矣乎、人而不爲周南召南、其猶正牆面而立也與。

CHAPTER IX. 1. The Master said, "My children, why do you not study the Book of Poetry?

2. "*The Odes* serve to stimulate the mind.

3. "They may be used for purposes of self-contemplation.

4. "They teach the art of sociability.

5. "They show how to regulate feelings of resentment.

6. "From them you learn the more immediate duty of serving one's father, and the remoter one of serving one's prince.

7. "From them we become largely acquainted with the names of birds, beasts, and plants."

CHAPTER X. The Master said to Pih-yu, "Do you give yourself to the Chow-nan, and the Chaou-nan. The man, who has not studied the Chow-nan and the Chaou-nan, is like one who stands with his face right against a wall. Is he not so?"

9. BENEFITS DERIVED FROM STUDYING THE BOOK OF POETRY. 1. 小子;—see V. 21; VIII. 3. I translate 詩 here by 'the Book of Poetry,' because the lesson is supposed to have been given, after Conf. had completed his compilation of the Odes. The 夫 is *that*, as in XI. 9. 1, *et al.* The descriptions in them of good and evil may have this effect. 3. Their awarding of praise and blame may show a man his own character. 4. Their exhibitions of gravity in the midst of pleasure may have this effect. 羣, as in XV. 21. 5. Their blending of pity and earnest desire with reproofs may teach how to regulate our resentments. 6. 草木, 'grasses and trees,'—plants generally.

10. THE IMPORTANCE OF STUDYING THE CHOW-NAN AND CHAOU-NAN. Chow-nan and Chaou-nan are the titles of the first two Books in the National Songs, or first part of the She-king. For the meaning of the titles, see the She-king, I. i. and I. ii. They are supposed to inculcate important lessons about personal virtue and family-government. Choo He explains 爲 by 學, 'to learn,' 'to study.' It denotes the entire mastery of the studies. 女 (for 汝) 爲云云 is imperative, the 乎 at the end, not being interrogative. 正面牆而立 is for 正面對牆而立. In such a situation, one cannot advance a step, nor see any thing. I have added—'Is he not so?' to bring out the force of the 與.—This chapter in the old editions, is incorporated with the preceding one.

十一子曰、禮云禮云、玉帛云乎哉、樂云樂云、鐘鼓云乎哉。

十二子曰、色厲而內荏、譬諸小人、其猶穿窬之盜也與。

十三子曰、鄉原、德之賊也。

十四子曰、道聽而塗說、德之棄也。

CHAPTER XI. The Master said, "'It is according to the rules of propriety,' they say.—'It is according to the rules of propriety,' they say. Are gems and silk all that is meant by propriety? 'It is Music,' they say.—'It is Music,' they say. Are bells and drums all that is meant by Music?"

CHAPTER XII. The Master said, "He who puts on an appearance of stern firmness, while inwardly he is weak, is like one of the small, mean, people;—yea, is he not like the thief who breaks through, or climbs over, a wall?"

CHAPTER XIII. The Master said, "Your good careful people of the villages are the thieves of virtue."

CHAPTER XIV. The Master said, "To tell, as we go along, what we have heard on the way, is to cast away our virtue."

11. IT IS NOT THE EXTERNAL APPURTENANCES WHICH CONSTITUTE PROPRIETY, NOR THE SOUND OF INSTRUMENTS WHICH CONSTITUTES MUSIC. 禮云—所稱爲禮者, 'as to what is called propriety.' The words approach the quotation of a common saying. So 樂云. Having thus given the common views of propriety and music, he refutes them in the questions that follow, 樂 and 禮 being present to the mind as the expressions of respect and harmony.

12. THE MEANNESS OF PRESUMPTION AND PUSILLANIMITY CONJOINED. 色 is here not the countenance merely, but the whole outward appearance. 小人 is explained by 細民, and the latter clause shows emphatically to whom, among the low, mean, people, the individual spoken of is like,—a thief, namely, who is in constant fear of being detected.

13. CONTENTMENT WITH VULGAR WAYS AND VIEWS INJURIOUS TO VIRTUE. See the sentiment of this chapter explained and expanded by Mencius, VII. Pt. II. xxxvii. 7, 8. 原, low. 3d tone, the same as 愿. See the dict., char. 原. 賊, as in XIV. 46, though it may be translated here, as generally, by the term 'thief.'

14. SWIFTNESS TO SPEAK INCOMPATIBLE WITH THE CULTIVATION OF VIRTUE. It is to be understood that what has been heard contains some good lesson. At once to be talking of it without revolving it, and striving to practise it, shows an indifference to our own improvement. 道 is 'the way' or 'road.' 塗 is the same way, a little farther on.—The glossarist on Ho An's work explains 德之棄 as meaning—'is what the virtuous do not do.' But this is evidently incorrect.

十五 一子曰、鄙夫、可與事君也與哉。二其未得之也、患得之、既得之、患失之。三苟患失之、無所不至矣。

十六 一子曰、古者民有三疾、今也或是之亡也。二古之狂也肆、今之狂也蕩。古之矜也廉、今之矜也忿戾。古之愚也直、今之愚也詐而已矣。

CHAPTER XV. 1. The Master said, "There are those mean creatures! How impossible it is along with them to serve one's prince!

2. "While they have not got their aims, their anxiety is how to get them. When they have got them, their anxiety is lest they should lose them.

3. "When they are anxious lest such things should be lost, there is nothing to which they will not proceed."

CHAPTER XVI. 1. The Master said, "Anciently, men had three failings, which now perhaps are not to be found.

2. "The high-mindedness of antiquity showed itself in a disregard of small things; the high-mindedness of the present day shows itself in wild license. The stern dignity of antiquity showed itself in grave reserve; the stern dignity of the present day shows itself in quarrelsome perverseness. The stupidity of antiquity showed itself in straightforwardness; the stupidity of the present day shows itself in sheer deceit."

15. THE CASE OF MERCENARY OFFICERS, AND HOW IT IS IMPOSSIBLE TO SERVE ONE'S PRINCE ALONG WITH THEM. 1. 與字作共字看, '與＝共,' i.e., 'together with.' 與哉是深慨其不可與意, '與哉＝a deep-felt lamentation on the unfitness of such persons to be associated with.' So, the 備旨. But as the remaining paragraphs are all occupied with describing the mercenaries, we must understand Confucius' object as being to condemn the employment of such creatures, rather than to set forth the impossibility of serving with them. 2. The 之 here, and in p. 3, are all to be understood of place and emolument.

16. THE DEFECTS OF FORMER TIMES BECOME VICES IN THE TIME OF CONFUCIUS. 1. 疾, 'bodily sickness,' here used metaphorically for 'errors,' 'vices.' 或是之亡 (woo),—'perhaps there is the absence of them.' The next par. shows that worse things had taken their place. 2. That 肆 is only 'a disregard of smaller matters,' or conventionalisms, appears from its opposition to 蕩, which has a more intense signification than in ch. 8. 矜, as in

十七 子曰、巧言令色鮮矣仁。

十八 子曰、惡紫之奪朱也、惡鄭聲之亂雅樂也、惡利口之覆邦家者。

十九 子曰、予欲無言。一 子貢曰、子如不言、則小子何述焉。二 子曰、天何言哉、四時行焉、百物生焉、天何言哉。

CHAPTER XVII. The Master said, "Fine words and an insinuating appearance are seldom associated with virtue."

CHAPTER XVIII. The Master said, "I hate the manner in which purple takes away *the lustre of* vermillion. I hate the way in which the songs of Ch'ing confound the music of the Gna. I hate those who with their sharp mouths overthrow kingdoms and families."

CHAPTER XIX. 1. The Master said, "I would prefer not speaking."

2. Tsze-kung said, "If you, Master, do not speak, what shall we, your disciples, have to record?"

3. The Master said, "Does Heaven speak? The four seasons pursue their courses, and all things are *continually* being produced, *but* does Heaven say anything?"

XV. 21, also with an interior meaning. 廉, 'an angular corner,' which cannot be impinged against without causing pain. It is used for 'purity,' 'modesty,' but the meaning here appears to be that given in the translation.

17. A repetition of I. 3.

18. CONFUCIUS' INDIGNATION AT THE WAY IN WHICH THE WRONG OVERCAME THE RIGHT. 紫之奪朱,—see X. 6, 2. 朱 is here as 'a correct' colour, though it is not among the five such colours mentioned in the note there. 紫 I have here translated—'purple.' 'Black and carnation mixed,' it is said, 'give 紫.' 'The songs or sounds of Ch'ing,'—see XV. 10. 'The ya,'—see on IX. 14. 國家 is a common designation for 'a state,' the 國, or kingdom of the prince, embracing the 家, 'families,' of his great officers.

19. THE ACTIONS OF CONFUCIUS WERE LESSONS AND LAWS, AND NOT HIS WORDS MERELY. Such is the scope of this ch., according to Choo He and his school. The older comm. say that it is a caution to men to pay attention to their conduct rather than to their words. This interpretation is far-fetched, but, on the other hand, it is not easy to defend Conf. from the charge of presumption in comparing himself to Heaven. 3. 天何言哉, 'Does Heaven speak,'—better than 'what does Heaven say?'

〔二十〕孺悲欲見孔子、孔子辭以疾、將命者出戶、取瑟而歌、使之聞之。〔廿一〕宰我問三年之喪、期已久矣。〇二君子三年不爲禮、禮必壞、三年不爲樂、樂必崩。〇三舊穀既沒、新穀既升、鑽燧改火、期可已矣。〇四子曰、食夫稻、衣夫錦、

CHAPTER XX. Joo Pei wished to see Confucius, but Confucius declined, on the ground of being sick, to see him. When the bearer of this message went out at the door, he took his harpsichord, and sang to it, in order that Pei might hear him.

CHAPTER XXI. 1. Tsae Go asked about the three years' mourning *for parents, saying* that one year was long enough.

2. "If the superior man," said he, "abstains for three years from the observances of propriety, those observances will be quite lost. If for three years he abstains from music, music will be ruined.

3. "*Within a year*, the old grain is exhausted, and the new grain has sprung up, and, in procuring fire by friction, we go through all the changes of wood for that purpose. After a complete year, the mourning may stop."

4. The Master said, "If you were, *after a year*, to eat good rice, and wear embroidered clothes, would you feel at ease?" "I should," replied Go.

20. HOW CONFUCIUS COULD BE NOT AT HOME, AND YET GIVE INTIMATION TO THE VISITOR OF HIS PRESENCE. Of Joo Pei little is known. He was a man of Loo, and had at one time been in attendance on Confucius to receive his instructions. There must have been some reason—some fault in him—why Conf. would not see him on the occasion in the text, and that he might understand that it was on that account, and not that he was really sick, that he declined his visit, the sage acted as we are told. But what was the necessity for sending a false message in the first place? In the notes to the 儀禮, III. 1, it is said that Joo Pei's fault was in trying to see the master without using the services of an internuncius. 將命者,—see XIV. 47. I translate the last 之 by *him*, but it refers generally to the preceding sentence, and might be left untranslated.

21. THE PERIOD OF THREE YEARS' MOURNING FOR PARENTS:—IT MAY NOT ON ANY ACCOUNT BE SHORTENED; THE REASON OF IT. 1. We must understand a 曰, either before 三, or, as I prefer, before 期, which is read *ke*, up. 1st tone, the same as 朞, XIII. 10. On the three years' mourning, see the 31st book of the Le-ke. Nominally extending to three years, that period

於女安乎。曰、安。五女安、則爲之、夫君子之居喪、食旨不甘、聞樂不樂、居處不安、故不爲也、今女安、則爲之。六宰我出。子曰、予之不仁也、子生三年、然後免於父母之懷、夫三年之喪、天下之通喪也、予也、有三年之愛於其父母乎。

5. The Master said, "If you can feel at ease, do it. But a superior man, during the whole period of mourning, does not enjoy pleasant food which he may eat, nor derive pleasure from music which he may hear. He also does not feel at ease, if he is comfortably lodged. Therefore he does not do *what you propose*. But now you feel at ease and may do it."

6. Tsae Go then went out, and the Master said, "This shows Yu's want of virtue. It is not till a child is three years old that it is allowed to leave the arms of its parents. And the three years mourning is universally observed throughout the empire. Did Yu enjoy the three years' affection for his parents?"

comprehended properly but 25 months, and at most 27 months. 2. 此以人事言之,—Tsae-go finds here a reason for his view in the necessity of 'human affairs.' 3. 此以天時言之,—He finds here a reason for his view in 'the seasons of heaven.' 燧 means either 'a piece of metal,'—a speculum,—with which to take fire from the sun, or 'a piece of wood,' with which to get fire by friction or 'boring' (鑽). It has here the latter meaning. Certain woods were assigned to the several seasons, to be employed for this purpose, the elm and willow, for instance to spring, the date and almond trees to summer, &c. 鑽燧改火—鑽燧以取火,又改乎四時之木, 'In boring with the 燧 to get fire, we have changed from wood to wood through the ones appropriate to the four seasons.' 4. Coarse food and coarse clothing were appropriate, though in varying degrees to all the period of mourning. Tsae-go is strangely insensible to the home-put argument of the Master. 稻 is to be understood here as 穀之美者 'the most excellent grain.' The 夫 are demonstrative. 7. 子之不仁也 responds to all that has gone before, and forms a sort of *apodosis*. Conf. added, it is said, the remarks in this par. that they might be reported to Tsae Go, lest he should 'feel at ease' to go and do as he said he could. Still the reason which the Master finds for the statute-period of mourning for parents must be pronounced puerile.

二十二子曰、飽食終日、無所用心、難矣哉、不有博奕者乎、爲之、猶賢乎已。

二十三子路曰、君子尚勇乎。子曰、君子義以爲上、君子有勇而無義、爲亂、小人有勇而無義、爲盜。

二十四子貢曰、君子亦有惡乎。子曰、有惡、惡稱人之惡者、惡居下流而訕上

CHAPTER XXII. The Master said, "Hard is the case of him, who will stuff himself with food the whole day, without applying his mind to anything *good!* Are there not gamesters and chessplayers? To be one of these would still be better than doing nothing at all."

CHAPTER XXIII. Tsze-loo said, "Does the superior man esteem valour?" The Master said, "The superior man holds righteousness to be of highest importance. A man in a superior situation, having valour without righteousness, will be guilty of insubordination; one of the lower people, having valour without righteousness, will commit robbery."

CHAPTER XXIV. 1. Tsze-kung said, "Has the superior man his hatreds also?" The Master said, "He has his hatreds. He hates those who proclaim the evil of others. He hates the man who, being in a low station, slanders his superiors. He hates those who

22. THE HOPELESS CASE OF GLUTTONY AND IDLENESS. 難矣哉,—XV. 16. 博 and 弈 are two things. To the former I am unable to give a name; but see some account of it quoted in the 集證 *in loc.* 弈 is 'to play at chess,' of which there are two kinds,—the 圍棋 played with 361 pieces and referred to the emperor Yaou as its inventor, and the 象棋 or ivory chess, played with 32 pieces, and having a great analogy to the European game. Its invention is attributed to the first emperor of the Chow dynasty, though some date its origin a few hundred years later. 爲之,—之 refers to 博弈. 賢, for 勝, as in XI. 15, 1.

23. VALOUR TO BE VALUED ONLY IN SUBORDINATION TO RIGHTEOUSNESS; ITS CONSEQUENCES APART FROM THAT. The first two 君子 are to be understood of the man superior in virtue. The third brings in the idea of rank, with 小人 as its correlate.

24. CHARACTERS DISLIKED BY CONFUCIUS AND TSZE-KUNG. 1. Tsze-kung is understood to have intended Confucius himself by 'the superior man.' 流 is here in the sense of 'class.' 下流=下位之人, 'men of low station.' In 君子亦有惡乎, the force of 亦 is to oppose 惡 to 愛, 'hatreds,' to 'loves.' 2. Hing Ping takes 子貢 as the nominative

者、惡勇而無禮者、惡果敢而窒者。曰、賜也、亦有惡乎。惡徼以爲知者、惡不孫以爲勇者、惡訐以爲直者。

二十五 子曰、唯女子與小人、爲難養也、近之則不孫、遠之則怨。

二十六 子曰、年四十而見惡焉、其終也已。

have valour *merely*, and are unobservant of propriety. He hates those who are forward and determined, and, *at the same time*, of contracted understanding."

2. *The Master then* inquired, "Tsze, have you also your hatreds?" *Tsze-kung replied*, "I hate those who pry out matters, and ascribe the knowledge to their wisdom. I hate those who are *only* not modest, and think that they are valorous. I hate those who make known secrets, and think that they are straightforward."

CHAPTER XXV. The Master said, "Of all people, girls and servants are the most difficult to behave to. If you are familiar with them, they lose their humility. If you maintain a reserve towards them, they are discontented."

CHAPTER XXVI. The Master said, "When a man at forty is the object of dislike, he will always continue what he is."

to 曰,—'He went on to say, *I, Tsze, also*,' &c. The modern comm., however, more correctly, understand 子, 'the Master,' as nom. to 曰, and supply another 曰 before 徼.

25. THE DIFFICULTY HOW TO TREAT CONCUBINES AND SERVANTS. 女子 does not mean women generally, but girls, *i.e.*, concubines. 小人, in the same way, is here boys, *i.e.*, servants. 養, 'to nourish,' 'to keep,'=to behave to. The force of 唯, 'only,' is as indicated in the translation.

26. THE DIFFICULTY OF IMPROVEMENT IN ADVANCED YEARS. According to Chinese views, at forty a man is at his best in every way. After 惡, we must understand 于君子,—'the object of dislike to the superior man.' 其終=其終于此, 'he will end in this.'—Youth is doubtless the season for improvement, but the sentiment of the chapter is too broadly stated.

BOOK XVIII. WEI TSZE.

微子第十八

[一章]微子去之、箕子爲之奴、比干諫而死。[二]孔子曰、殷有三仁焉。

[二章]柳下惠爲士師、三黜、人曰、子未可以去乎。曰、直道而事人、焉往而不三黜、枉道而事人、何

CHAPTER I. 1. The viscount of Wei withdrew *from the court*. The viscount of Ke became a slave *to Chow*. Pe-kan remonstrated with him and died.

2. Confucius said, "The Yin dynasty possessed *these* three men of virtue."

CHAPTER II. Hwuy of Lew-hea being chief criminal judge, was thrice dismissed from his office. Some one said to him, "Is it not yet time for you, Sir, to leave this?" He replied, "Serving men in an upright way, where shall I go to, and not experience such a thrice-repeated dismissal? If I choose to serve men in a crooked way, what necessity is there for me to leave the country of my parents?"

HEADING OF THIS BOOK.—微子第十八, 'The viscount of Wei—No. XVIII.' This Book, consisting of only eleven chapters, treats of various individuals famous in Chinese history, as eminent for the way in which they discharged their duties to their sovereign, or for their retirement from public service. It commemorates also some of the worthies of Confucius' days, who lived in retirement rather than be in office in so degenerate times. The object of the whole is to illustrate and vindicate the course of Confucius himself.

1. THE VISCOUNTS OF WEI AND KE, AND PE-KAN:—THREE WORTHIES OF THE YIN DYNASTY. 1. Wei-tsze and Ke-tsze are continually repeated by Chinese, as if they were proper names. But Wei and Ke were the names of two small states, presided over by chiefs of the Tsze, or fourth, degree of nobility, called *viscounts*, for want of a more exact term. They both appear to have been within the limits of the present Shan-se, Wei being referred to the district of 潞城, dep. 潞安, and Ke to 榆社, dep. 遼州. The chief of Wei was an elder brother (by a concubine) of the tyrant Chow, the last emperor of the Yin dynasty, B.C. 1153-1122. The chief of Ke, and Pe-kan, were both uncles of the tyrant. The first, seeing that remonstrances availed nothing, withdrew from court, wishing to preserve the sacrifices of their family, amid the ruin which he saw was impending. The second was thrown into prison, and, to escape death, feigned madness. He was used by Chow as a buffoon. Pe-kan, persisting in his remonstrances, was put barbarously to death, the tyrant having his heart torn out, that he might see, he said, a sage's heart. The 之 in 去之 is explained by 其位, 'his place.' Its reference may also be to 紂, the tyrant himself. On 爲之奴, comp. 爲之宰, V. 7, 3, *et al.*

2. HOW HWUY OF LEW-HEA, THOUGH OFTEN DISMISSED FROM OFFICE, STILL CLAVE TO HIS COUNTRY. Lew-hea Hwuy,—see XV. 13. The office of the 士師 is described in the Chow-

必去父母之邦。

[三] 齊景公待孔子、曰、若季氏、則吾不能以季孟之閒待之。曰、吾老矣、不能用也。孔子行。

[四] 齊人歸女樂。季桓子受之、三日不朝、孔子行。

[五] 楚狂接輿歌而過

CHAPTER III. The duke King of Ts'e, *with reference to the manner in which* he should treat Confucius, said, "I cannot treat him as I would the chief of the Ke family. I will treat him in a manner between that accorded to the chief of the Ke, and that given to the chief of the Măng family." He *also* said, "I am old; I cannot use *his doctrines*." Confucius took his departure.

CHAPTER IV. The people of Ts'e sent *to Loo* a present of female musicians, which Ke Hwan received, and for three days no court was held. Confucius took his departure.

CHAPTER V. 1. The madman of Ts'oo, Tsëě-yu, passed by Confucius, singing and saying, "Oh FUNG! Oh FUNG! How is your

in, XXXIV. 3. He was under the 司寇, or minister of Crime, but with many subordinate magistrates under him. 已, up. 3d tone, as in V. 19, XI. 5. We may translate 黜 'was dismissed from office,' or 'retired from office.' 人=或人.—Some remarks akin to that in the text are ascribed to Hwuy's wife. It is observed by the commentator Hoo (胡), that there ought to be another paragraph, giving Conf. judgment upon Hwuy's conduct, but it has been lost.

3. HOW CONFUCIUS LEFT TS'E, WHEN THE DUKE COULD NOT APPRECIATE AND EMPLOY HIM. It was in the year B.C. 516, that Confucius went to Ts'e. The remarks about how he should be treated, &c., are to be understood as having taken place in consultation between the duke and his ministers, and being afterwards reported to the sage. The Măng family (see II. 5) was in the time of Conf., much weaker than the Ke. The chief of it was only the 下卿, lowest noble of Loo, while the Ke was the highest. Yet for the duke of Ts'e to treat Conf. better than the duke of Loo treated the chief of the Măng family, was not dishonouring the sage. We must suppose that Conf. left Ts'e, because of the duke's concluding remarks.

4. HOW CONFUCIUS GAVE UP OFFICIAL SERVICE IN LOO. In the 14th year of the duke Ting, Conf. reached the highest point of his official service. He was minister of crime, and also, acc. to the general opinion, acting premier. He effected in a few months a wonderful renovation of the State, and the neighbouring countries began to fear that under his administration, Loo would overtop and subdue them all. To prevent this, the duke of Ts'e sent a present to Loo of fine horses and of 80 highly accomplished beauties. The duke of Loo was induced to receive these by the advice of the head of the Ke family, Ke Sze (斯), or Ke Hwan. The sage was forgotten; government was neglected. Confucius, indignant and sorrowful, withdrew from office, and for a time, from the country too. 歸 as in XVII. i, 1. 齊人, 'the people of Ts'e' is to be understood of the duke and his ministers.

5. CONFUCIUS AND THE MADMAN OF TS'OO, WHO BLAMES HIS NOT RETIRING FROM THE WORLD. 1. Tsëě-yu was the designation of one Luh T'ung

孔子、曰、鳳兮鳳兮、何德之衰、往者不可諫、來者猶可追、已而已而、今之從政者殆而。孔子下、欲與之言。趨而辟之、不得與之言。

六 長沮桀溺耦而耕。孔子過之、使子路問津焉。長沮曰、夫執輿者為誰。子路曰、為孔丘。曰、是魯孔丘與。曰、是也。曰、是知津矣。問於桀

virtue degenerated! As to the past, reproof is useless; but the future may be provided against. Give up *your vain pursuit*. Give up *your vain pursuit*. Peril awaits those who now engage in affairs of government."

2. Confucius alighted and wished to converse with him, but *Tsëë-yu* hastened away, so that he could not talk with him.

CHAPTER VI. 1. Ch'ang-tseu and Këë-neih were at work in the field together, when Confucius passed by them, and sent Tsze-loo to enquire for the ford.

2. Ch'ang-tseu said, "Who is he that holds the reins in the carriage there?" Tsze-loo told him, "It is K'ung K'ew." "Is it not K'ung K'ew of Loo?" asked he. "Yes," was the reply, to which the other rejoined, "He knows the ford."

3. *Tsze-loo then* enquired of Këë-neih, who said to him, "Who are you, Sir?" HE answered, "I am Chung Yew." "Are you

(陸通), a native of Ts'oo, who feigned himself mad, to escape being importuned to engage in public service. There are several notices of him in the 莊子, &c. It must have been about the year, B. C. 489, that the incident in the text occurred. By the *fung*, his satirist or adviser intended Confucius; see IX. 8. The three 而 in the song are simply expletives, pauses for the voice to help out the rhythm. 追, 'to overtake,' generally with reference to the past, but here it has reference to the future. In the dict., with reference to this passage, it is explained by 及, 'to come up to,' and 救, 'to save,' = to provide against.

6. CONFUCIUS AND THE TWO RECLUSES, CH'ANG-TSEU AND KEE-NEIH; WHY HE WOULD NOT WITHDRAW FROM THE WORLD. 1. The surnames and names of these worthies are not known. It is supposed that they belonged to Ts'oo, like the hero of the last chapter, and that the interview with them occurred about the same time. The designations in the text are descriptive of their character, and = 'the long Rester (沮者止而不出)' and 'the firm Recluse (溺者沉而不返).' What kind of field labour is

溺、桀溺曰。子爲誰。曰、爲仲由。曰、是魯孔丘之徒與。對曰、然。曰、滔滔者、天下皆是也、而誰以易之、且而與其從辟人之士也、豈若從辟世之士哉。耰而不輟。子路行以告。夫子憮然曰、鳥獸不可與同群、吾非斯人之徒與而誰與、天下有道、丘不與易也。

not the disciple of K'ung K'ew of Loo?" asked the other. "I am," replied he, and then Keě-neih said to him, "Disorder, like a swelling flood, spreads over the whole empire, and who is he that will change it *for you?* Than follow one who merely withdraws from this one and that one, had you not better follow those who have withdrawn from the world altogether?" *With this* he fell to covering up the seed, *and proceeded with his work*, without stopping.

4. Tsze-loo went and reported their remarks, when his master observed with a sigh, "It is impossible to associate with birds and beasts, as if they were the same with us. If I associate not with these people,—with mankind,—with whom shall I associate? If right principles prevailed through the empire, there would be no use for me to change its state."

have denoted by 耕 cannot be determined. 2. 執輿者, 'he who holds the carriage,'—執轡在車者, as in the transl. It is supposed that it was the remarkable appearance of Confucius, which elicited the inquiry. In 是知津, 是—'he;' i. e., he, going about every where, and seeking to be employed, ought to know the ford. 3. 滔滔者天下,—the speaker here probably pointed to the surging waters before them, for the ford to cross which the travellers were asking. Translating literally, we should say—'swelling and surging, such is all the empire.' 且而,—而—汝, 'you.' 辟人,辟世,—comp. XIV. 39. 耰, 'an implement for drawing the soil over the seed.' It may have been a hoe, or a rake. 4. 徒 is here—類, 'class.' 吾非斯人之徒與而誰與,—'If I am not to associate with the class of these men, i. e., with mankind, with whom am I to associate? I cannot associate with birds and beasts.' 丘不與易,—不與, it is said, 作無用,—'there would be no use.' Literally, 'I should not have for whom to change *the state of the empire*.'—The use of 夫子 in this paragraph is remarkable. It must mean 'his Master' and not 'the Master.' The compiler of this chapter can hardly have been a disciple of the sage.

七 子一路從而後、遇丈人、以杖荷蓧。子路問曰、子見夫子乎。丈人曰、四體不勤、五穀不分、孰爲夫子。植其杖而耘。二子路拱而立。三止子路宿、殺鷄、爲黍、而食之、見其二子焉。四明日、子路行以告。子曰、隱者也、使子路反見之、至、則行矣。五子路曰、不仕

CHAPTER VII. 1. Tsze-loo, following the Master, happened to fall behind, when he met an old man, carrying, across his shoulder on a staff, a basket for weeds. Tsze-loo said to him, "Have you seen my master, Sir!" The old man replied, "Your four limbs are unaccustomed to toil; you cannot distinguish the five kinds of grain:—who is your master?" With this, he planted his staff in the ground, and proceeded to weed.

2. Tsze-loo joined his hands across his breast, and stood *before him*.

3. The old man kept Tsze-loo to pass the night in his house, killed a fowl, prepared millet, and feasted him. He also introduced to him his two sons.

4. Next day, Tsze-loo went on his way, and reported *his adventure*. The Master said, "He is a recluse," and sent Tsze-loo back to see him again, but, when he got to the place, the old man was gone.

7. TSZE-LOO'S RENCONTRE WITH AN OLD MAN, A RECLUSE: HIS VINDICATION OF HIS MASTER'S COURSE. This incident in this chapter was probably nearly contemporaneous with those which occupy the two previous ones. Some say that the old man belonged to Shě, which was a part of Ts'oo. 1. 後, as in XI. xxii, 顔淵後. 丈人 is used for 'an old man,' as early as in the Yih-king, dia. 師. How the phrase comes to have that signification, I have not discovered. 蓧 is simply called by Choo He—竹器, 'a bamboo basket.' The 說文 defines it as in the translation—芸田器. 四體, 'the four bodies,' *i. e.*, the arms and legs, the four limbs of the body. 'The five grains' are 稻黍稷麥, and 菽, 'rice, millet, panicled millet, wheat, and pulse.' But they are sometimes otherwise enumerated. We have also 'the six kinds,' 'the eight kinds,' 'the nine kinds,' and perhaps other classifications. 2. Tsze-loo, standing with his arms across his breast, indicated his respect, and won upon the old man. 3. 食, *tsze*, low. 3d tone, 'entertained,' 'feasted.' The dict. defines it with this meaning, 以食與人, 'to give food to people.' 5. Tsze-loo is to be understood as here speaking the sentiments of the Master, and vindicating his course. 長幼之節 refers to the manner in which the old man had introduced his sons to him the evening before, and to all the orderly intercourse between old and

無義、長幼之節、不可廢也、君臣之義、如之何其廢之、欲潔其身、而亂大倫、君子之仕也、行其義也、道之不行、已知之矣。

八 逸民、伯夷、叔齊、虞仲、夷逸、朱張、柳下惠、少連。子曰、不降其志、不辱其身、伯夷叔齊與、謂柳下惠少連、降志辱身矣、言

5. Tsze-loo then said *to the family*, "Not to take office is not righteous. If the relations between old and young may not be neglected, how is it that he sets aside the duties that should be observed between sovereign and minister? Wishing to maintain his personal purity, he allows that great relation to come to confusion. A superior man takes office, and performs the righteous duties belonging to it. As to the failure of right principles to make progress, he is aware of that."

CHAPTER VIII. 1. The men who have retired to privacy from the world have been Pih-e, Shŭh-ts'e, Yu-chung, E-yih, Choo-chang, Hwuy of Lew-hea, and Shaou-lëen.

2. The Master said, "Refusing to surrender their wills, or to submit to any taint in their persons;—such, I think, were Pih-e and Shuh-ts'e.

young, which he had probably seen in the family. 何其廢之,—其 refers to the old man, but there is an indefiniteness about the Chinese construction, which does not make it so personal as our 'he.' So Confucius is intended by 君子, though that phrase may be taken in its general acceptation. 'He is aware of that;'—but will not therefore shrink from his righteous service.

8. CONFUCIUS' JUDGMENT OF FORMER WORTHIES WHO HAD KEPT FROM THE WORLD. HIS OWN GUIDING PRINCIPLE. 1. 逸民,—'retired people.' 民 is used here just as we sometimes use *people*, without reference to the rank of the individuals spoken of. The 備旨 quotes, upon the phrase, from the 說統 to the following effect:—'逸 here is not the 逸 *of seclusion*, but is characteristic of men of large souls, who cannot be measured by ordinary rules. They may display their character by retiring from the world. They may display it also in the manner of their discharge of office.' The phrase is guarded in this way, I suppose, because of its application to Hwuy of Lew-hea, who did not obstinately withdraw from the world. Pih-e, and Shuh-ts'e,—see V. 22. Yu-chung should probably be Woo (吳)-chung. He was the brother of Tae-pih, called Chung-yung (仲雍), and is mentioned in the note on VIII. 1. He retired with Tae-pih among the barbarous tribes, then occupying the country of Woo, and succeeded to the chieftaincy of them on his brother's death. 'E-yih and Choo-chang,' says Choo He, 'are not found in

中倫、行中慮、其斯而已矣。謂虞仲夷逸、隱居放言、身中清、廢中權。我則異於是、無可無不可。

九 大師摯適齊。亞飯干適楚。三飯繚適蔡。四飯缺適秦。鼓方叔、

3. "It may be said of Hwuy of Lew-hea, and of Shaou-lëen, that they surrendered their wills, and submitted to taint in their persons, but their words corresponded with reason, and their actions were such as men are anxious to see. This is all that is to be remarked in them.

4. "It may be said of Yu-chung and E-yih, that, while they hid themselves in their seclusion, they gave a license to their words, but, in their persons, they succeeded in preserving their purity, and, in their retirement, they acted according to the exigency of the times.

5. "I am different from all these. I have no course for which I am predetermined, and no course against which I am predetermined."

CHAPTER IX. 1. The grand music-master, Che, went to Ts'e. Kan, *the master of the band at* the second meal, went to Ts'oo. Leaou, *the band-master at* the third meal, went to Ts'ae. Keuĕh, *the band-master* at the fourth meal, went to Ts'in.

2. Fang-shuh, the drum-master, withdrew to *the north of* the river. Woo, the master of the hand-drum, withdrew to the Han.

the *king* and *chuen* (經 傳).' See, however, the 集證, in loc. From a passage in the Le-ke, XXI. i. 14, it appears that Shaou-lëen belonged to one of the barbarous tribes on the east, but was well acquainted with, and observant of, the rules of Propriety, particularly those relating to mourning. 3. The 謂, at the beginning of this paragraph and the next, are very perplexing. As there is neither 謂 nor 曰 at the beginning of par. 5, the 子曰 of p. 2 must evidently be carried on to the end of the chapter. Commentators do not seem to have felt the difficulty, and understand 謂 to be in the 3d pers.—'He, i. e., the master, said,' &c. I have made the best of it I could. 倫—義理之次第, 'the order and series of righteousness and principles.' 慮—人心之思慮, 'the thoughts and solicitudes of men's hearts.' 4. 'Living in retirement, they gave a license to their words,'—this is intended to show that in this respect they were inferior to Hwuy and Shaou-lëen, who 言中倫. 權,—see note on IX. 29. 5. Confucius' openness to act according to circumstances is to be understood as being always in subordination to right and propriety.

9. THE DISPERSION OF THE MUSICIANS OF LOO. The dispersion here narrated is supposed to have taken place in the time of duke Gae. When once Confucius had rectified the music of Loo (IX. 14), the musicians would no longer be assisting in the prostitution of their art, and so, as the disorganization and decay proceeded, the chief among them withdrew to other countries, or from society altogether. 1. 大—太, as opposed to 少, p. 5, 'grand,' and 'assistant.' 'The music-master, Che,'—see VIII. 15. 2. The princes of China, it would appear, had music at their meals, and a separate band performed at each meal, or, possibly, the band might be the same, but under the superintendence of a separate officer at each meal. The emperor had four meals a day, and the princes of States only three, but it was the prerogative of the duke of Loo to use the ceremonies of

入於河。四播鼗武、入於漢。五少師陽、擊磬襄、入於海。

十章 周公謂魯公曰、君子不施其親、不使大臣怨乎不以、故舊無大故、則不棄也、無求備於一人。

十一章 周有八士、伯達、伯适、仲突、仲忽、叔夜、叔夏、季隨、季騧。

Yang, the assistant music-master, and Seang, master of the musical stone, withdrew to *an island in* the sea."

CHAPTER X. The duke of Chow addressed *his son*, the duke of Loo, saying, "The virtuous prince does not neglect his relations. He does not cause the great ministers to repine at his not employing them. Without some great cause, he does not dismiss from their offices the members of old families. He does not seek in one man talents for every employment."

CHAPTER XI. To Chow belonged the eight officers, Pih-tă, Pih-kwŏh, Chung-tŭh, Chung-hwŭh, Shuh-yay, Shuh-hea, Ke-suy, and Ke-kwa.

the imperial household. Nothing is said here of the bandmaster at the first meal, perhaps because he did not leave Loo, or nothing may have been known of him. 3. 'The River' is of course 'the Yellow River.' According to the 四書釋地, art. LVI, the expressions 入於河, 入於漢, are to be taken as meaning simply,—'lived on the banks of the Ho, the Han.' The interpr. in the translation is after Choo He, who follows the glossarist Hing Ping. The ancient emperors had their capitals mostly north and east of 'the River, hence, the country north of it was called 河內, and to the south of it was called 河外. I don't see, however, the applicability of this, to the Han, which is a tributary of the Yang-tsze, flowing through Hoo-pih. 5. It was from Seang that Confucius learned to play on the 琴.

10. INSTRUCTIONS OF CHOW-KUNG TO HIS SON ABOUT GOVERNMENT; A GENEROUS CONSIDERATION OF OTHERS TO BE CHERISHED. 周公,—see VI. 5. The facts of the case seem to be that the duke of Chow was himself appointed to the principality of Loo, but being detained at court by his duties to the young emperor 成, he sent his son 伯禽, here called 'the duke of Loo,' to that state as his representative. 君子 contains here the ideas both of rank and virtue. 施 is read in the up. 2d tone, with the same meaning as 弛. Choo He, indeed, seems to think that 弛 should be in the text, but we have 施 in Ho An, who gives K'ung Gan-kwŏ's interpretation;—施易也,不以他人之親易已之親, 施 *is to change*. He does not substitute the relatives of other men in the room of his own relatives.' 以,—here=用, 'to use,' 'to employ.' 求備,—see XIII. 25.

11. THE FRUITFULNESS OF THE EARLY TIME OF THE CHOW DYNASTY IN ABLE OFFICERS. The eight individuals mentioned here are said to have been brothers, four pairs of twins by the same mother. This is intimated in their names, the two first being 伯, or *primi*, the next pair 仲, or *secundi*, the third 叔, or *tertii*, and the last two 季. One mother, bearing twins four times in succession, and all proving distinguished men, showed the vigour of the early days of the dynasty in all that was good.—It is disputed to what reign these brothers belonged, nor is their surname ascertained. 達, 适, 突, 云云, seem to be honorary designations.

BOOK XIX. TSZE-CHANG.

子張第十九

一 子張曰、士見危致命、見得思義、祭思敬、喪思哀、其可已矣。

二 子張曰、執德不弘、信道不篤、焉能爲有、焉能爲亡。

CHAPTER I. Tsze-chang said, "The scholar, *trained for public duty*, seeing threatening danger, is prepared to sacrifice his life. When the opportunity of gain is presented to him, he thinks of righteousness. In sacrificing, his thoughts are reverential. In mourning, his thoughts are about the grief *which he should feel*. Such a man commands our approbation indeed."

CHAPTER II. Tsze-chang said, "When a man holds fast virtue, but without seeking to enlarge it, and believes right principles, but without firm sincerity, what account can be made of his existence or non-existence?"

HEADING OF THIS BOOK.—子張第十九. 'Tsze-chang—No. XIX.' Confucius does not appear personally in this Book at all. Chu Hsi says:—'This Book records the words of the disciples, Tsze-hsia being the most frequent speaker, and Tsze-kung next to him. For in the Confucian school, after Yen Yuan there was no one of such discriminating understanding as Tsze-kung, and, after Tsăng Shăn no one of such firm sincerity as Tsze-hsia.' The disciples deliver their sentiments very much after the manner of their master, and yet we can discern a falling off from him.

1. TSZE-CHANG'S OPINION OF THE CHIEF ATTRIBUTES OF THE TRUE SCHOLAR. 士,—see on XII. 20, 1. Tsze-chang there asks Confucius about the scholar-officer. 見危,—the danger is to be understood as threatening his country. Hing Ping, indeed, confines the danger to the person of the sovereign, for whom the officer will gladly sacrifice his life. 致命 is the same as 致其身 in I. 7. 已 is not to be explained by 止, as in 而已. The combination 已矣 has occurred before, and 也已 in I. 14. It greatly intensifies the preceding 可.

2. TSZE-CHANG ON NARROW-MINDEDNESS AND A HESITATING FAITH. Hing Ping interprets this chapter in the following way:—'If a man grasp hold of his virtue, and is not widened and

〔三〕子夏之門人問交於子張。子張曰、子夏云何。對曰、子夏曰、可者與之、其不可者拒之。子張曰、異乎吾所聞、君子尊賢而容衆、嘉善而矜不能、我之大賢與、於人何所不容、我之不賢與、人將拒我、如之何其拒人也、

〔四〕子夏曰、雖小道、必有

CHAPTER III. The disciples of Tsze-hea asked Tsze-chang about the principles of intercourse. Tsze-chang asked, "What does Tsze-hea say on the subject?" They replied, "Tsze-hea says:—'Associate with those who can *advantage you*. Put away from you those who cannot *do so*.' Tsze-chang observed, "This is different from what I have learned. The superior man honours the talented and virtuous, and bears with all. He praises the good, and pities the incompetent. Am I possessed of great talents and virtue?—who is there among men whom I will not bear with? Am I devoid of talents and virtue?—men will put me away from them. What have we to do with the putting away of others?"

CHAPTER IV. Tsze-hea said, "Even in inferior studies and employments there is something worth being looked at, but if it be

enlarged by it, although he may believe good principles, he cannot be sincere and generous.' But it is better to take the clauses as coordinate, and not dependent on each other. With 執德不弘 we may compare XV. 28, which suggests the taking 弘 actively. The two last clauses are perplexing. Chou He, after Gan-kwŏ apparently, makes them equivalent to—'is of no consideration in the world' (猶言不足輕重).

3. THE DIFFERENT OPINIONS OF TSZE-HEA AND TSZE-CHANG ON THE PRINCIPLES WHICH SHOULD REGULATE OUR INTERCOURSE WITH OTHERS. On the disciples of Tsze-hea, see the 集證, *in loc.* It is strange to me that they should begin their answer to Tsze-chang with the designation 子夏, instead of saying 夫子, 'our Master.' 交,—see V. 16. In 可者不可者, the 可 is taken differently by the old interpreters and the new. Hing Ping expounds:—'If the man be worthy, fit for you to have intercourse with, then have it, but if he be not worthy,' &c. On the other hand, we find:—'If the man will advantage you, he is a fit person (是可者); then maintain intercourse with him.' &c. This seems to be merely carrying out Confucius' rule, I. 8, 3. Choo He, however, approves of Tsze-chang's censure of it, while he thinks also that Tsze-chang's own view is defective.—Paou Heen says,—'Our intercourse with friends should be according to Tsze-hea's rule; general intercourse according to Tsze-chang's.'

4. TSZE-HEA'S OPINION OF THE INAPPLICABILITY OF SMALL PURSUITS TO GREAT OBJECTS. Gardening, husbandry, divining, and the healing art, are all mentioned by Choo He as in-

可觀者焉、致遠恐泥、是以君子不為也。

五 子夏曰、日知其所亡、月無忘其所能、可謂好學也已矣。

六 子夏曰、博學而篤志、切問而近思、仁在其中矣。

七 子夏曰、百工居肆、以成其事、君子學以致其道。

attempted to carry them out to what is remote, there is a danger of their proving inapplicable. Therefore, the superior man does not practise them."

CHAPTER V. Tsze-hea said, "He, who from day to day recognizes what he has not yet, and from month to month does not forget what he has attained to, may be said indeed to love to learn."

CHAPTER VI. Tsze-hea said, "There are learning extensively, and having a firm and sincere aim; inquiring with earnestness, and reflecting with self-application:—virtue is in such a course."

CHAPTER VII. Tsze-hea said, "Mechanics have their shops to dwell in, in order to accomplish their works. The superior man learns, in order to reach to the utmost of his principles."

stances of the 小道, 'small ways,' here intended, having their own truth in them, but not available for higher purposes, or what is beyond themselves. 致 is imperative and emphatic,—推極, 'push them to an extreme.' What is intended by 遠, is the far-reaching object of the *Keun-tsze*, 'to cultivate himself and regulate others.' 泥, lower 3d tone, explained in the dict. by 滯, 'water impeded.'—Ho An makes the 小道 to be 異端, 'strange principles.'

5. THE INDICATIONS OF A REAL LOVE OF LEARNING:—BY TSZE-HEA.

6. HOW LEARNING SHOULD BE PURSUED TO LEAD TO VIRTUE:—BY TSZE-HEA. K'ung Gan-kwŏ explains 志 as if it were 識, 'to remember.' On 切問而近思, the 備旨 says—所問, 皆切己之事, 所思, 皆身心之要, 'what are inquired about are things essential to one's self; what are thought about are the important personal duties.' Probably it is so, but all this cannot be put in a translation. On 近思, comp. VII. 28, 4. 仁在其中,—comp. VII. 15; XIII. 18.

7. LEARNING IS THE STUDENT'S WORKSHOP:—BY TSZE-HEA. 肆 is here 所以陳貨鬻之物, 'a place for the display and sale of goods.' A certain quarter was assigned anciently in Chinese towns and cities for mecha-

八 子夏曰、小人之過也、必文。

九 子夏曰、君子有三變、望之儼然、卽之也溫、聽其言也厲。

十 子夏曰、君子信而後勞其民、未信、則以爲厲己也、信而後諫、未信、則以爲謗己也。

十一 子夏曰、大德不踰閑、

CHAPTER VIII. Tsze-hea said, "The mean man is sure to gloss his faults."

CHAPTER IX. Tsze-hea said, "The superior man undergoes three changes. Looked at from a distance, he appears stern; when approached, he is mild; when he is heard to speak, his language is firm and decided."

CHAPTER X. Tsze-hea said, "The superior man, having obtained their confidence, may then impose labours on his people. If he have not gained their confidence, they will think that he is oppressing them. Having obtained the confidence *of his prince*, he may then remonstrate with him. If he have not gained his confidence, *the prince* will think that he is vilifying him."

CHAPTER XI. Tsze-hea said, "When a person does not transgress the boundary-line in the great virtues, he may pass and repass it in the small virtues."

nies, and all of one art were required to have their shops together. A son must follow his father's profession, and, seeing nothing but the exercise of that around him, it was supposed that he would not be led to think of anything else, and become very proficient in it.

8. GLOSSING HIS FAULTS THE PROOF OF THE MEAN MAN:—BY TSZE-HEA. Lit., 'The faults of the mean man, must gloss,' i. e., *he* is sure to gloss. 文, in this sense, a verb, low. 3d tone.

9. CHANGING APPEARANCES OF THE SUPERIOR MAN TO OTHERS:—BY TSZE-HEA. Tsze-hea probably intended Confucius by the *Keun-tsze*, but there is a general applicability in his language and sentiments. 望之, 卽之,—lit., 'look towards him,' 'approach him.'—The description is about equivalent to our '*fortiter in re, suaviter in modo*.'

10. THE IMPORTANCE OF ENJOYING CONFIDENCE TO THE RIGHT SERVING OF SUPERIORS AND ORDERING OF INFERIORS:—BY TSZE-HEA. Choo He gives to 信 here the double meaning of 'being sincere,' and 'being believed in.' The last is the proper force of the term, but it requires the possession of the former quality.

11. THE GREAT VIRTUES DEMAND THE CHIEF ATTENTION, AND THE SMALL ONES MAY BE SOMEWHAT VIOLATED:—BY TSZE-HEA. The sentiment here is very questionable. A different turn however, is given to the chapter in the older interpreters. Hing Ping, expanding K'ung Gan-kwŏ says:—'Men of great virtue never go beyond the boundary-line; it is enough for those who are virtuous in a less degree to keep near to it, going beyond and coming back.' We adopt the more natural interpretation of

小德出入可也。

〔十二〕子游曰、子夏之門人小子、當洒掃、應對、進退、則可矣、抑末也、本之則無、如之何。〔二〕子夏聞之曰、噫、言游過矣、君子之道、孰先傳焉、孰後倦焉、譬諸草木、區以別矣、君子之道、焉可誣也、有始有卒者、其惟聖人乎。

CHAPTER XII. 1. Tsze-yew said, "The disciples and followers of Tsze-hea, in sprinkling and sweeping the ground, in answering and replying, in advancing and receding, are sufficiently accomplished. But these are only the branches *of learning*, and they are left ignorant of what is essential.—How can they be acknowledged as sufficiently taught?"

2. Tsze-hea heard of the remark and said, "Alas! Yen Yew is wrong. According to the way of the superior man *in teaching*, what departments are there which he considers of prime importance, and delivers? what are there which he considers of secondary importance, and allows himself to be idle about? *But* as in the case of plants, which are assorted according to their classes, *so he deals with his disciples*. How can the way of a superior man be such as to make fools of *any of* them? Is it not the sage alone, who can unite in one the beginning and the consummation *of learning*?"

Chao He. 閑, 'a piece of wood, in a doorway, obstructing ingress and egress;' then, 'an inclosure' generally, 'a railing,' whatever limits and confines.

12. TSZE-HEA'S DEFENCE OF HIS OWN GRADUATED METHOD OF TEACHING;—AGAINST TSZE-YEW. 1. 小子 is to be taken in apposition with 門人, being merely, as we have found it previously, an affectionate method of speaking of the disciples. The sprinkling, &c., are the things which boys were supposed anciently to be taught, the rudiments of learning, from which they advanced to all that is inculcated in the 大學. But as Tsze-hea's pupils were not boys, but men, we should understand, I suppose, these specifications as but a contemptuous reference to his instructions, as embracing merely what was external. 洒, read *shae* and *she*, up. 1st tone, 'to sprinkle the ground before sweeping.' 應, upper 3d tone, 'to answer a call.' 對, 'to answer a question.' 抑 = 'but,' as in VII. 33. 本之 is expanded by the paraphrasts = 若本之所在, 'as to that in which the root (or, what is essential) is.' This is, no doubt, the meaning, but the phrase itself is abrupt and enigmatical. 如之何 = 如之何其可哉, in opposition to the 則可矣 above. 2. The general scope of Tsze-hea's reply is sufficiently plain, but the old interpreters and new differ in explaining the several sentences. After dwelling long on it, I have agreed generally

十三 子夏曰、仕而優則學、學而優則仕。

十四 子游曰、喪致乎哀而止。

十五 子游曰、吾友張也爲難能也、然而未仁。

十六 曾子曰、堂堂乎張也、難與並爲仁矣。

十七 曾子曰、吾聞諸夫子、人未有自致者也、必也親喪乎。

CHAPTER XIII. Tsze-hea said, "The officer, *having discharged all his duties*, should devote his leisure to learning. The student, having completed his learning, should apply himself to be an officer."

CHAPTER XIV. Tsze-hea said, "Mourning, having been carried to the utmost degree of grief, should stop with that."

CHAPTER XV. Tsze-hea said, "My friend Chang can do things which are hard to be done, but yet he is not perfectly virtuous."

CHAPTER XVI. The philosopher Tsăng said, "How imposing is the manner of Chang! It is difficult along with him to practise virtue."

CHAPTER XVII. The philosopher Tsăng said, "I heard this from our Master:—'Men may not have shown what is in them to the full extent, and yet they will be found to do so, on occasion of mourning for their parents.'"

with the new school, and followed Choo He in the translation. 區 is explained in the dict. by 類, 'classes.'

13. THE OFFICER AND THE STUDENT SHOULD ATTEND EACH TO HIS PROPER WORK IN THE FIRST INSTANCE:—BY TSZE-HEA. 優,—有餘力, in I. 6.—The saying needs to be much supplemented in translating, in order to bring out its meaning.

14. THE TRAPPINGS OF MOURNING MAY BE DISPENSED WITH:—BY TSZE-YEW. The sentiment here is perhaps the same as that of Confucius in III. 4, but the sage guards and explains his utterance.—K'ung Gan-kwŏ, following an expression in the 孝經, makes the meaning to be that the mourner may not endanger his health or life by excessive grief and abstinence.

15. TSZE-YEW'S OPINION OF TSZE-CHANG, AS MINDING TOO MUCH HIGH THINGS.

16. THE PHILOSOPHER TSANG'S OPINION OF TSZE-CHANG, AS TOO HIGH-PITCHED FOR FRIENDSHIP. 堂堂 is explained in the dict. by 盛也, 正也, 'exuberant,' 'correct.' It is to be understood of Chang's manner and appearance, keeping himself aloof from other men in his high-pitched course.

17. HOW GRIEF FOR THE LOSS OF PARENTS BRINGS OUT THE REAL NATURE OF MAN:—BY TSANG SIN. 自 is said to indicate the ideas both of 自己, 'one's self,' and 自然 'naturally.' 自致, 'to put one's self out to the utmost,'

〔十八〕曾子曰、吾聞諸夫子、孟莊子之孝也、其他可能也、其不改父之臣、與父之政、是難能也。

〔十九〕孟氏使陽膚爲士師、問於曾子。曾子曰、上失其道、民散、久矣、如得其情、則哀矜而勿喜。

〔二十〕子貢曰、紂之不善、不如是之甚也、是以君子

CHAPTER XVIII. The philosopher Tsăng said, "I have heard this from our Master:—'The filial piety of Măng Chwang, in other matters, was what other men are competent to, but, as seen in his not changing the ministers of his father, nor his father's mode of government, it is difficult to be attained to.'"

CHAPTER XIX. The chief of the Măng family having appointed Yang Foo to be chief criminal judge, the latter consulted the philosopher Tsăng. Tsăng said, "The rulers have failed in their duties, and the people consequently been disorganized, for a long time. When you have found out the truth *of any accusation*, be grieved for and pity them, and do not feel joy *at your own ability*."

CHAPTER XX. Tsze-kung said, "Chow's wickedness was not so great *as that name implies*. Therefore, the superior man hates to

as we should say—'to come out fully,' *i. e.*, in one's proper nature and character. On the construction of 必也.親喪乎, comp. XII. 13. 吾聞諸夫子—諸 seems low 之, *i. e.*, so that 諸 and 夫子 are like two objectives, both governed by 聞.

18. THE FILIAL PIETY OF MANG CHWANG:—BY TSANG SIN. Chwang was the honorary epithet of Suh (速), the head of the Măng family, not long anterior to Confucius. His father, acc. to Choo He, had been a man of great merit, nor was he inferior to him, but his virtue especially appeared in what the text mentions.—Ho An gives the comment of Ma Yung, that though there were bad men among his father's ministers, and defects in his government, yet Chwang made no change in the one or the other, during the three years of mourning, and that it was this which constituted his excellence.

19. HOW A CRIMINAL JUDGE SHOULD CHERISH COMPASSION IN HIS ADMINISTRATION OF JUSTICE:—BY TSANG SIN. Seven disciples of Tsăng Sin are more particularly mentioned, one of them being this Yang Foo. 散 is to be understood of the moral state of the people, and not, physically, of their being scattered from their dwellings. 情 has occurred before in the sense of—'the truth,' which it has here.

20. THE DANGER OF A BAD NAME:—BY TSZE-KUNG. 如是之甚 'so very bad as this;'—the *this* (是) is understood by Hing Ping as referring to the epithet—紂, which cannot be called honorary in this instance. According to the laws for such terms, it means—殘忍捐

惡居下流、天下之惡皆歸焉。

二十一 子貢曰、君子之過也、如日月之食焉、過也、人皆見之、更也、人皆仰之。

二十二 衛公孫朝問於子貢曰、仲尼焉學。子貢曰、文武之道、未墜於地、在人、賢者識其大者、不賢者識其小者、莫不有文武之道焉、夫子焉不學、而亦何常師之有、

dwell in a low-lying situation, where all the evil of the world will flow in upon him."

CHAPTER XXI. Tsze-kung said, "The faults of the superior man are like the eclipses of the sun and moon. He has his faults, and all men see them: he changes again, and all men look up to him."

CHAPTER XXII. 1. Kung-sun Ch'aou of Wei asked Tsze-kung, saying, "From whom did Chung-ne get his learning?"

2. Tsze-kung replied, "The doctrines of Wăn and Woo have not yet fallen to the earth. They are to be found among men. Men of talents and virtue remember the greater principles of them, and others, not possessing such talents and virtue, remember the smaller. *Thus*, all possess the doctrines of Wăn and Woo. Where could our Master go that he should not have an opportunity of learning them? And yet what necessity was there for his having a regular master?"

殘, 'cruel and unmerciful, injurious to righteousness.' If the 是 does not in this way refer to the name, the remark would seem to have occurred in a conversation about the wickedness of Chow. 下流 is a low-lying situation, to which the streams flow and waters drain, representing here a bad reputation, which gets the credit of every vice.

21. THE SUPERIOR MAN DOES NOT CONCEAL HIS ERRORS, NOR PERSIST IN THEM.—BY TSZE-KUNG. Such is the lesson of this chapter, as expanded in the 日講. The sun and the moon being here spoken of together, the 食 must be confined to 'eclipses,' but the term is also applied to the ordinary waning of the moon.

22. CONFUCIUS'S SOURCES OF KNOWLEDGE WERE THE RECOLLECTIONS AND TRADITIONS OF THE PRINCIPLES OF WAN AND WOO;—BY TSZE-KUNG. 1. Of the questioner here we have no other memorial. His surname indicates that he was a descendant of some of the dukes of Wei. Observe how he calls Confucius by his designation of 仲尼 or 'Ne secundus.' (There was an elder brother, a concubine's son, who was called 伯

〔廿三〕〔一〕叔孫武叔語大夫於朝曰、子貢賢於仲尼。〔二〕子服景伯以告子貢。子貢曰、譬之宮牆、賜之牆也及肩、窺見室家之好。〔三〕夫子之牆數仞、不得其門而入、不見宗廟之美、百官之富。〔四〕得其門者或寡矣、夫子之云、不亦宜乎。

CHAPTER XXIII. 1. Shuh-sun Woo-shuh observed to the great officers in the court, saying, "Tsze-kung is superior to Chung-ne."

2. Tsze-fuh King-pih reported the observation to Tsze-kung, who said, "Let me use the comparison of a house and its *encompassing* wall. My wall *only* reaches to the shoulders. One may peep over it, and see whatever is valuable in the apartments.

3. "The wall of my master is several fathoms high. If one do not find the door and enter by it, he cannot see the ancestral temple with its beauties, nor all the officers in their rich array.

4. "But I may assume that they are few who find the door. Was not the observation of the chief only what might have been expected?"

尼.) 仲尼焉學, 'How did Chung-ne learn?' but the 'how'='from whom?' The expression below, however,—夫子焉不學, expounded as in the translation, might suggest, from 'what quarter?' rather than 'from what person?' as the proper rendering. The last clause is taken by modern commentators, as asserting Conf. connate knowledge, but Gan-kwŏ finds in it only a repetition of the statement that the sage found teachers everywhere.

23. TSZE-KUNG REPUDIATES BEING THOUGHT SUPERIOR TO CONFUCIUS, AND, BY THE COMPARISON OF A HOUSE AND WALL, SHOWS HOW ORDINARY PEOPLE COULD NOT UNDERSTAND THE MASTER. 1. 武 was the hon. epithet of Chow Kew (州仇), one of the chiefs of the Shuh-sun family. From a mention of him in the 家語, 顔回篇, we may conclude that he was given to envy and detraction. 賢,—used here as in XI. 15, 1. 2. Tsze-fuh King-pih,—see XIV. 38. 譬之宮牆,—宮 is to be taken generally for a house or building, and not in its now common acceptation of 'a palace.' It is a poor house, as representing the disciple, and a ducal mansion as representing his master. Many commen. make the wall to be the sole object in the comparison, and 宮牆=宮之牆. It is better, with the 合講, to take both the house and the wall as members of the comp., and 宮牆=宮與牆. The wall is not a part of the house, but one inclosing it. 3. 仞 means 7 cubits. I have translated it—'fathoms.' 4. The 夫子 here refers to Woo-shuh.

廿四 叔孫武叔毀仲尼。子貢曰、無以爲也。仲尼不可毀也。他人之賢者、丘陵也。猶可踰也。仲尼、日月也。無得而踰焉。人雖欲自絕、其何傷於日月乎。多見其不知量也。

廿五 陳子禽謂子貢曰、子爲恭也、仲尼豈賢於子乎。二 子貢曰、君子一言以爲知、一言以爲不知。言不可不愼也。三 夫子之

CHAPTER XXIV. Shuh-sun Woo-shuh having spoken revilingly of Chung-ne, Tsze-kung said, "It is of no use doing so. Chung-ne cannot be reviled. The talents and virtue of other men are hillocks and mounds, which may be stept over. Chung-ne is the sun or moon, which it is not possible to step over. Although a man may wish to cut himself off *from the sage*, what harm can he do to the sun or moon? He only shows that he does not know his own capacity."

CHAPTER XXV. 1. Tsze-k'in, addressing Tsze-kung, said, "You are too modest. How can Chung-ne be said to be superior to you?"

2. Tsze-kung said to him, "For one word a man is *often* deemed to be wise, and for one word he is *often* deemed to be foolish. We ought to be careful indeed in what we say.

3. "Our Master cannot be attained to, just in the same way as the heavens cannot be gone up to by the steps of a stair.

24. CONFUCIUS IS LIKE THE SUN OR MOON, HIGH ABOVE THE REACH OF DEPRECIATION:—BY TSZE-KUNG. 無以爲 is explained by Choo He (and the gloss of Hing Ping is the same) as =無用爲此, 'it is of no use to do this.' 他人之賢者,—他人 is to be understood, acc. to the 備旨, as embracing all other sages. 自絕,—I have supplied '*from the sage*,' after most modern paraphrasts. Hing Ping, however, supplies '*from the sun and moon*.' The meaning comes to the same. Choo He says that 多 here is the same with 祇, 'only.' Hing Ping takes it as =適, 'just.' This meaning of the char. is not given in the dictionary, but it is necessary here; see supplement to Hing Ping's 疏, *in loc.*

25. CONFUCIUS CAN NO MORE BE EQUALLED THAN THE HEAVENS CAN BE CLIMBED:—BY TSZE-KUNG. We find it difficult to conceive of the sage's disciples speaking to one another, as Tsze-k'in does here to Tsze-kung, and Hing

不可及也、猶天之不可階而升也。夫子之得邦家者、所謂立之斯立、道之斯行、綏之斯來、動之斯和、其生也榮、其死也哀、如之何其可及也。

4. "Were our Master in the position of the prince of a State or the chief of a Family, we should find verified the description *which has been given of a sage's rule*:—he would plant the people, and forthwith they would be established; he would lead them on, and forthwith they would follow him; he would make them happy, and forthwith *multitudes* would resort to *his dominions*; he would stimulate them, and forthwith they would be harmonious. While he lived, he would be glorious. When he died, he would be bitterly lamented. How is it possible for him to be attained to?"

Ping says that this was not the disciple Tsze-h'in, but another man of the same surname and designation. But this is inadmissible, especially as we find the same parties, in I. 10, talking about the character of their master. 1. 子爲恭, 'you are doing the modest.' 2. 君子 has here its lightest meaning. The 備旨 makes it=學者, 'a student,' but 'a man,' as in the transl., is quite as much as it denotes. Comp. its use in I. 8, et al. 4. 夫子之得邦家者 must be understood hypothetically, because he never was in the position here assigned to him. 斯,—as in X. 10, 1. 道 is for 導, as in I. 5. 來,—as in XVI. 1, 11. 動之,—as in XV. 32, 3. 之, *them*, 'the people' being always understood.

BOOK XX. YAOU YUE.

堯曰第二十

一章 堯曰、咨爾舜、天之厤數在爾躬、允執其中、四海困窮、天祿永終。舜亦以命禹。曰、予小子履、敢用玄牡、敢昭告于皇皇后帝、有罪不敢赦、帝臣不蔽、簡在帝心、朕躬有罪、無以萬方、萬方有罪、

CHAPTER I. 1. Yaou said, "Oh! you, Shun, the Heaven-determined order of succession now rests in your person. Sincerely hold fast the Due Mean. If there shall be distress and want within the four seas, *your* Heavenly revenue will come to a perpetual end."

2. Shun also used the same language in giving charge to Yu.

3. *T'ang* said, "I, the child Le, presume to use a dark-coloured victim, and presume to announce to Thee, O most great and sovereign God, that the sinner I dare not pardon, and thy ministers, O God, I do not keep in obscurity. The examination of them is by thy mind, O God. If, in my person, I commit offences, they are not to beattributed to you, *the people of* the myriad regions. If you in the myriad regions commit offences, these offences must rest on my person."

HEADING OF THIS BOOK.—堯曰第二十, 'Yaou said—No. XX.' Hing Ping says:—'This records the words of the two emperors, the three kings, and of Confucius, throwing light on the excellence of the ordinances of Heaven, and the transforming power of government. Its doctrines are all those of sages, worthy of being transmitted to posterity. On this account, it brings up the rear of all the other books, without any particular relation to the one immediately preceding.'

1. PRINCIPLES AND WAYS OF YAOU, SHUN, YU, T'ANG, AND WOO. The first five paragraphs here are mostly compiled from different parts of the Shoo-king. But there are many variations of language. The compiler may have thought it sufficient, if he gave the substance of the original in his quotations, without seeking to observe a verbal accuracy, or, possibly, the Shoo-king, as it was in his days, may have contained the passages as he gives them, and the variations be owing to the burning of most of the classical books by the founder of the Ts'in dynasty, and their recovery and restoration in a mutilated state. 1. We do not find this address of Yaou to Shun in the Shoo-king, Pt I., but the different sentences may be gathered from Pt II. ii. 14, 15, where we have the charge of Shun to Yu. Yaou's reign commenced B. C. 2356, and after reigning 73 years, he resigned the administration to Shun. He died, B. C. 2256, and, two years after, Shun occupied the throne, in obedience to the will of the people. 天之厤數,

罪在朕躬。四 周有大賚、善人是富。五 雖有周親、不如仁人、百姓有過、在予一人。六 謹權量、審法度、修廢官、四方之政行焉。七 興滅國、繼絕世、舉逸民、天下之民歸心焉。八 所重民、食、喪、祭。九 寬則得衆、信則民任焉、敏則有功、公則說。

4. Chow conferred great gifts, and the good were enriched.

5. "Although he has his near relatives, they are not equal to *my* virtuous men. The people are throwing blame upon me, the one man."

6. He carefully attended to the weights and measures, examined the body of the laws, restored the discarded officers, and the good government of the empire took its course.

7. He revived states that had been extinguished, restored families whose line of succession had been broken, and called to office those who had retired into obscurity, so that throughout the empire the hearts of the people turned towards him.

8. What he attached chief importance to, were the food of the people, the duties of mourning, and sacrifices.

9. By his generosity, he won all. By his sincerity, he made the people repose trust in him. By his earnest activity, his achievements were great. By his justice, all were delighted.

lit., 'the represented and calculated numbers of heaven,' i.e., the divisions of the year, its terms, months, and days, all described in a calendar, as they succeed one another with determined regularity. Here, ancient and modern interpreters agree in giving to the expression the meaning which appears in the translation. I may observe here, that Choo He differs often from the old interpreters in explaining these passages of the Shoo-king, but I have followed him, leaving the correctness or incorrectness of his views to be considered in the annotations on the Shoo-king. 3. Before 曰 here we must understand 湯, the designation of the founder of the Shang dynasty. The sentences here may in substance be collected from the Shoo-king, Pt IV. iii. 4, 8. Down to 簡在帝心 is a prayer addressed to God by T'ang, on his undertaking the overthrow of the Hea dynasty, which he rehearses to his nobles and people, after the completion of his work. T'ang's name was 履. We do not find in the Shoo-king the remarkable designation of God—皇皇后帝. For the grounds on which I translate 帝 by *God*, see my work on 'The notions of the Chinese concerning God and Spirits.' 后, now generally used for 'empress,' was anciently used for 'sovereign,' and applied to the emperors. Here, it is an adjective, or in apposition with 帝. The sinner is Kee (桀), the tyrant,

〔二〕子張問於孔子曰、何如斯可以從政矣。子曰、尊五美、屏四惡、斯可以從政矣。子張曰、何謂五美。子曰、君子惠而不費、勞而不怨、欲而不貪、泰而不驕、威而不猛。二子張曰、何謂惠而不費。子曰、因民之所利而利之、

CHAPTER II. 1. Tsze-chang asked Confucius, saying, "In what way should *a person in authority* act in order that he may conduct government properly?" The Master replied, "Let him honour the five excellent, and banish away the four bad, things;—then may he conduct government properly." Tsze-chang said, "What are meant by the five excellent things?" The Master said, "When the person in authority is beneficent without great expenditure; when he lays tasks *on the people* without their repining; when he *pursues what he* desires without being covetous; when he maintains a dignified ease without being proud; when he is majestic without being fierce."

2. Tsze-chang said, "What is meant by being beneficent without great expenditure?" The Master replied, "When *the person in*

and last emperor of the Hea dynasty. 'The ministers of God' are the able and virtuous men, whom T'ang had called, or would call, to office. By 簡在帝心, T'ang indicates that, in his punishing or rewarding, he only wanted to act in harmony with the mind of God. 無以萬方=萬方小民何預焉, as in the transl. In the dict. it is said that 以 and 與 are interchanged. This is a case in point. 4. In the Shoo-king, Pt V. iii. 8, we find king Woo saying 大賚於四海而萬姓悅服, 'I distributed great rewards through the empire, and all the people were pleased and submitted.' 5. See the Shoo-king, Pt V. i. sect. II. 6, 7. The subject in 雖有周親 is 受 or 紂, tyrant of the Yin dynasty. 周,—in the sense of 至. 過 is used in the sense of 咎, 'to blame.'—The people found fault with him, because he did not come to save them from their sufferings, by destroying their oppressor. The remaining paragraphs are descriptive of the policy of king Woo, but cannot, excepting the 8th one, be traced in the present Shoo-king. 任, par. 9, is in the low. 3d tone. See XVII. vi, which chap., generally, resembles this paragraph.

2. HOW GOVERNMENT MAY BE CONDUCTED WITH EFFICIENCY, BY HONOURING FIVE EXCELLENT THINGS, AND PUTTING AWAY FOUR BAD THINGS:—A CONVERSATION WITH TSZE-CHANG. It is understood that this chapter, and the next, give the ideas of Confucius on government, as a sequel to those of the ancient sages and emperors, whose principles are set forth in the last chapter, to show how Confucius was their proper successor. 1. On 從政 see VI. 6, but the gloss of the 備旨 says—從政只泛說行政, 不作爲大夫, '從政 here denotes generally the practice of government. It is not to be taken as indicating a minister.' We may, however, retain the proper meaning of the phrase, Confucius describing principles to be observed by all in authority, and which will find in the highest their noblest

斯不亦惠而不費乎、擇可勞而勞之、又誰怨、欲仁而得仁、又焉貪、君子無衆寡、無小大、無敢慢、斯不亦泰而不驕乎、君子正其衣冠、尊其瞻視、儼然人望而畏之、斯不亦威而不猛乎。三子張曰、何謂四惡。子曰、不教而殺、謂之虐、不戒視成、謂之暴、慢令致期、謂之賊、猶

authority makes more beneficial to the people the things from which they naturally derive benefit;—is not this being beneficent without *great* expenditure? When he chooses the labours which are proper, and makes them labour on them, who will repine? When his desires are set on benevolent *government*, and he realizes it, who will accuse him of covetousness? Whether he has to do with many people or few, or with things great or small, he does not dare to indicate any disrespect;—is not this to maintain a dignified ease without any pride? He adjusts his clothes and cap, and throws a dignity into his looks, so that, thus dignified, he is looked at with awe;—is not this to be majestic without being fierce?"

3. Tsze-chang then asked, "What are meant by the four bad things?" The Master said, "To put the people to death without having instructed them;—this is called cruelty. To require from them, *suddenly*, the full tale of work, without having given them warning:—this is called oppression. To issue orders as if without urgency, *at first*, and, when the time comes, *to insist on them with*

embellishment. The 日講 favours this view. See its paraphrase in loc. I have therefore translated 君子 by—'a person in authority.' 勞而不怨,—see IV. 18, though the application of the terms there is different. 泰而不驕,—see XIII. 26. 威而不猛,—see VII. 37. 2. 因民云云 is instanced by the promotion of agriculture. 擇可勞云云 is instanced by the employment of the people in advantageous public works. 欲仁云云 is explained:—'Desire for what is not proper is covetousness, but if, while the wish to have the empire overshadowed by his benevolence has not reached to universal advantaging, his desire does not cease, then, with a heart impatient of people's evils, he administers a government impatient of those evils. What he desires is benevolence, and what he gets is the same;—how can he be regarded as covetous?' 視

之與人也、出納之吝、謂之有司。

三 子曰、不知命、無以爲君子也。二不知禮、無以立也。三不知言、無以知人也。

severity;—this is called injury. And, generally speaking, to give *pay or rewards* to men, and yet to do it in a stingy way;—this is called acting the part of a mere official."

CHAPTER III. 1. The Master said, "Without recognizing the ordinances *of Heaven*, it is impossible to be a superior man.

2. "Without an acquaintance with the rules of Propriety, it is impossible for the character to be established.

3. "Without knowing *the force of* words, it is impossible to know men."

is explained here by 責, 'to require from.' We may get that meaning out of the char., which = 'to examine,' 'to look for.' A good deal has to be supplied, here and in the sentences below, to bring out the meaning as in the translation. 猶之 is explained by 均之, and seems to me to be nearly = our 'on the whole.' 出納,—'giving out,' *i. e., from this* and 'presenting,' *i. e., to that.* The whole is understood to refer to rewarding men for their services, and doing it in an unwilling and stingy manner.

3. THE ORDINANCES OF HEAVEN, THE RULES OF PROPRIETY, AND THE FORCE OF WORDS, ALL NECESSARY TO BE KNOWN. 1. 知 here is not only 'knowing,' but 'believing and resting in.' 命 is the will of Heaven regarding right and wrong, of which man has the standard in his own moral nature. If this be not recognized, a man is the slave of passion, or the sport of feeling. 2. Compare VIII. 8, 2. 3. 知 here supposes much thought and examination of principles. Words are the voice of the heart. To know a man, we must attend well to what and how he thinks.

THE GREAT LEARNING.

大學

子程子曰、大學、孔氏之遺書、而初學入德之門也、於今可見古人爲學次第者、獨賴此篇之存、而論孟次之、學者必由是而學焉、則庶乎其不

My master, the philosopher Ch'ing, says:—"The Great Learning is a book left by Confucius, and forms the gate by which first learners enter into virtue. That we can now perceive the order in which the ancients pursued their learning, is solely owing to the preservation of this work, the Analects and Mencius coming after it. Learners must commence their course with this, and then it may be hoped they will be kept from error."

TITLE OF THE WORK.—大學. 'The Great Learning.' I have pointed out, in the prolegomena, the great differences which are found among Chinese commentators on this Work, on almost every point connected with the criticism and interpretation of it. We encounter them here on the very threshold. The name itself is simply | the adoption of the two commencing characters of the treatise, according to the custom noticed at the beginning of the Analects; but in explaining those two characters, the old and new schools differ widely. Anciently, 大 was read as 太, and the oldest commentator whose notes on the work are preserved, Ch'ing K'ang-shing, in the last half of the second century, said that the book was called 大學, 以其記博學可以爲政, 'because it recorded that extensive learning, which was available for the administration of government.' This view is approved by K'ung Ying-tâ (孔穎達), whose expansion of K'ang-shing's notes, written in the first half of the 7th century, still remains. He says—大學, 至道矣, '大學 means the highest principles.' Choo He's definition, on the contrary, is—大學者大人之學也, '大學 means the Learning of Adults.' One of the paraphrasts who follow him says—大是大人, 與小子對, '大 means adults, in opposition to children.' The grounds of Choo He's interpr. are to be found in his very elegant preface to the Book, where he tries to make it out, that we have here the subjects taught in the advanced schools of antiquity. I have contented myself with the title—'The Great Learning,' which is a literal translation of the characters, whether read as 太學, or 大學.

THE INTRODUCTORY NOTE.—I have thought it well to translate this, and all the other notes and supplements appended by Choo He to the original text, because they appear in nearly all the editions of the work, which fall into the hands of students, and his view of the classics is what must be regarded as the orthodox one. The translation, which is here given, is also, for the most part, according to his views, though my own differing opinion will be found freely expressed in the notes. Another version, following the order of the text, before it was transposed by him and his masters, the Ch'ing, and without reference to his interpretations, will be

差矣。

一　大學之道、在明明德、在親民、在止於至善。二　知止、而后有定、定而后能靜、

THE TEXT OF CONFUCIUS.

1. What the Great Learning teaches, is—to illustrate illustrious virtue; to renovate the people; and to rest in the highest excellence.

2. The point where to rest being known, the object of pursuit is then determined; and, that being determined, a calm unperturbedness may be attained. To that calmness there will succeed a tranquil

found in the translation of the Le-ke.—子程子,—see note to the Ana. I. i. The Ch'ing here, is the second of the two brothers, to whom reference is made in the prolegomena. 孔氏, 'Confucius,' the K'ung, as 季氏 is found continually in the Analects for the Ke, i. e., the chief of the Ke family. But how can we say that 'The Great Learning' is a work left by Confucius? Even Choo He ascribes only a small portion of it to the Master, and makes the rest to be the production of the disciple Tsăng, and before his time, the whole work was attributed generally to the sage's grandson. I should be glad if I had authority for taking 孔氏 as=孔門, the Confucian school.

CHAPTER I. THE TEXT OF CONFUCIUS. Such Choo He, as will be seen from his concluding note, determines this chapter to be, and it has been divided into two sections (節), the first containing three paragraphs, occupied with the *heads* (綱領) of the Great Learning, and the second containing four paragraphs, occupied with the *particulars* (條目) of these.

Par. 1. The heads of the Great Learning. 大學之道,—'the way of the Great Learning,' 道 being=修爲之方法, 'the methods of cultivating and practising it,'—the Great Learning, that is. 在, 'is in.' The first 明 is a verb; the second is an adjective, qualifying 德. The illustrious virtue is the virtuous nature which man derives from Heaven. This is perverted as man grows up, through defects of the physical constitution, through inward lusts, and through outward seductions; and the great business of life should be, to bring the nature back to its original purity.—'To renovate the people,'—this object of the Great Learning is made out, by changing the character 親 of the old text into 新. The Ch'ing first proposed the alteration, and Choo He approved of it. When a man has entirely illustrated his own illustrious nature, he has to proceed to bring about the same result in every other man, till 'under heaven' there be not an individual, who is not in the same condition as himself.—'The highest excellence' is understood of the two previous matters. It is not a third and different object of pursuit, but indicates a perseverance in the two others, till they are perfectly accomplished.—According to these explanations, the objects contemplated in the Great Learning, are not three, but two. Suppose them realized, and we should have the whole world of mankind perfectly good, every individual what he ought to be!

Against the above interpretation, we have to consider the older and simpler. 德 is there not the *nature*, but simply virtue, or virtuous conduct, and the first object in the Great Learning is the making of one's-self more and more illustrious in virtue, or the practice of benevolence, reverence, filial piety, kindness, and sincerity. See the 故本大學註辨, *in loc.*—There is nothing, of course, of the *renovating of the people*, in this interpretation. The second object of the Great Learning is 親民=親愛於民, 'to love the people.'—The third object is said by Ying-tă to be 'in resting in conduct which is perfectly good (在止處於至善之行);' and here also, there would seem to be only two objects, for what essential distinction can we make between the first and third? There will be occasion below to refer to the reasons for changing 親 into 新, and their unsatisfactoriness. 'To love the people' is, doubtless, the second thing taught by the Great Learning.—Having the heads of the Great Learning now before us, according to both interpretations of it, we feel that the student of it should be an emperor, and not an ordinary man.

Par. 2. The mental process by which the point of rest may be attained. I confess that I do not well understand this par., in the relation of its parts in itself, nor in relation to the rest of the chapter. Choo He says:—'止 is the ground where we ought to rest;'—namely, the highest ex-

靜、而后能安、安、而后能慮、慮、而后能得。物有本末、事有終始、知所先後、則近道矣。古之欲明明德於天下者、先治其國、欲治其國者、先齊其家、欲齊其家者、先脩其身、欲脩其身者、先正

repose. In that repose there may be careful deliberation, and that deliberation will be followed by the attainment *of the desired end.*

3. Things have their root and their completion. Affairs have their end and their beginning. To know what is first and what is last will lead near to what is taught *in the Great Learning.*

4. The ancients who wished to illustrate illustrious virtue throughout the empire, first ordered well their own States. Wishing to order well their States, they first regulated their families. Wishing to regulate their families, they first cultivated their persons. Wishing to cultivate their persons, they first rectified their hearts. Wishing

excellence mentioned above. But if this be known in the outset, where is the necessity for the 慮, or 'careful deliberation,' which issues in its attainment? The paraphrasts make 知止 to embrace even all that is understood by 格物致知 below.—Ying-tâ is perhaps rather more intelligible. He says:—'When it is known that the rest is to be in the perfectly good, then the mind has fixedness. So it is free from concupiscence, and can be still, not engaging in disturbing pursuits. That still leads to a repose and harmony of the feelings. That state of the feelings fits for careful thought about affairs (能思慮於事), and thence it results that what is right in affairs is attained.' Perhaps, the par. just intimates that the objects of the G. L. being so great, a calm, serious, thoughtfulness is required in proceeding to seek their attainment.

Par. 3. *The order of things and methods in the two preceding paragraphs.* So, acc. to Choo He, does this par. wind up the two preceding. 'The illustration of virtue,' he says, 'is the *root*, and the renovation of the people is the *completion* (lit., *the branches*). Knowing where to rest is the *beginning*, and being able to attain is the end. The root and the beginning are *what is first*. The completion and end are *what is last*.'—The adherents of the old commentators say, on the contrary, that this par. is introductory to the succeeding ones. They contend that the illustration of virtue and renovation of the people are *doings* (事), and not *things* (物). Acc. to them, the *things* are the person, heart, thoughts, &c., mentioned below, which are 'the root,' and the family, kingdom, and empire, which are 'the branches.' The *affairs* are the various processes put forth on those things.—This, it seems to me, is the correct interpretation.

Par. 4. *The different steps by which the illustration of illustrious virtue throughout the empire may be brought about.* 明明德於天下 is understood by the school of Choo He as embracing the two first objects of the Great Learning, the illustration, namely of virtue, and the renovation of the people. We are not aided in determining the meaning by the synthetic arrangement of the different steps in the next par., for the result arrived at there is simply—天下平, 'the whole empire was made tranquil.'—Ying-tâ's comment is—章明己之明德使徧於天下, 'to display illustriously their own illustrious virtue (or, virtues), making them reach through the whole empire.' But the influence must be very much transformative. Of the several steps described, the central one is 修身, 'the cultivation of the person,' which, indeed, is called 本, 'the root,' in par.

其心、欲正其心者、先誠其意、欲誠其意者、先致其知、致知在格物。物格而后知

to rectify their hearts, they first sought to be sincere in their thoughts. Wishing to be sincere in their thoughts, they first extended to the utmost their knowledge. Such extension of knowledge lay in the investigation of things.

5. Things being investigated, knowledge became complete. Their knowledge being complete, their thoughts were sincere. Their

4. This requires 'the heart to be correct,' and that again 'that the thoughts be sincere.' Choo He defines 心 as 身之所主, 'what the body has for its lord,' and 意 as 心之所發, 'what the 心 sends forth.' Ying-tâ says:—總包萬慮謂之心 'that which comprehends and embraces all considerings is called the 心;' 爲情所意念謂之意, 'the thoughts under emotion are what is called 意.' 心 is thus the meta-physical part of our nature, all that we comprehend under the terms of mind or soul, heart, and spirit. This is conceived of as quiescent, and when its activity is aroused, then we have thoughts and purposes relative to what affects it. The 'being sincere' is explained by 實, 'real.' The sincerity of the thoughts is to be obtained by 致知, which means, acc. to Choo He, 'carrying our knowledge to its utmost extent, with the desire that there may be nothing which it shall not embrace.' This knowledge, finally, is realised 在格物. The same authority takes 物, 'things,' as embracing, 事, 'affairs,' as well. 格, sometimes=至, 'to come or extend to,' and assuming that the 'coming to' here is by study, he makes it=窮究 'to examine exhaustively,' so that '格物 means exhausting by examination the principles of things and affairs, with the desire that their uttermost point may be reached.'—We feel that this explanation cannot be correct, or that, if it be correct, the teaching of the Chinese sage is far beyond and above the condition and capacity of men. How can we suppose that, in order to secure sincerity of thought and our self-cultivation, there is necessarily the study of all the phenomena of physics and metaphysics, and of the events of history? Moreover, Choo He's view of the two last clauses is a consequence of the alterations which he adopts in the order of the text. As that exists in the Le-ke, the 7th par. of this chapter is followed by 此謂知本.此謂知之至也, which he has transferred and made the 5th chapter of annotations. Ying-tâ's comment on it is:—'*The root means the person.* The person (*i. e.* personal character) being regarded as the root, if one can know his own person, this is the knowledge of the root; yea, this is the very extremity of knowledge.' If we apply this conclusion to the clauses under notice, it is said that wishing to make our thoughts sincere we must first carry to the utmost our self-knowledge, and this extension of self-knowledge 在格物. Now, the change of the style indicates that the relation of 致知 and 格物 is different from that of the parts in the other clauses. It is not said that to get the one thing we must first do the other. Rather it seems to me that the 格物 is a consequence of 致知, that in it is seen the other. Now, 式, 'a rule or pattern,' and 正, 'to correct,' are accepted meanings of 格, and 物 being taken generally and loosely as=things, 在格物 will tell us that, when his self-knowledge is complete, a man is a law to himself, measuring, and measuring correctly, all things with which he has to do, not led astray or beclouded by them. This is the interpretation strongly insisted on by 臨仲遵, the author of the 古本大學註辨. It is the only view into any sympathy with which I can place my mind. In harmony with it, I would print 致至在格物 as a par. by itself, between the analytic and synthetic processes described in parr. 4, 5. Still there are difficulties connected with it, and I leave the vexed questions, regretting my own inability to clear them up.

Par. 5. *The synthesis of the preceding processes.* Observe the 致 of the preceding par. is changed into 至, and how 治 now becomes 治. low.

至、知至、而后意誠、意誠、而后心正、心正、而后身脩、身脩、而后家齊、家齊、而后國治、國治、而后天下平。

六 自天子、以至於庶人、壹是、皆以脩身爲本。

七 其本亂、而末治者否矣、其所厚者薄、而其所薄者厚、未之有也。

thoughts being sincere, their hearts were then rectified. Their hearts being rectified, their persons were cultivated. Their persons being cultivated, their families were regulated. Their families being regulated, their States were rightly governed. Their States being rightly governed, the whole empire was made tranquil and happy.

6. From the emperor down to the mass of the people, all must consider the cultivation of the person the root of *every thing besides*.

7. It cannot be, when the root is neglected, that what should spring from it will be well ordered. It never has been the case that what was of great importance has been slightly cared for, and, at the same time, that what was of slight importance has been greatly cared for.

3d time. 治 is explained by 政理, 'the work of ruling,' and 治 by 理效, 'the result.' 后 is used for 後, as in p. 2.

Par. 6. The cultivation of the person is the prime, radical, thing required from all. I have said above that the Great Learning is adapted only to an emperor, but it is intimated here that *the people* also may take part in it in their degree. 天子, 'Son of Heaven,' a designation of the emperor, 以其命于天, 'because he is ordained by Heaven.' 壹是＝一切, 'all.' Ch'ing K'ang-ch'ing, however, says:—壹是, 專行是也, '壹是 means that they uniformly do this.'

Par. 7. Reiteration of the importance of attending to the root. Chu He makes the *root* here to be the person, but accord. to the prec. par., it is 'the cultivation of the person' which is intended. By the 末 or 'branches' is intended the proper ordering of the family, the state, the empire. 厚薄, 'thick,' and 'thin,'—used here metaphorically. 所厚, acc. to Chu He, means 'the family,' and 所薄, the state and the empire, but that I cannot understand. 所厚 is the same as the *root*. Mencius has a saying which may illustrate the second part of the paragraph.—於所厚者薄, 無所不薄, 'He, who is careless in what is important, will be careless in every thing.'

右經一章、蓋孔子之言、而曾子述之、其傳十章、則曾子之意、而門人記之也、舊本頗有錯簡、今因程子所定、而更考經文、別爲序次如左。

傳一章

一 康誥曰、克明德。

The preceding chapter of classical text is in the words of Confucius, handed down by the philosopher Tsăng. The ten chapters of explanation which follow contain the views of Tsăng, and were recorded by his disciples. In the old copies of the work, there appeared considerable confusion in these, from the disarrangement of the tablets. But now, availing myself of the decisions of the philosopher Ch'ing, and having examined anew the classical text, I have arranged it in order, as follows:—

COMMENTARY OF THE PHILOSOPHER TSANG.

CHAPTER I. 1. In the Announcement to K'ang it is said, "He was able to make his virtue illustrious."

CONCLUDING NOTE. It has been shown in the prolegomena that there is no ground for the distinction made here between so much *king* attributed to Confucius, and so much 傳, or commentary, ascribed to his disciple Tsăng. The invention of paper is ascribed to Ts'ae Lun (蔡倫), an officer of the Han dynasty, in the time of the emperor Hwo (和), A.D. 89—104. Before that time, and long after also, slips of wood and of bamboo (簡), were used to write and engrave upon. We can easily conceive how a collection of them might get disarranged, but whether those containing the Great Learning did do so is a question vehemently disputed. 右經一章, 'the chapter of classic on the right;' 如左, 'on the left;'—these are expressions=our 'preceding,' and 'as follows,' indicating the Chinese method of writing and printing from the right side of a manuscript or book on to the left.

COMMENTARY OF THE PHILOSOPHER TSANG.

1. THE ILLUSTRATION OF ILLUSTRIOUS VIRTUE. The student will do well to refer here to the text of 'The Great Learning,' as it appears in the Le-ke. He will then see how a considerable portion of it has been broken up, and transposed to form this and the five succeeding chapters. It was, no doubt, the occurrence of 明, in the four paragraphs here, and of the phrase 明德, which determined Choo He to form them into one chapter, and refer them to the first head in the classical text. The old commentators connect them with the great business of making the thoughts sincere. 1. See the Shoo-king, V. ix. 3. The words are part of the address of King Woo to his brother Fung (封), called also K'ang-shuh (康叔; 康, the hon. ep.) on appointing him to the marquisate of 衛. The subject of 克 is king Wăn, to whose example K'ang-shuh is referred.—We cannot determine, from this par., between the old interpretation of 德, as ='virtuous,' and the new which understands by it,—'the heart or nature, all-virtuous.' 2. See the Shoo-king, IV. v. Sect. I. 2. Choo He takes 諟 as=此, 'this,' or 審, 'to judge,' 'to examine.' The old interpr. explains it by 正, 'to correct.' The sentence is part of the address of the premier, E-yin, to T'ae-këă, the 2d emperor of the Shang dynasty, B.C. 1753–1718. The subject of 顧 is T'ae-këă's father,

二 太甲曰、顧諟天之明命。三 帝典曰、克明峻德。四 皆自明也。

右傳之首章、釋明明德。

〔二〕一 湯之盤銘曰、苟日新、日日新、又日新。二 康誥曰、作新民。三 詩曰、周雖舊邦、其命維新。四 是故君子無所不用其

2. In the T'ae Këä, it is said, "He contemplated and studied the illustrious decrees of Heaven."

3. In the Canon of the emperor Yaou, it is said, "He was able to make illustrious his lofty virtue."

4. These *passages* all *show how those sovereigns* made themselves illustrious.

The above first chapter of commentary explains the illustration of illustrious virtue.

CHAPTER II. 1. On the bathing-tub of T'ang, the following words were engraved:—"If you can one day renovate yourself, do so from day to day. Yea, let there be daily renovation."

2. In the Announcement to K'ang, it is said, "To stir up the new people."

3. In the Book of Poetry, it is said, "Although Chow was an ancient state, the ordinance which lighted on it was new."

4. Therefore, the superior man in every thing uses his utmost endeavours.

the great T'ang. Choo He understands by 明命, the Heaven-given, illustrious nature of man. The other school take the phrase more generally,—the 顯道, 'displayed ways' of Heaven. 3. See the Shoo-king, I. 2. It is of the emperor Yaou that this is said. 4. The 皆 must be referred to the three quotations.

2. THE RENOVATION OF THE PEOPLE. Here the character 新, 'new,' 'to renovate,' occurs five times, and it was to find something corresponding to it at the commencement of the work, which made the Ch'ing change the 親 of 親民, into 新. But the 新 here have nothing to do with the renovation of the people. This is self-evident in the 1st and 2d parr. The heading of the chapter, as above, is a misnomer. 1. This fact about T'ang's bathing tub had come down by tradition. At least, we do not now find the mention of it anywhere but here. It was customary among the ancients, as it is in China at the present day, to engrave, all about them, on the articles of their furniture, such moral aphorisms and lessons. 2. See the *K'ang Kaou*, p. 7, where K'ang-shuh is exhorted to assist the emperor 'to settle the decree of Heaven, and 作新民,' which may mean to make the bad people of Yin into good people, or to stir up the new people, *i. e.*, new, as recently subjected to Chow. 3. See the She-king, III. i. Ode I. st. 1. The subject of the

極。

右傳之二章、釋新民。

[一]詩云、邦畿千里、惟民所止。[二]詩云、緡蠻黃鳥、止于丘隅。子曰、於止、知其所止、可以人而不如鳥乎。[三]詩云、穆穆文王、於緝熙敬止、為人君、止於仁、為人臣、止於敬、為人子、止於孝、為人父、止於慈、與國人交、止於信。[四]詩

The above second chapter of commentary explains the renovating of the people.

CHAPTER III. 1. In the Book of Poetry, it is said, "The imperial domain of a thousand le is where the people rest."

2. In the Book of Poetry, it is said, "The twittering yellow bird rests on a corner of the mound." The Master said, "When it rests, it knows where to rest. Is it possible that a man should not be equal to this bird?"

3. In the Book of Poetry, it is said, "Profound was King Wăn. With how bright and unceasing a feeling of reverence did he regard his resting places!" As a sovereign, he rested in benevolence. As a minister, he rested in reverence. As a son, he rested in filial piety. As a father, he rested in kindness. In communication with his subjects, he rested in good faith.

ode is the praise of king Wăn, whose virtue led to the possession of the empire by his house, more than a thousand years after its first rise. 2. 君子 is here the man of rank and office probably, as well as the man of virtue; but I do not, for my own part, see the particular relation of this to the preced. parr., nor the work which I does in relation to the whole chapter.

3. ON RESTING IN THE HIGHEST EXCELLENCE. The frequent occurrence of 止 in these paragraphs, and of 至善, in par. 4, led Choo He to combine them in one chapter, and connect them with the last clause in the opening par. of the work. 1. See the She-king, IV. iii. Ode III. st. 4. The ode celebrates the rise and establishment of the Shang or Yin dynasty. 畿 is the 1000 *le* around the capital, and constituting the imperial domain. The quotation shows, according to Choo He, that 物各有所當止之處, 'every thing has the place where it ought to rest.' But that surely is a very sweeping conclusion from the words. 2. See the She-king, II. viii. Ode VI. st. 2, where we have the complaint of a down-trodden man, contrasting his position with that of a bird. For 緡 here, we have 綿 in the She-king. 緡蠻 are intended to express the sound of the bird's singing or chattering. 'The yellow bird' is known by a variety of names. A com-

云、瞻彼淇澳、菉竹猗猗、有斐君子、如切如磋、如琢如磨、瑟兮僩兮、赫兮喧兮、有斐君子、終不可諠兮。如切如磋者、道學也、如琢如磨者、自脩也、瑟兮僩兮者、恂慄也、赫兮喧兮者、威儀也、有斐君子、終不可諠兮者、道盛德至善、民之不能忘

4. In the Book of Poetry, it is said, "Look at that winding course of the K'e, with the green bamboos so luxuriant! Here is our elegant and accomplished prince! As we cut and then file; as we chisel and then grind: *so has he cultivated himself*. How grave is he and dignified! How majestic and distinguished! Our elegant and accomplished prince never can be forgotten." *That expression*—"as we cut and then file," indicates the work of learning. "As we chisel, and then grind," indicates that of self culture. "How grave is he and dignified!" indicates the feeling of cautious reverence. "How commanding and distinguished," indicates an awe-inspiring deportment. "Our elegant and accomplished prince never can be forgotten," indicates how, when virtue is complete and excellence extreme, the people cannot forget them.

mon one is 倉庚, or, properly, 鶬鶊 *ts'ang kang*. It is a species of oriole. The 子曰 are worthy of observation. If the first chapter of the classical text, as Choo He calls it, really contains the words of Confucius, we might have expected it to be headed by these characters. 於止, lit., 'in resting.' 3. See the She-king, III. i. Ode I. st. 4. The stress is here all laid upon the final 止, which does not appear to have any force at all in the original, Choo He himself saying there that it is 語詞, 'a mere supplemental particle.' In 於緝, 於 is read *woo*, and is an interjection. 4. See the She-king, I. v. Ode I. st. 1. The ode celebrates the virtue of the duke Woo (武) of Wei (衛), in his laborious endeavours to cultivate his person. There are some verbal differences between the ode in the She-king, and as here quoted; namely, 奧 for 澳; 綠 for 菉; 匪 for 斐. 猗, here, *particle*, read *O*. 道 is used as = 言, 'says,' or 'means.' It is to be understood before 自修, 恂慄, and 威儀.—The transposition of this par. by Choo He to this place does seem unhappy. It ought evidently to come in connection with the work of 脩身. 5. See the She-king, IV. i. Sect. I. Ode IV. st. 3. The former kings are Wăn and Woo, the founders of the Chow dynasty. 於戲 are an interjection, read *woo hoo*. In the She-king we have 於乎. 烏呼 are found with the same meaning. I translate 其賢, 其親, by 'what they deemed worthy,' 'what they loved.' When we try to determine *what* that what was, we are perplexed by the varying views of the

也。五詩云、於戲前王不忘、君子賢其賢、而親其親、小人樂其樂、而利其利、此以沒世不忘也。

右傳之三章、釋止於至善。

四子曰、聽訟吾猶人也、必也使無訟乎。無情者、不得盡其辭、大畏民志、此謂之本。

右傳之四章、釋本末。

5. In the Book of Poetry, it is said, "Ah! the former kings are not forgotten." *Future* princes deem worthy what they deemed worthy, and love what they loved. The common people delight in what they delighted, and are benefited by their beneficial arrangements. It is on this account that the former kings, after they have quitted the world, are not forgotten.

The above third chapter of commentary explains resting in the highest excellence.

CHAPTER IV. The Master said, "In hearing litigations, I am like any other body. What is necessary is to cause the people to have no litigations?" *So*, those who are devoid of principle find it impossible to carry out their speeches, and a great awe would be struck into men's minds;—this is called knowing the root.

The above fourth chapter of commentary explains the root and the issue.

old and new schools. 沒世,—see Analects, XV. xix.—Acc. to Ying-tâ, 'this par. illustrates the business of having the thoughts sincere.' Acc. to Choo He, it tells that how the former kings renovated the people, was by their resting in perfect excellence, so as to be able, throughout the empire and to future ages, to effect that there should not be a single thing but got its proper place.

4. EXPLANATION OF THE ROOT AND THE BRANCHES. See the Analects XII. xiii, from which we understand that the words of Conf. terminate at 訟乎, and that what follows is from the compiler. According to the old commentators, this is the conclusion of the chapter on having the thoughts made sincere, and that 誠其意 is the *root*. But acc. to Choo, it is the illustration of illustrious virtue which is the *root*, while the renovation of the people is the *result* therefrom. Looking at the words of Confucius, we must conclude that *sincerity* was the subject in his mind.

傳五章 一此謂知本。二此謂知之至也。

右傳之五章、蓋釋格物致知之義、而今亡矣、閒嘗竊取程子之意、以補之曰、所謂致知在格物者、言欲致吾之知、在卽物、而窮其理也、蓋人心之靈、莫不有知、而天下之物、莫不有理、惟於理有未窮、故其知有不盡也、是以大學始教、必使學者卽凡天下之物、莫

CHAPTER V. 1. This is called knowing the root.
2. This is called the perfecting of knowledge.

The above fifth chapter of the commentary explained the meaning of "investigating things and carrying knowledge to the utmost extent," but it is now lost. I have ventured to take the views of the scholar Ch'ing to supply it, as follows:—The meaning of the expression, "The perfecting of knowledge depends on the investigation of things," is this:—If we wish to carry our knowledge to the utmost, we must investigate the principles of all things we come into contact with, for the intelligent mind of man is certainly formed to know, and there is not a single thing in which its principles do not inhere. But so long as all principles are not investigated, man's knowledge is incomplete. On this account, the Learning for Adults, at the outset of its lessons, instructs the learner, in regard to all things in the world, to proceed from what knowledge he has of their principles, and pursue his investiga-

5. ON THE INVESTIGATION OF THINGS, AND CARRYING KNOWLEDGE TO THE UTMOST EXTENT. 1. This is said by one of the Ch'ing to be 衍文, 'superfluous text.' 2. Choo He considers this to be the conclusion of a chapter which is now lost. But we have seen that the two sentences come in, as the work stands in the Le-ke, at the conclusion of what is deemed the classical text. It is not necessary to add anything here to what has been said there, and in the prolegomena, on the new dispositions of the work from the time of the Sung scholars, and the manner in which Choo He has supplied this supposed missing chapter.

不因其已知之理、而益窮之、以求至乎其極、至於用力之久、而一旦豁然貫通焉、則衆物之表裏精粗、無不到、而吾心之全體大用、無不明矣、此謂物格、此謂知之至也。

[六] 一 所謂誠其意者、毋自欺也、如惡惡臭、如好好色、此之謂自謙、故君子必慎其獨也。二 小人閒居爲不善、無所不至、見君子、而后

tion of them, till he reaches the extreme point. After exerting himself in this way for a long time, he will suddenly find himself possessed of a wide and far-reaching penetration. Then, the qualities of all things, whether external or internal, the subtle or the coarse, will all be apprehended, and the mind, in its entire substance and its relations to things, will be perfectly intelligent. This is called the investigation of things. This is called the perfection of knowledge

CHAPTER VI. 1. What is meant by "making the thoughts sincere," is the allowing no self-deception, as *when* we hate a bad smell, and as *when* we love what is beautiful. This is called self-enjoyment. Therefore, the superior man must be watchful over himself when he is alone.

2. There is no evil to which the mean man, dwelling retired, will not proceed, but when he sees a superior man, he instantly tries

6. ON MAKING THE THOUGHTS SINCERE. 1. *The sincerity of the thoughts obtains, when they move without effort to what is right and wrong, and, in order to this, a man must be specially on his guard in his solitary moments.* 自謙 is taken as if it were 自慊,=repose or enjoyment in one's-self. 慊, acc. to Choo He, is in the up. 4th tone, but the dict. makes it up. 2d. 2. *An enforcement of the concluding clause in the last paragraph.* 厭, up. 2d tone, the same as 黶, meaning 閉藏貌 'the appearance of concealing.' 人之視己,—人 refers to the superior man mentioned above,='the other.' 己=他, 'him,' and not=*himself*, which is its com-

厭然、揜其不善、而著其善、人之視己、如見其肺肝然、則何益矣、此謂誠於中、形於外、故君子必慎其獨也。曾子曰、十目所視、十手所指、其嚴乎。富潤屋、德潤身、心廣、體胖、故君子必誠其意。

右傳之六章、釋誠意。

to disguise himself, concealing his evil, and displaying what is good. The other beholds him, as if he saw his heart and reins;—of what use *is his disguise?* This is an instance of the saying—"What truly is within will be manifested without." Therefore, the superior man must be watchful over himself when he is alone.

3. The disciple Tsăng said, "What ten eyes behold, what ten hands point to, is to be regarded with reverence!"

4. Riches adorn a house, and virtue adorns the person. The mind is expanded, and the body is at ease. Therefore, the superior man must make his thoughts sincere.

The above sixth chapter of commentary explains making the thoughts sincere.

mon signification. 肺肝,—lit., 'the lungs and liver,' but with the meaning which we attach to the expression substituted for it in the translation. The Chinese make the lungs the seat of righteousness, and the liver the seat of benevolence. Compare 今予其敷心腹腎腸 in the Shoo-king, IV. vii. Sect. III. 8. 3. The use of 曾子 at the beginning of this paragraph (and extending, perhaps, over to the next) should suffice to show, that the whole work is not his, as assumed by Choo He. 'Ten' is a round number, put for many. The recent commentator, Lo Chung-fan, refers Tsăng's expressions to the multitude of spiritual beings, servants of Heaven or God, who dwell in the regions of the air, and are continually beholding men's conduct. But they are probably only an emphatic way of exhibiting what is said in the preceding paragraph. 4. This par. is commonly referred to Tsăng Sin, but whether correctly so or not cannot be positively affirmed. It is of the same purport as the two preceding, showing that hypocrisy is of no use. Compare Mencius, VII. Pt I. xxi. 4. Ching K'ang-shing explains 胖 (read *pwan*) by 大, 'large,' and Choo He by 安舒, as in the transl. The meaning is probably the same.—It is only the first of these parr. from which we can in any way ascertain the views of the writer on making the thoughts sincere. The other parr. contain only illustration or enforcement. Now the gist of the 1st par. seems to be in 毋自欺, 'allowing no self-deception.' After knowledge has been carried to the utmost, this remains to be done, and it is not true that, when knowledge has been completed, the thoughts become sincere. This fact overthrows Choo He's interpretation of the vexed passages in what he calls the text of Confucius. Let the student examine his note appended to this chapter, and he will see that Choo was not unconscious of this pinch of the difficulty.

一 所謂脩身、在正其心者、身有所忿懥、則不得其正、有所恐懼、則不得其正、有所好樂、則不得其正、有所憂患、則不得其正。二 心不在焉、視而不見、聽而不聞、食而不知其味。三 此謂脩身在正其心。

右傳之七章、釋正心脩身。

CHAPTER VII. 1. What is meant by, "The cultivation of the person depends on rectifying the mind," *may be thus illustrated*:—If a man be under the influence of passion, he will be incorrect in his conduct. He will be the same, if he is under the influence of terror, or under the influence of fond regard, or under that of sorrow and distress.

2. When the mind is not present, we look and do not see; we hear and do not understand; we eat and do not know the taste of what we eat.

3. This is what is meant by saying that the cultivation of the person depends on the rectifying of the mind.

The above seventh chapter of commentary explains rectifying the mind and cultivating the person.

7. ON PERSONAL CULTIVATION AS DEPENDENT ON THE RECTIFICATION OF THE MIND. 1. Here Choo He, following his master Ch'ing, would again alter the text, and change the second 身 into 心. But this is unnecessary. The 身 in 修身 is not the mere material body, but the person, the individual man, in contact with things, and intercourse with society, and the 2d par. shows that the evil conduct in the first is a consequence of the mind's not being under control. In 忿懥, 恐懼, 好樂 ([illegible]), 憂患, the 2d term rises on the signification of the first, and intensifies it. Thus, 忿 is called 'a burst of anger,' and 懥, 'persistence in anger,' &c., &c.—I have said above that 身 here is not the material body. Lo Chung-fan, however, says that it is:—身謂肉身, '身 is the body of flesh.' See his reasonings, *in loc.*, but they do not work conviction in the reader. 2. 心不在焉,—this seems to be a case in point, to prove that we cannot tie 心 in this work to any very definite application. Lo Chung-fan insists that it is 'the God-given moral nature,' but 心不在焉 is evidently = 'when the thoughts are otherwise engaged.'

傳八章 一 所謂齊其家、在脩其身者、人之其所親愛、而辟焉、之其所賤惡、而辟焉、之其所畏敬、而辟焉、之其所哀矜、而辟焉、之其所敖惰、而辟焉、故好而知其惡、惡而知其美者、天下鮮矣。二 故諺有之曰、人莫知其子之惡、莫知其苗之碩。三 此謂身不脩、不可以齊其家。

CHAPTER VIII. 1. What is meant by "The regulation of one's family depends on the cultivation of his person," is this:—Men are partial where they feel affection and love; partial where they despise and dislike; partial where they stand in awe and reverence; partial where they feel sorrow and compassion; partial where they are arrogant and rude. Thus it is that there are few men in the world, who love, and at the same time know the bad qualities of *the object of their love*, or who hate, and yet know the excellences of *the object of their hatred.*

2. Hence it is said, in the common adage, "A man does not know the wickedness of his son; he does not know the richness of his growing corn."

3. This is what is meant by saying that if the person be not cultivated, a man cannot regulate his family.

8. THE NECESSITY OF CULTIVATING THE PERSON, IN ORDER TO THE REGULATION OF THE FAMILY. The lesson here is evidently, that men are continually falling into error, in consequence of the partiality of their feelings and affections. How this error affects their personal cultivation, and interferes with the regulating of their families, is not specially indicated. 1. The old interpreters seem to go far astray in their interpretation. They take 之 in 之其所親愛, and the other clauses, as = 適, 'to go to,' and 辟 as synonymous with 譬, 'to compare.' Ying-ta thus expounds K'ang-ching on 人之其所親愛而辟焉:—'Suppose I go to that man. When I see that he is virtuous, I feel affection for, and love him. I ought then to turn round and compare him with myself. Since he is virtuous and I love him, then, if I cultivate myself and be virtuous, I shall so be able in like manner to make all men feel affection for and love me.' In a similar way the other clauses are dealt with. Choo He takes 之 as = 於, 'in regard to,' and 辟 (read *p'ih*) as = 偏, 'partial,' 'one-sided.' Even his opponent, Lo Chung-fan, interprets here in the same way. 親愛, and the other combinations are to be taken as if there were a 而, 'and,' between them. 敖 is here = 傲, 'proud,' 'un-

右傳之八章、釋脩身齊家。

九 1 所謂治國、必先齊其家者、其家不可教、而能教人者、無之、故君子不出家、而成教於國、孝者、所以事君也、弟者、所以事長也、慈者、所以使衆也。2 康誥曰、如保赤子、心誠求之、雖不中、不遠矣、未有學養子、而后嫁者也。3 一家仁、一國興仁、一家讓、一國興讓、一人貪

The above eighth chapter of commentary explains cultivating the person and regulating the family.

CHAPTER IX. 1. What is meant by "In order rightly to govern his State, it is necessary first to regulate his family," is this:—It is not possible for one to teach others, while he cannot teach his own family. Therefore, the ruler, without going beyond his family, completes the lessons for the State. There is filial piety:—therewith the sovereign should be served. There is fraternal submission:—therewith elders and superiors should be served. There is kindness:—therewith the multitude should be treated.

2. In the Announcement to K'ang, it is said, "*Act* as if you were watching over an infant." If a mother is really anxious about it, though she may not hit *exactly the wants of her infant*, she will not be far from doing so. There never has been *a girl* who learned to bring up a child, that she might afterwards marry.

3. From the loving *example* of one family, a whole State becomes loving, and from its courtesies, the whole State becomes courteous,

evil.' 2. 碩,—'great,' 'tall;' 苗之碩,—'the tallness (richness, abundance) of his growing crop.' Farmers were noted, it would appear, in China, so long ago, for grumbling about their crops.

9. ON REGULATING THE FAMILY AS THE MEANS TO THE WELL-ORDERING OF THE STATE. 1. *There is here implied the necessity of self-cultivation to the ruler, both of the family and of the State, and that being supposed to exist,—which is the force of the* 故,—*it is shown how the virtues that secure the regulation of the family, have their corresponding virtues in the wider sphere of the State.* 君子 has here both the moral and the political meaning; it is 治國之君子, 'the superior man with whom is the government of the state.'

戾、一國作亂、其機如此、此謂一言僨事、一人定國。(四節)堯舜帥天下以仁、而民從之、桀紂帥天下以暴、而民從之、其所令反其所好、而民不從、是故君子、有諸己、而后求諸人、無諸己、而后非諸人、所藏乎身不恕、而能喻諸人者、未之有也、(五節)故治國、在齊其家。(六節)詩云、桃之夭

while, from the ambition and perverseness of the one man, the whole State may be led to rebellious disorder;—such is the nature of the influence. This verifies the saying, "Affairs may be ruined by a single sentence; a kingdom may be settled by its one man."

4. Yaou and Shun led on the empire with benevolence, and the people followed them. Këë and Chow led on the empire with violence, and the people followed them. The orders which these issued were contrary to the practices which they loved, and so the people did not follow them. On this account, the ruler must himself be possessed of the *good* qualities, and then he may require them in the people. He must not have *the bad qualities* in himself, and then he may require that they shall not be in the people. Never has there been a man, who, not having reference to his own character and wishes in dealing with others, was able effectually to instruct them.

5. Thus we see how the government of the State depends on the regulation of the family.

It being once suggested to Choo He that 不可教 should be 不能教, he replied—彼之不可教,即我之不能教, 'The *impossibility* of that's being taught is just my *inability* to teach.' 2. See the Shoo-king, V. x. 7. Both in the Shoo-king and here, some verb, like *act*, must be supplied. This par. seems designed to show that *the ruler must be carried on to his object by an inward, unconstrained, feeling, like that of the mother for her infant.* Luh Chang-lan insists on this as harmonizing with 親民, 'to love the people,' as the second object propos-ed in the Great Learning. 3 *How certainly and rapidly the influence of the family extends to the State.* 一家 is the one family of the ruler, and 一人 is the ruler. 一人,='I, the one man,' is a way in which the emperor speaks of himself; see Ana. XX. i. 5. 一言=一句, as in Ana. II. ii. 一言僨事, 一人定國,—comp. Ana. XIII. xv. 仁 and 讓 have

夭、其葉蓁蓁、之子于歸、宜其家人、宜其家人、而后可以教國人。七詩云、宜兄宜弟、宜兄宜弟、而后可以教國人。八詩云、其儀不忒、正是四國、其爲父子兄弟足法、而后民法之也。九此謂治國、在齊其家。

6. In the Book of Poetry, it is said, "That peach tree, so delicate and elegant! How luxuriant is its foliage! This girl is going to her husband's house. She will rightly order her household." Let the household be rightly ordered, and then the people of the State may be taught.

7. In the Book of Poetry, it is said, "They can discharge their duties to their elder brothers. They can discharge their duties to their younger brothers." Let the ruler discharge his duties to his elder and younger brothers, and then he may teach the people of the State.

8. In the Book of Poetry, it is said, "In his deportment there is nothing wrong; he rectifies all the people of the State." *Yes;* when the ruler, as a father, a son, and a brother, is a model, then the people imitate him.

9. This is what is meant by saying, "The government of his kingdom depends on his regulation of the family."

reference to the 孝, 弟 (=悌), 慈, in par. 1. 4. *An illustration of the last part of the last paragraph.* But from the examples cited, the sphere of influence is extended from the State to the empire, and the family, moreover, does not intervene between the empire and the ruler. In 其所令, 其 must be understood as referring to the tyrants, Këë and Chow. Their orders were good, but unavailing, in consequence of their own contrary example. 諸=於. 所藏乎身, 'what is kept in one's own person,' i. e., his character and mind. 恕,—see Ana. V. xi; XV. xiii. Ying-tă seems to take 不恕 as simply='good.' 6. See the She-king, I. i. Ode VI. st. 3. The ode celebrates the wife of king Wăn, and the happy influence of their family government. 之子=是子. Obs. 子 is feminine, as in Ana. V. i. 歸, 'going home,' a term for marriage, used by women. 7. See the She-king, II. ii. Ode VI. st. 3. The ode was sung at entertainments, when the emperor feasted the princes. It celebrates their virtues. 8. See the She-king, I. xiv. Ode III. st. 3. It celebrates, acc. to Choo He, the praise of some *kwan-tsze*, or ruler. 四國,—not 'four states,' but the four quarters of the state, the whole of it.

右傳之九章、釋齊家治國。

〔一〕所謂平天下、在治其國者、上老老、而民興孝、上長長、而民興弟、上恤孤、而民不倍、是以君子、有絜矩之道也。〔二〕所惡於上、毋以使下、所惡於下、毋以事上、所惡於前、毋以先後、所惡於後、毋以

The above ninth chapter of commentary explains regulating the family and governing the kingdom.

CHAPTER X. 1. What is meant by "The making the whole empire peaceful and happy depends on the government of his State," is this:—When the sovereign behaves to his aged, as the aged should be behaved to, the people become filial; when the sovereign behaves to his elders, as elders should be behaved to, the people learn brotherly submission; when the sovereign treats compassionately the young and helpless, the people do the same. Thus the ruler has a principle with which, as with a measuring square, he may regulate his conduct.

2. What a man dislikes in his superiors, let him not display in the treatment of his inferiors; what he dislikes in inferiors, let him not display in the service of his superiors; what he hates in those who are before him, let him not therewith precede those who are behind him; what he hates in those who are behind him, let him

10. ON THE WELL-ORDERING OF THE STATE, AND MAKING THE WHOLE EMPIRE PEACEFUL AND HAPPY. The key to this chapter is in the phrase 絜矩之道, the principle of reciprocity, the doing to others as we would that they should do to us, though here, as elsewhere, it is put forth negatively. It is implied in the expression of the last ch.—所藏乎身不恕, but it is here discussed at length, and shown in its highest application. The following analysis of the chapter is translated freely from the 四書輯要:—'This ch. explains the well-ordering of the State, and the tranquillization of the empire. The greatest stress is to be laid on the phrase—*the measuring square*. That, and the expression in the general commentary—*loving and hating what the people love and hate*, *and not thinking only of the profit*, exhaust the teaching of the chap. It is divided into five parts. The *first*, embracing the two first paragraphs, teaches, that the way to make the empire tranquil and happy is in the principle of the measuring square. The *second* part embraces three paragraphs, and teaches that the application of the measuring square is seen in loving, and hating, in common with the people. The consequences of *losing* and *gaining* are mentioned for the first time in the 5th par., to wind up the ch. so far, showing that the decree of Heaven goes or remains, according as the people's hearts are lost or gained. The *third* part embraces

從前、所惡於右、毋以交於左、所惡於左、毋以交於右、此之謂絜矩之道。三詩云、樂只君子、民之父母、民之所好好之、民之所惡惡之、此之謂民之父母。四詩云、節彼南山、維石巖巖、赫赫師尹、民具爾瞻、有國者、不可以不愼、辟、則爲天下僇矣。五詩

not therewith follow those who are before him; what he hates to receive on the right, let him not bestow on the left; what he hates to receive on the left, let him not bestow on the right:—this is what is called "The principle, with which, as with a measuring square, to regulate one's conduct."

3. In the Book of Poetry, it is said, "How much to be rejoiced in are these princes, the parents of the people!" When *a prince* loves what the people love, and hates what the people hate, then is he what is called the parent of the people.

4. In the Book of Poetry, it is said, "Lofty is that southern hill, with its rugged masses of rocks! Greatly distinguished are you, O *grand*-teacher Yin, the people all look up to you." Rulers of kingdoms may not neglect to be careful. If they deviate *to a mean selfishness*, they will be a disgrace in the empire.

eight paragraphs, and teaches that the most important result of loving and hating in common with the people is seen in making the *root* the primary subject, and the *branch* only secondary. Here, in par. 11, mention is again made of *gaining* and *losing*, illustrating the meaning of the quotation in it, and showing that to the collection or dissipation of the people the decree of Heaven is attached. The *fourth* part consists of five paragraphs, and exhibits the extreme results of loving and hating, as shared with the people, or on one's own private feeling, and it has special reference to the sovereign's employment of ministers, because there is nothing in the principle more important than that. The 19th par. speaks of *gaining and losing*, for the third time, showing that from the 4th par. downwards, in reference both to the hearts of the people and the decree of Heaven, the application or non-application of the principle of the *measuring-square* depends on the mind of the sovereign. The *fifth* part embraces the other paragraphs. Because the root of the evil of a sovereign's not applying that principle, lies in his not knowing how wealth is produced, and employs mean men for that object, the distinction between righteousness and profit is here much insisted on, the former bringing with it all advantages, and the latter leading to all evil consequences. Thus the sovereign is admonished, and it is seen how to be careful of his virtue is the root of the principle of the *measuring-square*: and his loving and hating, in common sympathy with the people, is its reality.'

1. There is here no progress of thought, but a repetition of what has been insisted on in the two last chapters. In 老老, 長長, the first characters are verbs, with the meaning which it requires so many words to bring out in the translation. 弟=悌. 孤,—properly, '*la-*

云、殷之未喪師、克配上帝、儀監于殷、峻命不易、道得眾、則得國、失眾、則失國。○六 是故君子先慎乎德、有德、此有人、有人、此有土、有土、此有財、有財、此有用。○七 德者、本也、財者、末也。○八 外本內末、爭

5. In the Book of Poetry, it is said, "Before the sovereigns of the Yin *dynasty* had lost the *hearts of the* people, they could appear before God. Take warning from *the house of* Yin. The great decree is not easily *preserved*." This shows that, by gaining the people, the kingdom is gained, and, by losing the people, the kingdom is lost.

6. On this account, the ruler will first take pains about *his own* virtue. Possessing virtue will give him the people. Possessing the people will give him the territory. Possessing the territory will give him its wealth. Possessing the wealth, he will have resources for expenditure.

7. Virtue is the root; wealth is the result.

8. If he make the root his secondary object, and the result his primary, he will *only* wrangle with his people, and teach them rapine.

fatherless;' here, = 'the young and helpless.' 倍, read as, and = 背, 'to rebel,' 'to act contrary to.' 君子, here and throughout the ch., has reference to office, and specially to the imperial or highest. 絜矩之道,—絜 is a verb, read *hieh*, acc. to Choo He, = 度, 'to measure;' 矩,—the mechanical instrument, 'the square.' It having been seen that the ruler's example is so influential, it follows that the minds of all men are the same in sympathy and tendency. He has then only to take his own mind, and measure therewith the minds of others. If he act accordingly, the grand result—the empire tranquil and happy—will ensue. 2. *A lengthened description of the principle of reciprocity.* 先,—up. 3d tone, 'to precede.' 3. See the She-king, II. ii. Ode V. st. 3. The ode is one that was sung at festivals, and celebrates the virtues of the princes present. Choo He makes 只 (read *che*, up. 3d tone) an expletive. Ch'ing's gloss, in 毛詩註疏, takes it as = 是, and the whole is—'I gladden these princes, the parents of the people.' 4. See the She-king, II. iv. Ode VII. st. 1. The ode complains of the emperor Yew (幽), for his employing unworthy ministers. 節, read *tsëë*, meaning 'rugged and lofty-looking.' 具 = 俱, 'all.' 辟, read *p'ih*, as in ch. viii. 僇 is explained in the dict. by 辱, 'disgrace.' Choo He seems to take it as = 戮, 'to kill,' as did the old commentators. They say:—'he will be put to death by the people, as were the tyrants, Këë and Chow.' 5. See the She-king, III. i. Ode I. st. 6, where we have 宜 for 儀, and 駿 for 峻. The ode is supposed to be addressed to king Shing (成), to stimulate him to imitate the virtues of his grandfather Wan. 殷,—'the sovereigns of the Yin dynasty.' The capital of the Shang dynasty was changed to Yin by P'wan-kang, B. C.

民施奪。九節是故財聚、則民散、財散、則民聚。十節是故言悖而出者、亦悖而入、貨悖而入者、亦悖而出。十一節康誥曰、惟命不于常、道善則得之、不善則失之矣。十二節楚書曰、楚國、無以爲寶、惟善、以爲寶。十三節舅犯

9. Hence, the accumulation of wealth is the way to scatter the people; and the letting it be scattered among them is the way to collect the people.

10. And hence, the ruler's words going forth contrary to right, will come back to him in the same way, and wealth, gotten by improper ways, will take its departure by the same.

11. In the Announcement to K'ang, it is said, "The decree indeed may not always rest on *us*;" that is, goodness obtains the decree, and the want of goodness loses it.

12. In the Book of Ts'oo, it is said, "The kingdom of Ts'oo does not consider that to be valuable. It values, *instead*, its good men."

1400, after which the dynasty was so denominated. 配上帝, acc. to Choo He, means 'they were the sovereigns of the empire, and corresponded to (fronted) God.' K'ang-shing says:—'Before they lost their people, from their virtue, they were also able to appear before Heaven; that is, Heaven accepted their sacrifices.' Lo Chung-fan makes it,—'They harmonized with God; that is, in loving the people.' K'ang-shing's interpretation is, I apprehend, the correct one. 儀=宜, as in ch. iii. 4. 6. 愼乎德—德 here, acc. to Choo He, is the 'illustrious virtue' at the beginning of the book. His opponents say that it is the exhibition of virtue; that is, of filial piety, brotherly submission, &c. This is more in harmony with the first par. of the chapter. 8. 外 and 內 are used as verbs,=輕, 重, 'to consider slight,' 'to consider important.' 爭民,—'will wrangle the (*i. e.*, with the) people.' The ruler will be trying to take, and the people will be trying to hold. 施奪,—'he will give'—(*i. e.*, lead the people to, teach them)—'rapine.' The two phrases—he will be against the people, and will set them against himself, and against one another. Ying-tă explains them—'people wrangling for gain will give reins to their rapacious disposition.' 9. 財散, 'wealth being scattered,'—that is, diffused, and allowed to be so by the ruler, among the people. The collecting and scattering of the people are to be understood with reference to their feelings towards their ruler. 10. The 'words' are to be understood of governmental orders and enactments. 悖, read *pei*,=逆, 'to act contrary to,' 'to rebel,' that which is outraged being 理, 'what is right,' or, in the first place, 民心, 'the people's hearts,' and, in the second place, 君心, 'the ruler's heart.' Our proverb—'goods ill-gotten go ill-spent' might be translated by 貨悖而入者, 亦悖而出, but those words have a diff. meaning in the text. 11. See the *K'ang Kaou*, p. 23. The only difficulty is with 于. K'ang-shing and Ying-tă do not take it as an expletive, but say it=於, 'in,' or 'on;'—'The appointment of Heaven may not constantly rest on one family.' Treating 于 in this way, the supplement in the Shoo-king, should be 'us.'

曰、亡人、無以爲寶、仁親以爲寶。○十四節 秦誓曰、若有一个臣、斷斷兮、無他技、其心休休焉、其如有容焉、人之有技、若己有之、人之彥聖、其心好之、不啻若自其口出、寔能容之、以能保我子孫黎民、尚亦有利哉。人之有技、娼疾以惡之、人之彥聖、而違之、俾不通、寔不能容、以

13. *Duke Wăn's* uncle, Fan, said, "Our fugitive does not account that to be precious. What he considers precious, is the affection due to his parent."

14. In the Declaration *of the duke of* Ts'in, it is said, "Let me have but one minister, plain and sincere, not *pretending to* other abilities, but with a simple, upright, mind; and possessed of generosity, *regarding* the talents of others as though he himself possessed them, and, where he finds accomplished and perspicacious men, loving them in his heart more than his mouth expresses, and really showing himself able to bear them *and employ them*:—such a minister will be able to preserve my sons and grandsons, and black-haired people, and benefits likewise to the kingdom may well be looked for from him. But if *it be his character*, when he finds men of ability, to be jealous and hate them; and, when he finds accomplished and perspicacious men, to oppose them and not allow their advancement, showing himself really not able to bear them:—such a minister

道, as in p. 5. 12. The Book of Ts'oo is found in the 國語, 'National records,' a collection purporting to be of the Chow dynasty, and, in relation to the other states, what Confucius' 'Spring and Autumn' is to Loo. The exact words of the text do not occur, but they could easily be constructed from the narrative. An officer of Ts'oo being sent on an embassy to Tsin (晉), the minister who received him asked about a famous girdle of Ts'oo, called 白珩, how much it was worth. The officer replied that his country did not look on such things as its treasures, but on its able and virtuous ministers. 13. 舅犯, 'uncle Fan;' that is, uncle to Wăn, the duke of Tsin. See Ana. XIV. xvi. Wăn is the 亡人, or, 'fugitive.' In the early part of his life, he was a fugitive, and suffered many vicissitudes of fortune. Once, the duke of Ts'in (秦) having offered to help him, when he was in mourning for his father who had expelled him, to recover Tsin, his uncle Fan gave the reply in the text. The *that* in the translation refers to 得國, 'getting the kingdom.' 14. 'The declaration *of the duke of* Ts'in' is the last

不能保我子孫黎民、亦曰殆哉。(十五節)唯仁人放流之、迸諸四夷、不與同中國、此謂唯仁人、爲能愛人、能惡人。(十六節)見賢、而不能舉、舉、而不能先、命也、見不善、而不能退、退、而不能遠、過也。(十七節)好人之所惡、惡人之所好、是謂拂人之性、菑必逮夫身。(十八節)是故君子、有大道、必忠信以得之、

will not be able to protect my sons and grandsons and black-haired people; and may he not also be pronounced dangerous *to the State?*"

15. It is only the truly virtuous man, who can send away such a man and banish him, driving him out among the barbarous tribes around, determined not to dwell along with him in the Middle kingdom. This is in accordance with the saying, "It is only the truly virtuous man who can love or who can hate others."

16. To see men of worth and not be able to raise them to office; to raise them to office, but not to do so quickly:—this is disrespectful. To see bad men and not be able to remove them; to remove them, but not to do so to a distance:—this is weakness.

17. To love those whom men hate, and to hate those whom men love;—this is to outrage the natural feeling of men. Calamities cannot fail to come down on him who does so.

18. Thus *we see that* the sovereign has a great course *to pursue.* He must show entire self-devotion and sincerity to attain it, and by pride and extravagance he will fail of it.

book in the Shoo-king. It was made by one of the dukes of Ts'in to his officers, after he had sustained a great disaster, in consequence of neglecting the advice of his most faithful minister. Between the text here, and that which we find in the Shoo-king, there are some differences, but they are unimportant. 15. 仁人 is here, acc. to Choo He and his followers, the prince who applies the principle of reciprocity, expounded in the second par. Lo Chung-fan contends that it is 親民者, 'the lover of the people.' The par. is closely connected with the preceding. In 放流之, 之 refers to the bad minister, there described. The 四夷, 'four E;' see the Le-ke, III. iii. 14. 不與同中國=不與之同處中國, 'will not dwell together with him in the Middle kingdom.' China is evidently so denominated, from its being thought to be surrounded by barbarous tribes. 惟仁人能云云,—see Ana. IV. iii. 16. I have translated 命 as if it were

驕泰以失之。(十九節)生財有大道、生之者衆、食之者寡、爲之者疾、用之者舒、則財恆足矣。(二十節)仁者以財發身、不仁者以身發財。(二十一節)未有上好仁、而下不好義者也、未有好義、其事不終者也、未有府庫財、非其財者也。(二十二節)孟獻子曰、畜馬乘、不察於雞豚、伐冰

19. There is a great course *also* for the production of wealth. Let the producers be many and the consumers few. Let there be activity in the production, and economy in the expenditure. Then the wealth will always be sufficient.

20. The virtuous *ruler*, by means of his wealth, makes himself more distinguished. The vicious ruler accumulates wealth, at the expense of his life.

21. Never has there been a case of the sovereign loving benevolence, and the people not loving righteousness. Never has there been a case where the people have loved righteousness, and the affairs of the sovereign have not been carried to completion. And never has there been a case where the wealth in such a State, collected in the treasuries and arsenals, did not continue in the sovereign's possession.

22. The officer Măng Heen said, "He who keeps horses and a carriage does not look after fowls and pigs. The family which

慢, which K'ang-shing thinks should be in the text. Ch'ing E (頤) would substitute 怠, 'idle,' instead of 慢, and Choo He does not know which suggestion to prefer. Lo Chung-fan stoutly contends for retaining 命, and interprets it as = 'fate,' but he is obliged to supply a good deal himself, to make any sense of the passage. See his argument, in loc. The paraphrasts all explain 先 by 早, 'early.' 遠, up 3d tone, but with a hiphil force. 退 is referred to 放流 in last par., and 遠 to 不與同中國. 17. This is spoken of the ruler not having respect to the common feelings of the people in his employment of ministers, and the consequences thereof to himself. 夫, low. 1st tone, is used as in Ana. XI. ix. 4. or = the prep. 乎. *This par. speaks generally of the primal cause of gaining and losing, and shows how the principle of the measuring square must have its root in the ruler's mind.* So, in the 日講. The great course is explained by Choo He as—'the art of occupying the throne, and therein cultivating himself and governing others.' Ying-tă says it is—'the course by which he practises filial piety, fraternal duty, benevolence, and righteousness.' 驕 and 泰 are here qualities of the

之家、不畜牛羊、百乘之家、不畜聚斂之臣、與其有聚斂之臣、寧有盜臣。此謂國不以利爲利、以義爲利也。

廿三節 長國家、而務財用者、必自小人矣、彼爲善之、小人之使爲國家、菑害並至、雖有善者、亦無如之何矣、此謂

keeps its stores of ice does not rear cattle or sheep. *So*, the house which possesses a hundred chariots should not keep a minister to look out for imposts that he may lay them on the people. Than to have such a minister, it were better for that house to have one who should rob it *of its revenues*." This is in accordance with the saying:—"In a State, *pecuniary* gain is not to be considered to be prosperity, but its prosperity *will* be found in righteousness."

23. When he who presides over a State or a family makes his revenues his chief business, he must be under the influence of some small, mean, man. He may consider this man to be good; but when such a person is employed in the administration of a State or family, calamities *from Heaven*, and injuries *from men*, will befal it together, and, though a good man may take his place, he will not be able to remedy the evil. This illustrates *again* the saying, "In a State, gain is not to be considered prosperity, but its prosperity will be found in righteousness."

same nature. They are not contrasted as in Ana. XIII. xxvi. 19. This is understood by K'ang-hsi as requiring the promotion of agriculture, and that is included, but does not exhaust the meaning. The consumers are the salaried officers of the government. The sentiment of the whole is good;—where there is cheerful industry in the people, and an economical administration of the government, the finances will be flourishing. 20. The sentiment here is substantially the same as in parr. 7, 8. The old interpretation is different:—'The virtuous man uses his wealth so as to make his person distinguished. He who is not virtuous, toils with his body to increase his wealth.' 21. This shows how the people respond to the influence of the ruler, and that benevolence, even to the scattering of his wealth on the part of the latter, is the way to permanent prosperity and wealth. 22. Hien was the hon. epithet of Chung-sun Mäe (蔑?), a worthy minister of Loo, under the two dukes, who ruled before the birth of Confucius. His sayings, quoted here, were preserved by tradition, or recorded in some work which is now lost. 畜 (read *hü*) 乘馬,—on a scholar's being first called to office, he was gifted by his prince with a carriage, and four horses. He was then supposed to withdraw from petty ways of getting wealth. The 卿, or high officers of a State, kept ice for use in their funeral rites and sacrifices. 伐冰,—with reference to the *cutting* the ice to store it. 聚斂之臣,—see Ana. XI. xvi. 23. 彼爲善之,—善 is used as a verb,—以爲善, 'considers to be good.' 不以利爲利,以義爲利,—see Mencius, I. Pt. I. i, *et passim*.

國、不以利爲利、以義爲利也。

右傳之十章、釋治國平天下。凡傳十章、前四章、統論綱領指趣、後六章、細論條目工夫、其第五章、乃明善之要、第六章、乃誠身之本、在初學、尤爲當務之急、讀者不可以其近而忽之也。

The above tenth chapter of commentary explains the government of the State, and the making the empire peaceful and happy.

There are thus, in all, ten chapters of commentary, the first four of which discuss, in a general manner, the scope of the principal topic of the Work; while the other six go particularly into an exhibition of the work required in its subordinate branches. The fifth chapter contains the important subject of comprehending true excellence, and the sixth, what is the foundation of the attainment of true sincerity. Those two chapters demand the especial attention of the learner. Let not the reader despise them because of their simplicity.

中庸

子程子曰、不偏之謂中、不易之謂庸、中者、天下之正道、庸者、天下之定理、此篇乃孔門傳授心法、子思恐其久而差也、故筆之於書、以授孟子、其書始言一理、中散爲萬事、末復合爲一理、放

My master, the philosopher Ch'ing, says, "Being without inclination to either side is called CHUNG; *admitting of no change is called* YUNG. *By* CHUNG *is denoted the correct course to be pursued by all under heaven; by* YUNG *is denoted the fixed principle regulating all under heaven. This work contains the law of the mind, which was handed down from one to another, in the Confucian school, till Tsze-sze, fearing lest in the course of time errors should arise about it, committed it to writing, and delivered it to Mencius. The book first speaks of one principle; it next spreads this out, and embraces all things; finally, it returns and gathers them all up under the one principle. Unroll it, and it*

THE TITLE OF THE WORK.—中庸, 'The doctrine of the Mean.' I have not attempted to translate the Chinese character 庸, as to the exact force of which there is considerable difference of opinion, both among native commentators, and among previous translators. Ch'ing K'ang-shing said:—名曰中庸者, 以其記中和之爲用也, 'The Work is named 中庸, because it records the practice of the non-deviating mind and of harmony.' He takes 庸, in the sense of 用, 'to use,' 'to employ,' which is the first given to it in the dict., and is found in the Shoo-king, I. p. 9. As to the meaning of 中, and 和, see ch. i. p. 4. This appears to have been the accepted meaning of 庸, in this combination, till Ch'ing E introduced that of 不易, 'unchanging,' as in the introductory note, which, however, the dict. does not acknowledge. Choo He himself says—中者不偏不倚, 無過不及之名. 庸, 平常也, '*Chung* is the name for what is without inclination or deflection, which neither exceeds nor comes short. *Yung* means ordinary, constant.' The dict. gives another meaning of *Yung*, with special reference to the point before us. It is said—又和也, 'It also means harmony;' and then reference is made to K'ang-shing's words given above, the compilers not having observed that he immediately subjoins—庸, 用也, show-

之、則彌六合、卷之、則退藏於密、其味無窮、皆實學也、善讀者、玩索而有得焉、則終身用之、有不能盡者矣。

一 天命之謂性、率性之謂道、修道之謂教。道也者、不可

fills the universe; roll it up, and it retires and lies hid in mysteriousness. The relish of it is inexhaustible. The whole of it is solid learning. When the skilful reader has explored it with delight till he has apprehended it, he may carry it into practice all his life, and will find that it cannot be exhausted.

CHAPTER I. 1. What Heaven has conferred is called THE NATURE; an accordance with this nature is called THE PATH *of duty*; the regulation of this path is called INSTRUCTION.

ing that he takes *Yung*, in the sense of 'to employ,' and not of 'harmony.' Many, however, adopt this meaning of the term in ch. ii, and my own opinion is decidedly in favour of it here in the title. The work then treats of the human mind:—in its state of *chung*, absolutely correct, as it is in itself; and in its state of *ho*, or harmony, acting *ad extra*, according to its correct nature.—In the version of the work, given in the collection of '*Mémoires concernant l'histoire, les sciences, &c., des Chinois*,' vol. I, it is styled—'*Juste Milieu*.' Rémusat calls it '*L'invariable Milieu*,' after Ch'ing E. Intorcetta, and his coadjutors call it—'*Medium constans vel sempiternum*.' The book treats, they say, '*De* MEDIO SEMPITERNO, *sive de aurea mediocritate illa, quae est, ut ait Cicero, inter nimium et parum, constanter et omnibus in rebus tenenda*.' Morrison, character 庸, says, '*Chung Yung*, the constant (golden) medium.' Collie calls it—'The golden medium.' The objection which I have to all these names is, that from them it would appear as if 中 were a noun, and 庸 a qualifying adjective, whereas they are co-ordinate terms.

INTRODUCTORY NOTE. 子程子,—see on intro. note to the 大學. On Tsze-sze, and his authorship of this work, see the prolegomena. 六合 is a phrase denoting—'heaven, earth, and the four cardinal points,'=the universe. 善讀者,—not our 'good reader,' but as in the translation.—I will not here anticipate the judgment of the reader on the eulogy of the enthusiastic Ch'ing.

1. It has been stated, in the prolegomena, that the current division of the Chung Yung into chapters was made by Choo He, as well as their subdivision into paragraphs. The 33 chapters, which embrace the work, are again arranged by him in five divisions, as will be seen from his supplementary notes. The first and last chapters are complete in themselves, as the introduction and conclusion of the treatise. The second part contains ten chapters; the third, nine; and the fourth, twelve.

Par. 1. *The principles of duty have their root in the evidenced will of Heaven, and their full exhibition in the teaching of sages.* By 性, or 'nature,' is to be understood the nature of man, though Choo He generalizes it so as to embrace that of brutes also; but only men can be cognisant of the *taou* and *keaou*. 命 he defines by 令, 'to command,' 'to order.' But we must take it as in a gloss on a pass. from the Yih-king, quoted in the dict.—命者人所稟受, '*Ming* is what men are endowed with.' Choo He also says that 性 is just 理, the 'principle,' characteristic of any particular nature. But this only involves the subject in mystery. His explanation of 道 by 路, 'a path,' seems to be correct, though some modern writers object to it.—What is taught seems to be this:—To man belongs a moral nature, conferred on him by Heaven or God, by which he is constituted a

須臾離也、可離、非道也、是故君子戒慎乎其所不睹、恐懼乎其所不聞、莫見乎隱、莫顯乎微、故君子慎其獨也。喜怒哀樂之未發、謂之中、發而皆中節、謂之和、中也者、天下之大本也、和

2. The path may not be left for an instant. If it could be left, it would not be the path. On this account, the superior man does not wait till he sees things, to be cautious, nor till he hears things, to be apprehensive.

3. There is nothing more visible than what is secret, and nothing more manifest than what is minute. Therefore the superior man is watchful over himself, when he is alone.

4. While there are no stirrings of pleasure, anger, sorrow, or joy, the mind may be said to be in the state of EQUILIBRIUM. When those feelings have been stirred, and they act in their due degree, there ensues what may be called the state of HARMONY. This EQUILIBRIUM is the great root *from which grow all the human actings* in the world, and this HARMONY is the universal path *which they all should pursue.*

law to himself. But as he is prone to deviate from the path in which, according to his nature, he should go, wise and good men—sages—have appeared, to explain and regulate this, helping all by their instructions to walk in it.

Par. 2. *The path indicated by the nature may never be left, and the superior man*—體道之人, *he who would embody all principles of right and duty—exercises a most sedulous care that he may attain thereto.* 須臾 is a name for a short period of time, of which there are 30 in the 24 hours; but the phrase is commonly used for 'a moment,' 'an instant.' K'ung Ying-tâ explains 可離非道,—'what may be left, is a wrong way,' which is not admissible. 離, low. 3d tone,—去, 'to be, or go, away from.' If we translate the two last clauses literally,—'is cautious and careful in regard to what he does not see; is fearful and apprehensive in regard to what he does not hear,'—they will not be intelligible to an English reader. A question arises, moreover, whether 其所不睹, 其所不聞, ought not to be understood passively,='where he is not seen,' 'where he is not heard.' They are so understood by Ying-tâ, and the 大學傳, ch. vi., is much in favour, by its analogy, of such an interpretation.

Par. 3. Choo He says that 隱 is 'a dark place;' that 細 means 'small matters;' and that 獨 is 'the place which other men do not know, and is known only to one's-self.' There would thus hardly be here any advance from the last par. It seems to me that the secrecy must be in the recesses of one's own heart, and the minute things, the springs of thought and stirrings of purpose there. The full development of what is intended here is probably to be found in all the subsequent passages about 誠, or 'sincerity.' See 西河合集, 中庸說, in loc.

Par. 4. 'This,' says Choo He, 'speaks of the virtue of the nature and passions, to illustrate the meaning of the statement that the path may not be left.' It is difficult to translate the par.

也者、天下之達道也。致中和、天地位焉、萬物育焉。右第一章、子思述所傳之意、以立言、首明道之本原出於天、而不可易、其實體備於己、而不可離、次言存養省察之要、終言聖神功化之極、蓋欲學者於此、反求諸身、

5. Let the states of equilibrium and harmony exist in perfection, and a happy order will prevail throughout heaven and earth, and all things will be nourished and flourish.

In the first chapter which is given above, Tsze-sze states the views which had been handed down to him, as the basis of his discourse. First, it shows clearly how the path of duty is to be traced to its origin in Heaven, and is unchangeable, while the substance of it is provided in ourselves, and may not be departed from. Next, it speaks of the importance of preserving and nourishing this, and of exercising a watchful self-scrutiny with reference to it. Finally, it speaks of the meritorious achievements and transforming influence of sage and spiritual men in their highest extent. The wish of Tsze-sze was that hereby the learner should direct his thoughts inwards, and by searching in himself, there find these

because it is difficult to understand it. 謂之 is different from 之謂 in p. 1. That *defines*; this *describes*. What is described in the first clause, seems to be 性 'the nature,' capable of all feelings, but unacted on, and in equilibrium.

Par. 5. On this Intorcetta and his colleagues observe:—'*Quis non videt eo duntaxat collimasse philosophum, ut hominis naturam, quam ab origine sua rectam, sed deinde lapsam et depravatam passim Sinenses docent, ad primaevum innocentiae statum reduceret? Atque ita reliquas res creatas, homini jam rebelles, et in ejusdem ruinam armatas, ad pristinum obsequium veluti revocaret. Hoc f. 1. o. 1. libri Ta Hioh, hoc item hic et alibi non semel indicat. Etsi autem nesciret philosophus nos a prima felicitate propter peccatum primi parentis excidisse, tamen et tot rerum quae adversantur et infestae sunt homini, et ipsius naturae humanae ad deteriora tam pronae, longo usu et contemplatione didicisse videtur, non posse hoc universum, quod homo vitiatus quodam modo vitiarat, connaturali suae integritati et ordini restitui, nisi prius ipse homo per victoriam sui ipsius, eam, quam amiserat, integritatem et ordinem recuperaret.*' I fancied something of the same kind, before reading their note. Acc. to Choo He, the par. describes the work and influence of sage and spiritual men in their highest issues. The subject is developed in the 4th part of the work, in very extravagant and mystical language. The study of it will modify very much our assent to the views in the above passage. There is in this whole chapter a mixture of sense and

而自得之、以去夫外誘之私、而充其本然之善、楊氏所謂一篇之體要是也、其下十章、蓋子思引夫子之言、以終此章之義。

二 一 仲尼曰、君子、中庸、小人、反中庸。二 君子之中庸也、君子而時中、小人之中庸也、小人而無忌憚也。

truths, so that he might put aside all outward temptations appealing to his selfishness, and fill up the measure of the goodness which is natural to him. This chapter is what the writer Yang called it,—"The sum of the whole work." In the ten chapters which follow, Tsze-sze quotes the words of the Master to complete the meaning of this.

CHAPTER II. 1. Chung-ne said, "The superior man *embodies* the course of the Mean; the mean man acts contrary to the course of the Mean.

2. "The superior man's embodying the course of the Mean is because he is a superior man, and so always maintains the Mean. The mean man's acting contrary to the course of the Mean is because he is a mean man, and has no caution."

mysticism,—of what may be grasped, and what tantalizes and eludes the mind. 位, acc. to Choo He,=安其位, 'will rest in their positions.' K'ang-shing explained it by 正,—'will be rectified.' 'Heaven and Earth' are here the parent powers of the universe. Thus Ying-ta expounds:—'Heaven and Earth will get their correct place, and the processes of production and completion will go on according to their principles, so that all things will be nourished and fostered.'

CONCLUDING NOTE. The writer Yang, quoted here, was a distinguished scholar and author in the reign of 英宗, A. D. 1064–1085. He was a disciple of Ch'ing Haou, and a friend both of him and his brother. F. 體要, 'the substance and the abstract,'=the sum.

2. ONLY THE SUPERIOR MAN CAN FOLLOW THE MEAN; THE MEAN IS ALWAYS VIOLATING IT. 1. Why Confucius should here be quoted by his designation, or marriage name, is a moot-point. It is said by some that disciples might in this way refer to their teacher, and a grandson to his grandfather, but such a rule is constituted probable on the strength of this instance, and that in ch. XXX. Others say that it is the honorary designation of the sage, and=the 尼父, which duke Gae used in reference to Confucius, in eulogizing him after his death. See the Le-ke, II. Pt. I. iii. 43. Some verb must be understood between 君子 and 中

三 子曰、中庸其至矣乎、民鮮能久矣。

四 一 子曰、道之不行也、我知之矣、知者、過之、愚者、不及也、道之不明也、我知之矣、賢者、過之、不肖者、不及也。二 人莫不飲食也、鮮能知味也。

CHAPTER III. The Master said, "Perfect is the virtue which is according to the Mean! Rare have they long been among the people, who could practise it!"

CHAPTER IV. 1. The Master said, "I know how it is that the path *of the Mean* is not walked in:—The knowing go beyond it, and the stupid do not come up to it. I know how it is that the path of the Mean is not understood:—The men of talents and virtue go beyond it, and the worthless do not come up to it.

2. "There is no body but eats and drinks. But they are few who can distinguish flavours."

庸, and I have supposed it to be 常, with most of the paraphrasts. Nearly all seem to be agreed that 中庸 here is the same as 中和 in the last chapter. On the change of terms, Choo He quotes from the scholar Yew (游), to the effect that 中和 is said with the nature and feelings in view, and 中庸, with reference to virtues and conduct. 2. 君子而時中, is explained by Choo:—'Because he has the virtue of a superior man, and moreover is able always to manage the *chung*.' But I rather think that the *keun-tsze* here is specially to be referred to the same as described in l. 2, and 中 = 正中. Wang Suh, the famous scholar of the Wei (魏) dynasty, in the 1st part of the 3d cent., quotes 小人之中庸, with 反 before 中, of which Choo He approves. If 反 be not introduced into the text, it must certainly be understood. 忌憚 is the opposite of 戒愼, 恐懼, in l. 2.—This, and the ten chapters which follow, all quote the words of Confucius with reference to the 中庸, to explain the meaning of the first ch.; and 'though there is no connection of composition between them,' says Choo He, 'they are all related by their meaning.'

3. THE RARITY, LONG EXISTING IN CONFUCIUS' TIME, OF THE PRACTICE OF THE MEAN. See the Ana. VI. xxvii. K'ang-shing and Ying-tă take the last clause as—'few can practise it long.' But the view in the transl. is better. The change from 仲尼曰 to 子曰 is observable.

4. HOW IT WAS THAT FEW WERE ABLE TO PRACTISE THE MEAN. 1. 道 may be referred to the 道 in the first chapter; immediately following 中庸 in the last, I translate it here —'the path of the Mean.' 知者 and 賢者 are not to be understood as meaning the truly wise and the truly worthy, but only those who in the degenerate times of Confucius deemed themselves to be such. The former thought the course of the Mean not worth their study, and the latter thought it not sufficiently exalted for their practice. 肖,—'as,' 'like.' 不肖 following 賢, indicates individuals of a diff. character, not equal to them. 2. We have here not a comparison, but an illustra., which may help to an understanding of the former par., though it does not seem very apt. People don't

第五章 子曰、道其不行矣夫。

第六章 子曰、舜其大知也與、舜好問、而好察邇言、隱惡而揚善、執其兩端、用其中於民、其斯以爲舜乎。

第七章 子曰、人皆曰予知、驅而納諸罟擭陷阱之中、而莫之知辟也、人皆曰予知、擇乎中庸、而不能

CHAPTER V. The Master said, "Alas! How is the path of the Mean untrodden!"

CHAPTER VI. The Master said, "There was Shun:—He indeed was greatly wise! Shun loved to question *others*, and to study their words, though they might be shallow. He concealed what was bad *in them*, and displayed what was good. He took hold of their two extremes, *determined* the Mean, and employed it in *his government of* the people. It was by this that he was Shun!"

CHAPTER VII. The Master said, "Men all say, 'We are wise;' but being driven forward and taken in a net, a trap, or a pitfall, they know not how to escape. Men all say, 'We are wise;' but happening to choose the course of the Mean, they are not able to keep it for a round month."

know the true flavour of what they eat and drink, but they need not go beyond that to learn it. No, the Mean belongs to all the actions of ordinary life, and might be discerned and practised in them, without looking for it in extraordinary things.

5. Choo He says:—'From not being understood, therefore it is not practised.' Acc. to K'ang-shing, the remark is a lament that there was no intelligent sovereign to teach the path. But the two views are reconcileable.

6. HOW SHUN PURSUED THE COURSE OF THE MEAN. This example of Shun, it seems to me, is adduced in opposition to the knowing of ch. iv. Shun, tho' a sage, invited the opinions of all men, and found truth of the highest value in their simplest sayings, and was able to determine from them the course of the Mean. 執其兩端,—'the two extremes' are understood by K'ang-shing of the two errors of exceeding and coming short of the Mean. Choo He makes them—'the widest differences in the opinions which he received.' I conceive the meaning to be that he examined the answers which he got, in their entirety, from beginning to end. Comp. 扣其兩端, Ana. IX. vii. His concealing what was bad, and displaying what was good, was alike to encourage people to speak freely to him. K'ang-shing makes the last sentence to turn on the meaning of 舜, when applied as an honorary epithet of the dead, = 'Full, all-accomplished;' but Shun was so named when he was alive.

7. THEIR CONTRARY CONDUCT SHOWS MEN'S IGNORANCE OF THE COURSE AND NATURE OF THE MEAN. The first 予知 is to be understood with a general reference,—'We are wise,' i. e., we can very well take care of ourselves. Yet the presumption of such a profession is seen in men's not being able to take care of themselves. The applica. of this illustration is then made to

期月守也。

[八] 子曰、回之爲人也、擇乎中庸、得一善、則拳拳服膺、而弗失之矣。

[九] 子曰、天下國家、可均也、爵祿、可辭也、白刃、可蹈也、中庸、不可能也。

[十] 子路問强。子曰、南方之强與、北方之强與、抑而强與。寬柔以教、不報

CHAPTER VIII. The Master said, "This was the manner of Hwuy:—he made choice of the Mean, and whenever he got hold of what was good, he clasped it firmly, as if wearing it on his breast, and did not lose it."

CHAPTER IX. The Master said, "The empire, its States, and its families, may be perfectly ruled; dignities and emoluments may be declined; naked weapons may be trampled under the feet;—but the course of the Mean cannot be attained to."

CHAPTER X. 1. Tsze-loo asked about energy.

2. The Master said, "Do you mean the energy of the South, the energy of the North, or the energy which you should cultivate yourself?

the subject in hand, the second 予知 being to be specially understood, with reference to the subject of the Mean. The conclusion in both parts is left to be drawn by the reader for himself. 擭, read *hwo*, lower 3d tone, 'a trap for catching animals.' 期, read *ke*, like 朞, in Analects, XIII. x, though it is here applied to a month, and not, as there, to a year.

8. HOW HWUY HELD FAST THE COURSE OF THE MEAN. Here the example of Hwuy is likewise adduced, in oppos. to those mentioned in ch. iv. All the rest is exegetical of the first clause—回之爲人也, 'Hwuy's playing the man.' 一善 is not 'one good point,' so much as any one. 拳 is 'the closed fist;' 拳拳,—'the appearance of holding firm.'

9. THE DIFFICULTY OF ATTAINING TO THE COURSE OF THE MEAN. 天下,—'the empire;' we should say—'empires,' but the Chinese know only of one empire, and hence this name for it. The empire is made up of States, and each State of Families. See the Analects, V. vii.; XII. xx. 均, 'level;' here a verb,=平治, 'to bring to perfect order.' 刃,—'a sharp, strong, weapon,' used of swords, spears, javelins, &c. 不可能,—lit., 'cannot be ensured.'

10. ON ENERGY IN ITS RELATION TO THE MEAN. In the Analects we find Tsze-loo, on various occasions, putting forward the subject of his valour (勇), and claiming, on the ground of it, such praise as the Master awarded to Hwuy. We may suppose, with the old interpreters, that hearing Hwuy commended, as in ch. viii., he wanted to know whether Confucius would not allow that he also could, with his forceful character, seize and hold fast the Mean. 1. For 强 I have been disposed to coin the term 'forcefulness.' Choo He defines it correctly—力

無道、南方之强也、君子居之。四衽金革、死而不厭、北方之强也、而强者居之。五故君子和而不流、强哉矯、中立而不倚、强哉矯、國有道、不變塞焉、强哉矯、國無道、至死不變、强哉矯。

3. "To show forbearance and gentleness in teaching others; and not to revenge unreasonable conduct:—this is the energy of Southern regions, and the good man makes it his study.

4. "To lie under arms; and meet death without regret:—this is the energy of Northern regions, and the forceful make it their study.

5. "Therefore, the superior man cultivates *a friendly* harmony, without being weak.—How firm is he in his energy! He stands erect in the middle, without inclining to either side.—How firm is he in his energy! When good principles prevail in the government of his country, he does not change from what he was in retirement.—How firm is he in his energy! When bad principles prevail in the country, he maintains his course to death withot changing.—How firm is he in his energy!"

足以勝人之名, 'the name of strength sufficient to overcome others.' 2. 而(=汝)强 must be—'the energy which you should cultivate,' not 'which you have.' If the latter be the meaning, no farther notice of it is taken in Confucius' reply, while he would seem, in the three foll. paragraphs, to describe the three kinds of energy which he specifies. K'ang-shing and Ying-tâ say that 而强 means the energy of the Middle kingdom, the North being 'the sandy desert,' and the South, 'the country south of the Yang-tsze.' But this is not allowable. 3. That climate and situation have an influence on character is not to be denied, and the Chinese notions on the subject may be seen in the amplification of the 9th of K'ang-he's celebrated maxims (聖諭廣訓). But to speak of their effects as Confucius here does is extravagant. The barbarism of the South, accord. to the interpretation mentioned above, could not have been described by him in these terms. The energy of mildness and forbearance, thus described, is held to come short of the Mean; and therefore 君子 is taken with a low and light meaning, far short of what it has in par. 5. This practice of determining the force of phrases from the context makes the reading of the Ch. classics perplexing to a student. 居之,—see the Ana. XII. xiv. 4. 衽, 'the lappet in front of a coat;' also 'a mat.' 衽金革, 'to make a mat of the leather dress (革) and weapons (金).' This energy of the North, it is said, is in excess of the Mean, and the 故, at the beginning of p. 5, 'therefore,'=' these two kinds of energy being thus respectively in defect and excess.' 矯 is 强貌, 'the appearance of being energetic.' This illustrates the energy which is in exact accord with the Mean, in the individual's treatment of others, in his regulation of himself, and in relation to public affairs. 有道, 無道:—often in the Analects. I have followed Choo He in translating 塞. Ying-tâ paraphrases:—守直不變德行充實, 'He holds

〔十一〕子曰、素隱行怪、後世有述焉、吾弗爲之矣。二 君子遵道而行、半塗而廢、吾弗能已矣。三 君子依乎中庸、遯世不見知而不悔、唯聖者能之。

〔十二〕君子之道、費而隱。二 夫婦之愚、可以

CHAPTER XI. 1. The Master said, "To live in obscurity, and yet practise wonders, in order to be mentioned with honour in future ages;—this is what I do not do.

2. "The good man tries to proceed according to the right path, but when he has gone halfway, he abandons it;—I am not able *so* to stop.

3. "The superior man accords with the course of the Mean. Though he may be all unknown, unregarded by the world, he feels no regret.—It is only the sage who is able for this."

CHAPTER XII. 1. The way which the superior man pursues, reaches wide and far, and yet is secret.

to what is upright, and does not change, his virtuous conduct being all-complete.' A modern writer makes the meaning:—'He does not change through being puffed up by the fulness of office.' Both of these views go on the interpretation of 塞 as=實.

11. ONLY THE SAGE CAN COME UP TO THE REQUIREMENTS OF THE MEAN. 1. 素 is found written 索, 'to examine,' 'to study,' in a work of the Han dynasty, and Choo He adopts that character as the true reading, and explains accordingly:—'To study what is obscure and wrong (隱僻).' K'ang-shing took it as=傃, 'towards,' and both he and Ying-tâ explain as in the translation. It is an objection to Choo He's view, that, in the next ch., 隱 is given as one of the characteristics of the Mean. The 遯世云云, in p. 3, moreover, agree well with the older view. 2. 君子 is here the same as in last ch. p. 3. A distinction is made between 遵道 here and 依道 below. The former, it is said, implies endeavour, while the latter is natural and unconstrained accordance. 3. 君子 here has its very highest signification, and=聖者 in the last clause. 避世 is said to be diff. from 遯世, the latter being applicable to the recluse who withdraws from the world, while the former may describe one who is in the world, but does not act with a reference to its opinion of him. It will be observed how Confucius declines saying that he had himself attained to this highest style.—'With this ch.,' says Choo He, 'the quotations by Tsze-sze of the Master's words, to explain the meaning of the first chapter, stop. The great object of the work is to set forth wisdom, benevolent virtue, and valour, as the three grand virtues whereby entrance is effected into the path of the Mean, and therefore, at its commencement, they are illustrated by reference to Shun, Yen Yuen, and Tsze-loo, Shun possessing the wisdom, Yen Yuen the benevolence, and Tsze-loo the valour. If one of these virtues be absent, there is no way of advancing to the path, and perfecting the virtue. This will be found fully treated of in the 20th chapter.' So, Choo He. The student forming a judgment for himself, however, will not see very distinctly any reference to these cardinal virtues. The utterances of the sage illustrate the phrase 中庸, showing that the course of the Mean had fallen out of observance, some overshooting it, and others coming short of it. When we want some

與知焉、及其致也、雖聖人亦有所不知焉、夫婦之不肖、可以能行焉、及其至也、雖聖人亦有所不能焉、天地之大也、人猶有所憾、故君子語大、天下莫能載焉、語小、天下莫能破焉。詩云、鳶飛戾天、魚躍于淵、言其

2. Common men and women, however ignorant, may intermeddle with the knowledge of it; yet in its utmost reaches, there is that which even the sage does not know. Common men and women, however much below the ordinary standard of character, can carry it into practice; yet in its utmost reaches, there is that which even the sage is not able to carry into practice. Great as heaven and earth are, men still find some things in them with which to be dissatisfied. Thus it is, that were the superior man to speak of his way in all its greatness, nothing in the world would be found able to embrace it, and were he to speak of it in its minuteness, nothing in the world would be found able to split it.

3. It is said in the Book of Poetry, "The hawk flies up to heaven; the fishes leap in the deep." This expresses how this *way* is seen above and below.

precise directions how to attain to it, we come finally to the conclusion that only the sage is capable of doing so. We greatly want teaching, more practical and precise.

XII. THE COURSE OF THE MEAN REACHES FAR AND WIDE, BUT YET IS SECRET. With this ch. the third part of the work commences, and the first sentence,—君子之道費而隱, may be regarded as its text. If we could determine satisfactorily the signification of those two terms, we should have a good clue to the meaning of the whole, but it is not easy to do so. The old view is inadmissible. K'ang-shing takes 費 as = 佹, 'doubly involved,' 'perverted,' and both he and Ying-tâ explain:—'When right principles are opposed and disallowed, the superior man retires into obscurity, and does not hold office.' On this view of it, the sentence has nothing to do with the succeeding chapters. The two meanings of 費 in the dict. are—'the free expenditure of money,' and 'dissipation,' or 'waste.' Acc. to Choo He, in this passage, 費即用之廣也, '費 indicates the wide range of the *taou* in practice.' Something like this must be its meaning:—the course of the Mean, requiring everywhere to be exhibited. Choo then defines 隱 as 體之微, 'the minuteness of the *taou* in its nature or essence.' The former answers to the *what* of the *taou*, and the latter, to the *why*. But it rather seems to me, that the 隱 here is the same with the 隱 and 微, i. 4, and that the author simply intended to say, that the way of the superior man reaching everywhere,—embracing all duties,—yet had its secret spring and seat in the Heaven-gifted nature, the individual consciousness of duty in every man. 2. 夫婦=匹夫, 匹婦, Ana. XIV. xviii. 3. But I confess to be all at sea in the study of this par. Choo quotes from the scholar How (侯氏), that what the superior man fails to know, was exemplified in Conf. having to ask about ceremonies,

上下察也、君子之道、造端乎夫婦、及其至也、察乎天地。

右第十二章、子思之言、蓋以申明首章道不可離之意也、其下八章、雜引孔子之言以明之。

十三 子曰、道不遠人、人之爲道而遠人、不可以爲道。詩云、伐柯伐柯、其則不遠、執

4. The way of the superior man may be found, in its simple elements, in the intercourse of common men and women; but in its utmost reaches, it shines brightly through heaven and earth.

The twelfth chapter above contains the words of Tsze-sze, and is designed to illustrate what is said in the first chapter, that "The path may not be left." In the eight chapters which follow, he quotes, in a miscellaneous way, the words of Confucius to illustrate it.

CHAPTER XIII. 1. The Master said, "The path is not far from man. When men try to pursue a course, which is far from the common indications of consciousness, this course cannot be considered THE PATH.

2. "In the Book of Poetry, it is said, 'In hewing an axe-handle, in hewing an axe-handle, the pattern is not far off.' We grasp one axe-handle to hew the other, and yet, if we look askance from

and about offices, and what he fails to practise, was exemplified in Conf. not being on the throne, and in Yaou and Shun's being dissatisfied that they could not make every individual enjoy the benefits of their rule. He adds his own opinion, that wherein men complained of Heaven and Earth, was the partiality of their operations in overshadowing and supporting, producing and completing, the heat of summer, the cold of winter, &c. If such things were intended by the writer, we can only regret the vagueness of his language, and the want of coherence in his argument. In translating 君子語大云云, I have followed Maou Se-ho. 3. See the She-king, III. i. Ode V. st. 3. The ode is in praise of the virtue of king Wan. 察 is in the sense of 昭著, 'brightly displayed.' The application of the words of the ode does appear strange.

13. THE PATH OF THE MEAN IS NOT FAR TO SEEK. EACH MAN HAS THE LAW OF IT IN HIMSELF, AND IT IS TO BE PURSUED WITH EARNEST SINCERITY. 1. 人之爲道而遠人,—'When men practise a course, and wish to be far from men.' The meaning is as in the translation. 2. See the She-king I. xv. Ode V. st. 2. The object of the par. seems to be to show that

柯以伐柯、睨而視之、猶以爲遠、故君子以人治人、改而止。○三忠恕違道不遠、施諸己而不願、亦勿施於人。四君子之道四、丘未能一焉、所求乎子、以事父、未能也、所求乎臣、以事君、未能也、所求乎弟、以事兄、未能也、所求乎朋友、先施之、未能也、庸德之行、庸言之謹、有所

the one to the other, we may consider them as apart. Therefore, the superior man governs men, according to their nature, with what is proper to them, and as soon as they change *what is wrong*, he stops.

3. "When one cultivates to the utmost the principles of his nature, and exercises them on the principle of reciprocity, he is not far from the path. What you do not like, when done to yourself, do not do to others.

4. "In the way of the superior man there are four things, to not one of which have I as yet attained.—To serve my father, as I would require my son to serve me: to this I have not attained; to serve my prince, as I would require my minister to serve me: to this I have not attained; to serve my elder brother, as I would require my younger brother to serve me: to this I have not attained; to set the example in behaving to a friend, as I would require him to behave to me: to this I have not attained. Earnest in practising the ordinary virtues, and careful in speaking about them, if, in his practice, he has anything defective, the superior man dares not but

the rule for dealing with men, according to the principles of the Mean, is nearer to us than the axe in the hand is to the one which is to be cut down with, and fashioned after, it. The branch is hewn, and its form altered from its natural one. Not so with man. The change in him only brings him to his proper state. 3. Comp. Ana. IV. xv. 違 is here a neuter verb, 'to be distant from.' 4. Comp. Ana. VII. i, ii, xix, *et al.* The admissions made by Conf. here are important to those who find it necessary, in their intercourse with the Chinese, to insist on his having been, like other men, compassed with infirmity. It must be allowed, however, that the cases, as put by him, are in a measure hypothetical, his father having died when he was a child. In the course of the paragraph, he passes from speaking of himself by his name (丘), to speak of the *keun-tsze*, and the change is most naturally made after the last 能也. 庸德之行, 庸言之謹,—'in the prac-

不足、不敢不勉、有餘不敢盡、言顧行、行顧言、君子胡不慥慥爾。

十四 君子、素其位而行、不願乎其外。素富貴、行乎富貴、素貧賤、行乎貧賤、素夷狄、行乎夷狄、素患難、行乎患難、君子無入而不自得焉。在上位、不陵下、在下位、不援上、正

exert himself; and if, in his words, he has any excess, he dares not allow himself such license. Thus his words have respect to his actions, and his actions have respect to his words; is it not just an entire sincerity which marks the superior man?"

CHAPTER XIV. 1. The superior man does what is proper to the station in which he is; he does not desire to go beyond this.

2. In a position of wealth and honour, he does what is proper to a position of wealth and honour. In a poor and low position, he does what is proper to a poor and low position. Situated among barbarous tribes, he does what is proper to a situation among barbarous tribes. In a position of sorrow and difficulty, he does what is proper to a position of sorrow and difficulty. The superior man can find himself in no situation in which he is not himself.

3. In a high situation, he does not treat with contempt his inferiors. In a low situation, he does not court the favour of his

ties of ordinary virtues,' *i. e.*, the duties of a son, minister, &c., mentioned above, and in the carefulness or ordinary speech, *i. e.*, speaking about those virtues. To the practice belong the clauses 有所不足.不敢不勉. and to the speaking, the two next clauses. 爾, —as a final particle, = 耳, 'simply,' 'just.'

11. HOW THE SUPERIOR MAN, IN EVERY VARYING SITUATION, PURSUES THE MEAN, DOING WHAT IS RIGHT, AND FINDING HIS RULE IN HIMSELF. 1. Chu Hsi takes 素 as = 見在, 'at present,' 'now;' but that meaning was made to meet the exigency of the present passage. K'ang-shing takes it, as in ch. xi, as = 傃, 'towards.' Mao makes an attempt to establish this view:—素位者. 卽本來故有之位. '素位 is the proper station in which he has been.' The meaning comes to much the same in all these interpretations. 不願乎其外,—comp. Ana. XIV. xxviii. 2. 行乎富貴—行乎富貴所當行之道, 'He pursues the path, which ought to be pursued amid riches and honours.' So, in the other clauses. 自得,—lit., = 'self-possessing.' The paraphrasts make it—'happy in conforming himself to his position.' I consider it equivalent to what is said in ch. ii.—君子之中庸也.君子而時中. 3. 援 is explained in the

己而不求於人、則無怨、上不怨天、下不尤人、故四君子居易以俟命、小人、行險以徼幸。五子曰、射有似乎君子、失諸正鵠、反求諸其身。

十五 君子之道、一辟如行遠必自邇、辟如登高必自卑。二詩曰、妻子好合、如鼓瑟琴、兄弟既翕、和樂且

superiors. He rectifies himself, and seeks for nothing from others, so that he has no dissatisfactions. He does not murmur against heaven, nor grumble against men.

4. Thus it is that the superior man is quiet and calm, waiting for the appointments *of Heaven*, while the mean man walks in dangerous paths, looking for lucky occurences.

5. The Master said, "In archery we have something like the way of the superior man. When the archer misses the centre of the target, he turns round and seeks for the cause of his failure in himself."

CHAPTER XV. 1. The way of the superior man may be compared to what takes place in travelling, when to go to a distance we must first traverse the space that is near, and in ascending a height, when we must begin from the lower ground.

2. It is said in the Book of Poetry, "Happy union with wife and children, is like the music of lutes and harps. When there

dict., after K'ang-hsî, by 牽持, 'to drag and cling to.' The opposition of the two clauses makes the meaning plain. 上不怨天、下不尤人,—see Ana. XIV. xxxvii. 4. 易, acc. to K'ang-hsî, 猶平安, 'is equivalent to peaceful and tranquil.' Choo He says, 易平地也, '易 means level ground.' This is most correct, but we cannot so well express it in the translation. 幸, as used here, is often written 倖. 5. 正, up. 1st tone, and 鵠 are both names of birds, small and alert, and difficult to be hit. On this account, a picture of the former was painted on the middle of the target, and a figure of the latter was attached to it in leather. It is not meant, however, by this, that they were both used in the same target, at the same time. For another illustration of the way of the superior man from the customs of archery, see Ana., III. vii.

15. IN THE PRACTICE OF THE MEAN THERE IS AN ORDERLY ADVANCE FROM STEP TO STEP. 1. 辟 is read as, and = 譬. 2. See the Shih-ching, II. i. Ode IV. st. 7, 8. The ode celebrates, in a regretful tone, the dependence of brethren on one another, and the beauty of brotherly harmony. Mâo says:—'Although there may be the happy union of wife and children, like the music of lutes and harps, yet there must also be the harmonious concord of brethren, with its exceeding delight, and then may wife and

耽、宜爾室家、樂爾妻帑。子曰、父母其順矣乎。子曰、鬼神之爲德、其盛矣乎。視之而弗見、聽之而弗聞、體物而不可遺、使天下之人、齊明盛服、以承祭祀、洋

is concord among brethren, the harmony is delightful and enduring. *Thus* may you regulate your family, and enjoy the pleasure of your wife and children."

3. The Master said, "In such a state of things, parents have entire complacence!"

CHAPTER XVI. 1. The Master said, "How abundantly do spiritual beings display the powers that belong to them!

2. "We look for them, but do not see them; we listen to, but do not hear them; yet they enter into all things, and there is nothing without them.

3. "They cause all the people in the empire to fast and purify themselves, and array themselves in their richest dresses, in order to attend at their sacrifices. Then, like overflowing water, they seem to be over the heads, and on the right and left *of their worshippers*.

children be regulated and enjoyed. Brothers are near to us, while wife and children are more remote. Thus it is, that from what is near we proceed to what is remote.' He adds that anciently the relationship of husband and wife was not among the five relationships of society, because the union of brothers is from heaven, and that of husband and wife is from man! 3. This is understood to be a remark of Confucius on the ode. From wife, and children, and brothers, parents at last are reached, illustrating how from what is low we ascend to what is high.—But all this is far-fetched and obscure.

16. AN ILLUSTRATION, FROM THE OPERATION AND INFLUENCE OF SPIRITUAL BEINGS, OF THE WAY OF THE MEAN. What is said of the *kwei-shin* in this chapter is only by way of illustration. There is no design, on the part of the sage, to develop his views on those beings or agencies. The key of it is to be found in the last par., where the 夫微之顯 evidently refers to 莫顯乎微 in ch. i. This par., therefore, should be separated from the others, and not interpreted specially of the *kwei-shin*. I think that Dr. Medhurst, in rendering it (Theology of the Chinese, p. 22)—'How great then is the manifestation of *their* abstruseness! Whilst displaying their sincerity, they are not to be concealed,' was wrong, notwithstanding that he may be defended by the example of many Chinese commentators. The second clause of par. 5,—誠之不可揜如此, appears altogether synonymous with the 誠於中必形於外 in the 大學傳, ch. vi. 2, to which chapter we have seen that the whole of ch. i. pp. 2, 3, has a remarkable similarity. However we may be driven to find a recondite, mystical, meaning for 誠, in the 4th part of this work, there is no necessity to do so here. With regard to what is said of the *kwei-shin*, it is only the first two paragraphs which occasion difficulty. In the 3d par., the sage speaks of the spiritual beings that are sacrificed to. 齊,—read *chai*; see Ana. VII. xii. The same is the subject of the 4th par.; or rather, spiritual beings generally, whether sacrificed to or not, invisible themselves and yet able to behold our conduct. See the She-king, III. iii. Ode II. st. 7. The ode is said to have been composed by one of the dukes of Wei, and was repeated daily in his hearing for his admonition. In the context of the quotation, he is warned to be careful of his conduct, when alone as when in company. For in truth we are never alone. 'Millions of spiritual beings walk the earth,' and can take note of us.

洋乎、如在其上、如在其左右。詩曰、神之格思、不可度思、矧可射思。夫微之顯、誠之不可揜、如此夫。

十七 子曰、舜其大孝也與、德

4. "It is said in the Book of Poetry, 'The approaches of the spirits, you cannot surmise;—and can you treat them with indifference?'

5. "Such is the manifestness of what is minute! Such is the impossibility of repressing the outgoings of sincerity!"

CHAPTER XVII. 1. The Master said, "How greatly filial was Shun! His virtue was that of a sage; his dignity was the imperial

(思 is a final particle here, without meaning. It is often used so in the Shi-king. 度, read *tŏ*, lower 4th tone, 'to conjecture,' 'to surmise.' 射, read *yih*, low. 4th tone, 'to dislike.') What now are the *kwei-shin* in the first two paragraphs. Are we to understand by them something different from what they are in the 3d par., to which they run on from the first as the nominative or subject of 體? I think not. The precise meaning of what is said of them in 體物而不可遺 cannot be determined. The old interpreters say that 體 = 生, 'to give birth to;' that 可 = 所, 'that which;' that 不可遺 = 不有所遺, 'there is nothing which they neglect;' and that the meaning of the whole is—'that of all things there is not a single thing which is not produced by the breath (or energy: 氣) of the *kwei-shin*.' This is all that we learn from them. The Sung school explain the terms with reference to their physical theory of the universe, derived, as they think, from the *Yih-king*. Choo He's master, Ch'ing, explains:—'The *kwei-shin* are the energetic operations of Heaven and Earth, and the traces of production and transformation.' The scholar Chang (張氏) says:—'The *kwei-shin* are the easily acting powers of the two breaths of nature (二氣).' Choo He's own account is:—'If we speak of two breaths, then by *kwei* is denoted the efficaciousness of the secondary or inferior one, and by *shin*, that of the superior one. If we speak of one breath, then by *shin* is denoted its advancing and developing, and by *kwei*, its returning and reverting. They are really only one thing.' It is difficult—not to say impossible—to conceive to one's-self what is meant by such descriptions. And nowhere else in the Four Books is there an approach to this meaning of the phrase. Maou Se-ho is more comprehensible, though, after all, it may be doubted whether what he says is more than a play upon words. His explanation is:—'But in truth, the *kwei-shin* are 道. In the *Yih-king* the 陰 and 陽 are considered to be the *kwei-shin*; and it is said—*one* 陰 and *one* 陽 *are called* 道. Thus the *kwei-shin* are the 道, embodied in Heaven (體天) for the nourishment of things. But in the text we have the term 德 instead of 道, because the latter is the name of the absolute as embodied in Heaven, and the former denotes the same not only embodied, but operating to the nourishing of things, for Heaven considers the production of things to be 德.' See the 中庸說, *in loc.*

Rémusat translates the first par.:—'*Que les vertus des esprits sont sublimes!*' His Latin version is:—'*spirituum geniorumque est virtus: ea capax!*' Intorcetta renders:—'*spiritibus inest operativa virtus et efficacitas, et haec o quam praestans est! quam multiplex! quam sublimis!*' In a note, he and his friends say that the dignitary of the empire who assisted them, rejecting other interpretations, understood by *kwei-shin* here—'those spirits for the veneration of whom and imploring their help, sacrifices were instituted.' 神 signifies 'spirits,' 'a spirit,' 'spirit;' and 鬼, 'a ghost,' or 'demon.' The former is used for the *animus*, or intelligent soul separated from the body, and the latter for the *anima*, or animal, grosser, soul, so separated. In the text, however, they blend together, and are not to be separately translated. They are together equivalent to 神 in par. 4, 'spirits,' or 'spiritual beings.'

爲聖人、尊爲天子、富有四海之內、宗廟饗之、子孫保之。故大德、必得其位、必得其祿、必得其名、必得其壽。故天之生物、必因其材而篤焉、故栽者培之、傾者覆之。詩曰、嘉樂君子、憲憲令

throne; his riches were all within the four seas. He offered his sacrifices in his ancestral temple, and his descendants preserved the sacrifices to himself.

2. "Therefore having such great virtue, it could not but be that he should obtain the throne, that he should obtain those riches, that he should obtain his fame, that he should attain to his long life.

3. "Thus it is that Heaven, in the production of things, is surely bountiful to them, according to their qualities. Hence the tree that is flourishing, it nourishes, while that which is ready to fall, it overthrows.

4. "In the Book of Poetry, it is said, 'The admirable, amiable, prince, displayed conspicuously his excelling virtue, adjusting his people and adjusting his officers. *Therefore*, he received from Hea-

17. THE VIRTUE OF FILIAL PIETY, EXEMPLIFIED IN SHUN AS CARRIED TO THE HIGHEST POINT, AND REWARDED BY HEAVEN. 1. One does not readily see the connection between Shun's great filial piety, and all the other predicates of him that follow. The paraphrasts, however, try to trace it in this way:—'A son without virtue is insufficient to distinguish his parents. But Shun was born with all knowledge and acted without any effort;—in virtue, a sage. How great was the distinction which he thus conferred on his parents!' And so with regard to the other predicate. See the 日講 四海之內;—on this expression it is said in the encyclopedia called 博物志:—'The four cardinal points of heaven and earth are connected together by the waters of seas, the earth being a small space in the midst of them. Hence, he who rules over the empire (天下) is said to govern all within the four seas.' See also on Ana. XII. v. 4. The characters 宗廟 are thus explained:—'*Tsung* means honourable. *Meaou* means figure. The two together mean the place where the figures of one's ancestors are.' Choo He says nothing on 宗廟饗之, because he had given in to the views of some who thought that Shun sacrificed merely in the ancestral temple of Yaou. But it is capable of proof that he erected one of his own, and ascended to Hwang-te, as his great progenitor. See Mao's 中庸說, in loc. 饗,—'to entertain a guest;' and sometimes for 享, 'to enjoy.' So we must take it here,—'enjoyed him;' that is, his sacrifices. As Shun resigned the throne to Yu, and it did not run in the line of his family, we must take 保之 as in the translation. In the time of the Chow dynasty, there were descendants of Shun, possessed of the state of Ch'in (陳), and of course sacrificing to him. 2. The 其 must refer in every case to 大德;—'its place, its emolument,' &c.; that is, what is appropriate to such great virtue. The whole is to be understood with reference to Shun. He died at the age of 100 years. The word 'virtue,' takes here the place of 'filial piety,' in the last par.,

德、宜民宜人、受祿于天、保佑命之、自天申之。故大德者必受命。

〔十八〕子曰、無憂者、其惟文王乎、以王季為父、以武王為子、父作之、子述之。武王纘大王王季文王之緒、壹戎衣、而有天下、身不失天下之顯名、尊為天

ven the emoluments of dignity. It protected him, assisted him, decreed him the throne; sending from heaven these favours, *as it were* repeatedly.'

5. "*We may say* therefore that he who is greatly virtuous will be sure to receive the appointment of Heaven."

CHAPTER XVIII. 1. The Master said, "It is only king Wăn of whom it can be said that he had no cause for grief! His father was king Ke, and his son was king Woo. His father laid the foundations of his dignity, and his son transmitted it.

2. King Woo continued the enterprise of king T'ae, king Ke, and king Wăn. He once buckled on his armour, and got possession of the empire. He did not lose the distinguished personal reputation which he had throughout the empire. His dignity was the im-

acc. to Maou, because that is the root, the first and chief, of all virtues. 3. 材 and 篤 (acc. to Choo He,=厚, 'thick,' 'liberal') are explained by most commentators as equally capable of a good and bad application. This may be said of 材, but not of 篤, and the 生 in 天之生物 would seem to determine the meaning of both to be only good. If this be so, then the last clause 傾者覆之 is only an after-thought of the writer, and, indeed, the sentiment of it is out of place in the chapter. 栽 is best taken, with K'ang-ching, as=殖, and not, with Choo He, as merely=植. 4. See the She-king, III. ii. ode V. st. 1, where we have two slight variations of 假 for 嘉 and 顯 for 憲. The prince spoken of is king Wăn, who is thus brought forward to confirm the lesson taken from Shun. That lesson, however, is stated much too broadly in the last par. It is well to say that only virtue is a solid title to eminence, but to hold forth the certain attainment of wealth and position as an inducement to virtue is not favourable to morality. The case of Confucius himself, who attained neither to power nor to long life, may be adduced as inconsistent with these teachings.

18. ON KING WAN, KING WOO, AND THE DUKE OF CHOW. 1. Shun's father was bad, and the fathers of Yaou and Yu were undistinguished. Yaou and Shun's sons were both bad, and Yu's not remarkable. But to Wăn neither father nor son gave occasion but for satisfaction and happiness. King Ke was the duke Ke-lëih (季歷), the most distinguished by his virtues, and prowess, of all the princes of his time. He prepared the way for the elevation of his family. In 父作之,子述之, the 之 is made to refer to 基業, 'the foundation of the empire, but it may as well be referred to Wăn himself. 2. 大王,—this was the duke Tan-foo (亶父), the father of Ke-

子、富有四海之內、宗廟饗之、子孫保之。○三武王末受命、周公成文武之德、追王大王王季、上祀先公以天子之禮、斯禮也、達乎諸侯大夫、及士庶人、父爲大夫、子爲士、葬以大夫、祭以士、父爲士、子爲大夫、葬以士、祭以大夫、期之喪、達乎大夫、

perial throne. His riches were the possession of all within the four seas. He offered his sacrifices in his ancestral temple, and his descendants maintained the sacrifices to himself.

3. "It was in his old age that king Woo received the appointment *to the throne*, and the duke of Chow completed the virtuous course of Wăn and Woo. He carried up the title of king to T'ae and Ke, and sacrificed to all the former dukes above them with the imperial ceremonies. And this rule he extended to the princes of the empire, the great officers, the scholars, and the common people. Was the father a great officer and the son a scholar, then the burial was that due to a great officer, and the sacrifice that due to a scholar. Was the father a scholar, and the son a great officer, then the burial was that due to a scholar, and the sacrifice that due to a great officer. The one year's mourning was made to extend *only* to the great officers,

lih, a prince of great eminence, and who, in the decline of the Yin dynasty, drew to his family the thoughts of the people. 緒,—'the end of a cocoon.' It is used here for the beginnings of imperial sway, traceable to the various progenitors of king Woo. 壹戎衣 is interpreted by K'ang-shing:—'He destroyed the great Yin;' and recent commentators defend his view. It is not worth while setting forth what may be said for and against it. 'He did not lose his distinguished reputation;' that is, tho' he proceeded against his rightful sovereign, the people did not change their opinion of his virtue. 3. 末=老, 'when old.' Woo was 87 when he became emperor, and he only reigned 7 years. His brother Tan (旦), the duke of Chow (see Ana. VI. xxii: VII. v.) acted as his chief minister. In 追王, 王 is in the 3d tone, in which the character means—'to exercise the sovereign power.' 上祀先公云云,—the house of Chow traced their lineage, up to the emperor 嚳, B. C. 2433. But in various passages of the Shoo-king, king T'ae and king Ke are spoken of, as if the conference of those titles had been by king Wun. On this there are very long discussions. See the 中庸說, *in loc.* The truth seems to be, that Chow-kung, carrying out his brother's wishes by laws of State, confirmed the titles, and made the general rule about burials and sacrifices which is described. From 斯禮也 to the end, we are at first inclined to translate in the present tense, but the past with a reference to

三年之喪、達乎天子、父母之喪、無貴賤、一也。

十九 子曰、武王周公、其達孝矣乎。一 夫孝者、善繼人之志、善述人之事者也。二 春秋、脩其祖廟、陳其宗器、設其裳衣、薦其時食。三 宗廟之禮、所以序昭穆也、序

but the three years' mourning extended to the emperor. In the mourning for a father or mother, he allowed no difference between the noble and the mean."

CHAPTER XIX. 1. The Master said, "How far-extending was the filial piety of king Woo and the duke of Chow!

2. "Now filial piety is seen in the skilful carrying out of the wishes of our fore-fathers, and the skilful carrying forward of their undertakings.

3. "In spring and autumn, they repaired and beautified the temple-halls of their fathers, set forth their ancestral vessels, displayed their various robes, and presented the offerings of the several seasons.

4. "By means of the ceremonies of the ancestral temple, they distinguished the imperial kindred according to their order of descent. By ordering the parties present according to their rank, they

Chow-kung is more correct. The 'year's mourning' is that principally for uncles, and it did not extend beyond the great officers, because their uncles were the subjects of the princes and the emperor, and feelings of kindred must not be allowed to come into collision with the relation of governor and governed. On the 'three years' mourning,' see Ana. XVII. xxi.

19. THE FAR-REACHING FILIAL PIETY OF KING WOO, AND OF THE DUKE OF CHOW. 1. 達 is taken by Choo He as meaning—'universally acknowledged;' 'far-extending' is better, and accords with the meaning of the term in other parts of the work. 2. This definition of 孝, or 'filial piety,' is worthy of notice. Its operation ceases not with the lives of parents and parents' parents. 人 = 前人, 'antecedent men;' but English idiom seems to require the addition of our. 3. 春秋.—The emperors of China sacrificed, as they still do, to their ancestors every season. Reckoning from the spring, the names of the sacrifices appear to have been—祠, 禴 or 礿, 嘗, and 烝. Others, however, give the names as 礿, 禘, 嘗, 烝, while some affirm that the spring sacrifice was 禘. Though spring and autumn only are mentioned in the text, we are to understand that what is said of the sacrifices in those seasons applies to all the others. 祖廟,—'Halls or temples of ancestors,' of which the emperors had seven (see the next par.), all included in the name of 宗廟. 宗器, 'ancestral,' or 'venerable, vessels.' Choo He understands by them relics, something like our regalia. Ch'ing K'ang-shing makes them, and apparently with more correctness, simply 'the sacrificial vessels.' 裳衣,—'lower and upper garments,' with the latter of which the

爵、所以辨貴賤也、序事、所以辨賢也、旅酬、下爲上、所以逮賤也、燕毛、所以序齒也、右第四節 踐其位、行其禮、奏其樂、敬其所尊、愛其所親、事死如事生、事亡如事存、孝之

distinguished the more noble and the less. By the arrangement of the services, they made a distinction of talents and worth. In the ceremony of general pledging, the inferiors presented the cup to their superiors, and thus something was given the lowest to do. At the *concluding* feast, places were given according to the hair, and thus was made the distinction of years.

5. "They occupied the places of their fore-fathers, practised their ceremonies, and performed their music. They reverenced those whom they honoured, and loved those whom they regarded with affection. Thus they served the dead as they would have served them alive; they served the departed as they would have served them had they been continued among them.

parties personating the deceased were invested. 4. It was an old interpretation that the sacrifices and accompanying services, spoken of here, were not the seasonal services of every year, which are the subject of the prec. par., but the great 禘 and 祫 sacrifices, and to that view I would give in my adhesion. The emperor, as mentioned above had seven 廟. One belonged to the remote ancestor to whom the dynasty traced its origin. At the great sacrifices, his spirit-tablet was placed fronting the east, and on each side were ranged, three in a row, the tablets belonging to the six others, those of them which fronted the south being, in the genealogical line, the fathers of those who fronted the north. As fronting the south, the region of *brilliancy*, the former were called 昭; the latter, from the north, the *sombre* region, were called 穆. As the dynasty was prolonged, and successive emperors died, the older tablets were removed, and transferred to what was called the 祧廟, yet so as that one in the 昭 line displaced the topmost 昭, and so with the 穆. At the sacrifices, the imperial kindred arranged themselves as they were descended from a 昭, on the left, and from a 穆, on the right, and thus a genealogical correctness of place was maintained among them. The ceremony of 'general (旅=衆) pledging' occurred towards the end of the sacrifice. Choo He takes 旅 in the low, 3d tone, saying that to have anything to do at those services was accounted honourable, and after the emperor had commenced the ceremony by taking 'a cup of blessing,' all the juniors presented a similar cup to the seniors, and thus were called into employment. Ying-ta takes 爲 in its ordinary tone, 下爲上, 'the inferiors were the superiors,' *i. e.*, the juniors did present a cup to their elders, but had the honour of drinking first themselves. The 燕 was a concluding feast confined to the imperial kindred. 5. 踐其位, acc. to K'ang-shing, is—'ascended their thrones;' acc. to Choo He it is 'tread on—*i. e.*, occupied—their places in the ancestral temple.' On either view, the statement must be taken with allowance. The ancestors of king Woo had not been emperors, and their places in the temples had only been those of princes. The same may be said of the four particulars which follow. By 'those whom they'—*i. e.*, their progenitors—'honoured' are intended their ancestors, and by 'those whom they loved,' their descendants, and indeed all the people of their government. The two concluding sentences are

至也。六郊社之禮所以事上帝也、宗廟之禮所以祀乎其先也、明乎郊社之禮、禘嘗之義、治國其如示諸掌乎。

二十章 一 哀公問政。

6. "By the ceremonies of the sacrifices to Heaven and Earth they served God, and by the ceremonies of the ancestral temple they sacrificed to their ancestors. He who understands the ceremonies of the sacrifices to Heaven and Earth, and the meaning of the several sacrifices to ancestors, would find the government of a kingdom as easy as to look into his palm!"

CHAPTER XX. 1. The duke Gae asked about government.

important, as the Jesuits mainly based on them the defence of their practice in permitting their converts to continue the sacrifices to their ancestors. We read in 'Confucius Sinarum philosophus,'—the work of Intorcetta and others, to which I have made frequent reference;—*Ex plurimis et clarissimis textibus Sinicis probari potest, legitimum praedicti axiomatis sensum esse, quod eadem intentione et formali motivo Sinenses naturalem pietatem et politicum obsequium erga defunctos exercerent, sicuti erga eosdem adhuc superstites exercebant, ex quibus et ex infra dicendis prudens lector facile deducet, hos ritus circa defunctos fuisse mere civiles, institutos dumtaxat in honorem et obsequium parentum, etiam post mortem non intermittendum; nam si quid illic divinum agnovissent, cur diceret Confucius—Priscos servire solitos defunctis, uti iisdem serviebant viventibus.*' This is ingenious reasoning, but it does not meet the fact that sacrifice is an entirely new element introduced into the service of the dead. 6. I do not understand how it is that their sacrifices to God are adduced here as an illustration of the filial piety of king Wăn and king Woo. What is said about them, however, is important, in reference to the views which we should form about the ancient religion of China. K'ang-shing took 郊 to be the sacrifice to Heaven, offered, at the winter solstice, in the southern suburb (郊) of the imperial city; and 社 to be that offered to the Earth, at the summer solstice, in the northern. Choo He agrees with him. Both of them, however, add that after 上帝 we are to understand 后土, 'Sovereign Earth (不言后土者省文).' This view of 社 here is vehemently controverted by Maou and many others. But neither the opinion of the two great commentators that 后土 is suppressed for the sake of brevity, nor the opinion of others that by 社 we are to understand the tutelary deities of the soil, affects the judgment of the sage himself, that the service of one being—even of God—was designed by all those ceremonies. See my 'Notions of the Chinese concerning God and Spirits,' pp. 50–52. The ceremonies of the ancestral temple embrace the great and less frequent services of the 禘 and 祫 (see the Ana., III. x, xi.) and the seasonal sacrifices, of which only the autumnal one (嘗) is specified here. The old commentators take 示 as = 寘, with the meaning of 置, 'to place,' and interpret—'the government of the kingdom would be as easy as to place anything in the palm.' This view is defended in the 中庸說. It has the advantage of accounting better for the 諸. We are to understand 'the meaning of the sacrifices to ancestors,' as including all the uses mentioned in par. 4. I said above that I could not understand the connection between the first part of this par. and the general object of the chapter. Taking the par. by itself, it teaches that a proper knowledge and practice of the duties of religion and filial piety would amply equip a ruler for all the duties of his government.

20. ON GOVERNMENT: SHOWING PRINCIPALLY HOW IT DEPENDS ON THE CHARACTER OF THE OFFICERS ADMINISTERING IT, AND HOW THAT DEPENDS ON THE CHARACTER OF THE SOVEREIGN HIMSELF. We have here one of the fullest expositions of Confucius' views on this subject, though he unfolds them only as a description of the government of the kings Wăn and Woo. In the chapter there is the remarkable intermingling, which we have seen in 'The Great Learning,' of what is peculiar to a ruler, and what is of universal application. From the concluding paragraphs, the transition is easy to the next and most difficult part of the Work.

二 子曰、文武之政、布在方策、其人存、則其政擧、其人亡、則其政息。三 人道敏政、地道敏樹、夫政也者、蒲盧也。四 故爲政在人、取人以身、脩身以道、脩道以仁。五 仁者、人也、親親爲大、義者、宜也、尊賢

2. The Master said, "The government of Wăn and Woo is displayed in *the records*,—the tablets of wood and bamboo. Let there be the men and the government will flourish; but without the men, their government decays and ceases."

3. "With the *right* men the growth of government is rapid, just as vegetation is rapid in the earth; and moreover *their* government *might be called* an easily-growing rush.

4. "Therefore the administration of government lies in *getting proper* men. Such men are to be got by means of *the ruler's own* character. That character is to be cultivated by his treading in the ways *of duty*. And the treading those ways of duty is to be cultivated by the cherishing of benevolence.

5. "Benevolence is *the characteristic element of* humanity, and the great exercise of it is in loving relatives. Righteousness is *the accordance of actions with what is* right, and the great exercise of

This chapter is found also in the 家語, but with considerable additions.

1. 哀公.—See Ana. II. xix, et al. 2. The 方 were tablets of wood, one of which might contain up to 100 characters. The 策 were 簡, or slips of bamboo tied together. In 其人, 其=such, i.e., rulers like Wăn and Woo, and ministers such as they had. 3. K'ang-shing and Ying-tă take 敏 as=勉, 'to exert one's-self,' and interpret:—'A ruler ought to exert himself in the practice of government, as the earth exerts itself to produce and to nurture (樹=殖).' Choo He takes 敏 as=速, 'hasty,' 'to make haste.' 人道敏政,—'man's way hastens government;' but the 人 must be taken with special reference to the preceding par., as in the translation. The old comm. took 蒲盧 as the name of an insect, (so it is defined in the 爾雅) a kind of bee, said to take the young of the mulberry caterpillar, and keep them in its hole, where they are transformed into bees. So, they said, does government transform the people. This is in acc. with the paragraph, as we find it in the 家語,—天道敏生,人道敏政,地道敏樹,夫政者猶蒲盧也,待化以成. This view is maintained also in the 中庸說. But we cannot hesitate in preferring Choo He's, as in the translation. The other is too absurd. He takes 盧, as if it were 蘆=葦, which, as well as 蒲, is the name of various rushes or sedges. 4. In the 家語, for 在人, we have 在於得人, which is, no doubt, the meaning. By 道 here, says Choo He, are intended 'the duties of universal obligation,' in par. 8, 'which,' adds Maou, 'are the

爲大、親親之殺、尊賢之等、禮所生也。八在下位、不獲乎上、民不可得而治矣。九故君子、不可以不脩身、思脩身、不可以不事親、思事親、不可以不知人、思知人、不可以不知天。十天下之達道五、所以行之者三、曰君臣也、

it is in honouring the worthy. The decreasing measures of the love due to relatives, and the steps in the honour due to the worthy, are produced by *the principle of* propriety.

6. "When those in inferior situations do not possess the confidence of their superiors, they cannot retain the government of the people.

7. "Hence the sovereign may not neglect the cultivation of his own character. Wishing to cultivate his character, he may not neglect to serve his parents. In order to serve his parents, he may not neglect to acquire a knowledge of men. In order to know men, he may not dispense with a knowledge of Heaven.

8. "The duties of universal obligation are five, and the virtues wherewith they are practised are three. The duties are those between sovereign and minister, between father and son, between hus-

ways of the Mean, in accordance with the nature.' 5. 仁者人也, 'Benevolence is man.' We find the same language in Mencius, and in the Le-ke, XXXII. 16. This virtue is called *jin*, 'because loving, feeling, and the forbearing nature, belong to man, as he is born. They are that whereby man is man.' See the 中庸說, *in loc.* 殺,—upper 3d tone, read *shae*. It is opposed to 隆, and means 'decreasing,' 'growing less.' For 禮所生 we have, in the 家語, 禮所以生, which would seem to mean—'are that whereby ceremonies are produced.' But there follow the words—禮者政之本也. The 'produced' in the translation can only='distinguished.' Ying-ta explains 生 by 辨明. 6. This has crept into the text here by mistake. It belongs to par. 17, below. We do not find it here in the 家語. 7. 君子 is here the *ruler* or *sovereign*. I fail in trying to trace the connection between the different parts of this par. 'He may not be without knowing men.'—Why? 'Because,' we are told, 'it is by honouring, and being courteous to the worthy, and securing them as friends, that a man perfects his virtue, and is able to serve his relatives.' 'He may not be without knowing Heaven.'—Why? 'Because,' it is said, 'the gradations in the love of relatives and the honouring the worthy, are all heavenly arrangements, and a heavenly order, natural, necessary, principles.' But in this explanation, 知人 has a very different meaning from what it has in the previous clause. 親, too, is here *parents*, its meaning being more restricted than in par. 5. 8. From this down to par. 11, there is brought before us the character of the '*men*,' mentioned in par. 2, on whom depends the flourishing of '*government*,' which government is exhibited in parr. 12—15. 天下之達道,—'the paths proper to be trodden by all under heaven,

父子也、夫婦也、昆弟也、朋友之交也、五者、天下之達道也、知、仁、勇、三者、天下之達德也、所以行之者一也。九節或生而知之、或學而知之、或困而知之、及其知之、一也、或安而行之、或利而行之、或勉强而行之、及其成功、一也。十節子曰、好學近乎知、力行近乎仁、知恥近乎勇。

band and wife, between elder brother and younger, and those belonging to the intercourse of friends. Those five are the duties of universal obligation. Knowledge, magnanimity, and energy, these three, are the virtues universally binding. And the means by which they carry *the duties* into practice is singleness.

9. "Some are born with the knowledge *of those duties;* some know them by study; and some acquire the knowledge after a painful feeling of their ignorance. But the knowledge being possessed, it comes to the same thing. Some practise them with a natural ease; some from a desire for their advantages; and some by strenuous effort. But the achievement being made, it comes to the same thing."

=the path of the Mean. 知=智, is the *knowledge* necessary to choose the detailed courses of duty. 仁 (=心之公, 'the unselfishness of the heart') is the *magnanimity* (so I style it for want of a better term) to pursue it. 勇, is the *valiant energy*, which maintains the perseverance of the choice and the practice. 所以行之者一也,—this, acc. to Ying-ta, means—'From the various kings (百王) downwards, in the practising these five duties, and three virtues, there has been but one method. There has been no change in modern times and ancient.' This, however, is not satisfactory. We want a substantive meaning, for 一. This Choo He gives us. He says:—一 則誠而已, '一 is simply sincerity;' the sincerity, that is, on which the rest of the work dwells with such strange predication. I translate, therefore, 一 here by *singleness*. There seems a reference in the term to 獨, ch. I. p. 3. The singleness is that of the soul in the apprehension and practice of the duties of the Mean, which is attained to by watchfulness over one's-self, when *alone*. 行之 I understand as in the second clause of the paragraph. 9. Compare Ana., XVI. i. 10. 利,—comp. Ana. XV. ii. 强,—up. 2d tone, "to force," to employ violent efforts. Choo He says:—'The 之 in 知之, and 行之, refers to the duties of universal obligation.' But is there the threefold difference in the *knowledge* of those duties? And who are they

十一 知斯三者、則知所以脩身、知所以脩身、則知所以治人、知所以治人、則知所以治天下國家矣。十二 凡爲天下國家有九經、曰、脩身也、尊賢也、親親也、敬大臣也、體群臣也、子庶民也、來百工

10. The Master said, "To be fond of learning is to be near to knowledge. To practise with vigour is to be near to magnanimity. To possess the feeling of shame is to be near to energy.

11. "He who knows these three things, knows how to cultivate his own character. Knowing how to cultivate his own character, he knows how to govern other men. Knowing how to govern other men, he knows how to govern the empire with all its States and families.

12. "All who have the government of the Empire with its States and families have nine standard rules to follow;—viz., the cultivation of their own characters; the honouring of men of virtue and talents; affection towards their relatives; respect towards the great ministers; kind and considerate treatment of the whole body of officers; dealing with the mass of the people as children; encouraging the resort of all classes of artizans; indulgent treatment of men from a distance; and the kindly cherishing of the princes of the States.

who can practise them with entire ease? 10. Choo He observes that 子曰 is here superfluous. In the 家語, however, we find the last par. followed by—'The duke said, Your words are beautiful and perfect, but I am stupid, and unable to accomplish this.' Then comes this par.—'Confucius said,' &c. The 子曰, therefore, prove, that Tsze-sze took this chapter from some existing document, that which we have in the 家語, or some other. Conf. words were intended to encourage and stimulate the duke, telling him that the three grand virtues might be nearly, if not absolutely, attained to. 知恥,—'knowing to be ashamed,' i.e., being ashamed at being below others, leading to the determination not to be so. 11. 'These three things' are the three things in the last paragraph, which make an approximation at least to the three virtues which connect with the discharge of duty attainable by every one. What connects the various steps of the climax is the unlimited confidence in the power of the example of the ruler, which we have had occasion to point out so frequently in 'The Great Learning.' 12. These nine standard rules, it is to be borne in mind, constitute the government of Wan and Woo, referred to in par. 2. Comm. arrange the 4th and 5th rules, under the second; and the 6th, 7th, 8th, and 9th, under the third, so that after 'the cultivation of the person,' we have here an expansion of 親親 and 尊賢, in par. 5. 凡爲—爲=治, 'to govern.' The student will do well to understand a 者 after 家. 尊賢,—by the 賢 here are understood specially the officers called 師, 傅, and 保, the 三公 and the 三孤, who, as teachers, and guardians, were not styled 臣, 'ministers,' or 'servants.' See the Shoo-king V. xxi. 5, 6. 敬大臣,—by the 大臣 are understood

也、柔遠人也、懷諸侯也。○十三節 脩身、則道立、尊賢、則不惑、親親、則諸父昆弟不怨、敬大臣、則不眩、體群臣、則事之報禮重、子庶民、則百姓勸、來百工、則財用足、柔遠人、則四方歸之、懷諸侯、則天

13. "By the ruler's cultivation of his own character, the duties *of universal obligation* are set forth. By honouring men of virtue and talents, he is preserved from errors of judgment. By showing affection to his relatives, there is no grumbling nor resentment among his uncles and brethren. By respecting the great ministers, he is kept from errors in the practice of government. By kind and considerate treatment of the whole body of officers, they are led to make the most grateful return for his courtesies. By dealing with the mass of the people as his children, they are led to exhort one another to what is good. By encouraging the resort of all classes of artizans, his resources for expenditure are rendered ample. By indulgent treatment of men from a distance, they are brought to resort to him from all quarters. And by kindly cherishing the princes of the States, the whole empire is brought to revere him.

the six 卿,—the minister of Instruction, the minister of Religion, &c. See the Shoo-king, V. xxi. 7—13. 體羣臣,—the 羣臣 are the host of subordinate officers after the two prec. classes. K'ang-shing says,—體猶接納, '體=to receive,' to which Ying-tâ adds—與之同體, 'being of the same body with them.' Choo He brings out the force of the term in this way:—體謂設以身處其地,而察其心也, '體 means that he places himself in their place, and so examines their feelings.' 子庶民,—子 is a verb, 'to make children of,' 'to treat kindly as children.' 來百工,—來=招來, 'to call to come,'—'to encourage.' The 百工, or 'various artizans,' were, by the statutes of Chow, under the superintendence of a special officer, and it was his business to draw them out and forth from among the people. See the Chow-le, XXXIX. 1—4. 柔遠人,—Choo He by 遠人 understands 賓旅, 'guests or envoys, and travellers, or travelling merchants.' K'ang-shing understands by them 蕃國之諸侯, 'the princes of surrounding kingdoms,' *i. e.*, of the tribes that lay beyond the six *fuh* (服), or feudal tenures of the Chow rule. But these would hardly be spoken of before the 諸侯. And among *them*, in the 9th rule, would be included the 賓, or guests, the princes themselves at the imperial court, or their envoys. I doubt whether any others beside the 旅, or travelling merchants, are intended by the 遠人. If we may adopt, however, K'ang-shing's view, this is the rule for the treatment of foreigners by the government of China. 13. This par. describes the happy effects of observing the above nine rules. 道立,—by 道 are understood the five duties of universal obligation. We read in the 日講:—'About these nine rules, the only trouble is, that sovereigns

下畏之。○十四齊明盛服、非禮不動、所以脩身也、去讒、遠色、賤貨、而貴德、所以勸賢也、尊其位、重其祿、同其好惡、所以勸親親也、官盛任使、所以勸大臣也、忠信重祿、所以勸士也、時使薄斂、所以勸百姓也、日省月試、既

14. "Self-adjustment and purification, with careful regulation of his dress, and the not making a movement contrary to the rules of propriety:—this is the way for the ruler to cultivate his person. Discarding slanderers, and keeping himself from *the seductions of* beauty; making light of riches, and giving honour to virtue:—this is the way for him to encourage men of worth and talents. Giving them places *of honour* and large emolument, and sharing with them in their likes and dislikes:—this is the way for him to encourage his relatives to love him. Giving them numerous officers to discharge their orders and commissions:—this is the way for him to encourage the great ministers. According to them a generous confidence, and making their emoluments large:—this is the way to encourage the body of officers. Employing them only at the proper times, and making the imposts light:—this is the way to encourage the people. By daily examinations and monthly trials, and by making their rations in accordance with their labours:—this is the way to encourage the classes of artizans. To escort them on their departure and meet

are not able to practise them strenuously. Let the ruler be really able to cultivate his person, then will the universal duties and universal virtues be all-complete, so that he shall be an example to the whole empire, with its States and families. Those duties will be set up (道立), and men will know what to imitate.' 不惑 means, acc. to Choo He, '不疑於理,' 'he will have no doubts as to principle.' K'ang-shing explains it by 謀者良, 'his counsels will be good.' This latter is the meaning, the worthies being those specified in the note on the preceding par., their sovereign's counsellors and guides. The addition of 諸 determines the 父 to be uncles. See the 爾雅, I. iv. 昆弟 are all the younger branches of the ruler's kindred. 不眩 = 不惑, but the deception and mistake will be in the affairs in charge of those great ministers. 羣臣 and 士 are the same parties. 勸,—as in Ana. II. xx. Ying-ta explains it here—'They will exhort and stimulate one another to serve their ruler.' On 財用足, Choo He says:—來百工,則通功易事,農末相資,故財用足, 'The resort of all classes of artisans being encouraged, there is an intercommunication of the productions of labour, and an interchange of men's services, and the husbandman and the trafficker,' (it is this class which is designed by 末)

稟稱事、所以勸百工也、送往迎來、嘉善而矜不能、所以柔遠人也、繼絕世、舉廢國、治亂持危、朝聘以時、厚往而薄來、所以懷諸侯也、〇十五節 凡為天下國家有九經、所以行之者一也、〇十六節 凡事豫則立、不豫則廢、言前定、則不

them on their coming; to commend the good among them, and show compassion to the incompetent:—this is the way to treat indulgently men from a distance. To restore families whose line of succession has been broken, and to revive States that have been extinguished; to reduce to order States that are in confusion, and support those which are in peril; to have fixed times for their own reception at court, and the reception of their envoys; to send them away after liberal treatment, and welcome their coming with small contributions:—this is the way to cherish the princes of the States.

15. "All who have the government of the empire with its States and families have the above nine standard rules. And the means by which they are carried into practice is singleness.

16. "In all things success depends on previous preparation, and without such previous preparation there is sure to be failure. If what is to be spoken be previously determined, there will be no

'are aiding to one another. Hence the resources for expenditure are sufficient.' I suppose that Choo felt a want of some mention of agriculture in connection with these rules, and thought to find a place for it here. Maou would make 財=材, and 用=器物. See the 中庸說, in loc. Comp. also 大學傳, x. 19. K'ang-shing understands 四方 as meaning 蕃國, 'frontier kingdoms,' but the usage of the phrase is against such an interpretation. 14. After 天下畏之, we have in the 家語,—公曰, 爲之奈何, 'The duke said, *How are these rules to be practised?*' and then follows this par., preceded by 孔子曰, 'Confucius said.' 齊明盛服—comp. ch. xvi. 3. The blending together, as equally important, attention to inward purity and to dress, seems strange enough to a western reader. 勸, throughout,—'to encourage,' 'to stimulate in a friendly way.' I have translated 親親 after the 合講, which says 勸親親謂親之親我. The 1st 親 is the noun, and the 2d the verb, just the reverse of the phrase in its previous occurrences. The use of 忠 in reference to the prince's treatment of the officers is strange, but the translation gives what appears to be the meaning. K'ang-shing explained:—'Making large the emolument of the loyal and sincere;' but, according to the analogy of all the other clauses, 忠 and 信 must be descriptive of the ruler. 時使,—comp. Ana. I. v. For 既稟 we have in the 家語, 餼廩.

跲、事前定、則不困、行前定、則不疚、道前定、則不窮。○十七節在下位、不獲乎上、民不可得而治矣、獲乎上有道、不信乎朋友、不獲乎上矣、信乎朋友有道、不順乎親、不信乎朋友矣、順乎親有道、反諸身不誠、不順乎親矣、誠

stumbling. If affairs be previously determined, there will be no difficulty with them. If one's actions have been previously determined, there will be no sorrow in connection with them. If principles of conduct have been previously determined, the practice of them will be inexhaustible.

17. "When those in inferior situations do not obtain the confidence of the sovereign, they cannot succeed in governing the people. There is a way to obtain the confidence of the sovereign;—if one is not trusted by his friends, he will not get the confidence of his sovereign. There is a way to being trusted by one's friends;—if one is not obedient to his parents, he will not be true to friends. There is a way to being obedient to one's parents;—if one, on turning his

which K'ang-shing explains by 稍食, 'rations allowed by government.' See Morrison, char. 稍. Choo He follows K'ang-shing in this, but I agree with Maou, that 槩 and not 稍 is to be substituted here for 既. 稱, up. 3d tone, 'to weigh,' 'to be according to.' The trials and examinations, with these rations, show that the artizans are not to be understood of such dispersed among the people, but as collected under the superintendence of the government. Ambassadors from foreign countries have been received up to the present century, according to the rules here prescribed, and the two last regulations are quite in harmony with the moral and political superiority that China claims over the countries which they may represent. But in the case of travellers, and travelling merchants, passing from one state to another, there were anciently regulations, which may be adduced to illustrate all the expressions here. See the 中庸說, and the 日講 in loc. 繼絕世, 舉廢國,—see Ana. XX. i. 7. 15. We naturally understand 所以行之者一也, as meaning—'the means by which they are carried into practice is one and the same.' Then this means will be the 豫, or 'previous preparation' of the next par. This is the interpretation of K'ang-shing and Ying-ta, who take the two parr. together. But acc. to Choo He, 'the one thing' is *sincerity*, as in par. 8. 16. The 'all things' is to be understood with reference to the universal duties, the universal virtues, and the nine standard rules. 17. The object of this par. seems to be to show that the singleness, or sincerity, lies at the basis of that previous preparation, which is essential to success in any and every thing. The steps of the climax conduct us to it as the mental state, necessary to all virtues, and this sincerity is again made dependent on the understanding of what is good, upon which point see the next chapter. 不獲乎上, = acc. to Ying-ta, 不得於君上之意, 'do not get the mind—pleased feeling—of the sovereign.' We use 'to gain,' and 'to win,' sometimes, in a similar way. 18. Premare (*Not. Lin. Sin.*, p. 156) says:—'誠者 est in abstracto, et 誠之者 est in con-

身有道、不明乎善、不
誠乎身矣。○十八節 誠者、天之
道也、誠之者、人之道
也、誠者、不勉而中、不
思而得、從容中道、聖
人也、誠之者、擇善而
固執之者也。○十九節 博學之、
審問之、慎思之、明辨
之、篤行之。○二十節 有弗學、學
之弗能、弗措也、有弗

thoughts in upon himself, finds a want of sincerity, he will not be obedient to his parents. There is a way to the attainment of sincerity in one's-self;—if a man do not understand what is good, he will not attain sincerity in himself.

18. "Sincerity is the way of Heaven. The attainment of sincerity is the way of men. He who possesses sincerity, is he who, without an effort, hits what is right, and apprehends, without the exercise of thought;—he is the sage who naturally and easily embodies the *right* way. He who attains to sincerity, is he who chooses what is good, and firmly holds it fast.

19. "To this attainment there are requisite the extensive study of what is good, accurate inquiry about it, careful reflection on it, the clear discrimination of it, and the earnest practice of it.

20. "The superior man, while there is any thing he has not studied, or while in what he has studied there is any thing he cannot understand, will not intermit his labour. While there is any thing

ness.' This is not quite correct. For 誠者 is in the concrete, as much as the other, and is said, below, to be characteristic of the sage. 誠者 is the quality possessed absolutely. 誠之者 is the same acquired. 'The way of Heaven,'—this, acc. to Ying-tâ, = 'the way which Heaven pursues.' Choo He explains it 天理之本然, 'the fundamental natural course of heavenly principle.' Maou says:—此猶中庸之率性以爲道者也，本乎天也, 'this is like the accordance of nature in the Mean, considered to be THE PATH, having its root in Heaven.' We might acquiesce in this, but for the opposition of 人之道, on which Maou says:—此猶中庸之修道以爲道者也，成乎人也,—'this is like the cultivation of the path in the Mean, considered to be THE PATH, having its completion from man.' But this takes the second and third utterances in the Work as independent sentiments, which they certainly are not. I do not see my way to rest in any but the old interpretation, extravagant as it is.—At this point, the chapter in the 家語 ceases to be the same with that before us, and diverges to another subject. 19. There are here described the different processes which lead to the attainment of sincerity. The gloss in the 備旨 says that 'the five 之 all refer to the *what is good* in the last ch., the five universal duties, and the nine standard rules being included therein.' Rather it seems

問、問之弗知、弗措也、有弗思、思之弗得、弗措也、有弗辨、辨之弗明、弗措也、有弗行、行之弗篤、弗措也、人一能之、己百之、人十能之、己千之。廿一節 果能此道矣、雖愚必明、雖柔必強。

廿一章 自誠明、謂之性、自

he has not inquired about, or any thing in what he has inquired about which he does not know, he will not intermit his labour. While there is any thing which he has not reflected on, or any thing in what he has reflected on which he does not apprehend, he will not intermit his labour. While there is any thing which he has not discriminated, or his discrimination is not clear, he will not intermit his labour. If there be any thing which he has not practised, or his practice fails in earnestness, he will not intermit his labour. If another man succeed by one effort, he will use a hundred efforts. If another man succeed by ten efforts, he will use a thousand.

21. "Let a man proceed in this way, and, though dull, he will surely become intelligent; though weak, he will surely become strong."

CHAPTER XXI. When we have intelligence resulting from sincerity, this condition is to be ascribed to nature; when we have sincerity resulting from intelligence, this condition is to be ascribed

to me, that the 之, acc. to the idiom pointed out several times in the Analects, simply intensifies the meaning of the diff. verbs, whose regimen it is. 20. Here we have the determination which is necessary in the prosecution of the above processes, and par. 21 states the result of it. Choo He makes a pause at the end of the first clause in each part of the par., and interprets thus:—'If he do not study, well. But if he do, he will not give over till he understands what he studies,' and so on. But it seems more natural to carry the supposition in 有 over the whole of every part, as in the translation, which moreover substantially agrees with Ying-ta's interpretation.—Here terminates the third part of the Work. It was to illustrate, as Choo He told us, how 'the path of the Mean cannot be left.' The author seems to have kept this point before him in chapters xiii—xvi., but the next three are devoted to the one subject of filial piety, and the 20th, to the general subject of government. Some things are said worthy of being remembered, and others which require a careful sifting; but, on the whole, we do not find ourselves advanced in an understanding of the argument of the Work.

21. THE RECIPROCAL CONNECTION OF SINCERITY AND INTELLIGENCE. With this chap. commences the fourth part of the Work, which, as Choo observes in his concluding note, is an expansion of the 18th par. of the prec. chapter. It is, in a great measure, a glorification of the sage, finally resting in the person of Confucius, but the high character of the sage, it is maintained, is not unattainable by others. He realizes the ideal of humanity, but by his example and lessons, the same ideal is brought within the reach of many, perhaps of all. The ideal of humanity,—the perfect character belonging to the sage, which ranks him on a level with Hea-

明誠、謂之教、誠則明矣、明則誠矣。

右第二十一章、子思承上章、夫子天道人道之意、而立言也、自此以下十二章、皆子思之言、以反覆推明此章之意。

二十二 唯天下至誠、爲能

to instruction. But given the sincerity, and there shall be the intelligence; given the intelligence, and there shall be the sincerity.

The above is the twenty-first chapter. Tsze-sze takes up in it, and discourses from, the subjects of "the way of Heaven" and "the way of men," mentioned in the preceding chapter. The twelve chapters that follow are all from Tsze-sze, repeating and illustrating the meaning of this one.

CHAPTER XXII. It is only he who is possessed of the most complete sincerity that can exist under heaven, who can give its full

ven,—is indicated by 誠, and we have no single term in English, which can be considered as the complete equivalent of that character. The Chinese themselves had great difficulty in arriving at that definition of it which is now generally acquiesced in. In the 四書通 (quoted in the 匯參 中庸, xvi. 8), we are told that 'the Han scholars were all ignorant of its meaning. Under the Sung dynasty, first came 李邦直 who defined it by 不欺, *freedom from all deception*. After him, 徐仲車 said that it meant 不息, *ceaselessness*. Then, one of the Ch'ing called it 無妄, *freedom from all moral error*; and finally, Choo He added to this the positive element of 眞實, *truth and reality*, on which the definition of 誠 was complete.' Remusat calls it—*la perfection*, and '*la perfection morale*.' Intorcetta and his friends call it—*vera solidaque perfectio*. Simplicity or singleness of soul seems to be what is chiefly intended by the term;—the disposition to, and capacity of, what is good, without any deteriorating element, with no defect of intelligence, or intromission of selfish thoughts. This belongs to Heaven, to Heaven and Earth, and to the sage. Men, not naturally sages, may, by cultivating the intelligence of what is good, raise themselves to this elevation. 性 and 教 carry us back to the first chapter, but the terms have a different force, and the longer I dwell upon it, the more am I satisfied with Choo He's pronouncement in his 語類, that 性 is here 性之, 'possessing from nature,' and 教=學之, 'learning it,' and therefore I have translated 謂之 by—'is to be ascribed to.' When, however, he makes a difference in the connection between the parts of the two clauses—誠則明矣, 明則誠矣, and explains—誠則無不明, 明則可以至誠, 'sincerity is invariably intelligent, and intelligence may arrive at sincerity,' this is not dealing fairly with his text.

Here, at the outset, I may observe that, in this portion of the Work, there are specially the three following dogmas, which are more than questionable:—1st, That there are some men—sages—naturally in a state of moral perfection; 2d, That the same moral perfection is attainable by others, in whom its development is impeded by their material organization, and the influence of

盡其性，能盡其性，則能盡人之性，能盡人之性，則能盡物之性，能盡物之性，則可以贊天地之化育，可以贊天地之化育，則可以與天地參矣。

development to his nature. Able to give its full development to his own nature, he can do the same to the nature of other men. Able to give its full development to the nature of other men, he can give their full development to the natures of animals and things. Able to give their full development to the natures of creatures and things, he can assist the transforming and nourishing powers of Heaven and Earth. Able to assist the transforming and nourishing powers of Heaven and Earth, he may with Heaven and Earth form a ternion.

external things; and 3d, That the understanding of what is good will certainly lead to such moral perfection.

22. THE RESULTS OF SINCERITY; AND HOW THE POSSESSOR OF IT FORMS A TERNION WITH HEAVEN AND EARTH. On 天下至誠, Choo He says that it denotes 'the reality of the virtue of the sage, to which there is nothing in the world that can be added.' This is correct, and if we were to render—'It is only the most sincere man under heaven,' the translation would be wrong. 盡 means simply 'to exhaust,' but, by what processes and in what way, the character tells us nothing about. The 'giving full development to his nature,' however, may be understood with Maou, as='pursuing THE PATH in accordance with his nature, so that what Heaven has conferred on him is displayed without shortcoming or let.' The 'giving its development to the nature of other men' indicates the sage's helping them, by his example and lessons, to perfect themselves. 'His exhausting the nature of things,' *i.e.*, of all other beings, animate and inanimate, is, acc. to Choo He, 'knowing them completely, and dealing with them correctly,' 'so,' add the paraphrasts, 'that he secures their prosperous increase and development according to their nature. Here, however, a Buddhist idea appears in Choo He's commentary. He says:—'The nature of other men and things (=animals) is the same with my nature,' which, it is observed in Maou's work, is the same with the Buddhist sentiment, that 'a dog has the nature of Buddha,' and with that of the philosopher Kaou, that 'a dog's nature is the same as a man's.' Maou himself illustrates the 'exhausting the nature of things,' by reference to the Shoo-king IV. iii. 2, where we are told that under the first sovereigns of the Hea dynasty, 'the mountains and rivers, all enjoyed tranquillity, and the birds and beasts, the fishes and tortoises, all realized the happiness of their nature.' It is thus that the sage 'assists Heaven and Earth.' K'ang-ching, indeed, explains this by saying:—'The sage, receiving Heaven's appointment to the imperial throne, extends every where a happy tranquillity.' Evidently there is a reference in the language to the mystical paragraph in the 1st chapter—致中和.天地位焉.萬物育焉. 'Heaven and Earth' take the place here of the single term—'Heaven,' in ch. xx. par. 18. On this Ying-tă observes:—It is said above, *sincerity is the way of Heaven*, and here mention is made also of *Earth*. The reason is, that the reference above, was to the principle of sincerity in its spiritual and mysterious origin, and thence the expression simple,—*The way of Heaven*; but here we have the transformation and nourishing seen in the production of things, and hence *Earth* is associated with *Heaven*.' This is not very intelligible, but it is to bring out the idea of a *ternion*, that the great, supreme, ruling, Power is thus dualized. 參 is 'a file of three,' and I employ 'ternion,' to express the idea, just as we use 'quaternion,' for a file of four. What is it but blasphemy, thus to file man with the supreme Power?

〖二十三〗其次致曲、曲能有誠、誠則形、形則著、著則明、明則動、動則變、變則化、唯天下至誠、爲能化。

〖二十四〗至誠之道、可以前知、國家將興、必有禎祥、國家將亡、必有妖孽、見乎蓍龜、動乎四體、禍福將至、善、必先

CHAPTER XXIII. Next to the above is he who cultivates to the utmost the shoots *of goodness* in him. From these he can attain to the possession of sincerity. This sincerity becomes apparent. From being apparent, it becomes manifest. From being manifest, it becomes brilliant. Brilliant, it affects others. Affecting others, they are changed by it. Changed by it, they are transformed. It is only he who is possessed of the most complete sincerity that can exist under heaven, who can transform.

CHAPTER XXIV. It is characteristic of the most entire sincerity to be able to foreknow. When a nation or family is about to flourish, there are sure to be happy omens; and when it is about to perish, there are sure to be unlucky omens. *Such events are* seen in the milfoil and tortoise, and affect the movements of the four limbs.

23. THE WAY OF MAN;—THE DEVELOPMENT OF PERFECT SINCERITY IN THOSE NOT NATURALLY POSSESSED OF IT. 其次, 'the next,' or 'his next,' referring to the 自誠明者, of ch. xxi. 曲 is defined by Choo He—一偏, 'one half,' 'a part.' K'ang-hsi explains it by 小小之事, 'very small matters.' Maou defines it by 隅, 'a corner,' and refers to Ana. VII. viii, 舉一隅不以三隅反, as a sentiment analogous to the one in 致曲. There is difficulty about the term. It properly means 'crooked,' and with a bad application, like 偏, often signifies 'deflection from what is straight and right.' Yet it cannot have a bad meaning here, for if it have, the phrase,—致曲, will be, in the connection, unintelligible. One writer uses this comparison:—'Put a stone on a bamboo shoot, or where the shoot would show itself, and it will travel round the stone, and come out *crookedly* at its side.' So it is with the good nature, whose free development is repressed. It shows itself in shoots, but if they be cultivated and improved, a moral condition and influence may be attained, equal to that of the sage.

24. THAT ENTIRE SINCERITY CAN FOREKNOW. 至誠之道 is the quality in the abstract, while 至誠 at the end, is the entirely sincere individual,—the sage, by nature, or by attainment. 禎祥, 'lucky omens.' In the dict., 祥 is used to define 禎. 祥 may be used also of inauspicious omens, but here it cannot embrace such. Distinguishing between the two terms, Ying-ta says that unusual appearances of things existing in a country are 祥, and appearances of things new are 禎. 妖孽 are 'unlucky omens,' the former being spoken of 'prodigies of plants, and of strangely dressed boys singing ballads,' and the latter of prodi-

知之、不善、必先知之、故至誠如神。

第二十五章 誠者、自成也、而道、自道也。誠者、物之終始、不誠無物、是故君子誠之為貴。誠者、非自成己而已也、所以成物

When calamity or happiness is about to come, the good shall certainly be foreknown by him, and the evil also. Therefore the individual possessed of the most complete sincerity is like a spirit.

CHAPTER XXV. 1. Sincerity is that whereby self-completion is effected, and *its* way is that by which man must direct himself.

2. Sincerity is the end and beginning of things; without sincerity there would be nothing. On this account, the superior man regards the attainment of sincerity as the most excellent thing.

3. The possessor of sincerity does not merely accomplish the self-completion of himself. With this quality he completes *other men and* things *also*. The completing himself *shows his* perfect virtue.

gious animals. The subject of the verbs 見 and 動 is the events, not the omens. For the milfoil and tortoise, see the Yîh-king, App. I. xi. They are there called 神物, 'spiritual things.' Divination by the milfoil was called 筮; that by the tortoise was called 卜. They were used from the highest antiquity. See the Shoo-king, II. ii. 18; V. iv. 20-30. 四體, 'four limbs,' are by K'ang-shing interpreted of the feet of the tortoise, each foot being peculiarly appropriate to divination in a particular season. Choo He interprets them of the four limbs of the human body. 如神 must be left as indefinite in the translation as it is in the text.—The whole chapter is eminently absurd, and gives a character of ridiculousness to all the magniloquent teaching about 'entire sincerity.' The foreknowledge attributed to the sage,—the mate of Heaven,—is only a guessing by means of augury, sorcery, and other follies.

25. HOW FROM SINCERITY COMES SELF-COMPLETION, AND THE COMPLETION OF OTHERS AND OF THINGS. I have had difficulty in translating this chapter, because it is difficult to understand it. We wish that we had the writer before us to question him; but if we had, it is not likely that he would be able to afford us much satisfaction. Persuaded that what he denominates *sincerity* is a figment, we may not wonder at the extravagance of its predicates. 1. All the commen. of the Sung school say, that 誠 is here 天命之性 'the Heaven-conferred nature,' and that 道 is 率性之道, 'the path which is in accordance with the nature.' They are probably correct, but the difficulty comes when we go on with this view of 誠 to the next par. 2. I translate the expansion of this in the 日講:—'All that fill up the space between heaven and earth are things (物). They end and they begin again; they begin and proceed to an end; every change being accomplished by sincerity, and every phenomenon having sincerity unceasingly in it. So far as the mind of man (人之心) is concerned, if there be not sincerity, then every movement of it is vain and false. How can an unreal mind accomplish real things? Although it may do something, that is simply equivalent to nothing. Therefore the superior man searches out the source of sincerity, and examines the evil of insincerity, chooses what is good, and firmly holds it fast, so seeking to arrive at the place of truth and reality.' Maou's explanation is:—'Now, since the reason why the sincerity of spiritual beings is so incapable of being repressed, and why they foreknow, is because they enter into things, and there is nothing without them,—shall there be anything which is without the entirely sincere man, who is as a spirit?' I have given these specimens of commentary, that the

也、成己、仁也、成物、知也、性之德也、合內外之道也、故時措之宜也。

廿六 故至誠無息、不息則久、久則徵、徵則悠遠、悠遠、則博厚、博厚、則高明、博厚、所以載物也、高明、所以覆物也、悠久、所以成物也、博厚配地、高明配天、悠久無疆、如此者、

The completing *other men and* things *shows his* knowledge. *Both these are* virtues belonging to the nature, and *this is* the way by which a union is effected of the external and internal. Therefore, whenever he—*the entirely sincere man*—employs them,—*that is, these virtues*,—*their action will be* right.

CHAPTER XXVI. 1. Hence to entire sincerity there belongs ceaselessness.

2. Not ceasing, it continues long. Continuing long, it evidences itself.

3. Evidencing itself, it reaches far. Reaching far, it becomes large and substantial. Large and substantial, it becomes high and brilliant.

4. Large and substantial;—this is how it contains *all* things. High and brilliant;—this is how it overspreads *all* things. Reaching far and continuing long;—this is how it perfects *all* things.

5. So large and substantial, *the individual possessing it* is the co-equal of Earth. So high and brilliant, it makes him the coequal of Heaven. So far-reaching and long-continuing, it makes him infinite.

reader may, if he can, by means of them, gather some apprehensible meaning from the text. 3. I have translated 成物 by—'complete other men and things *also*,' with a reference to the account of the achievements of sincerity, in ch. xxii. On 性之德也, 合外內之道也, the 日講 paraphrases:—'Now both this perfect virtue and knowledge are virtues certainly and originally belonging to our nature, to be referred for their bestowment to Heaven;—what distinction is there in them of external and internal?' —All this, so far as I can see, is but veiling ignorance by words without knowledge.

26. A PARALLEL BETWEEN THE SAGE POSSESSED OF ENTIRE SINCERITY, AND HEAVEN AND EARTH, SHOWING THAT THE SAME QUALITIES BELONG TO THEM. The first six parr. show the way of the sage; the next three show the way of Heaven and Earth; and the last brings the two ways together, in their essential nature, in a passage from the She-king. The doctrine of the chapter is liable to the criticisms which have been made on the 22d ch. And, moreover, there is in it a sad confusion of the visible heavens and earth with the immaterial power and reason which govern them; in a word, with God. 1. Because of the 故, 'hence,' or 'therefore,'

不見而章、不動而變、無爲而成。天地之道、可一言而盡也、其爲物不貳、則其生物不測。天地之道、博也、厚也、高也、明也、悠也、久也。今夫天、斯昭昭之多、及其無窮也、日月星辰繫焉、萬物覆焉、今夫地、一撮土之多、

6. Such being its nature, without any display, it becomes manifested; without any movement, it produces changes; and without any effort, it accomplishes its ends.

7. The way of Heaven and Earth may be completely declared in one sentence.—They are without any doubleness, and so they produce things in a manner that is unfathomable.

8. The way of Heaven and Earth is large and substantial, high and brilliant, far-reaching and long-enduring.

9. The heaven now before us is only this bright shining spot; but when viewed in its inexhaustible extent, the sun, moon, stars, and constellations of the zodiac, are suspended in it, and all things are overspread by it. The earth before us is but a handful of soil; but when regarded in its breadth and thickness, it sustains

Choo He is condemned by recent writers for making a new chapter to commence here. Yet the matter is sufficiently distinct from that of the preceding one. Where the 故 takes hold of the text above, however, it is not easy to discover. The gloss in the 備旨 says that it indicates a conclusion from all the preceding predicates about sincerity. 至誠 is to be understood, now in the abstract, and now in the concrete. But the 6th paragraph seems to be the place to bring out the personal idea, as I have done. 無疆, 'without bounds,'=our *infinite*. Surely it is strange—passing strange—to apply that term in the description of any created being. 7. What I said was the prime idea in 誠, viz., 'simplicity,' 'singleness of soul,' is very conspicuous here. 其爲物不貳—爲 is the subst. verb. It surprises us, however, to find Heaven and Earth called '*things*,' at the same time that they are represented as by their entire sincerity producing all things. 9. This par. is said to illustrate the unfathomableness of Heaven and Earth in producing things, showing how it springs from their sincerity, or freedom from doubleness. I have already observed how it is only the material heavens and earth which are presented to us. And not only so;—we have mountains, seas, and rivers, set forth as acting with the same unfathomableness as those entire bodies and powers. The 備旨 says on this:—'The hills and waters are what Heaven and Earth produce, and that they should yet be able themselves to produce *other* things, shows still more how Heaven and Earth, in the producing of things, are unfathomable.' The confusion and error in such representations are very lamentable. The use of 多 in the several clauses here perplexes the student. On 斯昭昭之多, Choo He says—此指其一處而言之, 'This is speaking of it'—heaven—'as it appears in one point.' In the 中庸說, *in loc.*, there is an attempt to make this

及其廣厚、載華嶽而不重、振河海而不洩、萬物載焉、今夫山、一卷石之多、及其廣大、草木生之、禽獸居之、寶藏興焉、今夫水、一勺之多、及其不測、黿鼉蛟龍魚鼈生焉、貨財殖焉。詩云、維天之命、於穆不已、蓋曰、天之所以爲天也、於乎不顯、文王之德之純、蓋曰、文王之所以爲文也、純亦不已。

mountains like the Hwa and the Yoh, without feeling their weight, and contains the rivers and seas, without their leaking away. The mountain now before us appears only a stone; but when contemplated in all the vastness of its size, we see how the grass and trees are produced on it, and birds and beasts dwell on it, and precious things which men treasure up are found on it. The water now before us appears but a ladleful; yet extending our view to its unfathomable depths, the largest tortoises, iguanas, iguanadons, dragons, fishes, and turtles, are produced in them, articles of value and sources of wealth abound in them.

10. It is said in the Book of Poetry, "The ordinances of Heaven, how profound are they and unceasing!" The meaning is, that it is thus that Heaven is Heaven. *And again*, "How illustrious was it, the singleness of the virtue of king Wăn!" indicating that it was thus that king Wăn was what he was. Singleness likewise is unceasing.

out by a definition of 多:—多餘也，言少許耳，'多 is overplus, meaning a small overplus.' 日月星辰,—comp. the Shoo-king, I. 3. In that pass., as well as here, many take 星 as meaning the planets, but we need not depart from the meaning of 'stars' generally. 辰 is applied variously, but used along with the other terms, it denotes the conjunctions of the sun and moon, which divide the circumference of the heavens into twelve parts.

華嶽,—there are five peaks, or 嶽, worshipped in China, the western one of which is called 華 (low. 3d tone) 嶽. Here, however, we are to understand by each term a particular mountain. See the 集證 and 中庸說, *in loc.* In the 集證, the Yellow river, and that only, is understood by 河, but both it and 海 must be taken generally. 卷 read *k'üen*, lower 1st tone, is in the dict., with ref. to this

一 大哉聖人之道。二 洋洋乎發育萬物，峻極于天。三 優優大哉，禮儀三百，威儀三千。四 待其人而後行。五 故曰，苟不至德，至道不凝焉。六 故君子尊德性而道問學，致廣大，

CHAPTER XXVII. 1. How great is the path proper to the sage!

2. Like overflowing water, it sends forth and nourishes all things, and rises up to the height of heaven.

3. All complete is its greatness! It embraces the three hundred rules of ceremony, and the three thousand rules of demeanour.

4. It waits for the proper man, and then it is trodden.

5. Hence it is said, "Only by perfect virtue can the perfect path, in all its courses, be made a fact."

6. Therefore, the superior man honours his virtuous nature, and maintains constant inquiry and study, seeking to carry it out to its

passage, defined by 區, 'a place,' 'a small plot.' In the 中庸說, 龜 is defined as 介蟲之元 'the first-produced of the chelonia;' 龍 as 鱗蟲之長 'the chief of scaly animals;' 黿 as being a 'kind of 龜;' 蛟 as being 'a kind of 龍,' while the 鼉 'has scales like a fish, feet like a dragon, and is related to the 龜.' By 貨 are intended pearls and valuable shells; by 財, fish, salt, &c. 10. See the She-king, IV. i. Bk. I. Ode II. st. 1. The attributes of the ordinances of Heaven, and the virtue of king Wăn, are here set forth, as substantially the same. 純='fine and pure,' 'unmixed.' The dict. gives it the distinct meaning of 'unceasingness,' quoting the last clause here,—純亦不已, as if it were definition, and not description.

27. THE GLORIOUS PATH OF THE SAGE; AND HOW THE SUPERIOR MAN ENDEAVOURS TO ATTAIN TO IT. The chapter thus divides itself into two parts, one containing five par., descriptive of the 聖人, or SAGE, and the other two, descriptive of the 君子, or *superior man*, which two appellations are to be here distinguished. 1. 'This par.,' says Choo He, 'embraces the two that follow.' They are, indeed, to be taken as exegetical of it. 道, it is said, is here, as every where else in the work (see the 翼注, *in loc.*), '*the path which is in acc. with the nature.*' The student tries to believe so, and goes on to par. 2, when the predicate about *the nourishing of all things* puzzles and confounds him. 2. 極 is not here the adverb, but=至, 'reaching to.' 3. By 禮儀, we are to understand the greater and more general principles of propriety, 'such,' says the 備旨, 'as capping, marriage, mourning, and sacrifice;' and by 威儀 are intended all the minuter observances of these. The former are also 經禮, 禮經, and 正經; the latter, 曲禮, and 動禮. See the 集證, *in loc.* 300 and 3000 are round numbers. Reference is made to these rules and their minutiæ, to show how, in every one of them, as proceeding from the sage, there is a principle, to be referred to the Heaven-given nature. 4. Comp. ch. xx. 2. In '*Confucius Sinarum Philosophus*,' it is suggested that there may be here a prophecy of the Saviour, and that the writer may have been 'under the influence of that spirit, by whose moving the Sibyls formerly prophesied of Christ.' There is nothing in the text to justify such a thought. 5. 凝, 'to congeal;' then,=成, 'to complete,' and 定, 'to

而盡精微、極高明、而道中庸、温故、而知新、敦厚以崇禮。七是故居上不驕、爲下不倍、國有道、其言足以興、國無道、其默足以容、詩曰、既明且哲、以保其身、其此之謂與。

廿八子曰、愚而好自用、賤而好自專、生乎今之世、反古之道、如此者、烖及

breadth and greatness, so as to omit none of the more exquisite and minute points which it embraces, and to raise it to its greatest height and brilliancy, so as to pursue the course of the Mean. He cherishes his old knowledge, and is continually acquiring new. He exerts an honest, generous, earnestness, in the esteem and practice of all propriety.

7. Thus, when occupying a high situation, he is not proud, and in a low situation, he is not insubordinate. When the kingdom is well-governed, he is sure by his words to rise; and when it is ill-governed, he is sure by his silence to command forbearance to himself. Is not this what we find in the Book of Poetry,—"Intelligent is he and prudent, and so preserves his person?"

CHAPTER XXVIII. 1. The Master said, "Let a man who is ignorant be fond of using his own judgment; let a man without rank be fond of assuming a directing power to himself; let a man who is living in the present age go back to the ways of antiquity;—on the persons of all who act thus calamities will be sure to come."

8x.' The whole par. is merely a repetition of the prec. one, in other words. 6. 道 in both cases here, = 由, 'to proceed from,' or 'by.' It is said correctly, that 首句是一節頭腦 'the first sentence,—尊德性而道問學, is the brains of the whole paragraph.' 温故而知新,—See Ana. II. xi. 7. This describes the superior man, largely successful in pursuing the course indicated in the prec. par. 倍,=背. 詩曰,—See the Shi-king, III. iii. Ode VI. st. 4.

28. AN ILLUSTRATION OF THE SENTENCE IN THE LAST CHAPTER—'IN A LOW SITUATION HE IS NOT INSUBORDINATE.' There does seem to be a connection of the kind thus indicated between this chapter and the last, but the principal object of what is said here, is to prepare the way for the eulogium of Confucius below,—the eulogium of him, a sage without the throne. 1. The different clauses here may be understood generally, but they have a special reference to the general scope of the chapter. Three things are required to give law to the empire: virtue (including intelligence); rank; and the right time. 愚 is he who wants the virtue; 賤 is he who wants the rank; and the last clause describes

其身者也。○二非天子、不議禮、不制度、不考文。○三今天下、車同軌、書同文、行同倫。○四雖有其位、苟無其德、不敢作禮樂焉、雖有其德、苟無其位、亦不敢作禮樂焉。○五子曰、吾說夏禮、杞不足徵也、吾學殷禮、有宋存焉、吾學周禮、今用之、吾從周。

2. To no one but the emperor does it belong to order ceremonies, to fix the measures, and to determine the characters.

3. Now, over the empire, carriages have all wheels of the same size; all writing is with the same characters; and for conduct there are the same rules.

4. One may occupy the throne, but if he have not the proper virtue, he may not dare to make ceremonies or music. One may have the virtue, but if he do not occupy the throne, he may not presume to make ceremonies or music.

5. The Master said, "I may describe the ceremonies of the Hea dynasty, but Ke cannot sufficiently attest my words. I have learned the ceremonies of the Yin dynasty, and in Sung they still continue. I have learned the ceremonies of Chow, which are now used, and I follow Chow."

the absence of the right time.—In this last clause, there would seem to be a sentiment, which should have given course in China to the doctrine of Progress. 2. This, and the two next parr. are understood to be the words of Tsze-sze, illustrating the prev. declarations of Confucius. We have here the imperial prerogatives, which might not be usurped. 'Ceremonies' are the rules regulating religion and society; 'the measures' are the prescribed forms and dimensions of buildings, carriages, clothes, &c.; 文 is said by Choo He, after K'ang-shing, to be 書名, 'the names of the characters.' But 文 is properly the form of the character, representing, in the original characters of the language, the 形, or figure of the object denoted. The character and name together are styled 字; and 書 is the name appropriate to many characters, written or printed. 文, in the text, must denote both the form and sound of the character. 議, 'to discuss,' and 考, 'to examine,' but implying, in each case, the consequent ordering and settling. There is a long and eulogistic note here, in '*Confucius Sinarum Philosophus*,' on the admirable uniformity secured by these prerogatives throughout the Chinese empire. It was natural for Roman Catholic writers, to regard Chinese uniformity with sympathy. But the value, or, rather, no value, of such a system in its formative influence on the characters and institutions of men may be judged, both in the empire of China, and in the church of Rome. 3. 今, 'now,' is said with reference to the time of Tsze-sze. The par. is intended to account for Confucius' not giving law to the empire. It was not the time.

[廿九] 一 王天下有三重焉、其寡過矣乎。二 上焉者、雖善無徵、無徵、不信、不信、民弗從、下焉者、雖善、不尊、不尊、不信、不信、民弗從。三 故君子之道、本諸身、徵諸庶民、考諸三

CHAPTER XXIX. 1. He who attains to the sovereignty of the empire, having *those* three important things, shall be able to effect that there shall be few errors *under his government*.

2. However excellent may have been the regulations of those of former times, they cannot be attested. Not being attested, they cannot command credence, and not being credited, the people would not follow them. However excellent might be the regulations made by one in an inferior situation, he is not in a position to be honoured. Unhonoured, he cannot command credence, and not being credited, the people would not follow his rules.

3. Therefore the institutions of the Ruler are rooted in his own character and conduct, and sufficient attestation of them is given by the masses of the people. He examines them *by comparison* with those of the three kings, and finds them without mistake. He sets

軌, 'the rut of a wheel.' 4. 禮樂,—but we must understand also 'the measures,' and 'characters,' in par. 2. This par. would seem to reduce most emperors to the condition of *rois fainéants*. 5. See the Ana. III. ix., xiv., which chapters are quoted here; but in regard to what is said of Sung, with an important variation. The par. illustrates how Confucius himself 爲下不倍, 'occupied a low station, without being insubordinate.'

29. AN ILLUSTRATION OF THE SENTENCE IN THE XXVIITH CHAPTER,—'WHEN HE OCCUPIES A HIGH SITUATION, HE IS NOT PROUD;' OR RATHER, THE SAGE AND HIS INSTITUTIONS SEEN IN THEIR EFFECT AND TRUTH. 1. Different opinions have obtained as to what is intended by the 三重, 'three important *things*.' K'ang-shing says they are 三王之禮, 'the ceremonies of the three kings,' *i. e.*, the founders of the three dynasties, Hea, Yin, and Chow. This view we may safely reject. Choo He makes them to be the imperial prerogatives, mentioned in the last chapter, par. 2. This view may, possibly, be correct. But I incline to the view of the commentator Luh (陸氏), of the T'ang dynasty, that they refer to the virtue, station, and time, which we have seen, in the notes on the last ch., to be necessary to one who would give law to the empire. Maou mentions this view, indicating his own approval of it. 寡 is used as a verb, 'to make few.'—'He shall be able to effect that there shall be few errors,' *i. e.*, few errors among his officers and people. 2. By 上焉者 and 下焉者, K'ang-shing understands 'sovereign' and 'minister,' in which, again, we must pronounce him wrong. The translation follows the interpr. of Choo He, it being understood that the subject of the par. is the regulations to be followed by the people. 上焉者 having a reference both to *time* and to *rank*, 下焉者 must have the same. Thus there is in it an allusion to Confucius, and the way is still further prepared for his eulogium. 3. By 君子 is intended the 王天下者 in par. 1,—the emperor-sage. By 道 must be intended all his institutions and regulations. 'Attestation of them is given by the masses of the people;' *i. e.*, the people believe in such a ruler, and follow his regulations, thus attesting their adaptation to the general requirements of humanity. 'The three kings,' as mentioned above,

王而不繆、建諸天地而不悖、質諸鬼神而無疑、百世以俟聖人而不惑。四質鬼神而無疑、知天也、百世以俟聖人而不惑、知人也、五是故君子、動而世爲天下道、行而世爲天下法、言而世爲天下則、遠之則有望、近之則不厭、六詩曰、在彼無惡、在

them up before heaven and earth, and finds nothing in them contrary to their mode of operation. He presents himself with them before spiritual beings, and no doubts about them arise. He is prepared to wait for the rise of a sage, a hundred ages after, and has no misgivings.

4. His presenting himself *with his institutions* before spiritual beings, without any doubts about them arising, shows that he knows Heaven. His being prepared, without any misgivings, to wait for the rise of a sage a hundred ages after, shows that he knows men.

5. Such being the case, the movements of such a ruler, *illustrating his institutions*, constitute an example to the empire for ages. His acts are for ages a law to the empire. His words are for ages a lesson to the empire. Those who are far from him, look longingly for him; and those who are near him, are never wearied with him.

6. It is said in the Book of Poetry,—"Not disliked there, not tired of here, from day to day and night to night, will they per-

are the founders of the three dynasties, viz., the great Yu, T'ang, the Completer, and Wan and Woo, who are so often joined together, and spoken of as one. 繆=謬, and should be read in the low. 3d tone. I hardly know what to make of 建諸天地. Chou, in his 語新, says:—此天地只是道耳.謂吾建於此.而與道不相悖也. 'Heaven and Earth here simply mean right reason. The meaning is—I set up my *institutions* here, and there is nothing in them contradictory to right reason.' This, of course, is explaining the text away. But who can do anything better with it? I interpret 質諸鬼神, with ref. to sacrificial institutions, or the general trial of a sovereign's institutions by the efficacy of his sacrifice, in being responded to by the various spirits whom he worships. This is the view of a Ho He-chen (何屺瞻), and is preferable to any other I have met with. 百世以俟聖人而不惑,—compare Mencius, II. Pt. I. ii. 17. 6. See the She-king, IV. i. Bk. ii. Ode III. st. 2. It is a great descent to quote that ode here, however, for it is only praising the feudal princes of Chow. 在彼, 'there,' means their own States; and 在此, 'here,' is the imperial court of Chow. For 射, the She-king has 斁.

此無射、庶幾夙夜、以永終譽、君子未有不如此、而蚤有譽於天下者也。

〔三十〕仲尼祖述堯舜、憲章文武、上律天時、下襲水土。辟如天地之無不持載、無不覆幬、辟如四時之錯行、如日月之代明。萬物並育、而不相害、道並行、而不相悖、小德川

petuate their praise." Never has there been a ruler, who did not realize this description, that obtained an early renown throughout the empire.

CHAPTER XXX. 1. Chung-ne handed down the doctrines of Yaou and Shun, as if they had been his ancestors, and elegantly displayed the regulations of Wăn and Woo, taking them as his model. Above, he harmonized with the times of heaven, and below, he was conformed to the water and land.

2. He may be compared to heaven and earth, in their supporting and containing, their overshadowing and curtaining, all things. He may be compared to the four seasons in their alternating progress, and to the sun and moon in their successive shining.

3. All things are nourished together without their injuring one another. The courses *of the seasons, and of the sun and moon,* are pursued without any collision among them. The smaller energies

30. THE EULOGIUM OF CONFUCIUS, AS THE BEAU-IDEAL OF THE PERFECTLY SINCERE MAN, THE SAGE, MAKING A TERNION WITH HEAVEN AND EARTH. 1. 仲尼,—See ch. II. The various predicates here are explained by K'ang-shing, and Ying-tă, with reference to the 'Spring and Autumn,' making them descriptive of it, but such a view will not stand examination. In translating the two first clauses, I have followed the editor of the 參閱, who says:—祖述者,以爲祖而繼述之,憲章者,奉爲憲而表章之. In the 紹聞編, it is observed that in what he handed down, Confucius began with Yaou and Shun, because the times of Fuh-he and Shin-nung were very remote. Was not the true reason this, that he knew of nothing in China more remote than Yaou and Shun? By 'the times of heaven' are denoted the ceaseless regular movement, which appears to belong to the heavens; and by the 'water and the land,' we are to understand the earth, in contradistinction from heaven, supposed to be fixed and unmoveable. 律, 'a statute,' 'a law;' here used as a verb, 'to take as a law.' 襲=因, 'to follow,' 'to accord with.' The scope of the par. is, that the qualities of former sages, of Heaven, and of Earth, were all concentrated in Confucius. 2. 辟,—read as, and=譬. 錯, read ts'ŭh,=迭, 'successively,' 'alternatingly.'

流、大德敦化、此天地之所以爲大也。[三十一]唯天下至聖、爲能聰明睿知、足以有臨也、寬裕溫柔、足以有容也、發强剛毅、足以有執也、齊莊中正、足以有敬也、文理密察、足以有別也。溥博淵

are like river currents; the greater energies are seen in mighty transformations. It is this which makes heaven and earth so great.

CHAPTER XXXI. 1. It is only he, possessed of all sagely qualities that can exist under heaven, who shows himself quick in apprehension, clear in discernment, of far-reaching intelligence, and all-embracing knowledge, fitted to exercise rule; magnanimous generous, benign, and mild, fitted to exercise forbearance; impulsive, energetic, firm, and enduring, fitted to maintain a firm hold; self-adjusted, grave, never swerving from the Mean, and correct, fitted to command reverence; accomplished, distinctive, concentrative, and searching, fitted to exercise discrimination.

2. All-embracing is he and vast, deep and active as a fountain, sending forth in their due seasons his virtues.

'This describes,' says Choo He, 'the virtue of the sage.' 3. The wonderful and mysterious course of nature, or—as the Chinese conceive,—of the operations of Heaven and Earth, are described to illustrate the previous comparison of Confucius.

31. THE EULOGIUM OF CONFUCIUS CONTINUED. Choo He *says* that this chapter is an expansion of the clause in the last paragr. of the preceding,—'The smaller energies are like river currents.' Even if it be so, it will still have reference to Confucius, the subject of the preceding chapter. K'ang-hsing's account of the first paragraph is:—言德不如此、不可以君天下也、蓋傷孔子有其德而無其命. 'It describes how no one, who has not virtue such as this, can rule the empire, being a lamentation over the fact that while Confucius had the virtue, he did not have the appointment:' that is, of Heaven, to occupy the throne. Maou's account of the whole chapter is:—'Had it been that Chung-ne possessed the empire, then Chung-ne was a perfect sage. Being a perfect sage, he would certainly have been able to put forth the greater energies, and the smaller energies, of his virtue, so as to rule the world, and show himself the coequal of Heaven and Earth, in the manner here described.' Considering the whole chapter to be thus descriptive of Confucius, I was inclined to translate in the past tense,—'It *was* only he, who could,' &c. Still the author has expressed himself so indefinitely, that I have preferred translating the whole, that it may read as the description of the ideal man, who found, or might have found, his realization in Confucius. 1. 唯天下至聖,—see ch. xxi. 聖 here takes the place of 誠. Collie translates:—'It is only the most HOLY man.' Remusat:—'*Il n'y a dans l'univers qu'un* SAINT, *qui*... So the Jesuits:—'*Hic commemorat et commendat summe* SANCTI *virtutes*.' But *holiness* and *sanctity* are terms which indicate the humble and pious conformity of human character and life to the mind and will of God. The Chinese idea of the 聖人 is far enough from this. 臨,—以尊適卑曰臨, 'the approach of the honourable to the mean is called *lin*.' It denotes the high drawing near to the low, to influence and rule. 2. 淵泉, 'an abyss, a spring,' equal, acc. to Choo He, to—靜深而有本, 'still and deep, and having a root.' 時

泉、而時出之。溥博如天、淵泉如淵、見而民莫不敬、言而民莫不信、行而民莫不說。是以聲名洋溢乎中國、施及蠻貊、舟車所至、人力所通、天之所覆、地之所載、日月所照、霜露所隊、凡有血氣者、莫不尊親、故曰、配天。

唯天下至誠、為能經綸

3. All-embracing and vast, he is like heaven. Deep and active as a fountain, he is like the abyss. He is seen, and the people all reverence him; he speaks, and the people all believe him; he acts, and the people all are pleased with him. Therefore his fame overspreads the Middle kingdom, and extends to all barbarous tribes. Wherever ships and carriages reach; wherever the strength of man penetrates; wherever the heavens overshadow and the earth sustains; wherever the sun and moon shine; wherever frosts and dews fall:—all who have blood and breath unfeignedly honour and love him. Hence it is said,—"He is the equal of Heaven."

CHAPTER XXXII. 1. It is only the individual possessed of the most entire sincerity that can exist under heaven, who can adjust

出之, 'always,'—or, in season—'puts them forth,' the 之, 'them,' having reference to the qualities described in par. 1. 3. 見, 'he is seen;'—with reference, says the 備旨, to 'the robes and cap,' the visibilities of the ruler. 'He speaks;'—with reference to his 'instructions, declarations, orders.' 'He acts;'—with reference to his ceremonies, music, punishments, and acts of government.' 4. This par. is the glowing expression of grand conceptions. 蠻 the general name for the rude tribes south of the Middle kingdom. 貊 is another name for the 狄, or rude tribes on the north. The two stand here, like 夷狄 Ana. III. v. and like 四夷, in the 大學傳, x. 15, as representatives of all barbarous tribes. 隊, read chuy, low. 3d tone,=墜, 'to fall.'

32. THE EULOGIUM OF CONFUCIUS CONCLUDED. 'The chapter,' says Chu Hi, 'expands the clause in the last par. of ch. xxix., that the greater energies are seen in mighty transformations.' The sage is here not merely equal to Heaven;—he is another Heaven, an independent being, a God. 1. 經 and 綸 are processes in the manipulation of silk, the former denoting the first separating of the threads, and the latter the subsequent bringing of them together, according to their kinds. 天下之大經,—'the great invariabilities of the world;'

天下之大經、立天下之大本、知天地之化育、夫焉有所倚。二 肫肫其仁、淵淵其淵、浩浩其天。三 苟不固聰明聖知、達天德者、其孰能知之。

[illegible]詩曰、衣錦尚

the great invariable relations of mankind, establish the great fundamental virtues of humanity, and know the transforming and nurturing operations of Heaven and Earth;—shall this individual have any being or any thing beyond himself on which he depends?

2. Call him man in his ideal, how earnest is he! Call him an abyss, how deep is he! Call him Heaven, how vast is he!

3. Who can know him, but he who is indeed quick in apprehension, clear in discernment, of far-reaching intelligence, and all-embracing knowledge, possessing all heavenly virtue?

CHAPTER XXXIII. 1. It is said in the Book of Poetry, "Over

explained of the 達道 and 九經, in ch. xx, 8, 19. 天下之大本,—'the great root of the world;' evidently with reference to the same expression in ch. I. 4. 知 is taken as emphatic:—有默契焉,非但聞見之知而已, 'he has an intuitive apprehension of, and agreement with, them. It is not that he knows them merely by hearing and seeing.' 夫焉有所倚. This is joined by K'ang-hsi with the next par., and he interprets it of the Master's virtue, universally affecting all men, and not partially deflected, reaching only to those near him or to few. Choo He more correctly, as it seems to me, takes it as=倚著, 'to depend on.' I translate the expansion of the clause which is given in '*Confucius Sinarum Philosophus*.'—'The perfectly holy man of this kind therefore, since he is such and so great, how can it in any way be, that there is any thing in the whole universe, on which he leans, or in which he inheres, or on which he behooves to depend, or to be assisted by it in the first place, that he may afterwards operate?' 2. The three clauses refer severally to the three in the prec. paragraph. 仁 is virtuous humanity in all its dimensions and capacities, existing perfectly in the sage. Of 淵 I do not know what to say. The old Comm. interpret the second and third clauses, as if there were a 如 before 淵 and 天, against which Choo He exclaims, and justly. In the 紹聞編 we read:—天人本無二,人只有此形體,與天便隔,視聽思慮,動作,皆曰由我,各我其我,可知其小也,除卻形體,便渾是天。形體如何除得,只克去有我之私,便是除也,天這般廣大,吾心亦這般廣大,而造化無間於我,故曰浩浩其天. 'Heaven and man are not originally two, and man is separate from Heaven only by his having this body. Of their seeing and hearing, their thinking and revolving, their moving and acting, men all say—*It is from us.* Every one thus brings out his ego, and his smallness becomes known. But let the body be taken away, and all would be Heaven. How can the body be taken away? Simply by subduing and removing that self-having of the ego. This is the taking it away. That being done, so wide and great as Heaven is, my mind is also so wide and great, and production and transformation cannot be separated from me. Hence it is said—*How vast is his Heaven.*' Into such wandering mazes of mysterious speculation are Chinese thinkers conducted by the text:—only to be lost in them. As it is said, in par. 3, that only the sage can know the sage, we may be glad to leave him.

絅、惡其文之著也、故君子之道、闇然而日章、小人之道、的然而日亡、君子之道、淡而不厭、簡而文、溫而理、知遠之近、知風之自、知微之顯、可與入德矣。二 詩云、潛雖伏矣、亦孔之昭、故君子內省不疚、無惡於志、君子

her embroidered robe she puts a plain, single garment," intimating a dislike to the display of the elegance of the former. Just so, it is the way of the superior man to prefer the concealment *of his virtue*, while it daily becomes more illustrious, and it is the way of the mean man to seek notoriety, while he daily goes more and more to ruin. It is characteristic of the superior man, appearing insipid, yet never to produce satiety; while showing a simple negligence, yet to have his accomplishments recognized; while seemingly plain, yet to be discriminating. He knows how what is distant lies in what is near. He knows where the wind proceeds from. He knows how what is minute becomes manifested. Such an one, we may be sure, will enter into virtue.

2. It is said in the Book of Poetry, "Although *the fish* sink and lie at the bottom, it is still quite clearly seen." Therefore the supe-

33. THE COMMENCEMENT AND THE COMPLETION OF A VIRTUOUS COURSE. The chapter is understood to contain a summary of the whole Work, and to have a special relation to the first chapter. There, a commencement is made with Heaven, as the origin of our nature, in which are grounded the laws of virtuous conduct. This ends with Heaven, and exhibits the progress of virtue, advancing step by step in man, till it is equal to that of High Heaven. There are eight citations from the Book of Poetry, but to make the passages suit his purpose, the author allegorizes them, or alters their meaning, at his pleasure. Origen took no more license with the scriptures of the old and new Testament than Tsze-sze and even Confucius himself do with the Book of Poetry. 1. *The first requisite in the pursuit of virtue is, that the learner think of his own improvement, and do not act from a regard to others.* 詩曰,—see the She-king, I. v. Ode III. st. 1., where we read, however, 衣錦褧衣. 褧 and 絅 are synonyms. 惡 (op. 3d tone) 其云云 is a gloss by Tsze-sze, giving the spirit of the passage. The ode is understood to express the condolence of the people, with the wife of the duke of Wei, worthy of, but denied, the affection of her husband. 君子之道, 小人之道,—道 seems here to correspond exactly to our English way, as in the translation. 的然,—the primary meaning of 的 is 明, 'bright,' 'displayed.' 的然 'displayed-like,' in opp. to 闇然, 'concealed-like.' 知遠之近,—what is *distant*, is the nation to be governed, or the family to be regulated; what is *near*, is the person to be cultivated. 知風之自,—the *wind* is the influence exerted upon others, the *source* of which is one's own

之所不可及者、其唯人之所不見乎。三詩云、相在爾室、尚不愧於屋漏、故君子不動而敬、不言而信。四詩曰、奏假無言、時靡有爭、是故君子不賞而民勸、不怒而民威於鈇鉞。五詩曰、不顯惟德、

rior man examines his heart, that there may be nothing wrong there, and that he may have no cause for dissatisfaction with himself. That wherein the superior man cannot be equalled is simply this,—his *work* which other men cannot see.

3. It is said in the Book of Poetry, "Looked at in your apartment, be there free from shame, where you are exposed to the light of heaven." Therefore, the superior man, even when he is not moving, has *a feeling of* reverence, and while he speaks not, he has *the feeling of* truthfulness.

4. It is said in the Book of Poetry, "In silence is the offering presented, and *the spirit* approached to; there is not the slightest contention." Therefore the superior man does not use rewards, and the people are stimulated *to virtue*. He does not show anger, and the people are awed more than by hatchets and battle-axes.

5. It is said in the Book of Poetry, "What needs no display is

virtue. 知微之顯,—comp. ch. i. 3. 可與='it may be granted to such an one,' 與 being in the sense of 許. 2. *The superior man going on to virtue, is watchful over himself, when he is alone.* 詩云,—see the Shi-king, II. iv. Ode VIII. st. 11. The ode appears to have been written by some officer who was bewailing the disorder and misgovernment of his day. This is one of the comparisons which he uses;—the people are like fish in a shallow pond, unable to save themselves by diving to the bottom. The application of this to the superior man, dealing with himself, in the bottom of his soul, so to speak, and thereby realising what is good and right, is very far-fetched. 志, 'the will,' is here=心, 'the whole mind,' the self. 3. We have here substantially the same subject as in the last par. The ode is the same which is quoted in ch. xvi. 4, and the citation is from the same stanza of it. 屋漏, acc. to Choo He, was the north-west corner of ancient apartments, the spot most secret and retired. The single panes, in the roofs of Chinese houses, go now by the name, the light of heaven leaking in (漏) through them. Looking at the whole stanza of the ode, we must conclude that there is reference to the light of heaven, and the inspection of spiritual beings, as specially connected with the spot intended. 4. *The result of the processes described in the two preced. pars.* 詩曰,—see the Shi-king, IV. iii. Ode II. st. 2, where for 奏 we have 鬷. 假 read as, and=格. The ode describes the imperial worship of T'ang, the founder of the Shang dynasty. The first clause belongs to the emperor's act and demeanour; the second to the effect of these on his assistants in the service. They were awed to reverence, and had no striving among themselves. The 鈇鉞 were anciently given by the emperor to a prince, as symbolic of his investiture with a plenipotent authority to pun-

百辟其刑之、是故君子、篤恭而天下平。六 詩云、予懷明德、不大聲以色。子曰、聲色之於以化民、末也、詩曰、德輶如毛、毛猶有倫、上天之載、無聲無臭、至矣。

右第三十三章、子思因前章極致之言、反求其本、復自下學爲

virtue. All the princes imitate it." Therefore, the superior man being sincere and reverential, the whole world is conducted to a state of happy tranquillity.

6. It is said in the Book of Poetry, "I regard with pleasure your brilliant virtue, making no great display of itself in sounds and appearances." The Master said, "Among the appliances to transform the people, sounds and appearances are but trivial influences. It is said in another ode, 'His virtue is light as a hair.' Still, a hair will admit of comparison *as to its size*. 'The doings of the supreme Heaven have neither sound nor smell.'—That is perfect virtue."

The above is the thirty-third chapter. Tsze-sze having carried his descriptions to the extremest point in the preceding chapters, turns back in this, and examines the source of his subject; and then

ish the rebellious and refractory. The 鉞 is described as a large-handled axe, eight catties in weight. I call it a battle axe, because it was with one that king Woo despatched the tyrant Chow. 5. *The same subject continued.* 詩曰,—see the She-king, IV. i. Bk. i. Ode IV. st. 3. But in the She-king we must translate,—'There is nothing more illustrious than the virtue *of the sovereign*, all the princes will follow it.' Tsze-sze puts another meaning on the words, and makes them introductory to the next par. 君子 must here be the 王天下者 of ch. xxix. Thus it is that a constant shuffle of terms seems to be going on, and the subject before us is all at once raised to a higher, and inaccessible platform. 6. *Virtue in its highest degree and influence.* 詩云,—see the She-king, III. i. Ode VII. st. 7. The '*I*' is God, who announces to king Wăn the reasons why he had called him to execute his judgments. Wăn's virtue, not sounded nor emblazoned, might come near to the 不顯 of last par., but Confucius fixes on the 大 to show its shortcoming. It had *some*, though not *large* exhibition. He therefore quotes again from III. iii. Ode VI. st. 6, though away from the original intention of the words. But it does not satisfy him that virtue should be likened even to a *hair*. He therefore finally quotes III. i. Ode I. st. 7, where the imperceptible working of Heaven (載=事), in producing the overthrow of the Yin dynasty, is set forth as without sound or smell. That is his highest conception of the nature and power of virtue.

己謹獨之事、推而言之、以馴致乎篤恭而天下平之盛、又贊其妙、至於無聲無臭、而後已焉、蓋舉一篇之要、而約言之、其反復丁寧示人之意、至深切矣、學者其可不盡心乎。

again from the work of the learner, free from all selfishness, and watchful over himself when he is alone, he carries out his description, till by easy steps he brings it to the consummation of the whole empire tranquillized by simple and sincere reverentialness. He farther eulogizes its mysteriousness, till he speaks of it at last as without sound or smell. He here takes up the sum of his whole Work, and speaks of it in a compendious manner. Most deep and earnest was he in thus going again over his ground, admonishing and instructing men:—shall the learner not do his utmost in the study of the Work?

INDEXES.

INDEX I.

OF SUBJECTS IN THE CONFUCIAN ANALECTS.

A

Ability, various of Conf., IX. vi.
Able officers, eight, of Chow, XVIII. xi.
Abroad, when a son may go, IV. xix.
Accomplishments come after duty, I. vi.—blended with solid excellence, VI. xvi.
Achievement of government, the great, XIII. ix.
Acknowledgment of Conf. in estimating himself, VII. xxxii.
Acting heedlessly, against, VII. xxvii.
Actions should always be right, XIV. iv.—of Conf. were lessons and laws, XVII. xix.
Adaptation for government of Yen Yung, &c., VI. i.—of Tsze-loo, &c., VI. vi.
Admiration, Yen Yuen's, of Conf. doctrines, IX. x.
Admonition of Conf. to Tsze-loo, XI. xiv.
Advanced years, improvement difficult in, XVII. xxvi.
Adversity, men are known in times of, IX. xxvii.
Advice against useless expenditure, XI. xiii.
Age, the vice to be guarded against in, XVI. vii.
Aim, the chief, I. xvi.
Aims, of Tsze-loo, Tsang-sih, &c., XI. xxv.
An all-pervading unity, the knowledge of, Conf. aim, XV. ii.
Anarchy of Conf. time, III. v.
Ancient rites, how Conf. cleaved to, III. xvii.
Ancients, their slowness to speak, IV. xxii.
Antiquity, Conf. fondness for, VII. xix.—decay of the monuments of, III. ix.
Anxiety of parents, II. vi.—of Conf. about the training of his disciples, V. ii.
Appearances, fair, are suspicious, I. iii., & XVII. xvii.
Appellations for the wife of a prince, XVI. xiv.
Appreciation, what conduct will insure, XV. v.
Approaches of the unlikely, readily met by Conf., VII. xxviii.
Approbation, Conf., of Nan Yung, XI. v.
Aptitude of the *Keun-tsze*, II. xii.
Archery, contention in, III. vii.—a discipline of virtue, III. xvi.
Ardent and cautious disciples, Conf. obliged to be content with, XIII. xxi.
Ardour of Tsze-loo, V. vi.
Art of governing, XII. xiv.
Assent without reformation, a hopeless case, IX. xxiii.
Attachment to Conf. of Yen Yuen, XI. xxiii.
Attainment, different stages of, VI. xviii.
Attainments of Hwuy, like those of Conf., VII. x.
Attributes of the true scholar, XIX. i.
Auspicious omens, Conf. gives up hope for want of, IX. viii.
Avenge murder, how Conf., wished to, XIV. xxii.

B

Bad name, the danger of a, XIX. xx.
Barbarians, how to civilize, IX. xiii.
Beclouding of the mind, XVII. viii.
Bed, manner of Conf. in, X. xvi.
Benefits derived from studying the Odes, XVII. ix.
Benevolence, to be exercised with prudence, VI. xxiv.—and wisdom, XII. xxii.
Blind, consideration of Conf. for the, XV. xli.
Boldness, excessive of Tsze-loo, VII. x.
Burial, Conf. dissatisfaction with Hwuy's, XI. x.
Business, every man should mind his own, VIII. xiv., & XIV. xxvii.

C

Calmness of Conf. in danger, VII. xxii.
Capacity of Mang Kung-ch'o, XIV. xii.
Capacities of the superior and inferior man, XV. xxxiii.
Careful, about what things Conf. was, VII. xii.
Carriage, Conf. at and in his, X. xvii.—Conf. refuses to sell his, to assist a useless expenditure, XI. vii.
Caution, advantages of, IV. xxiii.—repentance avoided by, I. xiii.—in speaking, XII. iii., and XV. vii.
Ceremonies and music, XI. i.—end of, I. xii.—impropriety in, III x.—influence of in government, IV. xiii.—regulated according to their object, III. iv.—secondary and ornamental, III. viii.—vain without virtue, III. iii.
Character (s), admirable, of Tsze-yu, &c., XV. vi.—differences in, owing to habit, XVII. ii.—different, of two dukes, XIV. xvi.—disliked by Conf., and Tsze-kung, XVII. xxiv.—how Conf. dealt with different, XI. xxi.—how to determine, II. x.—lofty, of Shun and Yu, VIII. xviii.—of four disciples, XI. xvii.—of Kung-

shuh Wăn, XIV. xiv.—of Tan-t'ae Mee-ming, VI. xii.—various elements of in Conf., VII. xxxvii.—what may be learnt from, IV. xvii.
Characteristics, of perfect virtue, XIII. xix.—of ten disciples, XI. ii.
Claimed, what Conf., VII. xxxiii.
Classes of men, in relation to knowledge, four, XVI. ix.—only two whom practice cannot change, XVII. iii.
Climbing the heavens, equalling Conf. like, XIX. xxv.
Common practices, some indifferent and others not, IX. iii.
Communications to be proportioned to susceptibility, VI. xix.
Comparison of Sze and Shang, XI. xv.
Comparisons, against making, XIV. xxxi.
Compass and vigour of mind necessary to a scholar, VIII. vii.
Compassion, how a criminal-judge should cherish, XVIII. xix.
Complete man, of the, XIV. xiii.—virtue, I. xiv., and VI. xvi.
Concealment, not practised by Conf. with his disciples, VII. xxiii.
Concubines, difficult to treat, XVII. xxv.
Condemnation of Tsang Woo-chung, XIV. xv.—of Conf. for seeking employment, XIV. xli.
Condition, only virtue adapts a man to his, IV. ii.
Conduct that will be everywhere appreciated, XV. v.
Confidence, enjoying, necessary to serving and to ruling, XIX. x.
Connate, Conf. knowledge not, VII. xix.
Consideration, of Conf. for the blind, XV. xli.—a generous, of others, recommended, XVIII. x.
Consolation to Sze-ma New, when anxious about his brother, XII. v.
Constancy of mind, importance of, XIII. xxii.
Constant Mean, the, VI. xxvii.
Contemporaries of Conf. described, XVI. xi.
Contention, the superior man avoids, III. vii.
Contentment in poverty of Tsze-loo, IX. xxvi.—of Conf. with his condition, IX. xi.—of the officer King, XIII. viii.
Contrast of Hwuy and Tsze, XI. xviii.
Conversation, with Chung-kung, XII. ii.—with Tsze-chang, XII. vi.; vii.; XX. ii.—with Tsze-kung, XIV. xviii.—with Tsze-loo, XIV. xiii.; xvii.—with Tsze-new, XII. iii.—with Yen Yuen, XII. i.
Countenance, the, in filial piety, I. viii.
Courage, not doing right from want of, II. xxiv.
Criminal judge, should cherish compassion, XIX. xix.
Culpability of not reforming known faults, XV. xxix.

D

Danger, Conf. assured in time of, IX. v.
Dead, offices to the, I. ix.
Death, Conf. evades a question about, XI. xi.—how Conf. felt Hwuy's, XI. viii.; ix.—without regret, IV. viii.
Declined, what Conf., to be reckoned, VII. xxxiii.
Defects of former times become modern vices, XVII. xvi.
Defence, of himself by Conf., XIV. xxxvi.—of his own method of teaching, by Tsze-hea, XIX. xii.—of Tsze-loo, by Conf., XI. xiv.
Degeneracy, of Conf. age, VI. xiv.—instance of, XV. xxv.
Delusions, how to discover, XII. x.; xxi.
Demeanour of Conf., X. i., to v.; xiii.
Departure of Conf., from Loo, XVIII. iv.—from Tse, XVIII. iii.
Depreciation, Conf. above the reach of, XIX. xxiv.
Description of himself as a learner, by Conf. VII. xviii.
Desire and ability, required in disciples, VII. viii.
Development of knowledge, II. xi.
Differences of character, owing to habit, XVII. ii.
Dignity, necessary in a ruler, XV. xxxii.
Disciples, anxiety about training, V. xxi.
Discrimination of Conf. in rewarding officers, VI. iii.—without suspiciousness, the merit of, XIV. xxxiii.
Dispersion of the musicians of Loo, XVIII. ix.
Distinction, notoriety not, XII. xx.
Distress, the superior man above, XV. i.
Divine mission, Conf. assurance of a, VII. xxii.; IX. v.
Doctrine of Conf. admiration of, IX. x.
Dreams of Conf. affected by disappointments, VII. v.
Dress, rules of Conf., in regard to his, X. vi.
Dying counsels to a man in high station, VIII. iv.
Dynasties, Yin, Hea, and Chow, VIII. iv.; III. xx.—Yin and Hea, III. ix.—Chow, &c., III. xiv.—certain rules exemplified in the ancient,—eight able officers of the Chow, XVIII. xi.—three worthies of the Yin, XVIII. i.—the three, XV. xxiv.

E

Earnest student, Hwuy the, IX. xix.
Earnestness in teaching, of Conf., IX. vii.
Egotism, instance of freedom from, VIII. x.
Eight able officers of the Chow dynasty, XVIII. xi.
Emolument, learning for, II. xviii.—shameful to care only for, XIV. i.
End the, crowns the work, IX. xxi.
Enjoyment, advantageous and injurious sources of, XVI. v.
Equalled, Conf. cannot be, XIX. xxv.
Error, how acknowledged by Conf., VII. xxx.
Essential, what is, in different services, III. xxvi.
Estimate, Conf. humble of himself, VII. ii.; iii.; IX. xv.; XIV. xxx.—of what he could do if employed, XIII. x.
Estimation of others, not a man's concern, XIV. xxxii.
Example, better than force, II. xx.—government efficient by, &c., XII. xvii.; xviii.; xix.;—the secret of rulers' success, XIII. i.—value of, in those in high stations, VIII. ii.
Excess and defect equally wrong, XI. xv.
Expenditure, against useless, XI. xiii.
External, the, may be predicated from the internal, XIV. v.
Extravagant speech, hard to be made good, XIV. xxi.

F

G

H

I

J

Jealousy of others' talents, against, XV. x.; iii.
Joy of Conf. independent of outward circumstances, VII. xv.
Judgment of Conf. concerning Tsze-ch'an, &c., XIV. x.—of retired worthy, on Conf., XIV. xlii.

K

Keun-tsze, See Superior man.
Killing, not to be talked of by rulers, XII. xix.
Knowing and not knowing, II. xvii.
Knowledge, disclaimed by Conf., IX. vii.—four classes of men in relation to, XVI. ix.—not lasting without virtue, XV. xxxii.—of Conf. not connate, VIII. xix.—sources of Conf., XIX. xxii.—subserves benevolence, II. xxii.

L

Lament over moral error added to natural defect, VIII. xvi.—sickness of Pih-new, VI. viii.—persistence in error, V. xxvi.—rarity of the love of virtue, IV. vi.—the rash reply of Tsae Go, III. xxi.—the waywardness of men, VI. xiv.—of Conf., that men did not know him, XIV. xxxvii.
Language, the chief virtue of, XV. xl.
Learner the, I. i.; xiv.—Conf. describes himself as a, VII. xviii.
Learning and propriety combined, VI. xxv., & XII. xv.—Conf. fondness for, V. xxvii.—different motives for, XIV. xxv.—end of, II. xviii.—how to be pursued, VI. xi., & VIII. xvii.—in order to virtue, XIX. vi.—necessity of, to complete virtue, XVII. viii.—quickly leads to good, VIII. xii.—should not cease or be intermitted, IX. xviii.—substance of, I. vii.—the indications of a real love of, XIX. v.—the student's workshop, XIX. vii.
Lesson, of prudence, XIV. ix.—to parents and ministers, XIV. viii.—to rulers, VIII. x.—to Tsze-loo, XIII. i.
Lessons and laws, Conf. actions were, XVII. xix.
Libation, pouring out of, in sacrifice, III. x.
Life, human, valued by Conf., X. xii.—without uprightness, not true, VI. xvii.
Likings and dislikings of others, in determining a man's character, XIII. xxiv., & XV. xxvii.
Literary acquirements, useless without practical ability, XIII. v.
Litigation, how Tsze-loo could settle, XII. xii.—it is better to prevent, XII. xiii.
Love of virtue rare, IV. vi., & IX. xvii.
Love to learn, of Conf., V. xxvii.—of Hwuy, XI. vi.—rarity of, VI. ii.
Loving and hating aright, IV. iii.

M

Madman, the, of Ts'oo, XVIII. v.
Man, in relation to principles of duty, XV. xxviii.
Manhood, the vice to be guarded against in, XVI. vii.
Manner of Conf. when unoccupied, VII. iv.
Marriage-making, Conf. in, V. i.
Mat, rule of Conf. about his, X. ix.
Maturing of character, rules for, VII. vi.
Mean man, glosses his faults, XIX. viii. See Superior man.
Meanness of Wei-shang, V. xxiii.—not so bad as insubordination, VII. xxxv.
Mercenary officers, impossible to serve along with, XVII. xv.
Merit of Kung-shuh Wan, XIV. xix.—of Kwan Chung, XIV. xvii.; xviii.—virtue of concealing, VI. xiii.
Messenger, an admirable, XIV. xxvi.
Military affairs, Conf. refuses to talk of, XV. i.
Minding too much high things, XIX. xv.
Minister, the faithful, XV. xxxvii.
Ministers, great and ordinary, XI. xxiii.—importance of good and able, XIV. xx.—must be sincere and upright, XIV. xxiii.—should be strict and decided, XIV. viii.
Mission of Conf., Yen Yuen's confidence in, XI. xxii.
Model student, fond recollections of a, IX. xx.
Moral appliances to be preferred in govt., II iii.
Mourners, Conf. sympathy with, VII. ix.; & X. xvi.
Mourning, three years for parents, XVII. xxi.—government how carried on in time of, XIV. xliii.—the trappings of, may be dispensed with, XIX. xiv.
Murder of the duke of Ts'e, XIV. xxii.
Music, and ceremonies, vain without virtue, III. iii.—effect of, VIII. viii.—effect of on Conf., VII. xii.—influence of, in government, XVII. iv.—of Shun and Woo compared, III. xxv.—on the playing of, III. xxiii.—service rendered to, by Conf., IX. xiv.—the sound of instruments does not constitute, XVII. xi.
Musicians of Loo, the, dispersion of, XVIII. ix.
Music-master, praise of a, VIII. xv.

N

Name, danger of a bad, XIX. xx.—without reality, VI. xxiii.
Names, importance of being correct, XIII. iii.
Narrow-mindedness, Tsze-chang on, XIX. ii.
Natural-duty, and uprightness in collision, XIII. xviii.—case in ceremonies to be prized, I. xii.—qualities which are favourable to virtue, XIII. xxvii.
Nature of a man, grief brings out the real, XIX. xvii.
Neighbourhood, what constitutes the excellence of a, IV. i.
Nine subjects of thought to the superior man, XVI. x.
Notoriety, not true distinction, XII. xx.

O

Ode, (s), the *Chow-nan* and *Shaou-nan*, XVII. x.—the *Kwan-ts'eu*, III. xx.—the Yung, III. ii.—Pih-kwei, X. v.—of Ch'ing, XV. x.—the Nga, IX. xiv.; XVII. xviii.
Odes, the study of the Book of, XVI. xiii. &

XVII. ix.; x.;—quotations from the, I. xv.; III. viii.; IX. xxvi.; XII. x.—the pure design of the, II. ii.
Office, declined by Tsze-k'een, VI. vii.—desire for, qualified by self-respect, IX. xii.—Conf., why not in, II. xxi.—when to be accepted, and when to be declined, VIII. xiii.
Officers, classes of men who may be styled, XIII. xx.—mercenary, impossible to serve with, XVII. xv.—personal correctness essential to, XIII. xiii.—should first attend to their proper work, XIX. xiii.
Official notifications of Ch'ing, why excellent, XIV. ix.
Old knowledge, to be combined with new acquisitions, II. xi.
Old man, encounter with an, XVIII. vii.
Opposing a father, disapproved of, VII. xiv.
Ordinances of Heaven necessary to be known, XX. iii.
Ordinary people, could not understand Conf., XIX. xxiii.—ordinary rules, Conf. not to be judged by, XVII. vii.
Originator, Conf. not an, VII. i.

P

Parents, grief for, brings out the real nature of a man, XIX. xvii.—how a son may remonstrate with, IV. xviii.—should be strict and decided, XIV. viii.—three years' mourning for, XVII. xxi.—their years to be remembered, IV. xxi.
People, what may and what may not be attained to with the, VIII. ix.
Perfect virtue, caution in speaking, characteristic of, XII. iii.—characteristics of, XIII. xix.—estimation of, V. xviii., & VI. xx.—five things which constitute, XVII. vi.—how to attain to, XII. i.—not easily attained, XIV. vii.—wherein realized, XII. ii.
Persistence in error, lament over, V. xxvi.
Perseverance proper to a student, VI. x.
Personal attainment, a man's chief concern, I. xvi., & XIV. xxxii.—conduct, all in all to a ruler, XIII. xvi.—correctness, essential to an officer, XIII. xiii.
Perspicuity the chief virtue of language, XV. xl.
Pervading unity, Conf. doctrine a, IV. xv.—how Conf. aimed at, XV. viii.
Phoenix, the, IX. viii., & XVIII. v.
Piety, see Filial.
Pity of Conf. for misfortune, IX. ix.
Plans, what is necessary to concord in, XV. xxxix.
Poetry, benefits of the study of the Book of, VIII. viii., & XVII. ix.; x.—and music, service rendered to by Conf. IX. xiv.
Posthumous titles, on what principle conferred, V. xiv.
Poverty, happiness in, VI. ix.—harder to bear aright than riches, XIV. xi.—no disgrace to a scholar, IV. ix.
Practical ability, importance of, XIII. v.
Practice, Conf. zeal to carry his principles into, XVII. v.
Praise of the house of Chow, VIII. xx.—of the music-master Che, VIII. xv.—of Yaou, VIII. xix.—of Yu, VIII. xxi.
Praising and blaming, Conf. correctness in, XV. xxiv.
Prayer, sin against Heaven precludes III. xiii.—Conf. declines, for himself, VII. xxxiv.
Precaution, necessity of, XV. xi.
Preliminary study, necessity of to governing, XI. xxiv.
Presumption, &c., of the chief of the Ke family, XVI. i.—and pusillanimity conjoined, XVII. xii.
Pretence, against, II. xvii.—Conf. dislike of, IX. xi.
Pretentiousness of Conf. time, VII. xxv.
Prince, and minister, relation of, III. xix.—Conf. demeanour before a, X. ii.—Conf. demeanour in relation to, X. xiii.
Princes, Conf. influence on, I. x.—how to be served, III. xviii.
Principles, agreement in, necessary to concord in plans, XV. xxxix.—and ways of Yaou, Shun, &c., XX. i.—of duty, an instrument in the hand of man, XV. xxviii.
Prompt decision good, V. xix.
Propriety, and music, influence of, XVII. iv.—combined with learning, VI. xxv., & XII. xv.—effect of, VIII. viii.—love of, facilitates government, XIV. xliv.—necessary to a ruler, XV. xxxii.—not in external appurtenances, XVII. xi.—rules of, I. xii.; III. xv.—rules of, necessary to be known, XX. iii.—value of the rules of, VIII. ii.
Prosperity and ruin of a country, on what dependent, XIII. xv., & XVI. ii.
Prowess conducting to ruin, XIV. vi.
Prudence, a lesson of, XIV. iv.
Pursuit of riches, against, VII. xi.
Pusillanimity and presumption, XVII. xii.

Q

Qualifications of an officer, VIII. xiii.
Qualities that are favourable to virtue, XIII. xxvii.—that mark the scholar, XIII. xxviii.

R

Rash words cannot be recalled. III. xxi.
Readiness of Conf. to impart instruction, VII. vii.—of speech, V. iv., & XVII. xiv.
Reading and thought, should be combined, II. xv., & XV. xxx.
Rebuke to Yen Yew, &c., XVI. i.
Receptivity of Hwuy, II. ix., & XI. iii.
Reciprocity, the rule of life, XV. xxiii.
Recluse, Tsze-loo's encounter with a, XVIII. vii.
Recluses, Conf. and the two, XVIII. vi.
Recollection of Hwuy, Conf. fond, IX. xx.
Reflection, the necessity of, IX. xxx.
Regretful memory of disciples' fidelity, XI. ii.
Relative duties, necessity of maintaining, XII. xi.
Remark of an ignorant man about Conf., IX. ii.
Remonstrance with parents, IV. xviii.
Repentance escaped by timely care, I. xiii.
Reproof to Tsze-loo, XI. xxiv.
Reproofs, frequent, warning against the use of, IV. xxvi.
Reputation not a man's concern, XV. xviii.
Resentments, how to ward off, XV. xiv.
Residence, rule for selecting a, IV. i.

Respect, a youth should be regarded with, IX. xxii.—of Conf. for men, XV. xxiv.—of Conf. for rank, IX. ix.
Retired worthy's judgment on Conf., XIV. xlii.
Reverence for parents, II. vii.
Riches, pursuit of, uncertain of success, VII. xi.
Right way, importance of knowing the, IV. viii.
Righteous and public spirit of Conf., XIV. xxii.
Righteousness the *Keun-tsze's* concern, IV. xvi.—is his rule of practice, IV. x.
Root of benevolence, filial and fraternal duty is the, I. ii.
Royal ruler, a, could, in what time, transform the empire, XIII. xii.
Rule and prosperity dependent on what, XIII. xv., & XVI. ii.
Rule of life, reciprocity the, XV. xxiii.
Ruler, virtue in a, II. i.
Rulers, a lesson to, VIII. x.—personal conduct all in all to, XIII. xvi.—should not be occupied with what is the proper business of the people, XIII. iv.
Ruling, best means of, II. iii.
Running stream, a, Conf. how affected by, IX. xvi.

S

Sacrifice, Conf. sincerity in, III. xii.—the great, III. x.; xi.—wrong subjects of, II. xxiv.
Sagehood, not in various ability, IX. vi.
Scholar, attributes of the true, XIX. i.—his aim must be higher than comfort, XIV. iii.
Self-cultivation, I. viii., & IX. xxiv.—a man's concern, IV. xiv.—a characteristic of the *Keun-tsze*, XIV. xlv.—Conf. anxiety about, VII. iii.—steps in, I. xv.
Self-examination, I. iv.
Selfish conduct causes murmuring, IV. xii.
Self-respect should qualify desire for office, IX. xii.
Self-willed, Conf. not, XIV. xxxiv.
Sequences, of wisdom, virtue, and bravery, IX. xxviii.
Servants, difficult to treat, XVII. xxv.
Shame of caring only for salary, XIV. i.
Shaou, a name of certain music, III. xxv.
Sheep, the monthly offering of a, III. xvii.
Shoo-king, quotation from, II. xxi.; XIV. xliii.—compilation from, XX. i.
Silent mourning, three years of, XIV. xliii.
Simplicity, instance of, VIII. v.
Sincerity, cultivation of, I. iv.—necessity of, II. xxii.—praise of, V. xxiv.
Slandering of Tsze-loo, XIV. xxxviii.
Slowness to speak, of the ancients, IV. xxii.—of the *Keun-tsze*, IV. xxiv.
Small advantages not to be desired in government, XIII. xvii.
Social intercourse, qualities of the scholar in, XIII. xxiii.
Solid excellence blended with ornament, VI. xvi.
Son, a, opposing his father, against, VII. xiv.—Conf. instruction of his own, XVI. xiii.
Sources of Conf. knowledge, XIX. xxii.
Specious words, danger of, XV. xxvi.
Speech, discretion in, XV. vii.
Spirit of the times, against, III. xviii.
Spirits, Conf. evades a question about serving, XI. xi.—of the land, altars, of, III. xxi.
Stages of attainment, VI. xviii.—of progress, different persons stop at different, IX. xxix.
States of Ts'e and Loo, VI. xxii.
Strange doctrines, II. xvi.
Strength, not a fit subject of praise, XIV. xxxv.
Student's proper work, XIX. xiii.
Stupidity of Ning Woo, V. xx.
Subjects, avoided by Conf. VII. xx.—of Conf. teaching, VII. xxiv. See Topics.
Submission of subjects, how secured, II. xix.
Substantial qualities, and accomplishments, in the *Keun-tsze*, XII. viii.
Sun and moon, Conf. like the, XIX. xxiv.
Superficial speculations, against, XV. xvi.
Superior and mean man, II. xii.; xiii.; xiv.; IV. xi.; xvi.; VI. xi.; VII. xxxvi.; XVI. viii.—different air and bearing of, XIII. xxvi.—different in their relation to those employed by them, XIII. xxv.—different manners of, XIII. xxiii.—different tendencies of, XIV. xxiv.—how to know, XV. xxxiii.—opposite influence of, XII. xvi.
Superior man, above distress, XV. i.—changing appearances of, to others, XIX. ix.—cleaves to virtue, IV. v.—does not conceal, but changes, his errors, XIX. xxi.—firmness of, based on right, XV. xxxvi.—four characteristics of, V. xv.—is righteous, courteous, humble, and sincere, XV. xvii.—more in deeds than in words, XIV. xxix.—nine subjects of thought to, XVI. x.—rule about his words and actions, IV. xxiv.—self-cultivation, characteristic of, XIV. xlv.—talents and virtues of, VIII. vi.—thoughts of in harmony with his position, XIV. xxviii.—truth the object of, XV. xxxi.—various characteristics of, XV. xx.; xxi.; xxiii.—wishes to be had in remembrance, XV. xix.
Superiority of Hwuy, VI. ii.; v.
Superstition of Tsang Wan, V. xvii.
Supreme authority ought to maintain its power, XVI. ii.
Susceptivity of learners, teachers to be guided by, VI. xix.
Swiftness to speak, incompatible with virtue, XVII. xiv.
Sympathy of Conf. with mourners, VII. ix.—with sorrow, IX. ix.

T

Talents, men of, scarce, VIII. xx.—worthless without virtue, VIII. xi.
Taxation, light, advantages of, XII. ix.
Teacher, qualification of a, II. xi.
Teaching, effect of, XV. xxxviii.—Conf. earnestness in, IX. vii.—Conf. subjects of, VII. xxiv.—graduated method of, XIX. xii.—necessary to prepare the people for war, XIII. xxix.; xxx.
Temple, Conf. in the grand, XIII. xv., & X. xiv.
Thieves made by the example of rulers, XII. xviii.
Think, those who will not, the case of, hopeless, XV. xv.
Thinking without reading, fruitless, XV. xxx.
Thought and learning, to be combined, II. xv.
Three, errors of speech, in the presence of the great, XVI. vi.—families, of Loo, III. ii.—friendships advantageous, and three injurious, XVI. iv.—sources of enjoyment, *id.*, *ib.*, XVI. v.—things of which the superior man stands in awe, XVI. viii.—years' mourning, XIV. xliii.; XVII. xxi.—worthies of the Yin dynasty, XVIII. i.

Thunder, Conf. how affected by, X. xvi.
Topics, avoided by Conf., VII. xx.—most common of Conf., VII. xvii.—seldom spoken on by Conf., IX. i.
Traditions of the principles of Wăn and Wû, XIX. xxii.
Training of the young, I. vi.
Transmitter, Conf. a, VII. i.
Trappings of mourning may be dispensed with, XIX. xiv.
Treatment of a powerful, but unworthy officer by Conf., XVII. i.
True men, paucity of in Conf. time, VII. xxv.
Truthfulness, necessity of, I. xxii.
Two classes only whom practice cannot change, XVII. iii.—recluses, Conf. and the, XVIII. vi.

U

Unbending virtue, V. x.
Unextinguishableness of great principles, II. xxiii.
Unity of Conf. doctrine, IV. xv., & XV. ii.
Unmannerly old man, Conf. conduct to an, XIV. xlvi.
Unoccupied, Conf. manner when, VII. iv.
Unworthy man, Conf. responds to the advances of an, XVII. vii.
Uprightness, and natural duty in collision, XIII. xviii.—arrogance inconsistent with, V. xxiii.—necessary to true virtue, VI. xvii.
Usurped rites, against, III. i; ii; vi.
Usurping tendencies of the Ke family, XIII. xiv.
Utensil, Tsze-kung an, V. iii.—the accomplished scholar not an, II. xii.

V

Valour subordinate to righteousness, XVII. xxiii.
Various ability of Conf., IX. vi.
Vice, how to correct, XII. xxi.
Vices, of a father, no discredit to a good son, VI. iv.—which youth, manhood, and age have to guard against, XVI. vii.
Village, Conf. demeanour in his, X. i.; x.
Vindication, Conf., of himself, VI. xxvi.—of Conf. by Tsze-kung, XVIII. vii.
Virtue, alone adapts a man for his condition, IV. ii.—and not strength a fit subject of praise, XIV. xxxv.—ceremonies & music vain without, III. iii.—complete, I. i.—contentment with what is vulgar injures, XVII. xiii.—devotion of the Kuan-tsze to, IV. v.—exceeding, of Tae-pih, VIII. i.—few really know, XV. iii.—how to exalt, XII. x.; xxi.—in concealing one's merit, VI. xiii.—influence of, II. i.—knowledge not lasting without, XV. xxxii.—leading to empire, XIV. vi.—learning, necessary to the completion of, XVII. viii.—learning leading to, XIX. vi.—love of, rare, IV. vi.; IX. xvii.; XV. xii.—natural qualities which favour, XIII. xxvii.—not far to seek, VII. xxix.—the highest, not easily attained, and incompatible with meanness, XIV. vii.—the practice of, aided by intercourse with the good, XV. ix.—to be valued more than life, XV. viii.—true nature and art of, VI. xxviii.—without wealth, &c., XVI. xii.
Virtues, the great, demand the chief attention, XIX. xi.
Virtuous men, not left alone, IV, xxv.—only can love or hate others, IV. iii.
Vocation of Conf., a stranger's view of, III. xxiv.
Vulgar ways and views, against contentment with, XVII. xiii.

W

War, how a good ruler prepares the people for, XIII. xxix.; xxx.
Warning to Tsze-loo, XI. xii.
Waywardness, lament over, VI. xv.
Wealth without virtue, &c., XVI. xii.
Wickedness, the virtuous will, preserves from, IV. iv.
Wife of a prince, appellations for, XVI. xiv.
Will, the virtuous, preserves from wickedness, IV. iv.—is unsubduable, IX. xxv.
Wisdom and virtue, chief elements of, VI. xx.—contrasts of, VI. xxi.; IX. xxviii.
Wishes, different, of Yen Yuen, &c., V. xxv.—of Tsze-loo, &c., XI. xxv.
Withdrawing from public life, different causes of, XIV. xxxix.—of Conf., XVIII. v.; vi.—of seven men, XIV. xl.
Withdrawing from the world, Conf. proposes, V. vi.—Conf. judgment on, XVIII. viii.
Words, the force of, necessary to be known, XX. iii.
Work, a man's, is with himself, XIV. xxx.
Workshop, the student's, XIX. vii.

Y

Young, duty of the, I. vi.—should be regarded with respect, IX. xxii.
Youth, the vice to be guarded against in, XVI. vii.

INDEX II.

OF PROPER NAMES IN THE CONFUCIAN ANALECTS.

☞ *Names in Italics will be found in their own places in this Index with additional references.*

CH AND CH'.

Ch'ae, surnamed Kaou, and styled *Tsze-kaou*, a disciple of Conf., XI. xvii.

Chang, *Tsze-chang*, XIX. xv.; xvi.

Ch'ang-tseu, a worthy of Ts'oo, XVIII. vi.

Chaou, a prince celebrated for his beauty of person, VI. xiv.

Chaou, one of the three families which governed the state of Tsin, XIV. xii.

Ch'aou, the hon. epithet of Chow, duke of Loo, B.C. 540—509, VII. xxx.

Che, the Music-master of Loo, VIII. xv.; XVIII. ix.

Ch'ih, surnamed *Kung-se*, and styled *Tsze-hwa*, a disciple of Conf., V. vii.; VI. iii.; XI. xxv.

Ch'in, the state of, V. xxi.; VII. xxx.; XI. ii.; XV. i.

Ch'in K'ang, *Tsze-k'in*, a disciple of Conf., XVI. xiii.

Ch'in Shing, or Ch'in Hang, an officer of Keen, duke of Ts'e, XIV. xxii.

Chin Wăn, an officer of Ts'e, V. xviii.

Ch'ing, the State of, XV. x.

Chaou-chang, a person who retired from the world, XVIII. viii.

Chow dynasty, II. xxiii.; III. xiv.; xxi.; VIII. xx.; XV. x.; XVI. v.; XVIII. xi.; XX. i.

Chow, the last emperor of the Yin dynasty, XVIII. i.; XIX. xx.

Chow Jin, an ancient historiographer, XVI. i.

Chow-kung, or the duke of Chow, VII. v.; VIII. xi.; XI. xvi.; XVIII. x.

Chuen-yu, a small territory in Loo, XVI. i.

Chung-hwuh, an officer of Chow, XVIII. xi.

Chung-kung, the designation of Yen Yung, a disciple of Conf., VI. i.; iv.; XI. ii.; XII. ii.; XIII. ii.

Chung-mow, a place in the state of Tsin, XVII. vii.

Chung-ne, Confucius, XIX. xxii.—xxv.

Chung-shuh Yu, the same as *K'ung Wăn*, XIV. xx.

Chung *Yew*, styled Tsze-loo, a disciple of Confucius, VI. vi.; XI. xxiii.; XVIII. vi.

Chwang of Peen, XIV. xiii.

E

E, a small town on the borders of the State of Wei, III. xxiv.

E, a famous archer, B.C. about 2150., XIV. vi.

E-yih, a person who retired from the world, XVIII. viii.

E Yin, the minister of T'ang, XII. xxii.

F

Fan Ch'e, by name Seu, and designated Tsze-ch'e a disciple of Conf., II. v.; VI. xx.; XII. xxi.; xxii.; XIII. iv.; xix.

Fan Seu, the same as *Fan Ch'e*, XIII. iv.

Fang, a city in Loo, XIV. xv.

Fang-shuh, a musician of Loo, XVIII. ix.

G

Gae, the hon. title of Tseang, duke of Loo, B.C. 493—467, II. xix.; III. xxi.; VI. ii.; XII. ix.

Gan Ping, posthumous title of Gan Ying, principal minister of Ts'e, V. xvi.

H

Han, the river, XVIII. ix.

Hea dynasty, II. xxiii.; III. ix.; xxi.; XV. x.

Heen, the name of *Yuen Sze*, a disciple of Conf., XVI. i.

Hwan, the three great families of Loo, being descended from duke Hwan, are called the descendants of the three Hwan, II. v. note; XVI. iii.

Hwan, the duke of Ts'e, B.C. 683—642, XIV. xvi.; xviii.

Hwan Tuy, a high officer of Sung, VII. xxii.

Hwuy, *Yen Hwuy*, styled Tsze-yuen, a disciple of Conf., II. ix.; V. viii.; VI. v.; ix.; IX. xix.; XI. iii.; x.; xviii.; xxii.

Hwuy of Lew-hea, posthumous title of Chen Hwŏ, an officer of Loo, XV. xiii.; XVIII. ii.; viii.

J

Joo Pei, a man of Loo, XVII. xx.

K

Kan, the Master of the band at Loo, XVIII. ix.

Kaou-tsung, the hon. epithet of the emperor Woo-ting, B.C. 1323—1263., XIV. xliii.

Kaou-yaou, a minister of Shun, XII. xxii.

Ke, a small state in which sacrifices to the emperors of the Hea dynasty were maintained by their descendants, III. ix.

Ke, a small state in Shan-se, XVIII. i.

Ke family, the family of *Ke K'ang* of Loo, III. i.; vi.; VI. vii.; XI. xvi.; XVI. i.; XVIII. iii.

Ke Hwan, or Ke Sze, the head of the *Ke family* in the latter days of Conf., XVIII. iv.

Ke K'ang, the hon. epithet of *Ke-sun* Fei, the head of one of the three great families of Loo, II. xx.: VI. vi.: XI. vi.: XII. xvii.; xviii.; xix.: XIV. xx.

Ke-kwa, an officer of Chow, XVIII. xi.

Ke Loo, the same as *Tsze-loo*, V. xxv.: XI. ii.; xi.: XIII. xiv: XVI. i.

Ke-sun, the same as *Ke K'ang*, XIV. xxxviii; XVI. i.

Ke-suy, an officer of Chow, XVIII. xi.

Ke Tsze-jen, a younger brother of the Ke family, XI. xxiii.

Ke Wan, posthumous title of Ke Hang-foo, an officer of Loo, V. xix.

Ke-tseih, a worthy of Ts'oo, XVIII. vi.

Keen, a duke of Tse, XIV. xxii.

Keu-foo, a small city on the western borders of Loo, XIII. xvii.

Keu Pih-yuh, the designation of Keu Yuen, an officer of the State of Wei, XIV. xxvi.: XV. vi.

K'euch, the name of a village, XIV. xlvii.

Keueh, a musician of Loo, XVIII. ix.

Kew, brother of the duke Hwan of Tse, XIV. xvii.; xviii.

K'ew, Confucius' name, XIV. xxxiv.: XVIII. vi.

K'ew, the name of *Yen Yew*, a disciple of Conf., V. vii: VI. vi.: XI. xvi.; xxi.; xxiii.; xxv.: XVI. i.

Kih Tsze-shing, an officer of the State of Wei, XII. viii.

King, a duke of Tse, XII. xi.: XVI. xii.: XVIII. iii.

King, a scion of the ducal family of Wei, XIII. viii.

K'ung, Confucius, IX. ii.; XIV. xli.; XVIII. vi.

Kung-Ch'ŏ, *Măng Kung-ch'ŏ*, XIV. xiii.

Kung-ming Kea, XIV. xiv.

Kung-pih Leaou, a relative of the duke of Loo, XIV. xxxviii.

Kung-se Hwa, *Tsze-hwa*, a disciple of Conf., VII. xxxiii.: XI. xxi.; xxv.

Kung-shan Fuh-jaou, a confederate of Yang Ho, XVII. v.

Kung-shuh Wan, an officer of the State of Wei, XIV. xiv.; xix.

Kung-sun Ch'aou, of Wei, XIX. xxii.

K'ung Wan, posthumous title of Tsze-yu, an officer of Wei, V. xiv.

Kung-yay Ch'ang, the son-in-law of Confucius, V. i.

Kwan Chung, by name E Woo, chief minister to the duke Hwan of Tse, B.C. 683—643, III. xxii.: XIV. x.; xvii.; xviii.

K'wang, the name of a town, IX. v; XI. xxii.

L

Laou, surnamed K'in, and styled Tsze-k'ae or Tsze-chang, a disciple of Confucius, IX. vi.

Le, the name of T'ang, founder of the Shang dynasty. XX. i.

Le, a son Confucius, who died early, XI. vii.

Leaou, a musician of Loo, XVIII. ix.

Lin Fang, styled Tsze-kew, a man of Loo, supposed to have been a disciple of Confucius, III. iv. vi.

Ling, a duke of Wei, XIV. xx.: XV. i.

Loo, the native State of Conf., II. v. *xix*; III. xxiii: V. ii.: VI. xxii: IX. xiv: XI. xiii.: XIII. vii.: XIV. xv.: XVIII. iv.; vi.; x.

M

Măng Che-fan, named Tsih, an officer of Loo, VI. xiii.

Măng Chwang, the head of the *Măng family*, anterior to Conf. time, XIX. xviii.

Măng E, the posthumous title of *Măng-sun*, the head of the Măng family, II. v.

Măng family, one of the three great families of Loo, XVIII. iii.: XIX. xix.

Măng King, honorary title of Chung-sun Tsëë, son of Măng Woo, VIII. iv.

Măng Kung-ch'ŏ, the head of the *Măng* or Chung-sun *family*, in the time of Conf., XIV. xii.

Măng-sun, named Ho-ke, the same as *Măng E*, II. v.

Măng Woo, hon. title of Che, the son of Măng E, II. vi.: V. vii.

Min, the music-master of Loo, XV. xli.

Min, *Min Tsze-k'een*, XI. xii.

Min Tsze-k'een, named Sun, a disciple of Conf., VI. vii.: XI. ii.; iv.; xiii.

Mung, the eastern, the name of a mountain, XVI. i.

N

Nan-kung K'wŏh, supposed to be the same as *Nan Yung*, XIV. vi.

Nan-tsze, the wife of the duke of Wei, and sister of prince Chaou, VI. xxvi.

Nan-yung, a disciple of Conf., V. i.: XI. v.

Ngaou, the son of Han Tsuh, (B.C. 2100), XIV. vi.

Ning Woo, hon. ep. of Ning Yu, an officer of Wei, V. xx.

P

P'ang, an ancient worthy, VII. i.

Pe, a place in the state of Loo, VI. vii.: XI. xxiv.: XVI. i: XVII. v.

Pe-kan, an uncle of the tyrant Chow, XVIII. i.

Pe Sëin, a minister of the state of Ch'ing, XIV. ix.

Peen, the name of a city, XIV. x.

Peen, a city in Loo, XIV. xiii.

Peih Heih, commandant of Chung Mow, in the State of Tsin, XVII. vii.

Pih family, XIV. x.

Pih-e, hon. epithet of a worthy of the Shang dynasty, V. xxii.: VII. xiv.: XVI. xii.: XVIII. viii.

Pih-kwŏh, an officer of Chow, XVIII. xi.

Pih-new, the denomination of Tsze Kang, surnamed Yen, a disciple of Conf., VI. viii.: XI. ii.

Pih-tă, an officer of Chow, XVIII. xi.

Pih-yu, the eldest son of Conf., XVI. xiii.: XVII. x.

S

Seang, a musician of Loo, XVIII. ix.

Seŏ, the State of, XIV. xii.

INDEX III.

OF SUBJECTS IN THE GREAT LEARNING.

INDEX IV.

OF PROPER NAMES IN THE GREAT LEARNING.

C

Ch'ing, the philosopher, *Introductory note:* comm., v., *note.*
Chow, the State of, comm., ii. 3.
Chow, the tyrant, comm., ix. 4.
Confucius, *Concluding note to text.*

F

Fan, the uncle of duke Wăn, comm., x. 13.

K

K'ang, hon. epithet of Fung, brother of king Wan, comm., i. 1; ii. 2; ix. 2; x. 11.
Ke, the name of a river, comm., iii. 4.
Këë, the tyrant, comm., ix. 4.

M

Ming Hëen, hon. epithet of Chung-sun Mëë, a worthy minister of Loo, comm., x. 22.
Mencius, *Concluding note to text.*

S

Shun, the emperor, comm., ix. 4.

T

T'ae Këă, the second emperor of the Shang dynasty, comm., i. 2.
T'ang, the emperor, comm., ii. 1.
Tsăng, the philosopher, *concluding note to text;* comm., vi. 3.
Ts'in, the State of, comm., x. 14.
Ts'oo, the State of, comm., x. 12.

W

Wăn, the king, comm., iii. 3.

Y

Yaou, the emperor, comm., i. 3; ix. 4.
Yin dynasty, comm., x. 5.
Yin, an ancient officer mentioned in the She-king, comm., x. 4.

INDEX V.

OF SUBJECTS IN THE DOCTRINE OF THE MEAN.

A

Analects, quotations from the, iii.; xxviii. 5.
Ancestors, worship of, xviii. 2, 3; xix.
Antiquity, the regulations of, cannot be attested, xxviii. 5; xxix. 3
Archery, illustrative of the way of the superior man, xiv. 5.

B

Benevolence, to be cherished in treading the path of duty, xx. 4, 5.
Burial and mourning, xviii. 3.

C

Ceremonies, music, &c., can be ordered only by the emperor, xxviii. 2, 3, 4.
Common men and women may carry into practice the Mean in its simple elements, xii. 2, 4.
Completion of every thing effected by sincerity, xxv.

E

Emperor, certain exclusive prerogatives of the, xxviii. 2, 3, 4.
Emperor-sage, the, described, xxix.
Equilibrium, the mind in a state of, i. 4, 5.
Eulogium of Conf., xxx.; xxxi.; xxxii.

F

Fame of Conf. universal, xxxi. 4.
Filial piety, of Shun, xvii.—of king Wan, and the duke of Chow, xix.
Five duties of universal obligation, xx. 8.
Forcefulness, in its relation to the practice of the Mean, x.
Four things to which Conf. had not attained, xiii. 4.

G

Government, easy to him who understands sacrificial ceremonies, xix. 6.—dependent on the character of the officers, and ultimately on that of the sovereign, xx.

H

Harmony, the mind in a state of, i. 4, 5.—combined with firmness, in the superior man, x. 5.
Heaven, rewarding filial piety in the case of Shun, and virtue in the case of Wan, xvii.—Confucius the equal of, xxxi. 3.
Heaven and Earth, order of, dependent on the equilibrium and harmony of the human mind, i. 5.—the perfectly sincere man forms a ternion with, xxii.—Conf. compared to, xxx. 2.

I

Instruction, definition of, i. 1.
Insubordination, the evil of, xxviii.
Intelligence, how connected with sincerity, xxi.

K

Knowledge of duties come by in three different ways, xx. 9.

L

Lamentation that the path of the Mean was untrodden, v.
Law to himself, man a, xiii.

M

Man has the law of the Mean in himself, xiii.
Mean, only the superior man can follow the, ii. 1.—the rarity of the practice of the, iii.—how it was that few were able to practise the, iv.—how Shun practised the, vi.—men's ignorance of the, shown in their conduct, vii.—how Hwuy held fast the course of the, viii.—the difficulty of attaining to the, ix.—on forcefulness in its relation to the, x.—only the sage can come up to the requirements of the, xi. 3.—the course of the, reaches far and wide, but yet is secret, xii.—common men and women may practise the, xii. 2.—orderly advance in the practice of the, xv.—Conf. never swerved from the, xxxi. 1.
Middle kingdom, Conf. fame overspreads the, xxxi. 4.

N

Nature, definition of, i. 1.
Nine standard rules to be followed in the government of the empire, xx. 12, 13, 14, 15.

O

Odes, quotations from the, xii. 3; xiii. 2; xv. 2; xvi. 4; xvii. 4; xxvi; xxvii. 7; xxix. 6; xxxiii. 1, 2, 3, 4, 5, 6.

P

Passions, harmony of the, i. 4.
Path of duty, definition of, i. 1.—may not be left for an instant, i. 2.—is not far to seek, xiii.
Praise of Wăn and Woo, and the duke of Chow, xviii.; xix.
Preparation necessary to success, xx. 16.
Principles of duty, have their root in the evidenced will of Heaven, i. 1.—to be found in the nature of man, xiii.
Progress in the practice of the Mean, xv.
Propriety, the principle of, in relation to the path of duty, xx. 5.

R

Reciprocity, the law of, xiii. 3, 4.
Righteousness, chiefly exercised in honouring the worthy, xx. 5.

S

Sacrifices, to spiritual beings, xvi. 3.—instituted by Woo, and the duke of Chow, xviii. 2, 3.—to Heaven and Earth, xix. 6.—to ancestors, xviii. xix.
Sage, a, only can come up to the requirements of the mean, xi. 3.—naturally and easily embodies the right way, xx. 18.—the glorious path of, xxvii.—Conf. a perfect, xxxi. 1.
Seasons, Confucius compared to the four, xxx. 2, 3.
Secret watchfulness over himself characteristic of the superior man, i. 3.
Self-examination practised by the superior man, xxxiii. 2.
Sincerity, the outgoing of, cannot be repressed, xvi. 5.—the way of Heaven, xx. 17, 18.—how to be attained, xx. 19.—how connected with intelligence, xxi.—the most complete, necessary to the full development of the nature, xxii.—development of, in those not naturally possessed of it, xxiii.—when entire, can foreknow, xxiv.—the completion of every thing effected by, xxv.—the possessor of entire, is the co-equal of Heaven and Earth, and is an infinite, and an independent being,—a God, xxvi; xxxii. 1.
Singleness, necessary to the practice of the relative duties, xx. 8.—necessary to the practice of government, xx. 16, 17.—of king Wăn's virtue, xxvi. 10.
Sovereign, a, must not neglect personal and relative duties, xx. 7.
Spirit, the perfectly sincere man is like a, xxiv.
Spiritual beings, the operation and influence of, xvi.—the emperor-sage presents himself before, without any doubts, xxix. 3, 4.
Steps in the practice of the Mean, xv.
Superior man is cautious, and watchful over himself, i. 2, 3.—only can follow the Mean, ii. 2.—combines harmony with firmness, x. 5.—the way of, is far-reaching and yet secret, xii.—distinguished by entire sincerity, xiii. 4.—in every variety of situation pursues the Mean, and finds his rule in himself, xiv.—pursues his course with determination, xx. 20, 21.—endeavours to attain to the glorious path of the sage, xxvii. 6, 7.—prefers concealment of his virtue, while the mean man seeks notoriety, xxxiii. 1.

T

Three kings, the founders of the three dynasties, xxix. 3.
Three virtues, wherewith the relative duties are practised, xx. 8.
Three things, important to a sovereign, xxix. 1.
Three hundred rules of ceremony, and three thousand rules of demeanour, xxvii. 3.

V

Virtue in its highest degree and influence, xxxiii. 4, 5, 6.
Virtuous course, the commencement and completion of a, xxxiii.

INDEX VI.

OF PROPER NAMES IN THE DOCTRINE OF THE MEAN.

C

Ch'ing, the philosopher, *Introductory note.*
Chow dynasty, xxviii. 5.
Chow, the duke of, xviii. 3; xix.
Chung-ne, designation of Conf., ii. 1; xxx. 1.
Confucian school, *Introductory note.*

G

Gae, the duke of Loo, xx. 1.

H

Hea dynasty, xxviii. 5.
Hwa, the name of a mountain, xxvi. 9.
Hwuy, a disciple of Conf., viii.

K

Ke, a small State in which sacrifices were maintained to the emperors of the Hea dynasty, xxviii. 5.
Ke-leih, the duke, who received from Woo the title of king, xviii. 2, 3.

M

Mencius, *Introductory note.*

S

Shun, the emperor, vi.; xvii. 1; xxx. 1.
Sung, a state in which sacrifices were maintained to the emperors of the Yin dynasty, xxviii. 5.

T

T'ae, the duke, T'an-foo, who received from Woo the title of king, xviii. 2, 3.
Tsze-loo, a disciple of Conf., x. 1.
Tsze-sze, *Introductory note; concluding notes to chapters,* i.; xii.; xx.; xxxiii.

W

Wăn, the king, xvii. 4; xviii.; xx. 2; xxvi. 10; xxx. 1.
Woo, the king, xviii.; xix.; xx. 2; xxx. 1.

Y

Yaou, the emperor, xxx. 1.
Yin dynasty, xxviii. 5.
Yoh, the name of a mountain, xxvi. 9.
Yung, a distinguished scholar, A.D. 1004—1065, *Concluding note to ch. i.*

INDEX VII.

OF CHINESE CHARACTERS AND PHRASES;

INTENDED ALSO TO HELP TOWARDS THE FORMATION OF A DICTIONARY AND CONCORDANCE FOR THE CLASSICS.

A. stands for Analects; G.L.t., for The Great Learning, text; G.L.c., for The Great Learning, commentary; D.M., for The Doctrine of the Mean. In the references to the Analects, books are separated by a colon, and chapters of the same book by a semicolon.

THE 1st RADICAL 一.

一 *yih* *yi*. (1) One, sometimes = a. A., II. i.; IV. vi. 3; xviii. 3; VI. ix.; xxii.; *et alibi, saepe*. G.L.c., x. 18. D.M., viii.; xiii. 4; xxvi. 7, 9. (2) One and the same. D.M., xvii. 3; xx. 9. (3) Singleness, = sincerity. D.M., xx. 8, 18. (4) A unity. A., IV. xv. 1; XV. ii. (5) Adverbially, = by one effort. D.M., xx. 21. (6) As a verb, = to unite in one. A., XIV. xviii. 2. (7) 一人, the one man, a designation of the emperor. A., XX. i. 5. G.L.c., ix. 3. (8) 一...一, partly, now...now. A., XIV. xviii. 2.

七 *ts'ih* *ch'i*. Seven. A., II. iv. 6; XI. xxv. 5, 7, 10; XIII. xxix; XIV. xl.

三 *san*. (1) Three. A., I. xi; II. ii.; iv. 2; III. ii.; *et alibi, saepe*. D.M., xviii. 3; xx. 8, 11; xxvii. 3; xxix. 1. (2) Adverbially, = thrice. A., V. xviii. 1; VIII. i.; X. xviii. 2. Into three parts, A., VIII. xx. 4. But 三省, A., I. iv., on three points. (3) 二三子, ye, disciples. A., III. xxiv.; VII. xxiii.; IX. xi. 3; XI. x. 3; XVII. iv. 4. (4) 三王, three kings; *i.e.*, the founders of the three great dynasties. D.M., xxix. 3. (5) 三歸, the name of a tower. A., III. xxii. 2. (6) 三飯, A., XVIII. ix. 2, = the band-master at the third meal.

三 *san*. Up. 3d tone. Thrice. A., V. xix.; XI. v.; XVIII. ii.

上 *shang* *chang*. (1) He, she, it, this, that, which is above, with the corresponding plurals. A., I. ii. 1; III. xxvi.; *et saepius*. G.L.c., x. 1, 2, 21. D.M., xiv. 3; *et al.* (2) Adverbially, = upwards. A., XIV. xxiv.; xxxvii. 2. (In these instances the tone is low. 2d tone). D.M., xvii. 3; xxx. 1. (3) 在....上, in or on the above of.... A., VI. vii.; IX. xvi. D.M., xvi. 3. (4) 上下, above, below, in opposition, applied to heavens and earth. A., VII. xxx. D.M., xii. 3. (5) 草上之風, the grass, when the wind is upon it. A., XII. xix. (6) 上帝, God, the most High God. G.L.c., x. 5. D.M., xix. 6.

上 *shang* *chang*. Up. 3d tone. To ascend; proceeding upwards. 以上, A., VI. xix.; VII. vii.

下 *hea* *hsia*. Anciently, up. 2d tone. He, she, it, this, that, which is below, with the corresponding plurals; both positive, and superlative. A., IX. iii. 2; X. ii. 1; XVI. ix. G.L.c., x. 2, 20. D.M., xiv. 3; xix. 4; xx. 6. 17; xxix. 2. (2) 上下, see on 上. (3) 於 or 于.....下, in or on the beneath of...., XII. xxii. 1; XVII. xii. 1. (4) 天下, the world, the empire. A., III. xi.; xxiv.; IV. x.; *et al.* G.L.c., i. 4; c., viii. 1; ix. 4; x. 1, 4. D.M., i. 4; x. 1; *et al.* (5) Occurs in the proper name 柳下惠. A., XV. xiii.; XVIII. ii.; viii. 1, 2.

下 *hea* *hsia*. A verb, low. 3d tone. To descend. A., III. vii.; V. xiv.; *et al.* (2) 以下, downwards. A., VI. xix. (3) 下人, to humble one's-self to others. A., XII. xx. 5.

丈 *chang*. 丈人, an old man. A., XVIII. vii. 1.

不 *puh* *pu*. Not. *Passim.*

且 *ts'eay* *ch'ieh*. Moreover; and moreover. A., II. iii. 2; VI. iv.; VII. xv.; VIII. xi.; xiii. 3; IX. xi. 3; XI. xxv. 4; XVI. i. 4, 17; XVIII. vi. 3. D.M., xv. 2; xxvi. 2.

世 *she* *shih*. (1) An age, a generation. A., II. xxiii. 1, 2; VI. xiv.; XIII. xii.; XVI. i. 4; ii. 1; iii. D.M., XI. 1; xxviii. 1; xxix. 3, 4. (2) To all ages. D.M., xxix. 5. (3) 沒世, after death. A., XV. xix. G.L.c., iii. 5. (4) 絕世, interrupted generations; *i.e.*, families whose line of succession has been broken. A., XX. i. 1. D.M., xx. 14. (5) The world. A., XIV. xxxiv.: XVIII. vi. 3. G.L.c., xi. 3. (6) 世叔, as a proper name. A., XIV. ix.

丘 k'ew chiu. (1) A hillock. A. XIX. xx. (2) The name of Confucius. Used by himself. A., V. xxvii.: VII. xxiii.; xxx. 3; xxxiv.: et al. D.M., xiii. 4. Applied to him contemptuously. A., XIV. xxxiv. 1: XVIII. vi. 2, 3. (3) Part of a double surname. A., V. xxi.

並 ping. Properly written 竝. Together, alongside. A., XIV. xlvii. 2: XIX. xvi. G.L.c., x. 22. D.M., xxx. 3.

THE 2D RADICAL. 丨.

个 ko. 一个人, one man. G.L.c., x. 14.

中 chung. The middle. (1) 中, and 在 or 於...中, in, in the midst of. A., II. xviii. 2: V. i. 1: VII. xv.: X. xxii. 2: XV. xxi.: XVI. i. 4, 5. (2) The heart. G.L.c., vi. 2. (3) The Mean. A., VI. xxvii.: XX. i. 1. D.M., i. 4, 5; ii. 1, 2: et passim. (4) 中國, the Middle kingdom, China. G.L.c., x. 15. D.M., xxxi. 4. (5) 中道, midway, halfway. A., VI. x. (6) 中人, mediocre men. A., VI. xix. (7) 中門, to stand in the middle of the gateway. A., X. iv. 2. (8) 中行, to walk in the Mean, to act entirely right. A., XIII. xxi. Comp. D.M., xxxi. 1. (9). 中牟, the name of a place. A., XVII. vii. 2.

中 chung. Up. 3d tone. To hit the mark; hitting the mark; exact. A., XI. xiii. 5; xviii. 2: XIII. iii. 6: XVIII. viii. 3, 4. G.L.c., ix. 2. D.M., i. 4; xx. 18.

THE 3D RADICAL. 丶.

主 choo chu. (1) To count as chief or principal. A., I. viii. 2: III. xvi.: IX. xxiv.: XII. x. (2) A master, president. A., XVI. i. 4.

THE 4TH RADICAL. 丿.

乃 nae nai. To be. 無乃...乎 or 與, is it not...? A., VI. i. 3: XIV. xxxiv. 1: XVI. i. 2.

久 kew chiu. Long, for a long time. A., III. xxiv.: IV. ii.: et al. D.M. iii.; xxvi. 2, 4, 5, 6. After a long time. A., V. xvi.

乎 hoo hu. (1) A particle of interrogation. Found alone; preceded by another interrog. part.; prec. by 不亦. A., I. i.; iv.: II. vii.; viii.; xvii.: VI. xxviii.: VII. xiv. 1, 2: et al., saepe. G.L.c., iii. 2. (2) A particle of exclamation. A., VI. v.: VIII. xviii. 5; xix. 1, 2: IX. xx.: et al. D.M., xvi. 3; xxvii. 2. Foll. by 哉, giving emphasis. A., III. xiv.: VII. xxix.: et al. Prec. by 哉. A., XII. xxii. 5: XIV. xiii. 1, 2. (3) Partly interrog., partly exclam. In this usage it is sometimes preceded by 必也; it is often prec. by 其; and by 矣 immed. before it. A., II. xxi. 2: III. vii.; xi.: IV. vi. 2: V. xviii. 1, 2: et al., saepe. G.L.c., iv. 1; vi. 3. D.M., iii.; xv. 2; xvi. 2; xviii. 2; xix. 2: et al. (4) As a preposition, after verbs and adjectives,—in, to, &c. A., I. x. 2: II. xvi.: VIII. iv. 3: XVIII. x.; et al., saepe. G.L.c., ix. 4; x. 6. D.M., i. 3; vii.; xiv. 1, 2, 5: et al., saepe. (5) Than, in comparison. A., XI. xxv. 2: XVII. xxii.: XIX. xxv. D.M., i. 3, 莫...乎. (6) 惡乎, how. A., IV. v. 2. (7) Observe 異爾乎, A., VI. xii.; and 其庶乎, XI. xviii. 1.

乎 hoo hu. Up. 1st tone. Joined with 於. An exclamation. D.M., xxvi. 10.

之 che chih. (1) Of. A., I. ii. 2; v.; xi. 1: et passim. G.L.c., i. 4; c., iii. 1: et passim. D.M. ii. 2; viii.: et passim. In the construct state, the regent follows the 之, and the regimen precedes. They may be respectively a noun, a phrase, or a larger clause. (2) Him, her, it, them. A., I. vii.: XIV. xviii. 1; xix. 2: et passim. So, in G.L., and D.M. (3) It is often difficult to find the antecedent to 之, and it seems merely to give a substantive force to the verb. A., II. xiii.: III. xxiii.: XVII. ix. 6: XV. x. 2, 3: et saepe. D.M., xx. 18, 19, 20: et al. (4) 有之, G.L.c., viii. 2; x. 18, as in (2), but 有之 and 無之 are more like our use of impersonal verbs. G.L.c., ix. 1. A., IV. vi. 3. (5) Where 之 comes in a sentence with 未, it is generally transposed. G.L.c., 7. A., IV. vi. 3: et al. So, 莫之知避 D.M., vii.: et al. All negative adverbs seem to exert this attractive force. (6) 之謂, it is called. D.M., i. 1. G.L.c., vi. 1. A., XVI. xii. 2: et al. 謂之 is different, and comes under (2). So, 譬之, A., XIX. xxiii. 2. (7) Obs. the idiom in A., VI. iii. 2: XI. vii. 1, 2; xxv. 11: XVIII. i. 1. (8) 如之何, how. A., III. xix.: XI. xix.: et al. (9) 死之, died with, or for, him. A., XIV. xvii. 1.

(10) 末之難. A., XIV. xlii. 3. (11) =於, in regard to. G.L.c., viii. 1. (12) =此, this. G.L.c., ix. 6. (13) As a verb. To go, or come, to. A., V. xviii. 2; XIII. xix.: et al. (14) Part of a man's name. A., VI. xiii.

乘 shing ch'ing — To mount, to ride; spoken of horses, carriages, boats. A., V. vi.: VI. iii. 2: XV. x. 3; xxv.

乘 shing ch'ing — Low. 3d tone. (1) A carriage. A., I. v.: V. vii. 2, 3: et al. G.L.c., x. 22. (2) A team of 4 horses. A., V. xviii. 2.

THE 5TH RADICAL. 乙.

九 kiu chiu — Nine. A., VI. iii. 3: VIII. xxi. 3: XVI. x. 九夷, the nine rude tribes on the east. A., IX. xiv. 九經, the nine standard rules of govt. D.M., xx. 12, 15.

九 kiu chiu — Up. 1st tone. To collect. A., XIV. xvii. 2.

乞 k'ih ch'i — To beg. A., V. xxiii.

也 yé yeh — (1) A particle used at the end of sentences. Sometimes it might be dispensed with, and at others it is felt to be necessary, not only to the euphony and strength of the style, but also to give clearness and definiteness to the meaning. A., I. ii. 1; viii. 2: X. i.; ii. 1, 2; iii. 1, 2, 3, 4, 5: et passim. So also in G.L., and D.M. It closes also the diff. clauses in a long predicate, where we might use the ":" in English. D.M., xxv. 2: et al. (2) It is used after proper names, after some adverbs, and after a clause, in the first member of a sentence, and may be construed as—as to, the Latin quoad. A., I. x. 1, 2; xv. 3: VII. xxv. 1: XI. vi.; xii. 3; xiv. 2; xv.; xvi. 1; xvii. 1, 2, 3, 4: et passim. So, in G.L., and D.M. In these cases it is followed at the end of the sentence, by another particle,—itself, 矣, 焉, 乎. (3) As correlate of 者, in explanation of terms. G.L.c., iii. 4; vi. 1; x. 7. D.M., xxv. A., III. viii. 3: XII. xvii.: et al., saepe. (4) At the end of sentences, we find 者也, sometimes preceded by 者, sometimes not. In these cases, 者 may often be explained as imparting a participial or adjective power to other characters, but not so always. A., V. xxvi.: VI. ii.: VII. xix.: et saepe. So, in G.L., and D.M. (5) 也者 in the first member of a sentence, resuming a previous word, and followed by an explanation or account of it. A., I. ii. 2. D.M., i. 2, 4: et al., saepe. (6)—乎, interrog. A., III. xxii. 1: V. xvii.: VI. xxv. (7) As a final, it appears often followed by other particles:—也與; 也已; 也已矣; 也夫; 也哉.

亂 lwan luan — (1) To confound; unregulated; confusion, insurrection. A., VII. xx.: VIII. ii.; x.; xiii. 2: X. xiii. 4: XV. xxvi.: XVII. viii. 3; xviii.; xxiii.: XVIII. vii. 5. 作亂, to raise confusion, or insurrection. A., I. ii. 1. G.L.t., 7: c., ix. 3. D.M., xx. 14. (2) To put in order; able to govern. A., VIII. xx. 2. (3) The name of a certain part in a musical service. A., VIII. xv.

THE 6TH RADICAL. 亅.

予 yu yü — (1) I, me, my. A., III. viii. 3: VI. xxvi.; viii. 3; et al. D.M., vii.; xxxiii. 6. (2) Name of a disciple of Conf. A., V. ix. 1, 2: XVII. xxi. 6.

事 sze shih — (1) An affair, affairs; business. A., I. v.; xiv.: III. viii. 2; xv.: XV. i. 1: et al., saepe. G.L.t., 3: c., ix. 3; x. 20. D.M., xix. 2; xx. 16. 有事, having troublesome affairs. A., II. viii. Having an affair with. A., XVI. i. 2. 從事, to pursue business. A., VIII. v.: XVII. i. 2. 執事, to manage business. A., XIII. xvii. (2) Labours; the results of labour. A., XII. xxi. 3: XV. ix.: XIX. vii. D.M., xx. 14. (3) To serve. A., IX. xv. D.M., xix. 4: et passim. (4) 何事於仁 is probably=何有於仁, what difficulty has he in practising benevolence? so that it may be classed under (1). A., VI. xxviii. 1.

THE 7TH RADICAL. 二.

二 urh — (1) Two. A., III. xiv.; XII. vii. 2: ix. 2: et al. (2) 二三子, see 三 (3).

于 yu yü — In, on, to, from. A., II. iv. 1; xxi. 2: XX. i. 3: et al. G.L.c., iii. 2: et al. D.M., xvii. 4: et al.

云 yun yün — (1) Says, saying; gen., in quotations. A., II. xxi. 2: IX. vi. 4: XIV. xliii. 1: XIX. iii.; xxiii. 4. 詩云, often in G.L., and D.M. Observe A., XVII. vi. (2) Closing a sentence, and apparently = so. A., VII. xviii. 2; xxxiii.

五 wu wu — Five. D.M., xx. 8. A., II. iv. 1, 4: XX. ii. 1: et al.

互 hu hu — 互鄉, the name of a village. A., VII. xxviii.

井 *tsing* ching. A well. A., VI. xxiv. 1.

亟 *k'i* ch'i. Up. 3d tone. Frequently. A., XVII. i. 2.

亞 *ya* ya. 亞飯,—the band-master at the second meal. A., XVIII. ix. 2.

THE 8TH RADICAL, 亠.

亡 *wang*. (1) The dead. D.M., xix. 5; xx. 2. (2) To perish, to go to ruin. D.M., xxiv.; xxxiii. 1. (3) To cause to perish. A., VI. viii. (4) Not at home. A., XVII. i. 1. 亡人, a fugitive. G.L.c., x. 12.

亡 *wu* wu. Used as 無, not having, being without. A., III. v.; VI. ii.; VII. xxv. 3; XI. vi.; XII. v. 1; XV. xxv; XVII. xvi. 1; XIX. ii.; v.

亢 *k'ang*. 陳亢, a disciple of Conf. A., XVI. xiii. 1, 5. The same as 子禽.

交 *kiao* chiao. (1). Intercourse, to have intercourse with. A., I. iv.; vii.; V. xvi.; XIX. iii. G.L.c., iii. 3. D.M., xx. 8. (2) To give, to bestow. G.L.c., x. 2.

亦 *yih* yi. Also; even then. A., I. xii. 2; xiii.; III. xxii. 3; V. xi.; xx.; iv.; et saepe. G.L.c., iv. 2, 13, 22. D.M., xii. 2; et al. 不亦...乎, is it not? But the meaning of *also* may often be brought out. A., I. i. 1, 2, 3; XX. ii. 3; et al.

享 *hiang* hsiang. To offer, present. A., X. v. 2.

THE 9TH RADICAL, 人.

人 *jin* jên. (1) A man, other men, man,—humanity. A., I. i. 3; iv.; v.; x. 2; et passim. So, in G.L., and D.M. (2) As opposed to 民, meaning officers. D.M., xvii. 4. A., XI. xxiv. 3. (3) 爲人, playing the man, the style of man. A., I. ii.; VIII. xviii. 2. Obs. 人君, 人父, 人子, 人臣. G.L.c., iii. 3. (4) 小人, the mean man, opp. to 君子, passim. (5) 聖人, the sage. A., VII. xxv; XVI. viii. 1, 2; XIX. xii. 2. D.M., xii. 2; xvii. 1; xx. 18; xxvii. 1; xxix. 3, 4. (6) 門人, disciples. A., IV. xv. 2; VII. xxviii. 1; et al. (7) 庶人, all the people, the masses. A., XVI. ii. 3. G.L.c. 6. D.M., xviii. 3. (8) 善人, the good man. A., VII. xxvi. 2; et al. (9) 成人, the complete man. A., XIV. xiii. (10) 婦人, a woman. A., VIII. xx. 3. (11) 夫人, the designation of the wife of the prince of a State. A., XVI. xiv. (12) Used in designations of officers, like our word man in huntsman, 封人, the border-warden. A., III. xxiv. 行人, the manager of foreign intercourse. A., XIV. ix.

仁 *jin* jên. Is found passim. (1) Benevolence. (2) Perfect virtue.

今 *kin* chin. (1) Now; the present, modern, time. Saepe. (2) Used logically, by way of inference. A., XI. xxiii. 4; XVI. i. 6, 12. D.M., xxvi. 9.

仍 *jing* jing. According as. A., XI. xiii. 2.

仕 *sze* shih. To take—to be in—office. A., V. 5; xviii.; XV. vi. 2; XVII. i. 2; XVIII. vii. 5; XIX. xiii.

他 *t'o* t'a. Other, another. A., V. xviii. 2; X. xi. 1; XVI. xiii. 2; XIX. xviii.; xxiv. G.L.c., x. 13.

仞 *jin* jên. A measure of eight cubits. A., XIX. xxiii. 3.

代 *tai* tai. (1) Instead of, alternate. D.M., xxx. 2. (2) A dynasty. 三代, the three dynasties;—Hea, Shang, and Chow. A., III. xiv. 二代. A., XV. xxiv. 2.

令 *ling*. (1) To order. A., XIII. vi; XX. ii. 3. G.L.c., ix. 4. (2) Excellent. D.M., xvii. 4. (3) Specious, insinuating. A., I. iii.; V. xxiv. (4) 令尹, designa. of the chief minister of Tsoo. A., V. xviii. 1.

以 *i* i. (1) To do. A., II. x. 1. Rarely found in this sense. ? A., XI. xxv. 3. (2) By, with, according to, and perhaps other English prepositions. G.L.c., ix. 3. D.M., xviii. 3; xx. 4. A., I. v.; II. i.; iii. 1, 2; v. 3; et passim. To this belong 所以, therefore, that by which; 是以, hence; 何以, whereby;—which are found passim. (3) To take. This use is analogous to the preced., but the 以 precedes the verb, and is often followed by it, without an intervening object, as in 以告, 以與, &c. 以爲, to take to be, to consider, to be considered. Examples occur passim. We may refer to it the use of 以 sometimes at the beginning of a sentence,—considering, take it that. (4) To; so as to. G.L.c., 6; c., x. iii. D.M., x. 3; xxvii. 6, 7; xxix. 3, 4, 5. A., II. ii; ix: III. xxiii.; VII. I, 2; *et passim*. Sometimes we might translate in these cases by—*and thereby*. But not so in such cases as 以至, 以上, 以下, &c. (5) It is often found after 可. 可以, may, may be. (6) To use, to be used. A., III. xxi.; X. xvi. 2; XIII. xiv; XVIII. x. (7) The following instances are peculiar. G.L.c., iii. 5. D.M., xxviii. 5. A., XIV. xiv. 2; XV. xxx.; XIX. xxv. 4; XX. i. 3.

仰 *gang* To look up to. A., IX. x. 1; XIX. xxi.

任 *jăn* *jĕn* Low, 1st tone. 周任, a man's name. A., XVI. i. 6.

任 *jăn* *jĕn* (1) An office, a charge. A., VIII. vii. 1, 2. D.M., xx. 14. (2) To repose trust in. A., XVII. vi. 1; XX. i. 9.

伐 *fâ* *fa* (1) To attack by imperial authority. A., XVI. i. 1, 4; ii. 1. (2) To boast. A., V. xxv. 3; VI. xiii.; XIV. ii. 1. (3) To cut down, or out. D.M., xiii. 2. G.L.c., x. 22.

休 *hew* *hsiu* 休休, simple and upright. G.L.c., x. 14.

伊 *e* *i* 伊尹, the minister of the great T'ang. A., XII. xxii. 6.

伏 *fûh* *fu* To lie at the bottom. D.M., xxxiii. 2.

仲 *chung* The second of three; the second of brothers. Enters very commonly into designations, as in that of Confucius. D.M., ii.; xxx. A., XIX. xxii.; xxiii.; xxiv.; xxv. Of others. VI. i. 2, 3; iv.; XI. ii. 2; XII. ii.; XIII. ii.—III. xxii. 1, 2, 3; XIV. x. 3; xvii. 1, 2; xviii. 1, 2.—V. xvi. —V. xvii.; XV. xiii.—XIV. xiii.; xv.—XIV. xx. 2.—XVIII. viii. 1, 4.—XVIII. xi. A surname. A., VI. vi.; XI. xxiii.; XVIII. vi.

伯 *pih* *pi* The eldest of brothers. Enters into designations. A., XVI. xiii.; XVII. x.—XIV. xxvi.; XV. vi. 2.—II. vi.; V. vii.—V. xxii.; VII. ix. 2; XVI. xii.; XVIII. viii.—VI. i. 2.—XVIII. xi. *bis*.—XIV. xxxviii.; XIX. xviii. 2.—VIII. i. 1.—VI. viii.; XI. ii. 2. A surname. A., XIV. x. 3. 公伯 see 公.

似 *sze* *ssŭ* Like to, as. A., X. i. 1; iv. 3, 4. D.M., xv. 5.

位 *wei* Position, status. A., IV. xiv.; X. iv. 3, 5; *et al.* D.M., XIV. i. 2; *et al.* 天地位焉, Heaven and Earth get their places. D.M., i. 5.

佚 *yih* *yi* Idleness. A., XVI. v.

佑 *yew* *yu* To aid. D.M., xvii. 4.

何 *ho* What, what kind of, how. A., II. v. 3; vii.; xv.; xxii. 1; XVII. v. 2; ix.; xix. 2, 3; *et saepe*. G.L.c., vi. 2. (2) 如何, generally with 之 between. What, implying difficulty, indignation, or surprise. Other words are found also between the 如 and 何, and then the phrase=what has......to do with......? G.L.c., x. 22. A., III. xviii.; IX. v. 3; xiii. 2; xxiii.; *et saepe*. (3) 何如, what as?=what do you think of? how can it be said? A., I. xv. 1; V. iii.; xvii. 1, 2; *et saepe*. (4) 何有, gen., but not always,—will have no difficulty. A., VI. vi.; VII. ii.; XIII. xiii.; *et al.* (5) 何爲, gen.,=why. A., VI. xxiv.; IX. xv.; XIV. xxvi. 2; xxiv.; *et al.*

作 *tsoh* *tso* (1) To make, produce. G.L.c., ix. 2. A., I. ii. 2; XI. xiii. 2. To do. A., VII. xxvii. (2) To lay the foundation of, to be a maker or author. A., VII. i. D.M., xviii. 1. (3) To make,=to be. A., XIII. xxii. (4) To be begun. A., III. xxiii. (5) To rise, arise. A., IX. ix.; X. xvi. 4; xviii. 2; XI. xxv. 7; XIV. xl.

佞 *ning* Glib-tongued. A., V. iv. 1, 2; VI. xiv.; XI. xxiv. 4; XIV. xxxiv. 1, 2; XV. x. 6; XVI. iv.

佛 *pih* *pi* A surname. A., XVII. vii. 1, 2.

佾 *yih* *yi* A row of pantomimes. A., III. i.

使 *sze* *shih* Up. 3d tone. To send on a mission; to be commissioned. A., VI. iii. 1; XIII. v.; xx.; XIV. xxvi. 1, 2.

使 *sze* *shih* Up. 2d tone. (1) To cause. G.L.c., iv. D.M., xvi. 3. A., II. xx.; III. xxi.; XVIII. vi. 1; vii. 4; x.; *et al.* (2) To employ; to be employed. G.L.c., x. 22. D.M., xx. 14. A., V. vii. 2, 3, 4; VI. vi.; vii.; *et al.* (3) To treat, behave to. G.L.c., ix. 1; x. 2. A., II. xix.; V. xv. (4) Supposing that. A., VIII. xi.

依 *e* *i* To accord with. D.M., xi. 3. A., VII. vi. 3.

來 *lae* *lai* (1) To come. A., I. i. 2; *et al.* (2) To encourage, induce to come. D.M., xx. 12, 13. A., xvi. i. 11, 12; XIX. xxv. 4. (3) Coming, future. A., IX. xxii.; XVIII. v.; I. xv. 3.

儒 ju — A scholar. A., VI. xi.

儀 i — (1) Deportment. G.L.c., ix. 8. (2) Example. G.L.c., x. 5. (3) 禮儀, rules of ceremony. 威儀, rules of deportment. D.M., xxvii. 3. G.L.c., iii. 4. (4) The name of a place. A., III. xxiv.

優 yu — Abundant, more than adequate. A., XIV. xii.; XIX. xiii. 優優, D.M., xxvii. 3.

儺 no — Certain ceremonies to expel evil influences. A., X. x. 2.

儼 yen — 儼然, stern, dignified-like. A., XIX. ix.; XX. ii. 2.

THE 10TH RADICAL 儿.

允 yun — Sincerely. A. XX. i. 1.

兄 hsiung — An elder brother. 兄弟, elder and younger brothers. A brother. A., II. xxi. 2; V. i. 2; XII. v. 1, 4: *et al.* Also A. XIII. vii. G.L.c., ix. 7, 8. D.M., xiii. 4; xv. 2.

先 hsien — (1) First, former, before. A., II. xiii.; X. xiii. 1: *et al.* So, in G.L. and D.M. 先王, the ancient kings. A., I. xii. 1. =a former king. A., XVI. i. 4. (2) Ancestors. D.M., xix. 6. Comp. 先進, A., XI. i. (3) 先生, elders, II. viii.; XIV. xlvii. 2. (4) To make first, or chief. A., VI. xx.; XII. xxi. 3; XIII. ii. (5) 先之, A., XIII. i. To give an example to.

先 hsien — Up. 3d tone. To precede. Quickly. G.L.c., x. 2, 16.

克 k'o — (1) To be able, to attain to. G.L.c., i. 1, 2; x. 5. (2) To subdue. A., XII. i. 1. (3) The love of superiority. A., XIV. ii.

免 mien — (1) To escape, avoid. A., II. iii. 1; V. i. 2: *et al.* (2) To dispense with, have done with. A., XVII. xxi. 6.

兕 sze — A rhinoceros. A., XVI. i. 7.

兢 king — 兢兢, apprehensive and cautious. A., VIII. iii.

THE 11TH RADICAL 入.

入 ju — To enter. G.L.c., x. 1. D.M., xiv 2. A., III. xv.: *et al.* 出入, abroad, at home. A., I. vi.; IX. xv. 3. But in A., XIX. xi. 出入=to pass and repass. 入德, to enter into virtue. D.M., xxxiii. 1.

內 nei — Within, internal, internally. 四海之內, the within of—that which is within—the four seas; *i.e.*, the empire. D.M., xvii. 1: *et al.* Precedes the verb, =internally. A., IV. xvii.: *et al.* Obs. A., X. xvii. 2. As a verb G.L.c., x. 7, to make the internal, *i.e.*, of primary importance.

兩 liang — Two. D.M., vi. A., III. xxii. 3; IX. vii.

THE 12TH RADICAL 八.

八 pa — Eight. A., III. i.; XVIII. xi.

公 kung — (1) Public. A., VI. xii. (2) Just. A., XX. i. 2. (3) A duke, dukes. D.M., xviii. 3. A., III. ii.: *et al.* It often occurs in connection with the name and country of the noble spoken of. It enters also into double surnames. 公明, A., XIV. xiv. 1, 2:—公山, XVI. v.:—公西, VII. xxxiii.: XI. xxi.; xx. v.:—公冶, A., V. i. 1. Obs. 公子, A., XIII. viii.—XIV. xvii.; xviii.—公叔, A., XIV. xiv.:—公伯, A., xxxviii.: 公孫 A., XIX. xxii.: 公門, the palace gate. A., X. iv. 1. 於公, in the prince's *temple*. A., X. viii. 8.

六 lu — Six. A., II. iv. 5: *et al.*

兮 hsi — A particle of exclamation. O! how! Much used in poetry. G.L.c., iii. 4. A., III viii. 1; XVIII. v. 1. In G.L.c., x. 13, quoted from the Shoo-king, it appears for 猗.

共 kung — Together with, sharing with. A., V. xxv. 2; IX. xxix. 1.

共 kung — Up. 3d tone. To move towards. A., II. i.; X. xviii. 2.

兵 ping — Weapons of war. A., XII. vii. 1, 2; XIV. xvii. 2.

前 *tsʻien* chʻien. (1) Before, the front. G.L.c., x. 2. A. IX. x. 1.: X. iii. 2: XV. x. 3. (2) Formerly. A., XVII. iv. 4. (3) Beforehand. D.M., xx. 16; xxiv. (4) Former. G.L.c., iii. 5.

剛 *kang*. Firm, firmness. D.M., xxxi. 1. A., V. x.: *et al.*

割 *ko* ko. To cut. A., X. viii. 8: XVII. iv. 2.

創 *chʻwang* chʻuang. To make first. A., XIV. ix.

THE 19th RADICAL. 力.

力 *li* li. Strength, power; opportunity; strongly, strenuously. D.M., xx. 10; xxxi. 4. A., I. vi.; vii.; VII. 20: *et al.*

功 *kung*. Achievement, work done. A., VIII. xix. 2: XVII. vi.: XX. i. 9. D.M., xx. 2.

加 *kea* chia. To add. A., XIII. ix. 3, 4. To come upon, affect. IV. vi. To do to. V. xi. To lay upon. X. xiii. 8; to have in addition. XI. xxv. 4.

加 *kea* chia. Up. 2d tone, supposed to be for 假, if. A., VII. xvi.

助 *tsoo* chu. To help. A., XI. iii.

勃 *pŭ* po. 勃如, changing-like, spoken of the countenance. A., X. iii. 1; iv. 5; v. 1.

勇 *yung*. Valour, physical courage; bold. D.M., xx. 8, 10. A., II. xxiv. 2: XIV. v.; xiii.; xxx.; *et al.*

勉 *mëen* mien. To exert one's-self, use effort. D.M., xiii. 4; xx. 9, 18. A., IX. xv.

動 *tung*. To move, as a neuter verb. D.M., xx. 14; xxix. 5; xxxiii. 2. A., XII. i. 2. 知者動, the wise are active. A., VI. xxi. Obs. 動乎四體, D.M., xxiv. (2) To move, excite; as an active verb. D.M., xxiii.; xxvi. 6. A., VIII. iv. 3; XV. xxxii. 3. 動干戈, to stir up hostile movements. A., XVI. i. 13.

務 *woo* wu. To attend to earnestly, as the chief thing. G.L.c., x. 23. A., I. ii. 2: VI. xx.

勝 *shing* shêng. To exceed, surpass. A., VI. xvi.: X. viii. 4.

勝 *shing* shêng. Up. 1st tone. To be able for. A., X. v. 1. 勝殘, to transform the violent. A., XIII. xi.

勞 *laou* lao. (1) Toil, toiled, toilsome. A., II. viii.: IV. xiii.: VIII. ii. 勞之, to toil for the people. XIII. i. Comp. XIV. viii. (2) Merit. A., V. xxv. 3. (3) To make to labour. A., XIX. x.: XX. ii. 1, 2.

勤 *kʻin* chʻin. Laborious, accustomed to toil. A., XVIII. vii. 1.

勸 *keuen* chʻüan. (1) To encourage, advise. D.M., xx. 14. (2) To rejoice to follow, to exhort one another to good, i.e., to be advised. D.M., xx. 13; xxxiii. 14. A., II. xx.

THE 20th RADICAL. 勹.

勺 *chŏ* cho. A ladle, a ladleful. D.M., xxvi. 9.

勿 *wuh* wu. (1) Do not;—prohibitive. D.M., xiii. 3. A., I. viii. 4: *et al.* (2) Not;—negative, or the prohibition indirect. A., VI. iv.: XII. ii.: XIV. viii.

匏 *pʻaou* pʻao. A gourd. A., XVII. vii. 4.

THE 21st RADICAL. 匕.

化 *hwa* hua. To transform; to be transformed. Applied to the operations of Heaven and Earth, and of the sage. D.M., xxii.; xxiii.; xxx. 3; xxxii. 1; xxxiii. 6.

北 *pih* pei. The north, northern. D.M., x. 3, 4. A., II. i.

THE 22d RADICAL. 匚.

匡 *kʻwang* kʻuang. (1) To rectify. A., XIV. xviii. 2. (2) The name of a State. A., IX. v. 1.: XI. xxii.

匱 *kwei* kuei. A case, a casket. A., IX. xii.

THE 23d RADICAL. 匸.

匹 *pʻeih* pʻi. 匹夫, a common man. A., IX. xxv. 匹夫, 匹婦. A., XIV. xviii. 3.

匿 *nih* ni. To conceal. A., V. xxiv.

區 *kʻeu* chʻü. Classes, classified. A., XIX. xii. 2.

THE 24th RADICAL. 十.

十 *shih*. Ten. G.L.c., vi. 3. A., II. iv. 1, 2, 3, 4, 5, 6: *et al.* Adverbially, at ten times, by ten efforts. D.M., xx. 20.

THE 25TH RADICAL. 卜.

THE 26TH RADICAL. 卩.

THE 27TH RADICAL. 厂.

THE 28TH RADICAL. 厶.

THE 29TH RADICAL. 又.

al. Friendship. A., XII. xxiii.: XVI. iv. Friendly with, to make friends of. A., V. xxiv.; XV. ix. (2) Brotherly regard. A., II. xxi. 2.

反 *fan* (1) To be, or act, contrary to. G.L.c., ix. 4. D.M., ii. A., XII. xvi. (2) To turn round, on or to; to return. A., IX. xiv.; XVIII. vii. 4. D.M., xiv. 5. 反諸身, to turn round on and examine one's self. D.M., xx. 17. Observe A., VII. viii. 反坫, name of an ancient stand for cups. A., III. xxii. 3. (3) To repeat. A., VII. xxxi. (4) Up. 1st tone, for 翻. A., IX. xxx. 1. (5) 之反, a man's name. A., VI. xiii.

取 *tsen ch'ü* To take, to get. D.M., xx. 4. A., V. ii. Obs. V. vi.; VI. xxviii.: et al. 奚取, what application can it have? A., III. ii. 色取仁, assuming the appearance of virtue. A., XII. xx. 6.

娶 *tsen ch'ü* Up. 3d tone. To marry a wife. A., VII. xxx. 2.

叔 *shuh shu* A father's younger brother. In enumerating brothers, not the oldest nor the youngest. Used in surnames and designations. A., XIV. xx. 2.—XIX. xxii.; xxiv.—XIV. xiv. 1; xix.—V. xxii.: VII. xiv. 2; XVI. xiii.—XVIII. ix. 3. —XIV. ix. XVII. viii. 1, 2.—XVIII. xi. &c.

受 *show shou* To receive. D.M., xvii. 4, 5, xviii. 3. A., X. xi. 2; et al. To acquiesce in. A., XI. xviii.; 2. =to be intrusted with. A., XV. xxxiii.

THE 30TH RADICAL. 口

口 *k'ow k'ou* The mouth. G.L.c., x. 14. A., XVII. xviii. 口給, smartnesses of speech. A., V. iv. 2.

古 *koo ku* Antiquity. G.L.T., 4. D.M., xxviii. 1. A., III. xvi.; et al. 古者, the ancients; anciently. A., IV. xxii.: XVII. xvi. 1.

叩 *k'ow k'ou* (1) To tap, strike. A., XIV. xlvi. (2) To inquire about. A., IX. vii.

召 *chaou chao* To call, summon. A., VIII. iii.; et al. Read *shaou*, 召南,—see 南. 召忽, a name. A., XIV. xvii.

只 *che chih* Three. G.L.c., x. 3.

右 *yew yu* The right, on the right hand. G.L.c., x. 2. D.M., xvi. 2. A., X. iii. 2. Obs. X. vi. 5.

史 *she shih* (1) An historiographer. A., XV. xxv. (2) A clerk, a scrivener. A., VI. xvi.

司 *sze szŭ* (1) Always in the phrase 有司, the officers. A., VIII. iv. 3; xx. ii. 3. (2) 司馬, a double surname. A., XII. iii.; iv.; v. (3) 司敗, the minister of Crime. A., VII. xxx.

可 *k'o* May. Passim. As in English, the may may represent possibility, ability, liberty, or moral power, so with the char. 可. It is found continually in the combination 可以 = may (seldom, if ever, can), where we can't assign much distinctive force to the 以. 可也 is concessive, but does not indicate entire approval. A., I. xv. 1; II. xxiii.; VI. i. 2; et al. 可矣, however, is more concessive. A., V. xix.; VII. xxv. 1, 2; et al. Obs. A., XIV. xiii. 2; XVIII. viii. 5; XIX. iii.

各 *ko ko* Each, every one. A., IV. vii.; V. xxv. 1: IX. xiv.; XI. vii. 2; xxv. 7, 8.

名 *ming* (1) Name, names; to name. A., IV. v. 2: VIII. xix.; XIII. iii. 2, 5, 7; et al. (2) Fame, reputation. D.M., xvii. 2; xviii. 2; xxxi. 4. 習名. A., IX. ii.

合 *ho ho* To unite, assemble; united; a collection. D.M., xv. 2; xxv. 3. A., XIII. viii.; XIV. xvii. 2.

同 *t'ung* (1) The same. D.M., xxviii. 3. A., III. xvi.; et al. Together with. A., XIV. xix. As a verb, to be together in, to share. D.M., x. 14; xx. 14. (2) Applied to a certain imperial audience. A., XI. xxv. 6, 12.

后 *how hou* (1) Sovereign, a sovereign. A., III. xxi.: XX. i. 3. (2) Used throughout the G.L. for 後, afterwards.

吉 *keih chi* Fortunate. 吉月, the first day of the month. A., X. vi. 11.

君 *keun chün* A ruler, a sovereign. Passim. 君臣, Ruler and minister, the relation between. Sep. 君夫人. 小君, designations of the wife of the prince of a State. A., XVI. xiv. 君子, see on 子. 人君, &c. G.L.c., iii. 3. See 人.

齊 *lin* Niggardly, stingy. A., VIII. xi.: XX. ii. 3.

否 *fow fou* A negation, not. G.L.T., 1. =to do wrong. A. XI. xxvi.

吳 wu. The name of a State. A. VII. xxx. 2.

吾 wu. I. *Pассim.* In a few cases, *we*. Very rarely plural. Almost always in the nominative.

告 kao. To tell, report, announce to. A. I. xv. 5; II. v. 2; XIV. xxii. 2, 3, 4, 5. 告者, the reporters. A., XIV. xiv. 2.

告 kuh. To inform respectfully. A., III. xvii. 1; XII. xxiii.

味 wei. Taste, flavours. A., VII. xiii. D.M., iv. 2. G.L.c., vii. 2.

周 chow. (1) Catholic. A., II. xiv. (2) Explained by 至. A., XX. i. 5. (3) To assist, give charity to, syn. with 賙. A., VI. iii. 2. (4) Name of the Chow dynasty or of its original seat. *Pассim.* 周公, the duke of Chow. *Pассim.* 周任, a man's name. A., XVI. i. 6. 周南, one of the Books of the She-king. XVII. x. 1.

呼 hu. 嗚呼, alas. A., III. vi. 1.

命 ming. (1) To order, direct; what is appointed, spoken of what Heaven appoints,—the empire, our nature, and generally. G.L.c., i. 2; ii. 3, 5, 11. D.M., i. 1; xiv. 4; *et al.* A., II. iv. 4; VI. ii.; viii.; IX. i.; *et al.* (2) Spoken of a sovereign's ordering; a commission. A., VIII. vi.; X. iii. 4; xiii. 4; XIII. xx. 1; XVI. ii. 1; XX. i. 2. (3) Life. 致命, to devote life. A., XIV. xiii. 2; XIX. i. (4) Govt. notifications. A., XIV. ix. (5) Messages between host and guest. 將命, to convey such messages. A., XIV. xlvii. 1; XVII. xx.

命 ming. Used for 慢, *man*. Disrespectful. G.L.c., x. 16.

和 ho. Harmony, harmonious; natural ease, affable. D.M., i. 4, 5; x.; xv. 2. A., I. xii. 1, 2; XIII. xxiii.; XVI. i. 10; XIX. xxv. 4.

和 ho. Low, 3d tone. To accompany in singing. A., VII. xxxi.

咎 kew. To blame. A., III. xxi. 2.

哂 shin. To smile at. A., XI. xxv. 4, 6, 9.

咨 tsze. Ho! Oh! A., xx. i. 1.

哀 gae. (1) Sorrow, sorrowful, to feel sorry. G.L.c., viii. 1. D.M., i. 4. A., III. xxvi. *et al.* (2) Hon. epithet of a duke of Loo. D.M., xx. 1. A., III. xxi. *et al.*

哉 tsai. A particle of exclamation, expressing admiration or surprise. (1) It is often at the end of sentences. G.L.c., x. 13. D.M., xxvii. 3. A., III. xvii. 1; *et al.* (2) It is often used at the close of the first clause of a sentence, the subject exclaimed about following. D.M., x. 5; xxvii. 1. A., III. iv. 2; V. ii.; *et al.* (3) It often closes an interrogative sentence, being preceded by 何, 焉, 乎, and other interrog. particles, tho' the 乎 is itself sometimes more exclamatory than interrogative. A., II. x. 4; xxii.; VIII. xv.; IX. vii.; *et al.*

哲 che. Wise, prudent. D.M., xxvii. 7.

唐 t'ang. (1) 唐棣, a kind of tree. A., IX. xxx. 1. (2) A designation of the emperor Yaou. A., VIII. xx. 2.

哭 k'uh. To weep, wail. A., VII. ix. 2; XI. ix. 1.

唯 wei. Only. *Sæpe.* It stands at the beginning of the sentence or clause to which it belongs, such instances as A., II. vi.; D.M., xxxiii. 2, being only apparent exceptions. Observe. A., VII. xxviii. 2.

唯 wei. Low, 3d tone. Yes. A., IV. xv. 1.

問 wăn. (1) To ask, to ask about, to investigate; a question. *Pассim.* (2) To inquire for, to visit. A., VI. viii.; VIII. iv. 1. To send a complimentary inquiry. A., X. xi. 1.

啟 k'e. To open out; to uncover. A., VII. viii.; VIII. iii.

啻 ch'e. Simply, only. G.L.c., x. 14.

喻 yu. (1) To instruct. G.L.c., ix. 4. (2) To understand, be conversant with. A., IV. xvi.

善 shan. Good; the good:—in both numbers, and all persons. *Pассim.* (2) Skilful; ability. D.M., xix. 2. A., V. xvi.; VII. xxxi.; *et al.* (3) As a verb, to consider, or make good. G.L.c., x. 23. A., XV. ix.

嗅 heu. To smell. A., X. xviii. 2.

喜 *hsi* Joy, joyful, to be joyful. D.M., i. 4. A., IV. xxi. V. vi.; xviii. 1: XVI. xiii. 5; XIX. xix.

喟 *k'wei* 喟然, sighingly. A., IX. x. 1: XI. xxv. 7.

喪 *sang* To mourn, mourning: mourning clothes. D.M., xviii. 3. A., III. iv. 3; xx: VI. ix: XVII. xxi. 1, 5, 6: *et al.*

喪 *sang* Up. 3d tone. To lose. G.L.c., x. 5. To lose office, a throne. A., III. xxiv.: XIV. xx. 1, 2. (2) To let be lost, to destroy. A., IX. v. 3: XI. viii.: XIII. xv. 4, 5.

喧 *hsüan* 喧兮, how distinguished! G.L.c., iii. 4.

嘉 *chia* Admirable. D.M., xvii. 4. To commend, honour. D.M., xx. 14. A., XIX. iii.

嗚 *wu* 嗚呼, alas! A., III. vi.

喭 *yen* Coarse, rude. A., XI. xvii. 4.

嘗 *ch'ang* (1) To taste. A., X. xi. 2; xiii. 1. (2) Name of the autumnal sacrifice. D.M., xix. 6. (3) Indicates the present complete and past tenses, being often joined with 未. A., III. xxiv.; VIII. v.; *et al.*

器 *ch'i* (1) A vessel, a tool. D.M., xix. 3. A., XV. ix. Metaphorically. A., II. xii.: V. iii. (2) Capacity, calibre. A., III. xxii. 1. (3) To use according to capacity. A., XIII. xxv.

噫 *i* An exclamation of grief; of contempt. A., XI. viii.: XIX. xii. 2: XIII. xx. 4.

嚴 *yen* Severe, dignified. G.L.c., vi. 3.

THE 31st RADICAL. 囗.

四 *sze* Four. *Sepe.* Four things. A., VII. xxiv.: IX. iv. 四國, the four parts of the State. G.L.c., ix. 8. 四夷, the barbarians on the four sides of the empire. G.L.c., x. 14. 四體, the four limbs. D.M., xxiv. A., XVIII. vii. 四飯. A., XVIII. ix. 3.

因 *yin* (1) As a preposition. Because of, taking occasion from. D.M., xvii. 3. A., XX. ii. 2. (2) As a verb. To follow, succeed to. A., II. xxiii. 2: XI. xxv. 4. To rely on. A., I. xiii.

回 *hui* The name of Conf. favourite disciple. *Sepe.* 顏回. A., VI. ii.: XI. vi.

困 *k'wăn* (1) Distressed, reduced to straits. D.M., xx. 2. A., XX. i. 1. 酒困, overcome with wine. A., IX. xv. (2) Stupidity and the feeling of it. D.M., xx. 13. A., XVI. ix.

固 *ku* (1) Firm, strong. A., I. viii.: XVI. i. 8. ? XV. i. 3. (2) Obstinate, obstinacy. A., IX. iv.: XIV. xxxiv. 2. (3) Mean, niggardly. A., VII. xxxv. (4) Firmly. D.M., xx. 18. (5) Certainly, indeed. D.M., xxxii. 3. A., IX. vi. 2: XIV. xxxviii. 1: XV. i. 3; xli. 3.

圃 *p'u* A gardener. A., XIII. iv. 1.

圉 *yü* The name of an officer. A., XIV. xx. 2.

國 *kwo* A State. *Passim.* 中國, the Middle kingdom. D.M., xxxi. 4: *et al.* Only in this phrase is the term used for the empire. 千乘之國, one of the largest States, equipping 1,000 chariots. A., I. v.: *et al.* 為國, to administer a State. A., IV. xiii.

圖 *t'u* (1) To think, imagine. A., VII. xiii. (2) A map. A., IX. viii.

THE 32d RADICAL. 土.

土 *t'u* (1) The ground, ground, earth. D.M., xxvi. 9. A., V. ix. 1. (2) 水土, water and land. D.M., xxx. 1. (3) Comfort. A., IV. xi.

圭 *kwei* A precious stone, differently shaped, used as a badge of authority. A., X. v. 1: XI. v.

地 *ti* (1) The earth, the ground. D.M., xx. 3. A., IX. xviii.: XIX. xxii. 2. (2) Any particular country. A., XIV. xxxix. 2. (3) Throughout the Doctrine of the Mean, it occurs constantly as the correlative of 天, heaven, the phrase 天地 being now the component parts, and now the great powers, of the universe.

在 *tsai* (1) To be in, to consist in, depend on, the where and wherein following. *Passim.* (2) To be present. G.L.c., vii. 2. A., XI. xxi. (3) To be in life. A., I. xi.: IV. xix. 在 is followed not unfrequently by 上, 中, 內, with words intervening. Observe A., XIX. xxii. 2: XX. i. 6.

均 *chün* Level. An equally adjusted state of society. A., XVI. i. 10. As a verb; to adjust, keep in order. D.M., ix.

坐 *tso* To sit. A., X. vii. 2; ix. 1: *et al.*

THE 33D RADICAL. 士.

THE 35TH RADICAL. 夊.

THE 36TH RADICAL. 夕

THE 37TH RADICAL. 大.

THE 38TH RADICAL, 女.

如 ju. (1) As, and may often be rendered as when, as if. *Passim.* We find 如此, such, so; with the synonyms, 如斯, and 如是. 不如, not as, but sometimes meaning—there is nothing like, the best thing is to. We have also 譬如, and 辟如, may be compared to. (2) If. In this sense, it is often followed by 有. (3) 如何, and 何如, see on 何. (4) After adjectives, like, or our termination *ly.* See many instances in the Ana. Bk. X. (5) Or. A., XI. xxv. 10. (6) Obs. 如其仁. A., XIV. xvii. 2.

妖 yao. Prodigies, inauspicious appearances of plants, &c. D.M., xxiv.

妻 ch'i. A wife. D.M., xv. 2. A., XVI. xiv.

妻 ch'i. Up. 3d tone. To give to to wife. A., V. i. 1, 2: XI. v.

始 shih. The beginning; at first; to begin. G.L., v. 8. D.M., xxv. 2. A., I. xv. 3: III. viii. 3; xxiii: V. ix. 2: VIII. xv.: XIII. viii.; XIX. xii. 2.

姓 hsing. A surname, the patronymic of a family or clan. A., VII. xxx. 2. 百姓, a designation for the mass of the people. D.M., xx. 13, 14. A., XII. ix. 4: XIV. xlv.; xx. 1, 5.

威 wei. Majestic. A., VII. xxxvii.: XX. ii. 1, 2. To fear; to be feared. D.M., xxxiii. 4. A., I. viii. 1. 威儀, see 儀. G. L.c., iii. 4. D.M., xxvii. 3.

婦 fu. 夫婦, husband and wife. D.M., xii. 2, 4; xx. 12. A., XIV. xviii. 3. 婦人, a woman. A., VIII. xx. 3.

媚 mei. To flatter, pay court to. A., III. xiii. 1.

媢 mao. To be jealous. G.L.c., x. 14.

嫁 chia. To marry, be married to. Spoken of the woman. G.L.c., ix. 2.

THE 39TH RADICAL. 子.

子 tsze. (1) A son. G.L.c., viii. 2; ix. 2, 8. D.M., xiii. 4; xv. 2; xviii. 1, 3: xx. 1. A., III xv: VI. iv.; *et al.*, *saepe.* But in some instances, it is as much *child* as son. (2) A daughter, a young woman. G.L.c., ix. 6. A., V. i. 1, 2: VII. xxx. 2 (a play on the term): XI. v. 女子. A., XVII. xxv. (3) As a verb, to treat as children. D.M., xx. 12, 13. (4) Everywhere applied to Confucius,—the Master. (5) It follows surnames and honorary epithets. (6) It enters often into the designations of the disciples of Confucius, and others. (7) In conversation,—you, Sir, the gentlemen. 二三子, ye, my disciples, my friends. (8) Chiefs, officers. A., XIV. xxii. 3, 4, 5. (9) A title of nobility, viscount. A., XVIII. i. (10) 子孫, descendants, *Saepe.* (11) 君子. *Passim.* Generally, the superior man, with a moral and intellectual significance of varying degree. Often—a ruler. Sometimes, the highest style of man, the sage. (12) 天子, the emperor; see on 天. 弟子; see 弟. 人子; see 人. 小子; see 小. 童子; 童.

孔 k'ung. (1) Very. D.M., xxxiii. 2. (2) A surname. That of Confucius. 孔子. *Passim.* 孔氏. A., XIV. xli.; xlii. 1. 孔文子. A., V. xiv.

存 ts'un. To be preserved, to be alive, to continue, to be. D.M., xix. 5; xxii.; xxviii. 5. A., VIII. iv. 3.

孝 hsiao. Filial piety, to be filial. A., II. v. 1, 2; vi.; vii.; viii.; xx.; xxi. 2; xxii; xxviii. 5: *et al.*, *saepe.*

孟 mang, mêng. (1) The eldest. A., VII. iii. 2. (2) A surname, that of one of *the three families* of Lou. A., II. v. 2 (孟孫); XIX, xix.—II. v. 1.—XIX. xviii.—VIII. iv.—II. vi.; V. vii.: XVIII. iii.—VI. xiii.—XIV. xii.; xiii.—G.L.c., x. 22.

孤 ku. (1) Fatherless, an orphan. G.L.c., x. 1. A., VIII. vi. (2) Solitary, alone. A., IV. xxv.

季 chi. The youngest. Used in designations. A., XVIII. xi. A surname, that of one of the three families of Lou. A., III. i. (季氏), *et al.*: XIV, xxxviii.: XVI. i. 13. (季孫): XVIII. iii (季). 季康子, A., II. xx.: VI. i.: XI. vi.: XII. xvii.; xviii.; xix. 季子然, A., XI. xxiii. 季桓子, A., XVIII. iv. The disciple Tsze-lu was a 季. A., V. xxv.; *et al.*

孫 sun. (1) A grandson. 子孫, descendants. G.L.c., x. 14. D.M., xvii. 1; xviii. 2. A., XVI. i. 8; iii. (2) Used in double surnames. A., XIX. xviii.; xxiv.—XIV.

xxxviii.; XVI. i. 13.—II. v. 2.—III. xiii.; XIV. xx. 2.—XIX. xxii.

孫 *sun* Up. 3d tone, used for 遜. Complaisant, docile, obedient. A., VII. xxxv.; XIV. iv.; *et al.*

孰 *shuh shu* Who? which? D.M., xxxii. 3. A., III. xv.; xxii. 3.; *et al.*, *saepe*. What? A., III. i.

學 *hsio* To learn; learned; learning. G.L.c., i. D.M., xx. 2, 10, 12, 21. A., I. i. 1; vi.; vii.; viii.; xiv.; *et al.*, *saepe*.

孺 *ju* A surname. A., XVII. xx.

孽 *nieh* Unlucky omens of prodigious animals. D.M., xxiv.

THE 40TH RADICAL. 宀.

守 *shou* To keep, to maintain. D.M., vii. A., VIII. xiii. 1; XV. xxxii. 1, 2, 3; XVI. i. 12.

安 *an* (1) A condition of entire tranquillity. G.L.t., 2. A., XVI. i. 10. (2) Without any effort. D.M., xx. 9. A., III. xxxvii. (3) Comfort, at ease. A., I. xiv.; XVII. xxi. 4, 5. (4) To rest in. A., II. x. 3.; IV. ii. (5) To give rest to. A., V. xxv. 4; XIV. xlv.; XVI. i. 11. (6) An interrogative,=how, where. A., XI. xxv. 10.

宋 *sung* The name of a State. D.M., xxviii. 5. A., III. ix.; VI. xiv.

完 *wan* Complete. A., XIII. viii.

宗 *tsung* (1) Honourable, pertaining to one's ancestors. 宗廟, the ancestral temple. D.M., xvii. 1; *et al.* A., X. i. 2; *et al.* 宗器 D.M., xix. 3. 宗族, kindred. A., XIII. xx. 2. (2) To follow as master. A., I. xiii. (3) 高宗 an ancient emperor. A., XIV. xliii.

官 *kuan* An officer of government. D.M., xx. 14. A., III. xxii. 2; XIV. xliii. 2; XIX. xxiii. 3; XX. i. 6.

定 *ting* Determined, settled. G.L.t., 2. D.M., xx. 16. A., XVI. 7. To settle. G.L.c., ix. 3.

宜 *i* (1) Right, what is right. D.M., xx. 5; xxv. 3. (2) Reasonable, to be expected. A., XIX. xxii. 4. (3) As a verb, to regulate, discharge duty to. G.L.c., ix. 6, 7. D.M., xv. 2; xvii. 4.

客 *k'o* Strangers, guests. 賓客. A., V. vii. 4; XIV. xx. 2.

宮 *kung* A house. A., XIX. xxiii. 2. 宮室. VIII. xxi.

室 *shih* (1) An apartment, the inner rooms of a house. D.M., xxxiii. 3. A., IX. xxx.; XI. xiv. 2; xix. So, 室家, A., XIX. xxiii. 2. (2) A family. A., V. xii. 2; VI. xii.; XIII. viii. So 室家, D.M., xv. 2. 公室, the ducal house. A., XVI. iii. (3) 宮室, a house. A., VIII. xxi.

害 *hai* Injury, to injure. G.L.c., x. 22. D.M., xxx. 3. A., II. xvi.; XV. viii.

宰 *tsai* (1) Governor or commandant, of a town. A., V. vii. 3; VI. iii. 3; vii.; xii.; XI. xxiv.; XIII. xvii. (2) Head minister to a chief. A., XIII. ii. (3) 冢宰, a premier. A., XIV. xliii. (4) The surname of one of Conf. disciples. A., V. ix.; *et al.*

宴 *yen* Feasting. A., XVI. v.

家 *chia* (1) The family. G.L.t., 4, 5; c., viii. 1. 3; ix. 1, 3, 6. 家人, the household, c., ix. 6. 室家, D.M., xv. 2. (2) A family, the name for the possessions of the chiefs in a State. G.L.c., x. 22, 23. D.M., ix.; xx. 11, 12, 13; xxiv. A., III. ii.; V. vii. 3; XII. ii.; xx. 3, 5, 6; XVI. i. 10; XVII. xviii.; XIX. xxv. 4. (3) 室家, apartments. A., XIX. xxiii. 2.

容 *yung* (1) To bear, admit. A., X. iv. 1. (2) Forbearance, to forbear. G.L., x. 14. D.M., xxxi. 1. A., XIX. iii. To command forbearance. D.M., xxvii. 2. (3) Deportment. A., VIII. iv. 3; X. vi. 4. 容色, a placid appearance. A., X. v. 2. (4) 從容, easy, unconstrained. (5) A name. A., V. i. 2; XI. v.

宿 *su* (1) To stop over night. A., XIV. xli.; XVIII. vii. 3. To keep over night. A., X. viii. 8; XII. xii. 2. (2) Asleep and perching. A., VII. xxvi.

寄 *chi* To commit to one's charge. A., VIII. vi.

密 *mi* Concentrative. D.M., xxxi. 1.

富 *fu* Rich, riches. G.L.c., vi. 4. D.M., xvii. 1; xviii. 2. A., I. xv. 1; *et al.* Metaph., A., XII. xxii. 5. To enrich. A., XIII. ix. 3, 4; XX. i. 4. Often joined with 貴.

寒 *han* Cold, wintry. A., IX. xxvii.

往 *wang* — (1) To go, going. A., IX. xviii.; XVII. i. v.; VII. 1, 2; XVIII. ii. 1. D.M., xx. 14. 而往, and onwards. A., III. x. (2) The gone, the past. A., I. xv. 3; III. xxi. 2; VII. xxviii. 2; XVIII. v.

征 *ching* / chêng — 征伐, punitive military expeditions. A., XVI. ii.

待 *tai* / tai — (1) To wait, wait for. A., IX. xiii.; XIII. iii. 1. D.M., xxvii. 4. (2) To treat. A., XVIII. iii.

律 *luh* / lü — To imitate, follow as a model. D.M., xxx. 1.

後 *hau* / hou — (1) As a noun. That which is after, the back. *Sæpe.* 在後, A., IX. x. 1. Preceded by 之. A., XIV. xxii. 4, 5; *et al.* A successor. A., XIV. xv. (2) As an adjective. D.M., xl. 1; *et al.* 後死者, A., IX. v. 3. 後生, A., IX. xxii. (3) As an adverb, Afterwards. *Sæpe.* Often follows 然 and 而. (4) As a verb. To come after, fall behind, make an after consideration. A., III. viii. 2; VI. xiii.; and XI. xxii.; xxv. 5; XII. xxi. 3; XV. v. 3; xxvii.; XVIII. vii. 1.

徑 *king* / ching — A short, cross, path. A., VI. xii.

得 *tih* / tê — (1) To attain to, to be found. G.L.v., 2. D.M., xx. 18, 20. (2) To get, with an objective following. *Sæpe.* Without an objective, getting, anything as gain to be got. A., XVI. vii.; x. 1; XIX. i. (3) The auxiliary can often followed by 而. *Sæpe.* (4) Followed by an adjective, and often in the question 焉得 ……can how can be considered. A., IV. i.; V. x.; xviii. 1, 2; *et al.* (5) 不得已, could not but. A., VII. ii. 3. (6) 自得, to be himself. D.M., xiv. 2.

徒 *t'oo* / t'u — (1) On foot. A., XI. vii. 2. (2) Vainly, without cause. A., XVII. v. 3. (3) Disciple, associate. A., XI. xvi. 2; XVIII. vi. 3, 4.

徙 *se* / hsi — To move towards. A., VII. iii.; XII. x. 1.

從 *ts'ung* — To follow; to act according to. G.L.c., ix. 4; x. 2. D.M., xxviii. 5; xxix. 2. A., II. iv. 6; xiii.; *et al.*, *sæpe.* 從政, to be engaged in govt. Generally, in a subordinate capacity.—A., VI. vi.; XIII. xiii.; xx. 4; XVIII. v. 1. But not subordinate in—A., XX. ii. 1. 從事, to be engaged in affairs, to act. A., VIII. v. 1; XVII. i. 2.

從 *tsung* — Up. 3d tone. Proceeding on. A., III. xxiii.

從 *tsung* — Low. 3d tone. To be in close attendance on. Always 從者 or 從我者. A., III. xxiv.; V. vi.; XI. ii. 1; 6; 2.

從 *ts'ung* — 從容, naturally and easily. D.M., xx. 18.

御 *yu* / yü — To drive a carriage. A., II. v. 2; IX. ii. 2.

復 *fuh* / fu — (1) To make good. A., I. xiii. (2) To report a commission. A., X. iii. 4. (3) To return to. A., X. iv. 5; XII. i. 1. (4) To repeat. A., XI. v.

復 *fow* / fou — Again. A., VI. vii.; VII. v. As a verb. A., VII. viii.

循 *seun* / sun — (1) 循循然, by orderly method. A., IX. x. 2. (2) Tethered. A., X. v. 1.

微 *we* / wei — (1) That which is minute, minute. D.M., i. 3; xvi. 5; xxvi. 6; xxxiii. 1. Reduced. A., XVI. iii. (2) A negative particle, if not. A., XIV. xviii. 2. (3) 微子, the viscount of the State Wei. A., XVIII. i. (4) 微生, a double surname. A., V. xxiii.—XIV. xxxiv.

徵 *ching* / chêng — (1) To be evidenced. D.M., xxvi. 2, 3. (2) To attest, be attested. D.M., xxviii. 5; xxix. 2, 3. A., III. ix.

德 *tih* / tê — Virtue, virtuous. *Passim.* Energy, influence. D.M., xvi. 1. A., XII. xix.

徹 *ch'ĕ* — (1) To remove. A., III. ii. (2) Pervading, with reference to a law of tithe. A., XII. ix. 2, 3.

徼 *keaou* / hsiao — (1) To seek. D.M., xiv. 4. (2) To copy another's and pretend that it is one's own; to pry out. A., XVII. xxiv. 2.

THE 61st RADICAL. 心.

心 *sin* / shin — The heart, the mind;—denotes the mental constitution generally. Is not found in the Chung Yung. G.L.v., 4, 5; c. vi. 4; vii. 1, 2, 3; ix. 2; x. 11. A., II. iv. 6; VI. v.; XIV. xlii. 1; XVII. xxii.; XX. i. 6, 7.

必 *pih* / pi — Must, used as an auxiliary; often = will certainly, would certainly. Sometimes also with no verb following. *Passim.* 必也, what must,—what is necessary is……. Sometimes conditionally. G.L.c., iv. 1. A., III. vii.; VI. vii.; xxviii.;

VII. x. 3; XIII. iii. 2; xxi. 毋必, no arbitrary predeterminations. A., IX. iv.

忍 jin. To bear, forbear. A., III. i.; XV. xxvi.

忒 t'eh. To be wrong, in error. G.L.c., ix. 8.

志 chih. The will, aim. G.L.c., iv. 1. D.M., xix. 2; xxxiii. 2. A., I. xi.; *et al. saepe*. 志士, the determined scholar. A., XV. viii.

忌 chi. 忌憚, dread, caution. D.M., ii. 2.

忘 wang. To forget, be forgotten. A., VII. xviii. 2; XII. xxi. 3; XIV. xiii. 2; XIX. v. G.L.c., iii. 4, 5.

忠 chung. (1) Self-devotion, generous sincerity. Often in combination with 信. G.L.c., x. 18. D.M., xiii. 3; xx. 14. A., iv. xv. 2; V. xxvii.; *et al.* (2) Faithful, loyal. A., I. iv.; viii. 2; II. xx; III. xix.; V. xviii. 1; XII. xxiii.; XIV. viii.; XV. v. 2; XVI. x.

忿 fên. Anger, to be angry. A., XII. xxi. 3; XVI. x.; XVII. xvi. 2. G.L.c., vii. 1.

忮 chih. To dislike. A., IX. xxvi. 2.

念 nien. To think of, keep in mind. A., V. xxii.

忽 hwuh. (1) 忽焉=忽然, suddenly. A., IX. x. (2) In names. 召忽, A., XIV. xvii. 仲忽, A., XVIII. xi.

怍 tsoh. To be ashamed, modest. A., XIV. xxi.

怒 nu. Anger, to show anger. A., VI. ii. D.M., i. 4; xxxiii. 4.

思 sze. (1) To think, to think of; thought, thoughts, thinking. D.M., xx. 7, 18, 19, 20. A., II. ii.; xv.; IV. xvii.; *et al., saepe*. (2) A., final particle. D.M., xvi. 4. (3) 原思, a disciple of Conf. A., VI. iii. 3.

怡 i. 怡怡如, pleased-like. A., X. iv. 5; XIII. xxviii.

急 keih. The distressed, distress. A., VI. iii. 2.

性 sing. The nature (of man). G.L.c., x. 16. D.M., i. 1; xxi.; xxii.; xxv. 3; xxvii. 6. A., V. xii.; XVII. ii.

怨 yuen. (1) To murmur against, be murmured against. Resentment, in thought, word, or deed. D.M., xiv. 3; xx. 13. A., IV. xii.; V. xxii.; *et al., saepe*. (2) What provokes resentment, injury. A., XIV. xxxvi. 13.

怪 kwai. Extraordinary things. A., VII. xx. D.M., xi. 1.

恆 hăng. (1) Constantly; constancy. G.L.c., x. 19. A., VII. xxv. 2, 3; XIII. xxii. 1, 2. (2) 陳恆, an officer of Ts'e. A., XIV. xxii. 2.

恐 k'ung. To be afraid of, to be in danger of. A., V. xiii.; VIII. xvii.; XVI. i. 13; XIX. iv. 恐懼, G.L.c., vii. 1. D.M., i. 2.

恕 shu. The principle of reciprocity, making our own feelings the rule for our dealing with others. A., IV. xv. 2; XV. xxiii. G.L.c., ix. 4. D.M., xiii. 3.

恤 seuh. To commiserate, treat compassionately. G.L.c., x. 1.

恥 ch'ih. Shame, a sense of shame, what is shameful, to be ashamed of. D.M., xx. 10. A., I. xiii.; II. iii. 1, 2; IV. ix.; xxii.; V. xiv.; xxiv.; VIII. xiii. 3; IX. xxvi. 1; XIII. xx.; XIV. i.; xxix. 1.

恂 seun. Reverently careful. G.L.c., iii. 4. 恂恂如, simple-and-sincere-like. A., X. i. 1.

悔 hwuy. To regret, to repent, have occasion for repentance. D.M., xi. 3. A., II. xviii. 2; VII. x. 3.

息 seih. (1) To breathe. A., X. iv. 4. (2) To stop, cease. D.M., xx. 2; xxvi. 1, 2.

恭 kung. To revere, be reverential, sedate, reverence. D.M., xxxiii. 5. A., I. xiii.; V. xv.; xxiv.; VII. xxxvii.; VIII. ii.; XII. v. 4; XIII. xix.; XVI. x. = too modest. A., XIX. xxv. 1. 恭己, he made himself reverent. A., XV. iv.

悖 pei. Contrary to right, contradictory, to collide. G.L.c., x. 10. D.M., xxix. 3; xxx. 2.

悠 yu. Reaching far. D.M., xxiv. 3, 4, 6, 8.

患 hwan. To be grieved, anxious about. A., I. xvi.; III. xxiv.; IV. xiv.; XII. v. 4; xviii.; XIV. xxxii.; XVI. i. 10; XVII. xv. 2, 3. 憂患, G.L.c., vii. 1. 患難, distress and difficulty. D.M., xiv. 2.

悲 *pei*. A man's name. A., XVII. xx.

悱 *fei*. Unable to explain one's-self. A., VII. viii.

情 *ts'ing ch'ing*. Sincerity, the real state of a case. G.L.c., iv. A., XIII. iv. 3; XIX. xix.

惑 *hwo huo*. (1) To be deceived, deluded, delusion. D.M., xx. 13. A., XII. x. 1, 2; xxi. 1, 3; XIV. xxxviii. (2) To doubt, have misgivings. D.M., xxix. 3, 4. A., II. iv. 3; VII. xxviii; IX. xxviii; XI. xxi; XIV. xxx.

惜 *sih hsi*. 惜乎, alas! A., IX. xx.; XII. viii. 2.

惟 *wei*. A particle, generally initial, but sometimes in a clause. Sometimes it can hardly be translated. G.L.c., iii. 1; x. 1. A., II. xxi. 2. Often *to* *only*, especially when medial. G.L.c., x. 12. D.M., xviii. 1; xxxiii. 3. A., IV. iii; VII. x. 1; XIX. xii. 2.

悾 *k'ung*. 悾悾, simple. A., VIII. xvi.

惠 *hwuy hui*. Favours. A., IV. xi. Kind, beneficent; kindness. A., V. xv.; XIV. x. 1; XVI. x.; XX. ii. 1, 2.

惡 *ngo wu*. (1) Wickedness, what is bad. G.L.c., viii. 1, 2. D.M., vi. A., IV. iv.; V. xxii.; *et al.* (2) Bad, disagreeable, spoiled. G.L.c., vi. 1. A., IV. ix.; VIII. xxi.; X. viii. 2.

惡 *wu wu*. To dislike, to hate. G.L.c., vi. 1; viii. 1; x. 2, 3, 15, 11, 16. D.M., & A., *saepe*.

惡 *wu wu*. Up. 1st tone. How. A., IV. v. 2.

惰 *to*. Indolent. A., IX. xix. Rude. G.L.c., viii. 1.

愆 *k'ien ch'ien*. Fault, error. A., XVI. vi.

愈 *yu yü*. To be superior to. A., V. viii. 1; XI. xv. 2.

愉 *yu*. 愉愉如, pleased-like. A., X. v. 3.

意 *i*. The thoughts. G.L.t., 4, 5; c., vi. 1, 4. 毋意, no foregone conclusions. A., IX. iv.

愚 *yu yü*. Ignorant, stupid; stupidity. A., II. ix.; V. xx.; XI. xvii. 1; XVII. iii; viii. 3; xvi. 2. D.M., iv. 1; xii. 2; xx. 21; xxviii. 1.

愛 *ngai ai*. To love. G.L.c., viii. 1; x. 15. D.M., xix. 5. A., I. v.; vi.; III. xvii. 2; XII. x. 2; xxii. 1; XIV. viii; XVII. iv. 3. Love. A., XVII. xxi. 6.

慍 *wan wên*. To be angrily discomposed, dissatisfaction. A., I. i. 3; V. xviii. 1; XV. i. 3.

愧 *k'wei k'uei*. Ashamed. D.M., xxxiii. 3.

愬 *soo su*. To slander, slanderous statements. A., XII. vi; XIV. xxxviii. 1.

慎 *shin shên*. To be careful about, cautious, cautiously. Sometimes followed by the prepositions 乎 and 於. G.L.c., vi. 1, 2; x. 1, 6. D.M., i. 2, 3; xx. 19. A., I. ix.; xiv.; II. xviii. 2; VII. xii; VIII. ii.; XIX. xxv. 2.

愿 *yuen yüan*. Attentive, careful. A., VIII. xvi.

慄 *lih li*. 恂慄, cautiously reverent. G.L.c., iii. 4.

慈 *tsze tz'ŭ*. Kindness, to be kind. G.L.c., iii. 3; ix. 1. A., II. xx.

慧 *hwuy hui*. Shrewdness. A., XV. xvi.

慾 *yuh yü*. Passions, lusts. A., V. x.

慥 *ts'aou ts'ao*. 慥慥, entirely sincere. D.M., xiii. 4.

慝 *t'ih t'ê*. Cherished evil. A., XII. xxi. 1, 3.

慟 *t'ung*. To show excessive grief. A., XI. ix. 1, 2, 3.

慢 *man*. To be heedless, disrespectful. A., VIII. iv. 3; XX. ii. 2. Without urgency. A., XX. ii. 3.

慮 *leu lü*. To deliberate carefully. G.L.t., 2. A., XV. xi. Be anxious about. A., XII. xxv. What men are anxious about. A., XVIII. viii. 3.

憎 *tsang tsêng*. To be hated, disliked. A., V. iv. 2.

憂 *yew yu*. To feel sorrow or anxiety; to be anxious about; sorrow, cause of sorrow. G.L.c., vii. 1. D.M., xviii. 1. A., II. vi.; VI. ix.; VII. iii.; xviii. 2; IX. xxviii; XII. iv. 1, 2; v. 1; XIV. xxx.; XV. xi.; xxxi.; XVI. i. 6, 13.

THE 66TH RADICAL. 攴.

改 *kai.* To alter, to change. Both active and neuter. D.M., xiii. 2. A., I. viii. 4; xi.: V. ix. 2: VI. ix.; VII. iii.; xxi. (here it simply = to avoid): IX. xxiii.; xxiv.: XI. xiii. 2: XV. xxix.: XVII. xxi. 3. Obs. A., XIX. xviii.

攻 *kung.* To assail,—to reprove. A., XI. xvi. 2: XII. xxi. 3. = to study. A., II. xvi.

放 *fang.* (1) To drive, put away. G.L.c., x. 15: A., XV. x. 6. (2) To indulge, give license to. A., XVIII. viii. 4. (3) A name. A., III. iv.; vi.

倣 *fang.* Up. 3d tone. To accord with; having regard to. A., IV. xii.

政 *chêng.* Government; the principles of government; a govt. charge. *Passim*, *et al.* A., II. iii. 1. 爲政, to administer government, as supreme or subordinate. A., II. i.; xxi. 1: XII. xix. 從政, to be engaged in govt., as subordinate. A., VI. vi.: XIII. xiii. 1; xx. 1: XVIII. v. 1. Except, perhaps, A., XX. ii. 1.

故 *ku.* (1) Therefore. *Passim.* We have frequently 是故, with the same meaning, but perhaps a little more emphasis. Obs. A., III. ix, where 故 is at the end of the clause,—because, that's the cause. (2) Old, what is old. A., II. xi.: XVIII. x. D.M., xxvii. 6.

敏 *min.* To be earnest and active, earnest activity. A., I. xiv.: IV. xxiv. 1; V. xiv.: VII. xix.: XVI. vi.: XX. i. 2. Combining the idea of intelligence. A., XII. i. 2; ii. As a verb, to hasten, produce quickly. D.M., xx. 3.

教 *chiao.* To teach, instruct. G.L.c., ix. 1. 6. 7. D.M., x. 3. A., II. xx.; VII. xxiv.: VIII. ix. 1: XIII. ix. 4; xxix.: XV. xxxviii.: XX. ii. 3. 不教, uninstructed. A., XIII. xxx. Instruction. D.M., i. 1; xxi.

救 *chiu.* To stop, to save from. A., III. vi.

敖 *ao.* 敖惰, arrogant and rude. G.L.c., viii. 1.

敗 *pai.* (1) Gone, spoiled, as meat. A., X. viii. 2. (2) 司敗, minister of crime. A., VII. xxx.

敝 *pi.* To spoil; spoiled,—spoken of clothes. A., V. xxv. 2: IX. xxvi.

敢 *kan.* To presume, to dare. D.M., xiii. 4; xxviii. 4. A., V. viii. 2: VI. xiii.: *et al.*, *sæpe.* 豈敢, how dare I?—an expression of humility. A., VII. xxxiii. 1. In the 1st person, often = our 'allow me.' A., XI. xi.; xxi. 1: XII. xxi. 1: XIII. xx. 2. 3. Obs. A., XX. i. 3. 果敢, presumptuous. A., XVII. xxiv. 1.

散 *san.* To scatter, disperse. G.L.c., x. 9. To be scattered, disorganized. A., XIX. xix.

敦 *tun.* Liberal, generous, great. D.M., xxvii. 6; xxx. 3.

敬 *ching.* (1) To reverence, to respect; to be reverential, cherish the feeling of reverence. *Passim.* To be reverenced. D.M., xxxi. 1. In reference to business. A., I. v.: VI. i. 3: XIII. xix.: XV. xxxvii.: XVI. x. 畏敬, to be filled with awe and reverence. G.L.c., viii. 1. (2) As honorary epithet. A., VIII. iv.

數 *shu.* (1) Some, several. A., VII. xvi.: XIX. xxiii. 3. (2) 曆數, the determined time. A., XX. i. 1.

數 *so.* Frequently. A., IV. xxvi.

斂 *lien.* To ingather. Applied to imposts. G. L.c., x. 21. D.M., xx. 14. A., XI. xvi.

THE 67TH RADICAL. 文

文 *wên.* (1) The characters of the language. D.M., xxviii. 2. 3. A., XV. xxv. (2) Records, literary monuments. A., III. ix. (3) Literature, polite studies. A., I. vi.: VI. xxv.: VII. xxiv.; xxxii.: IX. x. 2: XI. ii. 2: XII. xv.; xxiv.: XVI. i. 11. (4) Accomplished, accomplishments, elegance. D.M., xxxi. 1; xxxiii. 1. A., III. xiv.: V. xiv.: VI. xvi.: XII. viii. 1, 3: XIV. xiii. 1; xix. 2. (5) = The cause of truth. A., IX. v. 2, 3. (6) 文章, elegant manners and discourses; elegant institutions. A., V. xii.: VIII. xix. 2. (7) Used as the honorary epithet, becoming in effect the name. D.M., xviii. 1, 2, 3: *et al.* G.L.c., iii. 3. A., IX. v. 2: XIX. xxii. 2.—A., XIV. xvi.—A., V. xiv.—A., V. xviii.: XV. xiii.—A., V. xviii. 2.—A., V. xix.—A., XIV. xiv.: xix. Used also in the name 子文. A., V. xviii.

文 *wăn.* Low. 3d tone. To gloss. A., XIX. viii.

斐 *fei.* Accomplished. G.L.c., iii. 4. 斐然. A., V. xx. 1.

THE 68TH RADICAL. 斗.

斗 *tou.* A peck. A., XIII. xx. 4.

THE 69th RADICAL. 斤.

斯 *sze* ssŭ — (1) This, these. *Passim.* Its antecedent is often a clause. (2) Forthwith. A., X. x. 1; xviii. 1; XIV. xliii. 2, and perhaps some other places.

新 *sin* hsin — To renovate. G.L.c., III. 1. New, what is new. G.L.c., iii. 2, 3. D.M., xxvii. 6. A., II. xi.; V. xviii.; XVII. xxi. 3.

斷 *twan* tuan — Up. 3d tone. 斷斷兮, plain and sincere. G.L.c., x. 14.

THE 70th RADICAL. 方.

方 *fang* — (1) A region, regions. D.M., x. 2, 3, 4. A., I. i. 2; xx. i. 3. 四方, the four quarters,=all parts of the empire, or of a State. D.M., xx. 13. A., XIII. iv. 3; XX. i. 6. =Any quarter. A., XIII. v.; xx. A settled definite place. A., IV. xix. (2) Tablets of wood. D.M., xx. 2. (3) An art, the way. A., VI. xxviii. 3. (4) Right rules. A., XI. xxv. 4. (5) Square. A., XI. xxv. 5, 11. (6) To compare. A., XIV. xxi. (7) Then. A., XVI. vii. (8) Used in a designation. A., XVIII. ix. 3.

於 *yu* yü — *Passim.* Its proper meaning is *in, at, on,* in regard to place. But after many verbs and adjectives we must translate by other prepositions, as *from, to,* &c. After the possessive 之, it=*in relation to.* With adjectives it forms the comparative degree, and=*than.* D.M., xxxiii. 4. A., XI. xvi. 1; XIX. xxv. 1. Observe 於我, A., X. xv. 1,=on me, be it mine.

於 *woo* wu — An exclamation. G.L.c., iii. 3, 5. D.M., xxvi. 10.

施 *she* shih — (1) To give, do, use. D.M., xiii. 3, 4. A., II. xxi. 2; XII. ii.; XV. xxiii. G.L.c., x. 12. (2) To make a display of. A., V. xxv. 3.

施 *she* shih — Up. 3d tone. To confer on, so as to reach to. D.M., xxxi. 4. A., VI. xxviii. 1. There is not much appreciable difference between the char. in this tone and the last.

施 *che* chih — For 弛, to treat remissly. A., XVIII. x.

旅 *leu* lü — (1) A body of 500 soldiers. 師旅, 軍旅, forces. A., XI. xxv. 4; XIV. xx. 2; XV. i. 1. (2) All, general. D.M., xix. 4. (3) The name of a sacrifice. A., III. vi.

族 *tsuh* tsu — The circle of relatives. A., XIII. xx. 2.

THE 71st RADICAL. 无.

既 *ke* chi — (1) A particle of past time,=have, having, having been. D.M., xv. 2; xxvii. 7. A., III. x.; xxi. 2; IX. v. 2; x. 3; *et al., saepe.* (2) Used adverbially. That done,=then, by-and-by. A., XIV. xliii. 2. (3) Used for 餼, or 槩 *ke.* Rations. D.M., xx. 14.

THE 72d RADICAL. 日.

日 *jih* — (1) The sun. D.M., xxvi. 9; xxx. 2; xxxi. 4. A., XIX. xxi.; xxiv. (2) A day, days. G.L.c., ii. 1. A., II. ix.; IV. vi. 2; VII. ix. 2; *et al., saepe.* (3) Adverbially. Daily. D.M., xx. 14; xxxiii. 1. A., I. iv. On some days. A., VI. v. 日日, every day. G.L.c., ii. 1.

旨 *che* chih — What is pleasant, spoken of food. A., XVII. xxi. 5.

昆 *kwăn* kuên — An elder brother. D.M., xx. 8. 昆弟, brothers; the younger branches of one's relatives, generally. D.M., xx. 13. A., XI. iv.

明 *ming* — (1) Clear, illustrious, brilliant; clearly. G.L.t., 1, 4; c., i. 2. D.M., xx. 19, 20; xxiii.; xxvi. 3, 4, 5, 8; xxvii. 6; xxx. 2; xxxiii. 6. A., XVI. x. (2) To illustrate. G.L.t., 1, 4; c., i. 1, 3, 4. (3) Intelligence, intelligent. D.M., xx. 21; xxi.; xxvi. 7; xxxi. 1; xxxii. 3. A., II. vi. (4) To understand. D.M., iv. 1; xix. 6. (5) To purify, purification; clean. D.M., xvi. 3; xx. 14. A., X. vii. 1. (6) 明日, next day. A., XV. i. 1; XVIII. vii. 4. (7) 公明, as a double surname. A., XIV. xiv. In names. A., V. xxiv.—A., VI. xii.

易 *yih* yi — (1) To change. A., I. vii.; XVIII. vi. 3, 4. (2) The name of the Yih classic. A., VII. xvi.

易 *e* i — Low. 3d tone. (1) Easy, easily. A., VIII. xii.; XIII. xv. 2; xxv.; XIV. xi; xliv.; XVII. iv. 3. Easily preserved, G.L.c., x. 5. Ease,=calmness, tranquillity. D.M., xiv. 4. (3) Minute attention to observances. A., III. iv. 3.

昔 *seih* hsi — Formerly. 昔者, A., VIII. v.; XVII. i. 4; XVII. iv. 3; vii. 2.

星 *sing* hsing — A star, stars. A., II. i. D.M., xxvi. 9.

春 *ch'un* ch'un — The spring. A., XI. xxv. 7. D.M., xix. 3.

昭 chao, ch'ao. (1) Bright; to be clearly seen; clearly. A., XX. i. 3. D.M., xxvi. 4; xxxiii. 2. (2) 昭穆, the tablets in the ancestral temple, acc. to the order of precedence. D.M., xix. 4. (3) Hon. ep. of a duke of Lu. A., VII. xxx.

是 shih. (1) This, these. *Passim.* It often resumes a previous clause, and often contains the copula,—this is. 如是, 若是, thus, such. 是故, 是以, therefore. Also 是用. A., V. xxii. (2) To be. A., IX. xxx. i; XI. xx.; XVI. i. 3, 4, 2; *et al.* (3) Right. A., XVII. iv. 4. (4) 之是, small. G.L.v, 6.

時 shih. (1) Time, times. A., XVI. vii. D.M., xxx. 1. Opportunity. A., XVII. i. 2. (2) The seasons. D.M., xxx. 2. A., XIX. iii. Seasonal. D.M., xix. 3. A., X. viii. 2; XVIII. 2. (3) Seasonably, at proper times. D.M., xx. 14; xxxi. 2. A., XIV. xiv. 2. 以時. A., I. v. (4) Always. D.M., ii. 2; xxv. 3. A., I. i. 1. (5) To time, watch. A., XVII. i. 1.

晉 chin. The name of a State. A., XIV. xvi.

晏 yen. (1) Late. A., XIII. xiv. (2) A surname. A., V. xvi.

晝 chau. The daytime; adverbially. A., V, ix. 1; IX. xvi.

晨 ch'ên. The morning. 晨門, style of a gate-keeper. A., XIV. xli.

晳 hsi. Designation of one of Conf. disciples. A., XI. xxv. 1.

暇 hsia. Leisure. A., XIV. xxxi.

暑 shu. Warm weather. A., X. vi. 2.

景 ching. An hon. epithet. A., XII. xi; XVI. xii; XVIII. iii. 景伯, an hon. designation. A., XIV. xxxviii; XIX. xxiii. 2.

暴 pao. (1) Violence, oppression. G.L.c., ix. 4. A., VIII. iv. 3; XX. ii. 2. (2) To attack, or strike, unarmed. A., VII x. 3.

曆 li. Calculated and represented. A., XX. i. 1.

THE 73D RADICAL. 曰.

曰 yüeh. To speak, to say, saying. *Passim.* Generally, the nominative is expressed, but not always, and then 曰=it is said. D.M., xxvii. 5; *et al.* Sometimes it=namely. D.M., xx. 8, 12; *et al.* 蓋曰, meaning, for it says. D.M., xxvi. iii.

曲 ch'ü. (1) Bent. A., VII. xv. (2) Shoots, what is small. D.M., xxiii.

更 kǎng. To change. A., XIX. xxi.

書 shu. (1) To write. A., XV. v. 4. Writing, writings, books. D.M., xxviii. 3. A., XI. xxiv. 3; XIV. xliii. 1. (2) The Shû-king, or classic of History. A., II. xxi. 2; VII. xvii. (3) 楚書, the name of a Book. G.L.c., x. 12.

曾 tsǎng. The surname of one of Conf. principal disciples, and of his father. G.L.c., vi. 3. A., I. iv.; *et al, saepe.* A., XI. xxv. 1, 8.

曾 ts'ǎng. Low. 1st tone. A conjunction,—then, but. A., II. viii; III. vi; XI. xxiii. 2.

會 hui. (1) To associate with. A., XII. xxiv. (2) Interviews of the princes with the emperor. A., XI. xxv. 6, 12.

THE 74TH RADICAL. 月.

月 yüeh. (1) The moon. D.M., xxvi. 9; xxx. 2; xxxi. 4. A., XIX. xxi; xxiv. (2) A month, months. D.M., vii. A., VI. v.; VII. xiii; X. vi. 11; XIII. x; XVII. i. 2. Monthly, from month to month. D.M., xx. 14. A., XIX. 5.

有 yu. (1) To have, possess. *Passim.* Followed by 者,—he who possesses, they who have. But sometimes the 者 is omitted, as in A., I. xiv.; VIII. iv.; XX. i. 1; *et al.* In this sense it not only governs nouns, but is used as an auxiliary to verbs, both active and passive. (2) The impersonal substantive verb, there is, there was. *Passim.* In very many instances, it is difficult to say whether the character is used thus, or as in 1. 有之, and the negative 未之有 at the end of sentences, are to be observed. G.L.v., A., I. ii. 1; IV. vi. 3; *et al.* 何有=there is no difficulty. A., IV. xiii; *et al.* But this not always. A., VII. ii; *et al.* Obs. A., XIX. ii. (3) The surname of one of Conf. disciples. A., I. ii. 1; xii.; xiii.; XII. ix. 1, 2. The name of another. A., III. vi.; VII. xiv.; *et al, saepe.*

有 *yew* yu — Low, 3d tone. And. A., II. iv. 1.; X. vi. 4.

朋 *p'ang* p'ăng — A fellow-student; a friend, friends. A., I. i. 2. 朋友, see under 友.

服 *fuh* fu — (1) To wear. A., II. xix.; XV. x. 4. Metaph. D.M., viii. Clothes. D.M., xvi. 3; xx. 14. A., VIII. xxi.; X. vi. 2, 11; *et al.* (2) To submit. A., XIII. iv. 3: XVI. i. 11, 12. 服事, to serve. A., VIII. xx. 4. 服勞, to undergo the labour. A., II. viii. (3) 子服, appr. a surname. A., XIV. xxxviii. XIX. xxiii. 2.

胡 *hoo* hu — How. D.M., xiii. 4.

朕 *ch'in* ch'ăn — The imperial *I*. A., XX. i. 3.

朔 *sŏ* so — The first day of the moon. A., III. xvi. 1.

望 *wang* — To look towards, admiring and expecting. D.M., xxix. 5. A., XIX. ix.: XX. ii. 2. =to compare one's self to. A., V. viii. 2.

朝 *chaou* chao — (1) Morning, in the morning. A., IV. viii.: XII. xxi. 3. (2) A name. A., VI. xiv.

朝 *ch'aou* ch'ao — (1) The court. A., V. vii. 4: XIV. xxxviii.: XIX. xxiii. 1. (2) To be in court, appear in court. A., X. ii. 1; vi. 1: XIV. xxii. 2. 退朝, to retire from court. A., X. xii.: XIII. xiv. (3) To hold a court, give audience. D.M., xx. 14. A., XVIII. iv. (4) Court, as an adjective. A., X. x. ii.; xiii. 3. (5) A name. A., XIX. xxii.

期 *k'e* ch'i — (1) A fixed time. A., XX. ii. 3. (2) A name. A., VII. xxx. 2, 3.

期 *ke* chi — A round year. D.M., xviii. 3. A., XVII. xxi. 1, 3. 期月, a round month. D.M., vii.

朞 *ke* chi — 朞月, a round year. A., XIII. x.

THE 75TH RADICAL. 木.

木 *muh* mu — (1) Trees. D.M., xxvi. 9. A., XVII. ix. 7: XIX. xii. 2. (2) Wood. A., V. ix. 1. (3) Wooden. A., III. xxiv. (4) Simple, plain. A., XIII. xxvii.

未 *we* wei — Not yet. *Passim*. We may sometimes translate by *not*, but the force of the *yet* is always to be detected. It is joined with 嘗. A., III. xxiv.; VI. xii.: VII. vii.; ix.: IX. xxx. 2. Its power, in common with other negatives, to attract 之 to itself, and make it precede the verb which governs it, is to be noted. G.L.v., 7; c., ix. 1. A., I. ii. 2; V. v. x.; xiii. *et al.*

末 *mŏ* mo — (1) The end, the product, result, in opp. to 本, the root. G.L.t., 3, 7: c., x. 7. (2) Small, trivial. D.M., xxxiii. 6. A., XIX. xii. 1. (3) In old age. D.M., xviii. 3. (4) Not, do not. A., IX. x. 3; xxiii.; XIV. xlii. 3: XV. xv.; XVII. v. 2.

本 *pun* păn — The root; what is radical, essential. G.L.t., 3, 6, 7: c., iv.; v.; x. 7. D.M., i. 4; xxxii. 1. A., I. ii. 2: XIX. xii. 1. What is first to be attended to. A., III. iv. 1. To be rooted. D.M., xxix. 3.

朱 *choo* chu — (1) Vermillion colour. A., XVII. xviii. (2) A surname. A., XVIII. viii.

朽 *hew* hsiu — Rotten. A., V. ix. 1.

杇 *woo* wu — To plaster. A., V. ix. 1.

杞 *k'e* ch'i — The name of a State. A., III. ix. D.M., xxviii. 5.

杖 *chang* chang — A staff. A., XIV. xlvi.: XVIII. vii. 1. 杖者, those who carried staves. A., X. x. 1.

束 *shuh* shu — (1) To bind, gird. A., V. vii. 4. (2) A bundle of dried flesh. A., VII. vii.

林 *lin* — A surname. A., III. iv. 1; vi.

東 *tung* — (1) The east, eastern. A., XVII. v. 3. To turn to the east. A., X. xiii. 3. (2) 東蒙, a mountain. A., XVI. i. 4. 東里, a place. A., XIV. ix. 1.

某 *mow* mou — So-and-so. A., XV. xli. 1.

松 *sung* — The pine tree. A., III. xxi. 1: IX. xxvii.

枉 *wang* — Crooked, used metaphorically. A., II. ix.: XII. xxii. 3, 4. With verbal force. A., XVIII. ii.

枕 *chin* — To use as a pillow. A., VII. xv.

材 *ts'ai* ts'ai. Qualities. D.M., xvii. 3. In A., V. vi., the meaning is uncertain.

果 *kwo* kuo. (1) Determined, decided. A., VI. vi.; XIV. xlii. 3. 果敢, A., XVII. xxiv. (2) To carry into effect. A., XIII. xx. 3. (3) Really. D.M., xx. 21.

柏 *poh* pai. The cypress tree. A., III. xxi. 1; IX. xxvii.

柙 *hea* hsia. A cage for wild beasts. A., XVI. i. 7.

柔 *jow* jou. (1) Gentle, mild. D.M., x. 3; xxxi. 1. To treat gently. D.M., xx. 12, 13, 14. (2) Weak. D.M., xx. 21. (3) Mild, soft, in a bad sense. A., XVI. iv.

析 *seih* hsi. To be split; divisions. A., XVI. i. 12.

柯 *ko* ko. An axe-handle. D.M., xiii. 2.

柳 *lew* liu. 柳下, the name of a place. A., XV. xiii; XVIII. ii; viii. 1, 3.

栖 *se* hsi. 栖栖者, one who keeps roosting, or hanging, about. A., XIV. xxxiv. 1.

栗 *leih* li. 戰栗, the appearance of being frightened. A., III. xxi. 1.

校 *keaou* chiao. To enter into altercation. A., VIII. v.

柴 *ch'ae* ch'ai. Name of one of Conf. disciples. A., XI. xvii. 1.

格 *kih* ko. (1) ? To investigate. G.L.t., 4, 5. (2) To come to, approach. D.M., xvi. 4. (3) To become correct. A., II. iii. 2.

桃 *t'aou* t'ao. The peach tree. G.L.c., ix. 6.

桀 *kee* chieh. The last emperor of the Hsia dynasty, a tyrant. G.L.c., ix. 4. 桀溺, a recluse. A., XVII. vi. 1, 3.

栽 *tsae* tsai. To flourish, as a tree. D.M., xvii. 3.

桓 *hwan* huan. (1) 桓公, a famous duke of Ts'e. A., XIV. xvi; xvii; xviii. (2) A surname. A., VII. xxii. (3) 三桓, the three principal families in Lû. A., XVI. iii.

桑 *sang* sang. 子桑 appy. a double surname. A., VI. i. 2.

桴 *fow* fu. A raft. A., V. vi.

梁 *leang* liang. A bridge. A., X. xviii. 2.

棁 *chuĕ* chüeh. Small pillars, supporting the rafters of a house. A., V. xvii.

棄 *k'e* ch'i. To abandon, throw away, neglect. A., V. xviii. 2; XIII. xix; xxx; XVII. xiv; XVIII. x.

棺 *kwan* kuan. An inner coffin. A., XI. vii. 2.

椁 *kŏ* kuo. An outer coffin. A., XI. vii. 1, 2.

棣 *te* ti. 唐棣, the aspen plum. A., IX. xxx. 1.

棘 *keih* chi. A surname. A., XII. viii.

棖 *ch'ang*. A name. A., V. x.

植 *chih*. To stick in the ground. A., XVIII. vii. 1.

極 *keih* chi. The very utmost, as a noun and adverb. G.L.c., ii. 4. D.M., xxvii. 2, 6.

楚 *ts'oo* ts'u. The name of a State. G.L.c., x. 12. A., XVIII. ix. 2; v.

榮 *yung* jung. Glorious. A., XIX. xxv. 4.

樂 *yŏ* yo. (1) Music. *Saepe*. 女樂, female musicians. A., XVIII. iv. (2) 大師樂, Grand music-master. A., III. xxiii.

樂 *lŏ* lo. Pleasure, joy; to rejoice in, find joy. *Saepe*.

樂 *gaou* yao. To find pleasure in. A., VI. xxi; XVI. v. 好樂, G.L.c., vii. 1.

樹 *shoo* shu. (1) Trees, = vegetation. D.M., xx. 3. (2) A screen. A., III. xxii. 3.

機 *ke* chi. A spring, source of influence. G.L.c., ix. 3.

權 *k'euen* ch'üan. A weight, weights. A., XX. i. 6. To weigh. A., IX. xxix. The exigency of the circumstances, as if determined by weighing. A., XVIII. viii. 4.

櫝 *tuh* *tu* A coffer, a repository. A. XVI. i. 7.

THE 76TH RADICAL. 欠.

次 *ts'ze* *tsze* (1) Next in order or degree. D.M., xxiii. 1; A., VII. xxvii.: XIII. xx. 2, 3: XVI. ix. In A., XIV. xxxix. 2, 3, 4, 其次 only = some. (2) 造次, in moments of haste.

欲 *yuh* *yü* (1) To desire, to wish. G.L.c., 4. A., II. iv. 6: III. x.; xvii. 1; *et al., saepe*. (2) To be covetous, = 貪. A., XII. xviii.: XIV. ii.; xiii. In A., XX. ii. 1, 2, 欲 is distinguished from 貪.

欺 *k'e* *ch'i* To deceive, impose upon; to be deceived. G.L.c., vi. 1. A., VI. xxiv.: IX. xi. 2: XIV. xxiii.

歌 *ko* To sing. A., VII. ix. 2; xxxi.: XVII. iv.; xx.: XVIII. v.

歎 *t'an* To sigh, with the idea of admiration. A., IX. x. 1: XI. xxv. 7.

THE 77TH RADICAL. 止.

止 *che* *chih* (1) To rest; where to rest. G.L.t., 1, 2: c., iii. 1, 2, 3. (2) To stop, desist. D.M., xiii. 2. A., IX. xviii.; xx.: XI. xxiii. 3: XII. xxiii.: XVI. i. 6: XIX. xiv. (3) To detain. A., XVIII. vii. 3.

正 *ching* *chêng* (1) To rectify, to adjust; be rectified. G.L.t., 4, 5: c., vii. 1, 3; ix. 8. D.M., xiv. 3. A., I. xiv.: VIII. iv. 3; *et al., saepe*. (2) Correct, correctness, correctly. G.L.c., vii. 1. D.M., xxxi. 1. A., X. viii. 3; ix.; xiii. 1; xvii. 1: In these examples, correct = square, straight. A., XIII. iii. 4, 5; vi.: XIV. xvi. (3) Just, exactly. A., VII. xxxiii. Observe A., XVII. x.

正 *ching* *chêng* Up. 1st tone. The bull's eye in a target. D.M., xiv. 5.

此 *ts'ze* *tz'ŭ* This. *Saepe*. 如此, thus. G.L.c., ix. 3. D.M., xvi. 5; xxvi. 6; xxviii. 1. 在此, here. D.M., xxix. 6. The character does not occur in the Analects.

武 *woo* *wu* (1) The honorary epithet of the first emperor of the Chow dynasty. D.M., xviii. 1, 2, 3. *Et al., saepe*. The name of his music. A., III. xxv. (2) The hon. ep. of others. A., XIV. xiii.; xv. A., V. xx.—A., II. vi.: V. vii.—A., XIX. xxiii.; xxiv. (3) A name. A., XVIII. ix. 4. (4) 武城, name of a place. A., VI. xii.: XVII. iv.

歲 *suy* *sui* The year, years. A., IX. xxvii.: XVII. i. 2.

歸 *kwei* *kuei* (1) To return. A., V. xxi.: XI. xxv. 7. (2) To revert to. A., I. ix.: XII. i. 1. (3) To turn to. D.M., xx. 13. To flow to. A., XIX. xx. 歸心, to turn to in heart. A., XX. i. 7. (4) To turn to, depend on. A., X. xv. 1. (5) To present. A., XVII. i. 1: XVIII. iv. (6) = to be married. G.L.c., ix. 6. (7) 三歸 see on 三.

THE 78TH RADICAL. 歹.

死 *sze* *ssŭ* To die; death; the dead. D.M., x. 4, 5; xix. 5. A., II. v. 3: IV. viii.: XI. vi.; vii. 1, 2; viii.; ix.; x.; xi.; xii. 2; xxii.: *et al., saepe*. 後死者, a future mortal. A., IX. v. 3.

殆 *tae* *tai* Dangerous;—both what is perilous, and being in peril. G.L.c., x. 3. A., II. xv.; xviii. 2: XV. x. 6: XVIII. v. 1.

殖 *chih* To be largely produced; to be amassed. D.M., xxvi. 9. A., XI. xviii. 2.

殘 *ts'an* Vicious, violently bad. A., XIII. xi.

殯 *pin* To coffin, = to bury. A., X. xv. 1.

THE 79TH RADICAL. 殳.

殺 *shă* *sha* To kill. A., XII. xix.: XIV. xvii. 1; xviii. 1: XV. viii.: XVIII. vii. 3: XX. ii. 2. = Capital punishments. XIII. xi.

殺 *shae* *shai* Gradually decreasing. D.M., xx. 5. A., X. vi. 9.

殷 *yin* The name of a dynasty. G.L.c., x. 5. D.M., xxviii. 5. A., II. xxiii. 2: *et al.*

殿 *tëen* *tien* Up. 3d tone. To bring up the rear. A., VI. xiii.

毀 *hwuy* (1) To blame excessively, revile. A., XV. xxiv.: XIX. xxiv. (2) To be broken. A., XVI. i. 7.

毅 *e* *i* Determined and enduring. D.M., xxxi. 1. A., VIII. vii. 1: XIII. xxv.

THE 80TH RADICAL. 毋.

毋 *woo* *wu* Do not, = do not do, do not have, &c. G.L.c., vi. 1; x. 2. A., VI. iii. 4: IX. xxiv.: XI. xxv. 2: XII. xxiii. In A., IX. iv., it is taken as = 無, the simple negative, but its ordinary meaning may be retained.

母 mu. A mother. A., VI. iii. 1. 父母, a parent, parents. G.L.c., x. 2. D.M., xv. 3; xviii. 3. A., I. vii: II. vi: IV. xviii; xix; xxi: XI. iv: XVII. xxi. 6: XVIII. ii.

每 mei. Every. A., III. xv: X. xiv.

THE 81st RADICAL. 比.

比 pi. To compare, be compared. A., VII. i.

比 pi. Low, 3d tone. (1) To follow. A., IV. x. (2) Partizanly. A., II. xiv. (3) Joined with 及, within, by the time of. A., XI. xxv. 4, 5.

THE 82d RADICAL. 毛.

毛 mao. The hair, a hair. D.M., xix. 4; xxxiii. 6.

THE 83d RADICAL. 氏.

氏 shih. A family. Follows surnames, and denotes particular individuals. A., III. i: et al.—A., III. xxi.—A., XIV. x.—A., 3. —A., III. xxii.—A., XIV. xli; xlii.—A., XIX. xix.

民 min. (1) The people, the multitude. Passim. (2) = 人, man, men. A., VI. xx: XV. xxxiv. And perhaps in some other places, as D.M., iii. A., VI. xxvii: XVI. ix: XVII. xvi.

THE 84th RADICAL. 气.

氣 ch'i. Breath. A., X. iv. 4. 血氣, blood and breath,=the physical powers. A., XVI. vii. 有血氣者, mankind. D.M., xxxi. 4. Observe 辭氣, A., VIII. iv. 3, and 食氣, A., X. viii. 4.

THE 85th RADICAL. 水.

水 shui. Water. D.M., xxvi. 9; xxx. 1. A., VI. xxi: VII. xv: XV. xxxiv.

永 yung. To perpetuate, perpetual. D.M., xxix. 6. A., XX. i. 1.

汎 fan. Universally. A., I. vi.

求 ch'iu. (1) To seek for; also to ask, request. G.L.c., ix. 2, 4. D.M., xiii. 4; xiv. 3, 5. A., I. x. 1, 2; xiv: IV. xiv: et al., saepe. (2) The name of one of Conf. disciples. A., V. vii. 3: VI. vi; x: et al., saepe.

汶 wăn. The name of a stream. A., VI. vii.

沂 i. The name of a stream. A., XI. xxv. 7.

沐 muh. 沐浴, to bathe. A., XIV. xxii. 2.

沒 mo. (1) To die, be dead. A., I. xi: IX. v. 2. 沒世, after death. G.L.c., iii. 5. A., XV. xix. (2) To exhaust, be exhausted. A., XVII. xxi. 3. 沒階, A., X. iv. 5. 沒齒, A., XIV. x. 3.

沛 p'ei. 顛沛, in danger, in confusion. A., IV. v. 3.

河 ho. Rivers, a river. D.M., xxvi. 9. A., VII. x. 3. The river, i.e., the Yellow river. A., IX. viii: XVIII. ix. 3.

治 chih. To regulate, manage, govern. G.L.t., 4: c., ix. 1, 6; x. 1. D.M., xiii. 2; xix. 6, 11, 14, 12. A., V. vii. 2: XIV. xxiii. 2.

治 chih. To be regulated, to be well governed. G.L.t., 5, 7. A., VIII. xx. 1: XV. iv.

沮 chü. 長沮, the designation of a recluse. A., XVIII. vi. 1, 2.

沽 ku. To sell. A., IX. xii. Retailed. A., X. viii. 5.

泥 ni. Low, 3d tone. To be obstructed, inapplicable. A., XIX. iv.

泉 ch'üan. A fountain, a spring. D.M., xxxi. 2, 3.

法 fa. (1) A model; to imitate. G.L.c., ix. 8. D.M., xxix. 5. (2) Law-like, =strict; laws. A., IX. xxiii: XX. i. 6.

泰 t'ai. (1) A dignified ease. A., VII. xxxvi. 3. Oppos. to 驕, A., XIII. xxvi: XX. ii. 1, 2. (2) Arrogant. A., IX. iii. 2. Coupled with 驕, G.L.c., x. 18. (3) 泰山, the name of a mountain. A., III. vi. 泰伯, hon. designation of an ancient worthy. A., VIII. i. 泰誓, name of a Book in the Shoo-king. G.L.c., x. 14.

洋 yang. 洋溢, to overflow. D.M., xxxi. 4. 洋洋乎, the appearance of vast swelling waters, grandly. D.M., xvi. 3; xxvii. 2. A., VIII. xv.

濟 *tsi* To help, benefit. A., VI. xxviii. 1.

洫 *hsü* A ditch. 溝洫, A., XIV. xviii. 3.

澳 *yü* A bank, the winding and curving of a river's banks. G.L.c., iii. 4.

濫 *lan* To overflow, exceed due bounds. A., XV. i. 3.

灌 *kwan* To pour out a libation. A., III. x.

THE 86th RADICAL. 火.

火 *huo* Fire. A., XV. xxxiv. 改火, 'to change the fire,' i.e., to get fire in all the diff. ways. A., XVII. xxi. 3.

烈 *lieh* Violent. A., X. xvi. 5.

烖 *tsai* i. q. 災, calamity. D.M., xxviii. 1.

焉 *yen* A final particle. *Passim.* (1) It is found at the end of clauses, when the mind expects the sequel. G.L.c., vii. 2. D.M., xi. 1; xiii. 1. A., V. xviii.; VI. vii. *et al., saepe.* (2) It is found at the end of sentences, and gives a liveliness to the style. D.M., x. 4; xiv. 2. A., I. xiv.; IV. xvii. *et al., saepe.* (3) It is found often at the end of correlative clauses and sentences. G.L.c., viii. 1; x. 13. D.M., i. 5; xii. 2; xxvi. 2. A., VIII. xiii. 3; XI. xxiv. 3; XIII. xx. 2; *et al.* (4) Observe D.M., xxix. 2. A., V. xii.

焉 *yen* Up. 1st tone. An interrogative particle, generally best translated by 'how.' It is placed at the beginning of the clause to which it belongs, unless where another particle, or the nominative, immediately precedes. D.M., xxxii. 1. A., II. x. 1; III. xxii. 2; IV. i.; V. ii.; iv. 2; x.; xviii. 1, 2; *et al., saepe.*

無 *wu* No, not, to be without, not to have. *Passim.* Joined to verbs, adjectives, and nouns. It is often followed by 所. A., III. vii.; IX. ii. 1; *et al.* The 所 must sometimes be understood. A., XX. iii. 1, 2, 3; *et al.* 無...不, a strong affirmation, often with 所 between. G.L.c., ii. 4; vi. 2; *et al.* So 末—無. A., VII. vii. 1. 無乃...乎, 無寧...乎, forms of interrogation. A., IX. xi. 3, VI. i. 3; *et al.* Opposed to 有, standing absolutely,—the state of being without. A., IX. xi. 2; VIII. v. 1. So 無之, there is not it, opposed to 有之. G.L.c., ix. 1. Observe 無以爲, it is of no use doing so. A., XIX. xxiv.

焚 *fen* To be burned. A., X. xii.

然 *jan* (1) So. A., III. viii. 2; VI. xxiv.; VIII. xx. 3; XIV. xiii. 2, *saepe.* A., XV. ii. 2; xii. 3; XVII. vii. 3; XVIII. vi. 3. 然則, so then, well then. 然而, so but. A., III. xxii. 3; XI. xiv. 2; xxiii. 5; XIX. xv. (2) To be right. A., XI. i. 1. (3) 然後, and afterwards. A., VI. xvi.; IX. xiv.; xxviii.; *et al.* (4) Added to adjectives, forming adverbs. G.L.c., vi. 2. D.M., xxxiii. 1. A., V. xxi.; IX. x. 1, 2; XX. ii. 2; XIX. ix.; *et al.*—Obs. A., VIII. xxi.; XI. xii. 2; XIV. vi. 1. (5) 子然, name of a member of the 季 family. A., XI. xxiii.

煥 *hwan* 煥煥乎, how glorious. A., VIII. xix. 2.

照 *chao* To enlighten, to shine on. D.M., xxxi. 4.

熙 *hsi* Bright. G.L.c., iii. 3.

熟 *shu* Cooked, to cook. A., X. xiii. 1.

燕 *yen* (1) A feast. D.M., xix. 4. (2) Easy and unoccupied. A., VII. iv.

燧 *sui* 鑽燧, to obtain fire by boring, or friction. A., XVII. xxi. 3.

THE 87th RADICAL. 爪.

爭 *tsăng* To wrangle, to strive. G.L.c., x. 8. D.M., xxxiii. 4. A., III. vii.; XV. xxi.

爲 *wei* To do, to make. G.L.c., vi. 2; x. 18. (1) D.M., xi. 1; xiii. 1; xvi. 1. A., III. xxvi.; XIV. xv.; xviii.; XIX. iv.; xv.; xvi.; *et al., saepe.* —to be in charge of, to administer, to govern. D.M., xx. 12, 13. A., II. i.; IV. xiii.; XI. xxv. 4, 5; XIII. iii. 1; xix.; *et al.* 何爲—why. A., VIII. xxiv.; XIV. xxxiv.; xxxvii. 2. (2) To be. G.L.c., x. 4. D.M., vi.; xvii. 1. A., I. ii. 2; xii.; VI. iii.; iii. 3; vii.; xi.; xiii.; *et al., saepe.* At the beginning of clauses, it may be often translated by which is. D.M., xxix.; xxxiii.; *et al.* (3) Before nouns

猗 *î* i — 猗猗, the appearance of luxuriance. G.L.c., iii. 4.

猛 *măng* mêng — Fierce. A., VII. xxxvii.; XX. ii. 1, 2.

猶 *yew* yu — (1) As. G.L.c., iv. A., V. xviii. 2; VII. xxxii.; XI. x.; xv.; XII. viii. 3; xiii.; XVII. x.; xii.; XIX. xxv. 3. (2) Still, yet. D.M., xii. 2; xiii. 2; xxxiii. 6. A., VI. xxviii. 1; VIII. xvii.; XII. iv. 3; XIV. xxxviii. 1; xiv.; XV. xxv. 1; XVII. xxii.; XVIII. v. 1; XIX. xxv.

獄 *yŭ* yü — Litigations. A., XII. xii.

獨 *tuh* tu — (1) Only. A., XII. xii. (2) Alone. A., XVI. xiii. 2, 3. 其獨, the being alone. G.L.c., vi. 1, 2. D.M., i. 3.

獲 *hwŏ* huo — To obtain; acquisition. A., VI. xx. To obtain the confidence of, to gain. D.M., xx. 6, 17. 獲罪, to sin, offend against. A., III. xiii. 2.

獻 *hëen* hsien — (1) Used for 賢, wise men. A., III. ix. (2) An honorary epithet. G.L.c., x. 22.

獸 *show* shou — Wild animals. D.M., xxvi. 9. A., XVII. ix. 7; XVIII. vi. 4.

THE 95TH RADICAL. 玄

玄 *heuen* hsüan — Dark-coloured. A., X. vi. 10; XX. i. 3.

率 *suh* lü — (1) To follow, accord with. D.M., i. 1. (2) 率爾, hastily. A., XI. xxv. 4.

THE 96TH RADICAL. 玉

玉 *yuh* yü — (1) A gem, gems. A., IX. xii.; XVI. i. 7; XVII. xi. (2) 伯玉, a designation. A., XIV. xxvi.; XV. vi. 2.

王 wang — (1) A king, kings. G.L.c., iii. 5. A., XIII. xii. 先王, the former kings. A., I. xii. 2. A former king. A., XVI. i. 4. (2) 王孫, a double surname. A., III. xiii.; XIV. xx. 2.

王 wang — Low, 3d tone. To exercise true, kingly authority. D.M., xviii. 3; xxix. 1. 追王, to carry up the title of king to. D.M., xviii. 3.

理 *le* li — Distinctive, discriminating. D.M., xxxi. 1; xxxiii. 1.

琢 *chŏ* cho — To cut, as jewels or gems. G.L.c., iii. 4. A., I. xv. 2.

琴 *k'in* ch'in — A harp, or lute. D.M., xv. 2.

瑟 *sih* shê — (1) Stern, majestic. G.L.c., iii. 4. (2) The harpsichord. A., XI. xiv. 1; xxv. 7; XVII. xx. 1. 琴瑟, D.M., xv. 2.

璉 *lëen* lien — A gemmed vessel, used in sacrifice. 瑚璉, A., V. iii.

瑚 *hoo* hu — Same as the above.

THE 97TH RADICAL. 瓜

瓜 *kwa* kua — A gourd, 匏瓜, A., XVII. vii. 4. Supposed to be instead of 必, A., X. viii. 10.

瓢 *p'eaou* p'iao — A calabash. A., VI. ix.

THE 99TH RADICAL. 甘

甘 *kan* kan — Sweet, to enjoy as sweet or pleasant. A., XVII. xxi. 5.

甚 *shin* shăn — Excessive, to an exceeding degree. A., VII. v.; xxviii. 3; VIII. x.; XV. xxxiv. 甚於…, more important than. A., XIX. xx.

THE 100TH RADICAL. 生

生 *săng* shăng — (1) To produce, to be produced. G.L.c., x. 19. D.M., xvii. 3; xx. 5; xxvi. 7, 9. A., I. ii. 2; VII. xxii.; XVII. xix. 3. (2) To be born. D.M., xx. 9; xxviii. 1. A., VII. xix. 生而知之, born with knowledge. A., XVI. ix.; VI. xvii. (3) To live. A., VI. xvii.; XII. x. 2; XVII. xxi. 6. The living, when living. D.M., xix. 5. A., II. v. 3; X. xiii. 1. Life. A., XI. xi.; XII. v. 3; XV. viii.; XIX. xxv. 4. 先生, elders. A., II. viii.; XIV. xlvii. 2. 後生, a youth. A., IX. xxii. 平生, the life-time. A., XIV. xiii. 2. (4) 微生, a double surname. A., XIV. xxxiv.—V. xxiii.

產 *tsan* ch'an — 子產, the designation of a statesman of Conf. time. A., V. xv.; XIV. ix.; x.

II. xxiii. 2. 百官. A., XIV. xliii. 2: XIX. xxiii. 3. 百物. A., XVII. xix. 3. 百姓 the people. D.M., xx. 13. 14. A., XII. ix. 4: et al. 百乘之家, a house of 100 chariots, the highest officer in a State. G.L.c., x. 22. A., V. vii. 3. 百里之命, authority over 100 li—a large State. A., VIII. vi.

的 teh ti 的然, seeking display. D.M., xxxiii. 1.

皆 kiai chieh All. At the commencement of clauses, with reference to preceding statements. If it have a noun with it, the noun always precedes. G.L.c., 6; c., i. 4. D.M., i. 4; vii. A., II. vii. 1; VII. xviii. XI. ii. 1; et al., saepe.

皇 hwang huang 3. Great, august. 皇皇后帝, most great and sovereign God. A., XX. i.

皦 kiao chiao Clear, distinct. A., III. xxiii.

THE 107TH RADICAL. 皮.

皮 p'i pi The hides of animals. A piece of skin or leather. A., III. xvi.

THE 108TH RADICAL. 皿.

盈 ying Full. A., VII. xxv. 3. To fill. A., VIII. xv.

益 yih yi (1) To add to: more. A., II. xxiii. 2; VI. iii. 1; XI. xvi. 1; XIII. i. 2. 益者, one who has made progress. A., XIV. xlvii. 1, 2. (2) Of advantage, profitable. G.L.c., vi. 2. A., XV. xxx.; XVI. iv.; v.

盍 ho ho Why not? A., V. xxv. 1; XII. ix. 2.

盛 shing sheng Complete, abundant, rich. G.L.c., iii. 4. D.M., XVI. i. 3. 盛服. D.M., xx. 14. A., VIII. xx. 3; X. xvi. 4.

盜 tau tao Robbing; a thief. G.L.c., x. 22. A., XII. xviii.; XVII. xii.; xxiii.

盡 tsin chin To carry out, give full development to; completely. G.L.c., iv. D.M., xiii. 1; xxii.; xxvi. 7; xxvii. 6. A., III. xviii.; xxv.; VIII. xxi.

監 kien chien To inspect, to view. G.L.c., x. 5. A., III. xiv.

盪 tang 盪舟, to push a boat on the dry land. A., XIV. vi.

盤 p'wan p'an A bathing tub. G.L.c., i. 1.

盧 loo lu Used for 蘆, a kind of rush. D.M., xx. 3.

THE 109TH RADICAL. 目.

目 muh mu (1) The eye. G.L.c., vi. 3. A., III. viii. 1. (2) An index, steps, processes. A., XII. i. 2.

盼 p'an The black and white of the eye well defined. A., III. viii. 1.

直 chih Upright, straight-forward. A., II. xix.; VI. xvii.; VIII. ii.; xvi.; et al., saepe. 直道, to pursue the straight path. A., XV. xxiv. 2; XVIII. ii. uprightness, justice. A., XIV. xxvi. 3.

相 seang hsiang Mutually, one another. D.M., xxx. 3. A., XV. xxxix.; XVII. ii.

相 seang hsiang Up, 3d tone. (1) To be observed. D.M., xxxiii. 3. (2) To assist. A., III. ii. To act as minister to. A., XIV. xviii. 1, 2; XVI. i. 12. (3) An assistant at interviews of ceremony. XI. xxv. 6. (4) To lead, guide, as the blind. A., XV. xli. 3.

省 sing hsing To examine, inspect. D.M., xx. 4; xxxiii. 2. A., I. iv.; II. ix.; IV. xvii.; XII. iv. 2.

眩 hiuen hsuan To be deceived. D.M., xx. 13.

衆 chung All, used absolutely. G.L.c., ix. 1; x. 5. A., I. vi.; VI. xxviii. 1; et al., saepe. Followed by a noun. A., II. i. Many, in opp. to 寡. G.L.c., x. 19. A., XX. ii. 2.

睨 i To look askance. D.M., xiii. 2.

睹 too tu To see. D.M., i. 2.

睿 jui jui Intelligent, perspicacious. D.M., xxxi. 1.

瞻 chen chan To look to. G.L.c., iii. 4. With reverence. G.L.c., x. 4. A., IX. x. 1. 瞻視. A., XX. ii. 2.

瞽 koo ku Blind. A., IX. ix.; X. xvi. 2. = blindness. A., XVI. vi.

XVIII. vii. 4; XIX. xviii. *et al., saepe.*—In all these cases the proper meaning of 者, as in case (1) is apparent. But (5) we find it where that can hardly be traced, and where sometimes we might translate it by *one* or *that*, and at other times by *as, such a thing*, with a ——, but there are cases where it cannot be translated. G.L.c., 7; c., ix. 4. A., VI. ii.; xiii.; XI. vi.; XII. viii. 2, 3; XVI. i. 5; xiii. 4; XVII. vi.; XIX. xxv. 4. (6) It forms adverbs with 昔 and 古. A., XVII. vii. 2; xvi. *et al.* Observe A., IX. xvi.; III. x.

THE 126TH RADICAL. 而.

而 *urh* *Passim.* A conjunction. (1) And. G.L.t., 2, 3; c., ix. 2, 4, 6, 7, 8. D.M., i. 4; ii. 2; xx. 6, 9, 12, 17. A., I. i. 1; ii. 2; iv.; v.; vi.; vii.; xii. 2; *et al., saepissime.* (2) And yet. G.L.t., 2; c., iii. 2; vii. 2; x. 13, 14. D.M., xxxiii. 1, 3, 4; *et al. saepissime.* The 'and yet' is often nearly, or altogether,=but. A., II. xiv: VII. xxvi.; XIII. xxv.; xxvi. *et al., saepe.* It may often be translated by if. A., III. xxii. 3; VII. xi.; xxv. 1, 2; xxx. 2; xxvi. *et al.* (3) It is used idiomatically, or for the rhythm, after adverbs. A., XI. xxv. 4; XIV. xx. 1; xlii. 3; XVII. iv. 2; *et al.* 然而. A., XIX. xv. 1. (4) After 得 and before a verb, it forms the passive of that verb. A., VIII. i.; XIX. xxiv.; xxv. 3; *et al.* (5) *sæpe.* A., XII. i. 1. (6) 而今而後, henceforth, both now and hereafter. A., VI. iii. (7) It is often followed by 已, 已也, 已矣. D.M., xxv. 3. A., II. xv. 2; XIV. xlv.; *et al.* (8) Used for 汝, you. D.M., ix. 2. (9) A., IX. xxx. 1, a mere expletive. 已而已而. A., XVIII. v. 1.

THE 127TH RADICAL. 耒.

耕 *kăng* *kêng* To plough; to do field-work. A., XV. xxxi.; XVIII. vi. 1.

耦 *gow* *ou* Two together. A., XVIII. vi. 1.

耰 *yew* *yu* To cover the seed. A., XVIII. vi. 3.

THE 128TH RADICAL. 耳.

耳 *urh* (1) The ear. A., II. iv. 5; VIII. xv. (2) A final particle,=simply. A., XVII. iv. 4. (3) An expletive. A., VI. xii.

耽 *tan* Yielding pleasure. D.M., xv. 2.

聘 *p'ing* The sending of envoys to one another, or to court, by the princes of the empire. D.M., xx. 11.

聖 *shing* *shêng* Intelligent, perspicacious. G.L.c., x. 11. D.M., xxxii. 3. Sage, possessing the highest knowledge and excellence. 聖者, a sage. D.M., xi. 3; xxxi. 1. A., VI. xxviii. 1; VII. xxxiii.; IX. vi. 1, 2.

聚 *ts'ü* *chü* To collect, be collected. G.L.c., x. 9. 聚斂, to collect imposts. G.L.c., x. 22. A., XI. xvi. 1.

聞 *wăn* *wên* To hear; to become acquainted with by report. *Passim.* 聽而不聞, to hear and not understand. G.L.c., vii. 2. D.M., xvi. 2.

聞 *wăn* *wên* Low, 3d tone. To be heard of, notoriety. A., XII. xx. 3, 4, 6.

聰 *ts'ung* Quick in apprehension. D.M., xxxi. 1; xxxii. 3. To hear distinctly. A., XVI. x.

聲 *shing* *shêng* A sound. D.M., xxxiii. 6. A., XVII. iv. 1.=Songs. A., XV. x. 6; XVII. xviii. 聲名, fame. D.M., xxxi. 4.

聽 *t'ing* To hear, to listen to. G.L.c., iv.; vii. 2. D.M., xvi. 2. A., V. ix. 2; XII. i. 2; xiii.; XVI. x.; XVII. xiv. 聽於, to receive instructions from. A., XIV. xliii. 2.

THE 129TH RADICAL. 聿.

肆 *sze* *ssŭ* (1) To expose a corpse. A., XIV. xxxviii. 1. (2) Unrestrained, a disregard of smaller matters. A., XVII. xvi. 2. (3). A shop, a stall for goods. A., XIX. vii.

THE 130TH RADICAL. 肉.

肉 *juh* *jou* Flesh, meat. A., VII. xiii.; X. viii. 2, 4, 8; xv. 2.

肖 *seaou* *hsiao* 不肖, not equal to, degenerate, worthless. D.M., iv.; xii. 2.

肝 *kan* The liver. 其肺肝, his lungs and liver,=his inward thoughts. G.L.c., vi. 2.

肸 *hih* *hsi* A name. A., XVII. vii. 1, 2.

肺 *fei* The lungs. See above.

A., XIX. xvii. To be carried to perfection. A., XIX. xiv. Observe 致期. A., XX. ii. 3. (2) 致身, 致命, to devote one's person, life. A., I. vii.; XIX. i.

臺 t'ai t'ai. 澹臺, a surname. A., VI. xii.

THE 134th RADICAL. 臼.

臾 yü yü. (1) 須臾, an instant. D.M., i. 2. (2) 顓臾, the name of a small State. A., XVI. i.

與 yü yü. Low, 2d tone. (1) With, along with; to be with, to associate with. G.L.c., iii. 3; x. 15. D.M., xxii. 1; xxiii. A., I. iv.; vii.; xv. 3: *et passim*. (2) And. A., IX. i; ix.; XI. xxiii. 2, 4, 6: *et al.* Sometimes it must be translated by *or*. A., XI. xv.; *et al.* (3) Followed by 寧, and by 豈若, than. G.L.c., x. 22. A., IV. iv. 3; xiii. 1; VII. xxxv.; IX. xi. 3; XVIII. vi. 3. (4) To give to. A., I. x. 1; V. xxiii.; VI. iii. 1, 3, 4. XX. ii. 3. (5) To grant, concede to, allow. A., V. viii. 3; VII. xxviii. 2; XI. xxv. 2. (6) To wait for. A., XVII. i. 2. 歲不我與. (7) Observe 與比. A., IV. x.; 巽與之言; A., IX. xxiii., 丘不與易. A., XVIII. vi. 4.

歟 yü yü. (1) Low, 1st tone. A final particle, sometimes interrogative, sometimes of admiration, and sometimes of doubt or hesitancy. As interrogative, it generally implies that the answer will be in the affirmative. As indicating doubt or hesitancy, we find it preceded by other final particles. It is followed also by other particles of exclamation. D.M., vi.; x. 2; xvii. 1; xxvii. 7. A., I. ii. 2; x. 1, 2; xv. 2: *et al., passim*. Observe A., V. ix. 1, 2; XII. xxviii. 2. (2) 與與, the appearance of dignity and satisfaction. A., X. ii. 2.

與 yü yü. Low, 3d tone. Sharing in; concerned with. D.M., xii. 2. A., III. xii. 2; VIII. xviii.; IX. v. 3; XIII. xiv.

興 hsing hsing. (1) To rise. A., XV. i. 2. = to become. G.L.c., ix. 3; x. 1. So, followed by 於. A., VIII. ii. 2. To be produced. D.M., xxvi. 9. To be aroused, stimulated. A., VIII. viii. 1; XVII. ix. 2. (2) To flourish. D.M., xxiv. A., XIII. iii. 6. To make to flourish; to raise. D.M., xxvii. 7. A., XIII. xv. 1, 3; XX. i. 7.

舉 chü chü. (1) To raise; employ, promote. G.L.c., x. 1. D.M., xx. 11. A., II. xix.; xx.; XII. xxii. 3, 4, 6; XIII. ii. 1, 2; XV. xxii.; XX. i. 7. To present; set forth (in discourse). A., VII. viii. Passive, to be established. D.M., xx. 2. (2) To rise. A., X. xviii. 1.

舊 chiu chiu. Old. G.L.c., ii. 3. A., V. xviii. 1; xxii.; XI. xiii. 2; XVII. xxi. 3. 故舊, old friends or ministers. A., VIII. ii. 2; XVIII. x. 舊惡, see 惡.

THE 135th RADICAL. 舌.

舌 shê shê. The tongue. A., XII. viii. 2.

舍 shê shê. Up. 2d tone, for 捨. (1) To reject. A., VI. iv. To neglect. A., XIII. ii. 2. To leave unemployed. A., VII. x. To lay aside. A., XI. xxv. 7. To omit; decline. A., XVI. i. 8. (2) To cease; give over. A., IX. xvi.

舒 shu shu. = economy. G.L.c., x. 19.

THE 136th RADICAL. 舛.

舜 shun shun. An ancient emperor. D.M., vi.; xvii. 1. A., VIII. xviii.; *et al.* 堯舜, G.L.c., ix. 4. D.M., xxx. 1. A., VI. xxviii.; XVI. xiv.

舞 wu wu. (1) Pantomimes. A., III. i.; XV. x. 4. (2) 舞雩, = the rain altars. A., XI. xxv. 7; XII. xxi. 1.

THE 137th RADICAL. 舟.

舟 chou chou. A ship, a boat. D.M., xxxi. 4. A., XIV. vi.

THE 139th RADICAL. 色.

色 shih shê. (1) Colour, appearance, especially as variously seen in the countenance; the countenance. G.L.c., vi. 1. D.M., xxxiii. 6. A., I. iii.; II. viii.; V. xviii.: *et al. saepe*. 顏色, A., VIII. iv. 3; X. v. 2; XVI. vi. 潤色, to give the proper finish. (2) Beauty, and the desire for its enjoyment. D.M., xx. 14. A., I. vii.; IX. xvii.; XV. xii.; XVI. vii.

THE 140th RADICAL. 艸.

芸 yün yun. In some copies for 耘. To weed. A., XVIII. vii. 1.

THE 141st RADICAL. 虍.

THE 142d RADICAL. 虫.

THE 143d RADICAL. 血.

THE 144th RADICAL. 行.

觀 kwan kuan. To look at; to mark. A., I. xi.; II. x. 2; III. x.; xxvi.; IV. vii.; V. ix. 2; VIII. xi.; XII. xx. 5; XIX. iv. 詩可以觀, the odes may be used for purposes of self-contemplation. A., XVII. ix. 3.

覺 kio chio. To apprehend. 先覺者, one who is of quick apprehension.

THE 148TH RADICAL. 角.

角 kiō chio. A horn; horned. A. VI. iv.

觚 ku ku. A drinking vessel, made with corners. A., VI. xxiii.

THE 149TH RADICAL. 言.

言 yen. (1) A word, words; a saying, a sentence. G.L.c., ix. 3; x. 2. D.M., vi.; xiii 4; xx. 6; xxvi. 7; xxvii. 7; xxxiii. 4. A., I. iii.; xiii.; xiv.; II. ii.; xiii.; et al., passim. To speak; to speak of; to tell. D.M., xxix. 5; xxxi. 3; xxxiii. 3. A., I. vii.; xv. 3; II. ix.; xviii. 2; et al., passim. meaning. D.M., xii. 3. (2) The surname of 子游, one of Conf. disciples. A., XIV. xii. 2.

訐 kie chieh. To expose people's secrets. A., XVII. xxiv. 2.

討 t'ao t'ao. (1) To punish. A., XIV. xxii. 2. (2) 討論, to examine and discuss. A., XIV. ix.

訒 jin jên. Words spoken slowly and cautiously. A., XII. iii. 2, 3.

訕 shan. To rail at, slander. A., XVII. xxiv.

託 t'o t'o. To entrust, be entrusted, with. A., VIII. vi.

訟 sung. Litigations. G.L.c., iv. A., XII. xiii. 自訟, to accuse. A., V. xxvi.

訥 nah na. Slow in speaking. A., IV. xxiv. Modest. A., XIII. xxvii.

設 shě shê. To set forth, display. D.M., xix. 3.

詐 cha. Deceitful. A., IX. xi. 2. Deceit. A., XVII. xvi. 2. Deception, attempts to deceive. A., XIV. xxxiii.

詠 yung. To sing. A., XI. xxv. 7.

試 she shih. (1) To try, examine. D.M., xx. 14. A., XV. xxiv. (2) To be used, have official employment. A., IX. vi. 4.

誄 lei. A collection of Prayers of Eulogy. A., VII. xxxiv.

誅 choo chu. To reprove. A., V. ix. 1.

詩 she shih. The Book of Poetry; the pieces in the B. of P. A., I. xv. 3; II. ii.; III. viii. 3; VII. xvii.; VIII. viii. 1; XIII. v.; XVI. xiii. 2, 5; XVII. ix. 1, 2. 詩曰, 詩云, says.

語 yu yü. To speak; to speak of. D.M., xii. 2. A., VII. xx.; X. viii. 9. Words, sayings. A., IX. xxiii.; XII. i. 2; ii.; XVI. xi. 1, 2.

語 yu yü. Low. 3d tone. To speak to; to tell. A., III. xxiii.; VI. xix.; IX. xix.; XIII. xviii. 1; XVII. viii. 2; XIX. xxiii.

誠 ch'ing ch'êng. To make, be made, sincere; sincerely. G.L.t., 1. 3; c., vi. 1, 2, 4. In the Doctrine of the Mean, the term has a mystical significance. D.M., xvi. 5; xx. 17, 18; xxi.; xxii.; xxiii.; xxiv.; xxv. 1, 2, 3; xxvi. 1; xxxii. 1. Really, sincerely. G.L.c., ix. 2. A., XII. x. 3. True. A., XIII. xi.

誦 sung. To repeat; hum over. A., IX. xxvi. 3. XIII. v.

說 shwŏ shuo. (1) To speak of; the speaking (what is said). D.M., xxviii. 5. A., III. xxi. 2; XII. viii. 2; XVII. xiv. (2) Meaning. A., III. xi.

說 yüe yueh. For 悅. To be pleased; pleased with; a matter of pleasure. D.M., xxxi. 3. A., I. i. 1; V. v.; VI. x.; xxvi.; IX. xxiii.; XI iii.; XIII. xvi. 2; xxv.; XVII. v. 2.

誥 kaou kao. To enjoin upon; instructions. 康誥, the name of a Book in the Shoo-king. G.L.c., i. 1; ii. 2; ix. 2; x. 10.

誨 hwuy hui. To instruct; teach. A., II. xvii.; VII. ii.; vii.; xxxiii.; XIV. viii.

誓 she shih. To declare solemnly; an oath. 泰誓, the name of a Book in the Shoo-king. G.L.c., x. 14.

誰 shwuy shui. Who, whom. A., VI. xv.; VII. x. 2; IX. xi. 2; XI. ix. 3; XV. xxiv.; XVI. i. 2; XVIII. vi. 2, 3, 4; XX. ii. 2.

誾 yin ên. The appearance of being bland, yet precise. A., X. ii. 2; XI. xii.

諂 chen ch'an. To flatter; flattering. A., I. xv. 1; II. xxiv.; III. xviii.

諟 *shih*. This, or to examine. G.L.c., i. 2.

諠 *hsüan*. To forget. G.L.c., iii. 4.

諶 *shän*. A name. A., XIV. ix.

諺 *yen*. A common saying, a proverb. G.L.c., viii. 2.

請 *ts'ing ch'ing*. To request; to beg. In the first person, sometimes merely a polite way of expressing a purpose. A., III. xxiv: VI. iii: VII. xxxiv: XI. vii. 1: XII. i. 2; ii: XIII. i. 2; iv. 1: XIV. xxii. 2: XVII. vi.

誣 *wû*. To delude; impose on. A., XIX. xxi. 2.

誘 *yu*. To lead on. A., IX. x. 2.

諒 *liang*. Sincere. A., XVI. iv. Simple and sincere. A., XIV. xviii. 3: XV. xxxvi.

諒 *liang*. Low, 1st tone. In the phrase 諒陰. A., XIV. xliii. 1.

謂 *wei*. (1) To say to. A., II. xxi. 1: III. ii: V. viii. 1; et al., saepe. (2) To say of. A., III. i; xx.; xxv.: XVIII. viii. 3, 4; et al., saepe. (3) To call; to be called. G.L.c., iv.; v.; vi. 1, 2: vii. 1, 3; viii. 1, 3; ix. 1, 3; x. 1, 12, 13, 22, 23. D.M. i. 4; xxi. A., I. vii; xi; xiv.; et al., saepe. Observe the idiom, 之謂. G.L.c., x. 2, 3. D.M., i. 1; xxvii. 7. A., I. xv. 2: XVI. xii. 2. 謂之 is different. 何謂 = what is meant? A., III. viii. 1; xiii. 1: IV. xv. 2: XX. ii. 1, 2, 3; et al., saepe.

論 *lun*. To discourse, discuss. A., XI. xx: XIV. ix.

諾 *no*. (1) Oh; yes. A., VII. xiv. 1: XVIII. i. 2. (2) A promise. A., XII. xii. 2.

諸 *chu*. (1) As a preposition,—in, to, from, &c., and sometimes cannot be translated. G.L.c., ix. 4; x. 15. D.M., vii.; xiii. 3; et al. A., I. xv. 3: III. xi: V. xi; xviii: XVII. i. 1, iv. 3; vii. 2; et al. (2) As an interrogative, = 之乎. A., VI. iv.: VII. xxxiv: IX. xii: XI. xxi: XII. xi. 3; et al. (3) Apparently = 此, this. A., VI. xxviii. 1: XIV. xlv. (4) Not merely one all. D.M., xx. 13. A., II. xix: XII. xxii. 3, 4. (5) Observe 其諸, A., I. x. 2; and 將諸. A., XVII. xii: XIX. xii. 2. (6) 諸夏, a name of China. A., III. v. (7) 諸侯, the princes of the empire, a prince. D.M., xviii. 3; xx. 12, 13, 14. A., XI. xxv. 11: XIV. xvii. 2; xviii. 2: XVI. ii.

諫 *chien*. To remonstrate with, reprove. A., III. xxi. 2: IV. xviii: XVIII. i; v. 1: XIX. x.

謀 *mau mou*. To plan; plan about; plans. A., I. iv.: VII. x. 3: VIII. xiv: XIV. xxvii: XV. xxvi; xxxi; xxxix: XVI. i. 13.

謹 *chin*. Earnestly careful. D.M., xiii. 4. A., I. vi.: X. i. 2. To give attention to. A., XX. i. 6.

識 *shih*. To know, become acquainted with. A., XVII. ix. 7.

識 *chih*. Up. 3d tone. To remember. A., VII ii; xxvii: XV. ii. 1: XIX. xxii. 2.

講 *chiang*. To discourse about. A., VII. iii.

謗 *pang*. To vilify. A., XIX. x.

譎 *chüeh*. Crafty. A., XIV. xvi.

謙 *ch'ieh*. 自謙 self-enjoyment. G.L.c., vi. 1.

譖 *tsan*. Slander. A., XII. vi.

證 *chäng*. To testify, bear witness to. A., XIII. xviii. 1.

譬 *p'i*. To compare; a comparison. A., VI. xxviii. 3. 譬如, may be compared to. A., II. i: IX. xviii. 譬諸, is like to. A., XVII. xii: XIX. xii. 2. 譬之, let me compare it. A., XIX. xxiii. 2.

譽 *yü*. Renown; to praise. D.M., xxix. 6. Read in the low, 1st tone, with the same meaning. A., XV. xxiv.

議 *i*. To discourse with, to discuss. A., IV. ix: XVI. ii. 3. To discuss and settle, to arrange. D.M., xxviii. 2.

讀 *tu*. To read, study. A., XI. xxiv. 3.

變 *pien*. To change; changes. D.M., x. 5; xxiii.; xxvi. 6. A., VI. xxii: X. vii. 2; xvi. 3, 4, 5: XIX. ix.

讓 *zang*. Courteous, humble. G.L.c., ix. 3. A., XI. xxv. 10. To decline, yield. A., VIII. i: XV. xxxv. 禮讓, the complaisance of propriety. A., IV. xiii.

讒 ch'an. Slander, or slanderers. D.M., xx. 14.

THE 151st RADICAL. 豆.

豆 tou. A wooden vessel in common use, and at sacrifices. 籩豆, A., VIII. iv. 3. 俎豆, A., XV. i. 1.

豈 ch'i. How. A. VII. xxxiii.: IX. xxx.: XIV. xiv. 2; xviii. 3. Followed by 哉, 也哉, and 乎. A., XVII. v. 3; vii. 4: XVIII. vi. 3: XIX. xxv.

THE 152d RADICAL. 豕.

豚 t'un. A small pig. G.L.c., x. 22. A., XVII. i. 1.

豫 yü. Preparation beforehand. D.M., xx. 16.

THE 153d RADICAL. 豸.

豹 pao. A leopard. A., XII. viii. 3.

貉 mo. The barbarous tribes of the north. 蠻貉. D.M., xxxi. 4. A., XV. v. 2.

貌 mao. Aspect, demeanour. A., VIII. iv. 3: XVI. x. 以貌, to use a ceremonious manner. A., X. xvi. 2.

貉 ho. The badger, or badger's fur. A., IX. xxvi.: X. vi. 7.

THE 154th RADICAL. 貝.

貞 chêng. Correct and firm. A., XV, xxxvi.

負 fu. To carry on the back. A., X. xvi. 3: XIII. iv. 3.

財 ts'ai. Wealth. G.L.c., x. 6, 7, 9, 20, 21, 23. 財用, means of expenditure. D.M., xx. 13. resources of wealth. D.M., xxvi. 9.

貢 kung. 子貢, one of Confucius' disciples. A., I. x. 1, 2; xv. 1, 2: II. xiii.: et al. saepe.

貧 p'in. Poor, being in a poor condition; poverty. D.M., xiv. 2. A., I. xv. 1: IV. v. 1: VIII. x.; xiii. 3: XIV. xi.: XV. xxxi.: XVI. i. 10.

貨 huo. Goods. G.L.c., x. 10. A., XI. xviii. 2. Riches D.M., xx. 14. Articles of value, D.M., xxvi. 9.

貪 t'an. To covet, desire. A., XX. ii. 1, 2. To be ambitious. G.L.c., ix. 3.

貫 kuan. To go through, pervade. A., IV. xv. 1: XV. ii. 3. It is difficult to assign its meaning in XI. xiii. 2.

貳 êrh. To repeat; repeated. A., VI. ii. 1. 不貳, without doubleness. D.M., xxvi. 7.

責 tsê. To require from. A., XV. xiv.

貴 kuei. (1) Noble, being in an honourable condition. Associated with 富. D.M., xiv. 2. A., IV. v. 1: VII. xv.: VIII. xiii. 3: XIV. v. 3. Contrasted with 賤. D.M., xviii. 3; xix. 4. Excellent, valuable. A., I. xii. 1: IX. xxiii. (2) To esteem noble. D.M., xx. 14. A., VIII. iv. 3.

費 fei. (1) Extended, reaching far and wide. D.M., xii. 1. (2) To expend largely. A., XX. ii. 1, 2.

費 pi. The name of a city. A., VI. vii.: XI. xxiv.: XVI. i. 1: XVII. v.

賊 tsei. To injure; injury. A., XI. xxiv. 2: XX. ii. 3. An injurious disregard of consequences. A., XVII. viii. 3. A pest. A., XIV. xlvi. Thieves or injurers. A., XVII. xiii.

賞 shang. To reward. D.M., xxxiii. 4. A., XII. xviii.

賈 ku, chia. A price. A., IX. xii. In op. 2d tone. A name. A., III. xiii.: XIV. xx.—A., XIV. xiv.

賢 hsien. (1) As an adjective, admirable, virtuous and talented. A., VI. ix.: XIII. ii. 1, 2: et al. As a noun, 賢 and 賢者, worthies, men of talents and virtue. G.L.c., x. 16. D.M., iv.; xix. 4; xx. 5, 8, 13, 14. A., I. vii.: IV. xvii.: XV. ix.: et al. saepe. As a verb, to treat as a hsien. G.L.c., iii. 5. A., I. vii. (2) To surpass, be better than. A., XI. xv. 1: XVII. xxii.: XIX. xxiii. 1: xxv. 1.

賓 pin. A guest, a visitor. A., X. iii. 4: XII. ii. 賓客, A., V. vii. 4: XIV. xx. 2.

賜 ts'ze. (1) To give; bestow. A., X. xiii. 1. Gifts. A., XIV. xviii. 2. (2) The name of 子貢, one of Conf. disciples. A., I. xv. 3: III. xvii. 2: et al. saepe.

THE 159TH RADICAL. 車.

車 *kü* chü. A carriage. D.M., xxviii. 3; xxxi. 4. A., II. xxii; V. xxv. 2; X. xv. 2; xvii. 1, 2; XI. vii. 1; XIV. xvii. 2.

軍 *kiun* chün. An army. 三軍, the forces of a great State. A., VII. x. 2; IX. xxv. 軍旅, A., XIV. xxiii; XV. i. 1.

軌 *kwei* kwei. The rut of a wheel, = size, standard. D.M., xxviii. 3.

軏 *yüeh* yueh. An arrangement for yoking the horses in a light carriage. A., II. xxii.

輅 *lu* lu. A state carriage. A., XV. x. 2.

輶 *yu* yu. Light. D.M., xxxiii. 6.

載 *tsai* tsai. (1) To contain. D.M., xii. 2, xxvi. 1, 9; xxx. 2; xxxi. 4. (2) Business, doings. D.M., xxxiii. 6.

輔 *fu* fu. To assist. A., XII. xxiv.

輕 *k'ing* ch'ing. Light. A., V. xxv. 2; VI. iii. 2.

輗 *i* i. The cross bar for yoking the oxen in a large carriage. A., II. xxii.

輿 *yu* yü. (1) A carriage. A., XV. v. 3; XVIII. vi. 2. (2) 接輿 a name. A., XVIII. v.

輟 *chwŏ* chueh. To desist, stop. A., XVIII. vi. 3.

THE 160TH RADICAL. 辛.

辟 *p'ih* pi. (1) Partial, perverse. G.L.c., viii. 1; x. 4. (2) Specious. A., XI. xvii. 3; XVI. iv.

辟 *pih* pi. A sovereign; applicable to the emperor as well as the princes. In the Ana. only of the princes. D.M., xxxiii. 5. A., III. ii.

辟 *pe* pi. I.q. 避. To escape; withdraw from. D.M., vii. A., XIV. xxxix. 1, 2, 3, 4; XVIII. v. 2; vi. 3.

辟 *p'e* pi. I.q. 譬. 辟如, may be compared to. D.M., xv. 1; xxx. 2.

辨 *pien* pien. To discriminate; to discover. D.M., xix. 4; xx. 19, 20. A., XII. x. 1; xxi. 1.

辭 *tsze* tz'u. (1) Language; speech. G.L.c., iv. A., XV. xl. 辭氣, = words and tones. A., VIII. iv. 3. 為之辭, to frame excuses for. A., XVI. i. 2. (2) To refuse, decline. D.M., ix. A., VI. iii. 3; vii; XVII. xx.

THE 161ST RADICAL. 辰.

辰 *shin* ch'ên. The constellations of the zodiac. D.M., xxvi. 9. 北辰, the north pole star. A., II. i.

農 *nung* nung. A husbandman. A., XIII. iv. 1.

辱 *juh* ju. Disgrace; to disgrace. A., [illegible] xiii; IV. xxvi; XII. xxiii; XIII. xx; [illegible]II. viii. 2, 3.

THE 162D RADICAL. 辵.

迅 *sün* hsün. Sudden. A., X. xvi. 5.

迂 *yu* yü. Wide of the mark. A., XIII. iii. 3.

近 *kin* chin. To be near to. G.L.t., 3. D.M., xx. 10; xxix. 5. A., I. xiii; et al. Nearness. D.M., xxxiii. 1. In what is near, i.e., one's self. A., VI. xxviii. 3; XIX. vi.

迎 *ying* ying. To meet. D.M., xx. 14.

述 *shuh* shu. To transmit; carry forward. D.M., xviii. 1; xix. 2; xxx. 1. A., VII. i; XVII. xix. 2. To be handed down to posterity. D.M., xi. 1. A., XIV. xl.

迷 *me* mi. To leave to error. A., XVII. i. 2.

适 *kwoh* kuo. A name. A., XIV. vi. —伯适. A., XVIII. xi.

追 *chuy* chui. To go back in thought, and act according to what may be required. D.M., xviii. 3. A., I. ix. To go forward in the same way. A., XVIII. v.

進 *tsin* chin. To advance, go forward. A., VI. xiii; VII. xxviii. 2; IX. xviii; xx; X. iii. 3; iv. 5; XIII. xxi; XIX. xii. Actively, to call, to urge, forward. A., III. xxv. 2; XI. xxi. 先進, 後進, = 先進, 後進. A., XI. i. 1, 2.

迹 *tseih* chi. Footsteps. A., XI. xix.

THE 167TH RADICAL. 金.

金 *kin* chin. Metal, arms. D.M., x. 4.

鈇 *foo* fu. An axe, a hatchet. 鈇鉞, D.M., xxxiii. 4.

鉞 *yud* yüeh. A battle-axe. See above.

釜 *foo* fu. A measure containing 64 shing. A., VI. iii. 1.

釣 *teaou* tiao. To angle. A., VII. xxvi.

錦 *kin* chin. Embroidered clothes. D.M., xxxiii. 1. A., XVII. xxi. 4.

銘 *ming*. To engrave; be engraved. G.L.c., ii. 1.

錯 *ts'ok* ts'o. Alternatingly. D.M., xxx.

錯 *ts'oo* ts'u. To set aside. A., II. xix.: XII. xxii. 3, 4.

鏗 *k'ang* k'ăng. 鏗爾, while it was yet twanging; spoken of the sound of a harpsichord. A., XI. xxv. 7.

鐸 *tok* to. 木鐸, a bell with a wooden clapper. A., III. xxiv.

鑽 *tsuen* tsuan. To bore; to penetrate. A., IX. x. 1. 鑽燧, to bore wood to procure fire. A., XVII. xxi. 3.

鐘 *chung*. A bell. A., XVII. xi.

THE 168TH RADICAL. 長.

長 *ch'ang*. (1) Long. A., X. vi. 5. 長府, the Long treasury. A., XI. xiii. 1. (2) Said of time. A., IX. ii. = always, A., VII. xxxvi. (3) 長沮, a recluse. A., XVIII. vi. 公冶長, a disciple, and son-in-law, of Conf. A., V. i.

長 *chang*. (1) Up. 2d tone. Old. A., XI. xxv. 2. Grown up. A., XIV. xlvi.: XVII. vii. 6. (長幼). Elders. G.L.c., ix. 1: x. 2. To treat as elders should be treated. G.L.c., x. 2. (2) To preside over, high in station. G.L.c., x. 23.

長 *chang*. Low. 3d tone. More than. A., X. vi. 6.

THE 169TH RADICAL. 門.

門 *mun*. (1) A door, a gate. A., II. xxii. 3: VI. xiii.: XII. ii.: XIV. xlii. Spoken by Conf. of his door, *i.e.*, his school. A., XI. ii. 1: XIV. i. 中門, to stand in the middle of the gate way. A., X. ix. 2. 門人, disciples. A., IV. xv. 2: VII. xxviii.: IX. xi.: XI. x. 1, 2; xiv. 2: XIX. iii.; xii. So, 門弟子, A., VIII. iii.: IX. ii. 2. (2) 石門, the name of a place, or barrier-pass. A., XIV. xli.

閑 *hëen* hsien. A boundary, or fending line. A., XIX. xi.

閒 *hëen* hsien. At leisure; retired. G.L.c., vi. 2.

間 *këen* chien. An interval. Used as a preposition, following its regimen, with 之 before it, = between. A., IV. v. 3: XI. xxv. 4; XVIII. iii. 病間, during an intermission of sickness. A., IX. xi. 2.

閒 *këen* chien. Up. 3d tone. To find a crevice or flaw. A., VIII. xxi.: XI. iv.

閾 *yih* yi. The threshold. A., X. iv. 2.

闇 *gan* an. 闇然, secret, concealed. D.M., xxxiii. 1.

闕 *k'euĕ* ch'üeh. (1) To put aside, exercise reserve. A., II. xviii. 2. 闕如. A., XIII. iii. 4. (2) 闕文, a blank left in the writing. A., XV. xxv. (3) The name of a village. A., XIV. xlvii.

關 *kwan* kuan. 關雎, the first ode in the She-king. A., III. xx.: VIII. xv.

開 *k'ae* k'ai. The name of one of Conf. disciples. A., V. v.

閔 *min*. The surname of one of Conf. disciples. A., VI. vii.: XI. ii.; iv.; xii.; xiii.

THE 170TH RADICAL. 阜.

防 *fang*. The name of a city in Loo. A., XIV. xv.

阼 *tsoo* tsu. The steps, or staircase, on the east. 阼階, A., X. x. 2.

THE 182D RADICAL. 風.

風 *fung* fêng — The wind. D.M., xxxiii. 1. A., X. xvi. 5; XII. xix. To enjoy the breeze; to take the air. A., XI. xxv. 7.

THE 183D RADICAL. 飛.

飛 *fei* — To fly. D.M., xii. 3.

THE 184TH RADICAL. 食.

食 *shih* — (1) To eat. G.L.c., vii. 2. D.M., iv. 2. A., I. xiv.; *et al., saepe.* = to consume. G.L.c., x. 19. = to enjoy. A., XI. xi. 3. To be eaten. A., XVII. vii. 4. 終食之間, a meal's time. A., IV. v. 3. = food. D.M., xix. 3. A., IV. ix.; VIII. xxi.; X. vii. 2; *et al.* (2) An eclipse. A., XIX. xxi.

食 *tsze* tsû — (1) Rice; food generally. A., II. viii.; VI. ix.; VII. xv.; X. viii. 1, 2, 4, 10; XIV. x. 3. (2) To give food to; to feast. A., XVIII. vii. 3.

飲 *yin* — To drink. D.M., iv. 2. A., X. x. 1. As a noun. A., VI. ix.; VIII. xxi.

飲 *yin* — Up. 3d tone. To give to drink. A., III. vii.

飪 *jin* jên — Meat over done. 失飪不食, he did not eat anything that was over-done. A., X. viii. 2. (This clause has slipt out of the translation.)

飯 *fan* — (1) to eat. 飯疏食. A., VII. xv.; XIV. x. 3. In these instances, perhaps 飯 = for food. To taste. A., X. xiii. 1. (2) 亞飯, 三飯, 四飯, see 亞, 三, 四. A., XVIII. ix.

飾 *shih* — To ornament. A., X. vi. 1. Obs. 修飾之. A., XIV. ix. 1.

飽 *paou* pao — To eat to the the full; satiety. A., I. xiv.; VII. ix.; XVII. xxii.

養 *yang* — To nourish; to bring up. G.L.c., ix. 2. A., V. xv. = to have about one; to manage. A., XVII. xxv.

養 *yang* — Low. 3d tone. To nourish, to support a superior. A., II. vii.

餘 *yu* yü — That which is over. 其餘, the others. A., II. xviii. 2; VI. v.; VIII. xi. Superabundant. A., I. vi. 有餘, having excess. D.M., xiii. 4.

餒 *nuy* nei — (1) Hunger, want. A., XV. xxxi. (2) Rotten, gone. A., X. viii. 2; spoken of fish.

餓 *go* o — Hungry. = to die of famine. A., XVI. xii. 1.

餲 *e* i — Rice sour, or with a bad odour. A., X. viii. 2.

餼 *he* ch'i — 餼羊, the sheep offered at the inauguration of the new moon. A., III. xvii. 1.

饌 *chwan* chuan — Provisions. A., X. xvi. 4. 先生饌, to set before one's elders. A., II. viii.

饐 *e* i — 食饐, rice injured by damp. A., X. viii. 2.

饑 *ke* chi — A famine;—specifically of the grain crop. A., XII. ix. 饑饉, a famine. A., XI. xxv. 4.

饉 *kin* chin — A famine;—specifically of vegetables. See 饑.

饋 *kwei* kuei — To present; anything presented. A., X. xi. 2; xv. 2.

饗 *heang* hsiang — To enjoy; to accept a sacrifice. D.M., xvii. 1; xviii. 2.

THE 185TH RADICAL. 首.

首 *show* shou — 首陽, the name of a mountain. A., XVI. xii. 1.

首 *show* shou — Upper 3d tone. The direction of the head. A., X. xiii. 3.

THE 187TH RADICAL. 馬.

馬 *ma* — (1) A horse, horses. G.L.c., x. 22. A., II. vii.; V. xviii. 2; xxv. 2; VI. iii. 2; xiii.; X. xii.; xv. 2; XV. xxv.; XVI. xii. 1. (2) 司馬, a double surname. A., XII. iii.; iv.; v. 巫馬, also a double surname. A., VII. xxx.

馮 *p'ing* — 馮河, to attempt to cross a river without using a boat. A., VII. x. 3.

駟 *sze* ssŭ — A team of four horses. A., XII. viii. 3; XVI. xii.

駕 *kea* chia — The yoking of a carriage. A., X. xiii. 4.

騂 *sing* hsing — Red. Spoken of a calf to be sacrificed. A., VI. iv.

驕 chiao — To be proud; pride. G.L.c., x. 18. D.M., xxvii. 7. A., I. xv.: VIII. xi.: XIII. xxvi.: XIV. xi.: XVI. v.: XX. ii. 1, 2.

驅 ch'ü — To drive. D.M., vii.

驥 chi — A horse that could go 1,000 le in a day, = a good horse. A., XIV. xxxv.

騫 ch'ien — 子騫, the designation of one of Conf. disciples. A., VI. vii.: XI. ii.; iv.; xiii.

騧 kua — 季騧 the name of an officer of the Chow dynasty. A., XVIII. xi.

駢 pien — The name of a town. A., XIV. x. 6.

THE 188TH RADICAL. 骨.

體 t'i — (1) The body. G.L.c., vi. 4. 四體, the four limbs. D.M., xxiv. A., XVIII. vii. 1. (2) As a verb. To treat with consideration. D.M., xx. 12, 13. To enter into, be incorporate with. D.M., xvi. 2.

THE 189TH RADICAL. 高.

高 kao — (1) High. D.M., xvi.; xxvi. 3, 4, 5, 9; xxvii. 6. A., IX. x. 1. (2) 高宗 the hon. epithet of the emperor 武丁. A., XIV. xliii. A name. (3) 微生高. A., V. xxiii.

THE 190TH RADICAL. 髟

髮 fa — The hair. A., XIV. xviii. 2.

THE 191ST RADICAL. 鬥.

鬭 tau — To contend; quarrelsomeness. A., XVI. vii.

THE 194TH RADICAL. 鬼.

鬼 kuei — Manes, the spirit or spirits of the departed. A., II. xxiv.: XI. xi. 鬼神, spiritual beings;—sometimes exclusively manes. D.M., xvi.; xxix. 3, 4. A., VI. xx.: VIII. xxi.

魏 wei — The name of a great family. A., XIV. xii.

魋 t'ui — 桓魋 a high officer of Sung, an enemy of Conf. A., VII. xxii.

THE 195TH RADICAL. 魚

魚 yü — (1) A fish, fishes, fish. D.M., xii. 3; xxvi. 9. A., X. viii. 2. (2) 魚子, an historiographer. A., XV. vi. (3) 伯魚, the designa. of Conf. son. A., XVI. xiii. 1: XVIII. x.

魯 lu — (1) Dull, blunt. A., XI. xvii. 2. (2) The name of a State. A., III. xxiii.: V. ii.: VI. xxii.; et al. 魯公, A., XVIII. x.

鮮 hsien — Up. 2d tone. Few, rare; seldom. G.L.c., viii. 1. D.M., iii.; iv. 2. A., I. ii. 1; iii.: IV. xxiii.: VI. xxvii.: XV. iii.: XVII. xvii.

鮀 t'o — An officer of Wei. A., VI. xiv.: XIV. xxii.

鯉 li — The name of Confucius' son. A., XI. vii. 2: XVI. xiii. 2, 5.

THE 196TH RADICAL. 鳥.

鳥 niao — A bird, birds. G.L.c., iii. 2. A., VIII. iv.: IX. viii.: XVII. ix. 7: XVIII. vi. 4.

鳳 fung — A fabulous bird, the phenix. A., IX. viii. Applied to Confucius. A., XVIII. vi. 1.

鳴 ming — (1) The cry of a bird. A., VIII. iv. 2. (2) To sound, to beat. A., XI. xvi. 2.

鳶 yüan — A kind of hawk. D.M., xii. 3.

鵠 ku — Used as = the bull's eye in a target. D.M., xiv. 5.

THE 198TH RADICAL. 鹿.

麑 ni — A fawn. A., X. vi. 4.

THE 200TH RADICAL. 麻.

麻 ma — Hemp; = linen. A., IX. iii. 1.

THE 201ST RADICAL. 黃.

黃 huang — Yellow. G.L.c., iii. 2. A., X. vi. 4.

THE 202D RADICAL. 黍

黎 *le* li — Black. 黎民, the black-haired people, = the people. G.L.c., x. 14.

THE 203D RADICAL. 黑.

默 *mih* mo — To be silent, silence. D.M., xxvii. 7. A., VII. ii.

黜 *ch'uh* chu — To be dismissed from office. A., XVIII. ii.

點 *tien* tien — The name of 曾晳, one of Conf. disciples. A., XI. xxv. 7.

黨 *tang* — (1) A village. A., IX. ii.: XIV. xlvii. 1. 鄉黨, A., VI. iii. 4: X. i. 1. (2) A class. A., VII. i. = school, pupils. A., V. xxi. 吾黨, we, among us. A., XIII. xviii. 1, 2. (3) A partizan, partizanly. A., VII. xxx. 2: XV. xxi.

THE 204TH RADICAL. 黹.

黻 *fuh* fu — An apron, belonging to the emperor's dress at sacrifices. A., VIII. xxi.

THE 205TH RADICAL. 黽.

黿 *yuen* yüan — A large tortoise. D.M., xxvi. 9.

鼈 *pie* pieh — A turtle. D.M., xxvi. 9.

鼉 *t'o* — An iguana. D.M., xxvi. 9.

THE 207TH RADICAL. 鼓

鼓 *koo* ku — (1) A drum, drums. A., XI. xvi. 2: XVII. xi. (2) Drum-master. A., XVIII. ix. 3. (3) To strike; to play on. D.M., xv. 2. A., XI. xxv. 2. Anciently, for the third of these senses the character 皷 was used.

鼗 *t'aou* t'ao — A kind of hand-drum. 播鼗, to shake the hand-drum. A., XVIII. ix. 4.

THE 210TH RADICAL. 齊.

齊 *ts'e* ch'i — (1) To regulate. G.L.T., 4, 5: c., viii. 1, 2; ix. 1, 5. To give uniformity to. A., II. iii. 1, 2. To equal; be equal with. A., IV. xvii. (2) The name of a State. A., V. xviii. 2: VI. iii. 1, 2; xxii.: VII. xiii.; XII. xi.: XVI. xii.: XVIII. iii.; iv.; ix. —XIV. xvi.; xvii.; xviii. (3) In 叔齊, it is the hon. epithet. A., V. xxii.: VII. xiv. 2: XVI. xii.: XVIII. viii. 1, 2.

齊 *chae* chai — To fast; religious adjustment. D.M., xvi. 3; xx. 14; xxxi. 1. A., VII. xii.: X. vii. 1, 2: viii. 10.

齊 *tsze* tzu — The lower edge of a garment. A., X. iv. 4. 齊衰, in mourning. A., IX. ix.: X. xvi. 2.

THE 211TH RADICAL. 齒

齒 *ch'e* ch'ih — The teeth. A., XIV. x. 3. Used for years, age. D.M., xix. 4.

THE 212TH RADICAL. 龍.

龍 *lung* — A dragon, dragons. D.M., xxvi. 9.

THE 213TH RADICAL. 龜.

龜 *kwei* kuei — A tortoise. D.M., xxiv. A., XVI. i. 7.

END OF VOL. I.

SBN

www.ingramcontent.com/pod-product-compliance
Lightning Source LLC
Chambersburg PA
CBHW020858020526
44116CB00029B/341

9783742822581